A KNIGHT IN POLITICS

Portrait of Sir Frederick by William Notman
Courtesy Library and Archives Canada

A Knight in Politics
A BIOGRAPHY OF SIR FREDERICK BORDEN

Carman Miller

McGill-Queen's University Press
Montreal & Kingston • London • Ithaca

© McGill-Queen's University Press 2010
ISBN 978-0-7735-3730-9

Legal deposit third quarter 2010
Bibliothèque nationale du Québec

Printed in Canada on acid-free paper that is 100% ancient forest free
(100% post-consumer recycled), processed chlorine free

This book has been published with the help of a grant from the
Canadian Federation for the Humanities and Social Sciences, through
the Aid to Scholarly Publications Programme, using funds provided
by the Social Sciences and Humanities Research Council of Canada.

McGill-Queen's University Press acknowledges the support of
the Canada Council for the Arts for our publishing program. We also
acknowledge the financial support of the Government of Canada
through the Canada Book Fund for our publishing activities.

LIBRARY AND ARCHIVES CANADA CATALOGUING IN PUBLICATION

Miller, Carman, 1940–
A knight in politics : a biography of Sir Frederick Borden /
Carman Miller.

Includes bibliographical references and index.
ISBN 978-0-7735-3730-9

1. Borden, F. W. (Frederick William), Sir, 1847–1917.   2. Politicians –
Canada – Biography.   3. Canada – Politics and government – 1867–1914.
I. Title.

FC551.B58M56 2010   971.05'6092   C2010-901845-1

Set in 10/12 Baskerville 10 Pro with Trade Gothic
Book design & typesetting by Garet Markvoort, zijn digital

Contents

Illustrations

Acknowledgments

I wish to acknowledge with thanks the generous assistance of several institutions and persons who facilitated the research and writing of this book.

Research grants from the Social Science and Humanities Research Council and from the former Faculty of Graduate Studies and Research at McGill University helped fund much of the research and writing of this study. This book has been published with the help of a grant from the Canadian Federation for the Humanities and Social Sciences, through the Aid to Scholarly Publications Program, using funds provided by the Social Sciences and Humanities Research Council of Canada.

The courteous and efficient assistance of staff at the Public Archives of Nova Scotia, Library and Archives Canada, the Inter-library Loans Department of McGill University's McLennan Library, the National Library of Scotland, the National Archives of the United Kingdom (formerly the Public Records Office), and the British Library (formerly the British Museum Reading Room) have assisted me on many occasions.

Over the years a number of persons have provided valuable criticism, counsel, and encouragement. Professor Peter Burroughs, the late Professor George Rawlyk, and the late Dr Phyllis Blakeley (subsequently provincial archivist of Nova Scotia) provided helpful direction, advice, and support at an early stage of this project. Subsequently, this study benefited from the critical scrutiny and advice of my colleague Professor Brian Young. Another colleague, Professor Sherry Olsen, generously gave up several of her research days to create a map of Sir Frederick's world in Kings County. The manuscript benefited from David McCall's careful reading and his various suggestions.

Several persons provided valuable information and assistance in recreating Sir Frederick's life and times, for all of which I am very grateful. Many years ago Mrs Lewis (Lou) Clarke recounted her very vivid memories of Lady Borden. More recently Joan Elizabeth (Starr) Murray, the great-granddaughter of Dr Jonathan Borden, shared her recollections of her family during a pleasant, informative lunch at her home, and subsequently provided copies of family photographs. Julia

Leslie Green MacKay (Sir Frederick's great-granddaughter) kindly
provided me with a detailed description of Borden Place and with her
recollections of Lady Borden and Elizabeth Hewitt; and on very short
notice Professor Kenneth MacKay responded to my request for a reproduction of Sir Frederick's coat of arms. Merritt and Wilma Gibson's
generous hospitality and instructive tour of their "Old Place" (Borden
Place) enabled me to visualize an aspect of Sir Frederick and Lady Borden's world. I wish also to thank Professor Glenys Gibson for providing me with better reproductions of several illustrations used in the
book. Over the years Kelvin and Roleen Ogilvie have assisted me in
various ways with their interest in and knowledge of the area. I am also
indebted to Ken Bezanson for generously providing me with reproductions of Borden family portraits and Dr Jonathan Borden's house, and
drawing my attention to other useful information.

The knowledge, counsel, and good humour of the staff of McGill-
Queen's University Press, Philip Cercone, Joan McGilvray, and Joanne
Pisano, have been much appreciated. I would also like to thank Judith
Turnbull, who copyedited the manuscript with patience, care, and
sensitivity.

Finally I offer a special thanks to Pamela, Danielle, Marc, Andrew,
Rolf, Elin, Carley, Marius, Lukas, Thea, Eva, and Alexandra.

A KNIGHT IN POLITICS

Introduction

Camp Borden, the Canadian Forces' largest permanent training base eighty kilometres northwest of Toronto, and Borden, Saskatchewan, a village some sixty-four kilometres southeast of Saskatoon,[1] are a long way from the birthplace of Sir Frederick William Borden, in Upper Canard, Nova Scotia.[2] Named to honour Sir Frederick Borden for his contribution to Canadian public life, these topographical tributes suggest the extent, nature, and significance of Borden's public career. A medical doctor and Nova Scotia entrepreneur, Borden served as Canada's minister of militia and defence from 1896 to 1911, a period that encompassed war (1899–1902), preparation for war, and intense debate on imperial reorganization. The longest-serving minister of defence in Canada's history, Borden reformed Canada's defence forces and acted as Canada's point man in London, a service to the Empire that his colleagues hailed at the time of his death as one of his greatest achievements – and one that Sir Wilfrid Laurier had intended to reward by appointing Sir Frederick Canada's high commissioner to the United Kingdom, to succeed the powerful Lord Strathcona. At the time, the high commissionership was the greatest award in the gift of the Canadian government.

Sir Frederick Borden has often been confused with his more illustrious first cousin, Sir Robert Laird Borden,[3] Canada's eighth prime minister, and historians have not always dealt kindly with the defence minister. His bad press began with contemporary political partisans and moralists, Tories with elephantine memories who remembered Sir Frederick as the Nova Scotia minister in Sir Wilfrid Laurier's Liberal government who was associated primarily with patronage and scandal. Many contemporary moralists nourished and promoted this partial and partisan characterization of Sir Frederick's public and private life. They decried his public career on grounds of his personal moral failings, his conflation of private and public interests, his weakness for "wine and women." One contemporary moralist, a Baptist clergyman who was also a disappointed political opponent, went so far as to describe Sir Frederick as a "stench in the nostrils of the right thinking people, from Halifax to Vancouver."[4] Another reverend gentleman,

Dr J. Pringle of Yukon renown, informed his Presbyterian colleagues attending their General Assembly in Kingston, Ontario, in June 1909 that, "the name of Sir Frederick was a synonym for lust."[5]

An earlier generation of military historians was no more charitable towards the long-serving minister of militia and defence. Busily chronicling the evolution of the Canadian forces, they cast Sir Frederick as an obstacle and retardant to military professionalization and reform. In their view, the minister, "an ignorant civilian," lacked any real knowledge or interest in the military and was concerned chiefly in turning the Department of Militia into a "military Tammany."[6] Their most eloquent authority was John Buchan, who in his commissioned biography of Lord Minto, the Canadian governor general (1898–1904), dismissed Borden as little more than "a country banker and physician from Nova Scotia, who ... had no serious knowledge of military affairs," who was "neither a courageous man nor an able man," and who "conceived his duties chiefly as a balancing of party patronage."[7] To clinch their damning assessment, Buchan and others assigned paternity for the impressive record of military reform that occurred during Borden's administration to the iterant professional "British" general officers on loan to and in command of the Canadian Militia.[8]

Perhaps no contemporary was more deeply offended by John Buchan's summary assessment of Sir Frederick than his Tory cousin, Sir Robert Borden.[9] When Canada's former prime minister read John Buchan's hastily written biography *Lord Minto: A Memoir* (London, 1924), he was outraged by the author's dismissive, unfair characterization of Sir Frederick. Sir Robert Borden had known Minto, the Canadian governor general, especially after Robert Borden had assumed the leadership of the Conservative Party in 1901. Indeed Sir Robert knew both the subject of the biography and its author.[10] Moved by his deep affection and respect for Sir Frederick and sensitive to his family's place in history,[11] Sir Robert immediately employed a clerk to document Sir Frederick's considerable contribution to Canadian public life. Armed with this arsenal of evidence, he wrote Buchan a lengthy, stinging letter of rebuke. Buchan, ever responsive to rank and influence, replied immediately and apologetically, attempting to explain his captious and perfunctory treatment of Sir Frederick. "Since that book was published," he pleaded to Sir Robert, "I have come to the conclusion that I have been unjust ... in many details and from what you write it is clear that I was unfair to Sir Frederick Borden ... I had no knowledge of the Canadian background to correct my views."[12]

Buchan might have explained to Sir Robert that the book's four offending chapters on Canada had been derived almost entirely from E.T.H. Hutton's self-promoting, unpublished manuscript, "John Gil-

bert, 4th Earl of Minto: A Narrative."[13] Hutton, a former general officer commanding the Canadian Militia who had been dismissed from
his office by the Laurier government upon Frederick Borden's recommendation, was a personal friend of Minto's and had begun a biography of the former Canadian governor general at the family's request,
a project that had been interrupted by Hutton's death in 1923. In this
highly partisan narrative, Hutton – ever the clever, self-serving propagandist – had used the Canadian chapters to settle old scores with Sir
Frederick and his Liberal colleagues. The result was a biased, partial
perspective that failed to recognize Sir Frederick's achievements or
appreciate the relationship of respect and confidence that developed
subsequently between Minto and Borden after Hutton's "recall" from
Canada in 1900.

Not all of Sir Frederick's contemporaries were as critical or censorious as Buchan or other partisan contemporary moralists. A popular
and entertaining guest at mess dinners or at the Canadian Press Gallery's raucous annual banquet, Sir Frederick appeared to others as a
talented, warm-hearted dandy, a welcome relief from some of his more
sober-sided colleagues.[14] In his reminiscences, Paul Bilkey, a former
editor of the Tory Montreal *Gazette*, remembered Sir Frederick affectionately as "tall, debonair, fruity of voice, a joyous old boy and something of a scamp, who could play the fiddle at a supper party if it was
the right kind of supper party, and who had other qualities which for
the sake of delicacy are usually called human. He was Minister of Militia and contributed to the gaiety of nations. I liked him."[15]

Similarly, Sir John French, viscount of Ypres and 1st Earl French,
during his address to Toronto's Empire Club on 29 May 1922, went
out of his way to praise the then deceased minister for his kindness
and courtesy, "whom he hailed as another great Canadian statesman"
whose prewar military reform could "be seen in the splendid fighting
efficiency that was manifested by the Canadian forces in the Great
War."[16] Other contemporaries, including Sam Hughes, Sir Frederick's
erratic, Tory friend, political "opponent" and successor as minister of
militia and defence, applauded Sir Frederick's many accomplishments
and generously ranked him "the best Minister of Militia to date" –
that is, until Sir Sam himself occupied the position![17] To demonstrate
his generous assessment of Sir Frederick and perhaps with an eye to
pleasing Prime Minister Borden and to undercutting his Liberal critics, in May 1916 Hughes named the new military base at Angus Plains
"Camp Borden" in honour of Sir Frederick, his friend and Liberal
predecessor.[18]

A second generation of military historians have confirmed French's
and Hughes' assessment of Sir Frederick's military contribution. Two

revisionist historians, Donald C. Gordon and Richard Preston, have
led the way. In Gordon's *The Dominion Partnership in Imperial Defence*,
the author's appreciation of the function and influences of patronage
and nationalism in "the more democratic Dominions" provided balance and perspective to his appraisal of the minister of militia and his
policies.[19] Unlike some previous writers who mistook purity for efficiency, Gordon focused on Borden's considerable contribution to the
formation of imperial defence policy. The second revisionist account,
R.A. Preston's *Canada and Imperial Defence*, distinguished clearly between imperial and British interests and underscored the close relationship between the development of self-defence and constitutional
autonomy. In this context, Preston considered Sir Frederick's insistence on imperial cooperation rather than integration more realistic and
more in line with the way the Empire/Commonwealth's structure of
defence was developing than Borden's critics appreciated.[20] Above all,
Preston praised Borden's careful defence preparations and his concern
to appoint only the best-qualified officers to command the Canadian
Militia, at times against considerable opposition from within his own
party. Similarly, Desmond Morton, in his careful, comparative analysis
of the relationship between minister and generals, has concluded that
Borden was the "most powerful force for [militia] reform in Laurier's
government."[21] Others have followed their lead, commending Borden
for his political and "moral courage," his attempts to end influence-
peddling in professional advancement, his development of a cooperative civil/military relationship, his "honest and effective financial management" of his department, and his open-minded approach to military
reform.[22] Altogether these revisionists describe quite a different Borden
than did an earlier generation of military historians. Their Borden is a
reforming, committed, informed public servant, a competent administrator with a well-defined agenda, the catalyst for a military renais-
sance[23] who presided over "the greatest peacetime expansion and mod-
ernization of Canada's military forces."[24]

But Borden was more than a public servant. He was an entrepreneur
and private person with ambitions, personal needs, and private aspirations. A singular focus on Borden's public service truncates our portrait of the man. It obscures the synergy between personal and public
life at the time, the dynamic and increasingly contested line between
personal material interest and public service.[25] Too narrow a focus on
Borden's public career deprives us of a privileged perspective on his
society, time, and place, and of an opportunity to appreciate how he
exercised power and how his behaviour reflected the changing culture
and social relationships of his era.

Although he was a medical doctor, and the son of a medical doctor of modest means, by the time of Sir Frederick's death in 1917, his estate was evaluated as worth at least $300,000, an amount equivalent to some $4.5 million in today's currency, an assessment that may well understate his real material assets.[26] While part of his wealth was accumulated during his years in Laurier's cabinet (1896–1911), a period of transition from family to corporate capitalism characterized by an incestuous relationship between business and politics, the foundation of his wealth had been established in Nova Scotia before 1896, during an era of regional socio-economic dislocation and transformation. While Borden was a moderately successful entrepreneur, his story was not a rags-to-riches saga, but a tale of how he skilfully maximized inheritance, family, and local networks to personal advantage.

An examination of Sir Frederick's entrepreneurial attitudes and strategies, of his capacity to translate circumstances into opportunities, provides insight into Maritime entrepreneurship and its relationship to regional (under)development. It is the tale of the interplay of family, business and politics, nepotism and patronage. While Borden's wealth and political influence remained grounded in the Maritime region, both operated within a national, transnational, and imperial context of interacting, overlapping spaces that Borden negotiated with remarkable skill and personal profit.

Borden's career demonstrates the symbiotic relationship between private and public life in late nineteenth and early twentieth-century Canada,[27] between business and politics, identity and belonging, class and culture. As a first-generation "Canadian," Borden came to belong to what H.V. Nelles has called a "national class" whose identity and allegiance subsumed locality and region. Uncomfortable with the separatist strategies of some of his Nova Scotia political fellow-travellers, Borden adopted a worldview that came to encompass region, nation, and empire. Equally instructive are Borden's social strategies and projection of power, his attempts to feudalize or gentrify his social relationships, expressed in terms of family, public service, titles, manners, memory, rituals, philanthropy, houses, hospitality, dress, language, and leisure, as well as the way these strategies reflected and helped him negotiate and cushion the transitions that characterized his life and time.

"The eighteenth-century knight," the Opposition's derisive characterization of Sir Frederick, playfully captures themes and ambiguities in Borden's life. His designation as a Knight Grace of the Venerable Order of the Hospital of St John of Jerusalem reminds us of his healing career, his concern for the sick, his informed commitment to public health, and his generous philanthropy. His other knighthood, the Most Distinguished Order of St Michael and St George (KCMG) evokes his role as "warrior," counsellor, and defender of the realm. His search for titles and honour through public service, with its material rewards, and his courtly, paternalistic manner seem both anachronistic and representative of his generation's anti-modernist re-enactment of "the age of Camelot," all in stark contrast to his fascination with technology and progress. Similarly, his promotion of professionalization (itself redolent of the medieval guild) seems at variance with his own occupational plurality, at once medical doctor, banker, entrepreneur, and politician, all reminding us of an individual's ability to reconcile apparent ambiguities and contradictions. Above all, these traits were a public affirmation of power, albeit soft power.

Biography has always been something of a staple of Canadian history, though for a time in the 1970s and 1980s biography became "a casualty of social history,"[28] as some professional historians focused on *la longue durée,* insisted on analysis rather than narrative, and saw social groups rather than individuals as the motors of social change. Within this perspective, biography was consigned to a "purgatory"[29] or, in gentler language, to a "cathedral belonging to another age."[30] More recently, the turn to a cultural-linguistic approach to historical meaning and representation, with its insistence upon subjectivity, contingency, voice, agency, the private sphere, feeling, and micro-narrative, has resuscitated biography as a site, medium, and mirror of historical expression and understanding. The desire to put a human face on history, however, ought not to be seen as simply a triumph of agency over hegemony, a divorce from the larger "history of society," but as a building block of history, a prism through which to view the "web of community, family, economic structures and political institutions," a medium of making sense of the complexity of material, social, cultural, and behavioural contexts.[31] In short, biography is a way to discern what it has meant to be human in diverse times and circumstances.[32] The new biography, then, is not simply a return to the "great man" theory, a past genre that favoured elite, male hagiography, but entails a recognition that biography may also be a form of social history, an opportunity to employ social and cultural insights and methods to biographical studies, a marriage of the macro- and micro-dynamics of history.[33]

A biographer's challenge is to tell a coherent story that recognizes the claims of narrative, character, and circumstance, of intention and convention, a story that provides contexts while recognizing a person's wilful and various capacities to domesticate circumstances to local and personal needs and conditions. It entails a balance of narrative and analysis. On occasion a biographer must "break from narration"[34] to join the micro and the macro, to identify the contemporaneous multiplicity of changing and often ambiguous factors that shaped a person's world over a lifetime (in the case of Borden, a span of almost seventy years), and to assess the significance of the subject's response, how the subject responded to, represented, or reflected his/her time, place, and circumstance. A biographer, like all historians, is a hostage to evidence, to a record that is usually arbitrary, fragmented, selective, partial and frequently mined with black holes that obscure vision and reduce the biographer to silence, inference, or conjecture. The Borden record, for example, is all but silent on his intimate family life, a casualty of family sensitivities.

My interest in Borden began when I was a master's student at Dalhousie University, researching a thesis focused entirely on Borden's federal political career. Since then, my curiosity has grown to include Borden's business and imperial career, his social strategies, including his management of family, business, and politics, and his conflation of private and public interests. This study has also been informed by my subsequent research and writing on regional, national, and imperial politics, biography, war, and society. A study of Frederick Borden, therefore, provides an opportunity to focus on the dynamic of local, regional, national, and imperial contexts, biography, politics, and military history, to explore the changing, overlapping, and interconnected worlds in which Borden and many Canadians lived in the nineteenth and early twentieth centuries.

This study is based on various collections of primary and secondary literature. Central to the study is the F.W. Borden fond (MG 2, volumes 63–223) deposited in the Public Archives of Nova Scotia (PANS), altogether some fifteen metres of records, a first instalment of which was deposited by Lady Bessie Borden in 1950. Henry D. Hicks, then premier of Nova Scotia, spotted additional papers while attending Lady Borden's funeral on 3 March 1956. Conscious of their potential historical value, he rescued them from the leaky shed to which they had been consigned, probably soon after Sir Fredrick's death in 1917. Water damage had obliterated some of the ink letter-books. Before being consigned to the shed, the papers seem to have been weeded by Lady Borden, who appears to have destroyed what she may have considered inappropriate, unnecessary, or incriminating evidence, including intimate and personal correspondence. As a young girl, Mrs Lewis (Lou) H. Clarke, to whom I spoke in 1989, visited Lady Borden soon after Sir Frederick's death; she remembered seeing Lady Borden seated by a fireplace burning letters and weeping, whether over her husband's recent death or his personal foibles she could not tell.[35] While the fond contains records ranging from 1849 to 1950, the bulk of the material is focused on his service as minister of militia and defence (1896–1911), bound letters-books containing ingoing and outgoing correspondence on political and administrative subjects. The fond also contains loose letters and financial records of his various business activities. Although it possesses some private and personal correspondence with his family, this record is limited and has been, it seems, carefully selected. Despite these deficiencies, the fairly extensive body of F.W. Borden papers in the PANS provides an indispensable source for a study of Sir Frederick's career. The papers have been supplemented by other important primary and secondary sources in Canada, England, and Scotland.

CHAPTER 1

Family

Family framed Frederick William Borden's world. In nineteenth- and early twentieth-century British North America/Canada this was not unusual, since family prescribed a person's material, social, and cultural boundaries. It provided physical, material, social, and emotional security. It formed an important ingredient of entrepreneurial success. It denoted religious, social, and ethnic identity. It was the site for the transmission of values and notions of authority, gender, and generational and social status, and of cultural conventions encoded in dress, manners, language, rituals, and obligations. Family purchased social recognition and standing and generated expectations. It relied upon reciprocity, loyalty, memory, kinship, and a sense of belonging, claims often sanctified by blood and exercised through property.

Given Frederick Borden's time, place, background, and upbringing, the practical utility of family seemed inescapable. Three generations after his first Yankee ancestor settled in Nova Scotia's fertile Cornwallis Valley, Borden grew up surrounded by a closely knit, extended, interdependent family that played an increasingly conspicuous role in Kings County's public life. Pervasive family networks defined and sustained the region's household and political economy, as well as its personal, religious, political, and professional relations. In this region of intersecting and overlapping political, economic, and ethnic worlds, its settlers required leaders – merchants of power and influence – to negotiate and mediate intra- and inter-community interests.

From the beginning, Borden's Yankee ancestors had figured prominently among those 8,000 "land-grabbing," opportunistic New England farmers who had been drawn to Nova Scotia by its mid-eighteenth-century promise of free fertile land, with its tempting prospects of place and profit. Planters they were called, and that said it all: like their seventeenth-century namesakes who occupied the lands seized in Ireland and elsewhere, these Yankee settlers were invited to occupy, cultivate, and defend the good soil from which some three-quarters (about 13,000) of the region's Acadian population had been deported between 1755 and 1762. And Planters they would remain, for in the years that followed, they and many of their fellow-Yankee migrants would *plant well*.[1] That deep, fertile land, with its long growing season of approximately 145 frost-free days, would sustain many of their industrious descendants for several generations. Few families were better served by that rich soil than the Borden family. Their good fortune began almost at once.

Although Samuel Borden, a prosperous farmer and land surveyor of Tiverton, Massachusetts, had been the first Borden to visit Nova Scotia, he had no intention of settling there. He had come to Nova Scotia in the spring of 1760, accompanied by his second-eldest son, Perry, at the invitation of Charles Lawrence, the colony's military governor. The architect of the Acadian deportation, Lawrence planned to resettle the land from which the Acadians had been forcibly expelled with Connecticut, Rhode Island, New Hampshire, and Massachusetts farmers.[2] One of a party of surveyors chosen by William Shirley, the governor of Massachusetts, Samuel Borden, with Perry, sailed to Nova Scotia to draw boundaries for Cornwallis, Horton, Falmouth, and Newport townships, four of the several projected English, Protestant townships to be resettled on both sides of the Fundy Basin.

The Nova Scotia government's plan envisaged the division of these four townships into shares, with each potential Yankee householder entitled to at least one share. A share consisted of 500 acres of diversified land that included "plough land," "grass land," and "woodland." Lawrence's offer proved an attractive incentive for an expanding number of Yankee farm families whose efforts to relieve demographic pressure through western expansion was at first discouraged and then formally blocked by imperial proclamation. In each proposed Nova Scotia township, space had been reserved for a church, school, and parade square or blockhouse, institutions that would serve and shape this area's non-conformist character, institutions in which the Bordens would occupy a prominent place.

The Yankee Planters' migration to the United Kingdom's "fourteenth colony" was more a movement *within* than *to* a new land, since the land had been known to and envied by many of its prospective settlers. The Planters brought with them their institutions, ideas, and culture, forged from their dissenting religious New England past. Yet, however democratic these "great levellers" may have been in rhetoric, prayer, and exhortation, especially during periods of revivalist fervour, a structured Calvinist order inevitably re-emerged to channel their excesses in a more hierarchical and deferential religious and social hierarchy. Consequently, as fortune, trade, and inheritance reshaped or reinforced the community's social order, a devout Samuel Chipman, with a thousand acres of land, a thriving mercantile business, and control of government patronage, did not meet on the same social level as

a man with but fifty or fewer acres. Moreover, the social experiment
of the fanatically devout Ebenezer Bigelow, the renowned shipbuilder
and wealthy nineteenth-century Canning merchant who attempted to
apply his faith to business practices, more especially his decision to
charge only a "just price," ended in bankruptcy and migration, and
served as a stern warning to those whose convictions threatened the
established social order or who sought to substitute social justice for
the "invisible hand" of supply and demand.

A social hierarchy was evident from the start. It began with the distribution of land, itself a recognized mark of a family's social standing and a means to social advancement. During the initial distribution, Samuel Borden was modestly favoured. He received two shares,
one in East Falmouth or Newport Township,[3] where he had done his
principal survey work, and another in Cornwallis Township, the township settled by many of his fellow Massachusetts migrants. Samuel, a
shrewd, fifty-five-year-old, fourth-generation Yankee farmer, however,
was too comfortably established in Tiverton to uproot his family and
begin life in a new land, however attractive its prospects.[4] This successful surveyor and farmer, however, recognized the land's social and
economic value, as well as its potential utility as a lucrative investment
and an opportunity to assure his family's future. Almost immediately
Samuel sought the governor's permission to sell a small portion of his
Cornwallis lands;[5] the rest he gave or bequeathed to his son, Perry,
who remained in Nova Scotia and in time became Frederick Borden's
great-grandfather.

Although Perry, just twenty-two years old when he came to Nova
Scotia with his father, obtained two shares in Newport (East Falmouth),
he sold a portion of these lands in 1765 and another portion in 1773
to secure sufficient capital to maintain his small family on his father's
lands in Cornwallis Township. There, in 1764, he had built his house
on Lot Number 8 in the First Division of the township, surrounded by
other Massachusetts Planters. With him was his wife Amy Percy, the
daughter of an English army officer whom he met and married in Nova
Scotia, and their two small sons, Samuel and Joseph. Unfortunately,
his wife's death in December 1765, soon after their settlement in Cornwallis, left Perry a widower for two years, until his marriage in October
1767 to Mary Ells, with whom he had nine more sons.

Perry needed every acre of his land to provide for his large family,
all of whom married and remained in the area except Samuel, the
eldest, who returned to Fall River, Massachusetts, where he became "a
successful business man."[6] While it is not clear what assets, livestock,
equipment, and other capital resources Perry had brought initially to
Cornwallis in 1764, there was little question of his subsequent business

acumen, managerial skills, and good fortune. The times were propitious. The American rebellion and the influx of Loyalists, provisioned and protected by the imperial government, raised land prices and created lucrative internal and external markets. In short order Perry established a prosperous farm that supported his large family and enabled him to sell his surplus corn, wheat, rye, cider, apples, bluenose potatoes, pigs, meat, cheese, tobacco, and candles.

So successful was Perry that when the time came for his sons to establish separate households, he provided generously for each of them. In 1797 he assisted four of his sons, Joseph, Lemeul, David, and Perry junior, to purchase a 1,402-acre farm in East Horton from John Fillis, Esquire, for £1,975. The terms required an initial £975 and seven equal instalments every two years thereafter, a debt that Perry's four sons relinquished in half the time.[7] Typical of their family relations, this cooperative endeavour proved profitable and congenial, and the Fillis farm was not partitioned until 1822.

Upon his death on 27 January 1805, Perry not only provided for the maintenance of his widow until her death but bequeathed his remaining lands in Falmouth – "besides what I have given him" – to his seventh-eldest son, Joshua, and divided the rest of his land, situated in Cornwallis Township, among his younger sons, William, Benjamin, Edward, and Abraham. In addition, the executors of Perry's estate were to pay £100 to his son Samuel and provide the earlier beneficiaries Joseph, David, Jonathan, and Perry junior, who had purchased the Fillis farm, with £20 a year for ten years.[8]

At the time of his father's death in 1805, Perry junior, Frederick Borden's grandfather, possessed both a claim to 350 acres of the Fillis farm and a ten-year annual income of £20. Meanwhile, international border tensions continued to create commercial opportunities. American president Thomas Jefferson's Embargo Acts of 1807 and 1809, forbidding British and later French vessels from entering American ports, fostered a lucrative licit and illicit Fundy trade in farm and other products.[9] Consequently, in 1809, four years after his father's death, Perry junior possessed sufficient capital or credit to purchase Jessie Harding's farm, a property of 750 acres that included a house at Grand Pre Corner, later known as the Borden House. The purchase coincided with his marriage that year to Lavinia Fuller, the daughter of Timothy Fuller, from Lower Horton; Perry was thirty-four years old at the time.[10] Here, at Grand Pre Corner, he established his family and lived until his death on 30 May 1862, at the age of eighty-nine, six months after the death of his second wife, Mary Dennison, whom he had married shortly after the death of his first wife.[11] Frederick and his cousin Robert Laird Borden, aged fifteen and eight respectively at the time of

Dr Jonathan Borden, MD (Harvard 1840), Frederick Borden's father, a "health professional" and advocate of public education. *Courtesy Joan Murray and Ken Bezanson*

their Grandfather Perry's death, retained vivid and affectionate memories of their grandfather and step-grandmother.[12]

Despite his initial success, Perry junior, like many second-generation Planters may not have had the opportunity to maximize his assets as rapidly as did his father. Nonetheless, his extensive farm enabled him to support a family of eight, maintain a place in his community, educate his children, and provide them with a modest inheritance. Lavinia's death in 1825, after sixteen years of marriage, left Perry with six children, four sons and two daughters, and placed an additional charge on his time and resources. His wife's untimely death also reinforced family solidarity and interdependence, a legacy of support and loyalty that Frederick and Robert would honour and from which they would benefit.

Frederick's father, Jonathan, Perry junior's eldest child, was born at Lower Horton on 14 June 1810. He was only fifteen when his mother died, and his youngest brother, Thomas, was not quite three. Relations between Jonathan and his brother Andrew, who was six years younger than Jonathan, were particularly close.[13] Jonathan and Andrew's mutual affection and respect extended to their sons, Frederick William Borden and Robert Laird Borden, fostering a friendship that Frederick's and Robert's prominent and contemporaneous public careers in opposing political parties failed to sever; in their case, blood remained forever thicker than politics.

After three generations, population growth and the influx of Loyalist refugees placed a strain on the Planters' accessible arable land. The growing economic and social diversification of their community, however, offered alternative employment to replace, or more often supplement, the opportunities available on its increasingly smaller land lots. Society's growing complexity required leaders who could negotiate and mediate the mutual and competing interests that were often created and resolved by the expanding presence of the state. The liberal professions, such as medicine and the law, provided one set of employment alternatives, and they often generated society's economic and political brokers. Perry's eldest son, Jonathan, chose to pursue a career in medicine. He was not the first Borden to obtain medical credentials from Harvard Medical School: in 1824 his cousin Adolphus Kinsman Borden, had graduated from the Harvard. Nor was he the last: his son Frederick followed his example. What was remarkable about the Bordens was their commitment to formal education.

Although, from our contemporary perspective, medical doctors at this time may have been generally "marginal men," uncertain of their authority and influence and facing a number of competitors in the medical marketplace,[14] Jonathan's decision to secure formal credentials, first from the College of Physicians and Surgeons in New York (1836–37) and then from Harvard Medical School, where he graduated in 1840 with an MD, suggests that he intended to make medicine more than a hobby. His decision set him apart, imbuing him with scientific authority within his community and the "profession." Jonathan's formal medical education made him one of only a handful of practising physicians in the province to hold a medical degree. The provincial secretary licensed both those with and those without formal educational credentials, the latter upon written testimony to their healing powers. The willingness of Jonathan's family to support his room, board, and the $200 per annum tuition fee for four years suggest their economic capacity, commitment to education, social standing, and aspirations within their community.[15]

Upon his graduation, Jonathan's professional commitment became even more evident when the thirty-one-year-old bachelor physician returned home to establish a medical practice in Londonderry, Colchester County. Londonderry was then an active mining town with family and commercial connections to the other side of the Minas Basin and a regular ferry service. Dr Jonathan Borden practised medicine for six years in Londonderry, where he became known as an affable, popular, but impecunious country doctor, reputed for his generosity to the poor, his passion for education, and his application of modern medical knowledge, more particularly for the vaccination of people against smallpox. His marriage on 24 September 1845 to Maria Frances Brown, the thirty-one-year-old daughter of Charles and Frances Lothrop Brown, prominent citizens in his home township of Horton, reflects his own social standing. It also imposed family obligations that made difficult his continued impecunious residence in Londonderry, despite the "numerously and influentially signed" petitions for him to remain. His patients' subsequent "pilgrimages ... to seek his advice" testify to Dr Jonathan's competence and/or affability.

Jonathan had no intention of abandoning medicine; he had decided to return to Cornwallis to open a medical practice in his Canard Street home in a village later known as Upper Canard. Shortly after his marriage he purchased the Dr Jacob Walton property, which included an elegant, spacious, ten-room Georgian-style house (constructed in 1790),[16] a visible and material reminder of his social status within the community. Here he received patients, and in the front of the house he built a small pharmacy to concoct his pills and potions. Here too he supplemented his income from his fifty-two-acre farm that backed onto his home, and where with a male and female servant he provided for his family. The consistency between the estimated value of his real and personal property entered for the 1851 Census and the stated value of his estate at the time of his death in 1875 suggests that his farm supported his family's requirements, which in themselves were considerable, given his subsequent extended family's demands and increasing social and community obligations.

A compassionate, sociable, cultivated, well-read person, Dr Jonathan established a reputation as a "gentleman of dignity and culture, and a distinguished person in the county"[17] who contributed modestly to the public life of his community. He enjoyed music and played his violin for personal pleasure, public entertainment, and occasionally as professional therapy, to quiet an overwrought patient! He was fond of debate and repartee, possessed a modest library, and was a keen advocate of public education. For twenty-two years he served as a school commissioner, along with his brother Andrew. Together they organized petitions to the provincial government calling for the creation of a provincial normal school, a county assessment to support free schools, and the annual inspection of county schools.[18] Both were members of the Scotia Masonic Lodge No. 28, a movement associated with enlightenment and free thinking. Jonathan also served as a surgeon in the 3rd Regiment of Kings County Militia from 1862 and in its reorganized embodiment as the 68th Battalion shortly after Confederation. Both Andrew and Jonathan were Reformers in politics, and in 1847 Jonathan

A present-day photograph of Frederick Borden's birthplace, built in 1790.
Courtesy Ken Bezanson

assisted Andrew in his first and only attempt to enter the legislature, a contest he lost "by about 14 or 15 votes," a loss Andrew attributed to his refusal to permit his committee to use "intoxicants in elections."[19] A public-spirited citizen, Dr Jonathan Borden served as a county coroner from 1847 until his death and as deputy postmaster in 1860, both politically sensitive offices that further supplemented his income.

Of Planter origin, Dr Jonathan Borden's wife, Marie Frances Brown, came from a prominent, entrepreneurial family that occupied a conspicuous place in the county's public life. Unfortunately, little documentary evidence survives to describe Marie Frances's formation and character, a casualty of our historical dependence on male-centred public records. Nor is there information on her relationship to her only son, Frederick Borden.[20] Many of the family's male members were professionals. Two of her eight brothers, Edward Lothrop Brown and John Lothrop Brown,[21] were members of the Nova Scotia House of Assembly. Edward was a Wolfville medical doctor with an MD from Pennsylvania (MD 1829), a school commissioner, and a surgeon in the 4th Regiment of Kings County Militia. John was a prosperous Horton farmer and merchant. A third brother, Samuel Denison Brown, was also a medical doctor. Another of her brothers, Charles Henry, was a prosperous farmer who died childless. Julia, one of Marie Frances's three living sisters, was married to a medical doctor, Harris Otis McLatchy, MD, who also resided in Horton. Marie Frances's youngest brother, Fred-

An early photograph of Frederick Borden's home. The man seated on the step resembles Frederick Borden but is not specifically identified. *Courtesy Ken Bezanson*

erick, a merchant known as a "gentleman of dignity and culture," later employed in the Mines Office in Halifax, was reputedly "among the best known men" in the county; his daughter married Robert Borden's brother, John William Borden. From her family's prominent public profile we may infer that Marie Frances shared her husband's commitment to education and public service.

Frederick William Borden was born into this comfortable, cultivated, public-spirited, and well-connected Annapolis Valley family on 14 May 1847. Named Frederick after his mother's youngest brother and William after his father's brother (who died a year later), Frederick William was an energetic, gregarious, and curious boy and for seventeen years his parents' only child, the focus of their care and attention. An incurable optimist, Frederick "detested inactivity and chafed at indecision."[22] He spent much time in the company of his father, absorbing his values and sharing his interests in education, music, medicine, the militia, and public life. Known in later life as a sociable "joyous old boy and something of a scamp"[23] who liked to dance and sing, Frederick learned from his father how to play the violin, a hobby that he enjoyed for the rest of his life. Frederick's violin became a prized possession and in later years an object of scandal to his sterner, sober-sided

contemporaries, who complained of his enjoyment of raucous social
gatherings where he readily "joined the boys playing accompaniments
to the singing."[24] Frederick was probably more ambitious and entrepreneurial than his father, and possessed greater opportunity to cultivate
his interests, ambitions, and entrepreneurial skills.

Much of Frederick's boyhood and early life seems to have been spent
predominately in a male world that included his father, his maternal
uncles, private schools, the military, business, and politics. His mother's lingering illness and early death (when Frederick was fifteen) may
explain partially the absence of documentary references to his relationship with her. It may also account for his loyal attachment to his
maternal family and their legatorial generosity towards him, a generosity that he reciprocated even before he entered the Canadian cabinet
(where soon there were more Browns than Panets in the Militia Department!). Whatever the reason, when Frederick was not in Canard, he
was in Horton at the prosperous farm of his childless Uncle Charles
Henry, where he was a great favourite of his aunt, or in Wolfville, at
the stately home (later occupied by the president of Acadia University
and now its alumni office) of his bachelor maternal uncle, Dr Edward
Lothrop Brown, Horton Township's Reform member of the Legislative
Assembly (MLA) from 1847 to 1859. Dr Edward was known as a "literary and poetical mentor,"[25] and he assisted Frederick with his studies,
especially Latin, and encouraged his interest in education, medicine,
the militia, and politics.

At home and at his uncle Edward's residence, Frederick could
scarcely have escaped the heated, infectious political discussions of
his time, especially since provincial politics in Horton Township had
become something of a family quarrel between his maternal uncles,
Edward and John. The latter, a wealthy local merchant and farmer
and the younger of the two,[26] had challenged and defeated Edward
in the South Division of Kings County in the election of 1859. In 1864
Dr Edward Brown, who had become a Conservative candidate, perhaps owing to Charles Tupper's free public school policy, returned
the compliment. Subsequently he broke with his party over Confederation and retained his provincial constituency in 1867 as a Liberal
Anti-Confederate.

In Britain and the colonies, education and the liberal professions,
especially law and medicine, were class markers, a preserve of the
gentry.[27] The choice and direction of Frederick's education, therefore,
suggest his family's values, social standing, and aspirations. Given his
family's commitment to public education, Frederick may have attended
a public primary school in Upper Canard before enrolling in Acacia
Villa Seminary. Founded in 1852 by Joseph R. Hea, Acacia Villa was a
privately funded institution that was attended later, then staffed briefly

Acacia Villa School, circa 1900. During Frederick Borden's tenure, the school was ruled by a Methodist disciplinarian charged with educating the region's elite. *From M.V Marshall,* A Short History of Acacia Villa School *(Wolfville, 1963)*

by his uncle Andrew's son, Robert Borden.[28] For an annual cost of about £30 a year, the school provided the sons of a local elite, especially sons of master mariners, with a basic academic education and instruction in "polite and gentlemanly habits and manners." The seminary was a small, rigorous boarding school, known until 1860 as Lower Horton Seminary. Located in Horton Township's central town plot and overlooking the Minas Basin, it housed ten to fifteen students, to whom it offered a broad, genteel, and "thorough scholastic training," especially in languages, including Greek and Latin. The school's founder offered students full fluency in French and insisted on conversation using the Ollendorff method.[29] From 1860 until 1907, the school was under the principalship of Arthur McNutt Patterson, MA, a graduate of Mount Allison University who had taught for several years in Lower Horton. Patterson was described as a practical man and a disciplinarian, and there was no doubt of the institution's strict Methodist orientation.[30] Rigorous, regimented, and disciplined, the school was designed to prepare boys for entry into business and "the several maritime provincial colleges."[31]

Life at Acacia Villa cushioned Frederick from his family's transformation. The deaths of his step-grandmother Mary in 26 October 1861 and his grandfather Perry on 30 May 1862 were only the beginning, though they were his first close encounters with death. More immediate and potentially traumatic was the death of his mother on 22 November 1862, followed by his father's rapid remarriage to Mrs Mary May Woodworth on 6 August 1863, and the birth of a half-sister, Maria Frances (named after Frederick's recently deceased mother) on 15 May 1864, just nine months later. Dr Borden's re-marriage (officiated by the Reverend William Sommerville, the Presbyterian minister, at the home of the bride's father, John M. Caldwell, high sheriff of Kings County from 1855 to 1881)[32] increased substantially the size of the Borden household, since the widowed Mary May Woodworth brought four children to the marriage.[33] Her recently deceased husband, John Bowles Woodworth, and four of their children had died during the great diphtheria epidemic that swept the area in the first three months of 1859, leaving her a widow with two daughters and two sons. Only the eldest daughter was older than Frederick. While his mother's death must have been a painful experience for a fifteen-year-old boy (the age at which Jonathan had lost his mother), no reminiscence or reference has been found of his reaction to her death. Frederick's absence at Acacia Villa, then at Kings, may have insulated him from some of the immediate effects of her death and of his father's suddenly enlarged family and altered household.

Encouraged and assisted by his father and his uncle Edward Brown, Frederick emerged at the age of sixteen from Acacia Villa well prepared for the spring matriculation examination that was required for entry to Kings College, the Church of England's University in Windsor that aspired to educate the province's elite. Of the twenty boys who sat the spring university entry examination at Windsor in 1863, including those who had attended the university's own Collegiate School, Frederick ranked fifth. Among the candidates from Acacia Villa was Henry Chipman, the son of Levrett de Veber Chipman, a prosperous Cornwallis farmer and hardware merchant and later a Liberal member of Parliament, from one of the county's most prominent families; Henry would accompany Frederick to Kings and later to Harvard Medical School. Frederick's family's choice of Kings College for their son underscores the family's social standing or/and aspirations.

Frederick's family's approach to religion was inclusive and ecumenical, an approach that would mark his own public life. Established in the province's evangelical heartland and swept periodically by religious revivals, beginning with Falmouth's own Henry Alline (1748–1784), Frederick's family is unlikely to have escaped the social and spiritual upheaval that ensued. As Free Will Baptists, though not particularly active or dogmatic adherents,[34] Frederick's parents might have been expected to send their son to the Baptists' Acadia College in Wolfville. Their eloquent choice, however, was the more reputable, elitist Church of England institution in the neighbouring community of Windsor.

Convocation Hall, Kings College, a space to educate the colonial gentry. *From F.M. Vroom,* Kings College: A Chronicle 1789–1939 *(Halifax, 1941)*

While it is tempting to see their decision as a case of class trumping religion, Frederick's Uncle Edward was a life member, generous supporter, and advocate of Kings; his advocacy and the institution's quality may have been sufficient reason to justify their choice. Although Kings remained an unapologetically Church of England institution, the college no longer barred dissenting students from graduation by imposing sectarian religious requirements; nor were dissenters obliged to attend either the Sunday morning or the afternoon services conducted according to Church of England rites, so long as a student supplied the university president each term with written certification from his pastor that he was in regular attendance at their "dissenting" services.[35]

In August 1863 Frederick, then only sixteen years old, strong, lanky, and tall for his age, arrived at Kings College to begin the regimented, highly structured, three-year program of studies required for a Kings bachelor of arts degree. He was one of the youngest of the nineteen male students in his first-year class. The youngest was fifteen and the eldest twenty-two; most, including Henry Chipman, were nineteen years old.[36] Situated on a sixty-nine-acre site, the university's newest building, Convocation Hall, was an impressive stone structure that served as both an assembly hall and a library.

Although Kings was much larger than Acacia Villa, the college's discipline, routine, hierarchy, and regimentation closely resembled that at Acacia Villa. In the college's barrack-like residence,[37] Frederick occupied a sparsely furnished bedroom in one of the building's several compartments, which consisted of two bedrooms opening onto a common study. From 15 August, when the first of the two academic terms began, until 15 June, when the second term ended, a student's life obeyed an almost unalterable routine, except for a welcome month's vacation at Christmas. The school day began with a wake-up bell at 6:30 a.m. and the arrival of a male servant who built a fire and prepared breakfast in the student's room, a daily reminder of the student's gentleman status. A half-hour later the still-drowsy boys were to be seated in the chapel for matins, after which classes began. At 3 p.m. the boys were more than ready for dinner in the common dining hall; prayers followed at 3:30 p.m. Then homework, recreation, and supper (taken in their study) preoccupied students until the ten o'clock bell announced lights out.

Kings' curriculum followed the familiar English pattern that was designed to develop manly, disciplined, taciturn, and cultivated gentlemen, natural and productive leaders of society. Five masters, steeped in the English grammar school tradition, instructed the students. Among the masters was a very reputable scholar, Dr Henry How, the author of *Mineralogy of Nova Scotia* (1869), then at the height of his career.[38] The college's strictly structured, though broadly based, curriculum required students to concentrate on five general subject areas, carefully organized into graduated levels, each area supervised by one of the five masters. These areas were the Humanities, which included the Greek and Latin languages and the translation of Euripides, Homer, Thucydides, Livy, and Horace; Mathematics and Physics, a course that began with arithmetic and advanced to the study of the binomial theorem, dynamics, hydrostatics, astronomy, and differential calculus; Theology, for which non-divinity students might substitute Art; Natural Sciences, principally chemistry and geology; and Modern Languages, an area that offered instruction in French, German, and Spanish but required students to specialize in one. Kings' broad classical curriculum fed Frederick's intellectual curiosity that included the historical, technical, and metaphysical. Altogether this English-inspired elite education was designed to create a transatlantic moral community of shared cultural and social habits and values.

Students sat three sets of examinations: at entry (matriculation), mid-program, and finals. Most students spent four years completing their program, but those who finished in three were obliged to wait until the fourth year to receive their degree. Frederick and his friend Henry Chipman completed their degree in three. Out of the twenty-nine students examined by the college masters in early April 1866, Frederick ranked third overall, and he tied with one other student for the top grade in Mathematics, a useful base for his future business endeavours. He received a second class in the Natural Sciences and Modern Languages (French having been his choice), a third class in Classics and a fourth in Theology; he appears not to have substituted Art for Theology.[39]

However disciplined, monastic, and otherworldly a Kings education may have appeared, it was far from insulated from its community and the turbulent times. After all, its mandate was to prepare the province's elite for public service. The Reverend Dr Robert Fitzgerald Uniacke, the evangelical Church of England social reformer, reminded his audience of their mission in his 1866 Encaenia address entitled "Progress: The Destiny of Man,"[40] an address that could only have fed Frederick's lifelong faith in progress and public service. Perhaps the troubled times in which they lived, the conclusion of the American Civil War, the rumours of Fenian invasions, and the emotive debate over the union of British North America, spoke to Kingsmen even more urgently than Uniacke on the need and importance of leadership, public service, and social commitment.

A sterner and immediate reminder of their civic obligations was the college's newly formed cadet corps. Frederick's decision to join Kings' Cadet Corps as a private immediately upon his entry to the college led to a long and distinguished military association. Sometimes seen as "the quintessential, patriarchal" institution, as a hierarchically structured, deferential family obsessed "with lineage, genealogy and continuity,"[41] the militia provided Frederick with the security of order, rank, and uniforms, a congenial combination of class, male culture, and civic responsibility that he shared with his father and his uncle Edward, both members of the local militia. Kings possessed a particularly active cadet corps, composed of forty of its fifty or so students. Cadets engaged in drill and rifle practice, the highlight of the year being the provincial rifle competition. Nothing, however, could match their excitement in March 1866 when their cadet corps, in which Frederick had been promoted to lieutenant, was called out on active duty during rumours of a Fenian raid, an engagement for which Frederick later received a Fenian service medal, created when he became minister of militia.

It was also during that same exciting spring, Frederick's last term at Kings, that he attended an anti-Confederation rally in Windsor, "almost the first meeting of the campaign," probably in the company of his uncle Edward, who was decidedly opposed to Confederation. There

Frederick would have heard William J. Stairs, A.G. Jones (a future House of Commons colleague), and "other Halifax men" denounce "Tupper's Confederation scheme,"[42] a political analysis doubtless reinforced by his uncle Edward, who broke with Charles Tupper on this divisive issue. Frederick left Kings with a lively interest in public life and a broad classical education that reinforced and encouraged a commitment to civic virtue, a family perspective overlaid with an "Anglican and hierarchical view of society,"[43] one that entailed duty and social obligation.

In August 1866, scarcely five months after he had been called out to defend his country against the Fenians, Frederick followed his father's footsteps to Harvard Medical School. Both Harvard and Boston offered a stark contrast to Kings and Windsor. Boston was a dynamic, bustling urban community of some 250,000 persons, whereas Windsor possessed only 3,300. And Harvard Medical School alone had six times more students than Kings. Yet for all these stark differences, neither Boston nor Harvard was entirely alien or unfamiliar to a descendant of *Her Majesty's Yankees*, especially with the familiar accents, growing bluenose population, and tall ships in port. Of the medical school's 306 students, 27 alone were from Nova Scotia, including his old Kings classmates Henry Chipman, Clarence David Barnaby from Cornwallis, James William Harris from Lower Horton, Charles Inglis Margeson from Wilmot, Augustus "Gus" Clarke (Frederick's future brother-in-law) from Canning, as well as his second cousin Henry Frances Borden (Dr A.K. Borden's son) from North Bridgewater.[44] (Dr Jonathan Borden's stepson, William Sommerville Woodworth, graduated from Harvard Medical School in 1873.)[45]

Harvard Medical School required candidates for the MD degree to be twenty-one years of age, to be of good moral character, to possess a bachelor's degree (or Latin and a course in experimental philosophy), to serve three years in professional studies under the supervision of a general practitioner, to complete eighteen courses, and to write a dissertation. Although the program consisted of "two short repetitive years" of study, it rewarded the graduate with the authority of science, and "a vehicle for social mobility," for an "entrepreneurial middle class."[46] For this, the university charged $200 per year in fees, plus $5 for matriculation and $30 for graduation. These charges, in addition to room, board, and travel, represented a considerable expense, indicating the commitment and financial capacity of families of students to support their children's education. This was an expenditure that Frederick's father would be obliged to cover for his stepson, William Sommerville Woodworth, who, as noted above, graduated from Harvard in 1873. Two months after his twenty-first birthday, Frederick returned to Canard with a Harvard medical degree, having graduated on 15 July

1868 with a dissertation on some aspect of *Historica medicale*.[47] His possession of a BA from Kings had enabled him to complete Harvard's requirements for the medical degree in two years. The medical school must also have credited him with a year's previous practical apprenticeship, perhaps with his father or uncle, or both.

Upon his return to Cornwallis Township, Frederick applied immediately for the required provincial licence to practise medicine in Nova Scotia, an application that required his personal appearance before the Provincial Secretary.[48] (Not until 1872 did the provincial legislature pass legislation to regulate the qualifications for the practice of medicine and surgery, granting control of entry into the profession to a provincial medical board.) The Provincial Secretary's certificate was granted promptly on 9 September 1868, upon Borden's presentation of his Harvard certificate.[49] By then, about half of the province's medical practitioners possessed medical degrees. Once licensed, he assisted his father for almost a year before beginning his own practice at Canning, about eight kilometres away, a community where he could apply his recently acquired medical knowledge and establish his autonomy while remaining well within the shadow of his prominent and supportive family.

In Canning Dr Borden secured an office where he received patients, heard their complaints, diagnosed their ailments, treated their maladies, and prescribed remedies, a mixture of sympathy, consolation, advice, pills, and plasters that he concocted on site. Treatment required a range of procedures: presiding over childbirth, extracting teeth, setting bones, and bandaging. In the process, the practice of medicine established privileged, confidential relationships and moral and financial obligations (patients often paid in kind) that bound patients to physicians. It gave physicians intimate knowledge of the community, imbued them with status and authority, and made them obvious spokesmen of community interests. On call day and night, and in all weather, medical practice meant travel and house calls, fluctuating demand, irregular hours, and uncertain compensation.[50] With four other practising physicians in the village vying for the limited medical trade, Canning was something of a saturated market. While Dr Borden continued to practise medicine in Canning for the next twenty-seven years or more,[51] at least until he entered the Laurier cabinet, he began shortly to seek other sources of revenue to supplement his income. One of the additional sources of income was trade, an occupation governed by confidence and trusted family networks.

CHAPTER 2

Business

Early in his career, Borden seems to have decided that medicine was not the only path to material comfort and social standing. However strong his professional commitment to medicine may have been, alone it offered very modest material and personal rewards. Had he restricted his income to the community's fragmented professional market, he might have enjoyed a livelihood no more lucrative than that of his father. Frederick's rising expectations and ambitions, perhaps whetted by his sojourn in Boston, encouraged him to seek means to supplement his relatively meagre income. A customary practice among contemporary physicians, occupational plurality was not confined to labourers and artisans at the time.[1] Much depended upon local opportunity and the ability to manage affairs, to profit from and contribute to the community's economic welfare.

When the young Dr Borden arrived in Canning in 1869, the village was in transition. A thriving, dynamic community of some 600 persons, Canning grew up on one side of the "narrow winding" bank of the Habitant River. On the other side of the Habitant stretched a broad, fertile meadow. Over time the village became an active market centre and tidal port that could accommodate as many as "eleven little 150 ton freighters,"[2] a political economy that married land and sea. When Borden settled in Canning, the village was probably at the peak of its local influence, reputed to be "one of the most flourishing and promising villages in Nova Scotia."[3] A casual visitor, however, might have dismissed this small, compact village as little more than a two-kilometre tree-lined street, running east and west, roughly parallel to the Habitant River. But Canning was more than that.

Upon inspecting the town more closely, a stranger could not help but be impressed by the large, well-constructed wooden houses that lined both sides of the often-muddy street, some in a Georgian and others in the popular gothic revival style, the houses connected by wooden sidewalks. The village's architecture was a monument to the skilled craftsmen who gave the community its reputation as one of the finest shipbuilding centres in the province. The shipyards, mill, forge, and two- and three-storey warehouses, shops, and commercial build-

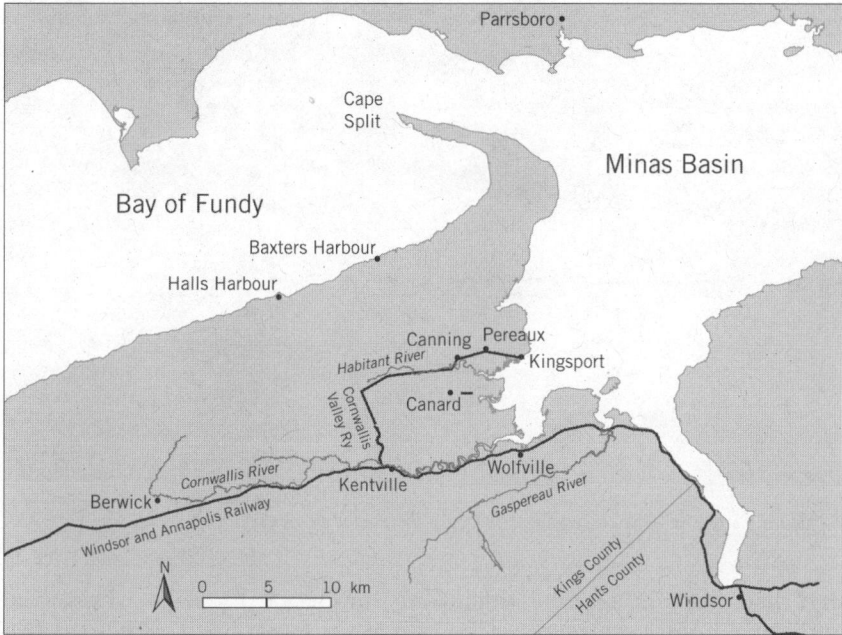

Map of the Kings County region. *Courtesy Sherry Olsen*

ings, many with tenants in upper flats, located largely on the Habitant side and concentrated along the eastern third of the street, closer to the Minas Basin, suggested the community's industry and commercial importance.[4] Three Protestant churches – the Wesleyan Methodist located in the east end, the Free Will Baptist in the west end, and the Regular Calvinist Baptist in the centre – testified to the centrality of religion in this reform Protestant village and to the broad consensus, rather than conflict, that described the community. Indeed, some of the "wealthy merchants" held "pews in all three" churches.[5] Canning also supported a school, situated close to the Free Will Baptist Church, four doctors, a hotel, a post and telegraph office, and a newspaper, the Kings County *Gazette*, at least until August 1866. In fact, the village seemed to posses all the amenities of a small town, all except "a fire engine or fire organization of any kind," not even "a hook and ladder company,"[6] an oversight that proved almost fatal to the community.

When the young Dr Borden began his practice in Canning in 1869, the village was recovering from the second of two devastating fires. The first had begun early Saturday morning, 15 July 1866, in the stores of Edward Harris, a conflagration that levelled Canning's thriving business section. In about three and a half hours, fifty-three build-

Canning, Nova Scotia, at low tide. *Courtesy Fieldwood Heritage Society*

ings had been consumed, including lumberyards, mills, shipyards, and seven homes on the opposite side of the street.[7] Altogether the fire had destroyed an estimated $120,000 worth of property, of which only $20,000 was insured.[8] The community, however, was so prosperous and confident of its continuing commercial potential that within two years "every store and house had been rebuilt," some with larger, better buildings.[9] Scarcely had the last building been restored than a second fire, on 1 July 1868, barely two years later, destroyed much of what had been reconstructed, this time levelling forty buildings, including twenty-six stores.

Although Canning had been called Apple Tree Landing before 1830,[10] the village's initial prosperity owed more to the potato than to the apple and to its relatively easy access to the Fundy.[11] Situated in the Annapolis Valley, a stretch of deep rich soil two to seven miles in width that ran from the Annapolis Basin to the Cornwallis River, the village was sheltered by the north and south "mountains." Most of the population of Kings County lived either along the Fundy–Minas Basin coast or in its five rich river valleys, particularly the Cornwallis river valley that stretched from Kentville to Kingsport. The valley's chief occupation was agriculture that produced a lucrative export market in livestock, hay, potatoes, and, later, apples. This trade was organized by a mercantile community composed of merchants, shipbuilders, and shipowners, loosely knit together by ties of family, business, and politics, a network of family capitalism.

While the 1844 New England potato blight created a lucrative market along the eastern seaboard for Nova Scotia potatoes,[12] Kings

County farmers soon discovered a more dependable market across the Fundy. Given New Brunswick's notorious neglect of agriculture during the high days of its great timber trade (its legendary potato culture arose later on the depleted timber lands), it was no coincidence that the potato, a low-cost cash staple, became king in the Annapolis Valley when New Brunswick was but "one vast lumber camp."[13] In 1861 Kings County, Nova Scotia's most productive potato growing area, alone harvested 858,551 bushels of potatoes, the equivalent of one-fifth of New Brunswick's total potato crop. Hay was in no less demand in the lumber camps and could be grown without fertilizer, with yields of two to three tons per acre, on the wide, flat dyked marshland of the Minas Basin. Backing onto the Cornwallis Valley, in a coastal area otherwise short of ports, Canning became the Cornwallis river valley's chief point of access to the Fundy and the city of Saint John, the destination for these exports and other produce that found a lucrative market among New Brunswick's voracious army of lumbermen.[14] To exploit that market Cornwallis Valley "farmers came for miles around, their ox-carts piled high with good Bluenose potatoes to load on vessels moored at the landing sometimes eleven deep."[15]

Many, if not most, of these vessels were built in Canning, renowned as a shipbuilding centre. There or nearby could be found all the principal resources for shipbuilding. The north ridge of Cape Split grew large stands of beech, birch, and maple, while its southern slope was covered with "a heavy growth of soft wood, spruce of various kinds and fir."[16] Canning also possessed some of the province's most renowned shipbuilders. The village's best-known shipyard belonged to Ebenezer Bigelow, a talented designer, merchant, and religious zealot, who constructed some of the largest and best vessels in the province. But Charles Northrup and the blacksmith Charles Lockhart had shipyards in Canning as well and built good vessels, as did W.H. Church at Kingsport, close to the government wharf, and Jonathan Steel at Scott's Bay.

In striking contrast to the people of Kentville (the county's seat of municipal government, with administrative offices, a courthouse, a regional post office, law offices, hotels, and inns), Canning's workforce was more skilled, commercial, and agricultural. Although Kentville counted twice the population of Canning in 1860, Canning possessed only eleven labourers as compared to Kentville's seventy-six. Canning's prosperous shipbuilding workshops, however, made it home to a hundred carpenters, in contrast to only thirty-five in Kentville. A community of merchants, Canning boasted at least twenty-seven, who were mostly commodity and wholesale distributors, whereas Kentville's ten merchants handled a wide range of retail goods. No barristers lived in Canning, while Kentville provided employment for six. Similarly, Canning had sixteen mariners, whereas Kentville had none. As the county's chief port, Canning was home to the county's chief collector of customs, with sub-collectors posted at Wolfville, Port Williams, Kingsport, Baxter's Harbour, Hall's Harbour, and other coastal outlets.

A profile of Canning's pluri-occupational workforce suggests the community's artisan and mercantile character even though the majority of its male workers were farmers, at least for part of the year, many with town lots backing onto prosperous farms. A discernible social hierarchy existed within the village, described roughly by occupation, wealth, and family, with shipbuilders "fewest and wealthiest," followed by well-travelled sea captains, merchants, then farmers. But in a place and at a time characterized by occupational pluralism and overlapping family ties, social distinctions were not always so clear-cut or decisive. Some families, like the Bigelows, were shipbuilders, captains, merchants, and farmers. Moreover, within the community, farmers, professionals (such as teachers and doctors), mariners, carpenters, and merchants owned shares in ships, although the ownership and management of vessels, here as elsewhere, was concentrated in the hands of merchants.[17]

In the absence of sharp social, economic, religious, or other ideological cleavages in this community, family largely defined a person's place in the community and governed his or her social, economic, and political relationships. Organizing the area's commerce were mercantile clans composed of merchants, shipbuilders, and shipowners, loosely knit together by family, business, and political interests. In Canning, the co-partnership of three brothers-in-law, Stephen Sheffield, John Leander Wickwire, and Edward M. Beckwith, constituted one discernible clan. Another was the merchant-shipping partnership of the Clem and Robert Dickie Company, which worked closely with the partners' uncle, David Matthew Dickie, a Canning merchant, shipowner and Liberal MLA for Kings County (1867–71), and they might join the Sheffield/Wickwire/Beckwith clan in a project such as the construction and ownership of the *Habitant*, an 1,800-ton sailing ship. A third clan consisted of Benjamin Baxter Woodworth; his half-brother Douglas Benjamin Woodworth, teacher, lawyer, Conservative MLA (1871–78), and member of Parliament (1882–87) who married a daughter of the wealthy Conservative Senator Ezra Churchill; and his other half-brother George Whitfield Woodworth, the editor and publisher of the Canning *Gazette* who married a Churchill daughter as well; they worked closely with J.E. and C.E. Eaton. In contrast to these clans, John Hopson Clarke, another respectable, prosperous Canning shipowner, community leader, merchant, justice of the peace, and Dr Borden's future father-in-law, occupied a more independent place in the community. He had married Elizabeth Tupper, Sir Charles Tupper's first cousin, and had been an unsuccessful Conservative candidate and had worked with any or none of the other mercantile clans.

In retrospect, Canning's two devastating fires were prophetic. The peak of the village's commercial growth and glory was over, less because of the fires, destructive and demoralizing as they had been, than owing to a restructuring of the county's economy, best symbolized by the arrival of the Windsor and Annapolis Railway (W&AR) in 1869, headquartered in Kentville, a line that bypassed Canning and drew trade and traffic along land lines. The railway heralded the slow decline of the region's old wind, wood, and water economy that had flourished so successfully at mid-century and from which Canning and other Fundy ports had profited so handsomely. Fuelled by the California gold rush, the Reciprocity Treaty of 1854, the Crimean War, and the American Civil War, this buoyant mercantile economy had drawn functional borders that had defied provincial and national boundaries and made the Fundy part of an eastern seaboard community of trade, people, ideas, and customs.

The arrival of the Windsor and Annapolis Railway (renamed the Dominion Atlantic Railway in 1894) one year after Confederation, however, announced the advent of a new land-based economy that created new borders and centres of gravity. Slowly but surely the railway restructured the Fundy's commerce, drawing people away from the coastal areas and funnelling the Cornwallis Valley's commerce from its Fundy ports to inland rail centres, principally Kentville, where the construction of the W&AR literally "changed the centre of the town."[18] Soon Kentville became the county's commercial as well as administrative centre. For example, during the decade of the 1870s, while the county's population grew 9.1 per cent (in contrast to the provincial average of 14 per cent), the population along the W&AR "increased by over 15%."[19] Between the years 1861 and 1891, the population of the rail stops grew phenomenally. Wolfville's population increased from 1,566 to 1,963, Berwick's from 872 to 1,738, and Kentville's from 1,488 to 2,526, whereas Canning's remained static.[20] And both Kentville and Wolfville were incorporated towns by 1893. Canning's merchants did not accept their eclipse passively. They were pragmatists and adapted to these realities as best they could, devising new strategies and exploiting new opportunities. Their construction of the Cornwallis Valley Railway (CVR) in 1885, a twenty-two-kilometre line connecting Canning to Kentville, was as much recognition of Kentville's centrality as an attempt to draw trade through its Fundy port.

In short, the W&AR was the instrument of a larger regional socioeconomic transformation in which the old sea-orientated mercantile economy of wind, wood, and sail gave way gradually to a land economy in some areas of the province based on coal, steel, and rails, but in Kings on commercial agriculture. The most visible and disturbing manifestation of that transformation in Kings was the exodus of its population, especially of its young and single residents, driven either by lack of opportunity at home or drawn by more attractive prospects abroad, especially to "the Boston states." Consequently, between 1871 and 1911 the county's population grew by only 426 persons.[21] While many of these migrants came from the coastal areas and initially moved inland and subsequently out of the region, others came from the county's small farms and woodlots, persons who were unable or unwilling to adapt to alternate, more specialized land uses dictated by opportunities and changing market demands.

The most obvious example of the county's changing land use was the remarkable growth of commercial fruit farming, more particularly pomiculture. In the wake of the collapse of the New Brunswick timber trade, the decline of Saint John, and the rise of the competitive New Brunswick potato culture, a growing transatlantic demand for apples offered a profitable alternative market for valley farmers, at least for those with sufficient land and capital to break into this large, lucrative market. Those who adapted to the new economy soon discovered that their relatively frost-free fertile valley soil produced a variety of durable species, Ribstons, Pippins, Blenheims, and Gravensteins, produce that was especially valued in the British market and a market that valley farmers practically came to monopolize up until the Second World War. In 1880 Nova Scotia exported about 20,000 barrels of apples, and by 1911 it was exporting 1.5 million barrels, largely to London and Liverpool.

The industry, however, required large acreages, relatively long-term capital investments, and knowledgeable managerial techniques, assets accessible to only a small number of landholders. Few could afford to wait the eight or so years for trees to mature and begin to produce. The reasonably good land prices offered by those who sought larger acreages gave small landholders an attractive incentive to sell their less competitive small holdings and seek opportunities elsewhere, within or increasingly outside the province. Small holdings were consolidated and held by fewer proprietors, and most were put to orchards. In 1889 over 100,000 trees were planted. Livestock, lumbering, small fruit, and market gardening offered other profitable, complementary employment. The county's economic transformation was not instantaneous, of course, and for years the old and new economies cohabited, often in apparent harmony. The economic transformation was a process of erosion rather than trauma, an opportunity that offered rich rewards to agile entrepreneurs.

Canning offered a good example of the dynamics of the transition, of the slow and graceful decline. Although its busiest, most prosperous period had been between 1850 and the great fire of 1868, subsequent alternative employment opportunities, changing land use, and the creation of small tertiary industries (such as the Kerr Vegetable Evaporating Company, which began production in 1884 with thirty employees)[22] helped sustain this community and cushion its decline. Moreover, the continued residence in this village of retired persons of means and regional entrepreneurs who demanded social amenities such as a seminary for young ladies,[23] a village library, a bank, and a weekly newspaper (the Canning *Gazette*) gave the community an air of industrious gentility. Consequently, Canning's stagnation appeared less obvious to contemporaries than it has to historians, largely because the decline was gradual, gracious, and non-linear. Those who knew how to manage the transition, to appreciate that landward and seaward industries could grow simultaneously and reciprocally, that good profits could still come from exploiting the short-run coastal trade, benefited handsomely from it.[24] The demand for shipbuilding, especially the construction of smaller craft, continued to grow until 1879 and perhaps later.[25] For example, Canning continued to construct medium-sized vessels, such as the 380-ton *Barteaux* (1909), the 408-ton *Cape Blomidon* (1919), and the 435-ton *Fieldwood* (1920), until after the Great War.

Few of Canning's citizens contributed more to or benefited more from the region's transformation than its new resident, the well-educated, versatile, restless, congenial young Dr Fred Borden, as he became known and who soon became "the leader in all local improvements."[26] An ambitious, imaginative, pragmatic person of versatile interests, personable, optimistic, decisive, and well organized, Borden discovered that the local economy's transformation created attractive and profitable opportunities. Aided by marriage and inheritance, he shrewdly identified his own interests with those of his community and mobilized the area's social, material, and political resources to their mutual benefit. Although he had been born into a nuclear family of relatively modest means, by the time of his death in 1917, his real and personal property was valued at some $300,000 ($4.5 million in today's terms), much of it made in and from the region before he became Canada's minister of militia and defence in 1896.

In Canning the most obvious way to begin a portfolio was to invest in the region's two principal securities, ships and land. Canning, like other regional ports and shipbuilding centres, offered a familiar means of sharing the risks and potential profits from shipowning through a simple partnership system, suited to an area where trust was embedded in extended family and friendship networks. In this system, farmers, teachers, doctors, and other local notables with small sums of accessible capital might purchase shares in ships; traditionally the total number of shares available was limited to sixty-four shares per ship. One trusted shareholder, called the master owner, held the purse, kept accounts, and distributed the profits. While the control of ships remained in the hands of small but recurring clans of local merchants whose number of shares may have determined the quantity of space their products might occupy in the outgoing and incoming voyage, non-merchants, as well as some merchants, held shares for purely speculative purposes.

Familiar with Canning's commercial culture, Borden began to place some of his spare capital and income in vessels. His choice of partners was significant. Initially he purchased shares in vessels controlled by Stephen Sheffield, John Leander Wickwire, and E.M. Beckwith, or the John and Clement Dickie families, or the Wolfville merchant Rufus Burgess, commercial clans with close Liberal and family ties. While it is difficult to identify the full extent of Borden's holdings, ten years after his arrival in Canning he possessed at least six shares divided equally between two trading vessels, one of which was the *Recovery*, a 1,012-ton barque whose principal shareholder was the Rufus Burgess. In 1885 he purchased two shares in the two-decked 1,618-ton vessel the *Habitant*, built by Jonathan Steele at Scott's Bay and sailed by his next-door neighbour, Captain Henry Potter, and in which Sheffield, Wick-wire, and Beckwith were the principal shareholders. The total esti-mated value of Borden's shares in ships by 1885 was $1,600.[27] By 1896 Borden owned or was the registered owner of two vessels, the *Amos Brown,* a 132-ton vessel,[28] and the *Harold Borden*, a 142-ton vessel named after his only son, and he held a controlling interest in a third vessel, altogether an estimated investment of $8,250 for the ships in which he was the registered owner or controlling shareholder.

Borden's other entrepreneurial obsession was land, an increasingly profitable asset that he began to acquire almost immediately after his arrival in Canning. Initially his land purchases were confined to Canning, especially along the northern side of the Habitant River, to provide an office and home and his home's subsequent extension and improvement. In April 1880 Borden shrewdly purchased a valu-able house and property on Main Street from Edward Harris for only $2,100, a property that Harris had bought for $4,000 and on which he had done some $1,000 worth of repairs. The "Old Place," as Borden initially named it, later bore the grander, more dynastic title "Borden Place." It is now a federal and provincial registered heritage property.

What was the source of Borden's investment capital? Although phys-icians possessed a privileged access to a community's trust and confi-dence, there is no evidence to suggest that Borden's medical practice generated much surplus income, though he continued to practise medi-cine until after he entered Laurier's cabinet in 1896.[29] Family inheritance and marriage, however, brought assets that enabled him to extend his property holdings beyond Canning, to include property in Cornwallis, Lower Horton, and Wolfville. His father's death on 15 January 1875, for example, brought Borden a small inheritance, roughly twenty-six acres of land in Upper Canard. The rest of his father's modest estate, estimated to be worth no more than $8,000, was required to provide for his father's second wife and their twelve-year-old daughter, Maria Frances, Frederick's half-sister and of whom he became a guardian. As an executor of his father's estate, along with his uncle Andrew, Frederick was obliged to defend claims against the estate lodged by his maternal uncle John L. Brown and James W. Caldwell,[30] the latter a first cousin of Borden's stepmother.

Much more profitable was his inheritance from two of his maternal uncles. In 1882 the death intestate of his childless Uncle Charles Henry Brown, in Wolfville, enabled Borden to procure about forty-five acres of mostly dyke land in Wolfville and Horton Township. His uncle's widow, who was especially fond of her nephew, sought the court's permission to have Frederick act on her behalf in settling the estate. In the process he not only secured claim to his deceased mother's portion of her brother's estate, but purchased the property rights from various other family claimants, a transaction that cost him $900 but which brought him property that he claimed before the Probate Court was worth about $1,500,[31] an example of his business acumen.

Two years later Borden received a more lucrative inheritance from his bachelor uncle Dr Edward L. Brown, with whom he had spent so much time as a small boy. Since Frederick's Uncle Edward had willed his entire estate to his two sisters, Frederick, as his deceased mother's only heir, had claim to half his uncle's property. This property included four acres of dyke land, an undetermined amount of upland, his uncle's well-appointed residence, and other buildings in Wolfville, as well as a farm on Gaspereau Mountain operated by John Atwell.[32]

Similarly, Borden's marriage in Canning's Wesleyan Church[33] on 1 October 1873 to the nineteen-year-old Julia Maude Clarke had enhanced his assets, standing, and opportunities within the town's influential commercial community. Julia's father, John Hopson Clarke, Esquire, was one of Canning's leading merchant shipowners; and her brother, Dr Gus Tupper Clarke, had been one of Frederick's Harvard classmates. Clarke's prominence in the community enhanced Borden's access to the confidence of a wide spectrum of the community's commercial elite.

Of more immediate material importance was his father-in-law's estate. When J.H. Clarke died on 4 May 1888, his estate, whose value in 1872 was estimated to be between $75,000 and $100,000, was probably closer to the upper limit. In his will, Clarke stipulated that his only living daughter, Bessie (whom Frederick married on 12 June 1884, four years after the death of her sister, Julia), receive $6,000. Moreover, Clarke's will specified that each of Borden's three children born of his first marriage receive $2,000, to be invested in real estate until their marriage or until they came of age. The Clarke inheritance gave Borden a large sum of working capital to be invested in land and in ship shares.[34]

In addition, Clarke's will established a comfortable legacy for Elizabeth, his sixty-year-old widow, who joined Borden's household following her husband's death, a legacy that Borden undoubtedly also managed. The remainder of Clarke's estate was left to his only son, Gus, then a medical doctor in Parrsboro, who later settled in Canon City, Colorado. Gus, however, had no interest in continuing his family's business, and when he failed to sell his father's stores, barns, and other property on the open market,[35] Borden offered to manage and later to purchase the properties. Possession of Clarke's Canning business gave Borden control of a substantial local enterprise, as well as standing in the community's commercial life comparable to that once occupied by his late father-in-law.

In addition to the roles played by marriage and inheritance, Borden's access to the working capital required to buy out Gus's claims, as well as those on his late Uncle Charles Henry Brown's estate, was almost certainly aided by his appointment as agent for the Bank of Nova Scotia in September 1882, the bank's first agency in Canning. Nova Scotia physicians frequently held bank agencies, perhaps because doctors were often educated and impecunious, and enjoyed the community's confidence. Although Borden himself received a generous annual fee of $1,000 and a commission on the business,[36] the bank's daily routine was handled by a junior clerk – and not always satisfactorily – who received $100 a year. Typically Borden filled the clerical position with relatives, first with Aubrey Melbourne Borden, from November 1885 until May 1886; then by Frederick Alexis Borden, from 1889 until May 1891; and then by John William Borden,[37] his uncle Andrew's son, whom he later brought to Ottawa to help manage the Department of Militia. Borden, however, took his banking sufficiently seriously that he became a member of the Canadian Bankers Association,[38] identified himself in legal documents as a physician and bank agent,[39] and when the Bank of Nova Scotia transferred its Canning agency to the Halifax Banking Company in 1891, he retained the agency until he entered Laurier's cabinet in 1896.

More important, the agency gave Borden access to credit and knowledge to complement his clinical intelligence of people and their financial standing, a power that enhanced his influence and material interests

within the Canning and district mercantile community. At least that is
the tenor of a bank supervisor's report to the district manager in 1888.[40]
With a paucity of evidence, it is difficult to determine precisely how he
managed affairs to his own advantage, but it is possible to imagine. His
access to the bank's financial resources, his privileged knowledge of
the credit constraints and potential of land buyers or sellers, his ability
to grant or withhold credit, all gave him an enviable access to information, trust, and advantage. Borden's later correspondence describes a
complex network of notes signed by him or by others for him,[41] and
suggests that in some instances he provided bank credit to needy farmers against his own account, probably with a lien on their property or
on a maturing crop,[42] on which he might foreclose or use at election
time to secure support.[43]

Whatever his means, shortly after Borden assumed command of the
Canning branch of the Bank of Nova Scotia he launched an extensive land-buying campaign. He had been defeated in the June 1882 federal election and was now free to pursue single-mindedly his business
plans. His subsequent purchases brought him property on the North
Mountain, Pereau, Cape Blomidon, Scott's Bay, Kingsport, Kentville, Grand Pre Dyke, and Gaspereau Mountain, purchases that often
included buildings, barns, and stores. Occasionally his purchases were
made in partnership with his Liberal friends, Robert C. and Clem B.
Dickie (Frederick's half-sister, Maria Frances, married Fred W. Dickie
on 28 November 1888),[44] or Delancy Sheffield. As a result of his land
purchases, by 1896 Borden possessed some four thousand acres of real
estate, but he had still not satiated his land hunger. During the year
1883 alone, he registered twenty-eight separate land transactions at the
Kings County Registry Office in Kentville, many to settle claims on his
uncle Charlie's estate.

Real estate offered various commercial opportunities. The county's
emerging pomiculture placed a premium on land prices. With acre-
age in great demand, land sales fetched cash. Accepting mortgages was
also profitable. Some shrewd land agents extracted mortgage rates as
high as 10 per cent. Borden's own lands could also be mortgaged for
investment capital. Exploiting this market, he placed some of his land
in mortgages. He dyked his marshlands and sold what he did not need
for $100 to $300 per acre, depending upon its proximity to the sea-
wall.[45] While some of his land purchases were speculative, held for a
better price, others were exchanged for adjacent properties to consolidate his holdings for more ambitious, productive purposes.

A portion of Borden's land purchases consisted of timberland to
feed his steam-driven lumber mill, which he had purchased in Lower
Blomidon and to which he added a door and sash factory. On other

land he planted extensive orchards and cash crops. At Pereau, he established a 150-acre farm, said to be one of the largest in the province, where he raised livestock and a dairy herd, grew wheat, planted an apple orchard, and maintained a cranberry bog. In an inventory that he compiled after fire devastated the 150-by-60-foot livestock barn in 1900, Borden claimed possession of 90 cattle, 15 horses, 100 sheep, and 50 acres of wheat, which, together with barns, machinery, and other farm produce (including 135 tons of hay and several thousand bushels of potatoes and turnips), he estimated to be worth $20,000.[46] To maximize income from his farm, Borden established the Cornwallis Creamery Company. His orchards were valued at $25,000 and his cranberry bog at $6,000. Nearby at Kingsport he owned a wharf, dyke, and dyke land valued at $100,000. There, working closely with Jonathan Steele, a shipbuilder and political ally, he grew potatoes and hay for export to the West Indies, probably shipped aboard his schooners. His ships, the *Harold Borden* and the *Amos Brown*, traded as far as the Caribbean. In a relatively short period, Borden came to own or hold an interest in a series of small, local, presumably profitable, loosely integrated land- and sea-based enterprises.

Meanwhile, in the late 1880s, Borden obtained two stores, one in Canning that had previously belonged to J.H. Clarke, his deceased father-in-law, and the other in Blomidon. Both were wholesale and retail outlets, operated in cooperation with Richard W. Kinsman, William R. Potter, R.D.G. Harris and C.V. Anthony, the latter a Scott's Bay farmer, lumberman, and agent. To manage the stores at Canning and Kingsport, which sold groceries, hardware, feed, and flour, Borden formed the Cornwallis Trading Company, which also operated a weekly freight and ferry service, the SS *Brunswick*, between Canning and Saint John. Borden held a controlling interest in the company.

Like many other "Maritime capitalists,"[47] Borden invested in a range of local public services and utilities, conveniently combining public service and personal profit and demonstrating a confidence in the "new" economy. Among these enterprises were the Valley Telephone Company and the Canning Water and Electrical Light Heating and Power Company (1893), whose board read like a directory of the county's Liberal hierarchy. Later, as his assets grew and his reach lengthened, Borden's holdings encompassed shares in the Nova Scotia Electric Light Company and the Nova Scotia Telephone Company.[48]

Finally, in October 1895, Borden decided to consolidate his various assets under the corporate name of F.W. Borden Company Limited, with an initial capital stock of $50,000, shortly increased to $250,000, of which $100,000 was paid up by 1897. The company's broad terms of incorporation describe both Borden's existing assets and his larger

The SS *Brunswick*, the property of Borden's Produce and Supply Company, leaving
Canning at high tide. *Courtesy Fieldwood Heritage Society*

entrepreneurial designs and aspirations. Under the terms of its incorporation, the F.W. Borden Company possessed the right to own, buy,
and sell lumber, real estate, and personal property, including vessels,
wharves, piers, scows, and telegraph, electrical, and telephone lines.
It had the right to construct and operate telegraph lines (the company
already owned thirteen miles of telegraph lines), telephone lines, railways, and tramways (clearly Halifax was within its purview) in connection with its business and to conduct a general commission business.
Two years after the company's incorporation, Borden raised a mortgage of $186,000 on the strength of its assets.

Borden's entrepreneurial success, then, was scarcely a "rags to riches"
tale. Family, marriage, inheritance, and social standing brought valuable material and social capital. Nevertheless, in building his local
business empire, Borden demonstrated a shrewd eye for opportunity, a
pragmatic flexibility, and the ability to coordinate and manage the old
and new economies, including the social relationships of family, business, and politics. In short, he demonstrated an awareness of the synergy of private and public interests. Although Borden had not abandoned his interest in medicine, by 1896 medicine had been eclipsed
by his business activities. After the June 1896 victory of the Laurier
Liberals, however, both business and medicine had to make place for
his increasingly active public life.

CHAPTER 3

Back Bench

In his 1866 encaenia address entitled "Progress the Destiny of Man," the Reverend Dr Uniacke had reminded Kingsmen that they constituted a provincial elite and that public service was a civic obligation. For an entrepreneurial, imaginative, articulate young man, raised in a prominent political family, steeped in a classical education, during the "heroic" age of politics, an age of "great" men and great causes, Borden needed little urging to engage in public service, especially as his own material interests increasingly became tied to those of his community. And as Thomas H. Ferns and Robert Craig Brown have pointed out, "Politics in 19th century Canada was about business."[1] Irresistible a magnet as material interests may have been, for Borden politics possessed other attractions. It offered access to a wider world of people, places, and ideas, an opportunity to negotiate and conciliate public and private interests, and it promised social advancement.

The health of a community's economy often depended upon commercial and transportation policy and the provision and maintenance of public works and services. In a community's pursuit of breakwaters, wharves, and lighthouses, customs and postal offices, tariffs, subsidies, and freight rates, contracts and government offices, its competitive advantage required the services of an effective public representative, a person who could articulate, negotiate, and advance its interests. The creeping power of the regulatory state, with its commitment to the development of infrastructure, created a political demand for persuasive power-brokers and lobbyists with inside knowledge and influence, men who could procure charters, franchises, subsidies, and service contracts. An informed, reliable community voice and lobbyist, Borden proved an effective representative of his community's interests in federal politics.

Even within a relatively homogenous community, various political visions and economic interests competed for recognition, a contest formally resolved through a political process familiar to a community of Planter origins and religious dissent. Effective local power, however, was more complex than this formal mechanism might suggest. Within the parliamentary system, not only did the bases of political power remain local, personal, and reciprocal, but economic and political interests were frequently fused.² Although agriculture was the principal occupation of Kings County, within "the free masonry of politics" effective political and economic power rested in the hands of its merchants, who were usually united by close family and business ties, a pattern familiar to contiguous communities in Canada and abroad.³ For example, of the nineteen men who represented one of the various Kings County constituencies in Halifax from 1784 until 1867, twelve were merchants, three were physicians, two were farmers, one was a barrister, and the occupation of the other is unknown. Similarly, of the fourteen men who represented Kings County in Halifax from 1867 until 1900, six were merchants, three were lawyers, two were farmers, one was a physician, and two were managers. Moreover, at least eleven of the fourteen post-Confederation representatives were related through birth or marriage to men who had previously held elected office.⁴

In other words, Kings, too, had its family compacts, not unlike other Canadian counties and regions.⁵ And no family had dominated Kings County's political life more consistently or effectively than the "Chipman Compact," as that family was known locally. Since 1784, a Chipman had held one of Kings' constituencies for sixty-three of the first hundred years. Patrician, prolific, and active in the economic, religious, Masonic, and social life of the county, the Chipmans had managed government patronage with a discerning skill, careful to retain as much as possible for their family and friends.

Chance and circumstance, however, could upset even the most entrenched local compact, as Borden's entry into federal politics demonstrated. Borden had resided in Canning scarcely four years, and had been married for less than four months, when duty, personal interests, community pressure, and opportunity, any or all of these possible influences, propelled him into federal politics, a world from which he never withdrew, even after his final defeat in 1911. The timing and narrow success of Borden's entry into federal politics in 1874 owed much to the confusion that characterized post-Confederation politics in Nova Scotia.

Nowhere was this confusion more apparent than in Kings County. There the county's patronage-hungry "Reform" incumbent, Leveret De Veber Chipman, the forty-three-year-old son of William Henry Chipman, the county's original anti-Confederation MP, had flirted with the governing Conservative Party ever since he succeeded to his father's seat by acclamation in 1870. At times he had voted with the government, on other occasions with the Reform party, as personal interest and patronage might dictate. Inter-community rivalry between Kentville and Canning, along with Chipman's crass political ambivalence, had created so much dissention within the ranks of the county's Reformers that an "independent" Reformer, J. Leander Wickwire, a prominent Canning merchant, had challenged Chipman in the 1872 federal election. A Kentville merchant and banker and the commanding officer of the 68th Battalion, Leveret De Veber Chipman had little difficulty defeating Wickwire by a significant margin of 604 votes, having obtained 64 per cent of the votes cast. So decisive was Chipman's victory that Wickwire refused to become the party's sacrificial lamb two year later, thereby opening a place for Dr Borden.

With Alexander Mackenzie's Reformers in power following the Pacific Scandal, Chipman had every intention of contesting Kings as a Reformer, ever appreciative of the benefits of office. His unexpected repudiation by the Reform hierarchy in Ottawa, less than three weeks before the election, however, changed all that. Since the party hierarchy was determined to find a candidate "who was a real friend of the Government,"[6] their intervention obliged Chipman to seek endorsement from the Conservative Party and Kings' Reformers to find an alternate candidate. When, ten days before the election, Wickwire refused to stand again for election. Canning's Reform merchants, led by J.L. Wickwire, Stephen Sheffield, Edward Beckwith, and Clem and Robert Dickie, persuaded Dr Fred Borden to be their candidate, his youth, energy, and family's political standing in the area being his most obvious credentials.

Borden's mandate was a formidable one, especially for a twenty-six-year-old novice, even one from a family with solid Reform credentials and the backing of Canning's Reform merchants. In less than ten days and in the dead of winter, he was expected to deliver what Wickwire had failed to secure two years earlier, to unseat Chipman, a man who seemed to view the constituency as a "hereditary right."[7] In more personal terms, the contest obliged Borden to confront the commanding officer of the 68th Battalion, the militia unit to which he, his father, and uncle belonged, and the brother of his old classmate Dr Henry Chipman. If he won, it would also mean leaving his recently married, and now pregnant, wife, Julia, the nineteen-year-old daughter of the prominent Canning merchant John Hopson Clarke. To make matters more difficult, soon after the election began, Borden, who seems to have been accident prone, slipped on the icy doorstep of his home and injured his knee sufficiently seriously that he was obliged to campaign on crutches. Meanwhile his opponents circulated the story that he had fallen because he had been completely intoxicated. This alleged personal failing would haunt his political career, even though, according to his own testimony, the young physician was then a total abstainer and still a member in good standing of the local Temperance Society.[8]

In Borden's favour were the county's traditional Reform sympathies, the spoils of office available to a government candidate, a weak and disorganized provincial Conservative Party, the tide of moral indignation elicited by the Pacific Scandal, and various local issues, the most damaging of which was the W&AR rate increase, decreed by Order-in-Council, thirteen days before Prime Minister John A. Macdonald's resignation. Making the most of this sensitive local issue, Borden blamed the rate increase on Chipman's complicity or negligence, a charge quickly repudiated by the railway's politically partisan general-manager, Peter Innis, a future provincial Conservative candidate. Borden may also have benefited from the support and standing of his father-in-law, the prominent Canning merchant.

Whatever the case for or against Chipman and/or his party, the electoral contest enabled Borden to secure a slender majority, though success was far from certain on the evening of the election of 5 February 1874. The electoral returns from the outlying areas were slow to come in, since roads were blocked by snow, and these votes were essential to his success. When the final tally was made, however, the county sheriff declared Borden elected by a slender margin of 98 votes, that is to say, he had secured 54 per cent of the votes cast. Chipman had performed well in the towns, particularly in his hometown of Kentville, but his success was more than offset by Borden's support in the rural and coastal areas. Borden also seems to have benefited from his party's general popularity, since Kings had replicated the provincial trend: nineteen of Nova Scotia's twenty-one constituencies had chosen Reform candidates.

Borden's slender margin, though sufficient, together with the exceptional circumstances surrounding his nomination and election, augured a tenuous political future. An unknown, inexperienced politician, Borden had not been called to Ottawa by his party's power-brokers. He had been the last-minute, almost desperate choice of a handful of Canning merchants, too uncertain of the outcome to risk their own candidacy. The county's constituents, however, had endorsed Borden. Although he was more the choice of those from the rural and coastal areas, the Canning merchants saw him no less as their agent. In the future, his success would depend upon retaining their confidence. But if he failed, he could expect no safe seat to be opened for him. He was on his own, and he accepted the challenge.

Borden was one of only a fraction of members of Parliament who were under thirty years of age.[9] A photograph of Borden taken four years after he arrived in Ottawa pictures the young physician as a sensitive, even delicate, balding young man, his face framed by mutton chops. Behind that gentle appearance was an energetic, optimistic

Dr Borden, a balding
thirty-year-old member of
Parliament, his face framed by
his trademark mutton chops.
*Courtesy Library and Archives
Canada, PA25597*

young man, entrepreneurial and versatile, and a cautious gambler. A
survivor by nature, he was a man who dared. Conciliatory and gregarious, he soon learned how to build bridges, purchase silence, and
conflate personal, public, and political interests; he was a power-broker
rather than a mere cipher. Above all, he knew his constituency well,
its family networks, personalities, and power structure. His political
approach was personal, practical, and reciprocal. And his political
durability owed much to his inclusive manner, his organizational and
executive ability, and his assiduous attention to constituency details,
including control of the locally generated electoral lists. In the thirty-
seven years between 1874 and 1911, including seventeen years in opposition, Borden suffered only two defeats, although in the words of one
of his contemporaries he never acknowledged defeat, he experienced
only "ups and downs."[10] During that time, Borden became an effective
constituency representative, the master rather than the agent of local
power. Through hard work and durability, he eventually became a
party figure of national standing, one whom Laurier did not hesitate to
make part of his winning team in his 1896 "cabinet of all the talents."
But that was all in the future.

Dr Borden's new career began immediately. Scarcely six weeks after
his election, the young doctor left Canning, leaving his pregnant wife
in the care of her parents, for a two-month stint in Ottawa, to take his

seat in the first session of Canada's Third Parliament. Canada's relatively inaccessible national capital, only a sixteenth the size of Boston
(the only other large city Borden knew), must have seemed raw and
alien at first, little more than a small, dirty lumber town. Apart from
Ottawa's recently constructed Parliament buildings, the architectural
pretensions of this city of sawdust and civil servants must have fallen
far short of Borden's eastern seaboard standards of civic splendour.
Lodged in a boarding house, away from his friends, wife, and family,
and unfamiliar with the rules and customs of the House of Commons,
he may have questioned his hasty decision to enter public life.

Borden, however, adapted relatively easily and quickly to the small,
male parliamentary fraternity. Among the other 205 members of the
Commons were men whom he would support and oppose for the
next several decades. They included the recently elected member for
Drummond-Arthabaska, Wilfrid Laurier, only six years Borden's senior, a man marked from the beginning (he would second the resolution in reply to the Speech from the Throne) and with whom Borden
would establish a close and lasting personal and political friendship;
James Domville, the loquacious, self-important, Conservative member
for Kings, New Brunswick, who would later give Borden more trouble
as a Liberal member of Parliament than he had as a Conservative; and
Sir Charles Tupper, the able, influential representative from Cumberland, one of the four Conservative members from Borden's province,
a former provincial premier, a father of Confederation, Macdonald's
closest colleague, and a first cousin once removed of Borden's wife.
There were few medical doctors in the House. Businessmen, however,
were well represented, though most of the members claimed more than
one occupation.[11]

Although a young, untried government backbencher, Borden asked
questions of the government and sought information on constituency
issues, notably the fate of the Windsor and Annapolis Railway, initiatives graciously endorsed by Tupper, who may have entertained hopes
of bringing the young member into his Conservative fold, given the
liquidity of post-Confederation politics in Nova Scotia.[12] Much united
the two men: both were ambitious, energetic, university-educated Nova
Scotia physicians committed to public health and education. Both
came to enjoy a national and imperial career. Although the member for
Cumberland extended every courtesy to his young colleague, on one
occasion intervening to assure him speaking rights, Borden retained
a distance from Tupper's political views, conscious of the fate of his
opportunistic predecessor, Leveret De Veber Chipman.[13]

Ottawa's political climate offered much to cheer an ambitious, gregarious government backbencher from Nova Scotia. As far as Borden

could see, Alexander Mackenzie's government had begun well. Even before Borden had reached Ottawa, the prime minister's close friend and confidant, George Brown, the trenchant editor of Toronto's *Globe*, had gone to Washington to negotiate a reciprocity agreement, and prospects for its success appeared encouraging at first. Had an agreement been concluded, it would certainly have been welcomed enthusiastically in Borden's Fundy-bordered county, "the largest agricultural constituency in Nova Scotia,"[14] and would have aided the young physician's chances of re-election; so too would his party's proposed electoral-reform agenda, especially his Baptist leader's commitment to temperance. In addition, the recent general election had given the Reform Party a comfortable majority of sixty seats in the House of Commons, thirty-five of them from the Maritime provinces. More encouraging still, across from Borden sat a temporarily discredited and demoralized Conservative opposition.

In the long run, however, the government's political prospects were less promising. All too soon the trade depression would deepen, the prospect of reciprocity would fade, and the Mackenzie cabinet, torn by conflict and indecision and weakened by defections, would appear less sympathetic to the claims of the Maritimes, a region Mackenzie's acerbic minister of finance, Richard Cartwright, unkindly dismissed as "the rags and patches" of Confederation. And that said it all. Despite the Maritime provinces' decisive support for the Reform government, the region was poorly represented in Mackenzie's cabinet, and the government's subsequent bungling of the tariff on shipbuilding tools, its abandonment of the promised Baie Verte Canal, and periodic insensitive pronouncements from George Brown's Toronto *Globe*, the government's voice and mentor, soon tarnished the party's reputation and standing in the region.

In contrast to the Reform Party's apparent lack of sympathy for the region, the ascendancy and power of Charles Tupper and Leonard Tilley in the Conservative Party, both fathers of Confederation and former premiers of their respective provinces of Nova Scotia and New Brunswick, made the Conservative Party appear to be a more responsive, effective guardian of Maritime interests, and in subsequent federal elections the Maritime electorate would respond with gratitude. While initially Borden may have benefited from his party's promise and his opponents' unsavoury reputation, his long-term political survival would depend largely on what happened in Kings, not in Ottawa; in other words, upon Borden himself.

That Kings generally resisted the subsequent regional Conservative ascendancy in federal politics during the next two decades was a tribute to Borden's personal and political skills and tenacity. Nonetheless, his hold on his constituency remained precarious. Every federal election between 1874 and 1896 was closely contested and decided by slender majorities. During these ritualistic contests, while the high electoral rhetoric focused on tariffs, rails, reciprocity, and regional resentments, personality, patronage, and local issues often determined the content of ballot boxes. In this battle, Borden's affable, conciliatory, inclusive manner, organizational skills, and conscientious attention to constituency details compensated for his lack of access to the federal spoils of office. Nonetheless, Borden was not entirely bereft of the benefit of public favours, since the provincial Liberals who held office from 1867 until 1925, except for the period 1878–82, provided competing compensatory rewards that helped recruit and retain Liberal partisans in Kings as elsewhere.

Warm, accessible, and efficient, Borden employed every means to win friends and influence people. Coroners, school commissioners, justices of the peace, postmasters, customs collectors, sub-customs collectors, and numerous other petty offices in the gift of government purchased or cemented partisan loyalties. Borden himself was appointed a provincial coroner in 1875. Since the Nova Scotia electoral law charged municipalities with the compilation of the federal and provincial electoral lists, the strategic battleground for the lists was the municipal government.[15] Throughout his career, Borden kept a vigilant eye on municipal elections, instructing his local political operatives, who were often business partners, to make certain that municipal councils were composed of "reliable men ... to look after the voters lists and do other things in accordance with the wishes and interests of party workers."[16] In short, his local political organization was a "neo-traditional machine" built largely upon a pre-existing local cluster of clientele networks.[17]

Seen from our contemporary perspective, Borden's most striking long-term electoral liability was his dependence on the declining coastal mercantile communities in his constituency, those areas that had supported him in 1874 and continued to constitute the backbone of his support in the years to follow. Unfortunately for Borden, an exodus from the coastal areas of the county to more favourable interior locations within it, such as Berwick, Wolfville, and Kentville, the strongholds of his political opponents, or farther afield, many to New England, threatened to sap his political strength. To make good this loss, Borden faced the political challenge of finding a way to expand his electoral base in the interior without alienating the support of his coastal constituency, a challenge that he met by bridging and reconciling the "two economies."

Throughout Borden's career, two large interrelated public issues dominated the political economy of his constituency: reciprocity and the w&ar. Conscious of the importance of the coastal economy's access to markets in the United States, the West Indies, and Latin America, Borden lectured the House relentlessly on the folly of Macdonald's protectionist strategy and lauded the virtues of reciprocity. In his view, reciprocity followed the "natural laws" of economics and geography, and he was confident that a restoration of the Reciprocity Treaty of 1854 would revive the towns and villages in his constituency "to the old prosperity which they enjoyed between 1854–66."[18] A policy of protection, he contended, was the most "obnoxious kind" of taxation, one that failed to shut out hard times but merely shut them in. In the House and during elections, Borden belaboured this conventional party doctrine, buttressed by local details, examples, and statistics. While the rhetoric was tediously familiar, it possessed an attentive and appreciative audience among farmers and those residing in the coastal areas of his constituency, for whom the exodus of the young was visible and real. It was also heartily endorsed by his merchant supporters and business partners.

Traditionally, a close companionship existed between farming and shipping, a relationship that the politically partisan w&ar increasingly challenged by drawing agricultural traffic away from the ports, though the railway's erratic performance often made it an undependable competitor. The railway's partisan character, however, was never in doubt. In fulfilment of an 1863 election promise, Charles Tupper's government had chartered the w&ar line, and Tupper remained one of the railway's principal shareholders, under the name of C.H.M. Black.[19] In Ottawa, he continued to advance the company's interests from his vantage in the federal cabinet, and after 1879 as the first minister of railways.

But the issue was more complicated than personal partisan benefit. Almost from the beginning, competing private interests, public ambivalence, and political machinations bedevilled the troubled railway's management and development. To provide the railway access to the lucrative Halifax market, in 1871 the Canadian government leased its publicly owned "Windsor to Halifax" line to the w&ar in return for a stipulated fee and its agreement to operate a specific number of trains and extend the line to Yarmouth, to serve the western counties of Annapolis, Digby, and Yarmouth. When the w&ar failed to meet these conditions by 1873 and was $30,000 in arrears to the federal government, Macdonald's government, just before it left office, passed an Order-in-Council, made law by the Mackenzie government on 24 May 1874, transferring the government's Windsor-to-Halifax line to a third party, the Western Counties Railway Company, which was committed to extending the line to Yarmouth by 1 October 1879. The same Order-in-Council authorized the cash-poor W&AR to increase its tariff, in itself an unpopular political decision in Kings.

While freight rates increased, service deteriorated, and the W&AR lobbied the government for compensation for the loss of its "rights" to the Halifax market. To make matters worse, when the marginally more successful Western Counties Railway Company failed to complete an eighteen-mile gap between Annapolis and Digby by October 1879, the government resumed control of the strategic, more lucrative Windsor-to-Halifax line. As a result, western county shippers and travellers to Halifax faced the inconveniences of negotiating alternative conveyance over the "missing link," as it was called, as well as the changing rates and timetables of three companies.

No one doubted the railway's growing economic importance to Borden's constituents who lived along its line, particularly in the market centres of Wolfville, Kentville, and Berwick. Nor was there any doubt of the railway's dependence on the government or the company's continuing, blatantly partisan political character. Both Barclay Webster, the W&AR's solicitor, and Peter Innis, its general manager, contested Kings at various times for the provincial Conservative Party. And during provincial and federal elections, the company made no secret of its patronage and endorsement of Conservative candidates; for example, during the 1896 federal election, a company locomotive ran from Kingsport through Canning to Kentville with a sign exhorting the electorate to "Vote for Bill," Borden's opponent.

Nonetheless, Borden pleaded the railway's case in the Commons, occasionally in defiance of his party's policy, conscious of the railway's importance to the economy of his county.[20] Although he was not in the House when the Mackenzie government enacted legislation transferring the Windsor-to-Halifax line to the Western Counties Railway Company, he worked and spoke against the transfer and argued for an amendment to the Act giving the W&AR a right of compensation for the transfer.[21] Above all, he persistently reminded the House of the cost and inconvenience of the missing link and the absurdity of three companies operating such a short line, especially for the valley farmers, an absurdity that cost "almost as much to bring freight from Montreal to Windsor Junction as it does from Windsor Junction to Bridgewater."[22] Similarly, he had no hesitation in denouncing the discriminatory rates that the government charged the W&AR for running cars to Halifax's new North Street terminus, that is, two dollars and fifty cents per car as opposed to the one dollar per car charged to the Intercolonial Railway's Eastern Extension that ran from Truro to Pictou, a discrepancy that was difficult to explain in terms other than partisan favouritism in return for electoral advantage.

A rhetorical proponent of competition, Borden remained a relentless critic of the waste and corruption associated with the government's Intercolonial Railway (ICR). His remedy was to sell the ICR to the Canadian Pacific (CPR) or the Grand Trunk Railway (GTR).[23] Although he preferred private ownership, he was a pragmatist. And on one occasion, so frustrated had he become with the W&AR and its failure to provide a dependable, efficient, and competitive service that he suggested government ownership of the entire line, as had occurred with the Eastern Extension Railway. This way, he explained to the House, the profits from the two valley lines (the W&AR was now making a profit) could be used to complete the missing link,[24] a proposal that spoke to the interests of his constituency, though not one that the W&AR might necessarily welcome, unless the price were right.

Important as local problems might be, Borden's public interests had never been entirely parochial. From the beginning of his parliamentary career and despite his youth and inexperience, he had not hesitated to rise from his backbench obscurity to address national issues; nor was he afraid, when necessary, to take positions contrary to those of his party. Two examples illustrate Borden's perspective. Troubled by the apparent unfairness of the restrictive 1871 New Brunswick School Act, Borden endorsed John Costigan's motion for a redress of Catholic grievances, despite his party's reservations. From the beginning of his public career, Borden maintained that fairness and respect for "different religious faiths" were essential to the country's growth and harmony,[25] a position that reflected his sense of tolerance and broad ecumenical formation at home and at school. Certainly it was not a cause pressed upon him by his overwhelmingly Protestant constituency!

On other issues, time and circumstances expanded his horizons. Fascinated by the possibilities of western expansion, peopling Canada's western territory, and exploiting its resources, in 1875 Borden rose in the House to articulate the classic "Maritime view" of the "pet fancy to connect the British provinces of the Atlantic with the Pacific at their expense."[26] Although he voted in the same year for the Mackenzie government's proposed piecemeal construction of the railway, at the time he made no secret of his view that, from a Maritime perspective, the attempt to bind the provinces together with bands of steel during a depression was premature, indeed seemed an "insane project" that would impose a heavy tax burden, one that would fall unfairly on the Maritime provinces and a project from which these provinces would scarcely benefit. In his view, it might be better to follow the American example and wait until a larger population demanded and could support the service.[27]

Not surprisingly, reciprocity and the W&AR were the principal rhetorical themes of the first test of Borden's parliamentary stewardship, or so Borden grandly explained on 10 September 1878 to the lively bipartisan crowd of an estimated three thousand people who had gathered in front of the Kentville County Courthouse to hear the candidates outline the issues of the federal election, after filing their nominations with the high sheriff of the county. The highlight of the local campaign, and a political ritual, was the opportunity given to the public to compare the constituency's two contestants. Competitive and genial, Borden enjoyed argument and controversy, and although a clear, concise, and forceful speaker, he was not best "until stirred"; and repartee had always been a cultivated family game.[28]

Borden was optimistic about the outcome of the election. Farmers listened approvingly as he denounced the evils of protection that Macdonald's Conservative Party threatened to inflict on the country, as opposed to his own party's continued commitment to reciprocity. Well-organized bipartisan meetings in Gapereau, Coldbrook, Grafton, and even Wolfville turned into Borden demonstrations, victories that his disappointed opponents dismissed as the work of "trained claquers from Canning and Wolfville," little more than a poorly clad, ill-mannered but powerfully lunged "rag, tag and bobtail," fortified by strong drink (a recurring political charge that he would face throughout his political career) and "officered by illustrious names and distinguished families in Wolfville"[29] – this last doubtless a reference to Borden's well-placed Brown relatives there.

Despite his confidence, Borden confronted a formidable opponent. The Conservative candidate, D.B. Woodworth, was the sitting member of the provincial legislature, a flamboyant lawyer, and a former teacher from Canning. He was also the son-in-law of the late wealthy Conservative senator Ezra Churchill, from neighbouring Hants County. Moreover, Woodworth's half-brother had married another of Churchill's daughters and edited the Canning Gazette. D.B. Woodworth also had a talent for invective, a penchant that led to his ejection from the House of Assembly for his refusal to withdraw unparliamentary remarks.

Borden's optimism had not been misplaced. If his opponents had hoped that Woodworth's candidacy would undermine Borden's support in Canning and district, they were mistaken. Borden had been an assiduous, solicitous representative who sought every benefit of office for his constituents. During his first parliamentary term, with his party in power, Borden had concentrated on a renovation of the county's dock facilities, breakwaters, wharves, and lighthouses,[30] for which the coastal regions demonstrated their gratitude. Borden learned the extent of their gratitude when the candidates met in Kentville on 17 September 1878 to hear the county's high sheriff announce the official results. Borden had passed his first performance review, beating his erratic opponent by a 265-vote margin, garnering 54 per cent of the votes cast. Given the national fate of his party, whose standing had been reduced from 138 members of Parliament to 64, and the drop in its representation from Nova Scotia, from 18 to 7, Borden had been lucky indeed. His opponents spitefully attributed his victory to Borden's "liberal use of money,"[31] as though Woodworth, the son-in-law of the late Ezra Churchill, lacked money or was restricted by scruples. If, however, government money had purchased Kings, presumably it had been available to other Reform candidates in the province but had failed to work its magic there. In fact, Nova Scotia Reformers would not increase their provincial representation above seven seats until 1896. To compound matters, the provincial election that had been held the same day had swept the Liberals from power, leaving them with only eight of the province's twenty-eight seats.

Although beaten, Woodworth had not been vanquished. Four years later Borden confronted him once again, and during this duel Woodworth returned the favour, defeating Borden by 350 votes, Borden's only defeat before 1911. During the 1882 contest, things were quite different and especially difficult, politically and personally, although at first Borden had some reason to feel confident. Early in the campaign, the Liberal *Daily Acadian Recorder* had pronounced Kings a safe seat for the Reform Party, and Edward Blake, who had become the party's new leader in 1880, had even visited Borden's constituency. More important, Woodworth's contested nomination had divided the Conservatives in Kings. Borden's prospects for success, therefore, looked very good at first.

Borden, however, faced some serious political obstacles. As an opposition candidate and with the provincial Liberals temporarily out of power, Borden lacked access to the spoils of office, provincial or federal. Well represented in the federal cabinet, his opponents controlled appointments to post offices, customs houses, lighthouses, and, more immediately, the electoral officers, and it was his opponents who awarded contracts for wharves, piers, and breakwaters. Moreover, his own party's association with the years of depression contrasted sharply with the country's current prosperity, a condition that contradicted Borden's dire denunciations of the folly of Macdonald's protective tariff; nor had Edward Blake's equivocations on free trade left Borden with a firm alternative trade policy. And when Sir Richard Cartwright, the Reform Party's financial critic, denounced the $150,000 fishing bounty resulting from the Halifax Award (which the Canadian gov-

ernment had secured in return for American access to the fisheries),
$87,000 of which had been earmarked for Nova Scotia (the first instal-
ment of which the government conveniently scheduled during election
year), Borden may well have wondered if his party was an asset or a
liability.

Borden's party may well have been a liability, but his own record in
the House and his electoral performance were far from stellar. During
the previous parliamentary term, pressing personal difficulties had distracted him from his parliamentary duties try as he might to balance
private and public demands. His twenty-six-year-old wife, Julia Maude,
had died of tuberculosis on 2 April 1880 after a prolonged illness, leaving him a widower with three small children, Elizabeth, Harold, and
Julia "Maude," aged six, three, and one respectively.[32] Preoccupied by
Julia's illness and the care of his small family, he had neglected his
constituency duties. In fact, during the 1880 parliamentary session
that had begun on 12 February and had terminated on 7 May, he had
spent very little time in the House.[33] His parliamentary interventions
had been confined largely to local issues, such as postal services in the
small communities of Greenwood and White Rock Mills, the "rights"
of the W&AR, or some of his constituents' objections to the blockage
of fish runs on the Gaspereau River caused by sawmills. Even the controversial debate on the repeal of the prohibition of marriage between
a man and his deceased wife's sister, which took place during the 1880
and 1882 sessions of Parliament, had failed to occupy much of his time,
though it was a subject in which he had a personal interest.[34]

The strains resulting from his personal life surfaced during the cam-.
paign when he was confronted by Cartwright's damaging utterance
on the fisheries bounty and responded that he was merely a "humble
follower." This careless justification handed his opponents an effective
weapon that they used mercilessly throughout the campaign. Nonetheless, Borden did what he could to counter the growing opposition, including soliciting the support of his cousin, Robert Borden,
then a Kentville barrister, who made his political debut with a speech
denouncing Macdonald's National Policy and supporting his cousin
Dr Borden.

Despite Borden's initial optimism, apprehension gradually eroded
his confidence. As decision day approached, Borden sensed an inescapable, unnerving indifference among his friends and neighbours and,
worse, the defection of some of his supporters. His most conspicuous
and damaging loss was the support of the Honourable Samuel Chipman, the patrician farmer and merchant from Cornwallis Township,
the county's former Reform leader, MLA, cabinet minister, legislative
councillor, and a devoted follower of Joseph Howe. At 92 years of age

(he lived until he was 101) and partially blind, Chipman canvassed the constituency on Woodworth's behalf.[35]

The 22 June election day began badly. Only two hours before the polls opened, one party worker informed Borden that he had changed sides and that Borden would have to find another person to work in his place.[36] And as the day proceeded, things only got worse. The next day Kings headed the Conservative Halifax *Morning Herald*'s list of "redeemed" constituencies. Two days later, on declaration day, Borden learned the extent of his defeat when the county sheriff announced the final official count to candidates and their supporters. Woodworth had defeated him by a large margin of 350 votes, having secured 56 per cent of those cast. Nowhere had Borden been more decisively beaten than in Kentville, where he garnered only 28 to Woodworth's 142 votes.[37] In an untypically bitter speech conceding defeat, Borden peevishly blamed his loss on unidentified "rings" that had bought up the whole Dominion, and he lashed out, not against those who had openly worked against him, but against those "contemptible snakes" who had "voted against him, while pretending to be his friends." After this bitter outburst, Borden announced that he would "go back to his pills and plasters" and hoped he would receive his fair share of the trade.[38]

CHAPTER 4

Front Bench

Borden had no intention of giving up politics or confining himself to pills and plasters. Instead he spent the next five crucial years rebuilding his family life, extending and diversifying his business interests, and restoring his political fortunes, determined in the future to be more than "a humble follower" within his party. Eight years of parliamentary service had expanded his horizons, whetted his ambitions, and suggested the possible synergies between business and politics. His most immediate challenge, however, was his home life, how he might fill the void created by the death of his twenty-six-year-old wife, find a companion who could also serve as mother to his three children, and establish a stability that would enable him to maintain his family's material welfare and social standing.

A convivial thirty-three-year-old widower with a marked interest in women, Borden could scarcely have been expected to remain a widower for long. All during his wife's drawn-out illness and after her death, his mother-in-law, Elizabeth Clarke, and his sister-in-law, Bessie Blanche Clarke, had cared for his three children. On 12 June 1884, over four years after Julia's death, Borden married the twenty-one-year-old Bessie.[1] Only two years before their marriage, on 17 May 1882, the Canadian Parliament had repealed the prohibition of marriage between a man and the sister of a deceased wife, legislation that was strongly opposed by the bishops of Canada's Church of England, who tried but failed to block the measure as their confreres had done in England.

According to local legend, an unrepentant Church of England, still smarting from its legislative defeat, refused to marry Frederick and Bessie. It is difficult, however, to understand why the couple would have sought the small local Church of England's services, given the denomination's public opposition. Moreover, both Bessie and her mother were devoted members of Canning's Wesleyan Methodist Church, and its minister, the Reverend R.A. Daniel, had no qualms about performing the service. If, indeed, the Church of England had refused the couple's request, the Bordens bore the church no resentment, as its small local congregation and the church continued to benefit from

Borden's generosity. Whatever the circumstances, Frederick and Bessie were married by their local Wesleyan minister, Rev. Daniel, on 12 June 1884, in the presence of the bride's parents and Borden's stepmother, with Robert Borden, Dr Borden's cousin, and Dr Augustus Tupper Clarke, the bride's brother, as witnesses.[2]

Seventeen years younger than her husband, Bessie was an attractive, lively, articulate companion, described some years later by a reporter as a woman with "dark brown hair, which she wears in a low soft coil. She has brown eyes, a fresh complexion, and that sweet womanly expression which painters give their madonnas."[3] Educated at Mount Allison Ladies' College as her sister had been (Mount Allison was a Canadian pioneer in the higher education of women), Bessie was intelligent, sophisticated, and ambitious, a person who appreciated and cultivated the social status afforded public prominence. Active in cultural, charitable, religious, and community activities, Bessie became an invaluable support to Borden in his public career and social advancement. Only ten years older than her niece and elder stepdaughter, she also became a devoted mother to his three children, ably assisted by her mother, who joined their household four years later upon the death of her husband. Elizabeth Clarke, then a sixty-year-old widow, would remain a family fixture for the next thirty-one years and would survive her son-in-law by two years.[4] Borden's second marriage brought a stability and security to his family life that freed him to establish his business career and pursue public life, to combine and develop these inseparable ingredients of his success.

The symbiotic relationship between Borden's business and political interests makes it difficult to give primacy to political or financial motivation in explaining his behaviour and strategies, nor is it necessary, for in many ways they were fused. It was during these years, 1882–87, that Borden laid the foundation of his successful business and political careers, concentrating his business projects in the growth areas of his constituency, conveniently enjoining private and political interests. As a physician, bank agent, farmer, merchant, and mill, factory and ship owner who traded in real estate and invested in public utilities, Borden created an elaborate, paternalistic, and politically useful network of dependency, a clientele system that was personal, multifunctional, unequal, and reciprocal, not unlike the Upper Canadian system described by S.J.R. Noel.[5] Borden's ability to employ men on his vessels, farms, woodlands, mills, stores, and public utilities, to market the produce of farmers and fishers, to provide credit at his retail and wholesale stores and bank agency, and to manage provincial patronage in cooperation with his partners in business and politics proved immensely advantageous during elections. These activities and his other diverse enterprises brought him into an ever-widening web of business and political associations within the county, especially within its growth areas, where he needed and intended to build his political support.

And nothing demonstrates more clearly the synthetic relationship between personal profit and political power than Borden's infiltration of the county's growth areas in this period, a long-term strategy that paid handsome political dividends in the years to come. Immediately after his electoral defeat in 1882, Borden not only acquired the bank agency but began purchasing land in Wolfville, Gaspereau, Kentville, and other growth areas, in the heartland of his political opposition, identifying himself with the new land-based economy. At the same time he invested in public utilities, telephones, electricity, and railways, projects that tied the old and new economies together and combined profits and public service.

The Cornwallis Valley Railway Company (CVR) provides a good example. A proposed twenty-two-kilometre rail line from Kingsport through Canning to Kentville, the CVR recognized Kentville's commercial importance and attempted to funnel trade through the Fundy ports of Canning and Kingsport, a project that linked Canning and Kentville merchants. The CVR's promoters (Stephen Sheffield, the company's president; David Matthew Dickie, its secretary and a former Liberal MLA; Brenton Haliburton Dodge, a Kentville merchant and future Liberal MLA; and Frederick Borden) left no doubt of the company's Liberal credentials. Given the promoters' political affiliations, they had no difficulty securing a provincial charter by May 1887, together with a provincial subsidy of $3,200 per mile and a legal right of way. A federal charter followed upon Borden's return to Ottawa in 1887, as well the Royal Mail contract for which he had lobbied successfully.[6]

The entrepreneurial success of the CVR was soon evident. Within two years of the rail line's completion, the "Conservative" W&AR purchased the line, and its new owners sought to maximize its traffic by chartering the Evangeline Navigation Company to offer a daily steamship service between Parrsboro and Kingsport, thereby emphasizing the continuing importance of Canning's sea-linked economy.[7] A keen supporter of the project, Borden had no politics where local interests were involved; in 1892 he petitioned the federal government for a subsidy for this daily steamship service, even though the CVR had passed into the hands of the politically partisan W&AR.

Politically far-sighted as Borden's concentration on the economic growth areas of his constituency may have been, his return to the House of Commons in 1887 was more the result of fortune than design. His Conservative opponent, Woodworth, might well have driven Borden from public life had the flamboyant incumbent kept out of trouble. But the public disclosure of Woodworth's sordid involvement in a land deal on behalf of Manitoba's proposed North West Central Railway proved his undoing, even for the son-in-law of the late wealthy Conservative senator Ezra Churchill. It seems that Woodworth, in conjunction with James Beatty, QC, a former mayor of Toronto, had agreed to sponsor a Commons bill to grant the North West Railway Company 6,400 acres of public land per mile to construct a ten-mile line from Brandon to Rapid City, Manitoba. In return, Woodworth and his Toronto partner were to receive stock concessions, buy extensively into the railway, and divide equally "emoluments and gain in and around the building and equipping the road."[8] That was the arrangement.

And all might have gone as planned had the partners not quarrelled over the spoils and Woodworth refused to proceed with the bill. At this point the deal's unsavoury details became public knowledge and were brought before the House of Commons Committee on Railways and Canals. When Woodworth was confronted with the evidence of his misdeeds, his retort that "they all do it" scarcely seemed persuasive to the electors of Kings County.[9] The rail scandal finished Woodworth and Borden defeated him in 1887 by 448 votes, obtaining some 56 per cent of the votes cast, before the "scoundrel" fled to California. Borden's electoral success was of even greater significance because the federal government now (since 1885) controlled the electoral lists.

While Woodworth's disgrace was probably Borden's greatest asset in the February 1887 election, Nova Scotia Liberals insisted that the election was also about policy, reform, reciprocity, and repeal. Given Woodworth's disgrace, reform possessed a particularly moral resonance in Kings. That was clear from the beginning of the campaign. Disgusted with Woodworth's performance, prominent Conservatives volunteered to sign Borden's nomination papers. Armed with copies of the Beatty-Woodworth exchange, Borden pursued Woodworth relentlessly. When Borden's own meetings conflicted with those of his opponent, Borden's chief organizer, Wentworth Eaton Roscoe, the able, young Kentville lawyer and former supporter and law partner of Woodworth, represented Borden and hounded and taunted the Conservative incumbent at every turn. At one Conservative meeting in Victoria, the chairman of the meeting was unable to control the irate audience, worked up by Roscoe's denunciations, and Woodworth fled from the hall, fearing for his safety.[10]

Quite apart from Woodworth's disgrace, Borden's growing entrepreneurial success, his rooted, reciprocal, and multifunctional relationships with his constituents, his business knowledge and experience, and his facility with numbers made him a credible voice for a county in the

throes of an increasing exodus of its young. Borden enjoyed addressing economic issues and rarely lost an opportunity to demonstrate his
business knowledge, reminding his audience of his own entrepreneurial success and illustrating his points with local examples of the evils of
protection and the need for reciprocity, whenever possible linking the
trade issue to his opponent's corruption. Woodworth's failure to vote
for Liberal motions calling for reciprocity, Borden charged, was the
price he had paid to bring off his land deal.[11]

A significant silence, however, marked Borden's response to repeal,
the other great 1887 electoral issue, a cause close to the heart of many
old-time Nova Scotia Liberals and pressed strongly by J.W. Longley,
the articulate and ambitious provincial member from the neighbouring
county of Annapolis, not to mention by the provincial premier, W.S.
Fielding, fresh from his successful provincial election on the repeal
issue. The repeal question had resurfaced during the 1884 session of
the provincial House of Assembly when James Fraser, the fiery Liberal
from Guysborough, introduced resolutions calling for better terms or
secession from Confederation.[12] The Fraser resolutions grew out of the
province's frustrations with the federal government's refusal in 1877 to
extend or renew the "better terms" for Confederation that had been
negotiated a decade earlier.

Borden did not share his Liberal colleagues' repeal sentiments or
their interest in commercial union with the United States, and he made
no secret of his preference for parliamentary over congressional institutions. In his view, congressional institutions were cumbersome retard-
ants to popular sentiment, especially the "defunct House of Representatives."[13] The fact that Borden had been on the government benches
when his province's initial request for renewal of the better terms had
been rejected may have made the issue a bit more sensitive for him than
for others. But there was more to his opposition to Nova Scotia separatism than this.

Furious at Borden's silence and his refusal to be framed in the repeal
issue, Halifax's Tory *Morning Herald* decided to flush him out by list-
ing him as a "grit secesher," simply because he had declined to declare
himself, "content to let them [him] pass as such."[14] If the Conservatives
had hoped to provoke Borden, they failed. That Borden's chief organizer, Wentworth Eaton Roscoe, was a declared repealer and one of its
most committed and articulate advocates during the recent successful provincial election, there could be no doubt; but Borden's studied
silence on the issue, the failure of W.S. Fielding to enter his constituency (though he held meetings in the bordering counties of Hants and
Annapolis), and a reading of Borden's Commons speeches suggest that
Borden had no difficulty with Confederation. He had little confidence

in repeal as a solution to his province's ills. Nor did he have to resort to repeal to regain Kings. Hard times and Woodworth's disgrace were sufficient to secure a margin of votes over his opponent, a remarkable turn of events since the last election.[15]

Whatever the cause of his electoral success in 1887, Borden returned to Ottawa with a strong local mandate and an ambitious personal agenda, resolved to remake his political career. More secure in his financial and personal life, he returned to the Commons determined to be more than a humble follower in his party. The timing could not have been more favourable, for he returned to a Liberal Party freed from the dour, censorious moral rectitude of Alexander Mackenzie and George Brown and the leadership of their aloof, quixotic, and didactic Ontario rival, "Master" Edward Blake. The Liberal Party's new leader, Wilfrid Laurier, represented a new generation with a wider, more inclusive vision, one that Borden could share and help to shape.

Borden felt a particular affinity with the party's new leader. He and Laurier had entered the Commons in 1874, both young men, Laurier thirty-three and Borden twenty-seven. For the next four decades or more they would work together in opposition and government. Both were courtly, mannered, well read, educated in the classics, broadly formed, and articulate. Moreover, Borden shared Laurier's pragmatic, inclusive approach to the economic, religious, language, and regional issues that bedevilled Canadian politics at the time. He appreciated Laurier's leadership style, which was more attuned to a regional perspective than was Blake's. Laurier was less aloof and more gracious, collegial, and consultative than his predecessor. Under his subtle leadership the party was unlikely to have its policies hijacked by *ex cathedra* pronouncements from the Toronto *Globe*. During these years, as they worked to open the party to a wider constituency that reflected the regional, religious, and linguistic character of the country, Borden and Laurier not only became colleagues, they soon became close personal friends.

Borden was perhaps more comfortable than Laurier in the contemporary male fraternity of public life. As the *Gazette* reporter Paul Bilkey recalled, Borden was a versatile and social animal and "something of a scamp."[16] At home in the freewheeling world of Macdonald's Ottawa, Borden was no longer a member in good standing of Canning's temperance society. Gregarious, conciliatory, a political entrepreneur by nature, Borden came to enjoy the camaraderie of Ottawa's social life during his eight weeks or so of parliamentary business. His social friendships crossed party lines. Nowhere were these cross-party personal relations more cordial and jovial than among the militia lobby, that bipartisan fraternity of parliamentarians devoted to the militia's well-being that Borden joined upon his return to the House in 1887. Borden soon realized that in Ottawa the quiet diplomacy of non-partisan friendship and private solicitation reaped greater personal and political returns than character assassination and public denunciations. His own unimpeded promotions within the militia, including his promotion to lieutenant-colonel in 1893, a reward sometimes reserved for party friends, proved a case in point.[17]

Borden's more ecumenical approach to politics was reflected in his approach to public policy. A curious and restless pragmatist, interested in wider horizons, Borden was an optimist, an advocate of progress who believed in technology and efficiency. His increasing fascination with the resources, growth, and potential of the West, blunted his earlier criticism of the Canadian Pacific Railway. And as time went on he became more preoccupied with the CPR's effectiveness as an instrument of national development than with the burdens it might place on the Maritime provinces.[18] Similarly, although he remained a staunch rhetorical supporter of free trade who came from a constituency that was not a "National Policy County," he recognized that "the Country as a whole has accepted the policy" and he was willing to live and let live.[19] His compliance reflected his party's increasingly more moderate stance on the National Policy. It also suggested his own evolution from a vigilant regional spokesman to a man with a wider national vision, a man who was coming to see himself as a member of a national class.[20]

Borden's national vision and proposed party strategy corresponded with those of his party's new leader. In the post-Riel era of cultural, religious, and linguistic bitterness, Laurier seemed to appreciate Borden's openness, fairness, and pragmatism. Laurier had not forgotten his young colleague's courageous stand on the New Brunswick school question. They agreed, too, on electoral strategy, on broadening the party's base and working more closely with its provincial power barons, Louis Davies, A.G. Blair, W.S. Fielding, and Oliver Mowat, the Liberal premiers of Prince Edward Island, New Brunswick, Nova Scotia, and Ontario, turning the party's provincial strength into a federal asset. For Laurier this strategy made good sense and possessed the additional advantages of strengthening his own leadership and loosening Toronto's yoke on the party. Borden insisted that this could be facilitated by a broader, more effective organization, and Laurier seemed to agree, impressed by Borden's capacity for hard work and organizational ability.

Altogether Laurier appeared to regard Borden as a more amiable, congenial, and cooperative colleague than the older generation of seasoned, doctrinaire Nova Scotia Liberals such as D.C. Fraser, L.G. Power and A.G. Jones. As late as 1887, for example, Jones was still haranguing the House of Commons on Nova Scotia separatism and reminding the House that he, like his hero Joseph Howe, was a Canadian only by Act of Parliament.[21] Laurier had wrestled with similar demons in his own province, with those who still resented the Confederation agreement. In contrast to Jones, Borden represented a new generation, a man whom Laurier considered, "un garcon intelligent, actif et dévoué,"[22] inclusive, pragmatic, organized, and energetic. Under Laurier's leadership, therefore, Borden's chances for political advancement were strong, that is, if he could retain his constituency, an assumption that was far from assured in 1887.

However expansive Borden's personal ambitions may have been, he appreciated the local bases of his power. Reinstalled in Ottawa, he used every opportunity to promote the welfare of his constituency, resolutely cultivating the growth areas of his county, particularly the recently chartered town of Kentville. Anxious to erase his self-inflicted characterization as "a humble follower" of his party, on several occasions Borden contradicted his party's senior regional spokesmen to support his opponents' agenda. "When loyalty to his party comes in conflict with loyalty to the best interests of his county," Borden explained in the House, "then I think loyalty to his party should give way to the interests of the county."[23] Nor did Borden attempt to deprive politically hostile areas of his constituency of public works or hesitate to back the local economic initiatives of his political opponents; and rarely did he persecute his defeated opponents or remember petty differences. The partisan W&AR was the most conspicuous beneficiary of his non-partisan interventions. Proof of the success of his strategy was the promise wrung from a reluctant Conservative government to construct a new post office for Kentville, in keeping with the town's needs and pretensions, even though the town remained the heartland of his political opposition.

Even in opposition quiet, back-room diplomacy, alliances and accommodations could purchase influence, favours, goods and services, and appointments in the gift of the government, especially if one possessed a family pipeline to power. His cousin Robert Borden's move from the small Kentville law firm of John Chipman to the large, influential, and Conservative Halifax law firm of Wallace Graham and Charles Hibbert Tupper (which until recently had included J.S.D. Thompson, the former premier, currently the powerful minister of justice, and the future prime minister) gave Frederick access to political influence that he never hesitated to use or that Robert hesitated to provide. For example, on at least one occasion during the Sixth Parliament (1887–91), Robert served as a mediator between Frederick and the ruling Conservative Party, to secure Liberal support from Maritime

Liberal members for the government's renegotiation of the terms for the expired Treaty of Washington in return for political patronage.[24] Frederick's ability to deliver patronage in opposition stiffened his supporters' loyalties and vindicated his practice of conciliation. Similarly his frequent intercessions on behalf of Conservatives and their sons in search of positions did much to neutralize his opponents and reduce the degree of personal rancour in electoral contests.[25] In Borden's view, the politics of accommodation was preferable to confrontation. Opponents who could not be wooed and won might be neutralized.

Nonetheless it was a delicate balance, especially at the local level. Occasionally his treatment with "the enemy" and his preoccupation with Kentville aroused resentment among his political friends, especially among his old clientele in the coastal areas of the county. In 1894 the son of Jonathan Steele, the large Scots Bay shipbuilder and Liberal partisan who had worked with Borden and the Canning merchants for more than three decades, complained to his father: "[A]s for Dr Borden I do not think a lie would stick in his throat very long especially during election times. It does seem hard. The man you have worked and slaved for the last thirty-five years, when we want a little help from them they should turn the cold shoulder and put business in the way of others."[26]

Borden's courtship of Kentville left little to chance. With a clear eye on the larger objective, in 1891 he and his Canning business cohorts and the Kentville Liberal merchant Brenton Haliburton Dodge formed a company, the Union Printing Company, that leased and then purchased the "independent but not neutral" Conservative newspaper the *Western Chronicle*, Kentville's largest weekly journal with a circulation of 1,750.[27] Under the editorship of Harold, Borden's only son, it campaigned relentlessly for the Liberal cause. When Harold left for Mount Allison University in 1895, the editorship passed to Fred Wickwire, the youngest son of J.L. Wickwire. In 1894 the Liberals chose J.L. Wickwire's eldest son, Harry Hamm Wickwire, a barrister who had opened an office in Kentville, as their provincial Liberal candidate. His running mate in this dual constituency was Brenton Haliburton Dodge, the Liberal Kentville merchant who had invested in the construction of the Cornwallis Valley Railway. In the years to follow, Borden, Wickwire, and Dodge constituted a team that worked assiduously to promote their mutual personal and political interests. This political marriage between Canning and Kentville began to pay solid political dividends, especially after Borden became a minister. Although Kentville did not fall immediately, after 1900 the Liberals could count on breaking even in Kentville. And in 1908 the Liberals emerged with a comfortable margin of forty-one votes, a stark contrast to the 1882 election when they had been beaten in Kentville by a five-to-one margin.

By that time Borden had been instrumental in moving Camp Alder-shot to Pine Woods, close to Kentville, and had laid the foundations for the federal experimental farm in Kentville.

In March 1891 Borden needed all the help he could get in an emo-tional electoral contest that pitched "the old man, the old flag and the old policy" against unrestricted reciprocity. Although his constituency had stubbornly resisted the province's pronounced preference for Con-servative members of Parliament (except for the 1882 election), Bor-den's hold on Kings remained tenuous. The exceptional circumstances of his return to Ottawa in 1887 provided little room for complacency, particularly given his party's failure to take more than seven of the province's twenty-one seats in that election. Moreover, in 1891 some of the Conservatives' most powerful spokesmen, Sir Charles Tupper, John S.D. Thompson, and George Eulas Foster, concentrated their efforts on the Maritime provinces and were rewarded with thirty-one of the region's forty-three seats, despite the region's vaunted free trade proclivities. According to Sir Richard Cartwright, only the "shreds and patches" of Confederation (Cartwright's unflattering characterization of the Maritimes) had saved the decrepit Conservative government from defeat.

Although Borden was among the Liberal survivors of the 1891 con-test, it was a very close call. In this election he defeated his Conserv-ative opponent, Caleb Rand Bill, a Wolfville customs collector, by a mere 161 votes, securing only 52 per cent of the total number of votes cast. A political neophyte, Caleb Bill came from a prominent political family. His father, William Cogswell Bill, had been a Liberal member of the House of Assembly until 1890 and was the grandson of a late Conservative senator after whom he had been named. Reciprocity was the dominant national issue in the 1891 election, but since both local candidates supported free trade, the debate turned on personality and on which party promised the more attractive menu of local favours. The offerings were generous and varied.

During the contest, Leveret de V. Chipman, whom Borden had defeated in 1874 and who served as Bill's ever-helpful bagman, was con-vinced that Kings could be purchased. To do so he raised $1,500 in the constituency and procured "$1,000 more (presumably from Ottawa)"; all he needed, he confided to his federal contact, was an additional $2,000, which he promised to raise himself on the condition that he receive the vacant Nova Scotia Senate seat. According to Chipman, the party's failure to agree to his offer cost the Conservatives the Kings constituency, which he was confident Bill could have won with a margin of "fifty to one hundred votes."[28]

To compensate for their failure to accede to Chipman's urgent request, two former provincial premiers, Sir Charles Tupper, who had family, personal, and political friends in the constituency, and J.S.D. Thompson, the federal minister of justice and the rising star in the federal party, visited Kings in an attempt to unseat Borden. Knowing the county's sympathy for reciprocity, they focused their speeches on loyalty and the "old flag" issue, a tactic that rankled Borden, not because his own loyalty was at issue but because he saw it as a veiled attack on Laurier, his leader and good friend.[29] Family loyalties, however, ran even deeper, and several members of Borden's family rallied to his support. Above all, his uncle Andrew joined a platform party to demonstrate his unmistakable and unshakeable support, and Andrew's son, Robert Borden, Thompson's former law partner and a future leader of the Conservative party, visited Kings as well to endorse his cousin's candidacy.[30] On these occasions blood ran thicker than politics.

Borden's electoral tribulations, though, were far from over. Shortly after the election the local Conservatives, buoyed by their success in Nova Scotia generally, charged Borden's agents with bribery and asked Robert Borden's Conservative law firm to press charges. When Robert refused to have his firm charge his cousin,[31] the Tory leaders were obliged to find other counsel to petition the court, and a trial was set for 16 November 1891. Meanwhile Dr Borden, taking the high road, "discovered" that several of his agents were indeed guilty, and he immediately informed the authorities and vacated his seat. A new election was set for 13 February 1892. It was perhaps the most difficult electoral contest of his career, and he survived by a reduced margin of only 131 votes.

During the required by-election, the re-elected Conservative government concentrated its attack on breaking Borden's hold on Kings in the hope of adding his constituency to the sixteen other Nova Scotia seats they had won in 1891. Wharves, breakwaters, post offices, mail routes, public buildings, railway repairs, and construction projects were lavishly promised in return for votes. The proposed Kentville post office, which had been dropped from the estimates following Woodworth's defeat in 1887 but restored after Dr Borden's extensive lobbying, now depended upon the election of a Conservative member. A much-needed breakwater at Pickett's wharf through which farmers could ship their goods, and for which Borden had petitioned the government for years, was promised (indeed the Conservative candidate himself, C.R. Bill, had been offered a contract for the breakwater); an engineer was sent to the area to demonstrate the government's serious intent. With Kentville, Berwick, and Wolfville responding with large majorities for Bill, only the faithful support of farmers and of citizens in Canning and the coastal areas of his constituency saved Borden from defeat. Upon the announcement of his victory work on Pickett's wharf stopped immediately.

To add insult to injury, during the campaign a temporary House of Commons messenger, Sam Moore, had attended Borden's meetings to contradict any assertion Borden made that Moore considered unfavourable to the government.[32] What offended Borden most about Moore's interventions was not that his own statements were challenged or contradicted (responding to such charges was all part of a politician's job description), but that he had to bear the insolence of a "mere messenger ... whom he had sent here and there with messages, carrying letters and parcels,"[33] a reaction that revealed Borden's class-consciousness. Subsequently Borden went to great and untypically petty lengths to have Moore dismissed from his minor post, a mission he was unable to achieve until the Liberals were elected in 1896.

Soon after the results of the by-election were announced, the Conservatives, having failed to unseat Borden but still determined to drive him from public life, launched a suit in the Supreme Court of Nova Scotia, alleging that Borden and his agents had violated statutes governing elections. In their appeal to the court, David Berteaux, the plaintiff, claimed that Borden and his agents had hired and promised to pay for horses, teams, carriages, and vehicles to convey voters to the polls; had offered meat, drink, refreshments, money, loans, and other promises to secure votes; and had intimidated and exercised undue influence to induce or compel voters to refrain from voting. Borden's able legal agent, W.E. Roscoe, a friend and sometime Liberal organizer, had little difficulty raising doubts as to the credibility of Berteaux's claims, although it is difficult to imagine that there was no substance to his allegations. Doubt was sufficient, however, to clear Borden and validate his right to represent Kings in the House of Commons.[34]

Borden's success, resilience, and public exposure only added to his political stature within his party and magnified his importance within his diminished regional caucus. Upon his return to the House, Laurier made him the party's Nova Scotia spokesman in the Commons, charged with raising questions of particular local concern, such as the representations of Cape Breton coal miners, petitions from the Halifax Board of Trade, the pollution of the LaHave River, fast Atlantic steamship service, and improvements for the Port of Halifax.[35] More important was Borden's organizational contribution. In December 1890 he and other prominent Nova Scotia Liberals founded the Nova Scotia Liberal Association, which Borden served as vice-president.[36] Supported both by federal and provincial politicians, the association employed a provincial party organizer to collect funds, make promises, resolve disputes, and coordinate party strategy, much as Oliver Mowat had done successfully in Ontario. Over the next few years the success of this strategy in Nova Scotia was undisputed. In 1891 Borden persuaded Laurier to visit Nova Scotia, and he organized his leader's successful first tour of the province.

Convinced of the power of organization, Borden welcomed Laurier's decision to hold a National Liberal Convention in Ottawa in June 1893, to determine policy, construct an organization, and give visibility to the party's charismatic leader. During the convention, Borden served on several of its committees and moved the nomination of New Brunswick premier A.G. Blair to one of the convention's vice-presidencies.[37] He also called and presided over a Maritime Liberal caucus that founded the Maritime Liberal Association and chose Louis Davies as its president; Borden and W.S. Fielding became its Nova Scotia representatives on the executive. In response to Borden's growing provincial stature, the provincial press gave his activities greater coverage and praised and defended his record. In 1893 the provincial Liberal government appointed him to the newly created provincial Board of Health. While this was a political appointment, it also recognized Borden's commitment to progressive causes such as public health, a cause he pursued later though membership in complementary organizations such as the Red Cross and the St John Ambulance Association.

In the Victorian language of the time, it was during these years that Borden came to be "recognised as one of the keenest critics of the Ministerial policy from the Eastern Provinces ... and scored in those days many a good point in the cause he championed."[38] Well prepared and reasoned, his parliamentary interventions were normally good natured, informed, illustrated by stories, laced with numbers, forceful, occasionally trenchant and acidic, but rarely eloquent.[39] Although careful to keep well within the bounds of parliamentary language, he could retaliate when he was provoked. For example, during the raucous closing session of the Sixth Parliament when the hypocrisy of the wealthy Conservative member for Halifax, Thomas Edward Kenny, proved too much to bear, Borden responded:

My honourable friend who really seems to be getting more and more loyal every hour of his life – if any man were to insinuate that his loyalty was in the slightest degree affected by the fact that he has a relative occupying a position of emolument in which he had $10,000 a year for a second term – I would be the last to make such an insinuation – or if any man were to stand on the

floor of this House and say that the hon. gentleman is connected
with an institution in the City of Halifax, which, at a critical
moment a year or so ago, by its good fortune in buying a large
quantity of sugar just before the duties were increased, made one
or two thousand dollars, and to insinuate that the hon. gentleman's loyalty has been stimulated thereby, would it not be base-
ness itself? And yet, Mr. Speaker, if the hon. gentleman persists in
his cause, someday someone may do that.[40]

Several times during the chaotic Seventh Parliament, Borden's
stinging arraignments of the crumbling Conservative administration
inflicted lasting scars on the government that impressed members of
his own party. During the April 1894 budget debate, Borden launched
a concerted attack on the bankrupt makeshift national policy, its failure to deliver prosperity, and the hypocrisy and contradictions of its
authors and defenders, targeting the language of Sir Charles Hibbert
Tupper, the minister of marine, and his father, whom Borden enjoyed
needling. Subsequently, the Liberal Party published Borden's hard-
hitting and confident partisan speech and distributed it among the
party faithful,[41] a sign of his growing stature within the party. Similarly, late in the 1894 session Borden orchestrated a devastating and
well-documented exposé of the government's manipulative, inflated,
and misleading 1891 Census returns, using his own constituency as a
prime example, reading into the record letters of residents of the United
States who had been enumerated and blacksmith shops that had been
designated industries created by the National Policy. Borden's exposure created a major sensation that led the government, in defence, to
close its files to further investigation.[42] Years later the Liberals' chief
financial critic, Sir Richard Cartwright, who had great respect for
Borden and developed a particular friendship with him, recalled Borden's singular success in discrediting the government on this issue.[43]

Another cause Borden championed with some success during the
dying days of Mackenzie Bowell's bungling administration was the
Liberal critique of the Manitoba Schools Question,[44] an issue that
threatened the unity of both parties. Borden, who had broken with
the party line in 1875 to defend the rights of New Brunswick's separate
schools, was careful not to deny the validity of separate religious or
linguistic schools. Instead he concentrated his attack on the coercive
nature of the Conservatives' remedial bill, its cynical electoral motives,
an argument completely in harmony with Laurier's position. In a
highly partisan speech Borden castigated Sir Charles Tupper, the new
prime minister, for his past sins as premier of Nova Scotia, likening
Tupper's coercive tactics against Manitoba to those he had employed

to force Nova Scotia into Confederation. Borden took special pleasure in reminding the House of Tupper's similar failure to demonstrate sensitivity toward minorities when, in 1864, as premier of Nova Scotia, he introduced the Free School Act that not only abolished Gaelic and French schools but deprived the province's sectarian schools of public support. Borden's provincially focused attack smacked of a family vendetta, and his speech ran for several days in the provincial party press.[45] It was published almost immediately and distributed during the June 1896 election as "the Nova Scotian interpretation of the remedial bill." Borden's speech was probably given more prominence because it had targeted Tupper, who had assumed the direction of the fumbling and divided Tory party.

Borden's growing prominence and his effective frontal assaults on the government during its final days made the Conservatives even more determined to defeat him in 1896 and drive him from public life. More than that, the 1896 contest in Kings soon turned into a duel that matched Borden against the prime minister and drew national attention to the constituency. Although the Conservatives' electoral strategy was "to run key veterans against Liberal chieftains,"[46] they were unable to persuade Sir Charles Hibbert Tupper, the prime minister's son, to leave the safety of Pictou to take on Borden in Kings; in place of the junior Tupper, they fielded William Cogswell Bill, the sixty-eight-year-old former Liberal MLA (1878–82; 1886–90) for Kings, the son of the late Conservative senator Caleb Rand Bill and the father of the man Borden had defeated in 1891 and 1892.[47] In the absence of a better candidate the Conservatives depended upon the power and prestige of the new prime minister, Sir Charles Tupper, and his representatives to rid Kings of Borden. Sir Charles Hibbert Tupper, the solicitor general, and George Eulas Foster, the minister of finance and a former classics professor at the University of New Brunswick, opened the campaign in Kings on behalf of Bill, denouncing Borden and threatening local retribution if the constituency failed to endorse their candidate.

Borden met his opposition head on, stimulated by the rigorous contest and the regional and national publicity it had generated, confident of the outcome despite the defection of one of his dynamic organizers, W.E. Roscoe, over the schools question.[48] In speech after speech Borden lambasted Tupper for his government's corruption, notably the Soulanges Canal Scandal and his coercive Manitoba Schools remedial legislation, linking the latter to the strong-armed methods Tupper had employed to carry his Free School Act and Confederation. In turn, the Conservatives called upon Kings' constituents to defeat Borden because he was "distasteful" to the Tuppers. The message was clear: Kings would be punished as long as it defied Tupper. Since Borden's

wife was Sir Charles Tupper's cousin, Borden countered Tupper's mal-
ediction with humour, explaining to a bemused audience that "he was
not distasteful to all the Tuppers. He had married into the Tupper
family and everything was lovely."[49] Borden reserved equal treatment
for Foster, castigating him for his changing economic ideas and policies that played havoc with the economy: "one day he would announce
a change and the next day he would say it was a clerical error."[50] Borden
enjoyed playing in the big leagues, measuring himself against the Conservatives' greats.

Conscious of the symbolic and strategic importance of Kings, the
Liberals sent former Prince Edward Island premier L.H. Davies, the
president of the Maritime Liberal Association, and Nova Scotia premier W.S. Fielding to assist Borden. Even Borden's eighty-year-old
uncle Andrew, ever loyal to his nephew, once more joined the platform
party to demonstrate where his vote would go on 23 June 1896, despite
the fact that his son was contesting a Halifax seat as a Conservative
candidate.[51] Well organized and confident, the Liberals had taken both
of the Kings County seats in the 1894 provincial election, a constituency now occupied by two of Borden's staunchest political allies and
business associates: H.H. Wickwire, a twenty-six-year-old Kentville
lawyer, and Brenton Haliburton Dodge, a Kentville merchant whose
father, a merchant and county treasurer, had represented Kings as a
Liberal in the legislature from 1882 to 1886.

The constituents of Kings County sensed the local and national
importance of this election. Meeting halls were packed to overflowing,
and on one occasion people "stood outside the doors and windows and
listened with deepest attention to the three hours and a half of speech-
making."[52] In the end Borden won his seat handily with a margin of
471 votes, taking 55.8 per cent of the votes cast. So clear was his victory that the Conservatives did not bother to contest the by-election
required by his appointment to the cabinet. His election was a great
personal victory,[53] enhanced by the news that his party had won the
election. Tupper was out and Borden's friend Laurier would be Canada's next prime minister.

CHAPTER 5

Minister

For two weeks after his party's electoral defeat on 23 June 1896, Tupper clung tenaciously to office, disputing the electoral results and attempting to foist last-minute appointments, judgeships, and senatorships on the reluctant and unsympathetic governor general, Lord Aberdeen. It was not until 9 July that Tupper publicly acknowledged his fate and submitted his resignation and the governor general asked Laurier to form a government. Meanwhile Laurier was busy choosing his cabinet, receiving lobbyists, answering correspondence, and interviewing prospective candidates. The new prime minister did not keep the public waiting long.

Three days after Laurier met the governor general (and after much speculation in the newspapers), he announced the composition of his first cabinet. The following day his sixteen-man cabinet was sworn in. This impressive executive, sometimes called the "ministry of all the talents," included five former provincial premiers (Oliver Mowat, Henri-Gustave Joly de Lotbinière, Andrew George Blair, Louis Henry Davies, and William Stephens Fielding) as well as other forceful provincial leaders such as Clifford Sifton, the real power in the Manitoba government; Sir Richard Cartwright, the party's relentless old "blue-ruin" financial critic whom Borden liked and respected; William Mulock, Toronto's wealthy "socialistic" gentleman farmer and Laurier's close friend, advisor, and financial supporter; Israel Tarte, the irrepressible, renegade Tory strategist who helped deliver Quebec to the Grits; and of course Frederick Borden. Altogether the cabinet represented an impressive array of talent and experience.

Borden's name was among the first to be announced. Although his appointment was not a surprise, it disappointed other provincial hopefuls such as D.C. Fraser, L.G. Power, and A.G. Jones, all experienced and able men. Each of the others, however, would be rewarded in good time, Jones with the lieutenant-governorship of Nova Scotia (1900–06); Fraser with a judgeship in the Supreme Court (1904–06), then the lieutenant-governorship of Nova Scotia (1906–10); and Power with the speaker-ship of the Senate (1901–05).[1] Borden was to be the minister of militia and defence. While he possessed interest, experi-

Dr Borden (seated at the table on far right), a member of Wilfrid Laurier's first "cabinet of all the talents." *Courtesy Library and Archives Canada*

ence, and knowledge of the defence portfolio, it may not have been his first choice. He had other public interests, including trade, commerce, and economic development; but these ministries had been reserved for more obvious claimants. Laurier acknowledged Borden's trade expertise and his regional status, however, by appointing him to the Tariff Commission, to work more closely with the minister of trade and commerce, Sir Richard Cartwright, who reciprocated Borden's respect.

But if Laurier's choice of Borden for Defence was proof of the prime minister's indifference to the portfolio or his desire for a passive military counsellor, as some authors have carelessly suggested, the prime minister had made a serious miscalculation, for Borden proved to be an expansive reforming minister who would make persistent claims on the government's time and resources. A measure of Borden's success as a minister was the Defence Department's annual budgetary increase during his fifteen-year tenure of office, from $1,136,714 to $8,143,450, a sevenfold increase at a time when the government's overall annual budget climbed from $36,949,142 to $87,774,198, a 2.3-fold increase.[2] Indeed, Borden's successive raids on the public treasury, "sometimes against the strong protests of his own party friends,"[3] became a source of sharp conflict with the Deputy Minister of Finance, J.M. Courtney, who monitored closely the Militia Department's organization and expenditures and sniped at its direction and administration.[4] Nor were these increases accidental or automatic, given the public's ambivalence toward defence and the hostility of some of Borden's colleagues toward military preparedness.[5] Twice Borden had to threaten to resign rather than accept cuts in his department's budget.[6] On other occasions he appealed to the Opposition or threatened to slash the militia's popular annual drill pay to get the government's attention and garner the political support he required to obtain his objectives.[7]

Moreover, Laurier might have chosen other candidates for the Defence portfolio. Among the self-promoting supplicants for the ministry none was more persistent or disagreeable than Colonel James William Domville, the feisty, born-again Liberal member for Kings, New Brunswick. An erstwhile Conservative who had defeated the influential Conservative minister of finance, George Eulas Foster (Foster had taken the precaution of contesting successfully the York County seat as well and thus remained a member of the House), Domville went to great lengths to lobby Laurier for the post[8] and seems never to have forgiven Borden for having been preferred. D.C. Fraser also informed Laurier of his interest in and qualifications for the position. Another obvious possibility was A.G. Jones, who had served briefly as minister of militia in Alexander Mackenzie's government.

Laurier's choice of Borden, however, was deliberate. The prime minister knew Borden well and appreciated his knowledge and interest in the welfare of the Canadian Militia. An active militia officer in Kings County's 68th (infantry) Battalion, Borden had continued to serve as a surgeon in his battalion and had never missed an annual militia camp since he had joined the battalion in 1869. Although Borden professed to believe it improper for serving officers to interfere in the militia's administration, these reservations did not exclude him from joining Parliament's militia lobby, a group that encompassed "between a sixth and a quarter of the House";[9] nor did it prevent him from asking questions and making suggestions.[10] Borden's knowledge and personal commitment to the force was no secret, and his appointment was bound to reassure the Commons' bipartisan militia lobby. Personal reasons may have influenced Laurier's choice as well. As a friend and colleague of long standing, Laurier had had ample opportunity to assess Borden's potential. He appreciated Borden's personal qualities, his intelligence, industry, organizational and political skills, his judgment, his open and conciliatory nature, and his capacity for hard work. He may also have seen Borden as a useful, loyal, and dependable personal friend in a cabinet composed of many unpredictable regional prima donnas. If so, he was not mistaken.

In 1896 no one would have described the Militia Department as a first-tier portfolio. Since the withdrawal of British regular forces from central Canada in 1871, however, the Active Militia had become the country's first line of defence, charged with the dual responsibility for the defence of Canada and aid to the civil power. As Canada's first line of defence, the Active Militia was designed to serve as auxiliary to British forces, which were still committed to the defence of Canada and were represented by the small British garrison remaining in Halifax to safeguard the British navy's installations there and by a similar post on the west coast at Esquimalt, British Columbia. Moreover, the British general officer commanding in Halifax was charged with command of all troops in British North America in time of war, with the added obligation to plan for that eventuality. To underscore the Halifax general's importance, he deputized for the governor general in the latter's absence.

Canada's Active Militia, an amorphous assembly of thirty-five thousand citizen soldiers, consisted of the usual fighting arms of infantry, cavalry, and artillery, organized into various designated units. In the case of the infantry, volunteers were grouped into companies, battalions, and regiments. Each volunteer citizen soldier signed a three-year agreement to train for twelve to sixteen days a year. In rural areas a community might contain one company of forty or so men; those who could get away might meet once a year with their regiment at annual camp, more often a social occasion than a rigorous training exercise, and frequently they might not meet at all.

In 1883 the Militia Act was amended to permit the creation of a small "permanent" active militia (to avoid confusion, hereafter the "Permanent Force" [PF]), consisting of no more than nine hundred men. Initially referred to as "schools," the PF served principally as garrison troops and as a "corps of school teachers" to educate and train the citizen volunteers in the Active Militia (hereafter the Militia).[11] Once created, however, the PF aspired to the status of a professional standing army with a combat capacity, an expectation that proved a point of contention between them and the Militia's civilian soldiers that would need resolution during Borden's watch. The PF also occupied an ambiguous position with respect to the British Army's presence in Canada, as it sought at once to emulate and replace their British comrades.

In these years, apart from a few capable career officers, the Permanent Force consisted of a very unimpressive lot. Low-paid and ill-housed, the PF tended to attract drifters, snowbirds in search of food and shelter during the harsh winter months. Far too many among their ranks were drawn more to the barroom than to the drill hall, and they were often viewed by respectable citizens as indolent barroom loafers, their officers little more than second-rate political hacks. Crime and desertion rates were high. Although some of their capable officers envied and tried to emulate their professional European equivalents and aspired to the status of professionals, as it stood Canada's PF offered a lamentable example to the gainfully employed civilian soldiers in the Militia.

The state of the civilian soldiers' force, however, was far from reassuring. While some of the urban Militia units were efficient and well run, and were populated by many intelligent, educated, industrious young citizens, others were predominantly social clubs whose primary activities were sport, recreation, ceremonial drill, and public entertainment.[12] A few managed to combine social and military activities. Unlike the urban units that could fulfil their allowable paid annual training obligations, many in commodious and well-appointed drill halls, during evenings or on weekends, many of the rural units were simply paper units whose training was subject to the vagaries of public funding and a sporadic annual summer camp. "Over sixty percent" of the Militia recruits "were new each year,"[13] a desertion rate that seemed to reflect a lack of challenge and opportunity rather than a want of commitment or patriotism, a condition that Borden hoped to remedy.

Perhaps the Militia's most useful and conspicuous function was its aid to the civil power. In the absence of capable municipal and provincial police forces at this time, the Militia provided a substitute police force to protect property and public order during civic disturbances, riots, and strikes. Of the twenty-four occasions in which the Militia was called upon to support the civil power during Borden's years as minister, nineteen were occasioned by strikes. Most entailed a commitment of a week or more, but one, the 1909 Dominion Coal strike in Glace Bay, lasted for nine months.[14]

Many contemporary critics dismissed the entire Militia as little more than a glorified police force, a substitute for incompetent municipal law enforcement, poorly organized and totally unprepared for war. The infantry, cavalry, and artillery, the fighting arms of the militia, were divided into units of unplanned and unequal strength. None of the fighting arms was equipped with adequate weapons, and none possessed the requisite service corps to transport, clothe, feed, and administer a fighting field force. Training was haphazard. During lean years only a third of the Militia trained, and in still leaner years cancellation of the annual camp deprived volunteers of that opportunity. Under these conditions a volunteer might complete his three-year contract with no training whatever. This was especially true of the rural units, whose only training opportunity was during the annual summer camp.

In peacetime, therefore, this "Cinderella" ministry might be relegated to the cinders of relative insignificance, ignored, ill-equipped, and underfunded. A measure of its political standing within the government was its all but static budget and its flux of ministers: between 1892 and Borden's appointment in 1896 the department had known six ministers. Yet with the advent of war, the threat of war, or domestic violence, real or apprehended, the Militia might assume importance and influence. Borden inherited a portfolio that had endured a long, sleepy period of neglect, starved for public funds especially during the recent years of economic stagnation and depression. The department was riddled by politics and often paralysed by conflict between the PF and the citizen soldiers and between civilian and military authority. In other words, the Militia Department was far from a prize portfolio.

Things would change during Borden's fifteen years as minister of militia. Above all the Canadian Militia would possess stability. It would be called upon to support the civil power, one of the most significant occasions being the Yukon gold rush expedition, and participate in its first overseas war, the South African War of 1899–1902. These commitments, together with a rapidly changing international context (the legacy of the Venezuela scare, American lawlessness in the Yukon, the Alaska boundary dispute, the German naval rivalry and the growing militarization of sectors of Canadian society), would give Borden's ministry a growing centrality in Canadian public life.

Altogether these events would raise thorny political questions about the prerequisites of Canada's defences and its commitment to imperial defence. Counter-currents during these years, such as the growth of anti-military sentiment contesting the need for a costly, redundant military force in North America, required of the minister equally careful political management and the ability to steer a reasoned middle course. Borden's public stature would grow with that of his ministry and with his ability to master his department, garner support for its projects, direct and shape its policy, and participate in imperial councils. All of this would take vision, time, energy, patience, and political skills, and would entail delays, failures, and disappointments.

More immediately, Borden's cabinet appointment required the resolution of a number of departmental and personal problems. Among his most pressing tasks was the choice of a competent, dependable private secretary, a person whom Borden could trust, someone bound by loyalties stronger than career aspirations. Predictably Borden turned to a family member, Harry Whidden Brown, his first cousin, his uncle John's son. A twenty-eight-year-old graduate of Acadia University (BA) and Dalhousie University (LLD), Harry Brown had practised law in Halifax before joining Borden's office in July 1896. As Borden's private secretary, he received a wide mandate, including the purview of Borden's personal, business, and departmental affairs. A devoted and capable assistant, Harry became more entangled in Borden's business affairs than public interest might dictate. Then again, Borden may well have supplemented the public service's allowable annual stipend of $600 for a minister's private secretary. In 1904 Borden promoted Harry to the position of chief clerk and director of contracts, a more lucrative permanent position within the department with a salary of $2,800 per year. By 1910 Harry Brown found himself surrounded by four more members of the Brown family. None was more prominent than Harry.[15]

In September 1897 Borden appointed another cousin, John William Borden (Robert Borden's forty-one-year-old younger brother, who had married Annie Frances Brown, the minister's maternal first cousin, in 1891), to the strategic position of departmental chief accountant. John William had begun his business career in Canning as Frederick Borden's agent of the Halifax Banking Company; subsequently he had moved to Kentville, where he had risen to the position of manager of the Union Bank. As a government employee with a salary of $2,400 a year, John William was the third-highest-paid civil servant in the Militia Department. Borden shortly placed him in charge of the politically sensitive contracts division, a clever assignment that made opposition criticism difficult, especially after Robert Borden became Conservative leader in 1901. When Borden made John William the financial member of the newly formed Militia Council in 1904 and the following year promoted him to the position of paymaster-general, he replaced him in the contracts division with Harry Brown.

Less successful was Borden's choice of Richard W. Kinsman, a business partner, friend, and member of a prominent local family, to administer the F.W. Borden Company. Although the name of the company had been changed to the R.W. Kinsman Company in 1897, probably a cosmetic change to avoid the appearance of conflict of interest, Borden remained "the sole owner of all the preferred stock of the Kinsman Company and by far the largest owner of debt stock in the new company."[16] Moreover, Borden's detailed daily letters from Ottawa to Kinsman instructing him on the minutiae of the company's management suggest the real locus of power. They also demonstrate Borden's hands-on administrative style. As Borden confessed to a friend, he liked to hold in his own hands "the real key" to a situation.[17] In today's language Borden was a micromanager who had difficulty relinquishing the administration of his business even to a trusted friend and partner. But in this case Kinsman needed close and constant supervision and this was not always possible from Ottawa, especially as departmental business absorbed more of Borden's time. Consequently, Borden's private business fell far too readily under the chaotic direction of Kinsman, whose administrative style brought the business to the brink of bankruptcy during the first few months of the South African War. In the end Borden, despite repeated remonstrance, had to dismiss Kinsman and replace him as general manager with Captain W.R. Potter, a prominent Canning merchant and shipowner and Borden's next-door neighbour.

Borden had also to make important personal decisions about his family life. This took longer than it might have done owing to an untimely accident, the subsequent uncertainty of his political career, and his ambivalence toward residence in Ottawa. Now that he was a minister, Parliament no longer meant simply a welcome break from the restraints and tedium of local business and politics, a twelve-to-fourteen week sojourn in Ottawa during the winter or early spring, living in a boarding house with congenial parliamentary friends and colleagues. His cabinet position entailed administrative and social responsibilities, greater public visibility, and a residence in Ottawa (as well as separation from his family and business) for which he received an annual salary of $7,000 and a $2,500 indemnity.

Borden was now forty-nine years old. His children were young adults. Elizabeth, his twenty-three-year-old daughter, had graduated from Mount Allison Ladies' College in 1893 and was living at home. An active, dynamic, restless person, she might have been happier in business or politics had she not been constricted by class and gender assumptions. His twenty-year-old son, Harold, whom he had brought into his business and political work, would graduate from Mount Allison University with a bachelor of arts in the spring of 1897. His younger daughter, Julia, would graduate that same spring from Mount Allison Ladies' College. (Frederick's third cousin, Byron Crane Borden, taught political economy and served as principal of Mount Allison Ladies' College before becoming president of Mount Allison University, a position he held from 1911 to 1923.) Harold planned to follow his father's and his grandfather's medical vocation and enrol in the medical program at McGill University. There he would be much closer to Ottawa than to Canning. As for his daughters, Elizabeth and Julia, their social opportunities would be immeasurably greater in Ottawa than in Canning, a consideration pressed strongly by his vivacious, socially conscious wife. Bessie could also be a great assistance in Ottawa, where she could employ her talent for social diplomacy. He also had the care of his mother-in-law, who had become an essential part of his household since the death of her husband. All things considered, Borden decided to rent and then purchase a house on Wilbrod Street in Ottawa and bring his wife and family with him. Nevertheless his letters reflect his initial ambivalence and dissatisfaction with residence in Ottawa, and the frequent press rumours of his early retirement suggest that he regarded Ottawa as but a temporary home. Meanwhile the family would spend as much time as they could spare at the "Old Place" in Canning.

Soon after the strenuous election and well before all these personal details could be settled satisfactorily, Borden was obliged to leave the relative cool of Canning for the sweltering heat of an Ottawa August to participate in an emergency meeting of Parliament. The session's singular pressing business was the approval of the proposed estimates that had become a dead letter when the House dissolved for the election. In the interim the Conservative government had been operating on Governor General's Warrants. The emergency August 1896 session, however, was mercifully short and deceptively easy. As Laurier announced through the Throne Speech, except for the appointment of a commission to consider the contentious tariff issue (he had named Borden one of the commissioners), the session's principal business was to approve the estimates. A temporarily dejected and decimated Conservative Opposition, unused to its new role, offered scant resistance; moreover, it had little alternative but to approve estimates that it had largely prepared.

Despite the perfunctory nature of the session, Borden used the occasion to announce his commitment to Militia reform. Although no supplies had been voted for the 1896 annual summer camp, Borden had refused the advice of his general officer commanding the Canadian Militia, Major-General N.Y Gascoigne, that drill be dropped for that year.[18] Training and education were to occupy a central place on Borden's reform agenda, and there could be no compromise, no hesitation. It was also a question of morale, of planting his standard, as well as a source of patronage. If money was short, it could and would be squeezed from the system. He knew how to do that too. Consequently, Borden rushed his estimates through the House in record time and had the men in camp before autumn. C.F. Hamilton, an early Canadian military historian, grasped the significance of Borden's decision, observing that it marked the end of the long period of "cool indifference" toward the Militia.[19] It was also a notice of more to come. After a few questions and some flattering comments from members of the militia lobby on both sides of the House, many of them militia colonels delighted with Borden's decisive rejection of Gascoigne's proposal to cancel their annual camps, Borden's estimates passed. His reception as a new minister was a deceptive preparation for what followed in the years ahead.

In recounting the impressive record of military reform during Borden's ministerial tenure, some authors have downplayed Borden's personal contribution to its achievement, praising instead the innovation and imagination of two of the more flamboyant general officers commanding the Canadian Militia, namely E.T.H. Hutton and Lord Dundonald. In fact, Borden had a fairly clear idea of the Militia's needs, informed by his personal experience, careful, intelligent reading, and discussions with professional and civilian soldiers. Moreover, few if any of the central recommendations of his general officers commanding were particularly original. Most were drawn from the repertoire of contemporary conventional military wisdom, including Garnet Wolseley's reforming agenda for the British Army, sometimes more easily tested by his disciples in the colonies than in Britain. For example, both of Hutton's predecessors, Major-Generals Ivor Herbert and N.Y. Gascoigne, had recommended reform of the Militia headquarters staff and the creation of a self-contained militia field force, complete in all its arms. More important still were the recommendations of the Canada Defence Committee report (1898), commissioned by the War Office and chaired by Major-General E.P. Leach, portions of which Hutton simply parroted in his 1898 report.[20] As Norman Penlington perceptively observed, the Canada Defence Committee report became "almost a blueprint of many of the reforms undertaken by Canada in the next two years."[21]

Mesmerized by the conflict between ministers and generals, historians have often overlooked the occasions when they worked in tandem to reform the Militia. Contrary to popular assumptions, ministers and generals were not always at cross-purposes; nor were their disagreements simply those between amateurs and professionals over corruption and purity, nation and empire, as some historians might lead one to believe. Ministers and generals frequently shared objectives and worked harmoniously and constructively to improve Canada's defences. Borden not only acknowledged his debt to the recommendations of the Canada Defence Committee report,[22] but he shrewdly used the report to lobby his parsimonious cabinet colleagues for resources to fund many of his administrative reforms.[23] After all, the target of the report's criticism of the Militia was largely a legacy of his political opponents. Similarly, he endorsed the recommendation of several general officers commanding the Canadian Militia (echoed in the Canada Defence Committee report) that Canada required a trained, well-equipped militia, complete and balanced in all its arms, as well as the requisite service and support corps to administer, feed, clothe, and transport an "army" in the field, all objectives that would guide his reform agenda in the years ahead and all part of Sir Garnet Wolseley's familiar agenda for the British Army.

Borden's chief role as minister, however, was to work within a parliamentary system to persuade a penny-conscious public of the importance of his objectives for the Militia, and to compete with his cabinet colleagues for the resources required to fund them. Borden believed that his strongest argument for more funds was to make better use of existing resources, improving soldiers' working conditions, raising morale, establishing and enforcing regulations, creating a competent, dependable headquarters staff, and, above all, educating and train-

ing men and officers, the leitmotif of his program. Altogether these
were ambitious goals along a tortuous path, mined with innumerable
obstructions. Unfortunately, few of his objectives could be realized as
quickly or in as tidy an order as many impatient military administrators wished. Borden's role as minister was to persuade, to create, and
to seize opportunities to achieve these ends. And he could also make
poor choices.

Determined to lead by example, Borden began his reforms within
his headquarters by redefining and reassigning duties and staffing
positions with capable persons. As an efficient, frugal administrator
with successful business experience, Borden believed in organization
and control and the need to secure "the maximum efficiency, with the
minimum of costs."[24] Consequently, he abolished the position of director of stores and transferred its duties to the quarter-master general.
He reorganized the accounting department under the able direction
of his cousin John William Borden and cut a number of civilian staff
positions, replacing them with military men, a practice suggested by
Major-General Herbert several years before and emulated by other
units within headquarters. Soldiers, who earned sixty cents a day,
replaced civilians who earned $1,700 a year. As a result, servicemen
acquired administrative experience and the department gleaned monetary savings that could be channelled into more productive military
activities. Of the thirty-four employees at headquarters, six were dismissed, four were replaced, and four more were promoted. Some positions were abolished or their lighter tasks transferred to other employees. Moreover, in his internal search for resources, Borden, who had
an interest in, knowledge of, and experience with railway administration, invoked section 264 of the Railway Act, which required the railways to carry military men and supplies at fixed rates. This item alone
netted a $20,000 saving on transportation. All these were small but
important initiatives that increased Borden's credibility with tax-shy
parliamentarians.

More concrete measures, however, were required to stem the attri-
tion of men in the Permanent Force and the civilian Militia. Borden's
frequently affirmed faith in a civilian militia implied no disrespect for
the PF.[25] On the contrary, he viewed the PF, the teachers of the civilian force, as essential to military reform, and he made every effort to
enhance the PF's effectiveness and make it an exemplary, educated,
professional force. Convinced that improved education and training
opportunities were required to recruit, form, and retain officers and
men, Borden began with the education of the officers of the PF.

Central to an educated officer corps was the mission and fate of the
Royal Military College (RMC), a hot potato inherited from his Con-

servative predecessor. Established in 1876 by a previous Liberal government, the RMC was in a sorry state by 1896, its decline coinciding with the appointment of Major-General D.R. Cameron, Sir Charles Tupper's son-in-law, to the position of commandant in 1888. Since Cameron's tenure, the number of cadets had fallen from eighty-one in 1888 to fifty in 1896. Staff and students were dissatisfied with the college's curriculum, morale was low, and the British military authorities complained of the quality of recent RMC graduates who had joined the British Army.

In 1895 the Conservative government had responded to the growing public criticism of the RMC by appointing a four-person Board of Visitors to report on the college. The board had submitted two reports, a majority report and a one-man minority report penned by Tupper's old friend, Sandford Fleming. The majority report recommended the replacement of Cameron by a capable British lieutenant-colonel on a limited-term appointment, the creation of a shorter school year, a more focused curriculum, and the establishment of more rigorous standards of admission and graduation. Although the majority report was endorsed by the new general officer commanding the Canadian Militia, Major-General N.Y Gascoigne, no action was possible while Tupper remained prime minister.

Borden was committed to education, and he had no brief for Tupper. Free to act, he did so as soon as he became minister, instructing Gascoigne to implement the Board of Visitors' recommendations, fully aware that his action would fuel his feud with Tupper. Cameron's successor, Lieutenant-Colonel Gerald Kitson, moved quickly to restructure the college's program, avoid competition with chartered colleges, and prepare cadets for service in the PF, the British Army, and the public service. Student fees were reduced, matriculation standards were raised, the minimum age of admission was increased to sixteen years of age, and the entire program was reduced from four to three years. The shorter revised curriculum focused on mathematics, civil surveying, and civil engineering, at the expense of the arts and pure sciences. Although Borden had strong personal reservations about Kitson's reduction of the college's academic program, he backed the new commandant's proposals and defended them in the House.[26] Within four years the RMC's reputation seemed to have been restored. The number of cadets had risen from fifty to eighty-seven, the quality and reputation of its students had improved, and its operating costs had been reduced, the saving being invested in overdue capital expenditures.[27]

Much more, however, was required to improve the quality and morale of the PF, especially among its officer corps. To attract better officers, a general military order (to be effective 1 July 1898, more than a month before the arrival of Hutton) raised the admission standards for an officer's commission. It imposed an age limit for admission of eighteen to twenty-five years of age; demanded a more rigorous medical examination; required a diploma from the RMC and matriculation from a chartered university or at least fifteen months of service as a commissioned officer in the Militia; and required attendance at two annual training camps and a long-course grade "A" certificate in the branch of the service to which the potential officer sought admission. A seven-month "long course" for officers had been instituted in 1886 but had been discontinued; Borden revived the course in 1897 to provide access to continuing education. Similarly, in 1899 military orders required instructors in the PF to learn French to enhance their communications with francophone units.

Borden saw the British Army as an important training ground, a means to extend the education and service experience of Canadian officer. In 1897 he approved an exchange between the British Royal Berkshire Regiment stationed in Halifax and the Royal Canadian Regiment of Infantry. That same year the first Canadian PF officer was selected for training at the Camberley Staff College in England. To remedy the disorganization in the Artillery, the branch of the service Borden thought most in need of attention, he authorized the recruitment of an imperial officer, Colonel F.G. Stone, charged with its reorganization and training. While not all of these initiatives were a success, nor was he solely responsible for their suggestion or implementation, all carried his full backing and underscored the new minister's strategy for the reform of the PF.

The civilian Militia faced similar difficulties. Many of its units were merely paper formations, others were demoralized, and turnover or "desertion" rates were alarmingly high. Many able young men or potential officers refused to join the PF or the civilian Militia. Many of those who did join soon left in discouragement because older officers, well past retirement age, monopolized command positions and blocked their careers. To overcome this impediment, in 1896 Borden authorized a new retirement age for all senior Militia officers. During the regulation's first year of enforcement, forty-two men and officers were superannuated and fourteen were retired on gratuities. In one instance the retired officer was eighty-one years old, doubtless past his most productive years.[28] This regulation alone revitalized the Militia's leadership and unblocked career paths.

Although Borden had insisted on an annual camp, in his view annual camps were not enough. They had to be supplemented by additional opportunities to improve military education. In 1897 Borden authorized the creation of provisional schools of infantry to bring training to the units wherever there was sufficient demand and where both men and officers could receive instruction. This measure reduced the cost of travel and the disruption of civilian employment, to the general benefit of a soldier's unit.[29]

After three years as minister, Borden might well review his record with some satisfaction. Although self-aggrandizing general officers commanding might date reform to their advent, Borden established the broad parameters of the agenda early in his mandate. He had made modest headway in reshaping the Canadian Militia, especially in the education, training, recruitment, and retention of good men in Canada's PF and civilian Militia. Opening civilian positions to military personnel and promulgating and enforcing rules and regulations on promotion and retention of command were steps designed to enhance morale and career opportunities. The more efficient administration of his department freed resources for other projects. Generally, the persons he employed were diligent, capable, and reliable. They were a nucleus around which he could build. Even his political opponents concurred: "I will say this, that I think the appointments the hon. Gentleman has made since he came into office, especially the appointments in headquarters staff, no minister could make better ones. He has surrounded himself with a most admirable staff of officers."[30] However impressive the aggregate of his early reforms may appear, his apprenticeship had been far from smooth. An ambitious, energetic minister, Borden sought immediate change, but progress had been painfully slow, his path mined with obstacles at every turn.

CHAPTER 6

Command

Command of Borden's department proved much more difficult than he had anticipated. Borden liked to manage and control, and during his first three years as minister of militia, he faced a number of administrative, personal, and political obstacles that frustrated and retarded his plans and challenged his authority. His problems began at the top, his efforts paralysed by lax and often incompetent departmental administrative structures, poorly defined lines of authority between military and civilian officials, and a history of conflict between the two.[1] A complete internal overhaul of his department's structures and procedures was long overdue, a condition much more easily diagnosed than remedied and that required resolution, sensitivity, political skills, and above all patience.

Nowhere was the need for change more obvious than at military headquarters. Borden's small military headquarters consisted of some thirty-four employees and was administered by a deputy minister, Charles-Eugene Panet. An ailing sixty-seven-year-old Militia colonel, Panet had resigned his seat in the Senate in 1875 to assume the more lucrative position of deputy minister of militia and defence. Although a pleasant old gentleman from a distinguished Quebec family and with a reputable record of performance in the position, Panet was now well past his prime.[2] Politically well connected, he exercised a highly personal and nepotistic leadership. At least three relatives, including his two sons, Charles-Louis and Arthur-Hubert, and his son's father-in-law, Colonel D.A. Macdonald, were on the headquarters' payroll. His resistance to Borden's efforts to replace him retarded the Militia Department's reform and efficient administration.

Panet's deficiencies were especially irksome to a conscientious new, hands-on administrator, anxious to restructure his department. Although Borden liked Panet and generously regarded him as a "[l]oyal and true friend" whose heart was "in the right place," he could see that the deputy minister was failing "lamentably" and was "no longer able to fill the position." Mistakes were "constantly being made" and his "forgetfulness and carelessness" were becoming "insufferable."[3] When Panet's failing eyesight obliged him to take a medical leave for treatment, Borden seized the opportunity to appoint Major Louis-Felix Pinault, a Liberal Quebec City journalist, as his temporary replacement. Deeply offended by the choice of Pinault, the haste of Borden's decision, and the feeling that the decision could scarcely have been taken without Laurier's complicity, Panet recovered sufficiently to reclaim his position, determined to delay Pinault's succession as long as possible. Moreover Panet's nepotic influence within the department made it that much more difficult to resolve the issue. Consequently, it was not until Panet's death in November 1898 that Borden was able to confirm Pinault in this strategic administrative post. Meanwhile Borden had simply to contend with Panet's growing incapacity, accept responsibility for his mistakes, and try to work around him, confiding his frustrations to Laurier and wondering how much longer he could continue with Panet's chaotic administration.

To add to Borden's difficulties a serious rail accident, six months after he assumed office, postponed his encounter with departmental realities. On 26 January 1897, on his way back to Ottawa from a meeting in Halifax of the Tariff Commission, a severe rail accident just outside Dorchester, New Brunswick, left Borden with a back injury that prevented him from returning to his office for a crucial six months.[4] During this trial, the prime minister was very supportive, enjoining him to take a year's leave if necessary.[5] In Borden's absence, Sir Richard Cartwright administered his department, answered questions in the House, and defended his estimates. Although Borden's private secretary, the deputy minister, the general officer commanding the Canadian Militia, and Cartwright all tried to keep Borden informed and sought his advice on questions of policy and pressing administrative decisions, departmental officials were left very much on their own. Meanwhile the press speculated upon Borden's retirement and replacement by D.C. Fraser or by the relentlessly ambitious James Domville, despite Borden's persistent denial of these rumours, hoping as he did to return to work within three months.

Perhaps no departmental problem was as immediate, pervasive, persistent, and troublesome as the patronage system, so central to the Canadian political process and so evident in Borden's department. John Buchan's partial assessment of Borden as a country physician with no knowledge of the Militia who saw his duty "chiefly as a balancing of party patronage,"[6] however, has created the distorted impression that patronage was not only peculiarly rampant in the department he inherited but that Borden had raised the system to new levels of refinement. In fact, if one can judge by Borden's private letters, public statements, and actions, and by the testimony of some of his political opponents, Borden made real efforts to curtail and regulate patronage in his department, often to the chagrin of many of his party's followers, some of whom complained for years after the Liberals' victory in 1896 that the Militia Department remained a "Tory hive," where "no Grit need apply."[7] Even Lord Minto, who became governor general in 1898 and whose political radar was especially sensitive to "colonial" corruption, admitted that imperial officials, notably disgruntled general officers commanding the Canadian Militia, were "too much inclined to attribute [political influence] to every move."[8]

Borden of course was not naive, nor was he averse to patronage and nepotism or his public career free from conflicts of interest. But certain areas were off-limits and others required regulation and management. Above all he resented the squandering of public funds and was alarmed and irritated by the voracious herd of party scavengers who surfaced on almost every occasion impatiently demanding personal consideration. Borden was surprised by the nature and persistence of the requests, frequently from persons who ought to have known better. Stories of past Tory abuses were legion and amusing. Borden's favourite entailed an incident involving the delivery of wood to the Royal Military College whereby the contractor drove in with wood, had it measured, drove it out by another route, and then repeated "the process as often as the contractor felt it necessary to be recouped for his heavy election contribution."[9] Past abuses, however, did not justify their continuance under Liberal auspices, a lesson that many of Borden's colleagues were reluctant to learn. One of the earlier and more unusual requests came from William Gibson, the Liberal member for Lincoln and Niagara, who asked Borden to send a man to pretend to survey the bank of a river on the eve of a municipal election. As Gibson explained, "Anyone would do providing he had a surveyor's instruments and would look wise and say nothing."[10] Borden rejected Gibson's absurd request out of hand.

Borden believed that there were areas where patronage could not and must not apply. Military appointments and promotion were a case in point. This sort of political interference sapped morale, denigrated merit, and offended his growing sense of professionalism. Moreover, his Tory opponents had always treated him fairly, even during the dark days of their dominance. In September 1883, for example, he had been promoted surgeon-major, and in October 1893 honorary surgeon lieutenant-colonel in the 68th Battalion. Besides, the efficiency of the force depended upon the maintenance of a merit system. "You know perfectly well," Borden wrote to the minister without portfolio, James Sutherland, in resisting his intercessions on behalf of a friend, "that military appointments differ essentially and necessarily from other patronage [appointments]."[11] He maintained this position in dealing with similar requests from others, including the prime minister, the minister of justice, and the minister of trade and commerce (Sir Richard Cartwright, Borden's friend and colleague had interceded on behalf of his son).[12]

Even in his constituency Borden resisted a wholesale dismissal of Tory office-holders in 1896. "[Do you think that I have] something else to do besides working up charges against so called offensive Tory office holders," he wrote angrily to a relative in his constituency who had called for a clean sweep of political opponents in the area.[13] While Elijah Borden, his distraught complainant, was rewarded shortly with a $300-a-year position as sub-customs officer for Kingsport, his position came from attrition, not from a wholesale purge of Tory office-holders. Similarly, C.R. Bill, Frederick's opponent during the 1891 election and the subsequent by-election, retained his $500-a-year position as the Wolfville sub-collector of customs, and Leveret de Veber Chipman, Borden's 1874 opponent and Bill's bagman (who attempted to purchase a Senate seat in 1892 at Borden's expense), maintained his postmaster's position in Kentville even after the Liberal victory in 1896. In a closely-knit constituency, where social relationships were face-to-face and personal, a live-and-let-live policy was also clever politics.

Nonetheless Borden was no innocent in the world of patronage. He made a clear distinction between professional and material resources, and between fair pricing and profiteering. Acutely aware that some $500,000 of his budget was spent on provisions, supplies, and the administration of annual militia camps, he defended openly the distribution of contracts to political friends so long as their prices were just and competitive. As he stated in the House, "[I]n every case, whenever I can do it fairly and justly, with all regard to the public exchequer, I am prepared to give the preference to my own political friends. I do not think that anybody expects different, and if they do, they will expect something which never happened in Canada before."[14] Significantly, no one rose to contradict his transparent definition of the rules of the long-established Canadian patronage system.[15] Consequently, in awarding repair and provisioning contracts he saw no reason why the RMC cadets should not eat Liberal bread, or the college's windows not be repaired by Liberal glaziers,[16] so long as it cost the public exchequer no more than Conservative bakers and glaziers; what was important was that the government received value for its money. Profiteering was another matter. "[I regret] very much if our Liberal friends are going to suffer in their loyalty to the party because they are not allowed to take out of the government more than they can get from ordinary purchasers," he wrote sarcastically to A.G. Blair, the minister of railways and canals, who seemed always to be begging for something.[17] As Borden explained to his secretary, public money must be treated with the same care as one's own.

Borden's doctrine provided ample room to accommodate the party faithful, silence the opposition, and purchase the support of others, a capacity especially important to a new government anxious to "reform" the system by combining cost savings with party advantage. One way to end some of the abuses, monitor the process, and open the system to Liberal bidders immediately was to substitute a competitive system of annual one-year contracts for the Conservatives' three-year policy, a measure Borden announced during the brief first session of Parliament. In doing so, he explained somewhat virtuously and perhaps disingenuously that the department would not "discriminate in favour of any particular class. I care not whether they are Liberals or Conservatives. I am here to act in the interests of the public, and I propose that other things being equal, the quality being the same, the people who can manufacture at the lowest figure whether Conservatives or Liberals, shall have these contracts in the future."[18] Conservatives would not be excluded from the ministry's bounty, at least those whom he might favour for personal or political reasons, providing they reciprocated with cooperation, neutrality, and goodwill.

In other words, while Borden's insistence upon fair prices and public tenders for supplies maintained the appearance of frugality and impartiality, between the principle and the practice there was ample room for manoeuvre and slippage. Much depended on the system's administration: How much notice was given of public tenders? To whom were they given? And how secret were the competitors' bids? Brenton Dodge, the Kentville merchant and Liberal MLA, was among the first to benefit from the new policy, winning a $2,000 or more contract to provision the annual militia camp in Kentville.[19] According to one scholar, Borden's talent lay in his ability to reconcile "honest and effective financial management" of his department with "the benefits of patronage";[20] at least that was his objective and the desired public image.

Not only did Borden's new one-year policy cut Liberal partisans in on lucrative militia contracts more quickly, it created its own problems. Many manufacturers required a longer production commitment or charged higher prices for one-year contracts than for three-year commitments; annual bidding inflated departmental administrative costs; and the inevitable political jockeying for favours was even more tedious and time-consuming. After a two-year trial Borden returned as quietly as possible to the Tory's three-year system. The Opposition gave him relatively little grief for this failed experiment, but when challenged he facetiously explained his retreat as a compliment to his opponents, and perhaps it was.[21]

The Opposition was less generous toward his department's selection of men for the Jubilee contingent. The June 1897 Diamond Jubilee of Queen Victoria's accession to the throne was a carefully planned pageant, staged by Joseph Chamberlain, the British colonial secretary, to demonstrate to an increasingly menacing world the diversity, power, and unity of an empire upon which the sun never set. In his plans and preparations, the colonial secretary had reserved a specially scripted role for Canada, the senior dominion, and Wilfrid Laurier, Canada's francophone and Roman Catholic prime minister, whose kinsmen had been in revolt when Queen Victoria had come to the throne but could now be represented as enjoying exemplary imperial prosperity and contentment in a country that was a living model of the Empire's unity in diversity. Chamberlain's pageant called for a North-West Mounted Police (NWMP) detachment and a contingent of two hundred Canadian militiamen, including twenty to thirty officers, to participate in this gigantic London celebration. The invitation elicited a predictable flood of hopeful, self-promoting begging letters, in fact two thousand in all, each pressing his professional, personal, or political claims for special favour.[22] It also brought predictable charges of personal and political favouritism from the disappointed applicants.

Although still recuperating from his back injury, Borden participated in the selection of the officers and men for the Jubilee contingent, careful to have all military branches and regions of the country represented (and his own constituency overrepresented with three successful candidates!).[23] Among those chosen was his son, Harold, a twenty-one-year-old medical student at McGill University and a popular and keen captain in the Kings County Hussars, whose candidacy was strongly pressed by the departmental selection committee. On merit alone, he was not an undeserving candidate, and he possessed the added advantage of representing his temporarily disabled father. But however defensible and well packaged his selection, it could not stifle suspicion of political favouritism; nor did it. The partisan press needled and carped, and Liberal counter-arguments and special pleading only kept the issue smouldering.

These criticisms, however, paled in comparison to the Opposition's assault on the manner in which Borden's department distributed provisioning contracts for the Yukon Field Force. In July 1897 the arrival in Seattle and San Francisco of ships laden with Klondike gold announced to the world the bonanza that had been discovered the previous summer. Almost immediately large numbers of men and women from all parts of the world converged on this remote and uncharted region, challenging borders, jurisdictions, laws, and authority. Within two years the small Dawson outpost had became a city of

20,000 people, but without any provision for municipal government or adequate law enforcement. According to J.B.B. Brebner, "no other event or combination of events occurring outside the battlefield had so profoundly affected the English speaking people and generally had so wide an influence in so short a time" as the Yukon Gold Rush.[24]

Uncertain of how populous the region might become or how long the gold madness would last, in 1898 the federal government recognized the Yukon as a special district and entrusted its governance to an appointed council, answerable directly to Ottawa. In September 1897 the government considered sending a Militia detachment to aid the civil power but it was too late in the season. The experience and proximity of the North-West Mounted Police made it easier to despatch a police detachment of three hundred men to the area, under the command of the legendary Sam Steele. It was not until March 1898 that the government, fearing that the police might not be able to cope with the anticipated lawlessness (and perhaps still undecided on the fate of the Tory-mined NWMP, which the Liberals had considered disbanding), issued an Order-in-Council authorizing the posting to the Yukon of two hundred and three officers and men of the Permanent Force, consisting of infantry, artillery, and cavalry, under the capable command of Lieutenant-Colonel T.D.B. Evans. After a year, half the military force was withdrawn, and the remaining men left a year later. As a benevolent "police state," the Yukon became an exemplary and orderly community, perhaps because of the visible presence of law and authority.

The responsibility for equipping, clothing, feeding, and freighting Evan's Yukon Field Force fell upon the shoulders of the very capable quartermaster-general of the Militia, Colonel Percy Lake, a Canadian-born British regular officer loaned to the Canadian government. His chief task was to secure a sufficient quantity of well-packed, serviceable matériel. What company supplied the matériel and at what cost was the concern of the civilian branch of the department. Since the detachment was to leave in ten days, there was some urgency in procuring the necessities for its immediate use; a second instalment, the reserve provisions, could be delivered later when the Yukon River became navigable.

News of the field force's despatch and its need of provisions elicited a crush of tenders from hopeful wholesale and retail merchants. Of these, the two lowest were accepted, the first from the Hudson's Bay Company, which possessed the advantage of a knowledge and experience of northern weather conditions; the second from the H.N. Bates Company, whose advantage was its location in Ottawa, where its work could be closely supervised by the Militia Department. The difficulty with the Bates contract was that many of the prices were inflated and

Bates was a conspicuous friend of the government who was rumoured to have offered to buy Laurier a house in Ottawa.

As soon as Borden rose to present his 1899 estimates, the Opposition demanded an explanation of the Bates contract. In pursuing the issue, the Opposition's primary target was the prime minister. The Conservatives had done their homework and had done it well. Striking a posture of reasonableness and understanding, they cleverly conceded the ministry's need to act expeditiously in awarding the first contracts for the goods required immediately by the force; they also acknowledged the convenience of choosing an Ottawa firm. But why, they insisted, had Bates been given the contract for the second allotment when there was sufficient time to secure more competitive prices elsewhere?

Poorly prepared by his deputy minister, Borden responded that he had saved the department money, since the prices on a number of items had increased owing to the outbreak of the Spanish-American War. Borden's response became a target rather than a shield. Thereafter member after member rose to read into the record comparative price lists that demonstrated that many of Bates's prices were indeed inflated.[25]

Despite Borden's stumbling, the Opposition's primary target remained the prime minister. Resentful of Sir Wilfrid's skilful command of the House and his growing reputation at home and abroad, enhanced by his warm reception in imperial London, the Opposition sought to reduce Sir Wilfrid to size. Particularly stung by the Opposition's insistence on linking the Yukon contract and Bates's rumoured attempts to buy him a house, Laurier rose to deny the allegation. His denial simply drove the insinuation underground. Playing Borden against Laurier, Opposition members facetiously excused Borden himself, commending him for his efforts to eliminate politics from the Militia, expressing confidence that "if he is not interfered with by the Prime Minister for political friends, the administration of Militia Affairs will, no doubt, bring credit to the Minister of Militia and benefit the country."[26] As the debate went on and Borden continued to fumble, other ministers came to his rescue. The Opposition, sensing Borden's weakness and discomfort, persisted, contesting practically every item of his estimates. George Eulas Foster, who had old scores to settle with the minister, was especially sharp and biting, lecturing and scolding Borden for thinking that his estimates could "slide through on grace and favour."[27] This would not be their last acrimonious exchange.

Borden was distraught with his poor performance and felt betrayed by the laxity and disorganization of his department, a legacy of his recently deceased deputy minister. The department clearly needed firmer ministerial control and direction. He was also furious with his Liberal friends, above all Bates and those who had promoted his claims. The "high prices which were paid for goods ... [for the Yukon Field Force] were simply outrageous, and not to be tolerated in the future," he indignantly lectured A.G. Blair, the minister of railways and canals, who Borden seemed to suggest bore some responsibility for Bates's contract.

Chastened by his brutal parliamentary mauling and determined to avoid its recurrence, Borden sought to staff his office with competent men whom he could trust. It was after this fiasco that he decided to place his first cousin, John William Borden, whom he had first employed in the Militia Department as an accountant, in charge of contracts, with the clear understanding that he was to protect the public purse from unreasonable charges. As Borden reiterated to his private secretary and his entire departmental staff, "public money should be treated as one's own."[28]

Borden's timely insistence upon fair market prices, coming as it did on the eve of the South African War, broke the thrust of the Opposition's subsequent criticism of his wartime administration, though their greater vigilance might have found much to criticize. It enabled him to manage his department's expanding and lucrative wartime business with due regard to public economy, as well as to party and personal advantage, and with a minimum of criticism. During the thirty-two-month period of the South African War, the Canadian government spent some $1,996,867 on the recruitment, clothing, equipment, and transportation of troops.[29] The British War Office spent an estimated additional $7.5 million in Canada on the purchase of supplies and provisions, horses, hay, and other necessities, procured largely through the Department of Militia or the Department of Agriculture,[30] whose ministers worked closely in tandem.

Although Borden might review his first three years with some satisfaction, far too much of his time had been engaged in damage control, coping with extraordinary public events, managing a weak department, his work disrupted by a protracted illness. For a minister in a hurry, the pace was painfully slow, much slower than he could have imagined, his time and energy dissipated in managing crises fuelled by his colleagues' avarice, his authority frustrated at every turn by his chief civilian and military advisors. Even greater personal, administrative, and political challenges remained ahead.

CHAPTER 7

Challenge

The most public and potentially damaging challenge to Borden's ministerial authority came not from the Opposition but from within his own department, from its most powerful official, the general officer commanding (GOC) the Canadian Militia, Major-General E.T.H. Hutton. The failure of the minister and the general to work in tandem frustrated military reform and delayed departmental reorganization. Borden's quarrel with Hutton was not unprecedented. The premature and acrimonious departure of several of Hutton's predecessors suggests that the periodic conflict between ministers and generals was structural, inherent in the position of GOC itself.[1] Whatever the structural problems, in Hutton's case conflict was almost assured by his abrasive personality and Borden's determination to establish ministerial control.

Borden had been in the House in 1875 when Parliament amended the Militia Act of 1868 to place the Canadian Militia under the command of "an officer who holds the rank of Colonel or rank superior thereto in Her Majesty's Regular Army, who shall be charged, under the orders of Her Majesty, with the military command and discipline of the Militia."[2] The theoretical purpose of this provision was to assure that the Canadian Militia remained abreast of modern warfare and capable of assisting the British military with Canada's defence. The practical logic of this objective was firmly grounded in Britain's ultimate responsibility for Canada's defence, even after Britain's land garrisons left central Canada in 1871. The general officer commanding the Canadian Militia was appointed by a Canadian Order-in-Council on the recommendation of the British War Office and paid from Canadian revenue, the duties of the position defined by Canadian statute. In accepting the command, the GOC assumed a Canadian rank, usually one step higher than his rank in the British regular forces, and became an officer of the Canadian Militia, subordinate to and under the instructions of the Canadian government through its minister of militia, a status that some generals and their supporters failed to appreciate.

Some people disagreed. They saw the position of GOC as different from that of other civil servants who were subordinate to a responsible minister. They claimed that the GOC possessed an authority derived from the position's direct responsibility to the Crown. In their view, the "under orders of Her Majesty" qualification of the Militia Act referred to a prerogative of the Crown that had been delegated to the governor general and that permitted vice-regal discretion, especially in areas of broad imperial interest.[3] In addition, they reasoned that the governor general's designation as commander-in-chief of the Canadian Militia signified his direct and personal authority over military affairs "for purposes of command not administration,"[4] a provision that appeared to hedge and mitigate the power of the minister. This more expansive interpretation of the governor general's powers assumed an extraordinary importance during Borden's quarrel with Hutton owing to Hutton's unusual personal friendship with Lord Minto, the governor general, whose political inexperience and constitutional naivety precipitated a constitutional crisis of significant dimensions during the early months of the South African War. Although the constitutional ambiguity assumed dramatic personal proportions during that crisis, it remained unresolved until well after Hutton's unceremonious departure in 1900.

The Militia's General Orders and Regulations, whose statutory authority derived from the Militia Act, were very explicit. General Orders and Regulations charged the GOC with the command, discipline, education, supervision, and administration of the Militia under the authority of the minister of militia, who answered directly to cabinet and Parliament. Moreover, the Militia Act specifically gave to the minister "the initiative in all affairs involving the expenditure of money," which in a parliamentary system formed "the very vitals of power," giving the minister a broad and pervasive jurisdiction.[5] Policy decisions, specifically those having financial implications (and most did), required the consent of the minister.

Like any other public servant, the general might advise, suggest, and warn, but if his counsels were rejected, he had but two alternatives: he must resign or submit. As the British prime minister Lord Salisbury reminded the British Parliament when facing a similar challenge from Lord Garnet Wolseley, the commander-in-chief of the British Army, "At the end we must have an Army governed by Parliament, governed by a Minister who is responsible to Parliament, and in any difference of opinion, whatever it may be, the Commander-in-chief must be a subordinate of the Secretary of State. Military men may not like that, but there it is ... any attempt to take the opinion of the expert above the opinion of the politician must, in view of all the circumstances of our constitution, inevitably fail."[6]

Many senior British officers loaned to the Canadian government had difficulty understanding that as general officer commanding the Can-

adian Militia they had only one master, the Canadian government. Yet
whatever the constitutional niceties, as a career officer on temporary
assignment in Canada, few GOCs could forget that their professional
advancement within the British Army depended on the continuing
good opinion of their British superiors. Most came to Canada with
little or no knowledge of the country and failed to appreciate the difference between a militia and a standing army.[7] Many lacked the personal
or political experience and talents so important to the position, having
been taught to command rather than persuade or lead.[8] A few regarded
the colonies as a laboratory for military experiments. Others were
simply "unfit by temperament and manners," to use the words of one
perceptive, senior Colonial Office official,[9] and were exiled to Canada,
or elsewhere, to get rid of them at home.[10] Some simply marked time
or promptly quarrelled with everyone who crossed their path. Much
depended upon the personality of the incumbent.

Borden was a fairly amiable person, ready and anxious to assist a conscientious GOC and defend him if necessary. When Borden assumed
responsibility for the Militia Department in 1896, General N.Y. Gascoigne was the GOC. Gascoigne's relations with the previous, Conservative minister of militia had been tense and troubled. The GOC's
support of the principal recommendation in the majority report of the
RMC Board of Visitors, namely the dismissal of its commandant, the
son-in-law of Sir Charles Tupper, earned him the permanent animos-
ity of the then prime minister, who thereafter had pursued Gascoigne
verbally with a rare vengeance.[11]

After a few months of adjustment Borden developed a pleasant, professional working relationship with Gascoigne. Gascoigne was blunt,
transparent, and outspoken, qualities Borden appreciated and encouraged. The GOC was a professional soldier willing to respect the minister's right of final decision.[12] Although he was no visionary, Gascoigne
worked assiduously, without fear or favour, to correct abuses within
the system and exact greater benefit from existing resources. In turn
Borden took the general into his confidence and shielded him from the
criticism of those whom the General had offended by his lack of tact
or indiscretion.[13] And Borden paid warm tribute to his work upon the
GOC's premature retirement for personal reasons in May 1898.[14]

Gascoigne's successor, Major-General E.T.H. Hutton, who arrived in
Canada in August 1898, was an unfortunate though not an unlikely
choice. Above all, he offered a stark contrast to his predecessor. Eton-
educated and the son of a middle-class banker, the fifty-year-old Hutton
was an ambitious, class-conscious career soldier who had served briefly
in Canada with the 60th Rifles, in which his stepfather had purchased
him a commission. An ingratiating disciple of the British Army's com-

mander-in-chief, Viscount Garnet Wolseley, Hutton shared his master's broad commitment to army reform and professionalism, as well as his dangerous disdain for politicians and parliamentary democracy. He lacked his master's political skills, however, though eventually even Lord Wolseley overplayed his hand and had to be called to order by the secretary of state for war, Lord Lansdowne.[15]

Hutton was a self-appointed missionary of imperialism, an imperialism based on race, language, and religion, an ideology ill-suited to a binational, bilingual country of mixed creeds. Increasingly fearful of the Empire's foes, especially the threat posed by Europe's conscript armies, Hutton sought to export Wolseley's formula for British home defence to the self-governing colonies, which he seemed to regard as a laboratory for military and political reform. What he grandly claimed was his cooperative system of imperial defence was a scheme to create a self-sufficient field force, complete in all its arms and ready for service at home or abroad.[16] In fact, this formula was neither original nor "his," but rather the conventional common property of many military reformers.

More alarming still was Hutton's belief that a soldier's primary loyalty was to Crown, Empire, and its "citizens," not to the elected government, and that "patriots" and professional soldiers had an obligation to participate in public debate and shape public events, to go public and force an issue if necessary.[17] Just how the soldiers' divergent voices were to be reconciled or channelled into political action the general never revealed, except perhaps through the army's hierarchical command structure, as Hutton demonstrated later in his treatment of Sam Hughes. Hutton was less happy, however, when things worked the other way, when he found himself on the wrong side of army politics, as he did during the South African War.

An energetic, though tactless, arrogant, and self-promoting officer, Hutton had commanded the New South Wales Militia from 1893 until 1896. He had quarrelled with the colonial government and had been obliged to return to Britain. Conscious of the general's unsuitability "by temperament and manners" for the Canadian position, the Colonial Office had objected to the recommendation of Hutton's War Office friends that he be appointed to the Canadian command and had tried to block his appointment. When these War Office friends "persisted," the Colonial Office conceded reluctantly on the condition that should Hutton get into trouble in Canada, he would be removed immediately, a promise they were obliged to honour later.[18] Conscious of their candidate's failings, two of Hutton's influential War Office supporters, Lord Garnet Wolseley and Sir Redvers Buller, both of whom had Canadian experience, warned Hutton before he left London to ride gently in Canada and to urge and flatter rather than drive and abuse.[19] Before long, however, Hutton had quarrelled with Borden, the minister of militia; Sam Hughes, the Opposition military critic; Lord William Seymour, the general officer commanding the British troops in Halifax; as well as other military and civilian persons of greater and lesser distinction.

Few shared the grandiose vision that Hutton had of himself as "the very humble instrument of an All-wise Providence" with a mission to reform the defences of the self-governing dominions. His immediate predecessor, Gascoigne, had warned Borden that Hutton was a "dangerous martinet." Borden soon found his new GOC to be an egocentric, selfish man, always playing to the galleries, carefully calculating the effect upon his name and fame: "It was Hutton first and the devil take whatever came afterward."[20] Later, the Canadian (and Australian) officers commanding battalions in Hutton's brigade during the South African War thoroughly hated the general, sentiments shared by many imperial officers.[21] According to H.O. Arnold-Forster, the British secretary of state for war, Hutton's principal difficulty was that he "[could not] keep his mouth shut" and, left to himself, "would talk us into difficulty every week."[22]

Initially relations between the minister and general were cordial. Hutton informed friends that he had "no reason to doubt the bona fides" of his minister or the government.[23] He found Borden "a particularly pleasant man to deal with," a man who possessed "a very sound grasp of the military requirement."[24] Borden went out of his way to encourage Hutton to be open and cooperative; he agreed with Hutton that the administration of his department was unsatisfactory and encouraged the general to suggest ways and means to reorganize and reform his department, still saddled as he was with Panet and the deputy minister's glaring administrative deficiencies. And when Hutton penned a critical report on the Militia's administration and needs, Borden defended the report fiercely in the cabinet, anxious to turn Hutton's criticism into material support for his department.

Hutton, however, soon decided to pursue his objectives by other means than through his responsible minister, especially after the arrival of Lord Minto, the new governor general. With well-placed protectors in the War Office and faced by what he misjudged to be a weak Canadian government and an inexperienced minister attempting to extricate his party from charges of patronage arising from the Yukon Field Force expedition, Hutton decided that the time was ripe to insist, assert, and reform, to make the Canadian Militia the reliable and effective force that the War Office required, capable of home defence and imperial assistance. In short, it was an opportunity to make the Canadian Militia an example to military reformers in Britain and the colonies, and in the process to make his name and fame as a military missionary of empire.

Hutton's close personal friendship with Lord Minto fed his pretensions. Having reached Canada in August 1898, two months before Minto, Hutton met the new governor general at Quebec, anxious to secure Minto's approval for his self-imposed mission to refashion the Canadian Militia. As a former Eton classmate and an old and faithful friend of the neophyte governor general, Hutton possessed privileged access to Rideau Hall and the information that flowed through its offices, as well as to a loyal and influential defender should he encounter difficulties. Very shortly relations between the minister and general began to deteriorate as each took the other's measure and attempted to define the borders of their increasingly uneasy relationship. Reform took second placed to the ensuing power struggle.

The timing of their initial encounter could scarcely have been worse. Borden was still recovering from the Opposition's searing attack on his department for its mishandling of the provisioning of the Yukon Field Force. He felt deceived by both the civilian and military sections of his department and was determined to establish a vigilant ministerial control over its affairs. At the same time Hutton seemed equally determined to reduce civilian "interference" and establish his own military authority over the Militia. The agendas of the minister and the general were on a collision path. The stage was set for a showdown.

Although anxious to reform the Militia and profit from Hutton's expert advice and give the general a chance, Borden soon realized that the general was unwilling to reciprocate. Hutton resented suggestions and mistook conciliation for weakness. Borden, not wishing to establish a legalistic relationship, first attempted to inform rather than instruct Hutton. He reminded the general that he as minister had a right to give instructions "from time to time as I may consider necessary," explaining to him the minister's political role and his need to answer "to Parliament and the people of Canada for everything pertaining to the administration including questions of discipline."[25] Borden had a clear view of his constitutional position. Moreover, he had been in Parliament and a member of its Militia lobby long enough to realize that the House held him and him alone responsible for every detail of the department's administration. Members wished to know why one officer was promoted, why another was chosen to attend the staff college, or why a cadet failed to obtain an imperial commission. Ultimately it was the members' goodwill, grace, and favour that would underwrite the resources required for reform and reorganization.

Moreover, Borden had no intention of serving merely as an accountant, cipher, and public relations officer for the general. As he explained in the House, he saw his position as comparable to that of the British secretary of state for war, as described by the Right Honourable Hugh C. Childers: "No act of discipline can be exercised, no appointment or promotion can be made, no troops can be moved, no payments can be made without the approval expressed or implied, of the Secretary of State."[26] But as time went on and Hutton became more expansive and verbose, it became increasingly difficult for Borden to defend in cabinet the general's controversial public statements, as he found himself obliged to do, more especially if he were not kept informed.

Borden soon realized, too, that Hutton would not be constrained. The general seemed intent on extending his authority at the expense of the minister. He seemed determined "to destroy existing conditions and substitute others with his own impress upon them, regardless of the consequences."[27] While the general lectured and scolded the minister on "their respective relations as to matters of discipline,"[28] he announced policy decisions without ministerial authority, in certain instances despite Borden's warnings,[29] and made financial commitments without the minister's consent or approval.[30] "[I am] exceedingly anxious to cooperate with you to the utmost," Borden wrote in some desperation to Hutton, "but I must draw the line somewhere, and I do it at the point of expenditure," and he went on to request that "in the future ... you will submit regulations to me in writing for matters involving expenditure of public money so that there may be no further misunderstanding."[31]

Despite Borden's pointed warnings, Hutton continued to appoint officers without the minister's knowledge, to ignore his instructions, and to "misunderstand" and deliberately defy and deform others. Hutton boasted of blocking Borden's recommendations,[32] but when his own suggestions were ignored or rejected, he cried political interference. Even Hutton's close friend and apologist, Minto, soon came to admit that Hutton tended to "exaggerate" and attribute political interference "to every move."[33] Hutton's lack of tact and discretion soon became notorious; even Minto could not defend his blunders. The general's use of the press embarrassed the government, and his unguarded bombast and boasting alienated his friends and enraged his opponents. His most notoriously menacing boast was his alleged claim that "he had upset one government in Australia, and that he would upset another in Canada if things did not go his way."[34] No responsible minister could tolerate this behaviour for long.

Perhaps Hutton's most serious strategic blunder, however, was to have misread his minister. In the words of Desmond Morton, Hutton's fault was his failure to understand that Borden was "the most powerful force for [Militia] reform in the Laurier government,"[35] to appreciate that the minister shared the general's commitment to empire and to the virtues of professionalism. Contrary to Hutton's superficial assessment, Borden was more than a simple country physician without knowledge of military affairs, interested only in patronage, however weak and floundering he may have appeared in the wake of the acrimonious debate on the provisioning of the Yukon Field Force. Although affable and accommodating and anxious to improve his department, Borden refused to relinquish control and responsibility of his department to an instant expert, no matter how impressive his military credentials. Furthermore, Borden could not be pushed, as the War Office itself soon learned. In short, Hutton misread Borden. He mistook Borden's initial cooperation for weakness. He also exaggerated the effective powers of the governor general. In both instances, he was to have a rude awakening.

Less than two weeks after Minto landed in Quebec, Hutton decided to test his influence with the governor general by bringing to Minto's attention a rather petty dispute that had turned into a contest of wills between himself and the minister. Borden had recommended the appointment of a Dr Napoleon Chevalier to the medical officer's post at the military school at St Jean, Quebec. He had sought Hutton's perfunctory approval, but when the general returned the appointment for further information, Borden ignored the request, which he saw as a challenge, and sent the appointment directly to the cabinet for approval. Annoyed by Borden's discourtesy, Hutton went at once to the governor general and asked him to refuse signature to the Order-in-Council until he himself had approved the appointment. When Minto raised this matter with the minister, which he had every right to do, Borden stiffly reminded Minto that in the end he must either accept his advice or request his resignation, and Minto, confused and uncertain of his authority, had capitulated.

Minto, however, had not abandoned the general; he made that public in an ill-advised speech to the Toronto Club in December 1898 when he acknowledged his personal friendship with Hutton (whom he described as a man of tact, knowledge, and competence), endorsed the general's reform program, and predicted his success if he were unhampered by "political influences."[36] Minto's gratuitous allusion to the Chevalier conflict not only raised the ire of many sensitive Liberals, but encouraged Hutton to ride less cautiously, confident of the governor general's public endorsement of his self-proclaimed imperial mission to reform the Militia and ready it for imperial service. It was not a good beginning for the governor general, the general, or the minister. And more was to follow.

The Domville affair, a tangled, eighteen-month comic opera, proved a dress rehearsal for the final break between Borden and Hutton. At first glance, the facts of the Domville case seem simple. Lieutenant-Colonel James W. Domville, the commanding officer of the 8th Princess Louise (New Brunswick) Hussars and a Liberal member of Parliament, was obliged to resign his command under General Order 90, an order issued by Hutton's predecessor (with Borden's full backing) that limited command of a unit to a five-year period. While the Tories, who had installed and retained their friends in battalion commands, saw General Order 90 as an attempt to rid the force of their friends, its primary purpose was to rejuvenate the command of Militia units and provide career mobility and experience. Only in exceptional circumstances could a command be extended to eight years. Ironically, the minister's greatest difficulty in enforcing the order came from a member of his own party, James Domville.

There was no disagreement between Borden and Gascoigne on the Domville case. Domville had been in command of his battalion for almost seventeen years. While there were rumours of the officer's fondness for alcohol and "commercial sharp practice,"[37] the longevity of his command was sufficient reason to persuade Borden and Gascoigne that Domville's time had come, despite the lieutenant-colonel's vociferous and persistent protests. At second glance, things were not that simple. Domville's claims for an extension had merit. Educated at the Royal Artillery Academy at Woolwich, Domville, who had then been a Conservative, had once been considered for the post of general officer commanding the Canadian Militia. And even in 1897, at the age of fifty-five, Domville was far from incompetent. In the opinion of the district officer commanding, Lieutenant-Colonel George J. Maunsell, Domville was well above the calibre of most commanding officers in his district, and on those grounds Maunsell had recommended him for a three-year extension.

Domville's primary reason for requesting an extension, however, was not military but political. He disliked the politics of his successor, Lieutenant-Colonel Alfred Markham, whose newspaper, the Saint John Sun, had opposed Domville's closely contested election to the House of Commons in 1896. By Domville's calculations, regimental patronage affected about five hundred votes, the difference between victory and defeat, votes that it would be foolish to transfer to a political opponent, particularly before a provincial election. A Conservative apostate, in 1896 Domville had contested the Kings County (New Brunswick) constituency for the Liberals, defeating the powerful minister of finance, George Eulas Foster. While his victory had enhanced Domville's reputation among the Liberals, encouraging him to believe he was entitled to a cabinet post, New Brunswick Conservatives remained bitter and vindictive.

Foster was especially anxious to destroy Domville's political influence in Kings, and he began his assault on Domville in the House of Commons by charging him with the misappropriation of Militia funds. According to the charge, Domville had cashed a cheque from the Department of Militia in the amount of $300 for the rental of his regimental armouries. When the auditor general had brought the error to Domville's attention, he had rectified it at once. Foster, undeterred by this clarification and his failure to sully Domville's reputation, used his parliamentary immunity to accuse Domville of other irregularities. These Gascoigne had investigated but, having found insufficient evidence to substantiate them, had recommended that Domville retire with honour.

Borden had backed Gascoigne fully and had insisted on Markham's right to succeed Domville, if for no other reason than to persuade the public "that politics was not at the bottom of it; and it is our duty as prudent men to take this into account."[38] Domville's feelings toward Borden, however, were far from cordial. He resented Borden's appointment to the Militia Department, a position he had canvassed for himself. Rejecting Borden's judgment, Domville appealed directly to Laurier. There the case rested until Hutton arrived, gathered the tangled threads of the dispute, and, without consulting Borden, ordered Domville to surrender the unit's regimental stores to his successor. Unable to await his victory, Markham foolishly ordered his agent to enter Domville's armouries (Domville's private property) and seize the military supplies. Markham's illegal actions gave Domville the excuse he sought to prolong the controversy and delay if not rob Markham of his victory. In an effort to end this comic opera, the district officer commanding suggested that both men ought to resign in favour of a third, more-neutral candidate. Borden immediately endorsed this compromise proposal, since it promised to rid the unit of further divisive controversy. Hutton, however, rejected the arrangement and Domville refused to retire.

In the face of this stalemate, Borden's first instinct was to negotiate. On several occasions he tried to reason with Domville and persuade him to retire voluntarily after the provincial election, and at one point he thought he had an agreement. But when the election was over, Domville refused to go until the Commons' Public Accounts Committee had investigated and reported on Foster's charges and cleared his reputation, a demand that Borden and even Hutton initially thought was reasonable. But to forestall the committee's report, Domville delayed appearing before the committee. Impatient with Domville's devious tactics, Hutton persuaded Foster to withdraw his accusations, and then, without Borden's approval, he put Domville on a leave of absence pending his retirement. Domville insisted, however, upon the committee's more-formal arm's-length repudiation of Foster's charges, and with reason.

At this point the minister and the general parted company. Borden had agreed to Domville's request that he await the report of the Public Accounts Committee; it was a point of honour. Hutton's deal with Foster, however, contravened Borden's agreement and placed him in the disagreeable position of defending Domville. Consequently he asked Hutton to withdraw his order pending the committee's report. But Hutton resisted; instead he sought the assistance of the governor general, who was fully conversant with all the details of this tangled dispute.

Initially Minto had assured Hutton of his "most thorough support," but upon closer examination of the situation Minto was less confident that he could back the general unequivocally.[39] The governor general was beginning to see his friend's limitations, his incorrigible vanity, tactlessness, and indiscretion. A brief conversation with Borden convinced Minto of Hutton's precipitate behaviour on this occasion, and he lost no time telling him so. Whatever the rights and wrongs of this case, Minto agreed with Borden that Domville should remain in command until the Commons committee had reported and Domville had had an opportunity to clear his reputation. But to end Domville's delaying tactics, Minto insisted that Hutton's cancellation of the order be conditional upon Domville stating in writing the date he intended to appear before the Public Accounts Committee. Then, following the committee's report, Domville was to retire and Markham to succeed him for a week, after which he would be replaced by a third man.[40] Since the terms of the settlement were essentially those Borden had proposed originally, following the advice of the district officer commanding, he had every reason to consent to the governor general's proposal. In retrospect, however, Minto's intervention may have set an unfortunate precedent, encouraging the governor general's claim to interfere.

Finally, in August 1899 the Commons' Public Accounts Committee reported. While it found financial irregularities in Domville's regimental administration, it cleared him of personal guilt or responsibility. That done, Domville retired as he had promised, and the long and ludicrous dispute might have ended had not Hutton, in contravention of the agreement, attempted to retain Markham in command during summer camp. Annoyed by the general's duplicitous behaviour, Borden insisted on Markham's immediate retirement, and Hutton capitulated.

Skilful propagandist that he was, Hutton promptly declared victory. In recounting the Domville affair to his friends and later in his self-serving "Memoirs," Hutton modestly labelled it Borden's Waterloo. He boasted that the Domville case constituted a great moral victory in his battle to purify the Canadian Militia from political interference, and that throughout his battle Minto had backed him "like a hero."[41] This battle, like so many others, was a combat against straw men of Hutton's lively imagination. In fact, Hutton, under vice-regal pressure, had been obliged to concede Borden's position and withdraw his order. Moreover, Domville's retirement might have been secured sooner had Hutton worked with, rather than against, Borden. But from the start he had cast Borden as the antagonist, as the corrupt, patronage-mongering colonial politician, a threat to his professional authority and the protector of Domville and the Liberal Party.

Hutton failed to realize that neither Borden nor his cabinet colleagues had any brief for Domville. They tended to regard Domville as a troublesome nuisance who inflated the political importance of his command.[42] Domville reciprocated Borden's personal dislike, viewing the minister as a professional rival, and made every effort to discredit him. In fact, their mutual dislike could be quite visceral, and during an earlier dispute, Domville had threatened to assault the minister. Oblivious to the machinations of Canadian politics and determined to establish and protect his professional territory, Hutton misread the partisan character of this dispute and Borden's part in it. His failure to regard Borden in this and other matters as the "most powerful force for [militia] reform in Laurier's government"[43] retarded rather than advanced reform.

Borden had no reason to feel that he had been singled out by Hutton's territorial sensitivities, nor that the dispute was simply a clash between ministers and generals or imperial dreams and colonial realities. As a friend of Lord William Seymour, the general officer commanding British troops in Halifax, Borden knew only too well that Seymour faced similar difficulties with Hutton. Despite Minto's and Hutton's efforts to exclude Borden from knowledge of the unseemly dispute between these two "imperial" officers, Borden was an interested, fully informed, and probably amused spectator to the professional rivalry and jurisdictional battle that poisoned relations between Hutton and Seymour.

The existence of two distinct military commands on Canadian soil created potential conflict. When the British withdrew their regular forces from central Canada in 1871, they retained sufficient imperial troops in Halifax, and later in Esquimalt, to protect the Royal Navy's installations on both coasts. The departure of all but the Halifax and later the Esquimalt garrison troops left the initial burden of Canadian defence to the recently created Canadian Militia, commanded by the general officer commanding the Canadian Militia. The presence of a senior and superior British regular officer in Halifax commanding British garrison troops, who was answerable directly to the War Office and (in the absence of the governor general doubled as administrator) was to assume command of Canadian and British troops in the event of war, made cohabitation and cooperation between the two commands essential.

To complicate matters further, not only was the GOC of the Canadian Militia a British regular officer on loan to the Canadian government, but he was only one of several British regulars borrowed by the Canadian government to improve the efficiency of Canada's small Militia force. In the past the War Office had asked the Halifax general to report annually on all British regular officers serving in Canada in his command and in the Canadian Militia. Seymour assumed, therefore, that he possessed command and authority over these regular officers, not in their role as temporary Canadian Militia officers, but as British regular officers, a somewhat tenuous distinction that Hutton haughtily rejected.

In Hutton's view, Seymour's request for information on the British officers serving in his Canadian command was more than a convenient, established, and practical reporting procedure. He feared that it was but the first instalment of Seymour's larger plan to subordinate the Canadian Militia to his authority. That seemed clear from Seymour's representations to the Canadian Defence Commission that had been despatched to Canada by the War Office in August 1898, under the presidency of Major-General E.P. Leach, to determine how the War Office's ultimate responsibility for the defences of Canada might be made more efficient and effective. While Hutton worked closely with the commission and later boasted that the Leach Report, which indicted Canadian defences, was made with his "direct collusion," he resented its discussion of how the two commands might work more closely together.

Hutton's unreasonable fears poisoned social and professional communications between the two British generals. Their personal encounters turned into confrontations, occasions for juvenile slights and injuries. At a vice-regal dinner in Ottawa for Seymour, Hutton's pliant chief of staff officer, Colonel Hubert Foster, himself a British regular on loan, insisted upon wearing civilian dress to make his point, a discourtesy that was not lost on Seymour. To make clear his claims upon British regulars loaned to the Canadian Militia, and not without a touch of malice, Seymour addressed them by their inferior British regular ranks rather than their more exalted Canadian Militia ranks. When Seymour asked Foster for a report on "Reconnaissance of the Eastern U.S. Frontier," Foster sent it through the Governor General's Office, which would have been an unusual though technically correct route had it first gone through the minister's office, which it had not. In April 1899 Seymour complained that Hutton had spoken publicly about naval defence of the Great Lakes, a subject under Seymour's jurisdiction. And with time the quarrel became more tense, petty, and personal.

Later the same month, when Seymour made his annual request for information on British officers serving in the Canadian Militia, Hutton flatly refused to comply and appealed directly to Minto, not Borden, to stop Seymour's intrusions. Although Minto reproached Hutton for being unduly sensitive, reminded him that these reports normally went to the War Office through the Halifax general, and urged him to be more cooperative, he gratuitously reminded Seymour that Canada was a self-governing colony and undertook to lecture him somewhat need-lessly on the constitutional separation between the two commands, a constitutional distinction Seymour fully understood and did not contest. In fact, on one occasion when Borden, in a moment of exas-peration, had appealed to Seymour to curb Hutton's insubordination, Seymour had declined to do so because he felt that any action on his part "as Lt. General was resented by Lord Minto as an unwarranted interference with the militia of Canada."[44] Moreover, to demonstrate that he appreciated the constitutional distinction between the two commands better than his would-be teachers, Seymour decided to call Minto and Hutton's bluff: he agreed to abandon the traditional informal mode of direct communication with Hutton and address him through the governor general and the minister of militia.

Seymour's ploy immediately exposed the illogic of Minto and Hut-ton's constitutional stance. The last thing they wanted was to admit Borden into the cosy confidence of imperial defence communications, much less expose him to this unseemly row between "imperial offi-cers." Alarmed by the implications of Seymour's suggestion, Minto wrote at once to Lord Lansdowne, the secretary of state for war, calling for a clearer definition between the two commands and a curb on the pretensions of the Halifax general. The War Office agreed to redefine Seymour's role, making clear the separation of the two commands, but also agreed with Seymour that official communications must pass through the minister of militia, a sentiment that the Colonial Office fully endorsement. It would "be anomalous to have one servant of the Dominion Govnt reporting on the services of another of its servants without the Dominion Govnt knowing anything about the matter," noted John Anderson, the powerful, perceptive, and experienced Col-onial Office official. "It is in one sense a mere matter of form but it involves a not unimportant principle."[45] As for Hutton, whose fears and suspicions had forced the issue, one War Office officer noted that he

was simply "constitutionally deficient in every atom of tact – and constitutionally incapable of even acquiring and exercising the elements
of it."[46] Minto and Hutton had called upon the imperial arbitrator; the
arbitrator had spoken and Minto and Hutton had lost. It would not be
the last time.

In the past, many vigilant Liberal partisans had noted the ease with
which Lieutenant-Colonel William White had extended his command
of the 30th Battalion, despite his public support for the Conservative
Party, while Domville faced considerable difficulty. They noted too
how closely Hutton worked with the Conservative senator Sir John
Carling in organizing the 7th Fusiliers of London, and commented on
the Conservative stranglehold on the organization of the Militia's new
medical corps. These were not concerns that Borden shared. Moreover,
Hutton's celebrated quarrel with Sam Hughes, the Conservatives' chief
military critic, demonstrated that the general respected no person's
politics if his actions threatened Hutton's personal and professional
ambitions. The Hutton-Hughes quarrel had long roots; indeed, it began
while Hutton was still battling Lord Seymour and Domville. Since the
story of this colourful encounter has been well told elsewhere, only the
barebones of the dispute need to be recounted.[47]

Initially Borden, who understood and liked Sam Hughes and played
the Conservative member like his violin, must have watched the sim-
mering Hughes-Hutton verbal duel with amused apprehension. During
the course of their increasingly acrimonious dispute, Hutton and
Hughes accused each other of insanity, and if one were to judge from
their language, correspondence, and subsequent behaviour, they were
both right. An ardent advocate of the Militia's civilian soldier, Hughes
resented Hutton's apparent scorn for civilian soldiers and his attempts
to subordinate them to the Permanent Force. In fact, this issue divided
the two men almost from their first encounter.

Personality, policy, and career ambitions combined to fuel their
doctrinal animosities. Both men were too similar to be compatible.
Although both were competent officers, they were also ambitious, vain,
impulsive, self-seeking, territorial, and intemperate. Both craved rank
and distinction and saw war as a means to advance their claims. It is no
coincidence that their conflicting ambitions surfaced publicly over the
issue of the leadership of the proposed Canadian South African War
contingent. In May and again in July 1899 Sam Hughes had offered to
raise and command a volunteer force of Canadian civilian soldiers in
anticipation of war in South Africa. Hutton, who had little respect for
the martial talents of Canada's civilian Militia, had personal reasons
to discourage private arrangements over which he would have no control and for which he would derive no professional credit. Hutton had

dreamed of, indeed he had offered to command, a brigade of colonial troops should war begin in South Africa; this was a role for which he believed his service in Australia and Canada had cast him. He thought, too, that his claim to command would be enhanced if he took a prominent part in organizing and despatching an official, government-sponsored Canadian contribution. And he feared that Hughes's private plans might deprive him of that opportunity, especially as the government, racked by political doubt and dissention on the issue, might prefer and promote Hughes's agenda, to avoid action and criticism. Hutton therefore made every effort to stop Hughes, make an example of him, and prevent similar private offers.

What Hutton failed to appreciate was that Hughes might be cajoled, flattered, and humoured but he would not be bullied, and Hutton was a bully. Unbeknown to Hughes, Hutton initially had planned to give Hughes a conspicuous place in his proposed official Canadian contingent; indeed he had slated him for the position of second in command, not a particularly discriminating military decision given Hughes's subsequent behaviour. Unaware of the general's plans and fearing the worst, in May 1899 Hughes formally offered to raise and command his own Canadian contingent, an offer designed to heighten his visibility and credibility. More insistent than he had been in May, in July Hughes sent his offer through three channels, the GOC of the Canadian Militia, the minister of militia, and the colonial secretary, Joseph Chamberlain. The first never got beyond Hutton's desk, and Hughes received not so much as a formal acknowledgment. The second Borden endorsed and sent to the cabinet, despite Hutton's objections. The cabinet, in turn, sent Hughes's offer to Minto and asked that he transmit it to the Colonial Office. After consulting with Hutton, the governor general returned the Privy Council minute covering Hughes's offer and explained to the cabinet that he considered Hughes incapable of serving with British officers.[48] As for the third offer, Chamberlain acknowledged it graciously and asked Minto to thank Hughes for his patriotism and loyalty. Hughes's success with Chamberlain infuriated Minto, and after discussing the matter with Hutton, the governor general foolishly asked the general to reprimand Hughes, a subordinate officer, for his unusual military behaviour in communicating directly with Chamberlain. Hutton was only too willing to inform Hughes of the governor general's "command," adding that all subsequent communications with governments must pass through the general's office.[49]

Hutton's communication stung Hughes into action, and he struck back with the recklessness of a doomed man. Extending his battle to the vice-regal front, Hughes questioned the governor general's authority to reprimand him and heaped abuse on British regulars for their historic stupidities in language that convinced Minto and Hutton that Hughes was slightly mad and certainly unfit to command troops in the field. Hutton's equally insulting and ill-advised response, claiming that Canadian troops were totally unprepared for war and "might as well try to fly to the moon as to take the field alongside of British regulars,"[50] only goaded Hughes into greater verbal excess. "You say I would be incapable to serve alongside British regulars," the enraged Hughes retorted. "Why, could I not retreat or surrender equally to the Boers? You are not infallible and you should know it."[51] (Ironically, Hutton's subsequent assessment of British leadership in South Africa echoed Hughes's analysis.)[52] To silence all who doubted that he could raise a contingent, Hughes wrote to several papers soliciting volunteers, whereupon Hutton retaliated by accusing Hughes with violation of the United Kingdom Army Act, which forbade unauthorized recruiting for the British regular army, and threatened to remove him from the command of his Militia battalion if he persisted.

While the initial Hughes-Hutton exchanges may have amused Borden, things had now come to a serious impasse and he moved at once to defend Hughes. Upon Borden's suggestion, the Canadian government rejected Hutton's contention that Hughes's press poll constituted recruitment for the British regular army, and consequently Hughes was not liable for Hutton's threatened punishment. Borden considered Hughes an efficient and popular militia officer, and he had no desire to see him humiliated. Moreover, as war approached, some cabinet members saw Hughes's private volunteer scheme as a convenient means of dodging official participation. They therefore did all they could to encourage Hughes and others to make private offers. Laurier made this position perfectly clear in his communications with the press,[53] to which Hutton replied indirectly through the *Canadian Military Gazette* that it was "a criminal act of folly to appoint an amateur militia officer without army experience to command a battalion."[54]

Although highly personal and acrimonious the Hutton-Hughes quarrel remained theoretical until the outbreak of war in South Africa. The beginning of military hostilities, however, seemed to unhinge Hutton and brought the Hughes dispute and others to a head. The war also precipitated Borden's final struggle with the contentious general for control of and authority over the Canadian Militia, a battle Borden was determined to win or fall in the process.

CHAPTER 8

War

A few days after Canada's first contingent of troops for South Africa sailed from Quebec City, Borden described Canada's first military expedition abroad as the "proudest moment of his life."[1] More than anything else, the war made Borden an imperial figure. Little did he know then how it would change his life for good and ill; in the short run it would bring more ill than good. Not only would it exact a terrible personal price, it would challenge his ministerial authority, his place in Laurier's cabinet, and his continuation in public life. Obliged to engage in the external military conflict with an unreformed Militia, Borden faced within his own department an uncooperative, quarrelsome, recalcitrant general determined to use the war to his own advantage, to contest the minister's power, and to push his own claims to their limits.

The causes and character of the war between Britain and the two Afrikaner republics, the South African Republic (popularly labelled the Transvaal) and the Orange Free State, that began on 11 October 1899, as well as the political controversy surrounding the despatch of Canadian troops, are too well known to justify detailed repetition here.[2] It is sufficient to note that historians have disagreed profoundly on the causes of the war. Some have seen it as an ethno-cultural conflict, a contest between Dutch-speaking Afrikaners and English-speaking inhabitants that began with the British purchase of the Dutch colony at the Cape of Good Hope in 1815. Others have viewed it as a socio-economic conflict, orchestrated by international financial capital following the discovery of diamonds in 1867 and gold in 1886. Still others have regarded it as a diplomatic chess game, a strategic manoeuvre in the nineteenth-century European partition of Africa. Few would still describe it as a "white-man's war," given the important role played by Africans. As one perceptive writer has observed, the South African War was many wars, depending upon the differing roles and objectives of its participants.[3] Canada, too, had its objectives.

Contemporary Canadians viewed the deteriorating relations between Britain and the South African Republic with interest and foreboding. At the time, their popular press represented the war largely as an ethno-linguistic conflict, one that challenged the enlightenment, honour, integrity, and religious mission of the Empire.[4] Pro-war advocates focused public attention on the human side of the conflict, the Afrikaners' or Boers' stubborn deprivation of basic civic rights to the "Uitlanders," those predominantly English-speaking inhabitants who had flooded into the two Boer republics following the discovery of diamonds (1867) and gold (1886). Dr Leander Jameson's abortive coup d'état in December of 1895, his bungled effort to seize Uitlander rights by force, however, so discredited the Uitlander cause that it was not until May 1899 that their grievances recaptured public attention.

By then Alfred Milner, the British high commissioner for South Africa, was well installed in Cape Town, determined to break the growing economic and strategic power of the interior Afrikaner republics and implicate the British government in his crusade. The Uitlanders' economic and political rights and privileges became his battle horse to achieve diplomatic advantage. In a highly publicized June 1899 conference with the Transvaal president, Paul Kruger, in Bloemfontein, the capital of the Orange Free State (the sister Afrikaner republic with which Kruger had a defensive alliance), Milner pushed Kruger further than he was prepared to go. In the months following the June meeting, Milner's decision to prepare for war hardened Kruger's intransigence. Finally, on 9 October 1899, Kruger, fearing the weakening of his military advantage as British troops steamed toward Cape Town, issued his famous forty-eight-hour ultimatum demanding that the British withdraw their military reinforcements, including those on the high seas. When the British failed to comply, Boer troops entered British territory and war began.

Just before its summer recess in July 1899, the Canadian Parliament had passed a carefully crafted resolution endorsing the Uitlanders' call for political liberty while scrupulously avoiding any promise of military aid. Meanwhile Militia officers, military institutes, patriotic societies, and other interest groups began to agitate for Canadian participation should war ensue. In anticipation of a federal election,[5] the political agitation, represented all too simplistically as a contest of wills between French and English Canadians, assumed a particularly divisive ethno-religious character, although the lines were much more complex that this.[6]

As early as May 1899, as he visited various summer militia training camps, Borden became aware of the intensity of the desire to participate in the anticipated conflict. It was not until early July, however, that he considered seriously the possibility of the despatch of Canadian troops. The occasion was Joseph Chamberlain's request that the governor general sound his Canadian government on the chances of a "spontaneous" Canadian offer of military assistance, more to demonstrate imperial solidarity than out of anticipated military need.

Borden maintained a close rapport with Militia officers and men. He scandalized the Opposition by attending summer camp as a serving medical officer for his first two summers as minister. He enjoyed the military fraternity, and even after he ceased to serve as a medical officer, he continued to visit the summer Militia camps across the country. Consequently, he appreciated the growing pressure from ambitious Militia officers, Militia units, and other well-placed interest groups to participate in the impending conflict. Borden himself, however, believed that if Canadians were to participate, they should be sent as an official, government-sponsored unit, a contingent of all arms, not simply as a point of Canadian pride, but in order for the Militia to benefit from their war experience; in this objective Borden's and Hutton's views were not at variance.

From the start Borden seemed to view the possibility of Canadian participation in the war largely in pragmatic terms, as an opportunity to promote his department, increase its estimates, secure resources for the much neglected Militia, test its organization and equipment, and give its men and officers valuable war experience and career opportunities. Nor did he hesitate to remind the reluctant prime minister of the patronage it would engender, something to consider on the eve of a general election.[7] The cause or justice of the war appeared not to preoccupy him; nor did he anticipate the war's duration and its human, material, and personal cost. Much less did Borden regard war as an opportunity for imperial integration. In fact, he seemed to see Canadian participation more as an opportunity to assert status, to establish Canada's place within the imperial family and the community of nations. He also understood the political consequences of resistance.

Although many Canadian historians assume that General Hutton, in response to a request from the governor general, prepared an unauthorized secret plan for the despatch of Canadian troops behind the back of his minister, in fact Borden authorized, contributed to, and approved Hutton's contingency plans. He was especially pleased with the proposal, drawn up largely by Hutton's chief of staff, Colonel Hubert Foster, for a balanced unit composed of one small infantry battalion, one battery of field artillery, and a hundred mounted rifles, with a total strength of 1,200 men, 314 horses, and six guns, all for an estimated cost of $300,000. Altogether it was to be a representative "little army" worthy of Canada.

Borden was no less happy with the general's choice of proposed senior officers, which he insisted then and subsequently be chosen for their military rather than their political merits.[8] The Opposition acknowledged and appreciated Borden's impartiality in the selection of officers, perhaps all too proud of the fact that their party boasted a larger number of officers than the Liberals. Even Hutton, in the midst of his acrimonious final struggle with Borden, admitted Borden's support and the impartiality of their selection. Borden had a great respect for Lieutenant-Colonel William Dillon Otter, tagged to lead the Canadian force, a respect that Otter seemed to reciprocate. Borden also approved the general's initial decision to name the Conservative member of Parliament, Sam Hughes, second-in-command of the proposed official contingent, a choice that had the advantage and intention of scotching Hughes's private recruitment plans. Nor was the Militia Department's choice of senior officers a well-guarded secret, especially among the senior officers whose services were being solicited.[9]

Borden never doubted the defensibility and the necessity of contingency plans, including plans for the provision of stores and supplies, if the department were to avoid the blunders and confusion that had surrounded the hasty despatch of the Yukon Field Force. Consequently, well before the war began, Borden placed orders with garment manufacturers to clothe a force of a thousand men to make good the anticipated shortage of uniforms in storage. The subsequent relative speed, fourteen days, and facility with which the first Canadian contingent was clothed and despatched owe much to this foresight.

Moreover, within the cabinet Borden assumed the role of chief advocate for an official Canadian contingent, a position made possible and necessary by Laurier's carefully cultivated, politically inspired ambiguity on the subject, firmly grounded on the prime minister's confidence that war would be avoided. While the Commons' unanimous July resolution had avoided any mention of Canadian military assistance, it did not exclude that possibility either. Borden felt free, therefore, to state his views publicly on 4 September at a banquet at Montreal's Windsor Hotel for Lieutenant-Colonel Percy Girouard, the rising French Canadian star in the British Army, promising that Canada would defend the Empire "wherever they may need such defence."[10] Laurier was not entirely happy with Borden's public statement and explained immediately to Borden his personal opposition "to sending an armed force to Africa, since we have too much to do in this country to go into military expenditures."[11] Nonetheless Borden refused to regard the case as closed, informing Laurier of the Militia Department's contingency plans and attempting to persuade him of the economic and political advantages that would accrue from participation on the eve of a general election.[12] But there their indecisive discussion ended for a time, lulled by the deceptive calm that had settled temporarily over the South Africa crisis.

When war came less than a month later, Borden found himself in the eye of a public storm, as the country and cabinet were racked by debate and conflict over the necessity of sending a Canadian military force to South Africa. Inspired by the news that Britain had despatched 10,000 more troops to South Africa and that other colonies were offering military assistance, on 30 September the Canadian Military Institute in Toronto called a public meeting, presided over by Sir Oliver Mowat, Ontario's aged Liberal lieutenant-governor, to press the government to offer troops. Copies of the institute's resolution were distributed to members of Parliament, commanding officers of Militia units, and associated military organizations. The resolution generated a rash of comparable meetings and resolutions from patriotic and voluntary associations across the country, accompanied by growing press coverage, especially from the Conservative press, whose party had declared itself favourable to sending Canadian troops two days before the Toronto meeting. Simultaneously, an influential section of the Conservative press launched an especially unscrupulous campaign to embarrass and discredit Laurier's government and force it to send troops. Perhaps no journal surpassed the antics of the "independent" *Montreal Star,* whose indecent and vitriolic campaign consisted of sensational, manipulative reports, "racial" invective, and threatening language, a scurrilous campaign that one author described as "unique in Canadian journalistic history."[13]

In the midst of this public clamour came the controversial cable of 3 October from the British colonial secretary, Joseph Chamberlain, thanking the people of Canada for their offers of military assistance and indicating the form their offers ought to take, despite the fact that the Canadian government had made no offer. To the pro-war Canadian press, Chamberlain's generic cable, sent to all the self-governing colonies, was a direct appeal, over the head of the Canadian government, to the Canadian people for help and a severe rebuke of their government's failure to offer assistance. Laurier's immediate denial of plans to send troops and his insistence that a decision would require the consent of the Canadian Parliament (not then in session), followed almost simultaneously by a rejection of his equivocations and the publication of the Militia Department's plan by the *Canadian Military Gazette* (an Ottawa journal close to military headquarters), convinced many pro-war advocates that Laurier's denial was merely a "subterfuge"[14] and that it was "not the law that is lacking, but the heart"[15] of a cowardly cabinet, afraid to offend its francophone colleagues.

Those cabinet ministers who were opposed to Canadian participation in the war, principally Israel Tarte, the controversial minister of public works, and Richard Scott, the wily, irascible old "Irish" secretary of state, were furious when they saw Chamberlain's cable and the Militia Department's plan. In their view, this was clear proof of a British conspiracy to coerce Canada into participation. Their chief suspects were Minto, the stiff, untried, pro-consular governor general, and his friend, Hutton, the GOC of the Canadian Militia, who they were convinced had made an unauthorized offer of troops and were responsible for the public release of Chamberlain's cable for the purpose of arousing public support for what was becoming a dangerously partisan political issue. In a lengthy cabinet meeting on 6 October, just before Laurier left Ottawa to participate in an international ceremony surrounding the opening of a post office in Chicago, Tarte and Scott laid their case against Minto and Hutton before a largely sympathetic cabinet. Neither the minister of finance, W.S. Fielding, Borden's provincial compatriot in Laurier's government, nor the powerful minister of the interior, Clifford Sifton, had much time for Minto or Hutton or for military expenditures for any purpose.

During this tense cabinet meeting Borden occupied centre stage. He defended the general and tried to placate his irate cabinet colleagues, assuring them that there had been no unauthorized offers of Canadian troops. He also volunteered to wire the general, who was suspiciously on a tour of inspection in the Northwest and British Columbia, to determine if he had had any communication with Chamberlain to this effect. (Borden had no reason to know that Hutton had corresponded with Chamberlain and Wolseley on the ministry's preparations and that on 5 September the general had informed the War Office privately of the probable composition of a Canadian military contribution; but this was not an offer.) In the end the cabinet agreed that Scott, the acting prime minister in Laurier's absence, would speak to Minto and secure confirmation from him as to his and the general's communications with the British government. Meanwhile Laurier left for Chicago, convinced that the storm would blow itself out.

But in Laurier's absence the Canadian storm intensified as South Africa moved closer to war. Scott's interview with Minto exacerbated rather than assuaged the governor general's relations with his government. When Minto refused to seek confirmation from Hutton on his communications with the British government, Scott asked Borden to do so. Hutton subsequently misinterpreted Borden's request, whereas in fact Borden was attempting to shield the general from the wrath of his detractors. Meanwhile the campaign of the pro-war press intensified, its tactics increasingly manipulative and its language more divisive and menacing. And as the large urban Liberal press, hitherto loyal to the government's non-committal stance, began to waiver and the independent press moved toward support of Canadian participation, cabinet solidarity began to fracture.

The cabinet's non-committal policy left ample space for difference of opinion within the government, a space that Borden filled, especially in Laurier's absence. Public speculation from one cabinet faction called for counter-speculation from the other. Consequently when Tarte's journal *La Patrie* assured its readers that Canadian troops would not go to South Africa, the Toronto *Globe* informed its readers that in fact the government had prepared a plan to despatch troops should they be required. The day Boer troops moved into British territory, the *Globe* assured the public that a Canadian contingent was ready to aid Britain, information that Borden had leaked to John Willison, the journal's editor.[16] The source of the leak was no secret. In an effort to exploit the cabinet divisions, the jubilant pro-war press praised Borden as the only minister who possessed the courage of his convictions.

Laurier first learned of the war's outbreak when his train reached London, Ontario, on his return from Chicago. As the train creaked and swayed its way towards Toronto, Laurier and his entourage debated the necessity of Canadian participation. Counsel was divided. His old friend John Willison, the influential editor of the *Globe*, was convinced that Laurier had no choice. He would have to send troops or leave office. In Montreal the disgruntled minister of public works, Israel Tarte, made clear his own and the Quebec caucus's opposition to sending troops. Odilon Desmarais, the Liberal member for St Jacques, had even threatened publicly to resign his seat should troops be sent, and Tarte warned that other members were certain to follow. Tarte also complained bitterly of Borden's and the *Globe*'s pro-war campaign. Laurier cautiously promised nothing, except that there would be a cabinet meeting the next day, where Tarte would have ample opportunity to make his case.

The next day a deeply divided cabinet met at 11 a.m. to debate Canadian participation. Ably assisted by the postmaster general, William Mulock, Borden made a strong case for a full official contingent, along the lines proposed by the Militia Department, a unit recruited, equipped, transported, and paid by the Canadian government. Above all Borden and Mulock pleaded against splitting the Canadian recruits into company-size units of 125 men and having them absorbed into British units, as Chamberlain's telegram of 3 October had suggested and Laurier seemed to favour. On the other hand, Tarte and Scott, who had promised their followers that "not a man, not a cent" would be sent to South Africa, were determined to keep their word. In an effort to rally support to their side, Tarte and Scott focused their attack on the alleged conspiracy of Hutton, Minto, and Chamberlain to force their hand, an issue that remained unresolved. Suspicion of the conspiracy had united the cabinet before Laurier had left for Chicago, and it gave Tarte and Scott a powerful weapon. When the cabinet rose at 5 p.m.

nothing had been resolved, except that they should meet the next day after Laurier had obtained answers from the governor general to the questions that Scott, while acting prime minister, had failed to obtain.

When the cabinet reassembled the following day, the political dynamics had changed. Minto, having agreed to do for Laurier what he had refused to do for Scott, had wired Chamberlain, and Chamberlain had replied that he had received only two offers of military assistance, one from Sam Hughes and another from the Province of British Columbia. Furthermore, Chamberlain made it clear that while the British government would welcome an offer of assistance, it had no intention of requesting, much less requiring, one; nor did the war's success depend upon a Canadian offer.[17] Meanwhile, in the interval between the two cabinet meetings, Laurier assessed the seemingly irrepressible public clamour of urban English Canadians for Canadian participation. The pressure seemed overwhelming. The previous evening two absent colleague, David Mills in British Columbia and Louis Davies in London, had wired Laurier advocating the despatch of a contingent; so too had Lord Strathcona, the powerful Canadian high commissioner in London. Increasingly, moderate journals, while rejecting the language of the fanatics, were demanding action, and even the Toronto *Globe*'s partisan support was beginning to crumble. Non-partisan organizations, such as the Canadian Club of Toronto, joined the growing call for troops. Reports that the Montreal Corn Exchange had interrupted its transactions to intone patriotic refrains and rumours that large public meetings were being planned in Hamilton, Toronto, and Montreal seemed even more ominous, especially in Montreal where a demonstration might degenerate into a physical confrontation between French and English Canadian hotheads. Even before his cabinet reconvened, Laurier realized that resistance was all but impossible.

Scott and Tarte, however, had not surrendered their arms. A compromise would be necessary, or at least the appearance of one. When the cabinet reconvened, Scott and Tarte renewed their unrepentant attack, but to an increasingly irritable and unreceptive audience. When William Mulock, a vociferous advocate of Canadian participation and acutely conscious of public passion in Toronto, could take it no longer, he stormed angrily from the meeting. At that point Laurier realized he could temporize no longer. He could not afford to lose an influential Ontario cabinet minister, a close friend and financial supporter, on so sensitive an issue on the eve of a general election.

Cabinet was recessed while Laurier met with the Quebec caucus to devise a compromise that would permit the government to recruit, equip, and transport "a certain number of volunteers by units of 125 men, with a few officers, not to exceed 1,000 men," who would thereafter be paid, maintained, and returned to Canada by the British government. Under no circumstance, the government maintained, were these terms and the necessary small expenditure of public funds "to be regarded as a departure from the well-known principles of constitutional practice, nor construed as a precedent for future action."[18] As soon as the cabinet had ratified this agreement, Laurier left for Rideau Hall to inform the anxious governor general. W.S. Fielding (instead of the sullen, unconvinced Richard Scott) announced the government's carefully worded compromise to the awaiting press, and Borden left jubilantly for his office to execute the cabinet's welcome decision.

Lights in the minister's office burned late that night as Borden and his new deputy minister, Colonel L.-F. Pinault, planned their organizational strategy. Early the next morning Borden was back in his office, a routine he maintained for the next two weeks, including weekends, with the exception of a trip to Montreal on 16 October and another to Toronto on the 17th (the latter to confer with his cabinet colleagues James Sutherland, the new minister without portfolio, and his pro-war advocate William Mulock), followed by a rapid trip to his constituency the following day – all the while, during these quick trips, working assiduously in the ministerial car. Borden's staff followed his example, working over time but claiming no extra pay. Subsequently, Borden liked to boast that the necessary work was accomplished in record time without hiring any additional clerical staff.[19] Borden's own correspondence increased exponentially, instructing, inquiring, and reminding his staff and responding to suggestions, requests, and complaints; and his consultations, interviews, meetings, and conversations seemed interminable.

Things went surprisingly smoothly despite (or perhaps because of) the absence of the GOC of the Canadian Militia and the adjutant-general. Hutton remained on tour in the Northwest and British Columbia until 25 October and would return to Ottawa only two days before the various companies began to congregate in Quebec, the port of debarkation. The adjutant-general, Colonel Matthew Aylmer, was still on staff course in England and unable to return in time. In their absence, much of the work fell upon the new deputy minister, Pinault, Hutton's chief of staff, Colonel Hubert Foster, and the heads of departments, especially the chief superintendent of stores, Lieutenant-Colonel D.A. Macdonald, in charge of the purchasing branch; Captain A. Benoit, the chief engineer; Captain Paul Weatherbe; and the departmental accountant, J.W. Borden. These men and others in Ottawa and in regimental headquarters across the country spared neither time nor energy in preparing the Canadian contingent to sail a day before the War Office's deadline of 31 October.

The task was formidable. To recruit, organize, lodge, feed, dress, equip, and transport 1,039 men, including 40 officers, from across Canada required proficiency, coordination, organization, cooperation, goodwill, and dedication. Accounts and a mountain of correspondence had to be maintained, contracts let, purchases made, and equipment and innumerable gifts, comforts, and other materials from organizations, "thoughtful friends and public-spirited citizens" itemized, packed, and shipped.[20] Fortunately, the contingent's strength closely approximated that of the PF, for which the department maintained the requisite supplies of uniforms, arms, and equipment; and the Department had had sufficient foresight to replenish the near-depleted stocks of clothing some weeks before war began.

Still stinging from the Opposition's attacks on his department for its mishandling of the provisioning contracts for the Yukon Field Force, Borden made every effort to avoid mistakes. Nevertheless mistakes were made, and inventories did not always match supplies, supposedly caused by Foster's bungling.[21] The shortage of smallpox vaccine and the insufficient quantity of khaki tunics (only 260), for example, were not remedied until the *Sardinian,* the first Canadian contingent's cramped old troop ship, reached Cape Town. Given the task, the inadequate support, the department's inexperience, and time constraints, it was less surprising that mistakes were made than that there were so few, and that none was irremediable.

One of Borden's most pressing and delicate political problems was to resuscitate the Militia Department's plan for an integrated, three-armed contingent and keep the Canadians together in one unit. Both of these objectives had been casualties of the cabinet compromise. Many cabinet members, even Richard Scott, strongly supported the idea of keeping the Canadians together and sending them in a mixed battalion of infantry, cavalry, and artillery. Canadians were especially keen to send artillery, allegedly Canada's best arm. At Borden's urging, and with Laurier's support, Minto wired the Colonial Office on 13 October seeking the War Office's permission to resuscitate the Militia Department's plan. Although the War Office, firmly instructed by Chamberlain, offered no objection to the eight Canadian infantry companies being grouped into a battalion, it did not see the need for cavalry and artillery. When Tarte learned of the communication, however, he insisted upon strict adherence to the cabinet's agreement,[22] and Laurier withdrew his support for an integrated force, at least officially.

Since Borden was confident that Tarte's opposition would melt eventually, the most he conceded was to delay, not abandon, his plan. This took political courage and administrative ingenuity. In principle, the first contingent of Canadian troops for South Africa consisted of eight infantry companies, under the temporary command of a lieutenant-colonel, who was instructed merely to lead the men to South Africa, after which he was free to return or seek employment with the British Army. In fact, the unit that left Quebec on 30 October possessed a supernumerary regimental command staff and was composed of sufficient cavalrymen and artillerymen in infantry uniforms to form an integrated contingent should it receive permission to reconstitute itself. An integrated, three-armed contingent never materialized and in some sense would have been redundant given the recruitment and composition of the second contingent, composed of cavalry (mounted infantry) and artillery.[23] Canada's first contingent, however, remained together as an infantry battalion, under the command of its lieutenant-colonel, W.D. Otter, owing to the Militia Department's quiet determination.

The mobilization of Canada's first contingent absorbed all of Borden's time and energy, tested his leadership, consolidated his control over his department, and demonstrated his administrative ability. Although it would have been easy to recruit the force from the overwhelming numbers of willing central Canadian volunteers, Borden insisted that the first contingent possess broad regional representation and reflect Canada's linguistic character. Favour seekers and influence peddlers were never more numerous and persistent, but Borden did not hesitate to deflate their pretensions. Partisan supplicants for war contracts who offered fair market prices received favourable and often preferential consideration, so long as they offered value for money. No less important was military competence, not politics, the primary qualification for selecting men and officers for the first contingent.[24]

Hutton's return from the Northwest five days before the first contingent sailed for Cape Town fractured departmental harmony and raised tension levels, adding to Borden's stress and workload and eroding the productivity of his department. Almost immediately the general began to find fault, disrupt working relationships, and quarrel with senior members of the headquarters staff. In his view, Lieutenant-Colonel D.A. Macdonald, the overworked chief superintendent of stores, had slighted him intentionally by the tone of his voice. Borden explained away this slight in terms of the strain of work and appealed to Hutton to try to ignore these unintentional mannerisms.[25] But Hutton remained unplacated, and even Minto had to intervene and urge him to be more reasonable. With Hutton's return, the department's chief staff officer, Colonel Foster, whose loyalties responded to immediate pressure and who worked best under instruction, could no longer be depended upon.

Unfortunately, too, Hutton's return brought to a head his absurd feud with Sam Hughes, the redoubtable member of Parliament for North Victoria. The quarrel placed an additional burden on Borden, as Hughes sought his protection from the general's abuse and anathemas.

In short, the triumph of Hutton's preference for an official Canadian contingent had left Hughes with the distasteful choice of making his bitter peace with Hutton or remaining at home. Hughes, however, was a gambler, and he had not played his last card. He knew he had a friend in Borden, and he went to see the minister to explain his predicament.

Although overburdened by work, Borden could not ignore Hughes's appeal and refused to see him humiliated. He liked Hughes and promised to assist him. The minister spoke at once to Richard Scott, an acerbic, brittle man, who had opposed the despatch of Canadian troops and in the course of the dispute had come to dislike Hutton intensely. In retrospect Borden's conversation with Scott was probably a mistake, since Scott's reaction was stronger than Borden had anticipated. Scott immediately summoned Hutton to appear before the cabinet, where he interrogated him on his efforts to pressure the government into sending troops and accused him of driving Hughes to insubordination.[26] Caught in the middle, Borden, despite his sympathy for Hughes, defended the general against Scott's wrath.

Meanwhile, outside cabinet, Borden tried his hand at peacemaking. First he spoke to Hughes and invited him to accompany him to Quebec, and once there to be ready to sail with the first contingent. Then, on the train down to Quebec, Borden, trading on Hutton's temporary goodwill arising from his defence of the general before the cabinet, suggested a compromise. According to Borden's plan, Hughes was to accompany the first contingent to South Africa, without a position and in civilian dress, where he might seek employment with the "incompetent" British regulars whom he had denounced, in return for a full written apology for his literary excesses, which had so deeply offended Hutton and his friend Minto.

Anxious to be off, Hughes impulsively agreed to apologize. Before he reached Father Point, however, he began to repent his thoughtless apology, resent his lack of official status, and demand to be uniformed and placed in a position of command in the Canadian contingent. Only then did Hughes appreciate how shallow his victory had been. In South Africa he found his career blocked at every turn: Minto and Hutton's screed had preceded him, where it had greater credence than in Canada. Unsatisfied with Hughes's initial, qualified apology, Hutton insisted that Hughes receive no post in the British Army until he complied fully with his demands. Similarly Minto wrote directly to Lord Roberts, the new commander-in-chief, describing Hughes's behaviour. Only after Hughes had penned a more abject apology did Minto and Hutton withdraw their objections to his employment, and on the condition that he never command Canadian troops. Hughes then obtained a post as a British intelligence officer, a position he held for five months, until Roberts ordered him home owing to Hughes's recidivistic press communications denouncing British military leadership. Ironically, by this time Hutton himself was in South Africa, having been relieved of his command of the Canadian Militia for insubordination.

The carnival mood of the estimated ten thousand people who came to Quebec City to see the troops depart belied the bitterness and recriminations among the official party that surfaced during the departure ceremonies. Borden's temporary credit with the general had all but been exhausted. During the final days of preparation for the despatch of Canadian troops to South Africa, Hutton's quarrel with Hughes had magnified Borden's stress and strain. Relations between the minister and general continued to deteriorate during the celebratory departure ceremonies at Quebec. Tired from overwork and increasingly irritated by the general's proprietary airs, Borden began to drink, which further weakened his patience and restraint.

Trouble began the first evening, during the Quebec Garrison Club's banquet for the officers of the contingent. Hutton, who could rarely resist an oratorical occasion, especially in the presence of the press, began his extended "few brief remarks" by directing saccharine, condescending comments toward the minister of militia, praising him for his generous and impartial administration of his department during the past few weeks (as though the general had been present to appreciate it), before moving to his loftier, more controversial promise that in the future Canada would send not simply 1,000 but 100,000 men to defend the Empire's integrity. While Hutton's insensitive and gratuitous prediction infuriated Laurier, whose "no precedent" promise had been the price of party unity, especially in Quebec,[27] Borden, an early, ardent, and unrepentant advocate of Canadian participation, was more offended by Hutton's pretension and condescension.

Borden himself did little to alleviate the growing tension between the general and the government. In the past he had played peacemaker and had defended Hutton against the harsh and exaggerated criticism of his colleagues, but he had had enough of the general's arrogance and presumption. The day after Hutton's Garrison Club speech the minister and the general had words on the parade square and Hutton stomped off in a huff. That evening, during the governor general's farewell reception at the Citadel for the contingent's senior officers, Minto's excessive praise of Hutton's contribution to the despatch of the Canadian contingent, describing the general as the best GOC of the Militia since Confederation, further irritated Borden. After all, had not Borden and his senior military and civilian staff at headquarters borne the brunt of the contingent's hectic mobilization while Hutton had continued his tour of the Northwest? Later that evening Borden went to the Garrison Club to continue the celebrations, and there, now in no condition to exercise reason, he expressed himself too freely in the presence of a retired officer of the 8th Royal Rifles. The officer defended the general's honour and an unseemly row ensued.

Even on the day of the departure while the "gallant" and long-suffering thousand volunteers stood on the Esplanade patiently await-ing their orders to board the *Sardinian*, civil and military spokesmen subtly continued their rancorous debate, each voicing his pointed views on the significance of the event. Borden was not an eloquent speaker, he knew that,[28] nor was he blind to the personal and political dangers of the soldiers' mission. Conscious of the historic, political, and per-sonal importance of the occasion, Borden described it as the "proud-est moment of his life." In his liberal imperialist credo, the despatch of Canada's first contingent overseas was a declaration of Canadian autonomy within the Empire. The Empire, he explained to his audi-ence, "is no longer a power with dependencies, but a power made up of several nations. The process of Empire building in this sense may have gone on slowly, but now it has come."[29] Canada was no longer a colony of the Empire; rather it was a part of that Empire and entitled to a voice in its direction. Borden saw himself as very much part of the process, as he would demonstrate later in his reform of the Canadian Militia and in his insistence upon cooperative imperial defence.

As the sound of departing cheers, sirens, and whistles from ship to shore faded and the overcrowded old *Sardinian* disappeared from sight, Borden must have felt a sense of satisfaction and relief. Canada's first, and presumably "only," contingent had been despatched to South Africa, after which it was to become the command responsibility of the British government. Borden had every reason to be proud of the recruitment and despatch of Canada's first expeditionary force abroad, especially the "decision" to keep the Canadians together in one bat-talion. Generally, things had gone well. The success of the effort owed much to his prodigious capacity for work, his exemplary enthusiasm, and his commitment and leadership. The task completed, his depart-ment could look forward to resuming its regular, more placid routine.

Borden, however, had little time to enjoy his success or to recover from the tension of the past four months, as he was soon confronted with the request for a second and third contingent. Indeed, the first contingent had scarcely departed when public demand, fired by the disappointment of a large surplus of eager volunteers for the first con-tingent, obliged the Canadian government to offer a second contin-gent. At the time, the overconfident British government had declined, or, technically, postponed, the offer. But the war had not gone as well as the British had expected. Consequently, by mid-December the Brit-ish government was only too willing to redeem the Canadian offer, par-ticularly to recruit mounted men and artillery. And this was only the

Dr Borden described the departure of Canada's first contingent of troops, seen here on the Esplanade in Quebec City prior to its departure for South Africa, as the proudest moment of his life. *Photograph in the author's possession*

beginning. The war's continuance and the demand for more Canadian recruits would severely tax his department and intensify its claim on his time and attention, keeping him and his department in the forefront of public interest.

Scarcely two weeks after the Canadian government had agreed to field a second contingent, Lord Strathcona, Canada's wealthy, Tory-appointed high commissioner to the United Kingdom, cabled Laurier offering to finance the recruitment of a small force of mounted scouts from the Canadian Northwest. Laurier agreed immediately to this offer and promised the Militia Department's full cooperation, as soon as it had completed its arrangements for the despatch of the second contingent.

Strathcona had initially requested that his offer remain anonymous, but this did not prevent him from insisting upon close supervision of the unit's recruitment, organization, equipment, and transportation. Above all, he insisted that no appointment be made to his battalion without the explicit consent of Major-General Hutton, gratuitously informing Laurier that his unit must "be entirely non political, the only qualification being fitness, suitability, and experience."[30] Strathcona's chief agent in Canada, Edward Clouston, the general manager of the Bank of Montreal, a Conservative, and a close friend of Lord Minto, had advised the high commissioner to insist that the recruitment and provisioning of the battalion be entrusted to Hutton and Minto. Stung by Strathcona's request, Laurier informed the high commissioner that, given the present unsatisfactory state of the general's relationship with his government, Hutton's cooperation could not be relied upon. Moreover, if Lord Strathcona wanted the department's assistance, then the ordinary administrative rules would apply and the general would act only under the minister's explicit instructions, a condition Strathcona readily conceded.

From mid-December Borden remained once again a virtual prisoner of his Ottawa office, immersed in the innumerable administrative and political details entailed in the despatch of additional Canadian troops, to be recruited in the dead of winter and shipped through the ice-free port of Halifax. The second contingent, a composite unit of mounted infantry and artillery, proved even more demanding to recruit, equip, maintain, and transport than the first, and much more expensive. The purchase, equipment, maintenance, and transportation of the requisite number of horses for the two additional contingents complicated the operation and taxed the resources of Borden's small department. But all this was not the minister's only concern. In fact, it was but the beginning of a veritable "annus miserabilis."

CHAPTER 9

Annus Miserabilis

Rest, relaxation, and self-congratulations would have to wait until Borden attended to more-demanding public and private duties. While the experience he had gained from the recruitment and despatch of the first contingent informed and facilitated the challenge, there were new and other complications, especially those associated with the season and the requirements of mounted units. Once again Borden led by example, by his energy and dedication, even though he was often distracted by personal problems, more especially his son's decision to enlist in the second contingent and the economic survival of his business. He had also to manage a succession of potentially damaging political crises. Altogether these preoccupations would tax his leadership, sap his confidence, and shake his will to continue in public life.

Borden was far from happy with his only son's decision to enlist, and he was haunted by a premonition that things might not go well. But Harold, a twenty-three-year-old, third-year medical student at McGill University and a major in the Kings County Hussars, felt that he had little choice. The day after the first contingent had sailed from Quebec the Conservative *Halifax Herald* had cruelly targeted him. Where, it had asked in large print, is the son of the minister of militia? Despite his father's remonstrance, Harold, a tall (six feet four inches), well-built, dark, handsome, and gregarious fellow, volunteered for service in the second contingent with B Squadron of the Royal Canadian Dragoons, under the command of Lieutenant-Colonel François Lessard, who assigned Harold the lieutenancy of Troop 4. The troop had recruited chiefly from Saint John, Sussex, and Canning. Ten of the forty men in Harold's troop came from his own unit, men only too anxious to serve under their dynamic, popular lieutenant.

Borden had still not reconciled himself to his son's decision when the *Milwaukee,* the ship bearing his son to South Africa, left its moorings in Halifax around noon on 21 February 1900. By this time the news of the first contingent's first bloody engagement at Paardeberg Drift had deepened the minister's apprehension. The *Milwaukee* was the last of three troopships commissioned to transport the second contingent's 1,289 men and a comparable number of horses to South Africa.

The departure of the 2nd Canadian Mounted Rifles from Ottawa on their way to Halifax. The South African War boosted the city's economy and helped rescue Borden's faltering business. *From E.S. Ridpath and J.C. Ellis,* The Story of South Africa *(Sydney, 1899)*

The presence of horses required three suitable vessels, a tall order on short notice; consequently, over a month separated the departure of the second contingent's first and last troopships.

Each time a vessel left Halifax for the war front, Borden came to the city to address the troops and participate in the elaborate departure celebrations. Each visit offered a welcome escape from the suffocating confines and incessant demands of his Ottawa office, as well as an opportunity to see Harold, who had remained in Halifax with his squadron, the last of the units to leave, training on the Commons while awaiting his departure. In retrospect, the sailing of the *Milwaukee* would claim a particular hold on Borden's memory, for it would be the last time he was to see his only son. The use of Halifax as the port of debarkation and for the quartering of troops brought lucrative business to the city, which Borden made certain would pass through Liberal hands and benefit the faltering R.W. Kinsman Company, a bounty that helped rescue his ailing enterprise, but did little for his reputation as an honest politician.

In the midst of all these competing political and personal demands and well before the *Milwaukee*'s departure Borden confronted another

The departure from Halifax of the ss *Milwaukee*, one of the four vessels required to transport the men and horses of the second continent. This would be the last time Borden would see his only son, Harold. *Courtesy the Public Archives of Nova Scotia*

"life and death" internal political battle: an unmistakable challenge by the general to his ministerial authority and his place in the cabinet. This volcano had been smouldering for a long time, but it could not have erupted at a worse moment. In the midst of all the preparation for the despatch of the two more contingents, Hutton's removal from the command of the Canadian Militia precipitated a tense, dramatic constitutional crisis that preoccupied Borden's days and nights for several weeks, owing largely to the governor general's ill-conceived decision to defend the general, embarrass the government, and remove Borden from his ministry. Had Minto's challenge succeeded it may have signalled the end of Borden's public career.

Since the outbreak of war in South Africa, relations between the minister and the general had deteriorated rapidly. The outbreak of war completely unsettled Hutton. Faced by administrative wars on several fronts and chaffing for active service, he had become even more irritable, peremptory, erratic, and unsettled. In Borden's view, Hutton had become a liability more than an asset in preparing the despatch of Canadian troops, and he encouraged the general to seek military service in South Africa.[1] Even Minto found Hutton impractical, quarrelsome, "theatrical," difficult, and at times "impossible" to deal with.[2]

Tired and strained by the increased work of his department and his personal preoccupations, Borden became less tolerant of the general's peculiarities. His cabinet colleagues, too, had had their fill of Hutton's pointed, provocative public statements, especially his prediction in Quebec during the despatch of the first contingent that Canada would send more troops, an explicit repudiation of the government's sensitive "no precedent" compromise. In the months that followed, relations between the minister and his general continued to deteriorate. In early December the *Quebec Mercury*, which had the ear of the minister or more especially his deputy minister, reported that Borden and Hutton had come close to blows over the appointment of an imperial inspector general. The question turned on a controversial order giving imperial officers seniority over a Canadian Militia officer of the same rank. Borden had ordered the general to issue no more Militia Orders without his explicit approval.[3] By January 1900 he had reached the end of his patience. He was tired of excusing and defending Hutton's behaviour to his colleagues. Moreover, that approach no longer worked. His colleagues realized that his defence of Hutton was a formality rather than a conviction. Even Hutton seemed to realize that he had overspent his minister's goodwill and tolerance. In the end he fancied Laurier his only "friend" in cabinet, but by mid-January even Laurier was convinced that Hutton would have to go.

Given the history of conflict between Borden and Hutton, Minto ought not to have been surprised when Laurier arrived at Rideau Hall on 17 January 1900 to demand Hutton's resignation. As Laurier explained to the governor general, the breaking-point between Borden and Hutton turned on a minor row over horse purchases. To avoid charges of patronage, corruption, and unreasonable prices in the purchase of horses for the mounted contingents, Borden had established boards of military officers in various regions to vet and purchase horses under the general supervision of the commandant of the Royal Military College, Colonel Gerald Kitson, a British regular officer on loan to the Canadian Militia and a close friend of Hutton's and Minto's. When Borden heard that some horses were below standard and unfit for service, especially those provided by a prominent Conservative horse dealer from Hamilton, Captain Hendrie, he spoke to Kitson.

The commandant denied the complaint, resented the insinuation, and reported the slight to Hutton. The general offered to speak to the minister, but before he did so, Borden, sceptical of the infallibility of military experts and not reassured by Kitson's reply, appointed Robert Beith, a respected farmer and horse breeder from Bowmanville, Ontario, and the Liberal member of Parliament for Durham West,[4] to go to London, Ontario, to oversee future purchases. Borden's provocative and discourteous appointment challenged the general's author-ity. When Beith arrived in camp, unannounced to Hutton, the general refused to permit him to inspect Kitson's horses. Beith immediately telegraphed Borden, and Borden ordered Hutton to purchase no more horses without Beith's approval and to permit Beith to inspect the horses. Surprised by Borden's firmness, Hutton complied with the minister's order, and according to Hutton, Beith found only five horses unfit and prices too high in only a few cases.

Although Hutton had no complaint with Beith's assessment, he resented Borden's interference and told him so in unmistakable terms on 12 January. The next day Borden, pushing his advantage, wrote Hutton requesting additional information on horse purchases. Insulted by the request, Hutton returned the letter unanswered, whereupon Borden wrote on it, "most unsatisfactory if not intentionally rude," and sent the letter back to Hutton. Although slow to anger and con-ciliatory by nature, Borden was tenacious and had his breaking-points; their relationship had reached that point. It had become a contest of wills, the lines now firmly drawn. Hutton had crossed Borden's line, and someone would have to submit or go. In assessing the political odds and determining his options, Borden realized that the general had few or no friends in the cabinet, and some ministers, Tarte, Scott, Sifton, and Cartwright, among them,[5] were active opponents. The only possible exception was the prime minister, whose chief concern was to avoid political damage so close to a general election. But neither the public nor the Opposition was likely to take up the general's cause, given his thinly veiled scorn for civilian soldiers and his vindictive pur-suit of the Opposition military critic Sam Hughes. The odds of win-ning a war with Hutton were in Borden's favour; taking up arms was a safe gamble.

As Borden had anticipated, Laurier initially believed that the dis-pute might be resolved, and for two days the prime minister tried to mediate. But when he failed, Borden laid the matter before the cabinet, requested its approval for Hutton's dismissal, and threatened to resign himself if he failed to receive its support. Borden had an easy case to plead, and with the cabinet now firmly of one opinion, Laurier had no choice but to visit Governor General Minto. Their meeting was long and stormy. The South African War had strained relations between the governor general and his government. In fact Minto had been expecting a "blow-up" for some time and was prepared for Laurier's request.[6] Sharing Hutton's sense of outrage and deploring the gratuit-ous slur on Kitson's judgment, Minto was determined to defend his friends, confident that no government could remove a high "imperial" official on so trivial and indecently petty an issue.

Laurier tried patiently to explain that the horse-purchasing row had been merely the last of a series of conflicts, a claim that Minto haughtily rejected as nothing but hearsay and gossip. The Canadian government, Minto insisted, had no grounds whatever for Hutton's dismissal. The horse row was simply a pretext trumped up by Tarte, Scott, Borden, and other cabinet ministers, perhaps even Laurier himself, to make Hutton a scapegoat, to mask his government's lack of imperial enthusiasm for the war, a vengeance that they had planned for months. And as governor general, he saw it as his responsibility to defend the imperial tie, especially during this time of imperial crisis.

Seizing the offensive, Minto informed Laurier that he had watched things closely and had quite made up his mind what ought to be done. In the governor general's view, Laurier ought to dismiss Borden, who was an intemperate, weak, and incompetent minister, a liability to the government and a man who viewed the Militia as little more than a patronage machine. Laurier, Minto speculated gratuitously, might even find Borden some other cabinet post, and someone such as James Sutherland, a minister without portfolio, might replace him in the Militia Department. Laurier replied that whatever Borden's faults, no other cabinet minister would accept the portfolio with Hutton as GOC, least of all James Sutherland, who thoroughly detested Hutton and had told Laurier that "he would have split with him long ago."[7]

Taken aback by Laurier's persistence, Minto inquired somewhat defensively just how Laurier planned to dismiss Hutton. When Laurier responded that either the general could be recalled quietly by the War Office for military service in South Africa, even lead the Strathcona Horse then being organized, or failing that, the government could take formal procedures and request his dismissal. Determined to use the occasion to reorder Canadian military structures, Minto rejected Laurier's suggestions as makeshift. Looking beyond the immediate issue to his own larger agenda, Minto informed Laurier that the time had come to redefine the office of GOC of the Canadian Militia. As for the government's proposal to dismiss the general, Minto threatened that he would withhold his signature from an Order-in-Council, at least until he received the advice of the Colonial Office. If the government wished to proceed formally, he continued, it must state its reasons in writing. He would then transmit the request to the British government, together with his own covering letter stating his strong opinions, in effect a recommendation to reject Laurier's request.

Furthermore and somewhat foolishly, Minto threatened to write an official memorandum to the Canadian government that could be laid before Parliament, stating his personal views on military administration in Canada, a draft of which he would send first to cabinet (a somewhat hazardous adventure that Laurier perhaps mischievously encouraged him to indulge). Meanwhile Laurier agreed to try to mediate the dispute once more, but he made it clear to Minto that if his efforts failed and Minto continued to block Hutton's dismissal, his government would resign. And there the interview terminated.

At first Minto seemed elated with the way things had unfolded. If Hutton was to go, he should not go quietly, of that the governor general was certain. Fully, though mistakenly, convinced of both Hutton's public popularity and his firm support by the British government, Minto now seemed determined to resist, to play the role of "patriot king" and defend the people from their capricious political leaders. Apart from the loss of Sir Wilfrid Laurier, he explained to Chamberlain later that day, "it would be a great thing for Canada generally if the govnt. resigned on the question." This way one could establish once and for all the correct position of the general officer commanding the Canadian Militia. If by chance Chamberlain disagreed with Minto's proposed plan of action, he ought to let him know immediately.[8]

Meanwhile Minto set about composing the unofficial memorandum he had promised Laurier, laying his case for the anticipated public outcry that he believed would ensue should the government persist. Minto's lengthy two-part document, the first part a constitutional treatise that David Mills, the minister of justice, claimed would have reduced Canada to the status of a Crown colony, and the second an exposé of the corruption in Laurier's government, especially in the Militia Department, infuriated the cabinet and placed the governor general himself in its direct line of fire. The minister of justice, a considerable constitutional authority, penned the reply, a document in which he attributed to Minto all the failings of a Stuart King; altogether it was a devastating constitutional blast that temporarily shook Minto's self-confidence. There was now no chance of compromise: the issue had grown into a confrontation between the governor general and his government, into a constitutional contest to establish who ruled Canada. Either Hutton must be recalled or the Canadian government would remove him. If Minto refused to sign, the government would resign.

Laurier, anxious to do nothing that might upset Canadian imperialist opinion so close to a federal election, revisited the governor general before Mills's constitutional counter-blast arrived, to restate the government's case for Hutton's recall. Minto misinterpreted the prime minister's conciliatory manner and his polite assurances that he continued to regard Hutton as nothing more than "a straight forward honourable officer."[9] Convinced that his firmness was working and that the government would back down, Minto decided to reaffirm his objections and intentions: he would submit his formal accusatory memorandum for parliamentary scrutiny and cover any request to the imperial government for a recall with a negative recommendation.

Minto had misread Laurier, as he would the British government and Canadian public opinion. Two days later Laurier returned with a despatch for the British government, formally requesting Hutton's recall. Caught off guard by the promptness of Laurier's return and the nature of his request, Minto objected that the despatch was too short and lacked a precise explanation for the request. A demand of this importance, he insisted, must be made by Order-in-Council, complete with explanation. If that was what Minto required, Laurier crisply responded, he would oblige but he warned Minto of the gravity of the matter and of the perils of the governor general's constitutional position. Laurier's new firmness unsettled Minto. He became even more unnerved when he learned that Laurier had circulated Minto's informal memorandum among the entire cabinet, even though Minto had insisted that the document had been written for the prime minister's eyes alone. In a bid for more time, Minto appealed to Laurier to make one final effort to "patch up the affair"; meanwhile he would speak to Hutton.

The next morning, before Minto had an opportunity to rethink his position, Laurier returned with an Order-in-Council requesting Hutton's recall. Surprised by Laurier's prompt action, Minto hesitated to sign the order, though he had previously agreed, even threatened, to do so. His refusal, he mused aloud, might be unconstitutional but the imperial crisis, the threat of Fenian raids, and the difficulty of replacing the general would surely justify his actions to the imperial government. After a regurgitation of his familiar threats and arguments, including a call for a cabinet reshuffle to remove Borden, Minto asked Laurier to withdraw the order for further consideration. But Laurier had had enough. He now had the measure of his man: the order must remain and he would represent Minto's views to the cabinet at his earliest convenience. Laurier had called Minto's bluff.

Minto was still not ready to quit. Confident of the British government's support, the governor general cabled Chamberlain the next day, explaining the serious turn of events. Minto made it clear that should the British government not recall the general, he would refuse to sign Laurier's dismissal order, thereby forcing the government to resign or submit. Alarmed by Minto's cable, Chamberlain replied immediately. The colonial secretary had no brief for Hutton and had opposed his appointment to Canada from the beginning. Moreover, he shared Laurier's desire to dispose of the matter quietly and promised to have Hutton recalled as soon as he could speak to the War Office and they could arrange Hutton's reassignment to South Africa. Meanwhile he warned Minto that it would be folly "to force an officer on your Governt. – who is distasteful to them."[10] Without Chamberlain's support and now in receipt of Mills's constitutional blast, Minto ought to have realized that he was defending a lost case.

He also had a hopeless client. For in the midst of the crisis Borden discovered evidence of Hutton's mischievous and gross insubordination, sufficient evidence in itself to warrant his recall or dismissal and seal the Canadian government's resolve to rid itself of the troublesome general. In December 1899, while checking a list of officers recommended for a staff course at the Royal Military College, Borden had asked Hutton to strike the names of Lieutenant-Colonels White and Vince, owing to their age and infirmity. White, whose command had been extended several times, was due to retire, and Vince was suffering from a physical disability. Borden wanted their places given to younger men whose training would benefit their battalions. Hutton had agreed and stated his approval in writing, adding that "it would be inadvisable to extend this officer's tenure of command."[11] Nevertheless Hutton instructed his pliant chief staff officer, Lieutenant-Colonel Foster, to inform White that he had been removed from the list, "by the honourable Minister," on the grounds that he had taken "an active part in politics on behalf of the opposition."[12] Since a week after Minto's receipt of Chamberlain's agreement to recall Hutton Minto had still not informed Laurier of Chamberlain's favourable response, the Canadian government, faced with Hutton's malicious behaviour, decided to exercise its second option and dismiss Hutton by Privy Council Order.

Minto welcomed this turn of events and signed the order immediately. This way Hutton would not disappear quietly with nothing accomplished. It was, he explained to the Colonial Office, so important, "in the public interest that my govnt. should accept responsibility" for the general's withdrawal.[13] It seems that despite the apparent hopelessness of both his case and his client, Minto counted on vocal public support for his position, if only he could find a means to expose his government and give the public the true facts of the case, which a quiet recall would not. Only a few days earlier, Minto had spoken to Hutton and persuaded him not to resign, advising the general that should the government move to dismiss him, Hutton should call for a royal commission into the Militia.

Minto had lost all perspective. The day after he signed Laurier's Privy Council Order, he cabled the Colonial Office to delay action "as to his [Hutton's] employment in South Africa ... till things further develop."[14] The Colonial Office, infuriated by Minto's behaviour, especially his failure to "tell his ministers that we were trying to get Hutton to S.A.," instructed Hutton the next day to return at once for service in South

Africa and, to avoid public debate, asked Minto to request Laurier to withdraw the Privy Council Order.[15] While Laurier would have been delighted to withdraw the order, the damage had been done. Hutton had already unleashed his public attack on the government. And, in his response to a question in the House, Laurier had admitted that the general had been dismissed. While Hutton's dismissal raised a brief, perfunctory debate in the House, much to Minto's disappointment it aroused no mass public outcry. Many who spoke in the House, notably friends of Sam Hughes, were hostile to the general. Domville, still stinging from his own encounters with Hutton and Minto, informed the House that he would rather have a Boer general as Canada's GOC than Hutton.[16]

In the midst of the crisis, Lord Seymour added his opinion, writing an official memorandum to the Canadian government condemning Hutton's conduct while in command of the Canadian Militia, a document that Minto refused to transmit to the Canadian government, though Borden himself, a close friend of the Halifax general, was fully aware of Seymour's devastating assessment of Hutton.[17] As some of Minto's close friends tried to explain to him, he had grossly overestimated Hutton's popularity. In time Minto came to realize how misguided Hutton's views of Canada and its government had been, and appreciate the folly of his own defence of the general. As he confessed to his wife a few years later, "I can understand Borden and Parsons [Seymour's Halifax successor], they talk sense though we may not agree with them."[18]

The dismissal of Hutton not only rid the Militia and the government of a distinct liability, it constituted a personal victory for Borden. Both Hutton and Minto had underestimated Borden's political skills, his standing within the cabinet, and his friendship with Laurier. For his part Borden had assessed his political probabilities shrewdly. He had chosen his ground, rallied his colleagues, put his position on the line, and won handily. The timing of Hutton's dismissal left something to be desired, burdened as the minister was with personal problems and the work, stress, and anxiety of preparing the despatch of two more contingents of Canadian troops for South Africa. But it had come to the point where the general's numerous slights and injuries and endless disputes had only added to the burdens of administering an overworked and understaffed department. In retrospect, Hutton's dismissal proved an important turning point in Borden's ministerial career. It established his authority in his department and earned him the respect of his cabinet colleagues as well as that of some of his former detractors, including the department's chief staff officer, Lieutenant-Colonel Hubert Foster, not to mention Lord Minto, who came to view Borden as one of the real strengths of the Laurier cabinet.

Borden moved at once to consolidate his position and establish his ministerial authority and control. Under Hutton, the Militia Department had operated like a British military district. All section heads reported to the general through his friend Chief Staff Officer Foster, the "Vulture" as he was called. Section heads were forbidden to speak directly to the minister: only the general enjoyed that privilege. This was not what Borden wanted or the way he was prepared to work and it was incompatible with his view of a responsible administration. Borden's discovery of Hutton's deliberate distortion of a ministerial instruction during the dying days of the general's administration convinced the minister of the need to open up the closed system. He immediately abolished the position of chief clerk and ordered all sections to report to him through the deputy minister. This enhanced his own control over his ministry and strengthened civilian authority. Although the governor general at first protested the change, he came shortly to concede that there was "a good deal to be said for Borden's desire to be directly informed."[19]

Borden's personal, financial, and political tribulations, however, were far from finished. For Borden, the first seven months of 1900 were a veritable *annus miserabilis*. Bad news came from all directions. On 28 March, less than six weeks after the firing of Hutton, his uncle Andrew, Robert Borden's aged father, died. Andrew had become something of a proxy father figure for Borden after his own father's death, and until he died at the age of eighty-five, he had remained a staunch, faithful, unshakeably loyal political supporter as well. Altogether Andrew's death marked a painful break with his father's generation. But worse news was to come.

Continuing public controversy, however, left little time for private grief. Scarcely had Borden recovered from the Hutton controversy than he faced another serious challenge to his administrative integrity, one that once again threatened to end his political career. The controversy focused on an adulterated emergency food ration that had been supplied to the second Canadian contingent for service in the South African War. The so-called Devlin emergency food-ration scandal stemmed from the failure of another unreformed area of his department but one for which he was obliged to assume ministerial responsibility.

The Opposition's assault began in June 1900, toward the end of the last session of the Eighth Parliament, when F.D. Monk, the Conservative member for Jacques-Cartier, rose to accuse the minister of militia of "gross and culpable negligence," a nineteen-point indictment made in the highly emotional atmosphere of war. The essence of Monk's charges was that the Militia Department had entered into a $4,660 contract with Dr F.E. Devlin, a friend of the government, for the delivery of

7,000 tins (2,333 pounds) of vegetable protein to be distributed to Canada's South African soldiers as an emergency food ration. The product, however, had turned out to be a worthless adulteration. According to Monk, the transaction had been riddled with fraud and deception from start to finish. He explained how the food ration contained only 17 per cent protein, was packed in small, unsterilized, and poorly sealed tins, had been manufactured in the United States, and had been shipped in large Saratoga trunks through customs on government orders, without payment of duties. Although Monk did not accuse Borden of personal profiteering, he held the minister responsible for the fraud and called for his resignation. In Monk's words, "If he did not know that the army contractors were swindling his department, he was not fit to be at the head of the department; if he did he was still less fit. In any case he should go."[20] In the overwrought partisan view of one Tory journal, the alleged offence was so serious a matter that it should be "regarded as treason and when found guilty the parties implicated should receive the severest punishment that the law will permit," presumably death![21]

Two months before Monk made his charges the *Military Gazette*, which was no friend of the minister, had hinted that there had been irregularities surrounding the emergency ration contract, insinuations that Borden had ignored, having been assured by his departmental officials that they were unfounded. Monk's devastating parliamentary charges, however, could not be ignored. Borden rose immediately to deny any knowledge of the charges and promised to place all papers connected with the transaction before a parliamentary committee. His apparent firmness and transparency initially unsettled the Opposition.

Some Opposition spokesmen, fearing Monk's indictment to have been overdone, attempted to soften the blow, but the government insisted upon the appointment of a bipartisan seven-member parliamentary committee to examine the evidence and report back to the House. The committee, chaired by Dr Benjamin Russell, a Dalhousie law professor and a Liberal member for Halifax, met for days, taking evidence and interviewing witnesses, including Borden, his deputy minister, Dr J.L.H. Neilson, the director-general of the department's medical corps, Dr F.E. Devlin, who had sold the emergency food ration to the department, and Dr Hatch, who had manufactured the substance, as well as various food analysts. Day after day journals reported the sensational details of the committee's deliberations and interpreted them from the perspective of party advantage.

Meanwhile Russell's parliamentary committee endeavoured to establish the facts upon which a judgment might be made. As the committee learned, in October 1898, a year before the South African War began, Dr Neilson, the newly appointed director-general of the medical corps, had asked Borden for permission to investigate the possibility of purchasing an emergency food ration for the men of the Yukon Field Force. Borden had been impressed by reports of a food powder concentrate, reputed to contain up to 80 per cent protein, developed by the Hatch Protose Company of Montreal and used successfully in some hospitals. Borden sought Hatch's permission to have Neilson test the compound on five men in the Royal Canadian Artillery in Kingston. In March 1899 Neilson had completed several weeks of tests and recommended that the Militia Department accept the compound, neglecting to note, however, that the Hatch product contained only 28 per cent protein. By this time the government had decided to recall the Yukon Field Force and consequently dropped its discussions with Hatch.

In July 1899, while Parliament was discussing the possibility of war in South Africa, Dr Devlin, Hatch's agent, requested an interview with Borden to discuss the sale of Hatch's emergency ration should the government send troops to South Africa.[22] Borden failed to respond to Devlin's request. In October when the Canadian government decided to send troops to South Africa, Hatch wrote directly to the minister offering to supply his recently tested emergency food ration. Borden declined the offer, however, on the grounds that the War Office had agreed to provision Canadian troops in South Africa. During the early days of the war, following the Canadian government's painful and controversial decision to send troops, Borden wished to remain well within the constricted financial limits of Canada's commitment. But by the time a second Canadian contingent had been authorized, the war had taken a more serious turn for the British, the public mood had changed, and the government, moving ever closer to a federal election, was anxious to obliterate their public image of reluctance and parsimony.

Borden decided, therefore, that the Canadian troops ought to carry a few days' supply of emergency ration as part of their kit, in case they were ever cut off from the main body of their contingent and were unable to secure food. And in the madly busy days of December 1899–January 1900 he instructed his department to solicit tenders for an emergency food ration. Since only Devlin responded, his offer was accepted, and a contract was drawn up on 4 January 1900 for the requisite quantity of food ration. Borden was confident that Devlin's food compound was identical to the substance that had been tested in Kingston.

Three weeks later Hatch informed the minister that Devlin was no longer in his employ and that the Devlin product was a poor and fraudulent adulteration of the Hatch "protose." Unfortunately Borden ignored Hatch's warning, convinced that it was little more than the cry of a disappointed competitor. Moreover, Borden knew the Devlin

family (his father had been a Liberal member of Parliament and a colleague), and at the time of the Kingston tests Dr Devlin had come
highly recommended by the Hatch Company, as well as by several
prominent Montreal doctors. Borden also trusted Lieutenant-Colonel
Neilson, in whose charge he had placed the matter, confident that he
would monitor the fulfilment of the contract and inform him of any
irregularities. Upon Devlin's delivery of the requisite quantity of food
ration in Halifax, and with Neilson having tested a sample of the ration
and found it in order, Devlin was paid and little more was heard of
the matter until Monk's exposé. When Canada's second contingent left
for South Africa (a unit that included Borden's only son), the men carried as part of their kit several days worth of the Devlin emergency
food ration.

After days of intensive investigation, several things became clear to
the committee appointed to look into Monk's charges. The men who
reportedly had been able to live for weeks on the ration in fact could
only use it to supplement their diet.[23] Furthermore, the Devlin food
ration was not the same as the Hatch food ration that had been tested
in Kingston. The Devlin product contained only 17 per cent protein,
whereas the Hatch product contained 28 per cent, itself well below the
60–80 per cent originally claimed, a finding that Neilson had failed to
report to the minister in recommending purchase of the Hatch product for the Yukon Field Force. Moreover, the sample Devlin had given
Neilson for testing upon his delivery of the food ration in Halifax was
not the same as the ration to be distributed to the troops, but had been
purchased from an American drugstore. And while initially Devlin had
attempted to avoid paying duty on the compound that he had imported
from the United States, falsely claiming that he had special permission
from the department to import it duty free, when his claim was challenged, Devlin paid the requisite duty.

Borden attempted to excuse himself by pleading overwork, and a
misguided confidence in his advisors. Both assertions were true. Devlin
had duped Neilson in Halifax. Neilson had failed to report to Borden
the discrepancy between Hatch's claims and the Kingston tests. Moreover, no precautions had been taken to prevent deception. And none of
this was reported to the minister. Devlin's duplicity and Neilson's naivety, however, could not be blamed for Borden's failure to heed Hatch's
warning, a costly mistake for which he alone was responsible. Even the
Opposition had not claimed that Borden had conspired to defraud
the public purse, enrich himself, or endanger the lives of the men
in the second contingent, including that of his own son. They did fault
his judgment, suspected political favouritism, and held him responsible
for his department's failures. They also believed that Neilson had been

careless and that Devlin had engaged in deliberate fraud and ought to be prosecuted. And the Opposition members of the Russell committee were determined to retain these points in the committee's report.

Only months away from a general election the government members of the Russell committee were equally determined to exonerate the minister and his department, and in their ill-advised partisan zeal found fault with no one, not even Devlin, an indiscriminate conclusion that some Liberals found excessive and politically not very astute. Consequently, when the committee reported, the Liberal-dominated majority report passed the Commons by a margin of only fourteen votes, the closest division of the session.[24] By finding no one guilty, the majority report cast suspicion upon everyone involved and left Borden as the responsible minister alone to bear the brunt of the Opposition's attacks. The government's mishandling of this issue gave the Opposition both a moral and a tactical victory, one that the Opposition intended to carry into the emotionally charged wartime khaki election that was to follow.

Ten days after the House cast its final vote on the infamous Devlin emergency ration fiasco the Conservatives' proposed electoral weapon was blunted by the tragic news that Lieutenant Harold Borden, the minister's only son, had died heroically in action on 16 July 1900.[25] He was killed during the Witpoort engagement when he and Lieutenant J.E. Burch, both in charge of Troop 2, stood up to discern the direction of fire and were struck at close range. Borden died instantly.

Before Harold left for South Africa, he had promised his men that he would never ask them to do anything he would not do himself; and he was as good as his word. A very competent and popular officer, Harold had earned the respect and confidence of his commanding officer, François Lessard, and even that of the brigade's general officer commanding, Major-General Hutton, his father's antagonist. Twice before Harold's tragic death, Hutton had brought his "intrepid and gallant service" to the notice of the commander-in-chief, Lord Roberts, who later claimed that had he known more of his contribution to the Vet River battle he would have recommended Harold for the Victoria Cross. In a moving torchlight ceremony the evening after his death, Canada's two mounted battalions of the second contingent and representatives from other units buried Harold near a farm at Rietvlei (he would be reinterred at Braamfontein, Johannesburg).

Borden was devastated by the news. He and his son had been unusually close. They had shared an interest in medicine, the military, business, and politics, and Borden had come to depend upon his son and entrust him with family and public responsibilities. Upon Harold's return from the war, Borden had planned to make him president of the Nova Scotia Supply Company (the renamed R.W. Kinsman Company), to clean up the confusion or worse created by R.W. Kinsman's chaotic administration.[26] In the words of Robert Borden, who shared his cousin's grief, Harold was a "splendid young man of great promise; of great stature ... dark handsome and of fine presence and manner," he was literally "the hope and delight of his father."[27]

Harold's death made headline news. Black-bordered photographs of him appeared in many dailies across Canada, including the *Halifax Herald,* whose cruel targeting had cut deeply.[28] Harold's prominence and popularity led to a great outpouring of public sympathy from his brigade in South Africa and in Canada.[29] Lord Roberts, the commander-in chief of British troops in South Africa who had recently lost his only son in the conflict, wrote a personal note to the minister. Lord Lansdowne, the British secretary of state for war, immediately announced the news in the House of Lords, praising Harold's gallantry, and Queen Victoria's secretary conveyed the queen's personal condolences and requested a photograph of his gallant son, all of which provided some consolation to Harold's father.

Lord Roberts's despatch to the governor general announcing Harold's death reached the minister's office about half past four in the afternoon while the minister was still in the House. The deputy minister, Major L.-F. Pinault, took the cable immediately to Laurier. And it was Laurier's sad task to call his close personal friend and colleague to his office to hear the tragic news. The news spread through the House like wildfire. When Laurier returned to the House to announce Harold's death to the Commons, the House was stunned. It adjourned immediately out of respect for the minister, after expressions of sympathy from all sides.[30]

This final blow, at the end of a monumentally trying session and just before a general election, shook Borden profoundly. After learning the shattering news, he left Laurier's office immediately and returned home and prepared to leave Ottawa for Canning with his wife and two daughters. Uncertain of his political future or of his own desire to continue in public life, and exhausted by overwork and emotional strain, he left Canada after several weeks, with his wife, for a holiday in England. There he hoped to relax, indulge his interest in travel, ancestry, and history, and reassess his uncertain future.

CHAPTER 10

Reform

Distance provided perspective, an opportunity to put unpleasant memories behind him, rethink his future, reimagine life without his son, and reassess his commitment to public life. Little could Borden have imagined how quickly and decisively things would turn about, how the war that had robbed him of his son and challenged his ministerial authority and political viability would make his reputation as a national and imperial figure. Borden would emerge from this war in full command of his department, an imperial figure, knighted for his service, and resolved to continue in public life, despite a faltering business and his irreparable personal loss. More than anything, the war created a context, impetus, and agenda for Canadian military reform. It gave Borden the opportunity to fashion a Canadian force that reflected Canadian needs and objectives. Essential to that agenda was the obligation to devise a cooperative imperial relationship that respected Canadian autonomy and guaranteed Canadian security.

Borden was an irrepressible optimist, and his decision to remain in public life was not a surprise. Federal politics had defined his life for over a quarter of a century. It had built a public persona whose continuance helped fill the void created by Harold's death. Nor could Borden have foreseen the extent to which his personal sacrifice would enhance his public image. Despite his relentless work, constant worry, contested authority, political conflict, and personal tragedy, the war had brought him and his ministry an unexpected national and imperial visibility. Each new consignment of Canadian troops for South Africa implicated him more deeply in national and imperial responsibilities. The war opened opportunities for military experimentation and the possibility of future personal advancement. The decision to remain in public office and pursue these possibilities was not entirely his own, however; it depended upon his ability to retain the confidence of his constituency and maintain his portfolio. Neither prospect seemed entirely certain to Borden in the late summer of 1900.

Borden's local political organization shared his apprehension. The day he and his wife boarded their transatlantic steamer for England, the county's Conservatives met in Kentville to choose Barclay Webster, an able and experienced solicitor, as their candidate for the imminent general election. Webster was the son-in-law of Borden's first political opponent, L. de Veber Chipman, the Conservative Party's local bagman, the would-be senator, and the current head of the powerful Chipman compact. Webster's candidacy bore all the marks of a political rematch. A graduate of Horton Academy, Dalhousie University, and Harvard University, where he received his LLB, Webster counted the Dominion Atlantic Railway and the Bank of Nova Scotia among his clients. A former warden of Kings County, he understood the importance of the municipal electoral list,[1] and he had represented Kings in the Nova Scotia legislature from 1890 until 1894. Nor could anyone fault his patriotism, with his son serving in the British Army in South Africa. Webster was clearly the most able, prominent, and experienced opponent Borden had yet faced.

The pugnacious, tireless old Tupper, however, was still leading the Conservative Party, ready to attack on all fronts and with any weapon in his implacable effort to unseat Laurier's Liberals. The wartime election promised to be a rude battle, a khaki contest fought on race, religion, and loyalty, and any other issue that Tupper thought might weaken his opponents. Apart from the treacherous national issues, including the government's initial vacillation on Canadian participation in the South African War, Tupper and his Tories had some local and personal scores to settle in Kings.

Borden's past four years in government provided Tupper with a broad target. The forced resignation of Tupper's son-in-law from the Royal Military College, the Militia Department's careless and questionable provisioning of the Yukon Field Force, the government's dismissal of Major-General E.T.H. Hutton, and the bungled purchase of the adulterated Devlin emergency food ration for the second contingent gave his opponents ample ammunition, an arsenal that the *Halifax Herald* called upon Tories to exhaust in their effort to rid Kings of Borden. So politically lethal did the *Halifax Herald* consider the emergency food fiasco that it charged the province's entire Liberal Party with its responsibility and its alleged cover-up. After all, Benjamin Russell, a Liberal member of Parliament for Halifax, had chaired the committee that had "whitewashed" the minister. In its endeavour to make the food ration scandal a central issue, the *Halifax Herald* not only implored the electors of Kings to defeat Borden but called on all provincial voters to punish "the rest of the Nova Scotia members who so dishonestly tried to whitewash him."[2]

Borden would also have to explain to his predominately Baptist electors the reasons for his party's failure to deliver on prohibition, despite the positive results of the 1898 referendum (Borden himself had endorsed prohibition during the referendum). Nor had Borden been able to bring reciprocity with the United States any closer than had his Tory predecessors, though he had fought every election on reciprocity since he entered politics. In view of all these considerations, Borden's closest political collaborator, Harry H. Wickwire, the local member of the Nova Scotia House of Assembly, was not at all confident that Borden could hold Kings. After close consultations with W.S. Fielding and H.W. Brown, Borden's private secretary, Wickwire cabled Borden asking him to return home immediately and prepare for the election, to be held on 7 November 1900.

Notwithstanding his personal grief, the minister of militia refused to back away from a fight, especially one that challenged his reputation and integrity and suggested that he had betrayed his country's citizen soldiers. Immediately upon his return from England Borden launched his campaign, determined to confound his opponent and silence his critics. Conscious of the depth of the temperance sentiment in his Baptist constituency, he reaffirmed his support for prohibition but argued that the 1898 plebiscite had demonstrated that the country as a whole was not ready for it; although the pro-prohibition forces had secured a majority of votes cast on the issue, the Liberals had decided that the slender majority of 13,687 votes was insufficient to warrant legislation. According to the *Halifax Herald*, this argument failed to convince the president of the county's Temperance Association. Perhaps that was why Borden decided to print and distribute Fielding's defence of the government's inaction, the temperate Baptist finance minister being a more credible advocate of this cause than he.[3]

The country's growth and prosperity, the Liberals' most potent weapon, made reciprocity a less grievous omission than Borden had anticipated, especially since the government had tried to secure freer trade with the Americans and had been rebuffed by Washington. The party's decision to turn what the Americans had refused into a Diamond Jubilee gift to Britain, in the form of an imperial trade preference, reaffirmed the Liberals' free trade commitment to farmers, strengthened their imperial credentials, and played well in Kings, a county increasingly in search of British capital and markets for its expanding and lucrative apple industry. Borden made all of these points by distributing hundreds of copies of government speeches and documents lauding the country's progress, prosperity, and budget surpluses, the most popular pamphlet being *Facts for Farmers*.[4]

Even the issue that Borden dreaded most and the one that challenged his integrity, the Devlin emergency food ration, with its rhetoric of betrayal and charges of waste of public funds, favouritism, and cover-up, proved less damaging than he had anticipated, though the Tories pressed the matter relentlessly and in the process probably overstated their case. The tragic death of Borden's popular son made it dif-

ficult for his own constituents to believe that the minister had know-
ingly imperilled the lives of Canada's soldiers; they knew too well how
close Borden had been to his son, how reluctant he had been to see him
enrol, how deeply he had felt his son's death. In fact, the issue cast him
more as a victim than a villain in this tangled affair. His opponents,
desperate to establish the minister's venality, turned to local issues and
accused Borden of misusing public funds in order to buy the Garland
Cox Farm in Canning. When G.W. Woodworth, the editor of the *Wedge*,
printed and circulated these accusations, Borden had him arrested on
charges of criminal libel.[5] This proved to be the turning point of his
campaign.

Quite apart from the political rhetoric, the Nova Scotia Liberals
were well organized; Borden had helped see to that. The previous year
he, Fielding, and George Murray, the provincial premier, had secured
financial commitments from political friends for an annual sum of
$2,000 to employ a permanent provincial organizer, the Lunenburg
barrister A.K. MacLean, to establish a network of constituency organizations, along the lines existing in Kings, that would report to them
fortnightly.[6] The Liberals also controlled patronage at both levels of
government. At the federal level Borden made certain that the annual
Militia camp was provisioned, repaired, and maintained by friends
of the government; that wharves, piers, and breakwaters remained
in good repair; and that the distribution of customs officers and sub-
customs officers, lighthouse keepers, postmasters and mail routes, and
the appointments of electoral constables, deputy returning officers,
and clerks all reaped maximum political returns. More important still,
their opponents' program was unfocused, lacked force and imagination, and was without any single significant issue. The Conservatives
had still not digested their 1896 defeat and appeared little more than a
"quarrelling collection of jealous, disorganized and dejected factions."[7]

Nevertheless Borden left nothing to chance. He made a house-to-
house canvass of his constituency, greeting old friends and reaffirming
alliances. When the polls closed on 7 November, the returns confirmed
the success of his party's efforts: the party had increased its national
representation by eleven seats, five of which came from Nova Scotia,
where the party had taken fifteen of the province's twenty seats. In
Halifax Robert Borden, assessing the returns of his party, considered
the election a "party disaster."[8] Some of Frederick Borden's stoutest
critics, such as George Eulas Foster and old Sir Charles Tupper himself, had gone down to defeat, Tupper's only personal defeat in public
life. Borden had no difficulty holding his seat, defeating Webster by
343 votes, taking 54 per cent of the votes cast. For Borden, the khaki
election proved a political watershed.

A more comfortable Ottawa greeted Borden's return to Parliament, an official life increasingly moulded by Laurier's courtly manners. In the House of Commons, Borden, as an experienced member of a secure and confident government, faced a chastised, disorganized Opposition, purged of many of the battle-hardened Tory veterans of the Macdonald era, such as Tupper, Foster, Joseph-Philippe-René-Adolphe Caron, and Joseph-Gideon-Horace Bergeron. More auspicious still, the Tories were now under the tentative leadership of Frederick's cousin Robert L. Borden. And that would count for much. Although Frederick was only seven years older than Robert, Frederick was a political veteran with some twenty-two years of parliamentary experience when Robert had entered the House in 1896.[9] The two men were bound by ties of mutual respect and affection, and in the months and years that followed, as they faced each other across the floor, their personal feelings seemed to trump political differences. Their relationship, it could be said, sheltered the minister from many personal attacks from irate Tory opponents. In Ottawa their families continued to meet socially. They shared investment advice and intelligence, often placing their money in similar ventures, such as gold mines, land, and telephone companies.[10]

In 1903 when a Liberal member of Parliament taunted the leader of the Opposition for his previous public interventions on behalf of his cousin and by implication the Liberal Party, Robert Borden responded defiantly and unrepentantly: "If I were not so actively engaged in public life, personal considerations might induce me to support him again." The following year Robert Borden went further. When a vigilant Conservative member attacked the minister of militia for his partisan distribution of patronage in Nova Scotia, citing chapter and verse, the leader of the Opposition, and sometime MP for Halifax, not only repudiated his colleague's accusation, but assured the House that he knew of no example of patronage involving the Militia in Nova Scotia.[11] Robert Borden may have found the issue of Militia patronage especially personal and painful, since Frederick had placed John William Borden, Robert's younger brother, in charge of the Militia's contracts department. Moreover, Robert never hesitated to recommend his party's adherents for patronage in the gift of Sir Frederick, requests that Sir Frederick had no hesitation honouring.[12]

If Robert knew of no example of Militia patronage in Nova Scotia, he was singularly poorly informed, since Frederick possessed an effective patronage system operating out of Halifax, Robert Borden's own constituency. The minister's Halifax agent was none other than the Liberal MLA for Kings, H.H. Wickwire. In 1905 Wickwire's partisan activities became a matter of public record when a Conservative member of Parliament called for information on the Militia Department's suspi-

cious land purchase the previous year to create a "new" Camp Aldershot in Pine Woods, Cornwallis, close to Kentville, to replace the "old"
Aldershot camp on the Aylesford plain, near the Annapolis County
line. According to the information the minister tabled in response to
the Conservative member's request, Wickwire and B.H. Dodge, the
other Liberal MLA for Kings County, both men Borden's close personal, political, and business friends, had purchased 640 acres of land
in the Kentville area at an average price of $6.20 an acre, which they
had sold subsequently to the Militia Department for $20.00 an acre,
a transaction that netted them a profit of $8,832.[13] Borden's political
influence was not confined to Militia patronage. Since Halifax was a
busy port and place of debarkation and reception of vast numbers of
immigrants requiring goods and services, the opportunities for influence and profit were many. It helped to have a myopic cousin as leader
of the Opposition.

The purchases of military goods and services that Borden made as
minister offered many murky and unregulated opportunities for political influence and personal favouritism within and outside Nova
Scotia. His large and growing Militia budget ($3 million in 1903) gave
him ample opportunity to make and maintain friends, and neutralize
grateful opponents, especially if transactions appeared bipartisan and
justifiable. Moreover, a simple analysis of partisan political patronage
based on an inventory of the division of spoils between Liberals and
Conservatives ignores the personal dynamic of patronage, especially in
an era of "ecumenical" interlocking business relations. In other words,
it fails to account for the favours that were distributed to advance
private interests, and in Frederick's case his private interests crossed
party lines.

Although large contracts were granted after public calls for tenders,
smaller lucrative contracts, such as for repairing, maintaining, provisioning, and serving summer camps, were awarded by soliciting competitive bids from "patronage" lists submitted by interested members
of Parliament on both sides of the House. For example, members of the
Commons Militia lobby, Liberal or Conservative, rarely suffered, the
minister's reward for their complicity. Even with larger, more formal tenders the success of partisan bids could be arranged by leaking information on a rival's offer. Aldershot, the military camp established in Borden's own constituency, commanded an annual expenditure of $4,000,
parcelled out to various persons, largely to Borden's political allies.

Moreover, the world of patronage, packaged in opaque arguments
of economy and fairness, often obscured more than it revealed. The
three-year contract system and the retention of the same suppliers were
often justifiable as a means to reward a firm's investment in a specialized market, to purchase security, and to encourage self-sufficiency and

production in Canada. Borden utilized both arguments for retaining two clothing companies as the Militia's principal clothing suppliers, Mark Workman's of Montreal (with whom he had close business relations)[14] and W.E. Sanford of Hamilton, the former a Liberal, the latter a Conservative company, contracts that might constitute a $500,000 annual expenditure. And although other Militia expenditures, such as the construction of armouries, were in the gift of the Department of Public Works, Borden's input could be determinant. In instances where there existed only one official supplier, artillery guns, for example, a minister's relationship with the company's agent might raise justifiable suspicions; but was there an alternative in this highly specialized production? Nor was it clear that partisan supplies were necessarily detrimental to the public interest. The system provided ample room for ministerial discretion that Borden rarely hesitated to employ.

Nothing demonstrated Borden's renewed commitment to public life more than his decision to purchase a large home in Ottawa. His choice of residence bore eloquent testimony to his political determination and social aspirations, a choice that reflected his wife's social ambitions. Stadacona Hall, a large, limestone "Gothic cottage,"[15] conveniently located next door to Laurier's residence, had been the home of John A. Macdonald from 1877 until 1883. Borden's vivacious, fashionable wife, the "mistress of Stadacona Hall" as one reporter labelled her, played a prominent role in the city's social and public life. Articulate, educated, and well-read, Bessie enjoyed discussing serious books with political friends. Active in clubs, organizations, and good works, she served as a director of the Young Women's Christian Association and as vice-president of the Victorian Order of Nurses, and belonged to several music clubs. Together Bessie and Frederick would make Stadacona Hall a lively centre of politics and social diplomacy.

Borden's residential proximity to Laurier cemented their friendship. They shared much. Educated, well-read, urbane, and gentrified, both men were liberal imperialists who practised the politics of tolerance and conciliation. Both were optimists, convinced that the "twentieth century belonged to Canada." They were infatuated with western Canadian development, its wheat fields "admitted to be the best in the world ... and practically without limit," and proud and boastful of the country's prosperous coast-to-coast rail lines. To hear Borden rhapsodize on the financial success of the Canadian Pacific Railway, "whose common stock is selling to-day at or around one hundred and fifty," one might have imagined that the railway had been a project of the Liberal Party.[16]

Laurier appreciated Borden's solid track record on language and religious contentions, especially Borden's inclusive, non-confrontational, conciliatory style, his search for reasonable accommodation, for ways

and means to diffuse religious and ethnic controversy. Even-handed
and ecumenical, Borden deplored the use of religion and language
as electoral weapons, a tactic his local opponents had employed unsuccessfully in 1891 and 1896, and would repeat in 1908. Although not
a particularly devout practitioner, Borden acknowledged the social
utility of religion. Soon after he became a minister in 1896, he lifted
the Conservative government's prohibition against the appointment of
chaplains to Militia units. He dismissed his opponents' fear that the
presence of military chaplains would fuel sectarian conflict, confident
that religious tensions could be managed. He began by authorizing the
appointment of chaplains as "special cases," then as honorary posts.
By 1897 he had approved some nineteen appointments, until shortly
each Militia unit possessed a chaplain.[17] Chaplains were particularly
welcomed in Catholic Quebec. And in Borden's view, Catholic Quebec
was important.

Similarly, in recruiting Canadian units for the South African War,
Borden authorized the appointment of Catholic, Presbyterian, Methodist, and Church of England chaplains, as well as an "evangelical"
YMCA representative to accompany the Canadian units. In subsequent
years he would go further. In 1905 the Militia Council authorized
padres to wear a "khaki drill service dress with a large Maltese Cross,
rank badges and the fashionable Sam Brown belt."[18] Goodwill alone,
however, failed to resolve bickering among Protestant denominations
in the Militia during the South African War and after. Vigilant Methodists and Presbyterians continued to resent what they perceived to be
the Church of England's attempt to monopolize the Protestant chaplain services and act as though it were an established church, a quarrel that Sir Frederick endeavoured to resolve by suggesting a rotation
among the principle Protestant denominations.[19]

Borden's religious tolerance coincided with his desire to make the
Canadian Militia more hospitable to French Canadians. "The Canadian people," Sir Frederick explained to a largely British audience,
"have sprung from different races and ... profess different faiths, but
they respect each other's differences none the less" and were united
in their allegiance and determination to defend their country. French
Canadians, he went on, had played a crucial role in defending their
country during both French and British regimes, beginning with Frontenac's organization of a militia, especially during various American
invasions. To make the Militia more accessible to French-Canadian
recruits, in 1899 he endeavoured to have Permanent Force officers,
the civilian Militia's instructors, learn French to facilitate their communication with francophones. Similarly, he insisted that all military
regulations, orders, and handbooks be translated, and in 1905 the Militia Council ordered that bilingual drill instructors be available in the

Quebec City military district.[20] And in organizing the first Canadian contingent for South Africa, Borden made every effort to field a franco-phone company with bilingual officers and non-commissioned officers (an experiment he tried to replicate within the 4th Canadian Mounted Rifles unit) as well as to appoint a bilingual padre and medical officer.

Borden's efforts did not stop there. Concerned that only about 18 per cent of the Militia's infantry battalions and 11 per cent of its officers were francophone,[21] in 1909 he sought to provide more space for franco-phone officers within the Permanent Force, including in his headquarters staff, where he had appointed a succession of French-Canadian deputy ministers. In 1898 he replaced Charles-Eugene Panet with L.-F. Pinault and in 1905 replaced Pinault with Eugene Fiset, the popular physician who had accompanied the first contingent to South Africa. In 1905 Borden also made Charles L. Panet his private secretary, a position of personal trust previously reserved for his own relatives.

In 1904, a year earlier, Borden had overturned the GOC Lord Dundonald's decision to block T.L. Boulanger's appointment to the Ottawa district headquarters and Boulanger's promotion to the rank of lieutenant-colonel. Just before Dundonald departed for a western tour, he had rejected the recommendation for Boulanger's promotion. In Dundonald's absence Sir Frederick asked the acting GOC, Lord Aylmer, to over-rule Dundonald's advice and approve Boulanger's promotion because he was a Boer War veteran and the only French-speaking Canadian in his unit and it was unfair to place him in an inferior rank.[22] The issue was further complicated by the state of "cold war" that had plagued the general's relations with the deputy minister, Colonel Pinault, whom Dundonald blamed for the reversal of his order. Dundonald and Pinault had clashed from the beginning, and there was no question which man Borden backed. Altogether, then, Borden's approach to religious and linguistic issues mirrored those of his leader, and this bond grew with time and circumstances.

Emblematic of Borden's changed political fortunes was his growing friendship with Governor General Minto. Within a very short time, their relationship underwent a remarkable transformation. While only two years earlier Minto had described Borden as a corrupt, incompetent, nonentity whom Laurier ought to dismiss or assign to another portfolio, he now viewed the minister as a thoroughly pleasant, agreeable man, "a very good friend," and "quite the best min. of Militia they have had here."[23] Harold's death had helped thaw the ice between Borden and Minto, especially after Minto went out of his way to have Harold's bravery recognized posthumously.

Borden's enhanced political and social standing in Ottawa fuelled rumours that he would shortly be knighted, rumours reinforced by the minister's growing friendship with the governor general, who jealously guarded his vice-regal role in the bestowal of honours. The rumours had substance. Convinced that "we shall not light upon a better Min. of militia,"[24] Minto began to work closely with Borden and press his claim for a knighthood, a well-deserved reward for his war work that might compensate for the British military's failure to honour his son's bravery. In the genteel campaign for recognition, Frederick and Bessie's social skills confirmed the governor general's confidence in Borden's eligibility and suitability for the honour.

Moreover, Borden's electoral victory had cleaned the slate of his early failures and left him in charge and control of his ministry, free to build on its strengths and address its weaknesses. Borden was especially pleased with Hutton's "temporary" replacement as GOC of the Canadian Militia. Major-General Richard O'Grady-Haly, a fifty-nine-year-old Irish-born infantry officer, had commanded the British garrison in Halifax from 1873 until 1878. A sensitive and diplomatic soldier, O'Grady-Haly had knowledge of Canada, was thoroughly versed in military law, and proved to be an excellent administrator who, in Borden's words, took, "a broad view of the whole Militia force."[25]

Borden and O'Grady-Haly did not always agree, but their differences were never a source of personal friction or public dispute.[26] Borden considered O'Grady-Haly one of the Canadian Militia's best GOCs and sought and obtained the extension of his term. And O'Grady-Haly might well have remained longer had Minto not petitioned the British government to send a more vigorous general, since he believed that O'Grady-Haly had become the compliant tool of the minister, permitting Borden to assume greater power within his ministry,[27] a view pressed upon Minto by O'Grady-Haly's spiteful predecessor.[28] Meanwhile, with a compliant general and a competent, experienced deputy minister in place, Borden was now well positioned to administer his department and reshape Canada's armed forces, capitalizing on the public's infatuation with the military, or so it appeared in the autumn of 1900.

The times were especially auspicious for military reform. The Boer War had created public momentum for an ambitious reform of the Canadian Militia, an opportunity that Borden exploited during the next decade to transform Canada's armed forces. Altogether Canada had recruited some 7,368 volunteers for military service in South Africa, and an additional 1,000 militiamen were raised to relieve the British troops garrisoned at Halifax for service in South Africa, which Borden regarded as a wartime version of the pre-war exchange program.[29] Of the Canadian contingents, only the first and second, however, were temporary members of the Canadian Militia, recruited under the authority of the Militia Act, organized, clothed, equipped, and transported (the second contingent paid partially) by the Canadian government at a total cost of $1,996,867.

Although the subsequent seven units that had been recruited in Canada by the Militia Department were staffed by Canadian officers and, with one exception (the South African Constabulary), bore Canadian regimental names, legally they were temporary units of the British Army raised under the authority of the United Kingdom's Army Act, the entire cost borne by the British government. The Lord Strathcona's Horse, a battalion of scouts financed entirely by Canada's wealthy high commissioner to the United Kingdom, was Canada's first "temporary British" unit. The other temporary British units were designated the 2nd, 3rd, 4th, 5th, and 6th Canadian Mounted Rifles. A somewhat exceptional unit was the contingent of 1,200 constables for Colonel Robert Baden-Powell's South African Constabulary, a hybrid military-police force.

Since the 3rd, 4th, 5th and 6th Canadian Mounted Rifles arrived too late to participate in the conflict, Canada's first two contingents, the Lord Strathcona's Horse, the 2nd Canadian Mounted Rifles, and the Canadian constables in the South African Constabulary were the only Canadian units to see military action in South Africa. All recruits, except members of the South African Constabulary, agreed to serve for one year or until the termination of the war, whichever came first. After a year's service some men demobilized in South Africa and joined other units, often irregular British units such as Howard's Canadian Scouts.[30]

Canadian popular support for recruitment was not unqualified. Although the Militia Department had no difficulty recruiting the requisite number of men for the various units, war enthusiasm began to decline after British troops entered Pretoria in June 1900, the six Canadian war correspondents returned home, and the war moved into its dirty guerrilla phase of drives, concentration camps, and farm burnings. In one instance, Baden-Powell's Canadian recruitment for his South African Constabulary aroused a storm of public criticism. Created in October 1900, this hybrid force, the child of Lord Milner, the dynamic British high commissioner to South Africa, was designed as a central piece in his plan for the pacification, resettlement, and reconstruction of South Africa. To encourage constables to settle in South Africa, recruits were required to sign a three-year contract, renewable for two years, with a generous land grant option at the end of their service. The Canadian press reacted negatively to the constabulary's terms of recruitment. Canadians were particularly critical of "detaching so many energetic young Canadians from the work of building up Canada."[31] More vociferous still was the *Canadian Military Gazette,*

which denounced recruitment as virtual "deportation of our best settlers and citizens."[32] Borden shared the *Canadian Military Gazette*'s
objections, and when Milner proposed doubling the number of Canadian constables, Borden wrote to Laurier protesting the transferral of
"actual settlers from Canada to South Africa."[33] The fact that married
officers were encouraged to bring their families confirmed his worst
fears.

Nonetheless, the Boer War was a defining moment for the Canadian
Militia, the crucible of the Canadian "army." Politicians and scholars
have long seen participation in war, along with patriotism and voting,
as an obligation of citizenship, a unifying force, especially in fragmented societies – as an occasion to forge lasting memories and bonds
of common experience. The Canadian public saw their Boer War soldiers, whatever their warrior status or terms of employment, as ambas-
sadors of their country whose battle experience ought to guide the formation and development of Canada's military. Their war experience,
its meanings and its lessons, became the subject of broad public discussion that Borden followed closely, seeking direction and confirmation
for his reform agenda.

Often the debate expanded into a discussion of the character and
future of the country itself. A broad consensus on the war's lessons
informed the discussions among Canadian military reformers. Most
agreed that the war's most conspicuous lesson had to do with national
confidence and self-consciousness. None suggested that the South African War created a sense of Canadian distinctiveness, since a Canadian
self-consciousness, various and inchoate as it may have been, predated
the war by several decades. At least three decades or more before the
war began, a small network of English-Canadian writers and intellec-
tuals had set out to reinforce and define the significance of the 49th
parallel, to map a nation from the fashionable contemporary notions of
race, environment, and institutions.[34] In their Darwinian view, Canada
was a country born and refined through a struggle, against nature, for
borders, popular institutions, and a distinctive place within its imperial family. It was a community bred from a Nordic environment, one
that had climatically attracted, selected, and refined particular European peoples. In Canada these peoples had been moulded by the British institutional heritage that framed their civil society, setting them
apart from their lawless southern neighbours. Whether the country's
British/American inhabitants had been formed more by their physical,
environmental, or institutional heritage, and thereby were more American or British, remained a debatable and often controversial question,
one that the war would highlight but not resolve. All this was baggage
that the recruits carried into battle, to be tested and refined during
their encounters with imperial troops.

Many soldiers and civilians agreed that whatever the British/American mix, Canada possessed a discernible identity within the British family, and they saw the South African war as an opportunity to assert that character and demand its recognition. Borden voiced their aspirations in clear and unmistakeable language during the departure ceremonies in Quebec City for the first Canadian contingent, describing Canada's participation in the South African War as nothing less than the voice of Canada announcing to the world that it was no longer a colony but a mature nation and member of the Empire.[35] Much of the contemporary press echoed the minister's rhetoric.

But Borden was determined to give substance to rhetoric. From the beginning, many Canadians had insisted that Canadian troops fight as Canadian units under Canadian officers, a demand that Borden and his colleagues insistently brokered against some difficult odds. Subsequently, Borden made every effort to enhance the contingent's importance, extend its autonomy, and affirm its Canadian character. To achieve these objectives, he made certain that each battalion's name, organization, kit, and clothing underlined its Canadian character. The first contingent's rather long and confusing title, the 2nd (Special Service) Battalion, Royal Canadian Regiment of Infantry, was chosen to associate it with its namesake in the PF, whose 1st Battalion remained at home. The same consideration accounted for the naming of subsequent contingents: the Royal Canadian Dragoons, the Canadian Mounted Rifles (a unit by this name had been amalgamated with the Canadian Dragoons in 1892), and the Royal Canadian Field Artillery. A British effort to have the 2nd Canadian Mounted Rifles named the "Canadian Yeoman" elicited a public storm and was successfully resisted; Canadians were equals of the British, not attendant yeomen to imperial masters!

Borden was no less attentive to the regional and linguistic personality of the first contingent, which consisted of eight regionally based companies, one of which was to be bilingual. Material distinctions were equally important. The Royal Canadians' brown canvass khaki uniforms, white helmets (later sensibly dyed coffee), heavy (and poorly made) black boots, Sam Browne belts, and heavy Oliver equipment, as well as other small distinctions of dress, kit, and insignia, underscored Canadians' desire for differentiation. The men greeted no mark of distinction with greater pride than the Maple Leaf "Canada" badge, surmounted by a crown, affixed to their helmets. Subsequent units possessed comparable distinctions in dress and equipment.

In South Africa, as the wear and tear of war obliterated material distinctions, Canadian soldiers became conscious of, and often sensitive to, the social and cultural distinctions that separated them from their imperial comrades; many became aware of their American culture.

They noted their difference in accents and expressions, in preferences for songs and sports, in attitudes and manners. Some of the Canadian units, such as the Strathcona's Horse (half of whom were British-born), under the command of the legendary Sam Steele of the North-West Mounted Police, went out of their way to construct an image of themselves as quintessential western Canadian frontiersmen, fearless, versatile roughriders of the plains comparable to Boer commandos, an elite somewhat indifferent to the more conventional rituals of warfare, an image that many of the senior British officers encouraged. Generally the Canadian volunteers professed to prefer to serve in Canadian units under Canadian officers. And they displayed little tolerance for Canadians who aped class-based British mannerisms.

Subsequently Canadian soldiers' memory and construction of the war and how it was fought further sharpened their sense of separateness and fed their self-confidence, especially as the British Army's initial difficulty coping with the Boers' unorthodox methods of warfare eroded their confidence in British military leadership, a style that one veteran described as often "heroic but damnably foolish."[36] Before the war Hutton and others had disparaged the martial capacity of Canada's poorly trained civilian soldiers, informing them that they could scarcely conceive of standing by seasoned British regulars. But the Canadian troops who had fought at Leliefontein, Rietfontein, and Harts River and had seen British regular units flee, leaving the Canadians alone to face overwhelming odds, developed other views of their comparative martial skills. And when imperial officers reminded Canadian Militia men that armies required organization and structure, many Canadian Boer War veterans remembered the British Army's pathetically inadequate medical service, dispensed according to rank and title rather than need, and their failure to provide the troops with adequate supplies of food and water. In the view of the redoubtable Colonel G.T. Denison and others, the South African War settled the question of the supposed inferiority of colonial troops, an assessment that cleverly ignored the fact that during the initial phase of the war the British Army, outnumbered, outgunned, and devoid of dependable reconnaissance, was not the best example of efficient organization.[37]

Intoxicated by their success at Paardeberg, Leliefontein, Harts River, and other engagements, many of Canada's Boer War soldiers became so confident of their own combat skills that they concurred with Lieutenant Richard Turner, one of Canada's three Victoria Cross recipients at the Battle of Leliefontein, who wrote in his diary that they "had taught the Regulars how to fight."[38] Another of Leliefontein's decorated Canadian veterans, the voluble, able gunner E.W.B. Morrison, spoke for many of his comrades when he expressed the hope that Canadians would fight the next war under Canadian officers and "in one division."[39] He and many of his comrades, including Turner, were to be part of that Canadian division largely because they and others used their Boer War experience to create a skeleton Canadian army capable of playing a larger, more autonomous role.

Many Canadian civilians shared their soldier-heroes' aspirations, and influenced by contemporary Darwinian social analysis, they drew self-serving conclusions from the soldiers' experiences and observations. They blamed the slowness, lethargy, and slovenliness of some British units on social and physical conditions, on what was popularly termed "race" deterioration caused by urbanization and industrialism and the British hidebound, class-cursed commitment to form, red tape, and "five o'clock tea principles," notions reinforced by tensions between Canadian and British troops in South Africa. This analysis was shared by other colonial troops, especially in Australia.[40] Indeed, Canadian criticism of British officers became so rampant during and after the war that Lord Minto and others vainly admonished returned Canadian soldiers to restrain "their criticism of their superior officers."[41]

Canadians were especially fond of Darwinian descriptions of their men as "taller and sturdier" than the British infantry, as "Lords of the Northland," grim, solid men as straight as poplars, products of their Nordic environment.[42] They supported their conclusions with selective statements from British authorities, such as the *Lancet*'s characterization of the Boers and colonials as physically larger, stronger, and fitter than the British Tommy, and "man for man ... incomparably superior to our workers in London or Manchester or Glasgow." Similarly, Canadians relished and repeated the Elgin Commission's description of Canadian and colonial troops as "half soldier by their upbringing, natural horsemen, observant scouts, whose officers share with their men mutual interests, and whose men are trained to think for themselves, with the result that they carry on should their leaders be killed," a theme validated and disseminated by popular British writers like Rudyard Kipling and Arthur Conan Doyle.[43] Even among working-class Tommies in South Africa the war created an appreciation of empire, a desire to emulate their colonial compatriots and secure civilian opportunities "denied this working class soldier back in England."[44]

In short, the war infused Canadian soldiers and civilians with a sense of distinctiveness, confidence, and power. It gave them the determination to take control of their own defences and ideas on how that might be done. "Canada for the Canadians really represents the root-sentiment of all sections far more accurately than Canada for the Empire," the popular British journalist Harold Spender concluded during his tour of Canada in 1900, a sentiment shared by John Hobson a few years later.[45] But for many, including Borden, this did not mean leaving the Empire; it meant reshaping it, even redeeming it, by example, a project that Stephen Leacock labelled "Greater Canada."[46] Jeanette Duncan captured this war-bred confidence in her novel *The Imperialist,* whose hero sees Canada as the future seat of imperial greatness, the new centre of the Empire.[47] More specifically the war strengthened the Canadian militia myth, the notion that a trained citizenry was preferable to the cost and sclerosis of a standing professional army. Above all, the war appeared to give reason, impetus, and direction to Canadian demands for distinctiveness and a trained citizenry. This leitmotif would inform and dictate the direction and nature of Borden's post-war Militia reform.

Borden followed this lively British and Canadian critique of the war closely, seeking confirmation of his personal preferences for Canadian military reform and searching for ideas, arguments, and opportunities to translate these into realities within the Canadian Militia. He read widely, especially official British investigations such as the Elgin and Esher reports for "lessons" applicable to Canada, lessons that may not always have been those that the British authorities or some professional soldiers intended him to draw. Borden focused on the Elgin report's criticism of the initial confusion and disorganization of the British military, paying careful attention to the record of conflict between the civilian and military authorities and pondering the report's proposed remedies. In his view, the Esher report's emphasis on organizational decentralization made good sense both within Canada and the Empire. He welcomed the report's proposal for a military council to resolve the perennial conflict between the civil and military authorities and reinforce civilian authority.

Altogether Borden shared his compatriots' confidence and their desire for a self-contained, decentralized civilian army, and he was determined to give the idea life and substance, a goal now more easily reached given his enhanced administrative control, political authority, and social standing. Above all he sought to create a force that reflected Canadian interests and objectives, one that did not exclude imperial cooperation; a force led by and accessible to qualified Canadians, one that answered the contemporary, war-fed call of "Canada for Canadians" and removed any reproach of inferiority.

CHAPTER 11

The Reproach of Inferiority

The return of confident, experienced Boer War veterans steeled Borden's pre-war determination to remove what he and others considered a "reproach of inferiority" within the Canadian Militia. As he explained at a military banquet in his honour in Toronto in December 1903, the issue of inequality between British regulars and Canadian Militia officers had rankled many Canadians for decades. Most of his own early piecemeal efforts to correct this defect had been frustrated by various political, legal, and constitutional objections and constraints, raised and vigilantly enforced by the GOC of the Canadian Militia, the governor general, the War Office, and the Colonial Office. Faced by these obstructions, Borden concluded that only a bold revision of the Militia Act, the possession of what he described as a "Canadian law, first, last and all the time,"[1] would give him the statutory authority he required to establish a truly "national Army, commanded by Canadians and that would stand on its own in North America."[2] This objective would bring him into direct conflict with the governor general and the GOC.

Although Borden's relations with Governor General Minto were soon to become remarkably cooperative, respectful, and cordial, in the months immediately following Hutton's dismissal their communications remained stiff and confrontational. Almost immediately after Hutton's tumultuous departure another jurisdictional quarrel demonstrated the gulf of tension and suspicion that separated the governor general from his ministers. A dispute ostensibly over military patronage constituted little more than a postlude to the earlier controversy over vice-regal interference in Canadian military affairs.

The quarrel began in March 1900 when Chamberlain cabled Minto informing him that the War Office would grant forty-four commissions to qualified Canadian officers who were currently serving in South Africa or were graduates of the Royal Military College. Determined to keep these awards in his own hands, Minto immediately wrote Chamberlain protesting the colonial secretary's suggestion that the coveted commissions be granted on the recommendation of the new GOC of the Canadian Militia, O'Grady-Haly, who was due to arrive in July. Since the new general would be unfamiliar with the Canadian Militia, his recommendations would simply reflect the preferences of his experienced, venial minister. To prevent this calamity, Minto suggested that he be entrusted with their selection in consultation with a small board of three senior imperial officers employed by the Canadian Militia, an arrangement that would prevent any possibility of personal or political pressure. Two of the three officers Minto proposed for his board, however, were his personal friends, Lieutenant-Colonel Gerald Kitson and Colonel Hubert Foster, and the third, "for appearances' sake," was Colonel Matthew Alymer, an imperial officer of Canadian descent who was a close friend of the minister's: such was Minto's peculiar version of impartiality.[3]

Borden welcomed news of the proposed career opportunities opened to Canadian officers in the British Army, seeing them as a vindication of his RMC reforms. Unaware of Minto's proposed selection board, the minister immediately published the notice, instructing candidates to report to designated bases for medical examination. Minto lost no time objecting to Borden's notice, determined to keep control of the process. In the face of Minto's objections, Borden withdrew the order. However, the government, reading Minto's communication as a continuation of his constitutional pretensions, made clear in a formal Minute of Council its opposition to Minto's proposed method of selection. All Militia officers recommended for commissions, the government insisted, must pass through the Militia Department, since the government could not countenance the creation of a board composed of subordinate officers in the employ of the Canadian government reporting directly to the British government.

Unmoved by the Minute of Council, Minto assured the Canadian government that the War Office would never consent to the Canadian procedure, despite the fact that the War Office had originally suggested that all recommendations pass through the Canadian ministry. Faced by Minto's intransigence, the government appealed directly to Chamberlain, insisting that it did not contest the War Office's right to recruit in Canada but that if that was its intention, it ought to appoint its own agents, not British officers employed by the Canadian Militia. Minto immediately seized upon this suggestion and put himself forward as an appropriate imperial recruitment agent.

Public disclosure of this dispute brought the predictable Canadian charges of Downing Street domination.[4] If judged by the Colonial Office's reaction, however, Downing Street seemed equally dismayed by Minto's pretensions. "The anxiety of Ld. Minto to eliminate his Ministers completely from this matter," John Anderson wrote, "is a bad sign." Ministers, he continued, "must have more knowledge than either the Gov. Genl. or the imperial authorities ... we cannot treat ministers as if they were totally unfit to be trusted. They are the Queen's ministers in Canada & we cannot ignore them."[5]

In an effort to diminish tension, the Colonial Office suggested that the commissions be treated as honours recommendations and that Minto submit the names of appropriate candidates suggested by his ministers together with his own comments, leaving the final decision to the British authorities. The point, however, was lost on Minto, and he immediately misinformed Laurier that the imperial government had asked him as governor general to recommend candidates for commissions.[6] He was shrewd enough, however, to realize that he required the assistance of the Militia Department. While Laurier restated his constitutional objections to Minto's proposed selection procedure, he did not push the issue further but agreed as a courtesy that the Militia Department might assist Minto informally. Unfortunately, Laurier's courtesy fed rather than appeased Minto's pretensions. Convinced that he had won "a valuable principle as regards appointments," Minto interpreted his "victory" as a clear vindication of his claim to a greater role in military administration.[7]

Contrary to the contentions of some "liberal-autonomist" historians, many of these perennial controversies over Canadian defence were less issues pitching Canadians against Britons, nationalism versus imperialism, than disputes over central or local control, more a quarrel over means than ends. And on these issues the Colonial Office and the Canadian government were often in agreement. Even so, there was much more that united the protagonists than divided them. Both believed firmly in the need for imperial defence, though they might disagree on the source and intensity of the danger and the best means of managing and controlling defence forces.

Neither nationalist nor imperialist advocates denied the desirability of satisfying the professional career ambitions of capable Canadian war veterans. Imperialists, or centralists, simply sought to meet these legitimate aspirations within an imperial rather than a Canadian framework. Of the imperialists, none was more convinced than the Canadian governor general of the folly of asking "Canadian officers to go on fighting for us in Impl. wars unless they share in Impl. professional awards." Minto himself went to great lengths to extract from the Colonial and War offices a promise that Lieutenant-Colonel Otter, the commanding officer of Canada's first South African War contingent, would receive a posting in the British Army worthy of his experience and abilities. Finally, with the War Office's permission, Minto jubilantly announced at Otter's homecoming reception that the imperial government would find a suitable imperial position for Otter, a promise the imperial authorities would fail to honour, despite Minto's repeated reminders.[8]

More interested in defence than defiance, Borden approached the challenge of rewarding Boer War veterans from a different perspective.

His general concern was how best to achieve his multiple objectives of raising morale, rewarding professional officers, and utilizing veterans' battle experience to improve Canadian land forces, goals he felt he might obtain more readily and appropriately within the Canadian PF than within the British Army. During the war Borden had pressed Otter to be more generous with his recommendations for decorations, especially among "non-commissioned officers and men" (Otter had made no recommendations for these ranks), since Borden was anxious to identify and reward leadership at all ranks).[9] Borden himself had attempted to make room for Canada's senior Boer War veterans within the Canadian PF, replacing imperial officers on loan to the Canadian government with battle-experienced Canadian officers.

In the autumn of 1900, for example, Borden proposed the appointment of Colonel William D. Otter, Lieutenant-Colonel Oscar Pelletier, and Major Robert Cartwright (assistant adjutant-general at military headquarters) to positions then occupied by three senior imperial officers on loan to the Canadian government, Lieutenant-Colonel Hubert Foster, the quartermaster-general; Colonel Gerald Kitson, the commandant of RMC; and Lieutenant-Colonel F.G. Stone, the officer commanding Canada's Permanent Artillery. "I am convinced," Borden wrote to Laurier in December 1900, just before the return of the first contingent, "that we owe it to our returning Permanent Force officers to make the best possible provision for them."[10]

Borden thought highly of Otter, a methodical, conscientious, professional officer with battle experience, and he frequently sought and respected his advice. Otter reciprocated Borden's friendship and worked closely and constructively with the minister. In fact, on one occasion his friendship with Borden drew the ire of Tories and the editor of the *Canadian Military Gazette*. In January 1904 the *Canadian Military Gazette* took umbrage at Otter's role in organizing a widely publicized Toronto banquet on 29 December 1903 to honour Borden, an initiative that Otter's critics claimed violated the King's Regulations.[11] Borden felt that the Militia needed officers like Otter and was convinced that Otter would make an excellent replacement for Gerald Kitson, whose limited term as commandant for the RMC had expired.[12]

Borden was intensely irritated, however, when he learned that the War Office had promised the RMC position to Major R.N.R. Reade, a decision made without consultation. The presumption of the War Office, its treatment of Canada as a subordinate command, had not only sabotaged Borden's plans to reward South African veterans but deprived the RMC of an excellent commandant. Although the Canadian government possessed the right to refuse the War Office's nominee because the RMC was a Canadian institution, Borden suppressed his anger and agreed to accept Reade after formally requesting an explanation of Reade's credentials and on the clear understanding that Foster's quartermaster-general's position would go to Otter. Otter, however, refused the position of quartermaster-general, preferring his pre-war position as the officer commanding Military District No. 2, still hoping for the imperial appointment he craved and had been "offered" by Minto. While he waited, his continued under-employment in Canada's PF remained a standing reproach to the system: an experienced Canadian professional whose career in the militia of his own country was temporarily blocked by the claims of imperial officers on loan to the Canadian Militia. Undeterred, Borden made every effort in the years to come to find a place for Otter and other veterans within the Canadian forces. He took great satisfaction in authorizing Otter's subsequent promotions: to the rank of general on 1 May 1905, to chief of the general staff in 1908, and to inspector general in 1910, all firsts for a Canadian Militia officer.

Consistent with his determination to find appropriate command positions for Boer War veterans, Borden insisted that Charles Drury, the commanding officer of the Royal Canadian Field Artillery, become the officer commanding the Maritime provinces (1905–11) and replace Sir Charles Parsons in command of the Halifax garrison. Similarly, Lieutenant-Colonel François Lessard, the commanding officer of the Royal Canadian Dragoons, was made the inspector of cavalry, then promoted to colonel in 1907 and appointed adjutant-general of the Militia; Lieutenant-Colonel Oscar Pelletier, who had served with Otter in South Africa, became the officer commanding the Militia's Fifth Division in 1908; Lieutenant-Colonel Sam B. Steel, upon his return from South Africa in 1907, became the commanding officer of Military District 13 (Alberta and Mackenzie District); Lieutenant-Colonel Robert Cartwright became commandant of the School of Musketry; Eugene Fiset, the first contingent's popular medical officer, became the director-general of Canadian Medical Services (1903–06) and then deputy minister of militia and defence (1906–22); Dr Guy Carleton Jones, second in command of the 10th Canadian Field Hospital, became director-general of Canadian Medical Services in 1910; in 1908 Georgina Pope became first matron of the Canadian Medical Corps; and Henri-Alexandre Panet, an officer in Canada's first two contingents, became Borden's trusted private secretary.

For many Canadian nationalists the most visible, irksome symbol of their military subordination was the 1875 amendment to the Militia Act reserving the position of general officer commanding the Canadian Militia for an officer of the British regular army. The putative purpose of this provision was to assure the Canadian Militia's quality, dependability, and compatibility with imperial forces, upon which Canadian security ultimately depended. Many Canadians, however, saw this objective as a condescending effort to save the Militia from ignorant civilians and patronage-mongering colonial politicians, in other words, to save Canadians from themselves! From the beginning, the Canada First Party and the third party movement had called for remedy of this disability, demanding that the post of GOC and "the principal positions in our military service" be opened to all Canadians.[13] In the 1890s even members of the Conservative Party pressed for the elimination of this irksome prohibition, especially when their personal or political agendas clashed with those of the "British" general officer commanding.

Borden was less dogmatic about the nationality of the GOC than many of its proponents or opponents. While he was convinced that the position ought to be open to any capable Canadian, he did not believe that it must be reserved for a Canadian PF officer, so long as it was open to any capable officer within the Empire, including those in the Canadian PF or the British regular army.[14] Consequently, soon after Hutton's controversial departure, Borden tested the governor general's frequently stated assurances that nothing prevented the appointment of distinguished Canadian officers in the British Army to the position of GOC of the Canadian Militia by proposing the appointment of Lieutenant-Colonel (Lord) Matthew Aylmer, a British Army officer born in India of Canadian parents, who had recently served as adjutant-general of the Canadian Militia.[15]

Although Aylmer's qualifications matched Minto's criteria, the governor general objected strenuously to his appointment for personal and political reasons: he considered Aylmer too weak and too close to the minister of militia. More to the point, when Aylmer was in Canada he had fallen afoul of General Hutton and the general had intrigued with his War Office friends to have Aylmer recalled from Canada for service "at home."[16] Unable to reveal his real objection to Borden's nominee, Minto invoked constitutional difficulties. When Borden responded by drafting an amendment to the Militia Act to overcome these difficulties, Minto persuaded the Colonial and War offices to ask Borden to withdraw the proposed amendment,[17] on the specious grounds that it would deprive the Militia of informed and capable British leadership. Borden acceded reluctantly to the request while he reconsidered his options, determined to find some other way to remove what he insisted was as an example of this "reproach of inferiority."[18]

All that Borden had sought was equality of opportunity for Canadian officers within their own force. In his view, equality was essential in order to retain, motivate, and reward capable Militia officers and train them for more senior positions. The existing structure simply institutionalized Canadian inferiority and prevented Canadians from taking charge of their own defence. The chief obstruction, though, was Canada's Militia Act, which had established a professional ceiling, limiting promotion within the Militia to the rank of lieutenant-colonel. To overcome this disability, Borden proposed amending the Militia Act to raise the highest Militia rank from lieutenant-colonel to colonel. Minto again objected to Borden's initiative, and in an effort to frustrate the minister's larger objective, he persuaded Borden to restrict the rank to honorary colonel, a restriction that vitiated the proposed higher rank, making it as something of a standing joke, as various public notables who had never seen a day's military service blossomed forth with more gold braid than Lord Roberts. Although Borden had unwisely caved in to the governor general's objections on this and the other issues, he had not abandoned the goal of placing Canadian PF officers on an equal footing with British regular army officers. Once again, his compliance was merely a strategic withdrawal while he considered his options.

Borden's more concerted offensive began with a small but significant confrontation with the governor general over paragraphs 68 and 69 of the Militia Orders and Regulations, which Hutton had abolished and Borden proposed to restore. According to these paragraphs, which had been promulgated in 1879 and designed to define the place of British officers loaned to the Canadian Militia, command of Canadian Militia troops was restricted to officers holding Canadian commissions. The paragraphs further stipulated that seniority within a rank was to be determined by the date of an officer's Canadian commission. In the past this regulation had caused little practical difficulty, since most British officers loaned to the Canadian Militia received a one-step promotion, that is, until Lieutenant-Colonel F.G. Stone was appointed to command the Canadian artillery in 1899. Since Stone's British rank was the highest rank permitted within the Canadian Militia other than that of GOC, he both failed to gain in rank and lost his seniority in assuming a Canadian rank. To resolve this exceptional difficulty, Hutton simply abolished sections 68 and 69 of the standing Militia Orders, insisting that they were in any case a violation of the Queen's Regulations, which granted imperial officers precedence over all colonial officers. In attempting to resolve Stone's personal grievance, Hutton created a great deal of resentment among Canadian Militia officers.

At the time Borden was furious with the general's peremptory actions. How could one instil pride and confidence within the Canadian Militia and provide senior training and experience when its officers were consigned to subordinate positions within their own Militia? Even Colonel Gerald Kitson, Hutton's friend and the British regular officer commanding the RMC, thought Hutton's action unwise and unfortunate,[19] despite the fact that Kitson's British junior officers at the RMC were direct beneficiaries of Hutton's measure. To remedy this situation, Borden restored paragraphs 68 and 69 immediately after Hutton's departure.

Borden's restoration of the paragraphs brought predictable howls of protest from junior imperial officers at the RMC who enjoyed both exalted ranks and seniority. Contrary to Kitson's advice, Minto backed the junior officers' case, convinced of its importance to Militia reform and insisted on what he and Hutton believed was a strict adherence to the Queen's Regulations. When Borden persisted, Minto asked the War Office to request that the Canadian government rescind "without delay" the two offending paragraphs of the Militia Order, which the War Office did, still smarting from its obligation to recall Hutton.[20] Less compliant this time, Borden rallied the cabinet to contest the War Office's peremptory request to rescind a Canadian regulation. Canada's Militia Orders and Regulations, he argued, were simply declaratory of the Militia Act, which lay clearly within Canadian jurisdiction, and the King's Regulations did not trump Canadian legislation. The Colonial Office, as often in the past, supported the Canadian contention as a "perfectly reasonable one" and sent the question to the law officers of the Crown for a legal opinion.[21]

Borden was delighted with the Law Court's final decision, rendered in February 1901, completely upholding the Canadian position, a decision that both Minto and the War Office accepted with ill grace.[22] In reporting the decision, the Colonial Office, aware of the War Office's insensitivity to the "colonial point of view," went even further than Borden and demanded that the War Office amend the King's Regulations that gave British colonels precedence in the command of colonial officers. Moreover, it refused to consider the War Office's not unreasonable counter-offer that in the future all imperial officers loaned to the colonies would receive an advance in rank.[23] Quite apart from the restoration of paragraphs 68 and 69, Borden's firmness on this issue meant that the Law Court's decision effectively settled the long-standing contention of GOCs that the Queen's/King's Regulations applied to the Canadian Militia. Borden could not have asked for more.

While this decision constituted an important victory for Borden, it scarcely compensated for his failure to overcome the various earlier vice-regal objections and obstructions. In almost all his earlier efforts to establish equality between the Canadian Militia and British regular troops serving in Canada, he confronted two persistent and determined obstacles: the objections of the governor general and the language of Canada's Militia Act. A soldier by aptitude with a distrust of politicians and impatient with democratic institutions, Minto took an extraordinarily active interest in military issues. He also possessed an expansive view of his constitutional powers as commander-in-chief, powers he used to justify his intrusion into military administrative matters. Yet, despite their considerable differences, Borden's relations with Minto remained frank, respectful, and cordial. In their various past encounters, Borden had remained patient, polite, consultative, and accommodating. He had accepted constraints, absorbed checks, and agreed to compromises. But Borden was also astute, tenacious, and politically adept. There were limits to his patience and tolerance of the obstruction of his proposed policies. In the months that followed, Borden's friendship with Minto would be severely tested as the minister pressed forward with his plans to remove "the reproach of inferiority." It is a tribute to the civility of both men that their friendship and mutual respect survived intact.

Borden realized that one of the governor general's most effective weapons in resisting his plans was Canada's own Militia Act and the restrictions it placed on a minister's ability to control his own department and implement a reform program unimpeded. Borden understood as well that any alteration of the Act meant persuading the cabinet and the Commons, as well as convincing or confronting the governor general and the GOC. Confident that he possessed the political credibility to manage the first two, he realized that he might have more difficulty confronting the governor general and the general, since they were unlikely to be persuaded.

Early in 1903, Borden made a bold move, aware of the risks. He had planned and prepared his move quietly for months in consultation with Otter, Lieutenant-Colonel T.D.B. Evans, and Colonel Henry Smith.[24] Confident of parliamentary and public support, Borden unveiled his plan, a comprehensive overhaul of the Militia Act designed to invest the Act with the legislative authority required to implement projects that had been frustrated and delayed by constitutional objections and administrative roadblocks. As he explained at the Toronto banquet on 29 December 1903, what he wanted was a Militia Act that was "a Canadian law, first, last and all the time."[25]

Many of the changes proposed by Borden's draft bill were bound, perhaps even intended, to receive the hearty support of the Commons' Militia lobby, a valuable ally in Borden's battle for the bill. His proposals included increasing the PF's establishment to 2,000 persons; doubling the number of permissible paid days of annual drill for the civilian Militia from sixteen to thirty; making more effective provision for the support of cadet corps in schools; confining riot control, in the first instance, to the PF; opening the rank of brigadier-general to Canadian officers; and establishing a graduated pay scale up to one dollar a day. Predictably, all these measures were applauded by the Militia lobby in the House of Commons, and Borden could count on the lobby's bipartisan support.

Three vital items in Borden's proposed revision of the Militia Act, however, aroused the immediate ire of the governor general. Minto's first objection centred on the Act's proposed section 3, which vested the position of commander-in-chief in the king rather than the governor general, a clause that the governor general invoked to justify his claim to meddle. The second significant change was to strike the existing Act's section 37, which restricted command of the Canadian Militia to an officer of the British regular army, thereby opening the position to alternative candidates, including an officer from the Canadian Militia. The third large "imperial" item, and one that troubled Minto immensely, was Borden's failure to include provision in the new Act for placing the Canadian Militia under the King's Regulations in the event of its service with British troops.

Minto lost no time demanding that Borden and Laurier delay legislation until they consulted the imperial authorities. Typically, the Colonial Office appeared more sympathetic to Borden's proposals than Minto had anticipated. Although it regretted Borden's failure to reserve the position of the GOC of the Canadian Militia for a British regular officer, it had no difficulty with the vesting of the position of commander-in-chief in the king rather than the governor general, since this simply brought the Militia Act into conformity with the British North America Act.[26] Nonetheless, in view of Minto's various objections, the Colonial Office prudently agreed with the governor general's suggestion that Borden delay action until he could consult the War Office in person, a meeting that the office scheduled for December 1903 in London.

Meanwhile Minto and Lord Dundonald, the GOC of the Canadian Militia who had replaced O'Grady-Haly in July 1902, bombarded the Colonial and War offices and any other well-placed British friend they felt might influence the outcome of the proposed December discussions with information, advice, and warnings. Their greatest objection centred on the position of the GOC of the Canadian Militia. Confident that Borden's visit to London would dissuade him from his folly, Minto provided the Colonial and War offices with a detailed, twelve-page, typescript memorandum outlining his views and recommendations. Above all he sternly warned against any of Borden's plans that would enlarge the Canadian government's field of patronage and corruption, a theme that was beginning to wear thin in the Colonial Office.[27] The Colonial Office was far from persuaded by Minto's objections. It realized that the existing system was so inadequate that it mattered little who commanded the Militia. "We know," one Colonial Office official noted, that Minto "is inclined to state a very unfavourable view of everything the Militia Dept. does. The Admiralty & W.O. are not so dissatisfied."[28]

Dundonald was no less generous and prolific with his opinion, advice, and counsel, but he was no more successful in convincing the recipients of the wisdom of his position. Scarcely a month before Borden's meeting in London, the GOC despatched a nine-page, typescript memorandum to Sir William Nicholson, director of military intelligence, part of the "fixed nucleus" of the Committee of Imperial Defence (CID) before whom Borden was to defend his proposed revisions of the Militia Act. Dundonald's memorandum outlined arguments designed to undermine all of Borden's proposals, along with points for compromise and other confidential material that might be useful to subvert Borden's plans.[29] In light of Minto's and Dundonald's frequent and exhaustive communications with the Colonial and War offices in the months leading up to Borden's December 1903 meeting, their subsequent complaint that the War Office caved in to Borden's demands because it was insufficiently informed lacks credibility.

Minto naively expected that Sir Frederick, once in London, would fall under the imperial spell and capitulate, an easy prey to the confident authority of imperial arguments and the intoxicating effects of social diplomacy designed "to turn weak men's heads."[30] Sir Frederick, however, proved more level-headed, headstrong, and successful than Minto and Dundonald had imagined. Three days before his meeting with the Committee of Imperial Defence, Borden met the British secretary for war, Hugh Oakeley Arnold-Forster, and explained his plans, and they agreed upon a settlement.[31] Borden's meeting with the committee on 11 December 1903, however, was more than a pleasant formality to rubberstamp the Borden–Arnold-Forster agreement. The committee members were well primed for the meeting and used the occasion to discuss a wide range of Canadian-Imperial defence issues and objectives, an exchange subsequently embodied in a significant and controversial eight-point resumé.

The committee readily approved Canada's right to name a Canadian to the post of general officer commanding the Canadian Militia, subject to the Crown's prerogative to appoint a "Senior General officer of the Regular Army to the supreme joint command" in time of war. The committee agreed as well that an imperial officer might from time to time make an "occasional inspection" of the Militia, at the invitation of the Canadian government, based on the imperial government's "need to know" in view of its continuing responsibility for Canadian defence. On the question of relative rank, the committee dropped the contention that imperial officers possessed "powers of executive command over Canadian troops by virtue of their Imperial Commissions," and granted reciprocal recognition of the commissions of Canadian Militia and British regular officers serving in North America. While the committee made it clear that it would prefer retaining the governor general as the commander-in-chief, it did not make this a requirement of its agreement. In what might appear as a gift, the British government offered to turn over the British garrisons at Halifax and Esquimalt to the Canadian government.

And in an effort to improve the quality of the Canadian forces, it consented to Borden's request that six imperial staff college positions be reserved annually for Canadian officers and that there be access to short-term staff positions in the British regular army for a selected number of Canadian officers. The committee also raised the possibility of sending a Canadian infantry battalion to India to serve and train with British troops.[32]

A reading of the detailed account of the conference proceedings horrified Minto. Not only had the committee failed to heed his warnings and follow his advice, it had gone well beyond Borden's agenda, offering to relinquish the British garrisons at Halifax and Esquimalt. Minto could not believe that the British government had been so shortsighted and stupid, and for a long time he used every pretext possible to upset the agreement and delay its implementation. "H.M. Govnt. by sheer idiocy," he fumed in his diary, "are ruining the military position here."[33] He placed most of the blame on the new colonial secretary, Alfred Lyttelton, who, friends told him, "behaved more stupidly even than I had imagined."[34]

Minto's analysis ignored Borden's contribution to the successful outcome of the conference, and he failed to appreciate the extent to which Borden had used the meeting to establish a "social beachhead" in London. Recently knighted, Canada's war minister had been well received in the imperial capital, where the death of his son was a subject of sympathetic commentary. Contrary to Minto's expectations, the minister's head had not been turned by social diplomacy. Borden himself had engaged in a certain amount of social diplomacy prior to meeting the committee, dining with persons of influence and establishing useful future contacts. Socially adroit, intelligent, and articulate, Borden knew his dossier and appeared receptive, conscientious, and committed to imperial defence. His hosts at the meeting were attentive, informative, and understanding, and sufficiently impressed with his knowledge and reliability to offer him "a place" on the CID, the first "colonial so honoured." Although the British prime minister, in explaining Borden's participation in the CID, described the Canadian minister as "of rather inferior quality," he regarded his presence on the committee as a precedent "of great significance" and the CID as having the potential to become an imperial council, an assessment shared by one contemporary scholar.[35] Borden himself valued the distinction (so much so that his family subsequently had chiselled onto his tombstone the fact of him membership), though it created a storm of criticism at home, where opponents feared that his membership was the precursor to some form of imperial governance.

In fact the honour was something of an empty shell. The committee's predecessor, the Colonial Defence Committee, created in 1895 to coordinate the interdepartmental intelligence, counsel, and policy required for military preparation, took on new life following the South African War.[36] Renamed the Committee of Imperial Defence in 1902, it became some enthusiasts' answer to imperial consolidation in the wake of the failure of other comparable schemes.[37] Since the committee was designed to advise the British prime minister and consisted of only those whom the prime minister summoned, technically it possessed no permanent places, though there were "regular" members, a privilege Borden could scarcely exercise from Ottawa.[38]

Sir Frederick's apparent success in London, however, had less to do with his personal qualities or Lyttelton's "stupidity" than with the committee's recent re-evaluation of Britain's strategic commitments in North America, in the wake of a British cabinet reorganization. Two months before Borden arrived in London, the British prime minister, Arthur Balfour, had reorganized his cabinet following Joseph Chamberlain's resignation to pursue his imperial preferential tariff campaign. The loss of Chamberlain, a powerful minister second only to the prime minister, and his replacement as colonial secretary by Alfred Lyttelton, a weaker, less effectual, and less experienced politician, diminished the Colonial Office's influence within the cabinet. The move of William St John Brodrick from the War Office to the India Office and his replacement by H.O. Arnold-Forster, an energetic, ambitious man with little tolerance for traditional court influence, permitted the settlement of an old argument over imperial defence strategy in North America.

In the past, Lord William Selborne, the First Lord of the Admiralty, had tried unsuccessfully to persuade the CID to reconsider Britain's burdensome colonial defence responsibilities in North America. Since the Admiralty dismissed the possibility of opposing the United States' navy in the Caribbean and the Atlantic, it proposed to withdraw the Atlantic squadron and concentrate its full strength in European waters.[39] With the support of the new prime minister, Arthur Balfour, who was also a strong advocate of War Office retrenchment and Anglo-American rapprochement, Selborne had favoured a withdrawal of the remaining imperial naval garrisons from North America.

According to Selborne, their two greatest opponents within cabinet to a withdrawal of the North Atlantic squadron and attendant garrisons had been the War Office Secretary St John Brodrick, who was "too sticky & not sufficiently resourceful," and Colonial Secretary Joseph Chamberlain, "who doesn't know all the facts & is impatient of those he doesn't like."⁴⁰ Chamberlain's departure from the cabinet and Balfour's recent cabinet shuffle removed both opponents from the decision-making council and tipped the cabinet balance in favour of the Balfour-Selborne option, especially since the new secretary of state for war, Arnold-Forster, agreed entirely with Balfour that a fight with the United States, "our cousins across the Atlantic is perhaps the most improbable."⁴¹

A week before Borden met with the Committee of Imperial Defence, the committee had convened to discuss Britain's North American defence commitments. It was during this timely meeting that Selborne and Balfour easily persuaded the committee to abandon the idea of defending Canada against an unlikely American attack and "to place the whole responsibility for the Militia upon the Canadian govnt."⁴² Once the fear of an American front ceased to preoccupy the minds of serious imperial strategists, the Canadian Militia's inefficiency no longer seemed the nightmare it had been. It mattered less, then, who commanded the Canadian Militia, and if Canada would take over the redundant imperial garrisons at Halifax and Esquimalt, so much the better. In other words, Borden had won his case largely by default. In addition, he had "received" the garrisons, a somewhat dubious, controversial bonus and one that would require a reordering of Canadian defences.

Unaware of the committee's strategic decision, however, Minto continued to play Don Quixote. As soon as Borden returned to Canada and reported his success to the governor general, Minto took perverse pleasure in what he saw as a discrepancy between Borden's version of the deliberations of the CID meeting and the War Office memorandum that Alfred Lyttelton had sent to him, a discrepancy with which Minto hoped to sabotage Borden's insidious agreements. When Borden met with Minto to discuss the discrepancy, he denied that he had agreed to take over the two garrisons at Halifax and Esquimalt or to send an infantry battalion to India. Moreover, Borden insisted that the War Office had consented to reserve six rather than two imperial staff training positions a year for Canadian officers. Above all, he rejected Minto's suggestion that he had bought a package plan: the War office had attached no preconditions to his proposed amendments to the Militia Act.⁴³

Dismayed by the apparent misunderstanding and fearing that Minto might exploit the discrepancies to his advantage, Borden wrote at once to Lyttelton for a clarification. Lyttelton responded almost immediately, agreeing entirely with Borden's recollection and regretting that the War Office secretary should have "composed the minutes on the theory that what he conceives ought to have been arranged was arranged."⁴⁴ Still, Minto remained unconvinced of Lyttelton's disclaimer until he received an official copy of the committee's minutes confirming Borden's version. This would take four months. Meanwhile he continued to bombard the Colonial Office with letters regurgitating all of his old objections and claiming wide public support for his opinions. His communications convinced no one in the Colonial Office, increasingly tired of the governor general's persistence. "Lord Minto will not understand," John Anderson, chief clerk in the Colonial Office, complained, "that a quasi-independent Commander-in-Chief is incompatible with complete Ministerial responsibility."[45] Another official added, "Lord Minto is evidently annoyed that his views have not been accepted and implies that H.M.G. are acting in ignorance."[46]

While Borden was unaware of the nature and extent of Minto's transatlantic correspondence, the governor general made no secret of his continuing opposition to Borden's proposed reforms. Consequently, when Borden reintroduced his amended Militia Act in March 1904, Minto renewed his battle to block or emasculate the proposed legislation. In Minto's view, Borden's bill violated the December "agreement" by omitting two important items: provision for the Crown to appoint a supreme commander in the event of war; and the right of British regular officers to command Canadian troops during joint manoeuvres in North America. Although Borden promised to insert the Crown's right to appoint a supreme commander in the event of war during second reading of the bill and to amend the Militia Orders and Regulations to permit British regular officers to command Canadian troops during joint manoeuvres, Minto remained sceptical and appealed once again to the colonial secretary to "insist" on their inclusion in the Act. While the Colonial Office shared Minto's concerns on both matters, it advised Minto to concentrate on the Crown's rights and to trust Borden to honour his promise on the issue of regular officers' claim to command Canadian troops. "I do not see how we can proceed on the assumption that Sir F. Borden is lying," one irritated official noted. "Lord Minto seems to be trying to force our hand."[47]

Although Borden had no idea of the Colonial Office's growing impatience with Minto's stubborn persistence, he may have sensed the governor general's exposed position, his splendid isolation within the imperial network. Minto, however, had counted on a second line of defence, namely Canadian opposition to the bill. Borden, of course, knew better. He realized that Minto's objections possessed little resonance within the Conservative party (their leader adopting a very judicial approach), which generally supported the bill,[48] with the exception of Borden's eccentric friend Sam Hughes, whose company the governor general was unlikely to cultivate. More important to Borden's future career was his success in London, which gave him an imperial visibility.

CHAPTER 12

Dundonald's Defiance

What really broke Minto's will to resist Borden's Militia Bill was the defiance of Lord Dundonald, the GOC of the Canadian Militia. Dundonald's deliberate decision to defy his civilian masters and appeal his case to the Canadian people left the government with little choice but to dismiss him from his command. Not only did Dundonald's dismissal break the governor general's will to resist the bill, it rid Borden of another troublesome GOC and enabled him to create his Militia Council. The council represented another fundamental change in the administration of the Canadian forces, one designed to tap the collective wisdom, end tensions between civilian and military authorities, and assure collegiality, continuity, and direction in the administration of the Canadian Militia. In addition, the Militia Council gave Borden the means to shape military policy, resolve conflicts, benefit from professional advice, and educate the military in Canadian political realities.

Irksome as Minto's dogged efforts to denature Borden's Militia Bill might have been, Borden soon faced a more serious public challenge to his authority from Lord Dundonald, the irate GOC of the Canadian Militia. This conflict would eventually kill Minto's will to resist the amendments to the Militia Act. Contrary to what some historians have assumed, the governor general's behaviour during Borden's confrontation with the 12th Earl of Dundonald was not a rerun of the Minto-Hutton fiasco. Minto had learned from his earlier blunder; besides, Minto and Dundonald were not friends. From the start Minto had taken a singular dislike to Dundonald. Ever since Hutton's dismissal Minto had begged the British colonial secretary to appoint as GOC a man of "repute, presence, capacity, wealth," tact, and with a wife with "social qualities" – all for $1,800 a year![1] He had even suggested the appointment of two popular British veterans of the South African War who had led Canadian troops, generals Horace Smith-Dorrien and E.A.H. Alderson, but they were unavailable.

Much to Minto's disappointment, Dundonald failed to fit the job description. During their first meeting in Ottawa Dundonald spent most of his time complaining to the governor general about the precedence table in Canada that placed him, the scion of a distinguished Scottish aristocratic family, after ministers of the Crown rather than after the governor general; this was perhaps a pointed way of reminding Minto of their relative social standings within the Scottish nobility. Despite Minto's unfavourable initial impression of Dundonald, he offered to help the general find a house in Ottawa and invited him to discuss Militia matters with him on any occasion and to seek his advice and counsel. Minto, however, did not wait for Dundonald to request advice. Well before Dundonald arrived in Canada, Minto had cautioned him "not to ride the horse too hard," especially in dealing with the minister, whom he described as "easy to work with ... really keen about his Depart ... most anxious to push on." There were, he suggested to Dundonald, more effective ways of handling the minister, who was "very sensitive to a little butter & with a judicious bestowal of it much friction would vanish."[2]

The general's quirks, however, could not be ignored, and they soon became the subject of mirth and dismay at Rideau Hall. Although Dundonald was reputed to possess many personal qualities, charm, imagination, eloquence, Minto and others found him egotistical, unbalanced, vindictive, and theatrical, anxious "to appear to the world as riding the storm and holding the gate."[3] In the privacy of his diary and correspondence with his family, the governor general began shortly to refer to the general as "Dundoddle," that "well-meaning faddist," that "dangerous demagogue," that "awful stick," that "vain, unreasonable creature," that "petulant baby," and that "crank with a brain the size of a fruit head."[4]

Borden himself had welcomed Dundonald as a popular Boer War hero who had commanded Canadian troops in South African and whose exploits had been favourably reported in the Canadian press. The general's younger son, a western Canadian prospector, had joined the Strathcona Horse and was the subject of much public curiosity. At first Borden saw Dundonald as energetic, inventive, open to change, and above all keenly committed to the creation of a civilian army, one of Borden's pet projects. Borden must also have been reassured by the suggestion that Dundonald appeared to those who had met him to be "rather quiet and reserved – not undesirable qualities."[5] But as Borden and others worked more closely with the new general, they soon came to share the governor general's view that Dundonald was a poor administrator who let stores rot for want of care, a faddist who engaged in expensive, dubious experiments, and a man generally indifferent to the state of the Canadian Militia, more interested in his own status, image, and popularity.

Obliged to defend his department's defence estimates and expenditures before the House of Commons, Borden soon became alarmed at the general's cavalier expenditures. Convinced of the pedagogical utility of instructional placards demonstrating commonplace activities such as the felling of a tree, the general seemed immune to advice and suggestions. As a result, much of the instructional material was risible or incorrect and the work had to be reprinted.[6] Other experiments were the object of public amusement and ridicule.[7] Although relatively small matters, they invited public and parliamentary scepticism and resistance to further military spending. Dundonald was no more careful about discipline.

A larger contention between the minister and the general concerned the selection of a central military training camp. If Borden were to realize the Boer War–inspired aspiration that in future wars Canadians would fight in Canadian units under Canadian officers rather than be broken up and serve in British units, what he needed was one large, accessible training base of sufficient size to mobilize and train a "self-contained citizen army complete in all its arms," under the command of Canadian senior officers and prepared to work as a unit. Apparently indifferent to cost, timing, advice, or the consideration of alternative sites, Dundonald decided that the proposed central camp ought to be established at Sharbot Lake, in Frontenac County, about ninety kilometres north of Kingston, Ontario. Borden, however, was determined to take his time, to make certain that he made "the best selection possible, in the public interest," conscious that he was "selecting a site for perhaps fifty years or more to come, and the question of annual cost in getting to and from the camp is most important."[8] In the end Borden's choice was Petawawa, but not until Dundonald had left Canada.

It took Dundonald little time to compile a long list of further grievances against the minister, three of which he identified as fundamental – at least they were represented as fundamental during his final engagement with the minister and in his subsequent reminiscences. The first of the aggrieved general's fundamentals was the minister's alleged suppression of the general's first annual report. According to the governor general, who held no particular brief for Borden, Dundonald's complaint was largely a figment of his lively imagination. The suppression consisted simply of Borden's request that the general transfer a defence plan from Part I of the report, which was to be made public, to Part II, which would not be submitted to Parliament. Even though Borden may not have been entirely credible in claiming that his request had been dictated solely by security considerations, at the time Dundonald was willing to live with the indignity and the issue only became active ammunition during the general's ultimate confrontation with the minister.

Whatever Borden's real or other motives may have been, the general's later charge that the minister simply wished to suppress criticism of the Militia seems preposterous given the familiarity and banality of Dundonald's criticisms and Borden's offer to include in Part I any "deleted" sections Dundonald himself thought appropriate.[9] In addition, Borden agreed to open the controversial unrevised Part II to any parliamentary committee to consider the report or to any interested member of Parliament.[10] Nonetheless Dundonald rejected Borden's offer out of hand and took his case to Sam Hughes, the opposition military critic. Hughes raised the question in the House of Commons, an action that neither surprised nor upset Borden, though it scandalized and further alienated the governor general, who thought Dundonald's behaviour improper and quite unacceptable, especially his truck with the disdained Sam Hughes!

Dundonald's second fundamental complaint was that the Militia was underfunded, a condition that had plagued it from its birth. Yet few ministers had done more than Borden to wring larger supplies from a reluctant government, even when doing so incurred the wrath of the tight-fisted Department of Finance and its deputy minister. Twice Borden had threatened to resign rather than reduce his estimates. He constantly badgered Laurier for increased funding, and he often secured what he wanted through supplementary estimates. During the past eight years the Militia had received nearly $24 million, twice the amount that had been spent during the previous eight years.[11] But this was not the point. The financial issue between the minister and the general often simply entailed differences of policy, administration, and timing. For example, neither Borden nor the Canadian or British government for that matter shared Dundonald's inordinate fear of an imminent American invasion, against which he proposed an expensive line of fortifications. According to Dundonald, the Canadian government's rejection of his expensive plans for enhanced border defences constituted a dangerous dereliction of duty that demanded public exposure and censure.

The third and central cause of the general's final, public explosion was Borden's plan to create a Militia Council that would obviate the general's position and establish civilian control once and for all. To Dundonald this was the last straw in their deteriorating relationship. Borden's proposed new Militia Bill had so deeply divided the two men that Borden had refused to take Dundonald to London for the December meeting with the CID for the understandable reason that the general had made no secret of his adamant opposition to Borden's plans, and he had made this known to the British authorities behind his minister's back. Borden's subsequent victory did nothing to improve their rapport, and from that time on, as Minto confided to his friend George Parkin, the former headmaster of Upper Canada College, the general "seemed to think he could upset the decision of the W.O. or render it ineffectual."[12]

The general's persistent obstructions persuaded Borden that the time had come for radical reform, for establishing civilian control of the military. To do so, he proposed to substitute a Militia Council that would subsume the position of GOC along the lines suggested for the British Army by Lord Esher's War Office (Reconstruction) Committee. Lord Esher's proposal, designed to improve communications between the British military and civilian authorities and reassert the primacy of civilian control over the British Army, seemed to Borden especially pertinent to Canada, given the long, troubled history of conflict between Canadian ministers and generals. The Canadian version of the Militia Council was to consist of four senior staff officers, the chief of the general staff, the adjutant-general, the quartermaster-general, and the master-general of ordnance; as well as three civilians, the minister as president, the deputy minister, and the departmental accountant. Altogether the proposed council was almost as important as the new Militia Act in transforming the administration of Canada's defence forces.

Quite apart from the problem of conflicting personalities, Borden saw something fundamentally wrong with a system that made an itinerate British GOC of the Canadian Militia his singular, formal channel of advice and counsel, a system based upon the fiction that ministers possessed neither military knowledge, interest, memory, experience, or common sense. An informed, well-read, and intelligent man, Borden maintained a network of communication with senior professional soldiers in Britain and Canada, officers such as Otter, Evans, Parsons, Seymour, Aylmer, and Lake; and he had no intention of becoming the captive of one man. Generals came and went; Borden had four in nine years. Each had to be educated to the local circumstances. Each brought a different scheme or emphasis. As Borden explained to a bemused Toronto audience, the GOC of the Canadian Militia possessed "great powers – perhaps not always as great as he imagined. He usually set out at once to prove that his predecessor was an ass – and he was oftentimes able to prove it without the slightest difficulty."[13]

Whatever Borden thought of the various generals' personalities (and in mellower moments he claimed he respected all with whom he had worked), he was convinced that the problem was structural. In his view, a Militia Council composed of senior military and civilian members would not only rid him of his organizational dependency on an itinerant, idiosyncratic incumbent and provide a forum for an exchange of information between civilians and military professionals, but it would reinforce civilian control and create a more adequate source of information, memory, continuity, and coordination in military affairs. Moreover, it would depersonalize decisions and reduce the friction between ministers and generals. For those who feared a deterioration of standards and requirements owing to the loss of input from the British regular army, Borden proposed naming an inspector general to the Militia Council (as he had agreed to do during the CID meeting in December 1903), normally a regular officer from the British Army, who would report and recommend, to assure the continuing quality of the Canadian Militia. Convinced of the deficiency of the existing system and the efficacy of his proposed remedy, Borden was determined to act. "[My mind is] made up to take the plunge," Borden wrote in April 1904 to Colonel T.D.R. Evans, the former officer commanding the 1st and 2nd Canadian Mounted Rifles in South Africa, "as I have all I can stand of the existing system and absurd condition of things."[14]

In proposing a Militia Council, Borden prepared for an acute passage of arms between himself and the GOC, as well as between himself and the governor general, a war on two fronts. (The Australians' adoption of a council in 1904 led to the resignation of their GOC, Major-General E.T.H. Hutton!) Anticipating a strong vice-regal reaction to his plan, the minister broke the news gently to the governor general in May 1904, explaining that while ultimately he favoured the creation of a Militia Council, the present time did not seem the appropriate moment. This was a far from forthright statement given his previous communication with Evans.

Borden was surprised and encouraged by Minto's calm response to the idea, a striking contrast to the reaction of Minto's military secretary, Major F.S. Maude, who explained to the Colonial Office the bases of his own objections. Minto's apparent equanimity, however, was based on an ulterior motive. He saw Borden's proposal as an opportunity to revive the vice-regal attempts to retain the British garrisons and maintain a British influence over the Canadian Militia by making the GOC of British troops in Halifax the permanent inspector general of the Canadian forces, a fanciful scheme for which neither the War Office nor the Colonial Office displayed any real interest.[15]

What broke Minto's will to resist Borden's new Militia Bill and proposed Militia Council, however, was not the bankruptcy of his proposal to bring the Canadian Militia under the Halifax general but Dundonald's theatrical reaction to the Militia Council. The general rightly saw Borden's Militia Council as an overt attack on the office of GOC and by extension on its incumbent, and he felt that a looming federal election was an opportune occasion to sound the alarm, or as Dundonald preferred, "to light the heather." Consequently, on 3 June 1904 the general launched a carefully planned public attack on the Canadian government during a Montreal Militia officers' banquet. Speaking before a large audience and in the presence of a press repor- ter, the general deliberately accused the government of gross political interference in Militia affairs. An example of flagrant political interfer- ence, he explained to a slightly embarrassed audience, had occurred only recently during recruiting for the Scottish Light Dragoons, a cav- alry regiment being formed in the Eastern Townships. Sydney Fisher, the minister of agriculture, whose constituency was in the area, had objected to the number of Conservative officers enrolled in the unit, and while he was acting minister of militia during Borden's absence, Fisher had struck some names from the list, notably that of Dr Wilfred Pickles, a well-known Conservative political partisan. The facts, though carefully selected, were much as Dundonald had related, although per- haps not as Sydney Fisher might have told them.

A vigilant politician with a lively appreciation of the power of patron- age and a close friend of the minister of militia, Sydney Fisher might have been more discreet had he not been embroiled in a heated political contest to re-elect the Quebec provincial secretary. Dundonald's appar- ent partiality and want of judgment in his choice of officers for the new unit had given Fisher cause for concern. In selecting an officer to com- mand the unit, Dundonald had appointed Colonel Charles A. Smart, a man who knew little of the area and who had depended on the advice of the Conservative senator G.B. Baker, Fisher's chief local opponent, in his selection of the unit's officers. When Smart submitted his proposed list of regimental officers, three of the persons were Senator Baker's relatives and another was Dr Wilfred Pickles, the Conservative mayor of Sweetsburg and Baker's chief political operative. Although he was the proprietor of a rifle range from which he stood to benefit, Pickles possessed no particular qualification for a senior military position, a fact he readily recognized. Given Dundonald's open flirtation with the Conservative Party, the general's behaviour appeared to Fisher to have all the appearances of blatant political provocation.

Borden and Fisher were colleagues, friends, and skilled politicians who understood the importance of timing. Urged on by Fisher, Borden continued to delay approval of Smart's list of officers. Then, just before the June Militia camp, Borden informed Dundonald that he was leav- ing Ottawa for a month, entrusting his department to Sydney Fisher. Borden's gesture needed no interpretation, especially for Pickles. Aware of the familiar rules of patronage, Pickles withdrew his name, not wishing to sabotage Smart's desire to train the men during the June camp. When Fisher learned of Pickles's decision he approved the list immediately, erasing Pickles's name. Fisher, however, failed to inform Dundonald of Pickles's request to have his name removed, leaving the general to draw the obvious conclusion.[16] Although technically above reproach, Fisher's conduct constituted a flagrant case of political intimidation, one in which Borden was complicit and that opponents might construe as the greater offence, especially on the eve of a federal election, a consideration not lost on Dundonald.

Despite his complicity, Borden, upon learning of Dundonald's public denunciation, seized the high road and asked the governor general to speak to Dundonald immediately and explain to him that no government "could possibly approve of an officer in his position publicly criticizing the actions of a Minister."[17] Although Minto took the opportunity to lecture Borden on Fisher's deplorable behaviour, the governor general agreed to speak to the general. During Minto's far from congenial interview with Dundonald, the governor general suggested that the general had but three options: resign, apologize, or bluff. In Minto's view, Dundonald provided no satisfactory justification for his action. He simply said that "he hated Laurier & wanted to do him all the harm he could."[18] Acutely aware of his own constitutional vulnerability, Dundonald begged Minto not to take too constitutional a line against him. Much to Minto's amazement, Dundonald seemed amused by the Canadian government's predicament and made no secret of his plans to exploit the issue, a prospect that alarmed the increasingly "constitutional" governor general, given Dundonald's unpredictability.

Whatever their differences had been over Canadian and imperial defences during the past year or more, Borden's relations with Minto remained remarkably open, respectful, and cordial throughout the Dundonald crisis. In sharp contrast to his myopic behaviour during the Hutton affair, Minto attempted to be impartial. Indeed his sympathy was probably more with the Canadian government than with the general, much to the alarm of many of his close friends and advisors. Although Minto insisted on speaking to Fisher as well as to Dundonald, his interview with the minister of agriculture evoked more viceregal sympathy than anger. Minto liked Fisher and considered him a sound, sensible man. During their discussion, Fisher, full of gratitude and contrition, almost wept on the governor general's shoulder. Convinced by Fisher's behaviour, Minto contented himself with lecturing him on the need for purity in Militia affairs. As Minto explained to his wife, Fisher's conduct "was more the action of a busy-body than having anything politically corrupt about it."[19] Nonetheless, Minto came under strong pressure from members of his household who sided with the general and pleaded with him to take a harder line with his ministers, advice that Minto shrewdly and firmly rejected.[20]

The Canadian government lost no time responding to Dundonald's speech. A cabinet subcommittee, consisting of Borden, Sifton and Fielding, met at once and agreed to dismiss Dundonald. When Laurier informed the governor general of the decision, Minto raised only a paper resistance, suggesting that in fairness Fisher ought also to resign, a proposal that Laurier rejected out of hand. Nor would Laurier agree to stay the dismissal and await Dundonald's recall. Given the general's public criticism of the government, Laurier insisted that no government "could do so with any sense of dignity," even if it were defeated in the House or at the polls.[21] The impending election was never far from the calculations of opponents and partisans of the general. Despite Borden's complicity, at no point did Minto fault the minister's behaviour, much less call for his resignation as he had done during the Hutton quarrel. As Minto confessed to his wife, he could understand Borden even if he did not always agree with him.

As a mark of Borden's standing within the cabinet and his continuing cordial relations with the governor, Borden rather than Laurier went to Minto's office with the Order-in-Council dismissing Dundonald. Minto signed the order without protest, even though he disapproved of its exaggerated justification of Fisher's actions. He made that sufficiently clear in a memorandum he composed after he had signed the council's order, the memorandum being the only concession he made to his more over-heated friends and staff. In the memorandum, Minto, mindful of his blundering behaviour during the Hutton conflict, was careful not to challenge his government's constitutional authority. Even so, when Laurier took exception to the vice-regal memorandum, solemnly asking Minto if he intended to dismiss his advisors, the governor general capitulated immediately and agreed to withdraw the offending document lest his actions be considered partisan and he "become a centre around which the political storm would rage."[22]

From the start Minto knew that dismissal would not silence the aggrieved general. Rumours were rife of a distraught Dundonald pacing his lawn, muttering to himself amidst a menagerie of "endless dogs and cats" that he kept "tied by separate chains to pegs on the grass."[23] The curious had not long to wait. With his usual dramatic flair Dundonald announced that he would remain in Canada and contest a constituency as a Conservative candidate.[24] He immediately published a manifesto explaining grandly that his struggle was not one between him and Borden but between "myself and the government of Canada."[25] In this contest he proposed to play the role of tribune of the people and stand between "the people" and their "civilian autocrats" who "were inclined to use their power not always with forbearance and kindness."[26]

On the eve of the general election, a partisan section of the English-Canadian press endorsed his cause, hoping to use Dundonald against their opponents by presenting him as a self-sacrificing hero, a mixture of Robert Bruce, Napoleon, and Wellington. The excitable general did not disappoint the large public meetings that greeted him. More level heads were alarmed at his incendiary rhetoric, more particularly his call upon all true Canadians to keep both hands on the Union Jack, which they saw as an attempt to trade on the racial conflict that had entered the controversy when Laurier had inadvertently used the word "foreigner" (*étranger*) to describe Dundonald.

Dundonald's political campaign destroyed any vestige of vice-regal support. In Minto's view, Dundonald had become little more than the cat's paw of the Conservative Party. During his last interview with Dundonald, Minto found the general "hopeless to deal with – mad – & abusive & a hard job to keep my temper."[27] Nothing, Minto felt, not even the undoubted political corruption in the country, could justify Dundonald's language and behaviour. The time had come to put an end to his mischief. Although earlier Minto had cautioned the British government to avoid interference in the dispute, he now advised them to recall the erratic general.

The War Office responded promptly to Minto's request. "I daresay," the British war secretary Arnold-Forster recorded in his diary after an interview with Dundonald upon the general's return, "he is quite right, but if he talked there as he talks here I do not wonder that he got into trouble."[28] As usual, the Colonial Office's reaction was even more sympathetic to the Canadian case. The "line taken by the Canadian Ministers in this O-in-C & their justification of Mr. Fisher's actions" were, according to the office's permanent undersecretary, "perfectly sound & unobjectionable."[29] Sir Frederick could not have asked for a more supportive assessment or a more favourable resolution of the larger conflict. Dundonald's dismissal and recall, together with the general election and the expiry of Minto's term of office, cleared the way for the creation of a Militia Council, a body that Borden would chair and employ as a source of informed counsel and within which civilian and military authorities would work harmoniously together to mould Canada's armed forces.

CHAPTER 13

A Civilian Militia

Even before the passage of the Militia Act or the creation of the Militia Council, Borden had unveiled an ambitious plan to revamp Canada's Militia, a blueprint for an effective, cost-efficient civilian defence force. Borden's plan called for the creation of a decentralized, self-sufficient civilian force, organized and instructed by a small, well-educated cadre of professional soldiers, a protective force at the service of the Canadian people at home and abroad. At home he envisaged a multipurpose militia, a didactic, integrative, civic academy that would be the means to instil patriotism, pride, health, loyalty, and discipline in its citizenry. It would be a pragmatic and regenerative institution whose community service would command public support and appeal to a cost-conscious progressive era. His task as minister was to identify and promote these objectives and enhance the Militia's presence in communities, schools, and universities across the country; allay his contemporaries' tight-fisted scepticism of the Militia's necessity; build public and political support; and secure the material resources required to realize his vision in the face of sceptics and critics.

Borden's initial challenge was to articulate an attractive, realistic defence doctrine tailored to Canada's needs, resources, and aspirations, and to find the language that would allay public apprehensions and rally and justify the support and confidence of Canadians. In articulating this doctrine, Borden appealed to the Boer War, a recent event that had assumed instant significance in museums, school texts, and public discourse.[1] He grounded his case within the general debate on the meaning and lessons derived from the war, more especially on the fears fuelled by Britain's initial apparent military deficiencies. Many contemporary British analysts spoke ominously of Britain's "loss of national power and virility," which they blamed on the softness of urban society, the undernourishment of its urban poor, and the indulgent affluence of middle-class urban living. These fears were reinforced by a library of popular literature that traded on racial assumptions and prophetic admonitions.[2] Their remedy was a social imperialism, a program of national efficiency, preparedness, and regeneration that the military would catalyze.

Within this gloomy critique of British degeneration, the success and example of colonial troops appeared to form the happy exception. Colonial troops were the flattering example of how to remedy the Empire's ills, a perspective that appealed particularly to Canadian commentators and corresponded to their troops' experience and self-image and the subsequent construction of their role in the war. During the war many British officers and writers had noted the colonials' superior physique, their stamina and initiative, as well as their adaptable, unconventional methods of warfare, a style that had seemed especially suitable to containing their unorthodox "amateur" opponents. Propagated by the juvenile press[3] and popular authors such as Rudyard Kipling, Conan Doyle, and Winston Churchill, this flattering assessment of colonial martial prowess singled out the colonial irregulars. According to Churchill, colonials were worth "three to five" British regulars,[4] an opinion endorsed by Lord Dundonald and Baden-Powell. Indeed the founder of the Boy Scout movement was convinced that his success at Mafeking represented the triumph of the kind of unconventional warfare he associated with colonial troops.[5] It was no coincidence that he had decreed that "Canada" would be the camp's password the first night after the liberation of Mafeking. Subsequently he sought to recruit even more Canadians for his South African Constabulary than were eventually enrolled.

Canadians savoured Baden-Powell's and others' flattering assessment of their soldiers' martial abilities. Proud of their warriors' success in battle, they were persuaded that their civilian soldiers possessed natural martial skills superior to the skills of the robotic British professionals. In their view, the most important lesson of the war was that every Canadian civilian was a potential soldier if given adequate resources and appropriate training; all that was required to create "the best army in the world" was courage, intelligence, initiative, firepower, and mobility.[6] If additional proof were needed, one had only to remember the resourcefulness and general effectiveness of the Boers and learn from them the lessons of the war. The Toronto *News* was so favourably impressed with the Boer system of defence and its applicability to Canada that it mischievously proposed that Boer generals Louis Botha or Christiaan De Wet be appointed to succeed General Hutton as GOC of the Canadian Militia.[7]

Although the republican ideal of a citizen soldiery was deeply rooted in Anglo-American history and mythology, it was the more contemporary Swiss example of a citizen army, of a nation in arms energized by commitment, mobility, and firepower, that had infatuated Canadian military advocates for several decades and which the Boer War appeared to validate.[8] (It is no coincidence that Australia followed a similar rhetorical line.) The Canadian advocates of the Swiss system, however, insisted on one important difference: Canada's civilian militia must remain a voluntary force, based on persuasion not compulsion. To Borden and the House of Commons' militia fraternity, an organized, voluntary citizen army was an idea whose time had come, so long as it possessed "sound administration" and "sufficient money."[9]

Several historians have attributed the paternity of Canada's citizen army to Lord Dundonald, who assumed command of the Canadian Militia on 20 July 1902.[10] Although Borden did not unveil his comprehensive blueprint for a civilian army until 8 October 1903, the plan's conception, design, and piecemeal implementation began long before Dundonald's arrival in Canada or Borden's subsequent policy statement. Only a few months after Hutton's dismissal, Borden had informed the House of Commons that he had made a close study of various European and American military systems and had concluded that Canada's needs would be best served by the Swiss model (minus its compulsory military obligation), a model capable of fielding a civilian force of 100,000 mobile sharpshooters and of defending the country from all comers.[11] Borden had grasped the Boer War's most salient lessons, that firepower and mobility were the two essential ingredients of modern warfare. Consequently, he determined that the rifle must become Canada's principal weapon of defence both for the infantry and the cavalry. Riding and rifle shooting were civilian skills easily perfected for military purposes at minimal time and cost – although Borden himself was not a rider.

With the strong backing and encouragement of Hutton's successor, O'Grady-Haly, whose support Borden publicly and generously acknowledged,[12] Borden returned to the House two years later with more precise plans for the formation of a citizen army composed of some 100,000 sharpshooters who were to belong to a network of rifle associations.[13] Essential to the plan's success was access to a dependable supply of rifles and horses, the creation of a School of Musketry (O'Grady-Haly's "excellent idea"), and preliminary provisions for cadet corps, the youth wing of his citizen army. To realize these objectives, Borden had initiated in 1901 a program to subsidize the organization of civilian rifle associations.[14] All these projects preceded the arrival of Lord Dundonald. Nonetheless no one could deny that Dundonald's appointment facilitated the development and implementation of Borden's plan. A passionate and articulate advocate of a citizen army for Great Britain, Dundonald publicly and enthusiastically endorsed Borden's plan and suggested ways and means to advance the project. The strategic support of a British professional soldier muted, even if it did not persuade or silence, some of Borden's potential critics and doubters at home and abroad.[15]

But it was only on 8 October 1903 that Borden revealed the full dimensions of his ambitious plan for a civilian army to an attentive House of Commons military fraternity. The occasion was the minister's presentation of his annual estimates. The usual vigilant bipartisan Militia lobby was in full attendance, from late morning until early evening, animated by the traditionally familiar, jovial, receptive, and largely non-partisan atmosphere. Borden was at his best, confident, informed, attentive, cordial, vigilant, and conciliatory, unapologetically making claim on public resources for his department to the applause of his friends on both sides of the House.

He began his well-prepared major policy statement by reminding his captive audience of the Militia's importance for the country's internal and external defence and lamenting how little the country spent on its security. Armed with a chart of historical statistics, Borden explained that while the country's expenditure on the Militia had doubled since 1895, per capita military expenditure still remained far less than it had been in 1871, though the government's general revenue had increased five to six times. Without disguising the need for and his intention of claiming more public funds, Borden promised the parsimonious House that his plan for a civilian army was designed first and foremost to be cost-effective and to provide maximum defence for a minimum of costs.

Borden's expansive plan envisaged a first line of defence composed of 100,000 civilian sharp shooters, two-thirds of whom were to be non-uniformed civilians and in some cases women.[16] The remaining one-third, carefully chosen to represent all military districts and all branches of the Militia, including commissariat, arms, medical, and transportation, together with their officers and non-commissioned officers, would be obliged to attend annual camp for instruction in the organizational, administrative, and tactical requirements of warfare. Staying well within the statutory establishment of 35,000 men, this "third" was to be enrolled, organized, trained, and assigned ranks, units, duties, and responsibilities. In Borden's medical language, this trained third was to form the skeleton of his citizen army. To improve the training of this important skeleton, he proposed to increase the number of eligible annual training day from sixteen to thirty. During war or the threat of war, this trained skeleton would embody, organize, and drill the remaining skilled citizen marksmen, what "Dr" Borden called the "flesh and blood" or "plastic material," thereby making the force "strong and stalwart and able to defend" the country, an organizational structure that could readily be expanded into a second 100,000-person line of defence.

Rifles were central to Borden's proposed civilian militia. To underscore their centrality, more ammunition would be distributed, especially to the infantry, and meets and competitions would be organized, subsidized, and encouraged with prizes. A musketry instructor would be assigned to each infantry regiment to supervise and assist with rifle training throughout the year.[17] To retain men and compensate good marksmen, in 1904 Borden would authorize an efficiency-pay system, and after 1909 a soldier's rifle performance would be the sole criterion for receipt of efficiency pay, a measure that could double a man's military income. Although traditionally the relatively well-equipped city units completed their annual service at their armouries and tended to concentrate on their social and ceremonial functions, in 1909 the Militia Council would require them to include more rifle shooting, tactical manoeuvres, and summer camp training.

The organization and content of military training would reflect the Militia's new objective. In 1905 the Militia headquarters' guidelines for summer camp training would require more rifle instruction, basic military manoeuvres rather than ceremonial drills, and military training that generally focused on more practical fieldwork. In 1906 Borden would insist that the Militia Council enforce the rule requiring units to train an annual minimum number of days, a measure that was aimed largely at the rural Militia and would require commanding officers to bring their units to annual camp.[18] As a result of these measures and other innovations, including a vastly improved commissariat, participation in summer training would rise to a high of 86 per cent of eligible participants in 1908,[19] whereas previously it had been as low as 33 per cent.

Members of the Militia lobby welcomed Borden's confirmation that the full burden of Canada's defence was to rest not on its PF but squarely on its productive citizens. Although the plan was designed to be cost-effective, Borden did not dissemble his need for additional resources to provide for training facilities, arms, and other incentives; free ammunition alone for this enlarged "peace establishment" would require some seven million rounds of ammunition, a sevenfold increase – good news for the Quebec cartridge factory located in his leader's constituency. In addition, the citizen soldiers would require rifles, ranges, armouries, and a large, convenient, central training ground of 20,000 to 30,000 acres, "somewhere in the interior," where they could be grouped and trained together in larger units, and which would facilitate their service under Canadian command. True to Borden's promise, two years later the Militia Department purchased a 30,770-hectare site at Petawawa, 166 kilometres northwest of Ottawa, a decision that J.D.P. French, who inspected the Canadian Militia in 1911, considered "the most important step which has yet been taken toward securing the efficiency of [Canadian] troops in war."[20]

To allay the fears of taxpayers, Borden assured the House that the full training costs would be spread out over time and would be mitigated through a network of private-public partnerships composed of subsidized armouries, rifle associations, and cadet corps. Nonetheless all of this would require major capital outlays over the next few years: notice to the tight-fisted guardians of the public purse in the Department of Finance that Borden would lead more raids on the public treasury; and good news for the politicians whose constituencies were to be favoured with armouries and rifle ranges, physical monuments to their political success.

While the Boer War had demonstrated the centrality of rifle training, it had equally underscored the importance of mobility, the need for trained horsemen and mounted infantry. In Borden's new model army, cavalry were to substitute their swords for rifles and become mounted infantry, a change strongly endorsed and promoted by the new GOC, Lord Dundonald. To meet the cavalry's numerical deficiency, Borden planned to recruit three to four times the number of uniformed mounted men and post them at strategic points along the Canadian-American border, notably in the Eastern Townships, Southern Ontario, and the Northwest.[21] To obtain this objective, priority was to be given to Western Canada, a decision subsequently ratified by the West's enthusiastic response to recruitment. While the cavalry never reached Borden's ambitious numerical objectives, in the next ten years the number of cavalry regiments more than doubled and were especially popular in Western Canada. As many as eighteen new cavalry units were formed in the West, where they soon outnumbered infantry units.[22] To capitalize on the cavalry's popularity in the West and provide for its instruction, Borden announced that he planned to reconstitute the Strathcona Horse, which had been disbanded after the Boer War, and make it part of the PF to replace the North-West Mounted Police in Calgary, as the police moved north. This measure was also designed to flatter Lord Strathcona, for whom Borden had additional plans important to the success of his citizen army. While the mounted police remained in Calgary, it was not until October 1909 that the reconstituted Lord Strathcona's Horse became part of the PF.

Similarly, Borden reassured the gunners, often considered Canada's best arm, especially its mobile field artillery, that he was equally committed to their training, education, and re-equipment. True to his promise, he subsequently authorized the organization of eight new batteries of field artillery; regrouped them into brigades to facilitate organization, training, and the production of senior officers; and re-armed them with quick firing British field guns. Between the years 1903 and 1912, the Department of Militia purchased from the British Vickers-Maxim Limited one hundred and thirty-six 18-pound field guns, twenty-four 13-pound horse artillery guns, twenty-four 4.5-inch howitzers, as well as heavy garrison coastal artillery, at the cost of $4 million.[23] The Garrison Artillery was also reformed and re-armed to deal with the country's coastal defences, especially after the Canadian Militia took over the British garrisons at Halifax and Esquimalt. And at the request of the Canadian Artillery Association (CAA), in 1905 Borden extended the number of minimum annual field training days from twelve to sixteen. As a result, successive military inspectors, Percy Lake, William Otter, and Ian Hamilton, would pronounce the cavalry and field artillery in relatively good shape.[24]

One of the pillars of Borden's civilian "army" was youth, as he had made clear in his 1903 Commons policy statement. The "young lads at school and college," Borden reminded the House, were "the material which will make up the future army of this country," the nursery for his citizen army.[25] He shared Dundonald's belief in the "military training of boys"; it was, in Borden's words, an opportunity to teach youth "physical orderliness and prompt obedience," to "bring up boys to patriotism, and to the realization that the first duty of a free citizen is to be prepared to defend his country."[26] As the nation's future defenders, they were the Militia's farm leagues, composed of impressionable, pliable youths who were more readily and economically trained than adults. All of these arguments capitalized on the era's growing obsession with notions of gender, youth, citizenship, physical fitness, order, and cost-efficiency. Cadet training was one of several youth movements that many progressives believed would help assure society's physical and social health and redeem it from urban rot, an agenda approved by social reformers, including public health reformers, such as Bor-den himself, and French-Canadian nationalists, such as Henri Bourassa.[27]

Cadet training was scarcely novel. The 1868 Militia Act had authorized the provision of arms and accoutrements for the instruction of boys over twelve in "every Normal School, University, College or School in Canada in which there shall be instituted classes of instruction in military drill and exercises." A lack of resources and competing priorities, however, had prevented the Militia from distributing arms and accoutrements to cadet corps, despite the ministry's efforts in 1879 to provide regulatory specificity to this provision of the Militia Act. In practice, the GOCs of the Canadian Militia, chronically short of funds, strenuously resisted efforts to siphon scarce resources from the adult forces. Those few cadet corps that existed before 1898, therefore, were normally associated with and nurtured by Militia units such as Montreal's 5th Royal Scots or confined to private schools, the latter subsidized by provincial governments, all operating outside the Militia Department's formal purview.

The most direct access to youth was through public schools, an institution that had been "captured by the state" during the last quarter of the nineteenth century through compulsory education and a fixed, supervised curriculum. Schools increasingly complemented and sometimes competed with the family and the church as society's "mind moulders and character builders."[28] Certainly Borden needed not to be persuaded of the power and importance of education or the value of cadet training; he had only to remember his own very positive cadet experience at Kings. Indeed one of his goals was to induce "every youth in the country, under twenty-one years of age ... to give to the State at least three annual trainings or their equivalent."[29] The challenge was how to promote cadet training through the provincially controlled school system.

Borden believed strongly in working with and through the provinces. In his view, only by "enlisting the co-operation of the various provinces of the Dominion" could one introduce "military physical training in the schools, and teach drill and rifle-shooting in the higher schools and colleges."[30] As early as 1898 he concluded an agreement with the premier of Ontario, George Ross, a former teacher, inspector, and minister of education and a general enthusiast. By this agreement the federal government pledged itself to work in cooperation with the Ontario government, whose High School Act of 1871 offered fifty dollars to every school board with a cadet corps of more than twenty-five boys.[31] To encourage schools to profit from this provision, Borden agreed to provide an eight-week summer course at Toronto's Stanley Barracks to educate teachers on the rudiments of military drill. Although Borden and Ross claimed that their primary purpose was to promote manly form and bearing, fresh air, and patriotism, defence not defiance as they liked to put it, neither disguised the provision's other purpose, to encourage fitness, drill, and military preparedness, and to train and arm a cadet corps. Borden eventually extended this initiative to other provinces.[32] But this was only the beginning.

To harness youth's potential for his citizen army, on December 1903, a month after his policy statement, Borden approved a special general order to incorporate schools or independent cadet corps into the military establishment and permit cadet instructors to hold the rank of second lieutenant in the Militia as long as they and their cadet corps remained efficient. The following year, the new Militia Act (1904) made provision for a more structured cadet organization. Cadets were divided into junior (age 12–14) and senior (age 14–18) corps, the latter "to be attached to any portion of the Active Militia for drill and training." In addition, the Act brought all cadet corps under the authority and orders of district officers commanding and provided for their provision with arms, ammunition, and equipment, including arcade rifle practice machines. As a concession to the peace lobby, cadet corps were not liable for service in the Militia in any emergency, "save only in the case of a Levee en masse."[33] In his cadet crusade Borden could count on the hardy backing of the GOC, Lord Dundonald, who believed that every boy in the country ought to belong to a cadet corps, a sentiment to which Borden would have added the proviso: "so long as it remained a voluntary system."

In 1905 Borden launched another voluntary federal-provincial initiative to tap youth's military potential. That year he announced in the House of Commons that he intended to work with provincial ministers of education to provide Canada's youth with a program of physical education, discipline, and patriotism, a program that would embrace but go beyond the cadet movement.[34] After several meetings and considerable communication with every provincial minister of education or premier, Borden obtained their support in principle for a broad program of physical education for all students, male and female, and one that included military drill for boys.

Only in 1907, however, did he announce his first concrete federal-provincial agreement, a physical education program to begin in Nova Scotia in September 1908 and to be refined as the system became fully operative. Using his influence with Nova Scotia's Liberal government, Borden had concluded an agreement with Dr A.H. McKay, the province's progressive superintendent of education.[35] The agreement provided the provincial Normal School with the federal resources, instructors, arms, equipment, books, examinations, and bonuses required to train every teacher, male and female, to qualify in physical training and drill, and male teachers to qualify for certification in advanced drill and shooting. Borden had a progressive attitude toward women's education and their participation in physical activities, encouraged by his wife and daughters. Certification of male teachers began in the summer of 1909 at the Wellington Barrack in Halifax. Successful completion of the course entitled male teachers to a commission in the Militia and the credentials to organize a cadet corps in any provincial public school. The framework of the Nova Scotia agreement, focused largely on the promotion of the cadet movement, provided a model for other provinces.

Borden's cadet program was an immense success, measured in terms of numbers and public support. In 1904 the Militia Department had reported 132 cadet corps, almost all located in Ontario and Quebec. By 1908 an estimated 9,000 boys were enrolled in 145 cadet corps; by 1910 about 21,000 boys were enrolled in 265 corps; and by 1911 the Militia Department supported 362 cadet companies. By 1914 some 9,000 male and female teachers had qualified as physical instructors under federal-provincial programs. To consolidate this initiative, in May 1909 Borden authorized a Corps of School Cadet Instructors, composed of qualified male public school teachers. The cadet movement was especially popular in Quebec, where the schools moulded the program to their cultural needs while benefiting from the support of the Militia Department and the Strathcona Trust, a fund designed o subsidize physical and para-military education. Nationalist leaders such as Henri Bourassa and Armand Lavergne gave both the cadet and the physical education programs their full support, seeing them as a means of teaching youth the virtues of self-control, discipline, manhood, and patriotism, apparently oblivious to federal intrusion in a provincial jurisdiction. So popular was the program in Quebec that by 1914 one-third of all of Canada's cadets came from that province.[36] Borden contemplated going further with his cadet training by establishing a school, a sort of junior college, under the auspices of the Strathcona Trust and administered by the Militia Department.[37]

Public leaders such as Hamilton Merritt, a founding member of the Canadian Defence League, a lobby committed to military preparedness, Maurice Hutton, principal of University College, University of Toronto, and Dr Albert Carman, the conservative general superintendent of the Canadian Methodist Church, applauded Borden's cadet and youth program, seeing it as a stepping stone to the popular Swiss system.[38] One Opposition MP, John W. Daniel, pronounced Sir Frederick's cadet program "the best move that the minister ever made."[39] The governor general, Lord Grey, was no less supportive. He shared Borden's faith in the patriotic, character-building potential of the program. To demonstrate his approval, Lord Grey donated a trophy to be given annually to the best cadet corps. The trophy depicted a strenuous young knight emerging from the folds of the Union Jack to save the Maple Leaf from the dragon of ignorance, sloth, and selfishness,[40] not an inappropriate symbol of Grey's version of Borden's citizen militia.

Altogether Borden's proposed civilian army promised to resolve a number of sticky military and political issues.[41] At first glance the projected number of trained citizen soldiers was impressive. The proposed numbers were a forceful response to those advocates of military preparedness who complained that Canada was inadequately defended. At the same time, Borden's civilian approach assured penny-pinching constituents who deplored funding an idle standing army that the civilian force was cost-effective: it required fewer uniforms, camps, and administrative expenses; and its training costs were shared by public-private arrangements. A civilian force dampened employers' objections to a large standing army that might drain productive workers at a time when economic expansion placed a premium on time and labour. In theory the plan offered the maximum defence for a minimum cost to the country and its citizens, a notion that appealed to the business-

minded minister, the country's parsimonious electorate, and the strong
Militia lobby in the House of Commons. Above all it steered a steady
course between the advocates of military preparedness and those who
denounced the folly of "taxing ourselves to a burdensome extent and
parading around the country for years on the off chance of something
occurring which is getting everyday more and more remote."[42]

In defending his blueprint amidst the enthusiastic applause of the
bipartisan Militia lobby, Borden appealed not only to the electorate's
pocketbooks, but to history, evoking "the militiamen of former days;
the men who put down the Red River uprising and the Northwest
rebellion; the men who volunteered for South Africa and won glory
for their country; the men who were second to none in heroism; the
men who never turned their backs upon the foe." Borden was confident
that "these men [and their fellow-citizens], if given an opportunity of
learning how to use a rifle would join the Militia and provide the flesh
and blood, the plastic material that would round out this skeleton and
make an army fit for duty whenever it is required." Altogether it was an
impressive performance.

Generally, the House of Commons' small,[43] friendly cross-party
Militia lobby applauded Borden's broad policy statement and praised
him for his accomplishments and plans and his bold and unapologetic
defence of the Militia.[44] Especially expansive was the Opposition's
chief defence critic, Sam Hughes, who commended both the minister
and his plan, saying that it would make Canada "invincible" against
the "entire forces of the United States."[45] Borden's plan, however, failed
to extinguish all criticism. Outside the House, pacifists denounced his
civilian army as a dangerous militarization of society. Imperialists worried about its singular obsession with the Canadian-American border
and its failure to prepare a credible expeditionary force for service
abroad, despite Borden's explicit assurance that his plan was readily
adaptable for overseas service. Others faulted its organizational weakness. General criticism, however, was blunted by the plan's enthusiastic
endorsement by many Boer War veterans, including the new GOC of
the Canadian Militia, who welcomed the opportunity to promote an
idea that he had advocated for the British Army and had made the core
of his controversial 1903 annual report.[46]

CHAPTER 14

The Politics of Persuasion

If Borden's civilian army were to be more than rhetoric, it would need to be packaged and sold to a penny-conscious Canadian public sharply divided on the issues of war and peace. It would require the minister to built a broad public consensus for his plan, especially among military advocates, manage its public opposition, and mobilize private and public resources to give substance to his vision. All this would require skilful political management, a formidable challenge in the decade following the Boer War. Borden, however, was adept at managing the growing and vigilant public sphere. He understood the power of the press, the pulpit, patronage, and personal persuasion, as well as the need to focus on the public's concerns, appealing to their material interests, and to address and manage their cultural and religious sensitivities.

Although Borden possessed the confidence of the Commons' bipartisan Militia lobby, this fraternity itself depended on public sentiment. In pitching his case to this larger constituency, Borden could count on what Desmond Morton and others have described as an unprecedented "moment of Canadian militarism,"[1] one fired by Canada's participation in the Boer War and fuelled by the growing European military rivalry. This moment of militarism created an increasingly organized and vocal public divided on issues of war and peace. Military enthusiasm expressed itself in military activities and rituals such as titles, uniforms, parades, mock battles, military pageants, and tattoos. It was represented in the language, literature, music, iconography, toys, games, sports, and public events of the period. And it was promoted by public and private schools, by patriotic, voluntary, and professional organizations, by historical and missionary societies, as well as by military and paramilitary organizations.

The urban public seemed particularly captivated by the Militia's visible and audible presence, by its ceremonial parades, martial music, uniforms (with their ranks and badges), athletic contests, and drills, especially on state-sponsored patriotic occasions. The opportunities were numerous during the early years of the new century: military pageants, industrial exhibitions,[2] Queenston Heights Day, Empire Day,

the King's Birthday, and Dominion Day, supplemented by special occasions such as the Duke of York's 1901 tour of Canada or the spectacular Quebec tercentennial, where the Militia's one-and-a-half-hour
"intricately choreographed parade of 15,000 men and more than 2,000
horses" seems to have stolen the show.[3] Other extravagant public dis-
plays included the 1909 Canadian National Exhibition's "Defence
Day"[4] and Henry Pellatt's 1909 celebration of the fiftieth anniversary of
the Queen's Own Rifles, complete with a historical pageant for 75,000
persons and a garden party for 10,000.[5]

Altogether, a plethora of focused pressure groups promoted military preparedness in the decade or more before World War I. They
included rifle clubs, organized sporting and hunting clubs, boy scouts,
les Guides Champlain (founded in 1894 in Quebec), and cadet corps
and boys' brigades nurtured by a cult of manliness, school drill, and
callisthenics. Men joined the Militia in increasing numbers, frequently
blessed and condoned by Catholic, Protestant, and Jewish religious
leaders. Other potential organizational allies in Borden's crusade to
obtain public support for his reforms included patriotic and voluntary
organizations such as the United Empire Loyalist Association, the
Sons of England, the Imperial Order of the Daughters of the Empire
(IODE), as well as professional and military preparedness pressure
groups such as the Navy League, the Canadian Defence League, the
Canadian Artillery Association, and the Military Institutes. All were
potential allies in building a civilian militia.

Borden could also count upon the broad and progressive constituency that viewed an active Militia as the answer to a spectrum of
contemporary social anxieties. These included many employers, who
endorsed the Militia as a school of order, punctuality, efficiency, discipline, and deference as well as a means of defending property during
industrial conflict,[6] and who encouraged their employees to attend
summer training camps.[7] Safely under the control and supervision
of its middle-class officers, a civilian militia promised to create cross-
class camaraderie and patriotism as a substitute for the growing class-
consciousness and American domination of organized labour in Canada. Similarly, many social reformers regarded the Militia as a character-
building institution, an antidote to hooliganism and disease, as well
as way to purge the fearful softness of urban living (round shoulders,
weak chests), race degeneration, and the feminization of the lives of
men and boys. To patriots, the Militia offered the virtues of courage,
loyalty, community, service, and citizenship, a means to create a strong
and healthy race capable of defending home, class, and homeland. To
nativists, the Militia provided a socializing institution, a means to Can-
adianize the growing and "dangerous" number of "strangers within

our gates." All these diverse groups required careful management if they were to aid Borden's specific agenda, since their support was often contingent on other things. He would also have to contend with the bipolarization of public opinion on questions of war and peace.

In opposition to the military lobby, a growing, organized, and vocal Canadian peace party viewed the Militia with scepticism and hostility. Many French Canadians had difficulty disentangling military preparedness from "British cultural imperialism," whose association with various ethnic, linguistic, and religious crusades made military preparedness suspect. They feared the human and material costs of war and the centralizing grasp and culturally monolithic agenda of imperialistic organizations. In English Canada a broad, "progressive" peace movement garnered wide support during these years, especially among Protestant churches, women's groups, farm and labour organizations, all uncomfortable with the militarization of their society.[8] Drill, guns, and uniforms, the symbols of militarism, and the indoctrination of youth were the targets of their criticism. None of their criticism was harsher than their objections to the cadet movement, since the moulding of youth had become the battleground of the era's nation builders. A growing number of Canadian Protestant leaders viewed militarism as un-Christian, the "ideals of Christ ... being replaced by those of paganism," and railed against placing guns in the hands of young boys.[9] Farm journals, such as the *Grain Growers Guide* and the *Farmers Sun*, the Methodist Epworth League, and trade union and socialist spokesmen such as James Simpson denounced the promoters of cadet training as "scaremongers and arrogant critics of honest farmers."[10] These persons and others questioned the Militia's necessity, especially on this continent, and deplored its waste of private time and public funds and its dangerous encouragement of big government, sentiments increasingly reflected within the Laurier government.

Perhaps none of these groups or organization was more consistently critical of the military than organized labour, owing largely to the Militia's use as strikebreakers. Labour was conscious, too, that the Militia constituted a potential class dissolvent, designed "as much toward building a quiescent labour force as a battle-worthy army."[11] While the conservative Trades and Labour Congress (TLC) periodically defeated radical resolutions calling for the disbandment of the Militia and a prohibition on members joining the force, it did not hesitate to condemn "war as a capitalist ploy" or advocate a general strike as the most effective means "to prevent the outbreak of war."[12]

Labour's opposition was matched by the powerful, articulate, and broadly organized temperance and prohibition lobby, represented by the Women's Christian Temperance Union (WCTU), which possessed a historic commitment to peace and arbitration, backed by the Dominion Alliance for the Total Suppression of the Liquor Traffic and the Lord's Day Alliance. All were appalled by what they believed to be wickedness and sin in the summer Militia camps. In their view, these wild weekends away from the constraints of community and parental scrutiny gave impressionable young recruits access to military canteens, with their cigarette smoking, drunkenness, brawling, and association with the worse elements of society. They saw the military camps as little more than dens of iniquity that eroded the moral fibre of young men. The temperance movement's price for its support of the Militia was closing the canteens. This was an especially sensitive and treacherous issue for Borden, for personal and political reasons, and one that he handled with great caution, not wanting to upset the increasingly vocal moral reform lobby, especially those he paternalistically described as "our Lady friends."

The founding of the Canadian Peace and Arbitration Society in 1905 created a more organized and focused voice for these and other historic conscientious objectors, such as the Quakers, Mennonites, Hutterites, and Doukhobors. Even the Liberal Party seemed mined by influential peace and arbitration advocates, whose number included the editors of Toronto's two Liberal journals, the *Globe* and the *Star*, as well as some of Sir Frederick's friends and cabinet colleagues, such as Sir William Mulock (1896–1905) and William Lyon Mackenzie King (1909–11), who dampened political support for ambitious military projects within the Laurier government. Meanwhile militarists, alarmed by the pacifism "sweeping the country," where it had become "almost a religion," decried pacifism's erosive effects on "national defence."[13]

By temperament Borden was well suited to the task of navigating these treacherous cross-currents of public opinion and securing the requisite support and resources for his civilian army. Generous, conciliatory, and reasonable, Borden knew how to negotiate, to reconcile small differences. Some would have called him a manipulator, though a successful one, who possessed a number of personal, political, and material assets. Whatever the means he employed, Borden was a shrewd manager of men. He knew how to persuade, flatter, and appeal to vanity and veniality. He also knew how to purchase useful friends and influence people, to neutralize opponents, to build and shape cross-party support, to select and manage his allies, and above all to make the most effective use of his access to federal largesse.

One of Borden's strongest institutional allies was the Dominion of Canada Rifle Association (DRA), a nationwide, decentralized coalition of civilian and military rifle clubs and provincial associations. Founded in 1868 to promote recreational and military rifle shooting

across the country, the DRA boasted a broad and influential membership. It also developed a vulnerable material dependency on the Militia Department. Favoured from its beginning with a generous federal
subsidy, authorized by the Militia Act of 1868, the DRA continued to
benefit from the Militia Department's generous subsidies under Borden's administration, subsidies that the minister increased and supplemented on occasion with grants-in-aid to the DRA and its provincial
associates.[14]

During much of Borden's tenure as minister, the DRA's president
was John Morison Gibson, an expert marksman and a well-connected
Ontario Liberal provincial cabinet minister and later lieutenant-
governor of Ontario, altogether a very useful ally.[15] Conscious of the
DRA's potential influence, Borden never missed its annual meeting,
which was a social and professional opportunity to cultivate and confirm bipartisan personal and political support. His gregarious presence
at the DRA annual competition and his acquiescence to the association's
various calls for aid (not to mention his personal donation of $500 for
a Harold Borden challenge cup in memory of his son) gave him a particular claim to the DRA's gratitude, one that he turned to political capital.[16] When Gibson became lieutenant-governor of Ontario in 1908,
Borden shrewdly threw his full personal support behind the candidacy
of Sam Hughes to succeed Gibson as DRA president. Hughes reciprocated immediately, insisting that Sir Frederick be named honorary
president of the DRA. Hughes and other DRA members would remain
among the minister's close friends and supporters.

Borden adopted a comparable tactic with other professional military associations, beginning with the Canadian Artillery Association.
Founded in 1876 and revitalized in 1904, the CAA promoted professional education and technical training, and lobbied government in
support of its interests. Like the DRA, it possessed a circulating library
for its members, published an annual journal, *The Canadian Artillerists*,
and organized an annual gunnery competition with cash prizes.

Although the DRA and the CAA were the senior professional groupings, they were not the only such associations. In the decade before the
Great War other, smaller professional associations were formed with
similar objectives: the Association of Officers of the Medical Corps,
the Guides Association of Canada, the Cavalry Association, and the
Canadian Army Service Corps Officers. Given their growing number,
interconnected interests, and overlapping memberships, in 1908 these
smaller professional associations decided to meet in Ottawa each February at the same time as the DRA and the CAA, to coincide with Paardeberg Day, the Boer War veterans' commemoration of the Canadians'
celebrated victory. During this annual rite, labelled "military week" by

the *Canadian Military Gazette*, members read and discussed papers and
lobbied government for pay increases, personal favours, and military
policy.[17] Borden made it a cardinal political rule to participate in these
meetings, address the gatherings, encourage their activities, seek their
counsel, and cultivate and lobby them for their support for his program. He also subsidized their activities, a practice he extended to private rifle clubs and military associations, including military bands and
militia institutes, with funds from an annual budget of some $50,000
and occasionally with small personal gifts, thereby creating a network
of golden political ties.

Borden also appreciated the power of the press. Able to mix pleasure with business, he was a favourite guest at the annual Press Gallery
dinner, where he was regarded as "one of the boys" and was "always
given a fine reception" and where he could be persuaded to entertain
with his violin long after the orchestra had departed.[18] He understood
the importance of managing the press, even at his constituency level,
and made the most of their goodwill. His deputy minister, a former
Quebec City newspaperman, had been chosen among other reasons for
his ability to secure good coverage for Borden's program. Ever mindful
of the power of the press, in the fall of 1905 Borden, accompanied by
Sir Percy Lake, his newly appointed chief of the general staff, undertook a cross-country speaking tour, from Ontario to British Columbia,
including the newly created provinces of Saskatchewan and Alberta
(passing through the newly named village of Borden, Saskatchewan,
named in his honour), to explain from the platform and the press his
plan to create "a chain of military depots stretching from ocean to
ocean."[19]

Equally important to Borden was personal diplomacy, favours, membership, and participation in advocacy groups such as the Canadian
Military Institute, of which he was a vice-president and to which he
donated two bronze field guns from the Napoleonic Wars. In Ottawa
he was a founding member and honorary vice-president of the Navy
League. Nor did he neglect historical societies and the establishment of
military monuments, one such example being the Stoney Creek Battlefield Monument, a project of the Women's Wentworth Historical Society.[20] Not only did Borden know how to oil the machine and cultivate
and consolidate support, he possessed an ability to tame his critics,
placate interest groups, and silence potential opponents such as the
powerful temperance movement.[21]

The temperance movement's obsessive objection to the Militia's wet
canteens was a potentially explosive political issue. Although military
regulations forbad the sale of "liquor," including wine and malt, in military camps, wet canteens continued to sell beer. Moreover, officers'

and non-commissioned officers' messes were customarily exempt from municipal laws prohibiting the sale of liquor; nor did anything prevent a person from purchasing or consuming liquor outside the camp or bringing it back to camp. Offended by "the sin" in the summer Militia camps, in 1908 the Women's Christian Temperance Union, the Dominion Alliance, and the Methodist Church launched a concerted campaign against the wet canteens, the Methodists threatening to discourage enlistment unless the Militia Department complied with its demands.[22]

Aided by well-publicized police raids on camps at Barriefield and London, where liquor was seized and charges laid, the campaign attracted wide public attention and led to a discussion in the House of Commons on the corrupting influence of the Militia on the youth of the country. Early the following year Borden, anxious to diffuse the issue, sought the advice of his Militia Council and later held a meeting with the Dominion Alliance, where he negotiated an agreement banning the sale and consumption of all spirits in Militia camp canteens and messes in return for the Dominion Alliance's silence on the continuing consumption of liquor in the canteens and messes of the PF. The agreement enabled Borden to assure irate correspondents that "no liquor is to be brought into camp by anyone."[23]

A successful though more venial means of purchasing parliamentary support and public approval for his civilian army was Borden's ambitious program of public works, subsidies, training, and capital expenditures, many of them joint private-public ventures that secured improved facilities for the Militia. Ever popular with both his Liberal colleagues and Opposition members was the construction of a network of armouries across the country and the subsidization of civilian rifle ranges, projects that appealed to civic pride and self-interest and that politicians, businessmen, and community leaders were likely to support, especially as they and their communities often benefited personally and materially. Borden's ultimate objective was to establish a rifle range within "commuting distance of every rifle club in Canada,"[24] beginning with all principal urban centres, including his own rural constituency. The model was Ottawa's Rockcliffe Rifle Range, "one of the best rifle ranges in the world," and one his department had generously subsidized. In launching his civilian army, Borden gave priority to the construction of armouries and rifle ranges, which he authorized "as fast as parliamentary grants [would] permit,"[25] creating a competition among constituencies for federal largesse, the price being their political support of his program.

At times, the process of arbitrating the competing demands for armouries created almost as many problems as it solved. Borden him-

self favoured the construction of small, low-cost drill sheds, so important to poorer rural units, but many of his parliamentary colleagues
sought grander civic monuments for their constituencies. To make matters more complex, responsibility for the construction of armouries lay
not with his department but with the Department of Public Works,
and it often approved the building of costly structures in cities like
Hamilton, Woodstock, and Guelph, against the advice of the minister of militia, his Militia Council, and a joint Militia–Public Works
coordinating committee. The Hamilton Armouries, for example, which
included bowling lanes and an indoor baseball diamond, cost some
$200,000.[26] As Borden complained in the House of Commons, "[I]nflu-
ences of all kinds are brought to bear to induce the government and
minister to make a handsome and pretentious building in certain ambitious towns," whereas his own preference was for "cheaper buildings
and more of them," facilities that "would answer the needs of the Militia very much better" than civic monuments.[27] To gain greater control
over these expenditures, in 1910 Borden finally took his case to cabinet,
where he persuaded Public Works to meet his requests for the construction of low-cost rural armouries. In the following year, cabinet gave his
department sole responsibility for all buildings under $15,000.[28]

Though a champion of modest rural armouries, Borden was not
opposed to handsome, pretentious armouries. He simply sought priority funding for those without access to alternative resources. Unlike
rural Militia units, many urban units could tap lucrative alternative
resources, including a cadre of wealthy patrons who in return for
ranks and titles funded social and recreational amenities within well-
appointed armouries. While Borden was anxious to encourage these
private sources, they were often difficult to manage and control, and
their support required matching public funds, occasionally a price he
was willing to pay. Too often, however, costs skyrocketed well beyond
initial estimates, and Public Works, under considerable political
pressure, ended up contributing more money than it had budgeted.
In Montreal alone the government was obliged to contribute some
$59,000 toward the Royal Scots' imposing $100,000 armoury and
$50,000 toward the 65th Carabiniers' $125,000 armoury.[29] Impressive
as these urban structures might appear, private-public ventures could
impose a heavy charge on the public purse.

Notwithstanding their difficulties Borden remained a convinced
advocate of private-public initiatives. He continued to offer public
incentives to attract private resources as a means to secure the necessary facilities for the formation of his civilian soldiers. Incentives
included cash subsidies, prizes (silver salvers), rifles, ammunition, and
arcade rifle machines for privately owned ranges and rifle clubs. To

receive rifles, ammunition, or subsidies for a private rifle range, civilian rifle associations were obliged to recruit at least forty but no more than eighty members; they then received an annual one hundred rounds of ammunition per member and one rifle for every four members. Private contractors could also profit from the government's provision of shooting gallery machines and mini-ranges in armouries and drill halls, procured from private suppliers such as the Ontario Sub-Target Gun Company, a firm closely associated with members of the government.

The subsidized private ranges were a great success and became so popular that they soon outnumbered the ranges owned by military units.[30] By 1911 the government counted 619 rifle associations on its payroll, 465 of which were private ranges.[31] So successful was Borden's subsidized private rifle training program that membership in the subsidized private rifle clubs grew from 11,830 in 1903 to 28,045 in 1911, whereas membership in Militia rifle associations increased from 11,105 to 19,583. The government-subsidized private rifle associations were especially popular in French Canada, where they provided an outlet for French-Canadian martial interests that was more autonomous and adaptable to French-Canadian culture than was permitted by the Canadian Militia.[32]

In amending the Militia Act in 1904, Borden had taken the opportunity to define and extend his department's legal control and management of existing rifle clubs and associations, whether they were or were not members of the Militia.[33] The new Act removed the earlier Act's restrictions against provision of clothing and allowances, and provided that "in case of emergency the members of rifle associations and clubs shall become members of the Militia and shall be under the command of the District Officer Commanding." Those who joined a designated subsidized civilian association became automatically members of the Militia for a three-year period, were given rudimentary military training, were assigned a nominal rank with the obligation to serve in time of war, and at the end of three years were placed on a reserve list to make room for new recruits.

Farmers (often sceptical of military endeavours), too, became interested suppliers, providing Borden's mobile civilian army with a sufficient number of reserve horses, wagons, and drivers to move his 100,000-man force of skilled sharp shooters during peace or war. To resolve this logistic challenge, in 1903 Borden authorized a registration system for horses, drivers, and wagons whereby military district officers commanding contracted with local horse owners for a reserve access to their animals, drivers, and wagons in return for an annual payment of one dollar for each horse, fifty cents for each wagon, and fifty cents for each driver. Although the horse register fell far short of the Militia's projected needs, the scheme's abandonment in 1911, and the failure to replace it with a better one, left the country less prepared for warfare in 1914 than would otherwise have been the case.

Philanthropy opened another source of funding for Borden's ambitious plan to promote military and physical training in the schools, schools being the most pervasive instrument of patriotism in the late nineteenth and early twentieth centuries.[34] Aware of Lord Strathcona's interest in youth, education, military training, and patriotism, and of the value of an endorsement from a wealthy patron, in 1908 Borden wrote to the high commissioner, with whom he had developed a close friendship, about his desire to promote "the moral physical and intellectual development" of Canadian youth.[35] Strathcona replied on 13 March 1909 expressing his support and willingness to establish a generous fund to finance Borden's proposed program. In announcing the good news to the Commons, Borden shrewdly suggested that the fund be known as the Strathcona Trust, even though Strathcona had expressed a desire for the gift to be anonymous. Borden recognized Strathcona's susceptibility to flattery; after all he had massaged the high commissioner's ego on a previous occasion, when he had expressed similar reservations regarding the naming of the Strathcona's Horse.

Anxious to persuade Strathcona to extend his generosity, Borden arranged that the House pass a unanimous resolution of thanks, proposed by the prime minister and seconded by the leader of the Opposition. The bipartisan commitment to the project helped dampen the opposition to "military training" in the schools expressed by some farmers' organizations, organized labour, the Toronto Methodist Conference, the Society of Friends, the Ontario Educational Association, the Peace and Arbitration Society, the Farmers Sun, and other bodies that "regarded peace as more important than power."[36] During Borden's visit to London in July and August 1909 to attend the Imperial Naval Conference, he met with Strathcona to discuss the trust's organization and terms of reference, to keep the wealthy high commissioner on side in anticipation of further support. Strathcona responded generously and predictably with additional funding.

A prestigious board consisting of the governor general as patron, the prime minister as vice-patron, Sir Frederick as chairman, and the ministers of education of all the participating provinces as vice-presidents gave the trust a visibility and public standing. An initial donation of $250,000, to which the wealthy high commissioner shortly added $50,000 and a final sum of $200,000 in October 1910, made a total endowment of $500,000.[37] Invested at 4.5 per cent, the fund generated an annual income of $22,500, to be divided among the participating provinces. Provincial committees chaired by the trust's vice-presidents administered the funds assigned to their province, largely through prizes to teachers and students for excellence in physical training, drill, and marksmanship: 50 per cent for physical training; 35 per cent for drill; and 15 per cent for marksmanship.

To give the program a national scope, in January 1909 Borden wrote again to all the provincial premiers, inviting them to participate in the defence of their homes and engage in "the bodily development of children of all classes and both sexes."[38] The Strathcona Trust program was open to private, public, and separate schools alike, and initially all the provinces except Prince Edward Island, Manitoba, and Saskatchewan signed on; in Quebec, agreements were signed easily with both the Protestant and Catholic school boards. Initially Prince Edward Island objected to placing guns in the hands of children and questioned the propriety of physical education for "ladies," whereas Manitoba and Saskatchewan misunderstood the voluntary character of the program.

Determined to overcome the apprehensions of the dissenting three Liberal premiers, Borden re-canvassed their support. As a dedicated health professional and public health advocate, he stressed the program's voluntary character and its physical benefits, including its "instruction in proper breathing and bearing, and the healthful exercise imparted to boys and girls alike," a regime helpful in combatting the scourge of tuberculosis and one of "inestimable value to our race in its effect upon future generations,"[39] a direct reference to the popular fresh air movement (which was endorsed by the minister-physician) and contemporary fears of racial deterioration. After further negotiations, the objections of the dissenting premiers were eventually overcome, so that by 1911 all provinces had joined the program.

Borden's partnerships were not restricted to governments, entrepreneurs, and the wealthy; they encompassed voluntary paramilitary youth organizations as well. Unlike many military men in Britain and Australia who found the Boy Scout movement "a troublesome rival of the cadets,"[40] Borden supported Baden-Powell's paramilitary youth movement. Although his primary loyalty was to the cadet movement, Borden did not fear competition from Baden-Powell's Boy Scout movement, whose goals paralleled those of the cadet movement. Moreover, Dr Charles Gordon Hewitt, the dominion entomologist, Sir Frederick's future son-in-law, and a strong in-house advocate of Baden-Powell's movement, dissipated any initial doubts Borden may have entertained; nor was Borden unaware of the fact that his friend and patron Lord Strathcona was a keen advocate of the Boy Scouts.[41] In his view, the Scouts and all other related youth training initiatives, including the Boys Bisley Competition, were means to encourage the cadet movement.[42] Consequently, as early as 1909 Borden had the Militia Council distribute copies of Baden-Powell's Boy Scout manual to cadet corps. Typically Borden's civilian Militia espoused an ecumenical and heterodox approach to military formation, an approach commended by Sir John French in his 1908 report on the status of Empire forces.

From the beginning of his tenure as minister Borden had contended that "the most serious problem with the Canadian Militia is the military education and training of its officers."[43] While the reformed RMC provided one solution to officer training, another was to tap the resources of civilian institutions: that is, to extend his cadet program to Canadian universities. He realized that many university students joined local Militia units during their studies to obtain access to social and recreational facilities as well as rudimentary military training,[44] and he sought to mobilize this social reality to secure qualified officers for his citizen army. Although the Canadian Officers' Training Corps (COTC) was not officially authorized until November 1912, in 1907 the Militia Department signed agreements with McGill, Toronto, Dalhousie, and Laval universities to subsidize university-based programs of military lectures, drill, musketry, and military manoeuvres, including two field days and the opportunity to qualify for a commission in the Active Militia, the precursor of the COTC.

Whatever its defects, Borden had articulated a comprehensive, attractive, and pragmatic plan for the creation of a citizen militia, a plan that tapped a wide spectrum of moral and material support. A master of political persuasion, he had dampened the fire of many of his opponents and built a broad-based, bipartisan network of support for his program. He had raised the Militia's public profile, provided a blueprint, and created a benchmark for its future development.

CHAPTER 15

A Made-in-Canada Militia

In Borden's view, the self-sufficiency, autonomy, and effectiveness of Canada's defences required administrative and support units to sustain its civilian soldiers in the field, a remedy that had been prescribed by many past GOCs of the Canadian Militia. No less important was an accessible, dependable, and secure source of weapons and ammunition. Like many Canadian military observers, Borden worried that Britain's loss of control of the seas, even for a short time, might imperil Canadian defences, a fear fed by Britain's strategic decision to concentrate its fleet in European waters.[1] Addressing this concern was difficult and controversial. No decision that Borden made during his fifteen years as minister was more controversial than his approval of a "Canadian" rifle for the Militia, a weapon different from the rifle used in the British Army. The story of the Ross rifle is tangled and tortuous, and best understood within the larger context of Borden's attempt to establish Canadian administrative and material self-sufficiency. Altogether, Borden's efforts to establish self-sufficiency challenged Canada's productive capacity, the uniformity of imperial weaponry, and Britain's singular control of imperial defence.

Borden realized that the country's war-fed confidence and sense of independence demanded more than simply equal career opportunities for its Militia officers within its own militia; it called for Canadians to assume a greater responsibility for their own defence. Greater responsibility for the defence of its territory meant the creation of an effective military infrastructure, greater self-sufficiency, and the capacity to plan, to move, and sustain its armed forces in the field. If Canadian troops were to be led by Canadian officers at home or abroad, Canada had to possess capable senior officers and the requisite material and administrative support. Greater responsibility also entailed a defence policy, organization, weapons, kit, and equipment that reflected Canadian needs and assumptions.

Borden had approached Canada's participation in the South African War from a multifunctional, instrumentalist perspective. He had seen participation as an opportunity to garner public backing for the Militia and combat experience for its officers and men, as well as an occasion to test its organization, clothing, kit, weapons, and equipment, and to learn from friend and foe. In organizing the first contingent, Borden had worked relentlessly to transform the cabinet's original eight-company offer into a regimental organization, to keep the Canadians together in one unit. Regimental status required a senior commanding officer at the rank of lieutenant-colonel, a senior second-in-command, two majors (one for each projected battalion), two battalion adjutants, a quartermaster, a paymaster, and a transport officer. It justified the addition of auxiliary staff, chaplains, medical officers, and nurses, as well as a historical recorder, instructional officers, and later the despatch of a small postal corps. By insisting upon an administrative and command structure that would justify the attachment of the appropriate administrative services, Borden had provided opportunities for senior leadership and battle experience, and senior leadership was a prerequisite for keeping Canadians together rather than having them broken up and employed as reinforcements for British units. In other words, Borden saw war experience as an opportunity to train a cadre of experienced officers in various branches, a cadre that might support a balanced "little army" and establish the requisite service corps to clothe, transport, feed, and care for a fighting field force. This was an ideal that several GOCs of the Canadian Militia shared with the minister.

Well before the war, Borden began to address the counsel of previous GOCs to establish appropriate service corps, starting with the medical service, the one he knew best. As a long-serving Militia medical officer Borden understood the need for a more effective medical service, and when he was a member of the Opposition, he had urged the Conservative government to take action. As minister he heeded his own counsel. Four months before the outbreak of the war in South Africa, Borden authorized the creation of the Canadian Militia Medical Department, a skeleton service consisting of two branches, the Militia Medical Staff Service and a regimental medical service, the progenitor of the Permanent Active Militia Medical Corps, as it was officially designated in July 1904.[2]

Borden had used the war to test and develop better medical equipment and to improve the delivery of services, including the training of personnel. Soon after the Canadian government decided to send an infantry battalion to South Africa, Borden asked the British authorities to sanction the recruitment of four nursing sisters and one doctor, A.B. Osborne, a captain from the Canadian Militia Medical staff,[3] to accompany the first contingent. To facilitate their despatch he had agreed to provide free transportation for them, though they were not attached to the first contingent and were forbidden by British regulation to care for

British troops at first. During the course of the war twelve other nurses were recruited and sent to South Africa with (but detached from) various Canadian contingents.[4] A more ambitious war experiment still was Borden's decision to send a fully equipped field hospital to accompany the 2nd Canadian Mounted Rifles. Placed under the command of Lieutenant-Colonel A.N. Worthington (in 1910 his second in command, Dr Guy Carleton Jones, became director-general of Canadian Medical Services),[5] the 10th Canadian Field Hospital, a sixty-four-man unit all ranks, included two doctors, one dentist, nine medical students, two chemists, twenty-two orderlies, fourteen drivers, and a hospital cook.

Apart from the commanding officer and his second in command, the Canadian Field Hospital counted a captain, four lieutenants, a quartermaster sergeant, and a paymaster sergeant. The unit also carried some distinctive medical equipment, such as a convertible transport/ambulance wagon, water carts, harnesses, saddle equipment, and a medical dispensing box, all of which were put to the test during two bloody engagements and much but not all of which Worthington reported to be superior to their British equivalent. Upon their return, veterans of the field hospital provided a pool of skilled military medical experience upon which a credible Canadian medical corps was built and staffed; a first instalment was the addition of a dental militia unit in 1902. Two years later Borden approved a Permanent Militia Army Medical Corps (re-designated the Canadian Army Medical Corps in 1909), composed of eight field hospitals and nine stretcher-bearer sections, and in 1906 he authorized its organization into sixteen field ambulances.

Similarly, Borden used the war and the success of the Canadian nursing sisters, notably the Canadian soldiers' preference for the Canadian nurses,[6] to establish a twenty-five-person Canadian military nursing service within the Canadian Medical Corps. Many of the service's initial recruits were themselves South African veterans, including its first and second matron. Initially the nurses' chief responsibility was to provide medical services for the Militia's annual summer camps,[7] but with the increased size of the Permanent Force establishment, especially after the Canadian government assumed control of the British garrisons in Halifax and Esquimalt in 1906, the nurses served garrison hospitals as well. Since nursing sister Georgina Pope had led the first and a subsequent consignment of Canadian nurses to South Africa, Borden recruited her into the Militia in 1904 and into the Permanent Force in 1906. In 1908 she became the first matron of the Canadian Army Medical Corps; her successor as matron was Margaret C. Macdonald, another South African War veteran.

Although Borden was anxious to learn from the British experience, he believed that service corps ought to be adapted to Canadian realities. One example of this attitude was his decision to give Canada's South African nurses officer status, a policy he formalized when he incorporated them into the Canadian Medical Corps and which he justified on the grounds that Canadian nurses came from a "better" social class and were better trained than their British counterparts. Canadian military nurses, therefore, carried officer ranks, a practice unheard of in the British Army at the time and one that caused considerable consternation among some British nursing sisters, especially when they served alongside the Canadian nurses.[8] Similarly, Borden authorized a distinctive Canadian uniform for Canadian nursing sisters, an attractive, serviceable uniform that they wore with pride. When Sir Ian Hamilton inspected the Canadian forces in 1913, he singled out the medical corps for special commendation, a tribute to Borden's commitment and foresight.

The medical service was just one of several service units Borden established in the wake of the Boer War. In 1903 alone he authorized the creation of the Canadian Engineer Corps, the Canadian Signalling Corps, the Canadian Militia Service Corps (re-designated the Canadian Army Service Corps in 1906), and the Ordnance Stores Corps (re-designated the Canadian Ordnance Corps in 1907). With the creation of the Canadian Army Pay Corps in 1907, the Veterinary Corps in 1910, and the Canadian Postal Corps in May 1911,[9] the Canadian Militia now possessed a full range of service corps.

Borden's reforms went well beyond replicating the British example, as he had demonstrated with the formation of the nursing sisters. For example, he had a particular interest in technical applications to warfare,[10] especially the military use of the telephone, telegraphy, the motorcar, and the airplane. He believed that civilian soldiers were especially well placed to transfer their technological and industrial knowledge and experience to warfare and overcome military conservatism and complacency. A director and first vice-president of Reginald Fesssenden's Wireless Telegraph Company of Canada since its founding,[11] in 1909 the minister persuaded his department to secure an experimental licence to permit radio-telegraphy training in military camps, convinced that the Militia would benefit from better forms of communication.[12] That same year he added telephone and telegraphy companies to the Corps of Guides.[13] The following year he authorized the establishment of a telephone and telegraph detachment for the Royal Engineer Corps.[14] As an enthusiastic pioneer automobile owner, he shared Sam Hughes's infatuation with their logistical and armoured use in warfare.

Likewise Borden recognized the military potential of "flying machines," especially their capacity for reconnaissance, and he closely followed reports of J.A.D. McCurdy and Alexander Graham Bell's flight experiments in Bedeck. He was present at Bell's speech in Ottawa two weeks after McCurdy's successful flight of the *Silver Dart* in February 1909.[15] That same summer he invited F.W. Baldwin and McCurdy to bring two of their flying machines to the Militia's new central training camp at Petawawa, at government expense, to demonstrate their military potential.[16] To facilitate the experiment, he authorized the construction of a shed to house the machines and provided the team with the services of two military engineers.[17] Unfortunately it was during one of those flights in early August 1909 that the Silver Dart was damaged beyond repair in the sands of Petawawa.

Apart from the practical benefits of these new technologies in the organization and training of the Militia, their technological application to warfare was a means of tapping civilian knowledge and experience, making the military service more attractive to young recruits who sought greater challenges than mastering the intricacies of the parade ground and the rifle range. Altogether these specialized service corps went a long way toward providing Canada's forces with the skeleton of service units required to maintain a Canadian fighting force in the field, thereby allowing Canadians to contribute more fully to their own national security, an important condition for Canadian military autonomy.

Not all the new service units were of equal quality, but several were marked successes. Few were more successful than the Canadian Army Service Corps, authorized in 1901 and charged with transporting and provisioning the Militia, especially during the summer camps. According to some military authorities, the "disgracefully" poor quality and quantity of food in the summer camps before 1901 accounted largely for the poor camp attendance, a complaint that Borden attempted to remedy. The subsequent success of the Ordnance Corps in improving the purchase, quality, and provisioning of food for the annual camp, which included making their own bread and butchering their own meat, was credited with the improved attendance at the annual training camps. The military competition also helped to "smarten up shoddy private suppliers" and reduce costs. The corps's capacity was demonstrated dramatically during the 1908 Quebec Tercentenary celebrations when it fed over fourteen thousand troops, a test that it acquitted with great distinction.

In the final analysis, however, the Militia's autonomy and effectiveness depended upon its access to a secure source of essential military materiel. Borden's answer to this requirement was a popular made-in-Canada policy that addressed the issue of security, garnered public support, attracted capital and technology, and retained the economic and political benefits at home. Determined to build a made-in-Canada militia force, Borden had used the South African War to test the quality of Canadian-made clothing, kit, and equipment. The khaki-coloured canvas suits, the heavy black ankle boots, the distinctively Canadian Oliver equipment – a white cross-belt, ball bag, and haversack – leather valises, bandolier, small water bottle, blankets, as well as the unfortunate adulterated emergency food ration that the second Canadian contingent carried to South Africa, were all subjected to the test of war. While some were found wanting, others provided Canadian forces with more effective materiel than was available from the British forces.

Borden made no secret of his plan to go further, to encourage the development of Canadian-made arms, kit, and equipment, even if it meant deviating from standard imperial patterns. Well before the war had ended Borden raised the issue of Canadian materiel in the House of Commons, calling upon his colleagues to support the adoption of a distinctive Canadian uniform whose cost would cease to be a barrier to service. Many members of the Militia lobby greeted his proposal with enthusiasm, though some attached the qualification that uniforms remain "something picturesque without being too expensive."[18] Picturesque was not exactly what Borden had in mind. Consequently, in 1904 he returned to the subject with a precise proposal for a simple Canadian khaki service uniform. "I do not know why in the world we should stick to these old uniforms," he explained, even if they "have a history in England" (and he was partial to history), but "so far as we are concerned [they] are useless importations," a sentiment seconded by other members of the Militia lobby.[19] By then even the British Army had adopted the khaki uniform for active service.

But Canadian sentiment was more difficult to change, as Borden learned when he first approved more serviceable dress. The "professional" PF offered stiff resistance, preferring prettier uniforms and arguing their cause in terms of morale. Faced by the PF's opposition, in 1907 Borden, a pragmatic politician who believed in erosion as a form of persuasion, modified his dress regulation, permitting the optional use of the coloured uniforms, confident in the gradual but persistent vindication of experience. His tactic worked: by 1909 rural corps were enjoying the lighter, simpler khaki shirts and trousers at summer camps; the following year the PF was clothed in khaki; and in 1911 even the city corps, who were especially attached to pretty uniforms, were persuaded, the comfort offered by the more serviceable uniforms having overcome their vanity.

Borden's made-in-Canada policy had a staunch ally in his friend and Opposition colleague Sam Hughes. Hughes shared the minister's interest in experimentation and invention and his preference for Canadian industry and design, a preference that could sometimes go awry. In 1897, well before Borden authorized the infamous Canadian emergency rations for Canada's second Boer War contingent, Borden enthusiastically approved the distribution of the Oliver pack harness to the Canadian Militia to replace the British web pattern in use at the time. Designed and manufactured in Canada, the Oliver equipment was tested and found wanting by Canada's Boer War soldiers, who complained about its awkward ammunition pouch and its stiff, sharp-edged buckles. Although the source of a great deal of complaint during and after the war, the Oliver equipment was not replaced by an improved British equivalent until 1909, and only after efforts failed to have the British web equipment manufactured in Canada.

Similarly, in 1905 Borden canvassed the possibility of manufacturing artillery in Canada, but he soon discovered that no Canadian foundries could produce artillery guns;[20] even Boer War monuments had to be cast in New York. Undeterred, in 1906 Borden attempted unsuccessfully to persuade Vickers to manufacture artillery guns in Canada. In 1897 Vickers had purchased the Maxim Gun Company, which produced an automatic machine gun, and Borden hoped to negotiate their manufacture in Canada. At first the company appeared interested, but after "careful investigation" it decided that the Canadian market was too small for economical production of its artillery guns, even with generous government support.[21] In the short run, therefore, Canada was obliged to procure its considerable artillery needs in Britain, except for a sizeable annual order of gun carriages manufactured by the Ottawa Car Company and Borden's decision to have the dominion arsenal retooled to produce twelve-pound and eighteen-pound ammunition.

Borden, however, had not given up on Vickers, or the gun company on Canada. But Vickers was more interested in securing the lucrative contracts for the construction of the projected Canadian navy. A committed advocate of the Canadian navy, Borden hoped that its construction projects would be centred in Halifax, but his enthusiasm remained unabated even after the Canadian government decided to centre Canada's shipbuilding industry in Montreal. Working closely with the British company's Canadian agent, Frederick Orr Lewis, a Montreal hardware merchant and his erstwhile business partner, Borden helped to persuade the company to incorporate the Canadian Vickers Company in June 1911, capitalized at $5 million, to build the Liberals' proposed Canadian navy (the Canadian company persuaded by generous government contracts and promises of subsidies and tax concessions). This arrangement, however, was imperilled by the election of a Conservative government in September 1911 with a different naval agenda.[22]

Added to the obvious material and political advantages of Canadian-made supplies was the perennial issue of security. What if Britain were to lose control of the seas? This was an old fear that grew in its intensity, especially after the British decision to withdraw its fleet to European waters and the subsequent German naval rivalry. It was the justification of the Canadian government's establishment of the Dominion Cartridge Factory in Quebec City in 1882. Designed to assure an independent supply of small-arms ammunition for the Canadian Militia, the Dominion Cartridge Factory was the first military arsenal to be established by any of Britain's self-governing dominions. Generally Borden preferred to use private suppliers, and he was prepared to go further than previous administrations in encouraging the Canadian manufacture of military clothing, kit, and equipment, even when it cost 40 per cent more than it would if purchased in Britain.

If Borden's decentralized citizen army of sharpshooters were to assume responsibility for Canada's defence, perhaps nothing was more critical to its success than a reliable access to rifles and ammunition. The South African War had underlined Canada's vulnerable dependency upon British rifle supplies. The arming of Canada's first three contingents with Lee-Enfields, the standard British service rifle at the time, had all but depleted the Militia Department's stores, leaving its Militia dangerously short of arms and crippling its capacity to respond to requests to outfit additional troops. To restore its depleted supply, Borden had ordered 10,000 Lee-Enfield rifles from the War Office soon after the departure of the first three contingents. Hard pressed to service its own troops in South Africa, the War Office could spare only 2,000 rifles for the Canadian Militia.[23] To address the deficiency, Borden asked two British companies, beginning with the Birmingham Small Arms Company, to establish a branch plant in Canada to supply the Canadian market.[24] When neither company agreed to produce the Lee-Enfield rifles in Canada, and when returned South African veterans complained that the Lee-Enfield was heavy, under-sighted at close to medium ranges, and threw constantly to the right,[25] Borden decided to explore other options, including the adoption of a different rifle, one that might be manufactured in Canada.

The tragic saga of the Ross rifle, labelled "our national arm" by its defenders,[26] is long, complex, and highly political. Suffice to say that early in 1901, while Borden was searching for a solution to his supply dilemma, Sir Charles Henry Augustus Frederick Lockhart Ross, the 9th Baronet of Balnagown, who had served on the war staff in South Africa with a hunting rifle of his own invention, sought an interview with Borden to demonstrate the virtues of his "new" rifle, a military version of his popular hunting rifle produced in Hartford, Connecticut. So impressed was Borden by the Scottish inventor's claims that he had drafted an agreement for an initial production of 12,000 rifles by 1902 and 10,000 per year for the next five years, at a cost of thirty dollars per rifle, subject to the rifle's thorough examination by a bipartisan committee of military experts.

In June 1901 Borden convened an impressive committee of military experts to advise him on the weapon's efficacy. The committee consisted of Colonel John M. Gibson, a prominent Militia officer, prize marksman, president of the Dominion Rifle Association, and Liberal member of the Ontario government; Major F.M. Gaudet, the superintendent of the Dominion Cartridge Factory in Quebec City; Colonel William Otter, the recently returned commanding officer of the first Canadian contingent for South Africa (he would chair the committee); Lieutenant-Colonel W.P. Anderson, the chief engineer of the Department of Marine and Fisheries; and Colonel Sam Hughes, the Conservative Party's military critic.[27]

The committee met in August to test the Ross against the Lee-Enfield. A pound lighter than the Lee-Enfield, the Ross performed well in ten of the twelve tests, but in the last two it jammed after repeated firing and was sensitive to dust and dirt, faults that Ross attributed to the type of cartridge that had been used, an explanation that subsequently became its defenders' stock excuse for the rifle's failures. Although Gaudet expressed doubts about the rifle's performance, doubts that he did not want to attribute to the cartridge manufactured by "his" Dominion Cartridge Factory,[28] Otter reported that overall his committee was favourably impressed with the rifle's accuracy and potential and unanimously recommended its adoption, confident that its "few" mechanical failures could be remedied easily. No one was more convinced of the Ross's superiority than Sam Hughes. Given his role as the Opposition's chief military critic and his subsequent position as minister of militia (1911–16), Hughes's almost blind support stifled criticism and prolonged the rifle's tragic employment by Canadian forces long after its defects as a weapon for mass fire had been demonstrated in active warfare.

The Canadian GOC, Major-General O'Grady Haly, was not persuaded by the committee's recommendation; nor was the governor general, Lord Minto; the British colonial secretary, Joseph Chamberlain; or the British secretary for war, St John Brodrick. Upon learning of the Canadian assessment, the War Office hurriedly ordered the British School of Musketry at Hythe to test the Ross against the Lee Enfield before pronouncing on the relative merits of the two weapons. Although the school's concern for the rifle's unresolved mechanical defects became the bases of British official opposition, its principal objection appeared to be the breach of imperial uniformity that would be entailed in the Canadian government's decision to adopt a rifle different from that used in the rest of the Empire. In deprecating the

Canadian government's assessment, the British director general of ordnance reminded Borden that only by maintaining a uniform pattern
could the imperial authorities guarantee a reliable and efficient supply
of rifles and ammunition "in time of war, when Imperial and colonial
troops are fighting side by side."[29] But since the Ross rifle possessed the
same bore and took the same ammunition as the Lee-Enfield, Borden
had no difficulty responding to that part of the argument. The question of interchangeable parts was not so easily answered, and Borden's
somewhat casual assurance that men could carry into battle the "two
or three parts which can possibly be damaged, and the rifle ... restored
without delay" was far less realistic or persuasive.[30]

Despite the imperial government's dire warnings, Borden persisted,
and at the June 1902 Colonial/Imperial Conference and elsewhere he
defended the superiority of the Ross over the Lee-Enfield and insisted
on the strategic importance of the local manufacture of arms.[31] By then
it was a little late to alter the decision, since two months before the
conference the Canadian government had signed a generous contract
with Ross for delivery of 12,000 Mark I Ross rifles by the end of 1903,
conditional upon the rifle's mechanical deficiencies being resolved.
According to the contract, the new rifle was to be issued to both the
Militia and the North-West Mounted Police, the latter under Laurier's
jurisdiction. Ross had agreed to establish a factory near Quebec City
to manufacture a "solely Canadian-made" rifle, upon which the Canadian government would have the first claim. The factory promised to
employ 1,000 workers in Laurier's constituency,[32] an important political consideration in a city whose traditional economy, based on the
square-timber trade and shipping, was in decline.

The government contract was more than generous to Ross. To facilitate the rifle's rapid and efficient production the government granted
Ross a ninety-nine-year lease to land on the Plains of Abraham for a
dollar a year, advanced him funds for the delivery of the initial order
of 12,000 rifles, and waived import duties on capital machinery. Ross
closed his Hartford, Connecticut, factory and invested $500,000 in his
Quebec City plant, confident that he could persuade other countries
to purchase his weapon. But despite Parliament's approval of the Ross
Rifle Company Act, the Ross Rifle Company was never incorporated
and Ross remained its sole owner and general manager.

Managing Ross proved as difficult as remedying his rifle's mechanical defects. Initially Ross denied Militia Department inspectors access
to his Quebec factory on the pretext of protecting his patent. Although
production of the rifle was behind schedule, early in 1904 Ross began
soliciting additional government orders: a contract with Marine and
Fisheries and a new contract with the NWMP. Twice Borden had to

remind him to "devote yourself exclusively to the carrying out of the terms of your contract with this Department."[33] Next Ross proposed a contract for the manufacture of artillery in Canada, and so it went. In 1905, already two years behind schedule, Ross finally pronounced the first instalment of rifles ready, but the master general of ordnance, Colonel W.H. Cotton, reported that the rifles he inspected were far from finished. In 1905 Borden was so frustrated with Ross's repeated failures that he considered asking the government to take over the factory.[34]

The mechanical and production deficiencies of the Ross rifle continued to haunt the minister. About eighty alterations were required in the original pattern to correct some of its more obvious deficiencies. Consequently it was not until August 1905 that Ross delivered the first instalment of the government order, 1,000 Mark I rifles, which was immediately distributed to the Royal North-West Mounted Police (RNWMP). Within a year the comptroller of the RNWMP complained discreetly to the prime minister, decrying the rifle's faulty workmanship, reporting accidents related to its use, and threatening to revert to the force's old Winchesters. So unsatisfactory did the rifle appear that a RNWMP board of inquiry, convened in 1907, recommended the rifle's withdrawal. In the board's opinion, the Ross rifle was unreliable and unsafe.

By then Ross's delivery of the remaining portion of the government's initial order simply amplified dissatisfaction. In January 1906, aware of the technical faults in the first instalment, the Militia delayed issuing the rifles to its men until Otter reconvened his committee to examine the Mark II and reported "no hesitation in saying that the changes ... embodied in the Mark II rifle are decided improvements and find that this rifle is an excellent arm."[35] But despite Otter's assurances, as soon as the Militia distributed the Mark II rifle, complaints of its defects, in a number of cases causing serious accidents, obliged the Militia Council to suspend acceptance of more rifles until Ross agreed to a thorough inspection.[36] Policemen and soldiers agreed that the rifle was too long, too heavy, was sensitive to dirt, jammed, and became overheated after repeated firing.

From the start, arguments in defence of the weapon were political, passionate, confused, and often convincing. The *Times* described the Ross as the rifle of the future, and for a time the Australians considered its adoption. Advocates of the Ross assumed that the next war would depend on marksmen and snipers, not on rapid mass fire. Moreover, the Ross rifle appeared to be an excellent target rifle, proven by several successful imperial rifle competitions. So confident were some of the rifle's supporters of its inherent virtues that they were convinced it was the answer to imperial uniformity of weapons, that it would eventually break the monopoly of the British arms manufacturers and capture the imperial market. The Canadian rifle would become *the* uniform imperial weapon, an example of Canadian imperial leadership![37] Could nationalists and imperialists ask for more? Tests in Britain, Canada, and the United States confirmed their confidence, comparing the Ross favourably with the Lee-Enfield, the American Springfield, and the Austrian and Swiss Mannlicher. The Ross rifle's rabid supporters dismissed their critics as being in the pocket of monopolistic British arms manufacturers. The rifle's critics responded in kind, accusing the rifle's advocates of being on the payroll of Sir Charles Ross.[38]

However passionate the rifle's supporters, by 1907 Borden was so discouraged with Ross's failure to correct the mechanical problems, and with the unconscionable delays in delivery, that he asked first Vickers-Maxim and then the Birmingham Small Arms Company to consider taking over Ross's Quebec City factory.[39] When these initiatives failed, Borden recommended to Laurier that the government invoke the twelve-month–notice termination clause in its contract with Ross and manufacture its own rifles using the administrative model of the Dominion Cartridge Factory. Laurier, however, was not convinced, though he did not discount the possibility entirely.[40] After all, the Ross rifle factory employed about five hundred workers, an estimated 10 per cent of Quebec City's industrial workforce, many located in his constituency; and political friends were pressing the prime minister to provide Ross with more land on the Plains of Abraham for expansion.[41] Ross had assured Laurier that he had every intention of increasing his factory's production in Quebec and of establishing a parts factory in Welland, Ontario, within another Liberal constituency.[42] Blocked in his efforts to find alternative solutions, Borden had to be content with Ross's promise to redress the weapon's deficiencies by improving the Mark II Ross rifle, but he continued to prod Ross, hoping to badger him into better behaviour. In 1909 he informed Ross's legal counsel that should the War Office approve a superior weapon, Canada might oblige Ross's company to manufacture it in Canada.[43]

Whatever Borden's personal reservation, he felt obliged to defend the rifle against vociferous Conservative criticism led by the member of Parliament for Sherbrooke, Colonel A.N. Worthington, MD, who had served with the Royal Canadian Artillery in South African and later commanded the 10th Canadian Field Hospital there, and was currently chief medical officer of the Quebec command. Elected to the House of Commons in a by-election in 1906 and returned during the general election of 1908, Dr Worthington constituted himself the Conservatives' military critic, effectively usurping Hughes's role, possibly because he believed Hughes too compromised by his friendship with Sir Frederick and his passionate, if not material, attachment to the Ross, a challenge to Hughes's position that heightened rather than diminished his defence of the weapon. Whatever the reason, during the 1907–08 parliamentary session Worthington, well primed with information and fearless, launched a concerted attack on the Ross rifle, condemning it as technically inferior, more costly than the Lee-Enfield, and responsible for various injuries, including the death of one militiaman and the blinding of one RNWMP officer. As for Ross's contract with the government, Worthington denounced it as "one of the most ridiculous and un-businesslike contracts ever entered into by a businesslike government and a totally one-sided affair," noting its ninety-nine-year lease of land, advance payments, guaranteed market, lack of penalty clause, and duty-free import privileges, not to mention the importation of parts from the country against which the rifle was intended to defend Canadians.[44]

In defence of his government's decision, Borden rehearsed the history of the Ross, his efforts to attract British manufacturers, and the country's need for a dependable supply of small arms, a policy recently endorsed by the Imperial Conference. He minimized the weapon's accidents, dismissing them as no greater than those of comparable weapons, and its technical problems as the inevitable difficulties of a new weapon. Similarly, he rejected Worthington's criticism of the rifle's cost and Ross's contract, pointing out that Ross had invested large sums of his own money and after seven years had still not realized a profit or retrieved the hundreds of thousands of dollars of debt he had incurred. Above all, Borden based his defence on Canada's need to become self-sufficient in arms and ammunition and end its risky dependence on British supplies, lest the sea link be severed. Whatever his real feelings about Ross and his rifle, and they were not always charitable, Borden could afford to keep to the high road, especially after Sam Hughes broke party ranks to second Borden's testimony and meet out rougher treatment to the rifle's critics in his own party. Hughes's passionate defence of the weapon helped spike the impact of Worthington's assault, whom Hughes savagely dismissed as "a patronage-hungry, jealous, debased politician with a bad military record in the Boer War"[45] and an agent of Ross's competitors.[46]

Borden and Hughes had a very special mutually beneficial, if at times clinical, relationship that transcended party loyalty. Borden recognized Hughes's somewhat mad qualities and knew how to flatter and placate him. The egotistical and idiosyncratic Hughes had an insatiable need of flattery, and Borden went out of his way to feed Hughes's addiction. Their friendship had a long history, and though frequently tested, it remained intact to the end. Not only had Borden defended Hughes against Hutton's vengeful punishment in 1899, he had negotiated Hughes's controversial passage to South Africa aboard the SS *Sardinian*. Upon Hughes's premature return from South Africa, Borden had named him to a committee to consider the adoption of the infamous Ross rifle. Subsequently Borden delayed enforcing a regulation obliging Hughes to relinquish command of his 45th Battalion, promoted him to brevet-colonel, created an unpaid military headquarters position of railway intelligence officer for him (as Hughes fancied himself an inventor with a special interest in railways), an appointment that permitted him to attend the spectacular military display at the 1908 Quebec Tercentenary celebration, and then placed him on the Board of Visitors of the Royal Military College. In 1911 Borden even took Hughes to London to attend the defence meetings of the Imperial Conference, more as an observer than an advisor, though Hughes predictably made more of it than Borden may have intended.[47] Borden frequently sought Hughes's counsel, even though he did not always heed it. They also shared business information and interests.[48] Hughes reciprocated Sir Frederick's friendship and rarely hesitated to praise Borden for his courage, kindness, accessibility, and goodwill.[49] The captive goodwill of the Opposition's chief military critic proved an invaluable asset for Borden, especially in paring down the Opposition's attacks on the Ross.

To forestall further controversy on the eve of a federal election, in October 1907 Borden created a nine-member parliamentary Small Arms Standing Committee (which included three senior Militia officers) to advise him on the suitability of the Ross as a "national" weapon. His clever appointment of Sam Hughes to chair the committee spiked the Tories' guns, stifled the possibility of a more objective assessment of the rifle, and precluded its abandonment as a national weapon, a possibility that Borden himself had been willing to contemplate. Still a passionate advocate of the Ross rifle, with a dangerous interest in mechanics and invention and an alleged financial relationship with Ross, Hughes once again turned on his own party's critics of the rifle. His committee pronounced the rifle a "serviceable weapon" in its current form, though it called for a number of Mark III improvements to make it "more nearly a perfect arm."[50] In the next eighteen months two additional committee meetings under Hughes's direction were convened to monitor the alterations to this "the near perfect weapon." Hughes's appointment as minister of militia in 1911 sealed the rifle's defence until its poor performance in war forced its abandonment.

In assessing the Ross rifle's deficiencies, many historians have concentrated on the weapon's tragic failure during the Great War and have blamed its promotion and retention as a national arm on its idiosyncratic and fanatical defender, Sam Hughes, and his skilful use of nationalist rhetoric, forgetting that the rifle had not been intended for mass fire but for a war between sharpshooters and that the contemporary authorities who defended it were more numerous, reputable, and professional than these historians have chosen to remember. On repeated occasions professional soldiers such as Otter approved the weapon. Moreover, professional endorsements were not restricted to Canadian soldiers blinded by venial and national considerations.[51] On Paardeberg Day, 1907, General Percy Lake informed the Dominion Rifle Association that he was convinced that the Ross was a sound rifle,[52] and the following year he linked the improvement in Militia rifle practice to the "excellent" Ross rifle, an opinion seemingly seconded by the British general Sir John French during his 1910 inspection of the Canadian Militia when he reportedly described it as a "splendid weapon of unsurpassed range and power."[53]

Canada's success at the annual Bisley rifle competition, beginning in 1909, seemed to confirm the Ross's prowess as a target rifle, as did the efforts of the British National Rifle Association to ban it from the competition, since it was too fine a weapon to be issued to the troops. (Even after the Canadian military abandoned the Ross as a general service rifle during World War I, snipers preferred to use the weapon.) Ross defenders could also quote the *Pall Mall Gazette*'s description of the rifle as "the very finest all-round small-arms weapon that has ever been evolved."[54] Little wonder that opposition to the Ross seemed to have all but disappeared by 1909, and that Canada entered the Great War with this arm. As one author has reminded us, the real problem with the Ross was that when it was adopted during the last year of the Boer War, its assessors were seeking "a sharpshooter's weapon ... for eventual war against the United States," not one for rapid firepower and the "mass attacks of the First World War."[55]

The Ross rifle's monumental failure as a national arm, especially in the tragic circumstances of the Great War, therefore, ought not to obscure the general success of Borden's program to create a citizen militia that was self-sufficient in support, services, and supplies. Although far from fully prepared to fight a European war, even critical inspectors general noted the "appreciable progress toward efficiency and readiness for the field" during Borden's watch.[56] The Ross rifle saga, a failed initiative to create a Canadian Explosive Company, and Montreal's Canadian Vickers remind us, however, that Borden's made-in-Canada strategy of self-sufficiency was only a partial success.[57]

CHAPTER 16

A Canadian Army

The Ross rifle debate was but part of a larger, often heated discussion on the nature and purpose of Canadian defences. In the years following the Boer War, Canadians came to think and speak of their Permanent Force as an army, an official designation that the Department of Militia attached to several of its service units. The growing official and unofficial use of the word *army* rather than *militia* to describe Canada's armed forces underscores the contemporary debate on the professionalization and appropriate use of its PF. An acrimonious debate characterized by misunderstanding, conflict, and confusion, the issue required resolution. As the South African War experience faded and many Canadian military advocates came to locate their defensive borders in Europe rather than the United States, they were obliged to reexamine their defence preparations, to consider the most effective ways and means to match their forces against Europe's professional armies.

Borden's ambiguous response to the "professionalization" of Canada's land force and the pressure to add a combative role to the PF's primary pedagogical duties mirrored the changing dynamics of this charged debate. While Borden continued to resist the principle of a standing army and insist upon the virtues of a civilian force, the inescapable logic of many of his assumptions, policies, and actions led ineluctably to an enlarged, more active administrative and combative role for Canada's PF in war and peace. A pragmatist, required to reconcile theory and practice, Borden found himself, somewhat ironically, presiding over the quiet transformation of Canada's armed forces, obliged to justify the PF's changing role within and outside the House of Commons.

After all, it was during Borden's tenure as minister that the PF more than tripled in number[1] and came to absorb a fourth of the departmental budget. Furthermore, Canada's professional soldiers were often the principal beneficiaries of his reforms, his replacement of civilians with soldiers at headquarters staff, and his insistence on equity of opportunity for Canadians within the Canadian Militia. More rigorous regulations and educational standards for career advancement enhanced the quality and reputation of the PF. Neither did Borden hesitate to employ British professional soldiers as a temporary measure until Canada could produce its own professional senior staff, nor shrink from the criticism of members of the Opposition and members of the Militia lobby who faulted him for employing "the old fossilized systems of Europe" and staffing the Militia with "useless" senior managers.[2]

The PF was no less the chief beneficiary of Borden's emphases on education, organization, technology, and specialization, as well as his insistence on professional rather than political criteria for appointments and promotions to senior positions in the Canadian Militia, all measures designed to enhance the PF's professional autonomy, prestige, and authority. Moreover, the logic of his professed desire to transform the Canadian forces into "a self-sufficient Canadian army," to substitute Canadian for British professionals, rather than continue as a mere auxiliary of the British Army, created a demand for senior commanders and planners that only the PF could fill. His insistence upon taking control of the British garrisons, his creation of PF "army" service units so as not to have to rely upon their militia equivalents, and his amendment to the Militia Act that obliged governments to call upon the PF in the first instance to support the civil power during a threat of civil disturbance, rather than upon the locally recruited citizen militia, extended the role and importance of the PF. In short, it was his policies that made it difficult to confine the PF exclusively to its traditional duties as garrison troops and teachers of the Militia.

Borden's insistence upon a degree of professional autonomy within the Militia (for example, his removal of military appointments and promotions from the reach of partisan politics) was largely a success and was acknowledged and applauded by supporters and critics alike, including the *Canadian Military Gazette*. While this policy applied both to the civilian Militia and the PF, in April 1905 the Militia Council privileged the PF when it decreed that not only would it permit no future political influence in the appointment of senior PF officers, but it would consider third-party representation on behalf of a candidate for appointment or promotion as unprofessional intervention that would be charged against the candidate's account.[3] Although the line between theory and practice remained blurred, there was no question of Borden's desire to create a cadre of senior, professional PF officers. Similarly, he sought to provide them a degree of professional autonomy and career development, free from political interference, to permit them to regulate their entry and advancement within the profession through education and training; and he did everything he could to enhance their opportunities for advancement within the senior ranks of the Canadian Militia.

Borden realized that his civilian army's success depended largely upon the 3,000 or so PF or professional soldiers who were to serve as "a corps of school teachers,"[4] a designation intended to underscore not denigrate the force's importance. As an educated physician (an occupation also in the process of professionalization), committed to education and medical research, and a man with a lively curiosity in science and a solid business background, Borden appreciated knowledge and expertise and endorsed the cult of efficiency and scientific management with its insistence on structure, method, and organization.[5] He understood and supported professional soldiers' need for a measure of autonomy, education, and training and was prepared to increase their numbers and visibility and give them a greater portion of the defence budget.

From the beginning of his tenure as minister, Borden had made military education and training the cornerstone of military reform, to address what he identified as the Militia's "most serious problem"[6] and establish what he inelegantly described as "the groundwork" for the "efficiency of our militia force." As he reminded his colleagues during his major policy statement to the House in 1903, that was why he had insisted on maintaining annual camps and intended to extend the number of days of paid annual training from sixteen to thirty. That was why he had insisted upon the immediate reform of the RMC, had authorized the creation of the School of Musketry, "one of the most valuable adjuncts of the Militia in Canada,"[7] and the formation of the School of Signalling, and had encouraged the growth of the cadet movement within schools and universities. That is why, too, he, himself an avid reader, had insisted on the creation of a staff library at headquarters with a budget to purchase books as well as foreign magazines, newspapers, and professional magazines.[8] If, he lectured the House, "we are to have educated men and up to date officers we must have books."[9]

But he did not stop there; education remained central to most of his plans. As he explained to his parliamentary colleagues, in the construction of armouries he intended that each Militia unit would possess not only a fixed physical space, or armoury, to accommodate a hundred or more men, but a social space, club room, and "training schools" equipped with lecture rooms, "blackboards and other means to educate them." Similarly, his blueprints for the large training base at Petawawa included an auditorium that could seat a thousand persons and was designed for nightly lectures, illustrated by lantern slides.[10] In his view, education was the primary method to create a more efficient and effective force, recruit and retain a better class of men, and instil professional pride, especially in the PF where only 50 per cent of the men re-enlisted for a second term of service and where indiscipline and desertion tarnished the force's image among Canadian taxpayers.[11] In short, Borden's was the language and strategy of professionalization, so popular during this period.

Precisely because of the PF's importance to the future of his civilian army, Borden searched for ways and means to recruit and retain good, dependable professional soldiers who would earn the respect of the Canadian public and its civilian soldiers. In his view, the best way to achieve this objective was through formal education and training, exchanges, career opportunities, and improved material conditions and financial incentives for service. Proud of the success of the reformed RMC as a source of good officers for the British Army and the Canadian Militia, Borden provided incentives to induce RMC graduates to enter the PF,[12] and in 1908 the Militia Council authorized the remission of college fees for those graduates who subsequently joined the PF.[13]

No less committed to continuing education, Borden sought access for Canadian career soldiers to more specialized professional and technical staff courses in Britain. During his meeting with the Imperial Defence Committee in December 1903, he had persuaded the War Office to reserve six staff positions annually for Canadian officers at the British staff college at Camberley and to permit access to "courses of instruction at Aldershot and elsewhere in various technical branches such as Engineering, the Army Service Corps, Army Medical Services etc."[14] To demonstrate his serious intent and to encourage good candidates, immediately after Dundonald's dismissal from the command of the Canadian Militia in July 1904, Borden announced, somewhat precipitously, that all future appointees to Canadian Headquarters Staff must conform to British training standards for appointment and promotion. This meant that all senior staff positions at headquarters or elsewhere must be filled by officers who had been educated at Camberley and possessed field experience.[15] This was an ambitious agenda and one that conflicted with Borden's attempt to provide senior service opportunities for Boer War veterans.

Exchanges constituted another form of practical continuing education. Although Borden and others promoted regimental exchanges, imperial exchanges entailed practical difficulties and aroused political hostility and suspicions. Borden's 1903 attempt to foster regimental exchanges with the British Army in India, for example, was nixed by the Canadian cabinet because of the fear that service in India was a precursor to imperial military obligations. Less visible and easier to arrange were individual, short-term staff positions in the British Army. In 1905 Borden concluded an agreement with the War Office that made Canadian PF officers who successfully completed their Camberley training eligible for exchange employment with officers of the British Army in India. This allowed Canadian officers to gain valuable practical experience and gave Canada access to the short-term services of experienced British officers.[16] This program was subsequently extended to Australia. In 1908 a total of twelve Canadian PF officers were enrolled in various British Army staff courses: at Camberley, the Ordnance College, the Artillery Staff course, the Military Engineers course, the Hythe School of Musketry, and the Royal Army Medical College.[17] Important as these initiatives might be, imperial exchanges were limited to a very small, select number of mobile professional soldiers.

Another means of recruiting and maintaining good PF men and officers was to improve the working conditions of Canada's professional soldiers, especially their financial compensation. Although Borden's efforts to improve their material conditions predate the South African War, after 1901 the minister initiated what Stephen Harris has described as a veritable "stampede" of regulations to ameliorate the lot of professional soldiers.[18] These included improved pay rates (1902 and 1904), bringing the per diem rate for PF soldiers from 40 to 75 cents; a pension scheme (1901); housing allowances for junior officers (1903); educational opportunities; and better medical and commissariat facilities and career opportunities.

The reorganization of the Militia's command and administration, the opening of senior positions, especially senior staff positions, to Canadian officers, and the creation of specialized support units offered important practical career opportunities, training, and experience for professional soldiers as well. All these initiatives underscored Borden's objective of creating a self-sufficient little Canadian army that would be capable of taking the field and would justify keeping Canadians together under Canadian officers and command. Decentralization had been one of the lessons of the recent war, demonstrated by the Boers' effective guerrilla tactics, a lesson retained and promoted by the Esher report for the British Army. Borden felt that decentralization was especially appropriate for Canada, given the country's size, regional configuration, and strategic vulnerabilities, including its "two" oceans. As a regional spokesman, he appreciated the importance of getting the senior decision-makers out of Ottawa so that they might understand regional realities. Moreover, decentralization entailed devising an appropriate and effective organizational structure for the administration, training, support, command, and deployment of Canada's civilian army.

Before 1905 the Canadian Militia had been organized into twelve geographically delineated military districts, commanded by district officers commanding, and composed of a hodgepodge of arms and units of unequal strength. In many rural districts, company-sized groupings were little more than paper phantoms. A district officer commanding possessed limited powers over the civilian soldiers' instruction, training, and mobilization. To facilitate more effective training and mobilization of the country's civilian military forces, in 1905 Borden regrouped the twelve districts into five regional commands, all with enhanced powers of initiative, command, and responsibility, including for equipment and training: Prairie (or North-West) Command, located in Winnipeg; Western Ontario Command, centred in Toronto; Eastern Ontario Command, based in Kingston; Quebec Command, headquartered in Montreal; and a Maritime Command, in Halifax.[19] The new regional structure charged each of its commands with the responsibility of organizing its citizen forces into integrated, coherent combat units, including the formation and maintenance of appropriate service corps. Five senior regional commanders were responsible for their force's maintenance and formation as well as for planning for their mobilization in the event of conflict. To facilitate education, PF units were stationed in each command to train the citizen soldiers. Military stores and supplies were relegated from headquarters in Ottawa to the new regional command depots, where they were more readily accessible in time of need than if stored in Ottawa.

The Militia's new decentralized command structure provided flexibility, enabling regional commands to mobilize and respond more quickly to military emergencies without waiting for detailed instructions or materiel from Ottawa. No less important in Borden's mind was the regional commands' function as a "school of experience" for senior officers, sensitizing them to regional exigencies. As he explained to Sam Hughes in the House, his goal was to staff Militia Headquarters with graduates of Staff College who had served in the regional commands, officers sensitive to regional capacities, perspectives, and needs.[20] Borden's decentralization of the Militia, the creation of regional centres of supply, training, and command, constituted another important pillar of his civilian army, one that provided a means of training and promoting senior PF officers and preparing them to assume responsibilities as might devolve upon them in time of war. It also served as a reward to Canada's Boer War veterans and enabled the Militia to benefit from their experience.

Divisional commands, of course, operated within national structures, directives, plans, and policies that were determined by defence headquarters in Ottawa.[21] The Militia Council's decision in 1906 to organize its various infantry and cavalry units into twenty trans-regional infantry and seven trans-regional mounted brigades crosscut divisional commands. As with the regional commands, the trans-divisional brigades required more senior PF commanders and administrators and provided command experience, especially when they were brought together to train at the central camp at Petawawa. This strategy of cross-regional organization and training was extended to the proliferation of specialized service corps, each with its national command structure, underlining the emergence of a nascent Canadian army.

Few decisions enhanced the strength and importance of the PF more than the Canadian government's decision to take over the British garrisons in Halifax and Esquimalt. Although the British government had withdrawn its land forces from central Canada in 1871, it had maintained a land garrison at Halifax and later established one at Esquimalt to protect its naval installations, which included a coaling station and dockyards. Continuing British command on Canadian soil created occasional jurisdictional tensions between the Canadian Militia and the British regular military authorities in Canada over the responsibility and command of Canada's defences. Since Canada's ultimate defence remained a British responsibility, in the event of war or the threat of war the GOC of British troops in Halifax possessed seniority and command over all land forces, including those of the Canadian Militia. The Canadian Militia GOCs, themselves British regular officers on loan to the Canadian government, had often resented the Halifax general's superior military, political, and social position. Sensitive Canadian nationalists regarded the continued custodial presence of British troops on Canadian soil as a reminder of their colonial dependency. And British authorities frequently grumbled about maintaining costly defences in Canada and pressed Canadians to make a larger (since it subsidized Esquimalt) monetary contribution to the maintenance of British forces in Canada.

Although Borden maintained very cordial personal relations with the officers commanding British troops in Halifax, enjoyed their company and their generous hospitality, and often sought their informal military advice and counsel, he made no secret of his own desire to have Canada take over the British garrisons. According to his own testimony, he had several reasons for wanting to patriate the garrisons, two being his desire "to foster a national spirit in Canada" and to relieve the "hardly pressed British tax payer."[22] Read another way, the removal of the British garrisons would give Canada undisputed control over its own forces; no longer would the Canadian Militia be seen as a mere auxiliary force of the British Army. At the same time, possession of the garrisons would respond to the perennial British reproach that Canada made little contribution to imperial defence, including the defence of its own territory. The Tory press detected another reason to explain Borden's interest in the garrisons: the existence of what the press called "graft chickens,"[23] a consideration that cannot be dismissed entirely given Borden's careless mixture of private and public interests.

Whatever his motives, from the time he became a minister Borden attempted to persuade the Canadian and British authorities that Canada ought to assume control of the British coastal garrisons, and on three occasions he proposed that Canada take possession. The first occurred during the Boer War when he persuaded the Canadian cabinet and the British government to replace the British regular unit garrisoning Halifax, the 100th Regiment, for service in the South African War with a Canadian Militia battalion, an arrangement that Borden hoped to make permanent at the end of the conflict. At the same time he agreed to increase Canada's contribution to the maintenance of the Esquimalt garrison from an annual sum of $76,500 to $140,000, to pay the British Army up to half the costs of maintaining their west coast garrison of some 320 men, including its replacement during the South African War by a local militia unit. The offer was designed to acknowledge Canada's financial responsibility for its own defences and lead to complete Canadian control at the end of the conflict.[24] To honour his offer to garrison Halifax, a third battalion of the Royal Canadian Regiment of Infantry was recruited to replace the British unit in Halifax during the war. When peace in South Africa terminated this arrangement in 1902, Borden took the first opportunity to claim control of the garrisons. The occasion was the Colonial/Imperial Conference of 1902, during which Borden countered the British authorities' call for a direct Canadian monetary contribution to support all imperial military installations in Canada with an alternative offer to take possession of the garrisons. The third occasion came a year and a half later during Borden's conference with the Imperial Defence Committee in December 1903. The time was ripe, since a week before its formal meeting with Borden the Imperial Defence Committee had decided to discount war with the United States and withdraw its fleet from Halifax. The committee therefore welcomed Borden's willingness to consider that Canada take over the garrisons, convinced that Canadian control of the garrisons might encourage Canada to proceed more quickly with its 1902 promise to make more effective provision for its own naval defences.

Borden's desire to take over the garrisons faced stronger opposition in Ottawa than in London, opposition on several fronts. Imperialists such as Minto and Dundonald rejected the proposal as beyond the practical competence of the Canadian military and another regrettable break in Canada's ties with Britain. Tories denounced it as a grab to secure military patronage. But the most vociferous and potentially damaging opposition came from within Borden's own party, led by Senator Raoul Dandurand, who regarded the arrangement as an effort to entangle Canada in costly imperial defence schemes, an argument taken up more publicly by Henri Bourassa. On the eve of a general election this dissident chorus of objections was sufficient to arrest the initiative, at least for a time.[25]

Borden's "membership" in the Committee of Imperial Defence became a special target of their criticism; it reinforced some of his Liberal colleagues' suspicions that membership was a thin edge of the imperial wedge. Even Laurier withheld his approval of Borden's membership in the CID and balked at his commitment to take over the garrisons. At first Borden tried to disarm his critics. He dismissed the importance of his membership in the committee and reassured his critics that the transfer of the garrisons brought no additional commitment. Even the argument that taking over the garrisons was a significant step toward military autonomy, rather than imperial entanglement, failed to convince his opponents at the time. Unable to persuade his colleagues and embarrassed by the opposition within his own party, Borden was obliged to write to the Colonial Office secretary, Alfred Lyttelton, to ask him to strike from the minutes any reference to the transfer of the imperial garrisons.[26]

Borden, the eternal optimist, had not capitulated; his was but a strategic retreat. Less than a year later, the federal election safely out of the way and Laurier's Liberals securely reinstalled in power, Borden learned that the British military authorities intended to withdraw the fleet and close the garrisons, come what may. Canada, therefore, had one last chance to take possession of the garrisons, to obtain valuable and potentially strategic military installations and assume greater responsibility for its own defence. Once again Borden turned to the press. On 8 December 1904 the *Globe* announced that Canada's reluctance to accept the garrisons was an affront to its autonomy. "National self-respect," its editorial declared, "demands that the Canadian people shall not be indebted to the home government in the maintenance of any soldier on the soil of Canada. Self-government must be accomplished by self-support." No statement could have summarized Borden's position more clearly. Few were deceived; they detected the fine hand of the minister, a skilful manager of the press.[27] Opposition melted within and outside the cabinet; even Henri Bourassa and the nationalists fell into line, making it clear that Canada had no need of "imperial military charity."[28]

Less than a month after the *Globe*'s intervention, Borden presented a carefully prepared proposition to a full cabinet meeting, arguing that control of the garrisons would play well with the Canadian public, especially if it were represented as another step "in the direction of complete Canadian nationhood."[29] At the same time, possession of the garrisons would silence those who called for a greater contribution to imperial defence, scotching British requests for direct monetary support. Borden had done his political homework well; he had found the language of persuasion and lined up his political support, and after a full cabinet discussion, the government agreed readily to an Order-in-Council offering to assume control of the garrisons.

Still, the minister had not cleared all the hurdles. The British used the occasion to try once again to extract a direct monetary contribution from the Canadian government. In acknowledging the Canadian government's offer in February 1905, the imperial government questioned Canada's capacity to assume immediate control of the garrisons given its paucity of experienced PF officers and men, a somewhat hollow objection given its decision to abandon the garrisons come what may. London's real agenda became clear when it suggested that Canada make a direct annual contribution of £200,000, exclusive of Canada's cash contribution to the defence of Esquimalt. The Canadian government swiftly rejected this proposal, reposting with a counter-offer to assume full responsibility for all current contracts incurred by the garrison, including the payment of its soldiers' wages: in other words, the British would transfer men and facilities to the Canadian Militia, thereby addressing the British concern for the paucity of experienced Canadian military personnel.

At first London declined the Canadian counter-offer on the grounds that army regulations prohibited the British from permitting another government to assume responsibilities for their contracts. A solution to London's objection required little imagination: in May 1905 Borden responded with an amended offer to borrow the requisite number of officers and non-commissioned officers from the British Army for periods of one to three years, depending on how long it took to recruit their Canadian replacements. This was an offer that the British government finally accepted, and arrangements were made for the transfer of the garrison and its fortification on 16 January 1906.

At the same time, Borden handily won the battle for public approval. The press hailed the transfer as a landmark in the growth of Canadian autonomy. According to one journal, "[N]o more significant one, we believe, has ever been taken."[30] The provincial partisan press lauded Sir Frederick for his role in this visionary, "epoch-making" event and extolled the minister's "energetic" and "intelligent management of the Militia generally," describing him as "the ablest and most useful Minister of Militia the Dominion has ever had."[31] Given Borden's persistence and his role in negotiating the transfer, the praise was not entirely misplaced.

A symbolic and strategic decision certainly it was. Of more immediate and practical significance was the enhanced role required of the

PF. Although the transfer of the garrisons occasioned no formal redefinition of the PF's functions as garrison troops and teachers, it did have significant practical repercussions on the force's size, place, and deployment within the Canadian Militia. The most obvious immediate effects were an increase in the PF's authorized establishment, from 2,000 to 5,000 men, and in its actual strength, from 2,000 to 3,500;[32] the addition of $1 million to the Militia Department's budget;[33] and the incorporation of five companies of garrison artillery and engineering troops into the PF establishment, including coastal guns. With the garrisons came PF service units, including a medical unit that had a base hospital with a laboratory; this unit was designed to service the concentration of permanent garrison troops, and Borden would later add a school of medical instruction to it. Recruiting Canadian replacements into the PF, however, proved a slow process owing to the uncompetitive incentives of military service during a period of national growth and prosperity. In the end the Militia met the recruiting deficit only by transferring to the PF some 431 officers and other ranks, largely other ranks, from the British regular army that had been stationed as garrison troops.[34]

The transfer of the garrisons dissipated the confusion over British responsibility for the command and financing of Canada's defences. It also left a void of senior staff to plan, organizes, and coordinate the country's defences, a void that only the PF could fill. If Borden were serious in his desire to transform Canada's armed forces from an auxiliary of the British Army to a self-sufficient Canadian army, however, he would have to plan the deployment of Canada's military resources effectively so that they could meet a threat to Canada's borders and participate in imperial defence. As Borden explained to the Commons' Militia lobby in 1908, in the past Canada had depended upon the senior British officers at the Halifax garrison for planning and leadership in the field. Their departure now made it imperative to establish a Canadian equivalent, a cadre of PF senior staff and field officers, as well as a Canadian general staff, to plan, educate, and advise the Militia Council.[35] In other words, an autonomous Canadian army brought with it additional PF responsibilities, including command and strategic planning, a challenge that Borden enthusiastically embraced.

Borden's most pressing priority was to secure capable leadership to prepare a blueprint for Canada's defences and educate a cadre of senior PF officers. What he needed was a credible expert who could champion his cause. Fortunately he knew the person for this task: Lieutenant-General Percy Lake. Scarcely had Borden rid himself of Dundonald than he requested and obtained the services of two senior British Army officers, Lake and Lieutenant-General Matthew Aylmer. Both were

Borden's personal friends. Indeed, Hutton and Minto believed that the minister's relations with these two British regular officers were far too friendly, since his direct correspondence with them on military matters provided an alternative source of professional advice that he might employ to contain or counter the counsel of overzealous GOCs of the Canadian Militia.

The War Office could not have been more helpful in facilitating Borden's request for their services, readily acquiescing to Lake's one condition of acceptance, namely his promotion over two hundred of his fellow regular officers. Upon Dundonald's dismissal on 14 June 1904 Borden immediately appointed the Canadian-born Matthew Aylmer as the acting general officer commanding the Canadian Militia, a position he would hold until the creation of the Militia Council on 31 October 1904, when he became the inspector general. The more important acquisition, however, was that of Percy Lake, a British regular officer of Canadian parentage who had served in Canada as quartermaster-general from 1892 to 1898 and whom Borden wanted as his chief of the general staff. Lake proved an excellent choice. In the years that followed Borden and Lake worked together closely and productively, even when they disagreed on issues.

Lake and Borden shared a faith in planning. Indeed, planning was Lake's professional expertise and Borden's primary reason for choosing him. In 1898 both men welcomed Major-General E.P. Leach's report on Canadian defences. Both saw the report as a coherent plan of action, a blueprint from which to work. Borden had cleverly used the Leach Report to extract resources from his reluctant cabinet colleagues, and subsequently he had used it as a reference in implementing military reform. Although Lake's new mandate included operations, structure, and policy, Borden asked him to give priority to devising a coordinated defence plan suitable to Canada's needs and capacity. What Borden wanted from Lake was a compelling, coherent plan for a balanced force, with appropriate support units, arms, and supplies, and an agreed, detailed procedure for orderly mobilization. In Borden's view, the plan ought to provide an integrated framework for divisional commands that could be rehearsed at the spacious new central training ground at Petawawa and would enable Canadian forces to serve as a unified, coordinated unit in times of need. Above all, he wanted a plan that he could defend before the Canadian public.

As soon as Lake arrived in November 1904, he began planning for the recruitment, organization, and orderly mobilization of Canada's land forces, working closely with the newly created regional commands and with Borden's full support and blessing. Lake assigned detailed planning to Lieutenant-Colonel Willoughby Gwatkin, an able British officer on loan to the Canadian Militia, whose work he watched and supervised closely. By June 1907 Gwatkin had a comprehensive plan in place, which the PF tested the following summer at Petawawa.

Borden's more ambitious objective, a fully-fledged Canadian general staff, a cadre of senior officers to advice the Militia Council on policy, military doctrine, and procedures, proved a more difficult and controversial order owing partly to the War Office's resistance (this subject will be addressed in a subsequent chapter). Suffice to say that the War Office continued to regard Canada as one of its "subordinate commands" and considered the creation of a separate Canadian general staff as "tantamount to a declaration of military independence" and a challenge to its control and authority.[36]

The War Office's answer to the Canadian initiative was an Imperial General Staff, a body under War Office control designed to educate key colonial staff officers, including those on exchange with the British Army or at the British staff college who upon their return to Canada would inform, advise, and direct their colonial military or civilian colleagues on policy. Initially Borden supported the creation of an Imperial General Staff, seeing it as another means to educate a cadre of senior Canadian officers who would advise him on strategy, operations, and policy. Once he appreciated the War Office's unidirectional pretensions, however, he contested and resisted its claims, a position he defended forcefully and successfully during subsequent imperial conferences. For Borden, cooperation was one thing, subordination another. His resistance tested but did not shake his friendships with Lake and Gwatkin. Both loyally backed their minister whatever they may have thought of his stubborn resistance to the War Office's designs.

A more remarkable exercise was Borden's approval of a detailed plan for the despatch of a Canadian overseas contingent, a decision that appeared to reverse Canada's singular commitment to the defence of its own territory. The novelty of Borden's commitment to an expeditionary force, however, has sometimes been overstated. As James Laxer has pointed out, well before the Boer War Canada possessed a bi-ethnic, non-partisan consensus on defence. It entailed a primary commitment to the defence of Canadian territory and by extension to the defence of Britain should its security be threatened, since Britain remained Canada's ultimate line of defence.[37] Laurier had enunciated this consensus in 1897 during the Diamond Jubilee festivities in his often misinterpreted "Let the fires be lit on the hills" speech. In this celebrated oration Laurier promised that if Britain itself were ever in danger, Canada would do whatever "can be done ... to help her" – a policy he had stated a year previous in the House of Commons, just before he became prime minister.[38] Canada's commitment to British defence, however, did not extend to brushfire wars on the periphery of the Empire, places where British supremacy was not threatened, as John A. Macdonald himself had made clear in 1885 when he refused to send troops to the Sudan.

Canada's participation in the Boer War, however, had extended the definition of Canadian defence in two significant respects. First, the despatch of the Canadian Militia forces beyond Canadian territorial waters (after all, the 2nd Battalion, Royal Canadian Regiment of Infantry, remained a Canadian Militia unit) had stretched the Militia Act's restriction of the Canadian Militia to the territorial defence of Canada (the restriction had become a constitutional issue that had agitated Canadian-imperial relations on the eve of the South Africa War).[39] Second, despite Laurier's insistence that the despatch of Canada's first contingent to South Africa had not created a precedent for Canadian contributions to future peripheral imperial conflicts, participation itself had created a precedent, as Henri Bourassa had so perceptively noted in response to Laurier's assurances.

Even before the Boer War Borden had tacitly endorsed an extension of Canada's defence obligations. Although the "idea" of commissioning a Canada defence report predated Borden's entry into cabinet, it was largely Borden, working closely with Major-General Sir Alexander Montgomery-Moore, who persuaded the cabinet to request a commission of British experts to advise on the defence of Canada's borders.[40] The result was the Leach Report, whose purpose was to prepare Canada for the more effective mobilization of its resources for the defence of its territory, and in doing so, the report made little distinction between local and imperial defence.

Borden shared Leach's vision. In his view, the line between Canadian and imperial defence was not always obvious. Consequently, in 1899 he tacitly endorsed General Hutton's addition of "imperial defence" to the list of the Militia's primary obligations. Borden's failure to disassociate himself from the Hutton report's commitment to imperial defence was no mere oversight. Moreover, three months before the start of the Boer War, Borden had condoned and abetted the Militia Department's preparation of rudimentary plans for an expeditionary force to serve in a potential brushfire war in South Africa. And when war began, Borden, a committed partisan of Canadian participation in that conflict, and William Mulock led the charge for an official Canadian contribution during a heated, two-day cabinet debate.

Similarly, during the 1902 Colonial/Imperial Conference, Borden had informed his colleagues that imperial defence had been added to Canada's traditional commitment to the defence of Canada's borders and aid to the civil power.[41] And he had reiterated this commitment during his House of Commons policy speech of October 1903. Conscious that a debate over the legality of moving the Canadian Militia beyond Canada had threatened to prevent the despatch of Canadian troops to South Africa in 1899, in 1904 Borden obtained parliamentary approval to alter the wording of section 79 of the old Militia Act to permit the Governor General in Council to deploy the Canadian Militia "beyond Canada for the defence thereof."[42] In Borden's view, Canadian and imperial defence were simply different sides of the same coin, though the deployment of Canadian troops remained the prerogative of the Canadian government. Only Canada could determine if and where it would deploy its forces.

Thus, to represent Borden's plan for an expeditionary force as a deathbed conversion to imperial military integration, as a clear rejection of his 1902 stand against the creation of a special colonial military reserve for imperial service, fails to appreciate the nature, evolution, and constraints of Borden's pragmatic expeditionary plan.[43] It also ignores the purpose and context of the plan and Borden's continuing insistence upon local control, including parliamentary consent to the despatch of Canadian troops abroad.[44] After all, a contingency plan for an expeditionary force constituted no automatic, binding commitment to the despatch of Canadian troops to any point of the globe at the behest of the British government, far from it. Borden had made that crystal clear during the Imperial Conference of 1909. Furthermore, the British government was "well aware" that Borden's planned expeditionary force constituted no automatic "guarantee that contingents of any strength or composition will be forthcoming … in the event of a great war."[45]

Borden's contingency plan for an expeditionary force, then, was remarkable less because it envisaged imperial service abroad than because it challenged Canadian contemporary military preparations and assumptions and raised the thorny issue of the function of professional soldiers. More important than the plan's alleged imperial novelty was its implications for the PF, especially if the site of the future conflict were to be Europe rather than North America. The prospect of a war in Europe against professional armies forced a debate and reconsideration of the PF's function. Were Canada's PF soldiers to remain simply a corps of schoolteachers, garrison troops, and the first line of support to the civil power during a civil disturbance or were they to be permitted to lead and engage in combat, to practise what they preached and become the staff and command structure, the nucleus of a standing army? Otherwise, how would Canada's civilian Militia fit within the ranks and leadership of Europe's professional armies?

While Borden welcomed the opportunity to transform the Canadian Militia "from an auxiliary force of the British Army into a self-sufficient army,"[46] he stalwartly defended the virtues of a civilian force, a position ever popular with the Commons' Militia lobby. Although sympathetic to the PF's desire to enhance their professional skills and place in the country's defences, he insisted that the PF not neglect its primary responsibility for the training and education of his civilian Militia. And on two occasions Borden called the PF to order in clear and unmistakable language, insisting that a PF officer be evaluated on his "performance as a teacher."[47]

But Borden was also a pragmatic realist, open to change and innovation. Gradually, if reluctantly, he came to see the logic of his own policies of professionalization and to accept an expanded combat role for Canada's professional soldiers. Consequently, though conscious of the discomfort of the Commons' Militia lobby with the growing importance of the PF, Borden was often obliged to explain and defend the PF's centrality in the planning, support, and command of Canada's armed forces in the field and plead with his fellow parliamentarians not to reduce the PF establishment, as some of his more committed militia enthusiasts suggested. "When an Army takes the field," he explained to his colleagues, it is required to assume duties "that are not required in peace, and which can only be performed by trained soldiers."[48] As Borden continued to explain in his 1909 annual report to Parliament, the removal of the British from Halifax and Esquimalt had created a vacuum in planning, support, and leadership that Canada was obliged to fill by creating a cadre of senior staff and field officers that only the PF could supply. Consequently, by 1909, largely as a result of his policies, the PF was responsible not only for garrison duty, teaching, and the primary support to the civil power, but for the support, equipment, supply, transport, and effective command of the active Militia in war and peace.[49]

Still the evolving role of the PF remained a moving target, a source of tension, ambiguity, and misunderstanding that Borden had to manage. In this debate the sensitive, crucial question of combat was determinant. What role was the PF to assume in the event of war? The PF's unmistakable desire for a combat role was fuelled not only by its growing size and influence, its access to improved training facilities, such as the large training base at Petawawa, and to more-sophisticated military technology, but by the military's plans for an expeditionary force and the prospect of military service with professional European armies. This issue remained unresolved until Major-General Colin Mackenzie, who replaced Lake as chief of the general staff in 1910, suggested a division of the PF into two rotating units, one for teaching and the other for combat, a compromise, hybrid solution to which Borden, the pragmatist, consented.

Ironically Borden, the articulate advocate and promoter of a civilian militia, found himself presiding over the professionalization of Canada's Militia, the creation of a nucleus of a standing Canadian army designed to lead Canadian forces into war. This quiet, ineluctable transformation, the PF's increasing numbers, the growth and quality of its support units, its expanding mission, including its responsibility for planning and leadership in the field, was inherent in the logic of Borden's policies, his commitment to education, professional development, specialization, and efficiency, and his determination to build an autonomous Canadian army, capable of taking the field. By 1910, the PF and Headquarters Staff's absorption of 41 per cent of his department's budget underlined the transformation facilitated by the larger, changing strategic context,[50] as the focus of Canada's defences shifted from North America to Europe, a theatre more appropriate to a professional army than to a civilian militia.

CHAPTER 17

Wise Autonomy

"Wise autonomy" is how Borden described his pragmatic vision of empire. Since Borden regarded "local defence and imperial defence" as "largely the same thing," imperial cooperation constituted an essential condition and guarantee of Canadian military and material security. As Borden explained to his imperial colleagues in 1909, "If the Empire falls, we fall as a result."[1] This was scarcely a novel or personal doctrine: it was the underlying assumption of Laurier's 1897 Diamond Jubilee promise, the Leach Report, and the Canadian justification for an expeditionary force. The challenge lay in making imperialism cooperative, in grounding these necessities on mutual respect, consultation, and cooperation rather than on paternalism, centralization, and integration,[2] and in building and maintaining a real partnership among partners of unequal size.

Some of Borden's contemporaries might not have agreed with his liberal imperialism, especially those imperialists and nationalists who saw colonial nationalism and imperialism as antithetical and the forty-ninth parallel as an impermeable barrier. In his embittered, self-serving manuscript *Memoir*, E.T.H. Hutton, the vindictive former GOC of the Canadian Militia, dismissed Borden as an imperial agnostic. According to Hutton, during the early months of the South African War Borden had "snarled at me across his table, 'I ask myself this question. Is it worth Canada's while to remain part of the Empire which can suffer such disasters as those of Methuen, Gataere and Buller?'"[3] If Hutton's two-decade-old memory transcribed Borden's imperial sentiments accurately at the time rather than an angry retort during an acrimonious verbal exchange between the two antagonists, the minister's subsequent actions and behaviour contradicted his alleged anti-imperialist sentiments.

Major-General Hutton was not the only person to have mistaken the nature and intensity of Borden's personal, political, and pragmatic imperial perspective and to have misread his transatlantic vision. Lord Dundonald entertained comparable illusions. In his published memoirs Dundonald denounced Borden's and Laurier's "irresponsible" reluctance to make adequate provision for the defence of the Canadian-

American border, and noted their misplaced confidence in the benefi-
cent intent of the Monroe doctrine as proof of their want of imperial
commitment. Yet Borden's and Laurier's carefully calculated gamble
on American goodwill was no less patriotic or irresponsible than their
British equivalents' faith in the Americans' benign, hemispheric military intentions, a faith represented by the British statesmen's subsequent decision to liquidate their naval garrisons in North America.
Borden and British Anglo-American well-wishers agreed that if the
Monroe doctrine was as good as its promise, it provided Canada with
an additional, not an alternative, guarantee of protection from European aggression.

Moreover, Dundonald, Hutton, and others frequently failed to appreciate the chameleon complexity of the triangular, transatlantic relationship at the time.[4] They failed to perceive or accept the emergence
of an Anglo-American community built on shared values and assumptions, a community that promised Canada security and status, one that
many Canadians believed was compatible with imperial allegiance and
neighbourly Canadian-American relations and in which Canada could
remain an active and important participant and beneficiary with a constructive role to play. In other words, Hutton and Dundonald failed
to recognize Borden's pragmatic imperialism as a form of Canadian
nationalism. Nor did they appear to appreciate that both Borden and
Laurier inhabited a British world governed by inclusive and pluralistic
ideas and values, that they believed in a liberal imperialism based on
diversity and self-government, what one author has called imperialism
"without the claws," an internationalism based on shared values and
reconciliation.[5] In short, they failed to appreciate Borden's personal
comfort within this transatlantic world.

Born of Planter ancestry, Borden had been raised in a region whose
demography and religious and economic life marked it as "New England's Outpost" and its inhabitants as "Her Majesty's Yankees."[6] Educated at Harvard, he possessed numerous trans-border family and
friends, many of them expatriates, the result of the out-migration from
his region during its recent great economic transformation. Throughout Borden's career he cultivated cross-border friendships, maintained
profitable business relations with Americans, and remained a persistent advocate of closer trade with the United States. No less proud of
his English ancestry, Borden grew up within an elitist British world,
nourished by its material values, cultural assumptions, and social
aspirations. His classical formation at Kings, whose memory, codes,
and symbols mirrored and imitated those of his British peers, encouraged a knowledge and appreciation of English society and culture,
an intellectual world he shared with Laurier, altogether a very useful

badge of social standing in a colonial society, especially among Canada's aspiring national class. Borden was a member of the first generation of national leaders whose identity and allegiance included a national perspective that subsumed locality and region and was not incompatible with empire.

Contemporary social and cultural anxieties, expressed in terms of race, class, language, and religion, reinforced transatlantic rapprochement and understanding. Perhaps nowhere were these cultural and social anxieties more visible than among the beleaguered New England elite, bewildered by their country's industrial transformation and changing class and ethnic composition, and as a consequence suffering from a perceived loss of place in society. To affirm their social and political standing, "old" New England families frequently appealed to the roots, history, and authenticity grounded in their English culture and heritage. Many Canadians shared their social and cultural anxieties and employed similar strategies to stake their claims to legitimacy and authority in their own changing society. This imagined transatlantic world bred among English-speaking peoples a feeling of cross-border community, of shared cultural values that transcended political borders. Borden understood and moved comfortably within this transatlantic world.

Contrary to Dundonald's assumption, Borden's comfort did not make him complacent or careless of Canada's border defences. That was clear from his broad policy statement to the House of Commons in October 1903 when he announced an increase in the number of mounted troops at strategic border points. This decision, together with his proposed civilian Militia, whose assumption was a war with the United States, was hailed by no less a patriot than Sam Hughes, the Conservatives' chief military critic, as making Canada "invincible" against the "entire forces of the United States."[7] Yet, however Borden may have welcomed Hughes's endorsement of his decision to defend the border, armed borders were not Borden's or Laurier's primary strategic defence. Apart from being reluctant to incur costly defence expenditures, both men sought more pacific mean to protect Canada's territorial integrity. In their view, the political resolution of border conflicts, the development of a community of mutually beneficial trans-border economic interests, and the cultivation of Anglo-American cultural understanding and cooperation were no less important and much more cost-effective. Skilfully employed, "soft" power could supplement and eventually replace more traditional defences. Borden did "not like the idea of shaking in the faces of our neighbours our war establishment if there is any way of avoiding it."[8] Nevertheless he realized that the Militia's principal *raison d'être* was defence against the United States, and he never hesitated to authorize modest military expenditures to maintain the integrity of the forty-ninth parallel.

Hutton simply failed to understand or accept the complexity, flexibility, plurality, and inclusiveness of empire or to appreciate that the imperial debate was not over the necessity of empire but over its nature and management and the equitable distribution of mutual responsibilities. As the minister of one of Canada's most British institutions,[9] and as defence assumed the dominant place on the imperial agenda, Borden became the minister to whom Laurier increasingly entrusted the task of articulating and defending Canada's place within a liberal empire. Contrary to a familiar liberal-autonomist reading of imperial relations that depicts imperial relations as a battle for colonial nationality against imperial allegiance, Laurier and Borden's pursuit of a just balance between Canadian responsibilities and imperial obligations proved less problematic and less heroic than this binary interpretation of Canadian constitutional evolution might suggest.

A cardinal weakness of this overly simplistic rendition of Canadian-imperial relations is its failure to appreciate the diverse and contradictory imperial dreams and interests available within Britain and its self-governing dominions at the time. Neither Borden nor Laurier suffered from this myopia. Aware of these alternative and conflicting imperial visions, Laurier cleverly exploited his position as head of Britain's senior dominion to champion a liberal imperialism and frustrate the agenda of Chamberlain and other imperial centralizers, adroitly turning the fluidity of these conflicting imperial dreams and interests to his advantage. As Chamberlain ultimately learned to his sorrow, Laurier was not a man with whom to go tiger hunting. Laurier was a seasoned politician, conscious of his strategic, senior position within imperial councils, aided by his faithful friend and colleague, the minister of militia and defence, whom he trusted to articulate and negotiate Canada's role within a liberal empire and whom he came to regard as a convinced, persistent, and dependable champion of Canadian autonomy, a confidence sealed by friendship and experience.[10] Borden had earned Laurier's confidence over time.

Borden's rail accident had prevented him from attending the great Colonial Conference in July 1897, the first comprehensive imperial gathering of the self-governing dominions. The conference was a central feature of the emotionally charged Diamond Jubilee celebration of Queen Victoria's reign, a spectacle elaborately staged by the new dynamic colonial secretary, Joseph Chamberlain, and designed to demonstrate the strength, solidarity, and diversity of her vast empire. In Chamberlain's blueprint this conference was an occasion to solicit support for his plans to reorganize the imperial estate to confront

European economic protectionism and its conscript armies. Although Chamberlain's agenda included discussion of a political, economic, and military union of the Empire, political union lacked any substantial support, especially among British Liberals for whom local autonomy remained a defining feature of their imperial vision. Chamberlain, however, had placed his cards on Canada's recently knighted prime minister.

During the jubilee celebrations Sir Wilfrid Laurier, the French-speaking, Catholic prime minister of Britain's senior dominion, became Chamberlain's emblem of Victoria's liberal empire. The Canadian prime minister's intellectual formation, theatrical talents, and carefully constructed self-image made him well cast for the role, and he cleverly exploited his stellar standing to remove political union from the conference agenda, insisting that the colonies were quite satisfied with their current enlightened political status within a liberal empire, committed as it was to liberty, diversity, and self-governance. More disturbing still to some ambitious empire-builders was Laurier's satisfaction with the current arrangements for imperial defence. To those who sought a greater Canadian contribution to the Empire's defences, Laurier confidently explained that Canada's defence of its own vast portion of the imperial estate and the construction and maintenance of strategic transcontinental rail and steamship communications to the Asian empire constituted his country's considerable and sufficient contribution to imperial security. This outcome was not exactly what the colonial secretary had planned.

Sir Wilfrid's case against political union and imperial defence integration proved an easier victory than many Liberal historians have imagined,[11] since Chamberlain and other British imperialists were never as insensitive to colonial nationalism as these liberal-autonomist historians have assumed. The colonial secretary himself had little difficulty describing the dominions as "independent sister nations" and was uncomfortable promoting the War Office's agenda of imperial defence integration; nor was Chamberlain convinced that political union and defence integration were the most appropriate ways to begin imperial reorganization. After five formal sessions of discussion, Chamberlain conceded that an organic political union of the Empire was indeed a very remote possibility.

What the colonial secretary had staked his hopes on was an imperial economic community, an imperial *zollverein* that would eventually require some form of shared defence and a concomitant coordinating, consultative means of governance. An appeal to material self-interest possessed the additional advantage of securing colonial support if one could judge from Sir Wilfrid's private and public rhetoric, especially his pre-conference gift of an imperial preference for British goods in Canadian markets. The gift had been accompanied by Canada's call for its reciprocity by the British government and its extension to other self-governing colonies. A protected imperial economic community, however, required a material British sacrifice and an ideological revolution. It required Britain to renounce its sacred commitment to free trade, a measure that proved an insurmountable political obstacle. The 1897 conference therefore accomplished little, except to establish the imperial agenda for the next decade and more.

The dominions' unanimous support of British arms in South Africa, however, resuscitated Chamberlain's dream of creating some functional, imperial consultative mechanism. The colonial secretary regarded the apparent success of British arms in South Africa and the premature prospects of peace in the late winter and early spring of 1900 as a propitious occasion to test the colonies' receptivity to an imperial consultative council. Before issuing invitations to a formal colonial consultation, however, Chamberlain sought a closer reading of colonial public opinion. On the pretext of consulting those self-governing colonies that had contributed arms on the terms of peace, principally Canada and the Australasian colonies, Chamberlain asked Lord Minto to act as his collecting agent in Canada.

The result of the governor general's thorough and perceptive canvass of Canadian official and representative public opinion, however, was so bleak that Chamberlain believed that Minto had frightened his respondents by excessive talk of military obligations.[12] At the time, Chamberlain and other British parliamentarians had placed great hope in Laurier's widely quoted Commons comment in March 1900: "If you want us to help you, call us to your councils." But Minto explained to Chamberlain that Laurier's famous retort to Henri Bourassa was not a call for imperial consultation so much as an exercise in logic.[13] In Minto's assessment, Canadian imperialism was limited to forms of profitable imperialism, schemes that promised some material benefit at no cost or obligation.[14] Faced with a lack of colonial support, Chamberlain dropped his plan for a colonial consultative conference in 1900.

Although checked, Chamberlain was not deterred. The end of the war in South Africa and the coronation of Edward VII in June 1902 appeared a more propitious time to re-chart the Empire's future, more especially if the colonial secretary could concentrate the colonies' discussion on the material benefits of an imperial trade community, an initiative the Birmingham industrialist had always believed was the thin edge of the wedge of imperial reorganization. Although trade was Chamberlain's principal agenda, and one on which he decided to stake his career, he invited the self-governing colonies to add any other items of interest to the proposed agenda.

Australia and New Zealand had more existential issues than trade on their agendas. Deeply apprehensive of the imperial government's "fortress Britain" strategy, its desire to concentrate its naval forces in European waters, the distant and insecure Pacific dominions could not neglect the topic of imperial defence. Closer to perceived danger and farther from help than Canada, Australia and New Zealand wanted some firmer imperial guarantee of security and were willing to purchase their demand with resources. Richard Seddon, the premier of New Zealand, not only insisted that imperial defence be placed on the agenda for the Colonial Conference scheduled to coincide with the coronation of Edward VII, but he arrived in London with a precise proposal that temporarily captured the empire-builders' imagination.

Preceded by Chamberlain's "weary titan" call for the self-governing dominions to help shoulder the burdensome cost of "their" empire's defence, Seddon proposed that each of "His Majesty's Dominions" establish units of an imperial reserve force, ready for employment in case of an emergency outside the dominion or colony in which the unit was raised. Seddon's proposal begged the question of consultation: who would determine the size of each colony's military commitment, its administration, deployment, and payment? A response to these questions required some agreed-upon, more-continuing, consultative coordinating mechanism. Seddon himself was a minimalist. As far as he was concerned, the size and cost of the military units could be determined through bilateral consultation between the imperial and colonial governments, or by regular "colonial conferences" of the self-governing dominions that he suggested be renamed "councils" and be designated as "imperial" rather than "colonial" gatherings.

Australia, however, sought a more structured system of consultation. Australia's long-standing discontent with the Colonial Office's perceived preoccupation with the Crown colonies, with its lack of knowledge and appreciation of the dominions, called for a more thorough reordering of the Colonial Office's mandate and management. What the Australians suggested was a separate Department of the Dominions within the Colonial Office or, better still, a separate Ministry of Dominion Affairs within the British government, complete with its own minister. In either case, what the Australians demanded was a greater commitment to genuine consultation and power sharing.

Australia's power-sharing proposal alarmed those imperial government departments potentially affected by its terms. Power sharing, even requests for additional information and more effective, systematic colonial consultation, aroused apprehension and resistance within various existing branches of the British government. Neither the War Office nor the Admiralty displayed any desire to share with the dominions its direction and authority over imperial defence, much less did the Foreign Office contemplate consultation.[15] The Colonial Office, especially sensitive to criticism of its administration, offered stiff and effective resistance to loss or diminution of its jurisdiction. After the 1902 Colonial/Imperial Conference, the formation of extra-parliamentary imperial ventriloquists, such as the Coefficients, the Compatriots, the Pollock Committee,[16] and later the Round Table movement, only magnified the Colonial Office's apprehensions that it might be dismantled or emasculated. In its defence of the status quo, the Colonial Office had no greater ally than Sir Wilfrid Laurier and the Canadian government.

Laurier did not disappoint the Colonial Office. He was only too willing to be the "stumbling block," the "obdurate figure," frustrating the various portentous plans for imperial reorganization, even those cloaked in the most autonomous garb. The prime minister's resistance played well back home. The tacit alliance between Laurier and the Colonial Office, however, was not quite as grotesque as it may appear.[17] Unlike several Australian prime ministers, Laurier had no particular quarrel with the Colonial Office's knowledge and understanding of Canada. Contrary to the Australian experience, the Colonial Office generally proved an informed, effective, and sympathetic defender of Canadian interests within the British government – more so than the War Office, Admiralty, and Foreign Office – although, ironically, liberal-autonomist historians such as O.D. Skelton, J.W. Dafoe, and L.-O. David have often charged the Colonial Office with the stupidities and blunders of the other government departments whose messages the Colonial Office had to transmit.

More importantly, Laurier failed to share the imperial re-organizers' objectives and methods. He simply could not see how their schemes could be reconciled with his liberal view of empire as a community of autonomous states, an imperial vision so important in a bi-national country such as Canada. However flattering or well packaged the imperial reorganizers' power-sharing proposals might appear, all raised serious constitutional issues. In Laurier's view proposals for a dominions office or an imperial secretariat without a responsible minister, a committee of dominion high commissioners appointed to the House of Lords, or a consultative council composed of appointed members, including representatives of colonial opposition parties, all seemed ill-suited to liberal parliamentary institutions. It was much better, Laurier contended, to continue on the familiar course than embark in the wrong direction. So effectively did Laurier checkmate the 1902 Colonial/Imperial Conference's political and military agenda that even Henri Bourassa publicly commended him on his accomplishment.[18]

Laurier had made it clear well before the 1902 conference that he opposed revisiting the subject of imperial defence and had no interest

in creating a consultative advisory council. Nevertheless he attended all
ten meetings of the conference, listened politely to the plans of others,
graciously conceded the obvious, exploited the divisions among the
participants, and resisted all substantive imperial proposals, except
one for the creation of a preferential trade zone. During the discussions
on defence and political union, Laurier simply reiterated and elaborated upon his earlier position. He continued to maintain that Canada's
commitment to the defence of its own territory and the building and
maintenance of the Canadian Pacific Railway, the great imperial highway, the all-red route to Asia, was his country's important and appropriate contribution to imperial defence.

While he appreciated Australia and New Zealand's insecurity and
their request for greater naval protection, Laurier saw no need for
Canada to go beyond the creation of a Canadian naval force under
Canadian control, along the lines of its land militia. He refused
therefore to countenance Seddon's proposed imperial reserve force,
explaining that its creation would be an "important departure from
the principles of colonial self-government." The creation of an advisory
council raised similar difficulties; he saw it as an impractical scheme,
a body with power but without responsibility, incompatible with parliamentary government. He agreed that one might hold more regular
and frequent conferences and call them imperial rather than colonial,
but the word *council* must be avoided, since it implied executive powers
that promised more than could be delivered.

The only conference topic Laurier considered seriously was preferential access to the British market, and here, too, he had his own agenda.
Until Britain renounced or renegotiated its trade treaties with Germany and Belgium, with their web of "most favoured nation" clauses,
it would be impossible for Britain to benefit from Canada's 1897 jubilee gift of preferential access to the Canadian market unless the same
access were granted to all "most favoured nations" triggered by these
treaties. During the 1897 conference Laurier had challenged Chamberlain to end the Belgian and German treaties, and Chamberlain had
responded by persuading his reluctant British cabinet colleagues to
comply, doing for Laurier what the British government had refused to
do for the Canadian Conservative government in 1894. The measure
freed Canada from its constraints and extended Canada's fiscal autonomy but did little to enhance Britain's access to the Canadian market.

Emboldened by his 1897 victory, Laurier sought to repeat his success
in 1902, to challenge Chamberlain to take the next step and repudiate
Britain's sacred free trade dogma and grant the colonies preferential
access to the British market. Since the 1902 Colonial/Imperial Conference had dashed Chamberlain's dreams of an advisory council and
rejected Seddon's imperial defence force, the colonial secretary feared

that his only real chance to reorganize the Empire was to accept Laurier's bold challenge. Otherwise, without Canada, whom the British saw as "the key to the imperial problem," and some greater agreement among the others, it was difficult to proceed.[19] Consequently, a year after the 1902 conference Chamberlain, having failed to convince his cabinet colleagues to breach their sacred free trade doctrine, quit the British cabinet to campaign for the chimera of an imperial preference. In the words of one author, Laurier had simply lured Chamberlain to his political doom.[20] If so, Laurier had proven a very effective tiger hunter!

Laurier had understood his country's strategic political role and had played his part well, loyally assisted by the ministers who accompanied him to the 1902 conference. Initially Chamberlain and other British politicians discounted Laurier's imperial views as unrepresentative of his country and as a function of his alleged "French Canadian antipathy to any Imperial measure."[21] Sensitive to these British suspicions, Laurier had brought four ministerial advisors with him to the 1902 conference, W.S. Fielding (Finance), William Patterson (Customs), and his two recently minted knights, Sir William Mulock (postmaster-general) and Sir Frederick Borden (Defence), all of whom were interrogated by doubting British statesmen and officials who failed to detect a discernible difference of opinion among them on any of the imperial issues. The ministers formed a solid Canadian front behind their leader.

During the conference Sir Frederick Borden proved a particularly faithful adherent to Laurier's imperial vision. He took every opportunity to elaborate, explain, and defend the prime minister's perspective in his private and public discussions in London. Borden was more than a mere messenger. He shared Laurier's vision of the Empire as an alliance of equal nations under the Crown and considered that less than "complete self-governance" in military affairs "was an anomaly" that "threatened friction" instead of creating "closer relations between Canada and the Mother Country." In his view, self-government was a matter of trust and it would be folly to "set about to substitute an effective co-operation [with] this semblance of coercion," to substitute "a wise autonomy" with a "well-meaning but fatal ... centralized control."[22]

Indeed, Borden went to some pains to promote the cause of "wise autonomy' and to justify its application to Canada's defence policy. Canada's defence of its own territory, he explained to his imperial colleagues, was not an escape from imperial responsibility but an appropriate and practical means to fulfil these responsibilities by assuming an even larger burden for its own defence, thereby relieving an overburdened British taxpayer. The best means of extending Canada's contribution to imperial defence, he suggested, would be to take possession of the British garrisons in Halifax and Esquimalt and assume responsibility for Canadian territorial waters. In his view, jurisdictional disputes over Canadian defence were mischievous and threatened relations "between Canada and the Motherland."[23] Solid imperial relations must be built on mutual trust, respect, and cooperation rather than on distrust, control, and centralization.

Moreover, Borden contended, practical political objections barred any other course. It was just not possible, he warned his British audiences, to persuade Canadians to contribute to the British Navy, given the country's sufficient protection by the Monroe doctrine. And since the Canadian Militia Act restricted jurisdiction and public defence spending to the defence of Canada, any contribution to imperial defence abroad would require public debate and parliamentary approval. And he doubted that Canadians were likely to "tax themselves to maintain the British Navy," not because they opposed imperial defence, but because they did not see how "money would be expended by a Committee in which Canada had no say." It was a question of accountability.[24] It would be better to trust Canadians to determine the nature and extent of their imperial responsibilities.

Borden and Laurier agreed on the nature and virtue of a liberal empire and the folly of centralization. Both believed that "Empire began at home," by Canada assuming full responsibility for the governance of its portion of the Empire.[25] In entrusting Borden with a growing role in imperial relations, Laurier had every confidence that his minister could and would defend their shared vision with intelligence, skill, courage, and tenacity. Laurier appreciated all too well the pitfalls of imperial diplomacy, of London's powerful, sophisticated, and "unrelenting" social dominance, the magnetic appeal of "royalty, aristocracy, and plutocracy" with their constant talk of "Empire, Empire, Empire," all designed to purchase conformity and turn "weak men's heads."[26] But Laurier had seen Sir Frederick in action in London, and he admired Sir Frederick's social skills and style, his tall, "handsome presence and immaculate attire that made him an outstanding figure in all Court and Parliamentary functions."[27] He knew Sir Frederick well, perhaps "more intimately than anyone else" in his cabinet, and respected his "common-sense and splendid executive ability"[28] and his capacity to withstand London's social pressures. In short, Laurier saw his minister as a dependable and effective point man who could defend the borders of the liberal empire.

Cabinet and non-cabinet colleagues soon acknowledged the prime minister's confidence in Sir Frederick and the latter's strategic role in managing the imperial dossier, especially as defence gained an imperative ascendance on the imperial agenda. Lord Minto was among the

first to acknowledge Borden's imperial potential. It was he who had
insisted on Borden's knighthood in 1902, confident of the minister's
imperial credentials. He had also tipped his successor, his brother-
in-law, Lord Grey, to Borden's strategic position within the imperial
nexus. Consequently, when Sir Frederick Pollock visited Ottawa in
October 1905 to solicit support for his "business plan" for imperial
reorganization, Grey invited Borden and Cartwright to a vice-regal
dinner to meet the imperial missionary, the two cabinet ministers he
tagged as the most likely to influence the prime minister on imperial
issues.[29] Although Borden shared Pollock's passion for efficiency and,
like Pollock, appreciated the need for a business-like administration of
the Empire, another imperial apostle, Richard Jebb, was holding court
in Ottawa at the same time, and Jebb's separatist approach to imperialism, his insistence upon partnership and alliance under British hegemony, appealed more to Borden than did Pollack's plan, as Borden was
to demonstrate in subsequent imperial encounters.

Borden's and Laurier's efforts to dilute, diffuse, and stall ambitious
imperial schemes were facilitated greatly by the return to power of the
British Liberals in 1905. Not only were British Liberals less committed
to imperial centralization, but they fielded a succession of well-placed
colonial secretaries, Lord Elgin (1905–08), Lord Crewe (1908–10), and
Lewis Harcourt (1910–15), ready and able to protect their department's
vested interests. Subsequent suggestions calling for the bifurcation
of the Colonial Office or the creation of an executive council chaired
by the British prime minister generated much debate but made little
headway. More difficult to resist were proposals to create a business-
like imperial secretariat to compile statistics within the Colonial Office
or convene functional "subsidiary" meetings on specific issues. Whatever the occasion, Canada could usually count on the Colonial Office's ability to scupper proposals that infringed on the Colonial Office's
administrative territory or on the self-governing dominions' absorption in their own internal affairs, to emasculate the best-laid plans for
a political reorganization of the Empire. Cooperative imperialism was
another matter.

CHAPTER 18

Cooperative Imperial Defence

The one vexatious item on the imperial agenda was defence, which for Canadian politicians was a heavily mined battlefield. In the decade before World War I, imperial defence became the central and most urgent imperial issue, an imperative that no imperial or colonial government could ignore, whatever its political colour. Within Canada, imperial defence was a controversial issue that required skilful management, made more treacherous since many imperialists, even those committed to political and economic union, believed that defence was key to imperial union, not an unreasonable assumption in view of the public's preoccupation with the arms rivalry and the patent need for collective security. Borden's challenge was how to manage a partnership composed of members of unequal power. According to Donald Gordon and R.A. Preston, Borden not only made an important contribution to the resolution of this thorny issue but read the future of imperial military relations more accurately than many of his contemporaries.

Many of Borden's contemporaries, including the British prime minister, Balfour, saw the Committee of Imperial Defence as an exemplary model of British interdepartmental cooperation that might be recast to include colonial representatives or transformed into an imperial council. Others saw it as a prototype Imperial General Staff charged with specific functional responsibilities such as defence planning and coordination.[1] Imperialists' speculations on the imperial potential of the CID fuelled strong opposition in the Canadian cabinet to Borden's CID "membership," which opponents considered another dangerous precedent. Whatever their motives and pretexts, defence became the most promising battleground for imperial integrationists, one in which Borden found himself on the front lines, especially during the imperial councils of 1907, 1909, and 1911.[2]

The battle over imperial governance focused on three interrelated imperial issues: the creation of a Canadian navy, the formation of an Imperial General Staff, and the debate on the uniformity of arms, equipment, and stores. Of these three topics, the creation of a Canadian navy dominated the national and imperial political agendas. Whatever

sympathy British Liberal governments may have felt for colonial autonomy, the maintenance of British military hegemony and its increasingly crippling cost made imperial defence an inescapable obligation
and its funding a pressing financial imperative, a priority that obliged
British governments, Liberal or Conservative, to consider a variety of
ways and means of financing their imperial responsibilities, including
tapping and managing colonial military resources. Their dilemma was
how to secure colonial resources without sharing power or control.

The Admiralty's sense of relative security following the renewal of
the Anglo-Japanese Alliance and the destruction of the Russian fleet
in 1905 was shattered in 1907 by Germany's dramatized ambitious
naval program and the growing realization that Germany's industrial capacity enabled it to outpace its British rival. The Admiralty's
subsequent demands for eight new dreadnoughts a year to maintain a
two-to-one ratio with Germany created a financial and political panic
in Britain that neither party could ignore. The British Liberal government was obliged, therefore, to do what it must to maximize its military resources and enable it to acquit its imperial responsibilities. One
obvious source of financial relief was the expanding, prosperous self-
governing dominions.

Borden sympathized with the British perspective. He believed that
Canada ought to do more to relieve the British taxpayer by assuming
greater financial responsibility for its own defence, an argument he
would repeat time and again to wring funds from his colleagues and
counter British requests for protection money. During the Toronto banquet that Otter had kindly organized in his honour on 28 December
1903 soon after he returned from London, Borden pledged to "relieve
the imperial British taxpayer of every dollar of expense for protecting
Canadian territory."[3] Control of the British garrisons was one means to
honour that pledge, one that was compatible with Canadian political
exigencies and entailed a larger commitment to naval defence. As a
Maritime politician, a shipowner, as well as an active member of the
Navy League, Borden was probably the most consistently committed
advocate for the creation of a "Canadian" navy within Laurier's cabinet, a point that the *Times* remembered in its obituary of Sir Frederick
in 1917.

Borden considered the creation of a naval militia the best way to
launch a Canadian navy. It seemed a manageable financial commitment and a logical extension and complement to Canada's land forces.
He was also fully aware of the anticipated material and political benefits of a navy to his region. Consequently, he endorsed enthusiastically
Laurier's promise during the 1902 Colonial/Imperial Conference to
create a Canadian navy. In his view, the prime minister's commitment

seemed an appropriate and consistent response to the British government's challenge to Canada to match Australia's direct monetary contribution to the Royal Navy.

The Canadian navy that Borden and Laurier imagined in 1902, however, was not the naval force that the subsequent European naval rivalry required, any more than the Ross rifle was the weapon for massive firepower during World War I. What Borden initially had in mind in 1902 was a naval extension of Canada's land forces: in his words, a Canadian "navy as complete as possible, first for local defence," more particularly to patrol the fisheries against American encroachment and to reinforce Canada's claims to territorial sovereignty, "and secondly to co-operate with the Imperial navy."[4] In other words he shared Laurier's assumption that the creation of a Canadian navy entailed a relatively low-cost financial commitment that required little more than the consolidation, reorganization, and extension of Canada's existing naval facilities and resources (the Fisheries Protective Service, docks, signal service, and hydrographical surveys) as well as the creation and development of a militia naval force as provided by the Militia Act of 1868, possibly under Borden's ministerial direction.

Even when it became clear, as it did very shortly, that Laurier's plan for a Canadian navy was to militarize the Department of Marine and Fisheries' Canadian Protective Fisheries Service under the ambitious, imperialistic direction of Raymond Préfontaine, Borden remained one of the Canadian navy's most persistent defenders and advocates. So closely did Borden become associated with the promotion of a Canadian navy within Laurier's cabinet that his political opponents playfully labelled him Canada's "First Lord of the Admiralty."[5] Moreover, he entertained no illusion as to a navy's ultimate use in time of war, given the symbiotic relationship between national and imperial defence. The real question for Borden was the form of governance, not whether Canada was to be responsible for its naval defence. His own preference was clear: a Canadian navy should be unmistakably under Canadian control and its governance should mirror its land defences. This was not an answer that the Admiralty wanted to hear.

After the 1902 Colonial/Imperial Conference, Laurier's government had endeavoured to honour its pledge to assume greater responsibility for its naval defence by creating a modest version of a navy for Canada. In 1902 the government added another cruiser to its Fisheries Protective Service, and in 1904 it ordered two more "modern, high-speed, steel-hulled cruisers, armed with quick firing guns," for its fleet of some twenty vessels, including icebreakers.[6] That same year Préfontaine announced the formation of a naval militia composed of young fishermen and devised a rudimentary training program for its volunteers; he even made plans for a naval academy. Préfontaine's sudden death in 1905, however, retarded further progress.

Although a staunch naval advocate, Louis-Philippe Brodeur, Préfontaine's successor, made little further progress at first in building a Canadian navy, preoccupied as he was by gaining control of his agitated ministry, then in the throws of liquidating the unsavoury legacy of scandal and misuse of money associated with his predecessor's extravagant administration, a nightmare that ended only in 1907 after Justice Walter Cassels's investigation forced the dismissal of the department's deputy minister and the suspension of three other civil servants. By this time Brodeur and his ministry had been overtaken by the rhetoric, the politics, and the technological prerequisites of naval defence, a sea change more radical than Canada or even the Admiralty had anticipated in 1902. Meanwhile Brodeur had failed to capitalize on the Canadian government's acquisition of the Halifax and Esquimalt garrisons to give naval issues a centrality and urgency. The only substantive naval asset derived from the transfer of the garrisons was the acquisition of the British dockyards in Halifax and Esquimalt.

One reason for Sir Frederick's continuing interest in the acquisition of the dockyards was his desire to see the Halifax dockyards transformed into a dynamic regional shipbuilding site. The transfer of the Halifax dockyards, however, was not completed until 10 October 1910, and those surrounding Esquimalt not until 4 May 1911; by this time, Sir Frederick had lost his battle to establish Halifax as the national centre for naval construction. Anxious to make his controversial naval bill more palatable to his Quebec colleagues, the prime minister had persuaded the British firm of Vickers, renamed Canadian Vickers, to locate its production in Montreal. The establishment of the Royal Naval College in Halifax in 1910 was Sir Frederick's consolation prize.

Meanwhile the dreadnought crisis had altered substantially the assumptions and requirements of imperial defence, underscoring the need for highly "specialized naval vessels, especially torpedo-boat destroyers and, before long, submarines,"[7] costly and sophisticated warships beyond the requirements of the Fisheries Protective Service. In this rapidly changing context, Canada's modest, desultory, and increasingly anachronistic naval efforts fell rapidly far short of the Admiralty's more exigent requirements for Canadian or imperial defence. Realistic, coordinated efforts, however, required close consultation and agreement on ships and their placement, as well as closer collaboration between the Royal Navy and its Canadian prototype. In short, these issues entailed questions of constitutional responsibility that only the politicians could resolve.

Sir Frederick Borden (BACK ROW, FAR RIGHT), Laurier's "point man" in London, at the Imperial Conference of 1907. *Courtesy Library and Archives Canada, c8013*

An opportunity to settle these issues came during the 1907 Imperial Conference. Initially Laurier thought the tediously familiar agenda for the proposed conference of so little importance that he considered not attending the meeting at all. He found imperial conferences exhausting, first "an uncomfortable voyage for a poor sailor" and then a social routine that "would wear down a body stronger than mine."[8] In his place he suggested that a few informed and dependable cabinet colleagues, such as Sir Frederick and Finance Minister W.S. Fielding, might attend and negotiate the more controversial and practical issues. The governor general, Lord Grey, however, pressed Laurier to attend the conference, representing it as the British Liberal government's first imperial conference, a "government to government" exchange, a significant moment for change, the conference to be opened by the British prime minister rather than the colonial secretary. In the end Laurier consented to go to London, persuaded that it was an opportunity to chart a new course for the Empire, an occasion when his prestige and authority might well make a difference.

Laurier, together with the Transvaal premier, Louis Botha, had little difficulty identifying and exposing the objections to and contradictions in the Australian-led initiative to remodel imperial governance.

The ensuing theoretical political discussion, with its liberal rhetorical rejection of subordination and its appeals to colonial nationalism, partnership, equality of status, and government-to-government relationships, proved a refreshingly congenial change from previous imperial gatherings. All agreed that specific imperial issues of urgent and collective interest, such as defence or trade, might best be negotiated by irregular, functional, subsidiary conferences rather than by an "irresponsible" council or ministry. The Imperial Conference, too, provided a propitious occasion for more focused discussions of imperial defence, in which Borden represented Canada.[9]

The wisdom of colonial navies was the central subject of the discussions on imperial defence. Borden's position remained unequivocal: Canadian control of its projected navy was non-negotiable. Laurier had made that crystal clear during the 1902 Colonial/Imperial Conference. Canada, Sir Frederick reminded his audience, had quadrupled its expenditures on its land forces during the past ten years and was prepared to do more for its land and naval defences, but on its own terms and in its own time. Throughout these engaged but polite discussions, Sir Frederick "withstood all pressure, much to the chagrin and disgust of the British government," effectively "torpedoing" their agenda.[10] Sir John Fisher, the tactless, remorseless First Sea Lord, was so furious with Canada's intransigence that when the Admiralty began to make plans for Canada's defence, he "would have none of it"; in his view, the Canadians should be left to their own devices, since he regarded them as "an unpatriotic, grasping people, who only stick to us for the good they can get out of us."[11]

Since Canada stuck stubbornly to its position, it was only Australia's discontent with its "unrepresented" monetary contribution to the Royal Navy that had put colonial navies back on the conference's agenda. The Admiralty's decision to assign most of its resources to European waters to protect the British Isles had irritated the Australians and fed their fears and sense of isolation. Determined to revisit Australia's earlier arrangement with the Royal Navy, Australian prime minister Alfred Deakin demanded greater control over the naval squadrons that had been consigned to its protection in return for a direct monetary contribution to the Royal Navy. The adamant Canadian insistence upon complete control of its naval forces made it easier for the Admiralty to concede the Australian demand for local squadrons within the Royal Navy, though it did so somewhat "grudgingly."[12] This concession was short of the Canadian position but still in harmony with the liberal tenor of the 1907 Imperial Conference.

Canada's adoption of the Ross rifle had raised the subject of local self-sufficiency and the uniformity of arms, equipment, and stores.

The War Office had never accepted the Canadian decision, at the time emphasizing the potential difficulties and inconveniences during joint operations, and Borden was obliged to defend that decision once again, which he did skilfully and convincingly. Borden cleverly chose a defensible stance, focusing on self-sufficiency and arguing the strategic wisdom of the dominions establishing a safe, dependable, local source of supplies, arms, and equipment, including the right of local manufacture. Placing his case within the broader context of colonial security, he pointed to the catastrophic colonial consequences should Britain temporarily lose control of the seas, a colonial fear enhanced by the Royal Navy's withdrawal to European waters. And in the end his position largely prevailed: the conference recognized the Empire's dependence on sea power, called upon colonies to maintain sufficient troops for their own self-defence, and endorsed cooperative defence planning, uniformity of ammunition, and the colonial manufacture of small arms.[13]

Even on the question of uniformity Borden imposed conditions for compliance. While he conceded the practical desirability of a uniformity of arms, equipment, and stores, he insisted that their choice be based upon consultation with the dominions, a formidable qualification and an effective barrier given the War Office's reluctance to share information and decision-making or to relinquish control. The War Office's reluctance may have entailed economic considerations, including loss of markets. After some fuller deliberation the War Office reluctantly endorsed the policy of local self-sufficiency for Canada and extended the policy to all the self-governing dominions. Borden had won his point, an apparent victory for the idea of a liberal empire. Nor was it difficult to reach agreement on the principle of uniformity of arms and equipment; more contentious was how to achieve the objective, given Borden's insistence upon consultation.

The War Office's apparent concession of self-sufficiency was made easier by Borden's and the other dominion representatives' agreement to establish an Imperial General Staff, a cadre of senior British and dominion officers that would be charged with planning and coordinating imperial defence requirements. Once again it was not difficult to concur on the obvious importance of planning and coordination and the need for military education and training. But the devil was in the details. Misunderstanding plagued the apparent agreement on the Imperial General Staff from the beginning, their conflicting motives disguised by lack of detail and precision.

In Canada's case the War Office regarded the Imperial General Staff as "a substitute for the service chain of command that had existed between the Canadian GOC and the British commander-in-chief" before Borden's suppression of the GOC position in October 1904 and Britain's abandonment of the Halifax and Esquimalt garrisons.[14] An Imperial General Staff was seen as a means of restoring the War Office's access to intelligence, on a need-to-know basis, as well as of its retaining control and influencing the composition, maintenance, and deployment of the dominion's military resources. An Imperial General Staff also provided an opportunity to educate and proselytize, all of which the War Office defended in the name of imperial unity of military doctrine and training. According to the agreement, five of the Imperial General Staff positions were reserved for incumbents of designated staff positions in the Canada Militia. Their only qualification was that they possess British staff college credentials and eight years of military service.

Borden's initial suspicions that the British plan was but another means to subordinate the Canadian Militia proved well founded. Nevertheless Borden had agreed to the plan, despite his initial reservations, far too precipitately as it turned out. In his view, planning and coordinating imperial defence only made good sense. But it could work only if it were based on understanding, cooperation, and two-way communication. Intelligently employed, an Imperial General Staff might provide Canada with valuable information and advice. It might also serve to educate the imperial authorities on Canadian defence needs and realities much as regional commands of the Canadian Militia were designed to get senior staff officers out of Ottawa.[15]

The Imperial General Staff's primary attraction for Borden, however, was its promise of education for Canadian senior military staff, an essential prerequisite for control and authority within the Canadian Militia and one of the PF's crying deficiencies. Conscious of the force's need for an educated, well-trained senior staff, at one time Borden had even toyed with the idea of creating a Canadian staff college or of mounting a fully-fledged senior staff program at the RMC, to which he was prepared to import imperial officers as instructors. But upon second thought he was convinced of the benefits, above all the cost-effectiveness, of sending Canadians to the British staff college at Camberley, and he was prepared to pay the British a reasonable service fee to cover the expenses of accommodation and instruction. What attracted Borden far too hastily to Canada's membership in the Imperial General Staff was its promise of guaranteed access to Camberley, since the possession of British staff college credentials was a prerequisite for membership in the Imperial General Staff.

Borden soon recognized the incompatibility of his and the War Office's objectives. While Britain and the dominions had all agreed on the desirability of an Imperial General Staff during the 1907 Imperial Conference, the question of how it was to work occupied relatively little of their attention. In his defence Borden contended that when he and Laurier had agreed to an Imperial General Staff to advise the imperial forces on the Empire's defence, their agreement had been conditional upon the War Office's respect for Canada's military autonomy.[16] But if this were so, it was not a condition that the War office had registered, understood, or accepted. On the contrary, the War Office saw the Imperial General Staff as a unit controlled and commanded by senior British Army officers who regarded colonial forces as a mere auxiliary to the British Army. Consequently, the War Office insisted upon the right to communicate directly with all members of the Imperial General Staff residing within the Empire, requesting information and offering counsel, short-circuiting their immediate colonial military superior and the civilian minister. Moreover, the War Office's requirement that membership in the Imperial General Staff be restricted to those who had been trained by their staff, namely those who possessed British staff college credential and eight years of service, limited whom Canada might appoint to the five designated, strategic positions within its Militia.

Borden's opposition to the War Office's assumptions was fundamental. He, like his compatriot Joseph Howe, saw Canadians as Britons overseas, with all their rights and responsibilities, willing to manage their own affairs and capable of doing so, asking for nothing more but satisfied with nothing less. Borden never tired of pointing out that he was ready to "work out in conjunction with the Home authorities and the representatives of other British Dominions" schemes for their common defence, but he adamantly refused to accept any "well-meaning but fatal return to a centralized control."[17] He had not fought for years to establish Canadian ministerial control over the Militia to have control subverted or short-circuited by myopic War Office officials. He had no intention of permitting the War Office to communicate directly with senior Canadian officers or of restricting the selection of this senior staff by denying them membership in the Imperial General Staff.

Initially Borden endeavoured to negotiate these issues by correspondence. Impatient with the painfully slow pace and rigidity of his correspondence with the War Office, Borden sought a political solution. A good sailor with indefatigable energy, he decided to go to London and appeal directly to the British secretary of war, Richard Haldane. On 15 January 1909 he met with Haldane, the Army Council, and Major-General John Charles Hood of Australia to discuss his "certain difficulties" with the administration of the Imperial General Staff. All agreed immediately on the obvious: that the mission of the Imperial General Staff was to ensure that all the forces of the Empire be organized on the same principles; that there be a uniformity of training; that Camberley be recognized as "the central school of military education for the Empire"; that there be uniformity in officers' curriculum and examination; and that there be comparable job descriptions for staff officers.[18]

More intractable was the issue of communications and credentials. The British soon learned, however, that on these issues they "could not push Borden too far."[19] Confident of his position, Borden realized that Canada held the key to the Imperial General Staff's success or failure: Canada's absence would emasculate the project; and what Canada did, others were likely to follow. He also knew that he had bipartisan support for his position. Consequently, faced by the War Office's intransigence, Borden broke the impasse by simply threatening to create a Canadian general staff, a threat that the War Office considered "tantamount to a declaration of military independence." To avoid this "frightful" eventuality, the War Office decided to compromise on the subject of communications.[20] The parties agreed that in the future all communications between the Imperial General Staff and its local members would be copied to the minister and that all information submitted by the Canadian Imperial Staff members to the War Office would require the minister's concurrence, a victory applauded by the Conservative Opposition, which shared Borden's concern to prevent the Imperial General Staff from issuing orders to its Canadian members. This arrangement, however, resolved only one of the two contentious issues. The War Office remained adamant on the credentials required for membership in the Imperial General Staff.

Borden was on shaky ground in pursuing the subject of credentials. After all, he had agreed to the staff college and military service qualification. For Borden, education had been one of the Imperial General Staff's most attractive features. At the time he had failed to appreciate its implications. However, as his deputy minister, Dr Eugene Fiset, forcefully reminded him upon his return from London, British and staff college service qualifications would limit the pool of eligible Canadian candidates for the senior positions designated for membership in the Imperial General Staff. These constraints, Fiset pointed out, were at variance with Borden's policy of opening senior positions to serving Canadian officers and especially Boer War veterans, since many potential candidates for the designated senior posts lacked these service and staff college credentials and were unlikely to secure them.

Unable to persuade the War Office to amend or violate the agreement, once again Borden resorted to direct action. He called the War Office's bluff by simply appointing "unqualified" Canadians to the designated imperial staff positions in the Canadian Militia, forcing the

War Office to accept his appointees or emasculate the Imperial General Staff. The War Office refused to give way, and in 1909 the issue reached ludicrous proportions when General William Otter, Canada's distinguished officer commanding Canada's first Boer War contingent, was appointed Canada's chief of the general staff, one of the designated positions for inclusion in the Imperial General Staff, but since Otter lacked the staff college qualification, the British refused to recognize him as a member of the Imperial General Staff. As a result of all these difficulties, the Imperial General Staff remained "stillborn," to use the words of the late C.P. Stacey.[21]

Although changing technological needs, more particularly the small and faster torpedo, might argue for local navies,[22] the Admiralty had as much difficulty accepting the reality and symbolism of a divided imperial fleet as the War Office had in seeing Canada and other dominions as anything but subordinate commands of the British Army. Despite the British Liberal politicians' endorsement of a liberal empire during the 1907 Imperial Conference, the War Office and the Admiralty remained unconvinced, and it was not until the 1911 Imperial Conference that the Admiralty accepted the principle of independent navies. In the months that followed the 1907 Imperial Conference, the Admiralty and the War Office simply sought other ways and means to retain control, dictate policy, and influence people, including an appeal to public sentiment. The dramatic dreadnought crisis provided a prime opportunity to feed public apprehension and corral and direct colonial opinion through fear and favour, a ploy that one author has described as a "game of brinkmanship with the Dominions."[23]

As H.V. Nelles has pointed out, the Royal Navy's powerful presence during the Quebec City tercentenary celebrations in 1908, notably the visit of eight of its impressive warships from the Atlantic fleet (among them the recently launched *Indomitable,* carrying the Prince of Wales), was a very "tangible way of inspiring greater Canadian awareness of the naval problem" and its urgency and of framing the crisis within an imperial context. The Royal Navy's dominant presence at the celebrations offered a stark contrast to the two French warships and the one American warship that were also present. Altogether the Royal Navy offered a naval spectacle at Quebec designed to advertise imperial power, instil pride, underline Canadian vulnerability and encourage some greater Canadian contribution to the maintenance of imperial power.[24] In March 1909 the Admiralty resorted to even more sensational methods, announcing publicly the extent of its growing disadvantage in its naval rivalry with Germany and emphasizing Germany's industrial capacity to outpace British naval construction. This challenge to British naval superiority threatened to cut Canada and the rest of the Empire from its chief line of security. New Zealand and Australia responded immediately with offers of direct material assistance; New Zealand was ready to contribute a dreadnought.

In contrast, Canada responded to the Admiralty's dire announcement with an artfully crafted parliamentary resolution that captured a temporary, fragile, bipartisan Canadian consensus on imperial defence. The resolution, moved on 29 March 1909 by George Eulas Foster, the venerable Conservative frontbencher, and seconded by Laurier, called for "any necessary expenditure designed to promote the organization of a Canadian naval service." Although the resolution pledged Canada's "loyal and hearty co-operation to maintain the integrity and honour of the empire," it rejected any monetary contributions to the imperial treasury as a limitation upon its responsible government.[25] In place of a monetary contribution Canada agreed to assume a larger portion of its own defence, "as its resources increase," and to create a naval service along the lines to be suggested by the Royal Navy. These commitments were designed to support British naval supremacy, which the parliamentarians unanimously agreed was a condition of Canadian security and the peace of the world, altogether a liberal imperialist credo. Encouraged by the Canadian resolution, the Admiralty and the War Office responded immediately, hoping to use the imperial moment to advantage.

To capitalize on the colonial reaction to the German scare, a few weeks after the Canadian resolution, the British government proposed calling a subsidiary imperial defence conference (as provided for by the 1907 Imperial Conference) to discuss the best means of implementing the Canadian resolution and employing the Australian and New Zealand offers of material assistance. Laurier agreed immediately to the proposed conference, on the condition that Borden and Brodeur, not he, represent Canada. Even before the imperial invitation, the Canadian ministers had planned to go to London as soon as possible to discuss with the Admiralty the best method of fulfilling the mandate of the Canadian parliamentary resolution. Although Borden and Brodeur had planned to meet with Admiralty officials in June, they had no difficulty postponing their visit until late July or early August 1909 in order to participate in the proposed subsidiary imperial conference.[26] Since the issues to be discussed were considered technical or quasi-technical, the Colonial Office agreed that other dominions might wish to follow the Canadian example and send their defence ministers as well.

Laurier had some apprehension about the outcome of the conference, fearful lest a "big effort will be made to bring us into the maelstrom." Nevertheless he was confident that Borden and Brodeur would "weather the storm successfully."[27] His confidence was not misplaced, but since the conference did not confine itself to naval issues, the ministers confronted a more onerous task than they had anticipated. The two ministers reached London on 16 July 1909, accompanied by their senior advisors, Major-General Percy Lake and Rear Admiral C.E. Kingsmill. Sir Frederick, as the senior defence minister, familiar with imperial men and issues and with a penchant for social diplomacy, led the Canadian delegation.

Conscious of his larger role and the power of public communications in setting the agenda, Borden sought every opportunity before and during the conference to create a sympathetic Canadian context for his "private and consultative" official discussions. As the guest speaker at the Guildhall banquet on 20 July, Borden praised the virtues of the liberal empire that "led nations along the lines of development of their own resources," explaining that Canada's imperial sentiment rested not "on material fiscal advantages" but on its commitment to rights and freedoms that could best be defended by preparing itself "for local defence."[28] Five days later he elaborated this theme during an interview with the London *Standard,* assuring the British public of Canada's desire to assume greater responsibility for its naval defences, including the control of the British dockyards at Halifax and Esquimalt, and repeatedly reminding his audience of the Canadian parliamentary bipartisan insistence on Canada's "absolute control over its own actions."[29] To reassure those who doubted Canada's military capacity for self-defence, Borden assured members attending the inaugural banquet of the British Empire Club, held at the United Service Club on 5 August, that Canada was capable of putting 50,000 men into the field immediately and within a few weeks another 50,000.[30] As a result of these public interventions, Borden had made Canada's position quite clear even before the meetings began.

The conference opened at the Foreign Office on 28 July 1909 with Lord Crewe, the colonial secretary, in the chair and in the presence of Reginald McKenna, the First Lord of the Admiralty, and Richard B. Haldane, the secretary of state for war. The British prime minister, Herbert H. Asquith, welcomed and addressed the delegates, inviting them to attend a meeting of the Committee of Imperial Defence to be briefed on the menacing German rivalry, a gesture designed to suggest a sharing of power.[31] During the first working meeting at the conference, Haldane seized the opportunity to revisit the question of imperial integration and focus the discussion, asking delegates to respond to three questions: Was each part of the Empire ready to coordinate its preparation for war? Ought an imperial war establishment be fixed and Britain and each of her dominions prepare its forces to enable it to mobilize for a common imperial purpose? And ought they to adopt uniformity of patterns for arms, equipment, and stores? After formal responses from each of the principal colonial delegates, a subcommittee chaired by the British Army's chief of the general staff, Sir William Nicholson, discussed the more detailed technical questions with the delegations' senior advisors.

From the opening of the conference until its closing, Sir Frederick deviated little from the classic Canadian position, frequently invoking the authority of Laurier and the language of the recent Canadian Commons motion. He assured his imperial colleagues that he realized that "local defence and Imperial defence are very largely one and the same thing," and if "the Empire falls, we fall as a result."[32] Consequently, his response to Haldane's first question was an enthusiastic yes; in his view, it was only common sense to organize Canadian defences in consultation with the imperial army. The proof of his faith in joint military planning and cooperation was his endorsement of Canada's membership in an Imperial General Staff. At the same time he reminded the War Office and the Admiralty that Canada's commitment to imperial defence meant largely the defence of its own territory (including its territorial waters), the construction of rails and docks, and fisheries protection. Moreover, as Canada's wealth permitted, Canadians intended to assume greater financial responsibility for the country's defences; Canada's military expenditures had already increased ten times during the past decade.

If Borden's response to Haldane's first question was positive and congenial, his reply to the second was forthright and blunt. He reminded the conference that during the 1902 Colonial/Imperial Conference, both he and Sir Wilfrid had opposed Sir Joseph Ward's resolution to create an imperial force composed of troops from Britain and its dominions. From the Canadian perspective the proposal was fraught with practical difficulties and constitutional objections. Since the 1902 conference, Canada's bipartisan Commons resolution had reinforced the country's position. While there was no question that Canada was ready to commit troops to Europe or to "any war in which the Empire is interested," Canada would do so only after parliamentary approval, since "we are not bound to take part if we do not wish to do so."[33]

The third question received a similar response. In 1907 Canada's support of the uniformity of arms, supplies, and equipment was conditional upon consultation and consent. Canada's position had not changed: Canada found unobjectionable the principal of uniformity of arms, supplies, and equipment so long as the War Office agreed to consult the dominions before adopting a particular design. Altogether Borden had articulated the classic Canadian case and defended it with skill and firmness, selectively employing the bipartisan Commons resolution to reinforce his case, one that the British could scarcely dismiss as unrepresentative of Canada.

Borden and Brodeur's chief business, however, was with the Admiralty, since that was their principal reason to be in London. The Commons resolution had called for the creation of a "real" Canadian navy in consultation with the Admiralty, and both men were anxious to lay its foundations. The Admiralty, however, possessed little faith in a Canadian navy, committed as they were to an undivided, paramount imperial fleet supported by direct colonial monetary contributions. Consequently, in its formal meeting with the colonial delegates on the 3rd, 5th, and 6th of August and before consenting to engage in specific bilateral discussions, the Admiralty, elated by colonial reactions to the naval scare, had disparaged the strategic wisdom of colonial navies. In pressing its case for an undivided imperial fleet, the Admiralty denigrated the utility of what it labelled "two-penny-half-penny" colonial navies, composed of small ships unable to "protect local interests if the main British fleet were destroyed," especially navies whose legal jurisdiction was confined to territorial waters, a political issue that was not resolved until 1911.[34] But despite the Admiralty's arguments neither Canada nor Australia relented, each stubbornly insisting upon control of its own naval forces.

The Imperial Defence Committee's briefing on the German situation never really convinced Borden. He shrewdly saw the naval scare as little more than a British "electoral device."[35] Still, his own vision of a Canadian navy had evolved well beyond that of a militarized fisheries protection service. Canada, he assured the conference, understood fully the requirements of specialized, modern naval warfare and was willing to assume its financial responsibilities for its own naval defence, not only by acquiring modern warships but also by constructing large docks and coaling stations, including docking facilities to accommodate dreadnoughts. Invoking the authority of Sir Wilfrid, Borden assured the Admiralty that imperial unity and local autonomy were not antithetical; in his words, they "must go hand and hand." Imperial unity could best be obtained through communications, consultation, and cooperation, not through centralization and control.[36]

In anticipation of Canadian and Australian objections to a direct contribution to the Royal Navy, the Admiralty held in reserve a plan B that envisaged colonial construction and control of fleet units that would be integrated into the Royal Navy in wartime, since colonial jurisdiction ended outside territorial waters. According to the Admiralty's plan, a fleet unit would consist of one dreadnought battle cruiser, three small cruisers, and six destroyers, including submarines. Altogether the unit would cost £3,695,000 to construct and about £172,000 per annum to maintain, figures designed to scare colonial legislatures into better behaviour. While its sense of insecurity made Australia more amenable to the compromise on the fleet unit, Canada rejected the Admiralty's plan B, determined to construct its own navy at its own pace. Only after the general discussion on the strategic wisdom of colonial navies reached this denouement did the Admiralty arrange a meeting with the Canadian ministers to discuss their specific requirements.

For the Canadian ministers, these meeting with the Committee of Imperial Defence and the Admiralty were the most useful. The Admiralty opened the conversation by reiterating its own one-fleet agenda, hoping that it might achieve through bilateral discussion what it had failed to obtain during the multilateral conference. Only after the Admiralty's suggestion that Canada might contribute a dreadnought died stillborn did the Admiralty reveal the "Canadian" version of its plan B, its fleet unit proposal. What it proposed was that Canada establish its own naval unit on the Pacific coast but entrust the protection of the Atlantic coast to the "great navy," without specifying precisely the nature of the protection that Canada might expect to receive. Borden and Brodeur immediately detected several major faults with the Admiralty's proposal. First and conspicuously, it failed to promise a precise, physical presence on the Atlantic coast, so essential to the protection of the fisheries and the maintenance of public support for naval expenditures, and given the Admiralty's preoccupation with European waters, its North Atlantic presence was unlikely to be very extensive or visible.[37] Second, whatever its size and composition, the British fleet's presence threatened to duplicate and create confusion on the Atlantic coast, where Canada was obliged to maintain an effective Fisheries Protective Service against American encroachment. Third, both Borden and Brodeur feared that the Admiralty's scheme implied a direct Canadian monetary contribution to the Royal Navy for its Atlantic services, an implication that flew in the face of the recent Commons resolution. Their fears were fed by the Admiralty's suggestion that Canada might consider building a dreadnought similar to the celebrated *Indomitable* (reputed to cost £231,500).[38] Consequently, Borden and Brodeur flatly rejected the Admiralty's proposal for practical, political, and constitutional reasons.

Only after the Canadians rejected its first proposal did the Admiralty revert to its final solution, a naval unit that could be integrated readily into the Royal Navy in wartime, a revised Canadian version of its plan B. The result was an ambiguous compromise of sorts. Borden and Brodeur recognized the strategic good sense of a coordinated, compatible imperial naval strategy, but continued to insist on a two-coast Canadian navy and Canadian command and deployment of its naval

forces, to mirror its land forces. In turn they accepted the Admiralty's proposed composition for a Canadian navy, namely a fleet unit of
three cruisers and four destroyers but preferably four cruisers and six
destroyers, a unit designed to form part of "an Imperial flying squadron of eight battleships and cruisers" during war, under the command
of the Royal Navy, since Canada as yet possessed no constitutional
jurisdiction beyond its territorial waters.[39] The Canadian ministers also
welcomed the Admiralty's offer to loan Canada two training cruisers,
the *Niobe* for the Atlantic coast and the *Rainbow* for the Pacific, until
the proposed full fleet unit was commissioned, vessels that they optimistically described as a "floating staff college for Canadian youth"
that would safeguard Canadian waters and be a visible presence in
Canadian ports.[40]

Similarly, to assure a seamless integration during wartime, the Canadian ministers accepted the Admiralty's offer to assist with the formation of Canada's naval personnel. This gift from the Admiralty gave the
Royal Navy greater influence in shaping the Canadian navy than either
minister might have anticipated or desired.[41] With these plans and
promises in hand, Borden and Brodeur returned to Canada ready to
translate their plans into realities. Although the primary responsibility
for this task belonged to Brodeur as minister for naval affairs, a title he
assumed in May 1910, Sir Frederick remained an interested accomplice,
and as it turned out, Brodeur needed all the help he could muster.

Borden and Brodeur's battle with the Admiralty was child's play
compared to the struggle they and their party faced at home when Laurier moved a second reading of the naval bill in February 1910, a bill to
build a navy "if possible in Canada." The bill proposed a naval force
of eleven ships to be built over five years, four Bristols, one Broadicea,
and six destroyers. In introducing the bill, Laurier concentrated his
remarks on the political and constitutional context and implications
of the proposed legislation, exploiting as best he could the political
divisions that had fractured the Conservative Party since the parties
reached a fragile, bipartisan parliamentary unanimity on the subject,
unable to resist taunting the Conservatives for their apparent change
of policy.

Assuming the rhetoric of a liberal imperialist, Laurier described
Canada as "a nation within the British empire," a "daughter nation of
England," ready to assume its responsible place within the imperial
family,[42] along the lines unanimously agreed upon in the bipartisan
resolution of almost a year ago. In Laurier's view, experience and
authority suggested the wisdom of a decentralized, autonomous body
as opposed to a centralized force concentrated in European waters. In
choosing autonomy, the prime minister reminded his colleagues of the

Australian experience, how they had abandoned their 1902 agreement to make a direct contribution to the Royal Navy in favour of creating their own naval squadron, and reinforced his case by citing Lord Milner's preference for "individual defences."[43]

A week later came Sir Frederick's turn. His intervention occupied the better part of the afternoon and evening session. Since Brodeur was ill, Sir Frederick, whom the Opposition liked to call Canada's "First Lord of the Admiralty and Minister of Militia," seconded Laurier's motion, and thoroughly briefed by the Ministry of Marine and Fisheries, he responded to the more technical, military, and financial issues. Borden's intervention deviated little from that of his chief, whom he applauded for his "well known devotion, loyalty and unswerving patriotism," and whose vision of Canada he shared, "one of the great dominions that make up the galaxy of nations constituting this great empire." In a very personal reference he also reminded the House that he, too, had "made sacrifices for Empire."[44] Then, following Laurier's lead, Borden needled the Opposition, chiding them for the "domestic infelicity in their political home" since the bipartisan parliamentary resolution.

According to Sir Frederick, the bipartisan parliamentary resolution calling for the "speedy organization of a Canadian naval service" had remained intact until the Conservative leader, Robert Borden, returned to Canada from London in the summer of 1909. During his sojourn in the imperial capital, the Conservative leader had consistently and tenaciously defended the parliamentary resolution. But during his absence fractures began to appear in his party's unity. Some Conservative imperialists, spooked by the naval panic, believed that Britain's need was real and immediate; others, such as Frederick Monk and some of the Conservative Quebec nationalists, increasingly working in tandem with Henri Bourassa, felt that anything more than a fisheries protection service would create a target rather than a shield and render any Canadian naval unit liable for imperial service. Upon his return from London, Robert Borden had established temporary peace and order in his party by enunciating a new gloss on his naval policy on 3 February 1910. In moving a parliamentary motion deploring the government's refusal to commit Canada's naval forces to those of the Empire, Robert Borden called upon Canada to confine itself to the maintenance of an effective fisheries protective service until the more ambitious project of a Canadian navy was submitted to the people; meanwhile Canada ought to make a monetary contribution to the Royal Navy. Conscious of his cousin's sore spots, his political and emotional commitment to a Canadian navy (especially popular in his Halifax constituency), his fondness for consistency, and his insistence on fiscal accountability, Sir Frederick chided the Conservative leader for changing his mind, backtracking on a Canadian navy, and wishing to contribute $25 million to the British treasury without any control, altogether a policy contrary to the language and spirit of the bipartisan resolution.

Sir Frederick's participation in the Imperial Naval Conference the previous summer enabled him to respond with precision and authority to his opponents' charge that Canada's policy ran counter to effective imperial defence. His detailed account of the proceedings of the "private and consultative" meetings with other colonial delegates and his and Brodeur's meetings with the Admiralty were accurate renditions though not entirely forthright, since he chose to report the conclusions reached in the discussions rather than the preferences of the imperial authorities, leaving the impression that the Canadian decision was "consistent with the Admiralty's desires."[45] And when the Opposition endeavoured to exploit discrepancies in the cost estimates provided by Sir Frederick and the prime minister during the debate on the bill and later in the Commons' Committee of Supply, Laurier playfully dismissed the objection, assuring the House that "[m]y hon. Friend [Sir Frederick Borden] is always right. I am likely to be the one in the wrong"; and on questions of figures, the prime minister was probably correct.[46]

Controversy over the naval bill, however, intensified. While Brodeur's recovery and return to the House shifted the onus for its defence from Borden to Brodeur, Borden retained an unwavering political interest in the creation of a Canadian navy, continuing his losing crusade to make Halifax the national centre for naval construction, a project in which he possessed the hearty support of his cousin, the Conservative leader. Robert Borden's support, however, may have been a liability, since Halifax was his constituency and few Liberals had any interest in aiding his re-election.

Sir Frederick's last imperial conference had all the appearances of a personal coronation, a recognition and reward for a decade or more of imperial service. Called for the summer of 1911 on the occasion of the coronation of George V, the Imperial Conference was opened by British Prime Minister H.H. Asquith. His celebratory remarks on the health and power of the Empire set the self-congratulatory tone of the gathering, a tone that offered a striking contrast to the frightening rhetoric of the two previous imperial conferences. The British prime minister's cheerful optimism appeared to vindicate Borden's refusal to be stampeded by the naval scare and the government's deliberate insistence on cooperative imperialism rather than control and centralization.

The Imperial Conference's familiar agenda and the distinction of its chief participants enhanced its congenial nature. In attendance was Laurier, at the height of his power and influence, who had little dif-

ficulty managing the agenda. By now a familiar figure in the imperial
capital, Sir Frederick moved with ease and assurance among the influential men of the government and the city. During the preceding fifteen
years he had presided over a significant reform of Canada's land forces,
preparing them for home defence and imperial service. He and his colleagues had honoured their promise to create a Canadian navy. So confident and entrenched in power did he appear that he had brought his
friend, the Conservatives' chief military critic, Sam Hughes, "not quite
captive" to the imperial capital, as an advisor. During the conference,
the legal status of the Canadian navy, whose jurisdiction was confined
to the three-mile territorial limit, was finally resolved with the decision
to permit its deployment outside territorial waters.

For Sir Frederick the crowning event of his 1911 visit to England
was the Dominion Day eve celebrations at Canada House, the occasion Laurier chose to announce publicly Lord Strathcona's resignation
as high commissioner and his choice of Sir Frederick Borden to succeed him. For years Sir Frederick had coveted this position.[47] Twice
he had refused the lieutenant-governorship of Nova Scotia, content to
wait for this, the most important post in the gift of the Canadian government. The high commissionership was an opportunity to combine
social advancement, public service, and business, to be more removed
from the harsh, harrying, and tedious realities of partisan scrutiny.
And it was a position that placed a strong premium on gentlemanly
credentials.

CHAPTER 19

Gentleman Capitalist

Sir Frederick's long-sought reward of the high commissionership not only recognized his political service, but his knowledge of and ability to manage the sensitive imperial agenda, including its demanding ceremonial and social obligations. At the same time it provided Sir Frederick with an opportunity to advance his personal, social, and economic interests. Lord Strathcona's illustrious career created expectations and suggested the possibilities, but Sir Frederick was no Lord Strathcona, whose wealth and influence purchased silence, complicity, and influence in the imperial capital. Sir Frederick's wealth and career pattern were closer to that of his old political rival, Sir Charles Tupper, who had preceded Strathcona in the office of high commissioner. An examination of Sir Frederick's motives to succeed Strathcona and the strategies he employed to obtain the high commissionership reveals the scope of his ambitions. It also suggests the character and chemistry of social and economic power in the imperial capital.

As David Cannadine has written, the British Empire was "first and foremost a class act,"[1] an ordered, layered, hierarchical social structure designed to replicate British society. It consciously pursued its objectives after the loss of the thirteen colonies through constitutional arrangements, land and immigration policies, titles, ceremonies, and other forms of "ornamentalism." Increasingly during the late nineteenth and early twentieth centuries, the creation and/or revival of coded English forms and customs and their export to the Empire were designed to bridge the centre and periphery to create a transcendent sense of community and imperial belonging. Valued and pursued by colonial politicians, the use and meaning of imperial recognition and titles were adapted to personal needs and local realities.

Few would dispute that wealth was a primary condition of power and influence in Sir Frederick's real and created British world. A relatively successful regional entrepreneur, Borden's entrepreneurial success nevertheless paled in comparison to the exceptional business careers of some contemporary Canadian business tycoons such as Sir Henry Mill Pellatt, Sir Joseph Flavelle, Sir William Mackenzie, Sir Donald Mann, and Sir Max Aitken. At the time of his death Sir Frederick's real and personal wealth had an estimated value of $300,000.[2] If one were to assume that $300,000 was an accurate measure of his material legacy, this amount is less than double the dollar value that he had placed upon his total assets about twenty years before, that is to say $186,000. In other words, between the years 1895 and 1917 the value of Borden's assets appeared to grow at an annual rate of only 2.4 per cent; whereas the annual gross national product during these years grew at an average of 4.2 per cent.

What makes Sir Frederick's apparent financial failure particularly striking is that he had been minister of militia and defence during fifteen of these years, a period of unprecedented economic expansion and opportunity, punctured by recessions in 1903, 1907, and 1913–15. Characterized by incestuous relationships between business and politics, this period offered a venial politician ample opportunity to maximize his assets. Indeed, W.S. Fielding, Borden's fellow Nova Scotia cabinet colleague, considered political morality so low during these years that he informed the governor general that several of his colleagues deserved jail sentences rather than positions of public trust.[3] It is unclear whether Fielding had Borden in mind. Certainly virtue does not explain Borden's apparent lack of success.

Borden himself often spoke, even boasted, of his chronic "impecuniousness," sometimes as a means to purchase sympathy for a deferred payment or to deflate expectations.[4] His estimated worth at death, however, may be misleading: it may be only a partial indication of his wealth and assets, and a crude measure of his success as an entrepreneur. For example, his estimated wealth takes no account of his personal expenditures, the costs of public life, his transfer of assets to his wife and daughters before his death, or the property that may have fallen outside the purview of estate executors. As Michael Bliss points out in his biography of George Albertus Cox, a political and business associate of Sir Frederick's, the $870,000 evaluation of Cox's estate at his death in 1914 is scarcely a "true indicator of real wealth he had accumulated."[5] One measure of Borden's personal expenditures is his car, which cost between $1,200 and $1,400, the equivalent of a school principal's annual salary;[6] Borden's was one of only 3,033 privately owned automobiles in Canada in 1908. Similarly, Borden's disposal of his interest in the New Brunswick Cold Storage scheme, which he turned over to his son-in-law, reminds us that he distributed assets to members of his immediate family before his death. Among these assets were his daughters' Ottawa residences.[7] In short, Borden's failure might have been more apparent than real and have disguised or understated his entrepreneurial success.[8] Precisely how much wealth he acquired is less important than how he used it and what its employment reveals of his self-image, values, and aspiration.

Implicit in the notion of Borden's business failure is the assumption that a businessperson's single objective is the maximization of assets. But as P.L. Payne pointed out many years ago in his study of the failure of British nineteenth-century entrepreneurs, the "pig principle"[9] fails to account for a person's values and goals and the price a person will pay to obtain non-material objectives. Even Adam Smith recognized that it "was not wealth that men desire, but the consideration and good opinions that wait upon riches."[10] While many Canadian public men at the time may have agreed that politics was about business, for others it was about something more than business. It was about what Thorstein Veblen called "human nature," about purchasing recognition, power, and position.[11]

Borden, for one, regarded politics as much more than business. In his very British world, he, like many nineteenth-century British entrepreneurs, sought recognition and status, an enhanced place in his society, which he and they displayed through a process of gentrification. And he, like they, employed many strategies to achieve that objective, including conspicuous consumption, gracious living, philanthropy, and public service, the material and the symbolic bonds and attributes of class. Among their goals, values, and attributes were titles, landed estates, great houses, political power, and other "non-economic ends," all forms of "symbolic capital."[12] In Britain and elsewhere a strategic display of wealth constituted an important means to establish, maintain, and remind others of one's credentials within the gentry, a material means to demonstrate one's power and claim to deference, even when it constituted a constraint and drain on an aspirant's financial resources. Although Sir Frederick may well have envied the wealth of the Toronto magnates Pellatt, Mackenzie, and Mann, he spent little time agonizing over his own comparative failure. He realized that ostentation alone, "even fake chateaux overlooking the smoky sprawl of a great Canadian city," might not purchase social standing.

Complementary attributes were important and often essential to gentrification.[13] Non-economic ends, education, social and cultural obligations, comportment, language, dress, manners, and pedigree also mattered as reminders of and a means to purchase a person's place and power. If education and the liberal professions, especially law and medicine, were class markers in nineteenth-century British society,[14] Sir Frederick's credentials were impeccable. Sir Frederick, his father, both his wives, all three of his children, and his two sons-in-law possessed formal secondary education, and he, his father, and his son were educated as physicians, an occupation enjoying an enhanced status within society.

Another class marker was public service. Since Britain's vaunted genius for self-governance and the rule of others remained the monopoly of its ruling class, in the late nineteenth century its aspiring gentry regarded public service as a means to exercise power and purchase, claim, justify, and display recognition and social legitimacy, values that had been instilled in Borden at home and at school.[15] But as Payne has pointed out, public service was a vocation that required commitment, time, and resources, and "inevitably involved a haemorrhage of entrepreneurial talent,"[16] choices that Borden and other aspiring gentry chose to make, in Borden's case encouraged by his Anglican hierarchical formation and admonition.

Public service became a form of patriotism in the nineteenth-century British world. In Canada an expanding, protected national economy and a growing positive state that increasingly subsumed limited identities fuelled a more comprehensive sense of belonging, one that enhanced the visibility, valorization, and conflation of the state and public service, making civic participation a form of patriotism. As Anthony D. Smith has pointed out, patriotism's conflation with nationalism provided many nineteenth-century persons with non-material objectives, including self-fulfilment, identity, and a sense of community and belonging. To them a nation or an empire constituted a "superfamily," a secular substitute for religion, and a "way to surmount the finality of death."[17]

In their desire to transcend "oblivion through posterity,"[18] people sought continuity through commemoration, public memory, and "historicism."[19] They were fascinated by genealogy, by a search for roots that offered authenticity, legitimacy, and authority, represented by titles, heraldry, customs, ceremonies, rituals, and traditions, the forms of "Victorian medievalism" so popular among members of the British ruling class before the Great War and often seen as the ruling class's means to bind the newly enfranchised classes to itself to legitimate their natural right to rule.[20] Rich aspiring gentry revelled in titles, built country estates, dressed in courtly attire, collected art and armour, and read romantic history and tales of knights and chivalry.

Borden, too, possessed a special interest in family genealogy, his own and others. According to one of his eulogists, Sir Frederick "knew more of the genealogy of the older families of his native county than any living man, and hour after hour he would trace out genealogies."[21] One of the highlights of his visit to Britain in 1900 to recover from his son's death was his pilgrimage to the ancestral village of Burden, in Kent, where his first English ancestor reputedly had received land in

The "AUSPICIUM
MELIORIS AEVI"
[omen for a better time]
on Sir Frederick's coat of
arms may have referred
to life after Harold's
death. *Courtesy Kenneth
MacKay and Julia Leslie
Green MacKay*

the wake of William the Conqueror and where the "de Burdens" of Sit-
tingbourne, Kent, had built "the original family mansion in the 1300s."
It was during this pilgrimage that Borden, intrigued by his family's
"noble origins," commissioned a family pedigree from a Mr J.A. Glen,
a copy of which he sent to his childless cousin Robert Borden, who
appeared to share his cousin's interest in family genealogy and to
accept Sir Frederick's family hegemony.[22] In this reconstituted late
nineteenth-century age of Camelot, Norman pedigree was particularly
desirable for those who aspired to rule!

In 1908 Sir Frederick went further and obtained his family coat of
arms from the Herald of Arms. Subsequently he had the family coat
of arms reproduced as nameplates for the books in his extensive personal library.[23] Whether Borden's interest in ancestry was shaped by a
post-Darwinian respect for genetics, status anxiety, a quest for continu-

ity and order in a disordered world, the commercial class's self-feudal-ization, or some other explanation, he went to considerable lengths to establish his lineage and through it to affirm and reinforce the legitim-acy of his enhanced social standing.[24] Given his "highly familiar polit-ical style," based on recognition, reminiscences, and recollections, Sir Frederick's genealogical knowledge also proved an effective political instrument during election time, a means to acknowledge, retain, and reaffirm identity with his community.

History consecrated memory. As a national referent and "a site of identity formation," history was an especially important instrument in fragmented societies. National holidays, monuments, museums, and historical societies established, maintained, and sanctified claims to belonging and recognition.[25] History books occupied a prominent place in Sir Frederick's personal library. He shared this intellectual interest with Lady Borden, who read history and employed its wisdom and justification for contemporary politics. He enjoyed Canadian and British history, with their contemporary emphasis on biography, consti-tutional development, continuity, and progress, and he frequently cited historical examples in defence of his policies and decisions. Signifi-cantly, one of Elizabeth's last Christmas gifts to her father was volume three, the most recent volume, of William Monypenny and George E. Buckle's popular multi-volume *The Life of Benjamin Disraeli* (volumes that Borden's contemporary R.B. Bennett also "read and re-read" for inspiration and example).[26]

Borden regarded Canada's history as the story of a distinctive but inclusive community within the British family, secured through the struggle, sacrifice, public service, and heroic actions of "great men." Perhaps no public institution was more redolent of family and patriot-ism than the military, with its emphasis on regimental lineage, gene-alogy, uniforms, battle honours, and decorations.[27] In a twelve-page article on the contemporary Canadian Militia solicited by the editor of the *United Service Magazine,* Borden spent a third of the space locating the Canadian Militia within a historical continuum, beginning with New France.[28] Conscious of the Boer War's historic significance and its patriotic potential, Borden had been careful to appoint a historical offi-cer, F.J. Dixon, to accompany Canada's first contingent. Subsequently he authorized public funds for battlefield commemorations, collective markers, and sites of veneration, to memorialize not only the Boer War but the War of 1812 and the Fenian raids as well. He enjoyed unveil-ing historical monuments and had ample opportunity to indulge this pleasure and reflect upon its historical lessons after the Boer War. In 1899 he had a special Fenian raid medal struck and distributed to those who helped repel the Fenians in 1866; as a participant, he was also a recipient. He purchased historical relics and artefacts and occasionally donated them to public institutions; the best example was his purchase in England in 1900 of two bronze nine-pounder smooth-bore field guns from the Napoleonic Wars, which he donated to the Canadian Military Institute in 1900 (they were subsequently installed outside the Toronto institute's doors).

In an era characterized by a cult of individualism and hero worship, Borden was aware of his own historical importance and endeavoured to paint his own public portrait, to shape the public memory of him and his family. At the time, great persons were valorized by their possession of public office, their sacrifices, their participation in great events, and their honours and titles, and the public's memory of them was perpetuated by portraits and monuments. Borden's numerous portraits of himself in oil, charcoal, and photography, in court uniform, formal attire, or with "dundreary whiskers, freshly laundered and brushed, clutching an umbrella in kid-gloved hand,"[29] standing, seated, holding a book, all suggested an imposing, distinguished public servant, a man of substance, sophistication, elegance, learning, and public importance. Despite (or perhaps because of) the absence of a male heir, Sir Frederick sought immortality by memorializing himself and his family.

Many of Sir Frederick's memorials focused on Harold, his irreparable sacrifice. On several occasions Borden interceded with Lord Minto on behalf of his son's memory, asking why his son's courage had not been recognized, confident that the governor general would understand "a father's zeal on behalf of the memory of an only son who gave up his life for his country."[30] Although Harold's death in battle at Witpoort made him ineligible for the Victoria Cross, during an earlier engagement at Vet River he and Richard Turner had courageously swum the river to scout safer locations for their troops, an action that earned Turner the Distinguished Service Order.[31] Minto shared Borden's disappointment with the War Office's failure to recognize Harold's service, and he solicited the advice of his friend Lord Roberts on how to address the failure. Roberts responded that young Borden's heroism had not been brought to his attention (Borden and Turner had been mentioned in despatches), otherwise he would have been "delighted" to recommend him for the Victoria Cross.[32]

Sir Frederick's inability to secure redress from the British military authorities fired his determination to perpetuate his son's memory. In South Africa and in the family burial plot in Canning, Nova Scotia, memorials marked Harold's tragic death in combat. In addition, on 21 January 1903 a tablet was dedicated to his memory in the chapel at Mount Allison University.[33] Five years later Sir Frederick unveiled a marble plaque in memory of Harold in McGill's new Strathcona Med-

Harold Borden, killed in South Africa in July 1900. *Courtesy Joan Murray and Ken Bezanson*

(LEFT) To memorialize Harold, a bust sculpted by Hamilton McCarthy was unveiled in the centre of Canning in 1903. *Courtesy Ken Bezanson*; (RIGHT) Marble tablet commemorating Harold's death and that of another soldier, Strathcona Medical Building, McGill University.

ical Building. In 1908 he donated the Harold Borden Memorial Cup (worth $500) to the Dominion Rifle Association, a silver cup with medallions bearing Harold's portrait that Sir Frederick had commissioned from a London engraver shortly after his son's death.[34] But the most visible, celebrated public memorial to his son was a bronze, life-size bust of Harold, sculpted by Hamilton MacCarthy (who also lost a son in the war), which was unveiled during an elaborate public ceremony in the centre of Canning on 23 September 1903.[35] A commemorative coloured plate (now considered very rare) and a special postcard of the memorial marked the event. Guests were identified with special memorial ribbons, and Lady Borden was presented with a Union Jack. Well after Sir Frederick's death, members of his family continued to memorialize Harold through scholarships at Mount Allison University.[36] Altogether these monuments constituted tangible public reminders of the family's standing, service, and sacrifice for Canada and the Empire.

The ultimate accolades in the structured world of the nineteenth-century gentry were titles, the symbols of recognition and power. They

Postcard showing the elaborate ceremony accompanying the unveiling of Harold
Borden's monument in Canning. *Courtesy Ken Bezanson*

bestowed public status, commanded deference, signified leadership,
and entailed social obligations. In a colonial society transatlantic titles
were an important additional recognition and seal of social approval.
Within Borden's British world, title identified the recipient as an exem-
plar and leader; in Canada it signified membership within a nascent
national class that transcended local and regional borders.[37] Implicit in
the notion of a national class was the assumption of community, social
hierarchy, and responsibility, asserted and reinforced by manners,
material trappings, and social obligations. Social obligations included
the obligation to entertain, travel, participate in cross-regional associations, and patronize artistic, recreational, educational, philanthropic,
and religious institutions. Much like Payne's gentrifying British
entrepreneurs of the time, Canadian aspirants to membership in this
national class were all too willing to pay the price: "to substitute leisure
or political power, or prestige from philanthropic works, for income
maximization after a certain conventionally acceptable level had been
attained."[38]

In Borden's chivalric Edwardian world, military titles possessed a
special cachet, particularly those signifying imperial or royal approval.
They were symbols of power and legitimacy, reinforced by hierarchical
ranks and uniforms. Borden appreciated the British Army's decision
in 1901 to name him an honorary colonel of the British Army Medical
Corps, and he took even greater pride in his honorific title of Honorary
Surgeon-General to the King. After 1902 no introduction or biograph-

ical reference was complete without mention of his title, Knight of Grace of the Venerable Order of the Hospital of St John of Jerusalem. Originally a Catholic chivalrous fraternal order of "warrior monks" that dated its founding to 1113, by the nineteenth century it possessed an English Protestant branch under royal patronage. The order was devoted to the care of the sick and the alleviation of suffering, its most visible work being that of St John Ambulance. Knights were entitled to wear vestments and an eight-point cross insignia, and were eligible to register their family coat of arms with heraldic authorities.

No honour gave Sir Frederick and Lady Borden greater satisfaction than Sir Frederick's admission to Britain's Order of Chivalry, his "real" knighthood, the Most Distinguished Order of St Michael and St George (KCMG), granted on the occasion of King Edward's coronation in June 1902. Established in 1818, the Order of St Michael and St George was one of several late eighteenth- and early nineteenth-century titles created, extended, or codified to promote a layered sense of place, hierarchy, and belonging.[39] Initially Borden attributed his KCMG to the king's desire to recognize Canada's South African War contribution. (It might also have been a way for the imperial government to compensate for its failure to recognize Harold's heroism.) Soon, however, Borden came to regard his title as a mark of personal esteem and social recognition, social capital that constituted a valuable calling card, one that he and Lady Borden did all in their power to maximize. Earlier he had responded to rumours of his impending knighthood with the disclaimer that he was "too poor and too democratic" to accept a knighthood. Once rumour became a reality, neither consideration restrained him.

Domestic and social space confirmed a person's status and invited and reinforced deference and projected power. Two large houses, "Stadacona Hall" in Ottawa and "Borden Place" in Canning, provided conspicuous genteel sites for Sir Frederick and Lady Borden to dispense hospitality, to receive and entertain a growing number of distinguished guests. They were places for dinners, luncheons, and teas, for pictures, gardens, music, and conversation. In 1901 when Borden first learned of his nomination for honours, he immediately engaged William Critchlow Harris, from a prestigious firm of Halifax architects, to plan and supervise an extensive renovation of the "Old Place," his Canning home. The result was a large wooden mansion constructed (or reconstructed) in the popular Queen Anne revival style, a style marked by ornamentation, irregular or asymmetrical form, hipped roofs, towers, and verandas, one that "appealed to the burgeoning, prosperous middle classes in England and in Canada who were looking for affordable houses that were also showy."[40] Once the renovations were

Photograph of the renovated Borden Place. *Courtesy Library and Archives Canada,*
PA20750

completed, the deliberately dynastic title, Borden Place, replaced the
Old Place's more rustic designation.

Borden Place commanded a spacious lot between the steep-banked
Habitant River and Canning's tree-lined Main Street. Access from the
highway to the "cottage" was through an elegant circular driveway
carved through well-manicured hedges and gardens that were later
embellished by his son-in-law, Charles Gordon Hewitt, the dominion
entomologist and a devoted gardener and conservationist.[41] The gardens contained apple, pear, plum, and quince trees, and the house was
surrounded by peonies, poppies, and hollyhocks.[42] Out-of-town visitors
usually arrived by rail; a spur from the Cornwallis-Kingsport Railway that passed "between rows of apple trees"[43] along the east side
of the Habitant gave direct access to Borden Place. On the grounds
there were two ice houses, a carriage house, stables, and tennis courts.
At least seven servants were required to care for the household; without access to precise records, one might imagine that they included a
driver, stable hand, groundsman, personal servant, stoker, as well as
persons to cook and clean. On the third floor were servants' quarters.[44]

Sir Frederick and Lady Borden's renovated "stately cottage contained a wood-panelled dining room, a drawing room, a library, hall-
ways, a kitchen, a pantry, and seven bedrooms heated by large stone
fireplaces. Many of the receiving rooms had stained-glass windows and

This postcard shows Borden Place with its renovations completed. The Canning residence soon became a town landmark. *Courtesy Library and Archives Canada*

were decorated with paintings, vases, and *objets d'art* collected during their various European travels. Sir Frederick liked appearance and was "notorious for buying cheap or getting a bargain, so many things looked impressive but were of little value."[45] In the hall of Borden Place hung a full-length oil portrait of Sir Frederick in court uniform, reminding visitors of their host's title and social standing. In the formal dining room, where Lady Borden presided over a table graced by an impressive array of knives, forks, and spoons (which she wielded with dexterity and a strict eye for propriety), hung an oil portrait of a scholarly Sir Frederick, seated reading. Adjacent to the dining room was a large library, with a fireplace, and shelves well stocked with books, many of them history books but also poetry and books on science and travel, each book containing a nameplate bearing the Borden family coat of arms. In 1910 the Borden Place was insured for $20,000 and its contents for $11,000, altogether a far from modest dwelling.[46] Although a domestic space, it constituted a monument to his success, at once a source of local pride, curiosity, and envy. Contemporary postcards of the "Home of Sir Frederick Borden" and the "Residence of Sir Frederick Borden" underscored the community's pride in Borden Place.

In Ottawa Sir Frederick and Lady Borden held court in an even grander residence, Stadacona Hall. This large stone house had been built in 1871 by John Cameron, the Ottawa lumber baron, and had been John A. Macdonald's home from 1873 to 1883. Valued, with its land, at $75,000 in 1912, this property strategically adjoined Laurier's home.[47]

A present-day photograph of Stadacona Hall, Sir Frederick's Ottawa residence, next door to the residence of Sir Wilfrid Laurier. *Wikipedia. Photograph by Simon P.*

The furnishings alone in Borden's Ottawa residence were valued at $4,000 in 1908.[48] A reporter who interviewed Lady Borden in her morning room at Stadacona Hall informed her readers that the sunlight that "streams through the large window facing South is a delightful experience, but perhaps the room looks even more cheery in the late afternoon, when the light comes from huge logs burning in the wide old-fashioned fireplace, and when she serves her guests with fragrant cups of tea. There are always plenty of flowers and books in this pleasant room."[49]

From these two well-appointed residences, Sir Frederick and Lady Borden dispensed their legendary courtly and generous hospitality, including teas, at homes, and formal dinners. Dinner guests at Stadacona Hall might include the young, ambitious Mackenzie King, with whom Borden established a close friendship; Sydney Fisher, his very political colleague, the bachelor minister of agriculture who lived on the same street about three houses away on the other side; Sir Wilfrid and Lady Laurier, who lived in the adjacent property; or Sir Henry Pellatt, the athletic, eccentric Toronto capitalist, military enthusiast, and sometime business partner, with Lady Pellatt (the couple usually stayed at the Bordens as house guests when they were in Ottawa).[50] All were treated to entertaining conversation and generous, baronial hospitality. During their London visit in 1911 Laurier was sufficiently impressed by the Bordens' gastronomic discernment that he charged Sir Frederick and Lady Borden with assisting him in finding "a suitable cook for his home in Ottawa."[51]

Leisure, vacations, and travel were also class markers, as were dress and language, the latter an important "companion of Empire."[52] Lady Borden shared her husband's passion for travel, as did their children. They had visited London at least twice before Borden had joined Laurier's government in 1896. When they travelled, as they did frequently, membership in some twenty private clubs in Canada, the United States, and Britain offered facilities that allowed them to enjoy and reciprocate hospitality. These clubs included the Rideau Club, the Laurentian Club, the Ottawa Hunt Club, the Ottawa Country Club, the Ottawa Golf Club, the Belmont Country Club, the Halifax Club, the Quebec Garrison Club, the Petawawa Camp Fish and Game Club (to which Borden was elected patron in 1911), the Royal Automobile Club, the Calumet Club (New York), the Intercolonial Club (Boston), and the Canadian Club (Boston).[53]

Lady Borden invariably accompanied Sir Frederick on his annual political/business pilgrimage to Britain, occasions that offered opportunities for private travel, including excursions to the Continent, to Paris, the Riviera, Rome, Naples, and Florence. Lady Borden developed a particular affection for Florence, and after her husband died, she spent most of her winters there until World War II. Sir Frederick's "approved" biographical references underscore what he considered the memorable social highlights of their various European tours: attendance at the coronation of Edward VII in 1902; dining with the king and queen and the colonial premiers in 1907; an audience with Pope Pius X in January 1909; and the coronation of George V in June 1911, with the additional bonus of photographs of Sir Frederick and Lady Borden appearing in the *Court Journal* (14 July 1911).

London visits entailed an exhilarating round of entertainment and social obligations, country home weekends, teas, luncheons, dinners, the theatre, concerts, and public engagements. Increasingly the *Times* announced the Bordens' arrival in London,[54] and there a flood of invitations awaited them from titled persons and other notables. A generous, hospitable network of old Canadian hands, expatriates, former governors general and their entourage, as well as other distinguished imperial officials rarely missed an opportunity to recognize the Bordens' presence in London. Heading the list was Lord Strathcona, renowned for his lavish entertainment and assiduous attention to wining and dining visiting Canadian dignitaries. During the Bordens' visit to Britain to recover from the death of their son, Lord Strathcona had thoughtfully invited them to his country home at Glencoe for a weekend,[55] an invitation invariably repeated on subsequent visits. Lord William Seymour, the former GOC of the Halifax garrison and a friend of Sir Frederick's, and Lady Seymour were no less hospitable.

Sir Frederick, photographed in London by William Downey. Downey was known as the "Royal" photographer. *Courtesy Joan Murray and Ken Bezanson*

Lady "Bessie" Borden, Sir Frederick's second wife. *Courtesy Joan Murray and Ken Bezanson*

To reciprocate this hospitality Sir Frederick held honorary member-ships in at least six of the city's gentlemen's clubs (others offered him temporary membership during his London visits, such as the Royal Automobile Club and the Travellers' Club).[56] In London Sir Frederick patronized a number of organizations and participated in their delib-erations. He was elected an honorary member of the Cobden Club, the United Empire Club, the Royal Colonial Institute, the United Service Club, and the British Empire Club, and he served as a vice-president of the British Empire League, as vice-president of the Imperial Com-mercial Club, and as a director of the Home Scholarship Fund (whose some sixty scholarships encouraged study in Britain "to keep the Empire and motherland together").[57] He also accepted invitations to speak at the Guildhall, the British Empire League, the Imperial Insti-tute, the Anglo-Saxon Union, and the United Service Club.

Lady Borden herself was more than up to these occasions. A poised, vivacious, well-read, articulate, and intelligent woman with a flair for fashion and an eye for costume and jewellery, she appreciated the importance of comportment, dress, and speech. Seventeen years her husband's junior, she made every effort to remove any telltale sign of parochialism and to project a sophisticated image appropriate to the emerging national class. Educated at Mount Allison Ladies' College (1871–73), she shared her husband's interest in history and politics. And she cultivated what she referred to as an Ottawa accent and encour-aged promising relatives to follow her example, to facilitate their social advancement![58] On state occasions in Britain or on very special occa-sions in Ottawa she wore a tiara, with various jewels, which she had reset as the event required. From Stadacona Hall or from Borden Place, the spacious "brown mansion above the Habitant," the queen, as she was called in Canning, ruled "in stately fashion her little empire."[59]

The Bordens' social obligations and philanthropy, their generous support of education, music, religion, and charity, complemented their conspicuous consumption, hospitality, and public visibility. Among the several national and international organizations that Sir Frederick sup-ported were the Field Naturalist Club, the American University Asso-ciation, the Order of St John, and the Canadian Association for the Advancement of Science. He also served as a director of the YMCA, the Red Cross, and the Tuberculosis Association of Canada; as vice-president of the Canadian Patriotic Fund, the Canadian Militia Insti-tute, and the Navy League; and as an honorary patron of the Dominion Rifle Association, not to mention his involvement with various imper-ial organizations that adhered to Canadian identity within a British world. Seconding her husband's aspirations, Lady Borden undertook various artistic endeavours and good works. She served as a director of the Ottawa YWCA and as vice-president of the Victorian Order of Nurses and subscribed to various music clubs, including the Canadian Conservatory of Music. Clearly they were a couple whose intellectual and social horizons extended well beyond region.

Philanthropy created goodwill, bonds, and obligations. It revealed and enforced the donor's values and self-image and invited reciprocity. Predictably, public education possessed a high priority on Sir Frederick's philanthropic agenda. An inveterate reader, a passion he shared with Lady Borden, he had belonged to a reading club when he was young; and over the years he amassed a good personal library. Within his constituency he contributed regularly to the public libraries in Kentville and Canning. A director, donor and ardent promoter of the Home Scholarship Fund, in 1910 he created the Sir Frederick Borden scholarship fund for high school graduates from Kings County, "to encourage young people of small means to take a course at college."[60] In 1913 he responded generously to a request from his cousin Dr Byron Borden, the recently installed president of Mount Allison University, his son's alma mater, with a contribution of $3,000 to Mount Allison University's Fund. Two years before he had donated $1,000 to his own alma mater, King's College. Acadia University, McGill University, and the University of New Brunswick received smaller but substantial donations. In recognition of his generosity and commitment to higher education, both King's College (1910) and the University of New Brunswick (1913) awarded him an honorary doctorate of civil law.

An amateur musician, Sir Frederick had a special passion for music, especially the violin. His treasured violin had been made in London in 1790, and he went to considerable pains to have it restored in Washington in 1898. He continued to play for his own and others' enjoyment, although the occasion and accompaniments were often a cause of scandal for some of his more straight-laced contemporaries. His prized possession could also be used to entertain and charm the Press Gallery and other more worldly gatherings.[61] His appreciation of music was well known, as was his generosity. When a mother wrote to him requesting a loan of twenty-five dollars for her daughter's musical education, Borden responded with a sum of fifty dollars, to be returned only and if the family could afford it. Well before he became a cabinet minister Borden had patronized Ottawa's various musical concerts. Subsequently he became an associate member and vice-patron of the Ottawa Amateur Orchestral Society and a vice-president of the Ottawa Choral Society, and he subscribed generously to the Ottawa Symphony Orchestra's guaranteed fund.

Although Sir Frederick was not a particularly devout Methodist, he appeared to appreciate the social function of religion, and he could scarcely have been oblivious to its political influence. Whatever his motives, he donated generously to religious and benevolent causes. Regardless of the denomination soliciting his assistance, Sir Frederick responded with a contribution of $100. Special circumstances elicited a larger contribution, such as the 1909 reconstruction of his Methodist church in Canning ($1,500) after its destruction by fire; the Baptist church in his "childhood village" of Cunard ($500), notwithstanding its pastor's active political opposition; or the construction of the All Saints Church of England cathedral in Halifax ($500), despite the denomination's disapproval of his second marriage. That he bore the Church of England in Canada no rancour is evident from his generosity toward the local congregation whose Canning church, St Michael and All Angels, began as a carriage house on his property before being moved in 1904 to Main Street and consecrated the following year.

Benevolent organizations, especially those designed to care for the sick and needy, benefited from Sir Frederick's professed belief that social responsibilities ought to be "in proportion to our blessings."[62] Judged by his generosity, his blessings were considerable. Beneficiaries of his philanthropy included the Salvation Army, the Ottawa General Protestant Hospital, the Halifax and Ottawa YMCA (the latter received $1,000 toward its building fund), the Red Cross Society, the Tuberculosis Association. Other recipients were more closely associated with his ministry, such as the Patriotic Fund and the Toronto Veterans Association, and the list may be extended. On many occasions Sir Frederick's benevolence was direct and personal. At Christmastime he instructed his agents to provide gifts of food for "all cases of special hardship."[63] Lady Borden, too, who possessed income of her own, supported various endeavours, not least of which was her church in Canning, to which she provided generous support (including the donation of chimes in memory of her devout but eccentric stepdaughter Elizabeth) during her lifetime and a legacy upon her death.

There was something oddly dynastic in Sir Frederick's social strategy, odd because it seemed to intensify after the untimely death of his only son, a dynastic aspiration inspired by his knighthood. Cut from his father's cloth, Harold had been an intelligent, dynamic, and charismatic young man, cast to assume the family mantle. Educated at the nation's leading medical school rather than at one in the region or abroad, Harold had shared his father's interest in medicine, the militia, business, and politics. He had represented his father in London during the 1897 Diamond Jubilee and had assisted him in politics, editing for a time Kentville's Liberal weekly, the *Western Chronicle*. Sir Frederick had entrusted Harold with all aspects of the family business and had planned to name him the managing president of Sir Frederick's floundering business, the R.W. Kinsman Company, upon his return from South Africa. But Harold's death sabotaged Sir Frederick's plans and severed the patrilineal continuity.

Sir Frederick's dynastic aspirations, however, were not entirely extinguished with Harold's death. Although he, like Lord Strathcona, lacked a male heir, he had two daughters. The marriage of his younger daughter, Julia Maude, to Leslie Stuart Macoun and the birth of their only child, Elizabeth Rosamond, in 1907 promised a family continuity through the female line. It also provided him with a son-in-law, someone to assist him in managing and anchoring the family assets and who became something of a substitute for Harold. Leslie Macoun had been born in Ireland in 1872, the son of a wealthy linen manufacturer, John Macoun of Hollywood, near Belfast, and had been educated at King William College on the Isle of Man. He had come to Canada as a young man and secured a position as an accountant at the Horticultural Experimental Station in Ottawa, where his uncle William Macoun was the dominion horticulturist. Later he entered business on his own as a venture capitalist. In Ottawa he joined the Princess Louise Dragoon Guards and attained the rank of captain.[64] Anxious to assist his son-in-law, Borden provided Macoun with useful introductions, engaged his services, and brought him into business deals, where he often served as a convenient proxy and cover for some of Sir Frederick's public projects.

Titled and prominent in public life in Canada and Britain, with a cousin who was leader of His Majesty's Opposition, both men living in Ottawa in comfortable circumstances, Sir Frederick might not have found it too difficult to imagine himself as the head of some emerging Canadian family dynasty. The British world in which Borden lived has been described as one of titles, hierarchy, and social obligation, "the node at which the metropolitan culture of outreach and replication converged with the colonial culture of aspiration and assimilation."[65] This system, however, was not monolithic; it was flexible and could be tailored to personal needs and local realities. Borden, for example, did not emulate some of his more anglophile compatriots' riding to hounds; he was not a hunter, not even a rider. And he did not disdain commerce, industry, and finance, but remained a gentleman capitalist. In fact his claim to gentility resulted from a material base. That status, however, entailed high maintenance. The question remains: how did Sir Frederick secure the material means to sustain his and Lady Borden's social aspirations while remaining in public life and how were his personal, material interests related to his proposed London appointment?

CHAPTER 20

Maritime Entrepreneur

To assess the nature and magnitude of Sir Frederick's wealth and appreciate his material interest in London, one must understand how a regional entrepreneur's material interests came to encompass national and imperial dimensions. More especially, how did Borden negotiate the transition from a small community–based family capitalism to the more impersonal financial, managerial capitalism that was reordering his world? In addressing this vexed question, scholars have focused on three principal sources of regional disparity: physical resources; private and public policy; and human capital, principally labour and leadership.[1] While answers to the question of the region's alleged economic retardation can scarcely be derived from a single biographical case study, Borden's experience is instructive in evaluating the role of Maritime entrepreneurship.

In his comparative study of Nova Scotia, Quebec, and Ontario, Roy George concluded that entrepreneurship strategies played a determining factor in explaining Nova Scotia's comparative economic failure, specifically its entrepreneurs' cautious, conservative, constrictive investment preferences.[2] According to Borden's contemporary Max Aitken, the future Lord Beaverbrook, who worked in and knew the Maritime region thoroughly, Maritime investors were notoriously conservative, persons with limited identities who preferred "local issues nine times out of ten."[3] Others have explained the region's economic failure by pointing to the haemorrhaging, or "decapitation," of entrepreneurial talent owing to the out-migration of its more dynamic business leaders, who would obtain subsequent fame and fortune elsewhere, such as Lord Beaverbrook.

Borden, however, was not a migrant. He remained in the region even when his world came to encompass national and imperial dimensions. Moreover, he derived his initial economic success from the skilful management of the region's community-based resources, and he retained a firm faith in the region's economic potential. Nor can Borden's entrepreneurial career be faulted for its conservatism and parochialism. During the latter part of his career Borden endeavoured to adapt to the new managerial capitalism, diversify and depersonalize his portfolio, and invest in speculative opportunities outside the region. Over time Borden came to possess interests in some seventy companies, largely in Canada, but also in Britain, the United States, and Cuba.

Initially, Borden's early business career conformed to a certain regional pattern. He owned a small family firm, with limited capital, and he worked with traditional mercantile families within a subregional geography.[4] Most of his more profitable enterprises were located in the region. They possessed a productive, value-added purpose or offered a service, enjoyed a sizeable local market, and were governed by personal and/or familial arrangements. His produce, real estate, orchard, dairy farm, small mill, ship, utility, banking, and merchandising companies were based in the region (as would be those he dreamed of creating, such as hydroelectricity, pulp and paper, and linen production). Most of his value-added enterprises began as and remained small community-oriented forms of family capitalism that an imaginative, energetic entrepreneur could organize and direct and from which the entrepreneur and community might profit. And during a period of demographic, economic, and corporate transition, Borden, an educated professional from a prominent local family, shrewdly managed a web of family, business, and political relationships to create a modest personal fortune, based principally on regional resources and services.

Something of a captive of his own success, for a long time Borden appeared wedded to the values and habits of community-based family capitalism. In his world of familial capitalism, his confidence, trust, and obligations were based on his knowledge of the enterprise, its potential benefits, risks, and limitations, as well as the local social dynamics, institutions, politics, and culture. Trust and an intimate knowledge of his constituency and clientele played an important role in the creation and the maintenance of his local, multi-faceted mercantile business. Through direct loans, the extension of credit, and the endorsement of notes, Borden established an elaborate web of credit relationships to bind people to him. In fact, he often complained that he had become a "professional money lender."[5] This system worked well enough on a local, personal level where Borden knew the debtor's family, character, and credit rating. The loans were never large and there were multiple mutual benefits, especially at election time.

A similar hands-on strategy characterized his management of his business and public affairs. During his temporary absences in Ottawa and elsewhere, he left things in the hands of trusted friends and family members who understood and accepted his status and authority. In staffing his ministerial office in Ottawa, he assigned strategic positions to family and trusted friends. This was more than simply a system of patronage; it was a success formula that implied and entailed trust, a system based on the same methods and assumptions that he had employed to create the F.W. Borden Company. This system allowed him to retain control and guide the direction of his enterprises. In short, he was more comfortable in what one author has described as a "culture of confidence."[6]

During the last decade or more of the nineteenth and early twentieth centuries, however, Canadian capitalism "underwent a dramatic metamorphosis" from "traditional family capitalism" to "modern financial and managerial business methods ... no longer limited to ... personal interaction."[7] While some of the familial managerial values and techniques were transportable to the new capitalism, many were not. Transition to the new, impersonal, corporate capitalism often required new values, methods, and strategies that were based on other assumptions. In the larger world of corporate business the stakes were higher, the risks greater, and the rewards more diffuse. For all of Sir Frederick's confidence in technology, innovation, change, progress, and economic success, his old personal habits died slowly.

Less comfortable in the more impersonal world of corporate enterprise, Borden initially approached the new capitalism with a degree of caution and suspicion. Early in the management of his produce company, for example, he warned his more speculative partners not to pay clients with stock options and insisted upon staying within the confines of the law and maintaining the "bona fides of the whole business."[8] Indeed, so wedded was Borden to the values and habits of the passing world of family capitalism that his transfer of the old habits to the new corporate world occasionally compromised his own material interests. For instance, his endorsement of notes for sums of $3,000 or more for men such as B.F. Pearson, the Halifax editor and businessman; Rufus Henry Pope, the Eastern Townships farmer and businessman; and C.A. Henderson, a New York financier,[9] sometimes compromised his credit rating.

Similarly, although Borden promoted professionalism and the virtue of expertise in medicine and the Militia, he had difficulty relinquishing control to others and adapting to the more impersonal, specialized, indirect world of corporate business, where ownership was diffused and effective control rested in the hands of career administrators. In short, Borden was an incurable micromanager, even though his virtual permanent residence in Ottawa after 1896 and the regional nature of his business made micromanagement of his Maritime affairs increasingly difficult. Like Norman W. Taylor's French-Canadian industrialists, whose individualism expressed itself in a strong sense of independence, Borden tried to maintain control of his business. While working with family, friends, and familiar partners was one way of maintaining control, these relationships could entail material liabilities, including difficulty in securing external financing for his projects.

Illustrative of Borden's entrepreneurial style was his tumultuous relationship with R.W. Kinsman, the managing director of his produce company. If Borden's assessment of his "delinquent" general manager was accurate, it is difficult to understand why he retained Kinsman in a position of trust and responsibility for six years despite Kinsman's "scandalous behaviour," "outrageous and intolerable" business habits, bad judgment, chaotic bookkeeping, failure to collect bills, misleading information, procrastination, and refusal to answer letters.[10] In the end Borden replaced Kinsman only *in extremis,* when George Cox and other Toronto financiers made Kinsman's removal a condition of their investment in the floundering Nova Scotia Supply Company. Although Borden and Kinsman's acrimonious parting entailed threats of legal action, Borden accusing Kinsman of misappropriation of funds and Kinsman charging Borden with slander, Borden continued to lend money to members of the Kinsman family, and six years after their vitriolic parting Borden found Kinsman a position in the Militia Department.[11] Borden's reluctance to establish less personal, more professional relations with Kinsman and his willingness to retain an allegedly incompetent, but pliable, administrator were more than the proclivities of a self-confessed micromanager; they were also the tribute extracted by the family capitalism imbricated in the local political culture.

Although the family-based political economy, with its familiar assumptions and habits and its web of beneficial social and political relationships, had served Borden well, he was a realist and enjoyed a new challenge, and was not averse to a calculated risk. He was also an inveterate conciliator. Consequently, he attempted to reconcile the two capitalisms, to negotiate a profitable coexistence, a marriage of convenience, between the new and old economy, as he had done with the changing land and sea economies of his constituency, or with the claims of the amateur and professional soldier in his Militia Department; retaining as much of the old as was possible and profitable. His efforts to adapt to the new world, to profit from the golden age of corporate Canadian capitalism, are evident from his diverse, speculative, and growing inter-regional investments.

Necessity and opportunity fashioned and facilitated Borden's adaptation to the new capitalism. Necessity came in the form of the near death of his Produce Company that obliged him to diversify his assets and secure the capital he required for their more profitable development. Diversification diffused control, it reduced the time and attention he could devote to any one enterprise, and it created a need for financial capital. Opportunity came with his daughter's marriage to Leslie S. Macoun, an investment banker. The marriage provided an occasion and an incentive to assist and benefit from his son-in-law's profession, while retaining and assuring continuing family oversight, control, and management of his assets, a strategy designed to enable him to inhabit both worlds and ease the transition from the old to the new.

The near death of the Produce Company served as a wake-up call. By 1899 his R.W. Kinsman Company Limited was in serious trouble. In 1895, the year before Borden joined Laurier's cabinet, he had incorporated the greater part of his assets under his own name. In its corporate capacity the F.W. Borden Company Limited possessed an initial capital stock of $50,000 and a broad mandate. In 1897 the company changed its name to the R.W. Kinsman Company Limited, presumably to avoid the perception of conflicts of interest. At the same time the company's capital stock was increased to $250,000, of which only $100,000 had been paid up by 1897. That same year the company raised a mortgage of $186,000 on the strength of its assets, to exploit other projects permitted by the broad terms of the company's incorporation. Although Richard Kinsman, Borden's business partner and prominent Canning merchant, became the company's managing director and namesake, Borden retained "all the preferred stock of the Kinsman Company and [was] by far the largest owner of the debt stock" of the new company.[12] His weekly, sometimes daily, detailed and peremptory advice and instructions to Kinsman and his eventual dismissal of Kinsman leave little doubt of the minister's controlling interest in the company.

That Borden feared for the company's health well before 1899 is clear from his increasingly pressing, apprehensive, and carping communications with Kinsman, whose poor performance (detailed above) played havoc with the minister's best efforts to keep the company solvent.[13] It is not clear to what degree the company's difficulties were the result of Kinsman's careless management or of overexpansion, luck, or poor markets. Borden himself seemed convinced that Kinsman's "outrageous and intolerable" business habits were the primary source of the company's problems. Nonetheless Borden did what he could to keep the company afloat, inveigling orders from political friends, a shipload of deals for Alfred Dobell and Company of London, an order of wheat for Archibald Campbell from Chatham, Ontario, and favourable wholesale prices from A.E. Bates & Company, a recipient of government contracts. Still, Kinsman's ineptitude and delay in honouring these commitments eroded the company's credit and credibility, despite Borden's almost desperate remonstrances.[14] Under Kinsman's direction the company was losing money.

Things reached a crisis in the last six months of 1899, unfortunately in one of the most tense and trying periods of Borden's personal and public life. Although Borden's accountant estimated that the company's farm lands, capital goods, and other fixed property, exclusive of personal accounts, were worth $286,000, the R.W. Kinsman Company was cash poor and its credit overextended. With the company in desperate need of cash or credit to meet its contractual obligations, Borden warned Kinsman in June 1899 that "things cannot go on as they have been going for the past year. You must manage in some way to get money out of the business. It is no use to buy goods simply for the purpose of scattering them among the impecunious. We have been running a benevolent institution about long enough."[15]

To stave off an immediate credit crisis Borden authorized Kinsman to draw upon the minister's personal credit, a portion of which may have come from his ministerial salary. But there was a limit to his personal credit, and he was soon obliged to remind Kinsman that he had reached that limit. Moreover, Borden was anxious to launch other projects, including an ambitious scheme to harness the Gaspereau and Curel rivers. By December the Kinsman Company's two principal creditors, the Halifax Banking Company and the Temperance and General Life Insurance Company, had become menacing, the latter threatening to place the matter of an unpaid loan in the hands of its solicitors. In addition to having to deal with these pressures, the Kinsman Company owed a mortgage payment to H.H. Wickwire and Alfred Cogswell, business and political partners; they, too, needed to be placated in some way or other.

To ward off disaster, Borden offered bonds in the company, an offer initially refused by the general manager of the Temperance and General Life Insurance Company, who insisted instead on legal action. At this point Borden went over the general manager's head to the company president, Hon. G.W. Ross, the Liberal Ontario premier, and George Cox, the Liberal senator who held a controlling interest in the company. Obligingly they persuaded the general manager to delay action and extend the loan for another thirty days while the Kinsman Company attempted to salvage its credit. So desperate had things become that Kinsman decided to sell the company's 142-ton schooner, the *Harold Borden*. On 28 December 1899, just before they could arrange the sale, the vessel was lost at sea during a voyage from Kingsport to Havana, Cuba, with a loss of six men, a harbinger of Borden's subsequent personal loss. Then, early the next year, a fire destroyed Borden's livestock barn in Pereau, the loss estimated to be $20,000. Borden planned to rebuild the barn, but in the meantime the ready cash from his insurance claims for the vessel and the devastating fire may have offered temporary relief from his impatient creditors. The company still lacked a dependable source of revenue.[16]

As it turned out, the South African War gave Borden an opportunity to rescue his ailing business. In mid-December 1899, scarcely two weeks before the loss of the *Harold Borden,* the government agreed to recruit a second contingent of soldiers for South Africa. Borden's decision to send the second and subsequent contingents through the ice-free port of Halifax invigorated the city's sluggish winter economy, fuelled by the large expenditure of private and public money on the housing, equipping, feeding, and entertaining of the troops and provisioning the three ships that had been hired to despatch the men and horses for the second contingent. Even before the second contingent left Halifax, the government had agreed to recruit and provision a third contingent, the Strathcona's Horse. That unit, too, would pass through Halifax, as would all subsequent units destined for South Africa, and all would require comparable goods and services.

Borden's designation of H.H. Wickwire as his Halifax agent, charged with supervising the letting of contracts, required little interpretation. An able lawyer, Wickwire was one of the Kinsman Company's creditors and shareholders; he was also Borden's business partner and perhaps the minister's closest political ally.[17] So confidential and political were Borden's communications with Wickwire during this period that they were transmitted frequently by cipher.[18] Initially Borden explained Wickwire's appointment as a measure to prevent the payment of unreasonable prices and thus avoid a repetition of the political embarrassment surrounding the provisioning of the Yukon Field Force. Wickwire's appointment accomplished this to a certain extent, but more important to party contractors, his placement gave the friends of the government an interested, strategically located advocate and judge in the court of public favours.

Not surprisingly the R.W. Kinsman Company was one of the first to benefit from Wickwire's grace and favour. Materially interested in the company's immediate cash crisis, Wickwire advised Borden to divide the contingent's demands for forage, meat, and vegetables among a very limited number of firms.[19] Arrangements were made to place orders with the R.W. Kinsman Company for this and subsequent calls to feed the troops stationed in Halifax and provision the ships with beef, horses and fodder during the war. On occasion the minister himself advised Kinsman on competitive offers.[20] Borden was no less direct in his communications with private companies doing business with the government, such as the steamships lines, insisting that in provisioning their ships they were to work through Wickwire, a practice that the companies understood and that there is no reason to believe that they did not honour.[21]

While Borden's political intervention averted immediate disaster, the Kinsman Company's near collapse called for new, long-range management strategies. To bring Kinsman under stricter control, Borden named his cousin Harry Brown (his private secretary and government employee) president of the R.W. Kinsman Company, a temporary arrangement pending a larger reorganization and refinancing of the company. In April 1901 the company was renamed the Nova Scotia Produce and Supply Company Limited, its capital stock increased to $500,000, and George Esson Boak, the Scottish-born president of the Nova Scotia Legislative Council and a prominent Water Street merchant, was made president. Boak's company held a lucrative contract with the Militia Department to supply coal and hardwood.[22] Meanwhile Borden searched for other means to obtain additional working capital, offering $25,000 preferred stock in the new company to Thomas White, the Liberal president of the Toronto-based National Trust Company at that time.[23] At first Borden had high expectations for his new company, optimistically promoting it among his friends and potential clients as "the largest general business in western Nova Scotia."[24]

But things did not work out quite as Borden had planned. Relations between Borden and Kinsman continued to deteriorate. Unhappy with the new corporate arrangement, effectively a form of trusteeship, Kinsman threatened to sell the company's real and personal property, its franchises and "good name," as well as his own preferred stock, which amounted to some $13,900. Nor did the company's makeshift "new" management instil confidence, as only a small portion of the new stock was taken up. Finally, when Senator George Cox made Kinsman's departure a condition of his investment in the new company, Borden dismissed Kinsman and replaced him with Borden's Canning neighbour, Captain Alfred Potter, an experienced merchant and sea captain. Meanwhile Borden doubled his efforts to secure business, reminding political friends and beneficiaries of public contracts to accept orders from the Nova Scotia Produce and Supply Company and provide "favourable rates."[25] To escape the stigma of mismanagement, the company was reorganized the following year; Nova Scotia was dropped from its name; and its capital stock was reduced to $200,000. Thereafter the National Trust, directed by Thomas White, one of Cox's protégés, handled the company's bonds, and Cox's Manufacturers Life Insurance Company held $10,000 of the company's $100,000 worth of outstanding bonds.[26]

The Produce and Supply Company's reduced capitalization was more than a belated recognition of the company's failure to attract investors; it represented Borden's recognition that he needed a more effective, alternative entrepreneurial strategy for managing his diverse assets. In retrospect Borden's decision in 1895 to consolidate his entrepreneurial activities into one corporate structure had not been prudent; the company's failure might threaten all his assets, making them liable in the event of misfortune or mismanagement. Consequently, Borden decided upon a new strategy, to diversify and shelter these assets in more specialized corporate structures, spreading the risk rather than having his assets sequestered in one corporate body, dependent upon the unforeseen circumstances or the (mis)management of one person. Single-function enterprises might also facilitate his closer scrutiny, and Borden liked to retain control.

In fact, Borden had tested the new diversification strategy well before 1903. As early as the spring of 1899 he had initiated a project to electrify the counties of Annapolis, Kings, Hants, and Halifax (excluding the city of Halifax and the town of Dartmouth) by purchasing existing local coal-generated power companies and replacing coal power with cheaper hydroelectricity, to be produced by harnessing the Gaspereau (Kings County) and Curel (Annapolis County) rivers. Rather than pursue this entrepreneurial objective under the broad terms of his Produce and Supply Company's charter, Borden had formed a separate company, the Nova Scotia Electric Light Company Limited, with an authorized stock of $50,000 and with himself as president.[27] This project would become more ambitious and controversial in the years following his defeat in 1911.

Similarly, the Produce and Supply Company's thirteen miles of telephone lines, together with their local franchise, were traded to the Valley Telephone Company in return for stock and a directorship in the larger company. A "firm believer in co-operation" and the future of the region's fruit industry, Borden also became a member of the Maple Leaf Fruit Company, a subsidiary of the United Fruit Company of Nova Scotia, to market the produce of his orchards.[28] The Produce and Supply Company's mining assets were incorporated into the Eastern Mines Limited, chartered in 1912 and capitalized at $3 million.[29] Its real estate and mortgage business eventually became part and parcel of the Harbourville Realty Company, then the King's Reality Company, incorporated under a federal charter in 1910 and capitalized at $500,000, with Borden as president.[30] Stripping the Produce and Supply Company of its various assets and developing them through other appropriate corporate instruments meant that the Produce Company's annual profits remained marginal and in some years it operated at a loss, but it was no longer Borden's principal source of corporate profits and liabilities.[31]

The marriage between Sir Frederick's younger daughter, Julia, and Leslie Macoun on 26 May 1906 provided him with an opportunity to unite the two capitalisms, to entrust the management of his business to an interested family member while he negotiated more speculative corporate ventures. Very shortly after the wedding, Borden began working closely with his son-in-law. He appreciated Macoun's financial knowledge, managerial skills, industry, and dependability. In turn Macoun respected Borden's need to be informed, consulted, and advised. In 1905, even before Macoun's marriage to Julia, Borden had sent Macoun, an investment banker, to the United States, Britain, and Germany in search of capital for his revived hydroelectrical project. Three years later, when Borden faced charges of conflict of interest, he transferred his interests in the New Brunswick Cold Storage Company to his son-in-law, who subsequently managed "their" interests under Sir Frederick's close scrutiny. At the same time he made Leslie the managing director and president of his Produce and Supply Company, the position he had hoped Harold would occupy upon his return from South Africa. Shortly afterwards, Leslie became director and president of the Cornwallis Trading Company Limited.[32] In addition to their home in Ottawa, Macoun and his family purchased a farm in Woodside, near Canning, where Macoun could monitor Borden's business interests more closely. By then he had become the general factotum of Borden's various local economic interests, plans, and projects. The relationship between the two men would remain frank, forthright, and respectful, though not free from tensions.[33]

Although Macoun may have been hot-tempered, Borden's confidence in him seems to have been well placed. It enabled Macoun to take difficult decisions to make the troubled Supply Company more attractive to investors. In 1911 he persuaded Sir Frederick to extract some $40,700 of watered stock from the company, an operation that entailed the cancellation of 407 shares, 355 of which belonged to Sir Frederick, representing a nominal loss to Borden of $35,500.[34] Once this was accomplished Macoun secured the National Trust Company's permission to issue an addition $50,000 worth of the company's bonds. Up to this point, only $100,000 of the $200,000 allowable bond limit had been issued, of which Sir Frederick held $85,000 worth and Lady Borden $500.[35] Nor did Macoun hesitate to warn Sir Frederick of questionable business practices. In 1910, for example, he had to remind Borden that paying dividends on preferred stock in the Cornwallis Trading Company, a company that had declared an annual loss, was "strictly against the Nova Scotia Companies Act."[36]

Typical of their relationship was Macoun's involvement in the incorporation of the Blomidon Railway Company Limited, a stillborn enterprise incorporated in 1912, capitalized at $250,000, and designed to construct a railway from Canning through Woodside, North Corner, Upper Pereau, and Delhaven (formerly Middle Pereau) to the top of Cape Blomidon, where Sir Frederick hoped to persuade the federal government to establish a park, then continuing on to Scott's Bay and Cape Split. Ever responsive to emerging commercial opportunities, Borden intended the project to profit from the public's growing interest in tourism, its fashionable, idealized search for natural beauty and tranquility, especially in the land of Evangeline. The company commissioned the recently founded Nova Scotia Technical College to prepare a report on the railway's feasibility and make recommendations on the location of termini. The company then circulated a community petition that Sir Frederick presented to the government in support of his own project.[37] In the Blomidon project as in others (for example, the Union Printing Company, designed to purchase and operate journals favourable to their various economic and political projects),[38] few people doubted that Leslie Macoun was anything but Sir Frederick's proxy, the guardian of Borden's personal and public legacy.[39] Ultimately he served as administrator of Sir Frederick Borden's estate.

Borden's confidence in Macoun's capable management of his regional interests enabled the minister to explore more speculative ventures, to exploit the opportunities offered by a growing circle of successful businessmen who hounded prominent politicians for favours. Many of these ventures brought Borden into contact with members of Canada's capitalist "clans" in Halifax, Montreal, and Toronto, described by Christopher Armstrong and H.V. Nelles in their book *Southern Exposure*.[40] While many of these men were Liberal friends and associates (for example, E.A. Robert, H.M. Pellatt, T. White, G. Cox, and B.F. Pearson), Borden's business interests crossed political lines and included prominent Conservatives (Edward Clouston, Frank Stanfield, Rufus Pope, R.J. Forget, and John Nesbitt Kirchhoffer, among others).

A speculator by nature, Borden enjoyed calculated risk in his entrepreneurial endeavours as well as in his private life. Confident of his country's unlimited potential, he placed money in mines (coal, gold, silver, copper, cobalt, and aluminum, especially in Ontario), as well as in banks, trusts, mortgages, insurance, utilities, cold storage, and manufacturing, often drawn into the market by his friend Henry Pellatt. Soon Borden's economic assets entailed investments in some seventy companies. His investment in the Reddick Larder Company, a cobalt mining company, was a risky decision that many "conservative business prophets" advised against, and by 1912 it had failed.[41] The Butte Central Copper Company, of which he was president, was also a long shot, chronically in need of money; it, too, eventually failed. Few of Borden's investments, though, were more "purely speculative"[42] than his investment in the Beaver Valley Oil Company, which was listed on the somewhat notorious Vancouver Stock Exchange. Nor did Borden hesitate to secure large demand loans from banks or mortgage companies to finance his speculation.[43] In other words, his investment strategy was neither parochial nor unduly cautious, and sometimes his adventures risked both material resources and personal reputation.

Indeed, at times Borden seemed to be running with a very fast crowd, if we can judge from his involvement in the Butte Central Copper Company.[44] To secure capital for Borden's Butte Central Copper Company, not only did Borden's broker Freeman I. Davison touch the minister's network of friends and patronage supplicants for investment funds, but he also worked the curb market, a world of unregulated exchange. To persuade Borden's contacts to invest in Butte Central, Davison promised to "manage the market" to guarantee a substantial profit.[45] As he explained to Borden in the fall of 1910, he intended to create a market for Butte Central and thus "enable everyone that is now in the syndicate to realize on any holdings they may wish to part with." Davison was confident that "when the public starts in – as they are sure to do – we will distribute all our holdings at a big profit. This would give all hands plenty of money, and the feeling of people with money in their pocket will go a long way to make Butte Central look as good as it did when we sat down and figured it out."[46] In short, Davidson planned to cut and run!

Borden's immediate response to this familiar trick of unscrupulous promoters was eloquent: "I am afraid you will have to manage your stock affairs without reference to me as I am not at all well."[47] That Borden's doctors advised him in the fall of 1910 to slow down there is no doubt, but in no other activity did he heed his doctor's advice or use it to escape obligations or decline opportunities. Borden, though speculative, was not entirely reckless. Deeply committed as he was to promoting Butte Central, Borden's diplomatic illness seems to have been more an effort to avoid complicity, to wash his hands of a questionable venture, an unwillingness to pay the price of public exposure.

Overall, Borden's investments tended to be in preferred stocks, bonds, and stock debentures that yielded a fixed income and possessed a prior equity claim on the company's assets, something to provide security on outstanding loans and mortgages. His common stock holdings were usually minimal, enough to demonstrate his faith in the enterprise, or were penny and promotional stocks. How profitable these assets were is difficult to say without access to more extensive and systematic documentation. The Reddick Larder mine, of which he was a director, failed in 1912. The Spanish River Pulp and Paper Company was "ravaged" by the 1913 recession.[48] Butte Central Copper was another failure as a productive mine. Still, unloading promotional stock in an internally managed market (the sort of activity that Davison suggested) and other sharp practices could be profitable, though risky and unethical. Although he was a cautious gambler, Borden's interest in mining ventures was not entirely speculative. He participated in their direction as well. He served as president of both the Silver Crown Mining Company and the Butte Central Copper Syndicate and was a director of the Canadian Cobalt Company and the Reddick Larder Mine Company.

Borden also retained an insatiable curiosity and faith in technology and in launching more productive enterprises. Telephone and telegraph companies and hydroelectric development attracted his interest and investments, as did the possibility of harnessing the Fundy tides. Moreover, these investments were not confined to the Nova Scotia Light and Power Company, the Nova Scotia Telephone Company, and other parochial endeavours. He was a director and vice-president of the Fessenden Wireless Telegraph Company, which sought licences in Newfoundland, Bermuda, and the West Indies.[49] Similarly, the Ontario Spanish River Pulp and Paper Company's promise to grind mechanically and hydraulically press pulp into paper captured his entrepreneurial imagination, and he endeavoured to replicate the process on his Gaspereau lands in Nova Scotia.

Another example of Borden's entrepreneurialism was his effort to establish the Canadian Linen Fibre Company, an industry that had enriched Macoun's family in Ireland. Capitalized at $2.5 million, the company was to work in cooperation with the Honourable William Pugsley, briefly premier of New Brunswick but then Borden's colleague in the federal cabinet as minister of public works. Their plan was to purchase from the American Linen Fiber Company of Philadelphia the patent rights to a machine to separate flax fibre from flax straw in "one continuous operation," an industry that might be located in his constituency and for which Macoun was to seek capital.[50]

Although it would be hazardous to draw conclusions on Maritime entrepreneurship from one case study, Sir Frederick did not lack the entrepreneurial talent to translate the region's resources into profitable enterprise. Nor was Borden's investment strategy marked by a parochial conservatism. His Canadian portfolio had a broad geographic distribution that included investments in Ontario, Manitoba, Alberta, and British Columbia.[51] While his portfolio contained holdings in safe conservative enterprises such as land, banks, railways, insurance, and utilities, he also held industrial stock (the Stanfield Company and the Spanish River Pulp and Paper Company, for example), as well as shares in at least eleven mining companies, by nature speculative.[52] During the first decade of the twentieth century, necessity and opportunity enabled Sir Frederick to negotiate a comfortable accommodation between family and corporate capitalism. His material interests now extended well beyond the region to encompass both nation and empire, an economic network that sought the services and resources of a compliant and regulatory state, nourished by an imperial connection.

CHAPTER 21

Political Business

Although Borden often complained that politics constrained his ability to make money, as a prominent politician with access to entrepreneurial men and resources, he found that it offered opportunities to accumulate wealth as well. If the strategic strength of pre–World War I Canadian capitalism rested upon its access to British capital, American technology, and its skilful management of a compliant state, as Christopher Armstrong and H.V. Nelles have observed, a politician occupied a strategic brokerage position from which he could negotiate policy and obtain favours, a role made more important by an increasingly active and regulatory state. In other words, the growth of the state enhanced a politician's status and utility, especially the status and utility of those who possessed influence with and the political dexterity to manage municipal, provincial, federal, and imperial governments, as Borden's career amply demonstrates.[1]

Borden's own constituency suggests the useful intersection of imperial, national, and personal interests. The reorientation of the Annapolis Valley's economy during these years made imperialism a very profitable venture for the region's farmers. Faced by the collapse of the New Brunswick timber trade, the decline of Saint John, and the rise of New Brunswick's competitive potato industry, the valley's apple farmers possessed a lucrative British market for their product, a market they came to dominate until World War II.[2] Britain had also become a useful source of the capital required to develop this market's potential, since commercial farmers required long-term capital investment while awaiting full fruition of their orchards.

With some 15 per cent of his total assets invested in commercial orchards, Borden recognized Britain as an important source of funds for these and other enterprises. After all, this was the golden age of British capital, a period from 1902 to 1914 when "Canada replaced the United States" as Britain's single largest borrower, "absorbing perhaps a third of British lending."[3] Many of Borden's and his partner's endeavours sought British capital, notably for mining and land companies. Two of Borden's investments, the Nichola Lake Horticultural Estates and the British Columbia Development Company, even denoted their shares in sterling. Similarly, several of Borden's land, mining, and utility endeavours worked closely with British companies such as the Imperial Trust Company, the Dominion of Canada Trust Company, and Empire Construction Company.[4]

Letters of introduction opened doors and facilitated access to British capital investment.[5] "Social capital" in the form of titles and public office purchased entrée, confidence, and credibility among the gentlemen capitalists in the imperial capital. In this world, appearance, dress, bearing, speech, and manners mattered, and Sir Frederick and Lady Borden could play that role convincingly. Indeed the prospect of cultivating these resources weighed heavily on Borden in his desire to succeed Lord Strathcona as Canada's high commissioner in London.

Whatever the constraints of public life, and there were constraints, office provided ample opportunities to advance private interests. The process began with membership in Parliament, itself a small, exclusive male club that gave access to a network of Canadian men of means and influence within and outside the House, a bipartisan world of interlocking interests where members might exchange favours and negotiate silence and complicity. Membership in this small club served as a magnet for those seeking favours (personal, public, or political) or promises of future considerations. The benefits to parliamentarians were multiple, great and small, from lucrative passes on rail and other forms of transportation for a member, his family, and friends to new clients, investment opportunities, and endorsements of promissory notes, opportunities from which Borden benefited.[6] Equally important to Borden was the parliamentarian's access to inside information, government officials, and services that could be used in the pursuit of private ends; for example, Department of Agriculture experts advised Borden on his dairy herds and on the value of a proposed cold storage project. Similarly, he had no qualms in soliciting and securing sales and discounts for his private business from persons seeking and receiving public contracts.[7]

Few members of Parliament possessed independent wealth. Most pursued several occupations. Moreover, the line between personal and public interests was often ambiguous, both creating unfair suspicion and masking personal benefit. One could ask, for example, whether Borden's successful lobbying of the Department of Agriculture (whose minister Sydney Fisher was his colleague, friend, and Ottawa neighbour) to establish an eighteen-hectare experimental research station in Kentville in 1910 to serve his constituency's lucrative apple and dairy industry was in the public interest or his own. The answer is that his lobbying probably served both ends and generated multiple benefits, including an opportunity for his political friends to negotiate a profitable land deal.

Similarly, the Conservative Opposition had reason to suspect the motives behind a federal expenditure of $33,867 on the construction of a wharf in Canning, tellingly called "Borden wharf," to accommodate the Dominion Atlantic Railway's spur line that ran along the Habitant River, partly bordering the minister's own property. The railway served the Canning port facility of which Borden's Produce and Supply Company was a chief beneficiary but which Borden defended as a public work designed to facilitate trade with Saint John and the West Indies. In addition, the line permitted Borden to build a rail spur to bring his ministerial railcar to Borden Place. While he defended these expenditures and others as community projects designed to stimulate the region's economy, his personal stake in the regional economy made him a principal beneficiary as well as a conspicuous object of suspicion in the eyes of vigilant, crusading progressives determined to expose conflicts of interest.[8]

Other instances of conflict of interest were less ambiguous. Three flagrant examples of Borden's conflation of public and private interests were his rescue of the R.W. Kinsman Company in 1899–1900, discussed in the previous chapter; his efforts to extract tax concessions, port access, and subsidies for the New Brunswick Cold Storage Company in Saint John; and his role in negotiating a scheme to electrify Halifax in which he and his friends possessed material interests.[9]

The New Brunswick Cold Storage Company, one of the offshoots of Borden's new diversified entrepreneurial strategy, proved a costly political blunder. At first glance, his cold storage venture resembled others: it was a bold, imaginative scheme to exploit the region's resources, a plan that combined public need and personal profit. Since reorganizing his Produce and Supply Company in 1903, Borden sought a more efficient means of developing and managing his extensive farm holdings, particularly his large apple orchards. In 1906 he considered making his entire farm operation a subsidiary of an American company, the American Farm Produce Company, backed by New York interests,[10] in which he would hold shares and a place on its board. But while he was assessing this idea, a larger, more adventuresome proposal, one that was closer to home, caught his attention. R.J. Graham, a Belleville, Ontario, fruit dealer and cold storage expert, proposed that he and the minister seek a federal charter to incorporate a company entitled the Canada Lands and Farm Products Limited with an authorized stock of $1 million.[11] The proposed company's purpose was to buy and store farm produce, especially fruit, while awaiting a favourable price on the English market. According to the plan, both men were to turn over their farms and orchards to the Canada Lands and Farm Products Limited in return for stocks and bonds in the new company. Borden was to go to England to float the company and secure sufficient capital during the spring and summer of 1907 to commence operations.

Although a private venture, this project addressed a pressing regional need. As early as October 1895 the *Maritime Grocer* had campaigned for more adequate cold storage facilities to aid local farmers.[12] The United Fruit Growers' Association and the regional United Boards of Trade, popular organizations among Annapolis Valley commercial farmers, had endorsed the campaign. But over a decade later their efforts had achieved little. As the extensive plantings of commercial orchards in the 1880s came to fruition, the need for proper cold storage facilities reached crisis proportions. By 1901 apple production in the three valley counties of Annapolis, Kings, and Hants amounted to 1,370,798 bushels. Poor storage facilities in the Annapolis Valley, Saint John, and Halifax entailed waste and loss of market advantage. J.W. Bigelow, the president of the Nova Scotia Fruit Growers' Association in 1901, estimated that valley farmers lost as much as $100,000 during that year owing to inadequate storage and shipping facilities.[13] Their inability to store the product while awaiting more favourable market conditions in London compounded their loss. Borden's projected large, well-equipped, and modern storage facilities at Saint John, Halifax, and an unspecified location in Prince Edward Island promised to change all this, providing both a public good and a private benefit.

From Graham's perspective, Borden brought more to Canada Lands and Farm Products Limited than his farmlands and social standing among England's gentlemen capitalists. Since Graham was a Conservative, he realized that Canada Lands and Farm Products would benefit from Sir Frederick's political knowledge and influence, especially given Borden's close personal friendship with Minister of Agriculture Sydney Fisher. Graham was not mistaken. From Borden's vantage within the Laurier cabinet, he learned that Fisher intended to launch a generous program of federal subsidies to encourage the construction of cold storage facilities. Confident that this policy was close to a certainty, Borden left for England to promote Canada Lands and Farm Products. The British mission, however, was not a success. In the end, the English promoters quarrelled among themselves and were unable to deliver the funds they had promised,[14] and Borden was obliged to settle for a more modest proposal, the creation of the New Brunswick Cold Storage Company, to be located in the thriving city of Saint John, whose ambitions to become a national port had been enhanced by A.G. Blair's tenure as Laurier's minister of railways and canals from 1897 to 1903.

Although the more modest New Brunswick Cold Storage Company lacked the grandiose proportions of Canada Lands and Products Limited, it promised ample scope for profits, especially if it possessed the support of political friends. Apart from Graham and Borden, the more modest proposal had attracted another helpful fixer, George McAvity, a prominent Liberal businessman from Saint John. In charting their strategy, Borden and Graham calculated that a cold storage plant could be constructed in Saint John for $75,000 to $80,000 (Borden later claimed the real costs ran to $160,000; this larger sum may have included refrigeration equipment). The federal government would pay one-third of the cost of the construction and equipment;[15] the New Brunswick government would guarantee the principal and interest on bonds to the amount of $60,000; the City of Saint John would offer municipal tax exemptions; and the government-run Intercolonial Railway, not to be outdone by the others' generosity, would lease to the Cold Storage Company a site close to its terminus, described as "one of the most desirable in the city," for $250 a year, tax exempt, for sixty-three years. (The ICR had purchased the site for $8,415 and had invested $4,000–$5,000 in improvements.) In other words, by placing little or no personal capital in the company, the promoters would obtain a very valuable property, if not an immediately profitable business. In fact, in its first year of operation, the company lost $15,000 owing to technical malfunctioning and questionable managerial decisions.[16] Nor had Borden and Graham anticipated the political costs.

In 1906 a Liberal competitor, F.E. Williams, was planning a comparable but more modest cold storage business in Saint John for fish, meat (principally pork), and fruit. He decided to apply for a subsidy from the Department of Marine and Fisheries under provisions in the Frozen Bait Act. Before making his application, Williams took the precaution of seeking the political endorsement of Henry Robert Emerson, Laurier's minister of railways and canals and a former premier of New Brunswick. Emerson not only endorsed Williams's application but suggested that he apply directly to the minister of agriculture, whose cold storage program was even more generous, inclusive, and appropriate to Williams's application.

After several inquiries at the Department of Agriculture, Williams discovered that he faced a competing application. Given Borden's close friendship with Fisher, Williams quickly and probably correctly concluded that his own application stood little chance of success against that of Borden's company, especially as his chief advocate in Laurier's cabinet, Emerson, has just been obliged to resign from the cabinet owing to Opposition charges of "wine, women and graft." Efforts to reconcile the contestants, to bring Williams into Borden's scheme, failed. Williams was so furious that he refused to comply with the department's request that he file an application with "proper specification." Instead he decided to go public.

He began with an anonymous letter to the Saint John *Globe* on 26 August 1907 in which he complained of the gross conflicts of interest. Then he addressed the Saint John City Council, which had offered the New Brunswick Cold Storage Company tax exemptions, denouncing Borden as interested only in securing government grants and construction and promotional profits; ironically, these were incentives that Williams himself had sought through political influence. Nevertheless Williams's indictment of Borden, though partial, was an accurate enough description of Borden's interest in the project. In May 1908 George Eulas Foster, the self-appointed chief of the Conservatives' morality squad, former member of Parliament for Saint John, and no friend of Borden's, raised the subject in the House of Commons. With all the rhetorical dexterity that the experienced parliamentarian could muster, Foster read into the records the correspondence between Borden and various interested parties, making the appropriate insinuations and ending with a charge of complicity that later he was obliged to withdraw.[17]

Just before the storm broke, Sir Frederick's family and friends had persuaded him to withdraw from the New Brunswick Cold Storage Company in favour of his son-in-law, L.S. Macoun. It was not an easy decision or one that he executed with good grace or, perhaps, even in good faith, since he continued to involve himself in the company's business. But as a result of his formal withdrawal, Borden could respond somewhat tendentiously to his accusers in the House, saying, "I do not own one dollar of stock. I have never received one dollar of benefit. I never expect or intend to hold one dollar of stock. I do not expect to receive one dollar of benefits."[18]

In the course of the debate Sir Frederick minimized his initial association with the cold storage project, which he represented as little more than a disinterested effort to advance the public good of his constituents from "the great Annapolis and Cornwallis Valley" by providing them with a long-sought essential facility. He dismissed his competitor's "hypocritical" complaints, pointing to Williams's own efforts to solicit political support and his subsequent failure to make an application for funds. Denying any personal material interest in the project or influence in the company's current direction, Borden took the offensive, rejecting the notion that his son-in-law ought "to be prevented from engaging in legitimate business because he happened to be connected to my family."[19] Then, carrying the battle into enemy territory, Borden ended his lengthy defence by reminding his chief accuser,

George Eulas Foster, of the Conservative critic's own less than spot-less record of public probity, a reference to criticism levelled at Foster by the 1906 Royal Commission on Life Insurance for his questionable management of the Independent Order of Foresters' investment funds.

Borden's clever but far from forthright retort obliged Foster to with-draw the charge of complicity, limited debate on the issue, and silenced, but failed to convince, his parliamentary critics. After all, Borden had invested considerable time, as well as financial and political credit, in promoting the cold storage project; he had been prepared to place his own farm properties in the pool; he had gone to England in search of capital for the earlier project; he had used his inside knowledge and influence to advantage; and he had withdrawn reluctantly (and with ill grace) from the project only under pressure from friends and family. Few could believe that he had no expectation of some material return. Indeed, Borden's private papers demonstrate the validity of their suspicions. Macoun, for example, continued to seek Borden's advice and approval for all decisions affecting the financial health of the company.[20] While Borden might cite his forced withdrawal from this scheme as an example of the constraints of public life on his entre-preneurial activities, it also demonstrated the potential benefits of pol-itical power, as well as his confusion over public and private interests.

Another example of the synergy between personal advantage and political power was Borden's role in a scheme to electrify Halifax. For years Borden fancied the economic potential of hydroelectricity that could be produced in the rivers and tides that traversed and bordered his constituency. These dreams were captured by the F.W. Borden Company's expansive act of incorporation in 1895, which included the right to own and operate electrical lines. In the spring of 1899, Borden incorporated the Nova Scotia Electric Light Company Limited to exploit this potential. His plan was to electrify Kings, Hants, and Hali-fax (excluding the city) with hydroelectricity generated from the Gas-pereau and Curel rivers. A prestigious Montreal hydraulic engineering firm, R. Pringle and Son, prepared a detailed survey of the potential of these rivers, together with cost and profit estimates. Its report cal-culated that the company might realize annual profits of 17 per cent on the $41,660 estimated capital costs for the erection of the hydroelec-tric facility. But for Borden the timing could scarcely have been worse, faced with an imminent South African War, the dismissal of Hutton, the food ration scandal, the death of his only son, and the precarious finances of his R.W. Kinsman Company. Overwhelmed by his finan-cial, political, and personal troubles, Borden failed to proceed with the project, and as a result the charter of the Nova Scotia Electric Light Company lapsed at that time.[21]

As it turned out, the project was merely postponed. Very shortly the rising price of pulp and paper and its dependence on cheap energy revived Borden's appetite for developing the abundance of water and woodlands on his Gaspereau property. As an early investor in the Spanish River Pulp and Paper Company, headquartered in Orillia, Ontario, Borden could not see why he could not replicate its apparent potential with his Gapereau proprieties. Convinced of the future and interdependence of pulp and power, in December 1906 he incorporated the Gaspereau Power Company Limited, capitalized at $50,000, designed to own, construct, and operate telegraph and telephone lines and generate hydroelectricity for domestic, municipal, and industrial use.[22] At the same time he incorporated the Gaspereau Lumber Company (later renamed the Borden Lumber Company) and, with the assistance of Macoun, sought investment capital to realize his property's potential.

The following year Borden persuaded W. George A. Lambe, a Montreal businessman, to join his project. To attract other potential investors, Lambe and Borden borrowed $80,000 from the Albany National Bank to purchase an additional 30,000 acres of largely spruce timberland along the Gaspereau River. In February 1909 Borden, having failed to interest American, British, or German capital in their power and pulp-and-paper project, persuaded Edmund Arthur Robert, a prominent Montreal Liberal and vice-president and managing director of the Canada Light and Power Company (and shortly to become, in 1910, president of the Montreal Street Railway), to invest in the project, along with the Montreal investment broker John Wilson McConnell.[23] This verbal agreement, however, was not signed and sealed until October 1910.

The Montreal investors' primary interest was not pulp and paper but an ambitious scheme to electrify the city of Halifax and take over the city's street tramway system and later its electric light and gas franchise.[24] Their plan followed a familiar contemporary corporate strategy. A syndicate would incorporate a company to own and develop the Gaspereau property and to supply adjacent communities with hydroelectricity, including the city of Halifax, which was to be their primary market target. There they intended to purchase the recently electrified Halifax Tramway Company, which they anticipated would consume an estimated 5,000 horsepower and whose annual earnings ($190,000) and surplus fund ($460,000) would be used to pay dividends on the syndicate's inflated (watered) capital securities. Sir Frederick's role in this project was twofold, to sell the syndicate his Gapereau property rights and to use his political credit to secure the necessary legislative authority to execute their plan. According to a formal memorandum of agreement, Robert promised Borden and Lambe $50,000 in cash each for their share of the property, as well as $50,000 worth of bonds and $50,000 in capital stock in the proposed company.[25]

Lambe possessed far less confidence in the scheme and in the integrity of its promoters than Borden. Pressed by the Albany Bank for repayment of his half of the $80,000, Lambe began to worry about Robert's delay in signing the final agreement as well as about the value of the stock, preferring bonds to the shares in the proposed company. Borden tried to reassure Lambe, explaining to his skittish partner that the stock would be valuable, "the same as that of which Mr Robert and his associates expect to make their money."[26] So confident was Borden in the value of the scheme that he informed Lambe he would prefer stock to bonds[27] and would gladly buy Lambe out if he had the money to do so.[28] There was little Robert could do to meet Lambe's concerns, however, until his proposed project possessed a legal corporate structure that would allow it to hold property and issue bonds and stock.

Borden's confidence in the Hydro project possessed a firmer material base than Lambe's.[29] Long before Robert signed the formal memorandum of agreement with Borden and Lambe in October 1910, Borden and Robert had negotiated a side agreement for repayment for Borden's Gapereau properties and/or his political services. In November 1909 Borden agreed to underwrite $100,000 worth of bonds in Robert's Canada Light and Power Company, for which Borden paid only 20 per cent of the principal in two instalments, a total of $20,000, and for which he received a bonus of $100,000 in stock in Robert's Canada Light and Power. In March 1910 Borden transferred the $100,000 worth of bonds and $60,000 (600 shares) worth of stock back to Robert's company, leaving himself with $40,000 (400 shares) of stock in Canada Light and Power. Borden then cashed his remaining 400 ($40,000) shares and used $20,000 to cover the outstanding amount in his transaction with Robert. With the remaining amount ($20,000) he purchased 500 shares in the Montreal Street Railway.[30]

More lucrative profits awaited the success of the electrification of Halifax. Anxious to realize these rewards, Borden immediately attempted to resuscitate the charter of his Nova Scotia Electric Light Company. But when this failed, in 1909 he instructed his legal advisor, W.E. Roscoe, to seek incorporation of a new company, the Nova Scotia Power and Pulp Company, capitalized at $6 million and with sweeping powers. This request immediately aroused the apprehensions of Halifax city councillors. To allay their fears and avoid the scrutiny of the province's new Board of Public Utilities, the promoters of the proposed new company agreed that the city of Halifax would be excluded from the company's reach and that the company would refrain from owning shares and franchises of other companies. Once the company was incorporated, Robert honoured his agreement with Borden and Lambe. Since they had borrowed $80,000 of their $100,000 reward from the Albany National Bank, each would have realized a profit of $10,000, less costs.[31] So confident was Borden of the larger project's material success that he underwrote an additional $25,000 worth of bonds in the Nova Scotia Power Company.[32]

Borden's need to secure and enhance the value of his investments kept him actively engaged in the tumultuous politics that ensued, a task that placed a premium on his political services. Success required both access to the Halifax power market and the right to purchase the city's tramway company, with its exclusive franchise. Consequently, in April 1911 Borden's political ally, H.H. Wickwire, the recently re-elected member of the legislature for Kings, introduced a private member's bill in the provincial legislature to change the name of Borden's former company, the Nova Scotia Power and Pulp Company, to the Nova Scotia Power Company, making it clear that the company's single objective was hydroelectricity, not pulp, and giving it access to the Halifax market and the right to own shares in other companies. In short, the private member's bill was a clear repudiation of the company's previous agreement and an open declaration of war against the Halifax Electric Tramway Company and those campaigning for municipal ownership, a cause promoted by William Dennis, the English-born city counsellor and owner of the *Halifax Herald*, soon to become a Conservative senator.

Initially the battle for the bill, both in the Nova Scotia House of Assembly and the Legislative Council, appeared little more than a partisan political dispute between Liberals and Conservatives. But it was more complicated than that. It was also what the *Canadian Annual Review of Public Affairs* grandly described as "a fight for the financial supremacy of Halifax,"[33] as well as a dispute over notions of progress, the efficacy of public ownership, and the community's resistance to outsiders, in this case the "Montreal carpetbaggers." In fact, neither Liberals nor Conservatives were entirely united. Two of the Liberals' four Halifax representatives in the provincial legislature, Robert Finn and George Faulkner, broke political ranks to oppose the bill, and others were sufficiently restless that Sir Frederick was obliged to despatch several stiffly worded telegrams to Liberal premier George H. Murray to get the charter through the legislature.[34] Whatever the reason, the bill passed in the legislature quickly and with a comfortable majority.

But the battle had just begun. No sooner had the bill passed the legislative hurdle and had the Robert "syndicate" begun to buy shares in the Halifax Electric Tramway Company than Robert's group faced a bipartisan corporate rival, the Nova Scotia Hydraulic Company, led

by local businessmen such as B.F. Pearson, the owner of the Liberal
Halifax *Morning Chronicle,* and Frank Stanfield, the underwear manufacturer and the recently elected Conservative MLA for Colchester. (Sir
Frederick had business relations with both men, having loaned money
to Pearson and invested in the Stanfield Company.) Pearson and Stanfield and their associates envisaged electrifying Halifax with power
from the Mersey River, and like their rivals they were anxious to gain
control of the city's lucrative tramway company. To confront the tramway company's resistance to takeover by either group and to respond
to a growing demand for public ownership, Sir Frederick, W.S. Fielding, and Premier Murray persuaded the rival business groups to join
forces. In fact, Robert's syndicate effectively absorbed its business
rivals, buying them out for $250,000.[35] The union silenced a corporate
rival, but more important it purchased valuable Conservative political
support that weakened the Conservatives' opposition to Robert's plan.

Even corporate unity, however, could not stifle resistance. The
president of the Halifax Electric Tramway Company, the seventy-three-
year-old Conservative senator David MacKeen, a stockbroker and
former general manager of the Dominion Coal Company, headed the
opposition. In renegotiating the tramway's franchise with the city in
January 1912, MacKeen tried to spike Robert's guns by offering Halifax city a deal it could not resist. This suicidal deal offered more generous financial returns to the city by limiting the company's dividends to
its shareholders, freezing the issue of further securities, and providing
the city with a veto over the purchase of hydroelectricity from outside
the city. So generous to Halifax city were the company's financial terms
that the aggrieved shareholders immediately cried "confiscation" and
organized a movement to remove the tramway company's directors and
management before the proposed new contract received the required
legislative approval.

Delighted by the division in the ranks of his opponents, Robert
immediately sought and received federal incorporation of the Nova
Scotia Development Company, into which the Robert syndicate and
other unhappy shareholders placed their shares. With these and any
additional shares they could purchase, by February 1913 the Nova
Scotia Development Company possessed a sufficient number of shares
to rid itself of MacKeen and his friends and install Robert as president
of the Halifax Electric Tramway Company. By this time Robert's group
controlled the electric light and gas franchise as well.[36]

The only way to block Robert now was to municipalize the tramway.
To do so, the Halifax City Council announced that it would seek public
approval by referendum to purchase the tramway. But this measure
required legislative consent. Before a referendum could be organized,

Robert's group retaliated by seeking legislative authority to increase its tramway company's authorized capital from its modest limit of $1.5 million to $5 million to develop "Borden's" Gaspereau property, which its detractors dismissed as "150,000 acres of 'blueberry barrens.'"[37] A fierce newspaper war ensued, led by the recently created Senator Dennis and his *Halifax Herald*. A sometime advocate of public ownership, Dennis was determined to defend the province from the depredation of the Montreal carpetbaggers, so determined that he was ready to back a rival Montreal private initiative so long as it was Conservative![38] His opponents generously reciprocated the senator's charges of betrayal, political treachery, and character assassination. Occasionally, however, the debate rose to a higher level, to discuss the nature of progress and the economies and merits of public ownership.

The public debate that preceded and accompanied the introduction of the rival private member's bills, one from the city and the other from Robert's group, made these private bills "the most discussed" and controversial issues of the 1913 legislative session, a story that has been recounted humorously elsewhere by Christopher Armstrong and H.V. Nelles. Although Sir Frederick was not a central actor in this public drama, he remained an interested and influential senior member of the stage crew. In the end, the legislature approved neither of the opposing private bills, despite the Liberals' comfortable majority in both houses.[39] As a result, the city failed to secure authority to expropriate the tramway; and Robert's tramway group lost its bid to increase its authorized capitalization. Even the Liberal premier cast his vote against Robert's request; all that the Liberal-dominated legislature provided the Robert group was a modest consolation prize, a bill permitting the tramway to increase its capitalization from $1.5 million to $2 million.

The following year, the last pre-war session, Robert's group returned to the legislature with an even more grandiose proposal, backed by accrued political support. Robert's new private member's bill requested the incorporation of a Nova Scotia tramways and power company, capitalized at no less than $20 million. The new bill was designed not only to control the city's tramway, electric light, and gas franchise, but also to develop other hydroelectric facilities, notably at West River, Sheet Harbour. The Robert group's purchase of the Sheet Harbour property the previous year from the newly named Conservative senator Nathaniel Curry and his nephew, Edgar Nelson Rhodes, the Conservative MP for Cumberland, was more than a straightforward business deal. It crippled the efforts of provincial Conservative leader Charles Elliott Tanner to make his opposition to Robert's new bill simply a party issue. Inspired by Ontario Conservative premier James P. Whitney's popular nationalization of hydroelectricity and Robert Borden's verbal flirtation with "government ownership or operation" of public resources and franchises,[40] Tanner, backed by Senator Dennis, led a spirited battle for public ownership, against Robert's reinforced bipartisan coalition.

Although once again the provincial legislature would be the central stage for the subsequent drama, Ottawa became the site of important, intense backstage lobbying. This was almost inevitable given the Nova Scotia Development Corporation's federal charter, the inextricable relationship between provincial and federal politics, and the fact that one of Halifax's two members of Parliament was the prime minister of Canada, Robert Borden. To no one's surprise the contending parties focused their lobbying on the prime minister owing to his ambiguous attitude toward public ownership and his personal interest in the potential political fallout, not to mention his relationship with his cousin, one of the Robert syndicate's interested parties.

As the Conservatives, Rhodes and Curry, made their rounds soliciting support for Robert's syndicate, one of Sir Frederick's defeated Conservative opponents, Caleb Rand Bill, warned Rhodes that he was running with a fast crowd and that "Robert and Sir Fred" had "no love for you and your uncle." While Bill's general advice seemed to be "a plague on both your houses," a warning to Rhodes against trusting either side, more significantly Bill seemed to see "Sir Robert and Sir Frederick" as a unit.[41] Suffice to say that in the end Robert Borden, for whatever reason, effectively threw his support behind the Robert syndicate by making it clear that he did not oppose the syndicate. That was all that was needed. After an intense heated debate within and outside the legislature, the Robert bill passed largely along party lines, Tanner's Conservatives maintaining a facade of unity except for the conspicuous absence of two Conservative members, Frank Stanfield and Robert Hamilton Butts, and for a Conservative member of the Legislative Assembly who explained privately that he had only voted with his party under very strong pressure.[42]

The new company was incorporated as the Nova Scotia Tramways and Power Company in June 1914, with Sir Frederick as one of its fifteen directors. Borden was now one step closer to his repeatedly expressed desire to live "to see the power of the Gaspereau utilized in a manner that would supply electricity for the whole length and breath of the Valley as well as for Halifax."[43] Over a year passed before the province's Public Utilities Board approved the new company's principal objective of taking over the Halifax tramways. Consequently, it was not until January 1917 (the month Sir Frederick died) that the Nova Scotia Tramways and Power Company purchased from itself, namely its Nova Scotia Development Company, the Montreal-based holding company, its controlling shares in the Halifax Electric Tramway

Company. Had Sir Frederick lived longer, however, he would not have *seen* his dream realized, the dream of the Gaspereau's power electrifying Halifax, since soon after his death the syndicate chose alternative hydro sources to supply the city's power needs.

The extent and value of Sir Frederick's holdings in the new corporate structure as it made its tortuous way through its various corporate incarnations cannot be determined precisely. But if the "grab" was as profitable to its promoters as has been suggested, then Sir Frederick's last large regional speculative venture may have been the most lucrative of his career.[44] In addition to his $40,000 side deal with Robert and the $10,000 profit on his Gaspereau property, Borden had received $50,000 worth of bonds and $50,000 worth of common stock in the Nova Scotia Power and Pulp Company.[45] At the time of his death he may have held as much as $250,000 in common stock in the company, stock that at one time he had optimistically estimated could realize $250,000 to $270,000 on the open market.[46]

Clearly public life, whatever its constraints, had its rewards. Moreover, the complicity between political power and personal profit helped keep Borden interested and active in public life. This complicity, however, was not unrestrained. An increasingly vigilant public sphere shaped by "press and pulpit" contested this complicity, determined to hold its public representatives to a higher standard of personal and public behaviour. Theirs was a crusade in which Borden soon became a conspicuous and vulnerable target.

CHAPTER 22

Political Purity

Just before the 1904 federal election Sir Frederick had toyed with the idea of retiring from public life. After nine elections and thirty-one years of active political service, elections had "become a commonplace event." Perhaps, he mused, it was time to leave politics. But unfinished business detained him on this and subsequent occasions.[1] In 1904 Lord Dundonald's uncertain intentions, their possible electoral repercussions, and Laurier's personal plea that Borden remain and face another election overcame Sir Frederick's initial hesitations.[2] As colleagues from Laurier's first "cabinet of all the talents," provincial leaders such as Mowat, Blair, Davies, and Tarte, had been replaced by younger men, Laurier depended more and more on the loyalty of his old guard. And as an incentive for Borden to remain, the prime minister promised to name him lieutenant-governor of Nova Scotia or Canadian high commissioner to the United Kingdom, should the aged Strathcona ever retire, both tempting prospects that Borden realized might be redeemed more readily within than outside the cabinet.

Furthermore, the party's electoral success seemed almost certain. At the height of his power and popularity, Laurier was in full command of his party. The country was prosperous. The Ninth Parliament's productive legislative record argued strongly for the government's re-election. No major scandal marred the government's record. The only uncertainty was Dundonald's theatrics, and that problem soon faded once the aggrieved general had been recalled. But while the general remained, Borden felt a personal responsibility, the need to defend his central role in the drama. Fearing the issue's centrality in the campaign, the party printed 10,000 copies of Borden's speech to the Commons explaining the circumstances surrounding Dundonald's dismissal. As for the Opposition, its fortunes seemed to have fled. Demoralized, divided, and disorganized, it was unlikely to put up a strong fight.

Sir Frederick's own chances of success seemed indisputably strong. Well entrenched in Kings, freshly titled, and increasingly prominent in national and imperial affairs, he enjoyed access to the largesse of both the federal and provincial governments. His cousin's leadership of the Conservative Party removed the personal antagonism between

Sir Frederick and the Conservative Party leadership that had enlivened previous recent contests. And nowhere were the Conservative Party's disorganization, demoralization, and ill fortune more visible than in Kings County. Conscious of the difficulty of dislodging Sir Frederick, the Conservative Party had nominated a Dr Miller, a former mayor of Kentville, to represent them, but much to their embarrassment Miller had declined the nomination. Then a successor, Peter Innis, the general manager of the Dominion Atlantic Railway, agreed to stand, more out of a sense of party loyalty than conviction. But Innis was a very ill man and was soon obliged to withdraw to consult a physician in Boston. The party tried again, and finally James W. Ryan, a merchant and another former mayor of Kentville, agreed to be the party's sacrificial lamb.[3]

Borden's comfortable self-assurance and popularity contrasted sharply with the Conservatives' uncertainties and tribulations. The Liberals' meeting in Kentville on 8 October to acclaim Sir Frederick as their candidate was well attended, the delegates confident and enthusiastic. In responding to the partisan meeting's endorsement of the government's record and his own success, Borden thanked the audience and regaled it with humorous stories of past elections, demonstrating his ease and confidence. So confident was he of the outcome of the election that he spent relatively little time campaigning in Kings. He returned to his constituency only for the essential meetings with his opponent. The party, sharing Borden's optimism, decided to employ him elsewhere, charging him with the oversight of the counties of Cumberland, Colchester, and Pictou, where he canvassed and spoke on behalf of the Liberal candidates in those localities. As a recognized regional and national leader, he also assisted the Liberals in New Brunswick.[4]

Borden did not neglect his constituency entirely. Although his public meetings were few, he employed other electoral tactics. Signed photographs of the minister in court attire reminded friends and supporters of the eminence of their candidate. Maps sent to schoolteachers for use in their classrooms underscored Borden's support for education and his growing reputation in the larger imperial world painted red, a world increasingly important to his constituency's economy. To others he addressed friendly, anecdotal, personalized letters, admonishing them to "vote the right way," the sort of letters that could easily have been drafted by a knowledgeable, sensitive assistant and signed by Sir Frederick; after all, his private secretary, Harry Brown, knew the constituency well.[5]

The result was overwhelming. In 1904 not a Conservative candidate was elected in Nova Scotia, not even his cousin, the leader of the Opposition. Kings led the party's provincial success: Sir Frederick received a margin of 1,167 votes over his unfortunate opponent, taking 64 per cent of the votes cast, the largest majority of any candidate in the province and the largest of his career. As his victory was announced, an enthusiastic crowd, led by a band, gathered in front of Borden Place, Sir Frederick's grand renovated house on the Main Street of Canning, to serenade and cheer their candidate's success. Sir Frederick was drawn by his supporters through the streets to the centre of town, where the impressive monument to his son had been unveiled scarcely a year before. There he addressed the large audience and thanked them for his success. Despite the magnitude, ease, and personal nature of his 1904 victory, Sir Frederick had difficulty enjoying the occasion. As he explained to a friend, he was beginning to lose his appetite for elections.[6]

The 1904 election ended the relative calm that had marked Canada's Ninth Parliament. In the Tenth Parliament public and private morality became the Conservatives' progressive battle cry, their response to a growing, organized public crusade to legislate morality and reform society. Organized moral regulators inside and outside Parliament demanded laws to remedy a wide spectrum of perceived social ills. Temperance, Sunday observance, family values, the banishment of impure books, the abolition of racetrack gambling, and the end of civic corruption fuelled their reforming zeal. Given the state's strategic role in delivering this progressive program of public ownership and regulation, the crusaders riveted their gaze on public life and its prominent participants, insisting on political and personal purity and on the need to put an end to bribery, corruption, and conflicts of interest. While the Conservatives concentrated their fire on the departments of the Interior, Marine and Fisheries, Railways and Canals, and Customs, they soon found that they "were much better at alleging than confirming wrongdoing in the Canadian government" and that their strategy incurred liabilities, including a growing public distrust of all politicians.[7] Often they had difficulty distinguishing between corruption and an inefficiency that was the result of archaic administrative procedures.

At first Sir Frederick seemed shielded from the Opposition scrutiny owing to his friendship with Sam Hughes and his kinship with the leader of the Opposition. Sir Frederick's family shield, however, was far from impermeable. Robert and Sir Frederick were professional politicians, consenting adults, occupying prominent positions on opposing teams in an adversarial public sport. While their public exchanges were always civil, respectful, and restrained, their mutual respect failed to prevent them from airing their policy differences, at least for the record. Robert questioned Sir Frederick on his military estimates, and

Sir Frederick teased Robert about conflicts and contradictions within his somewhat fractious party. Even so, some Conservatives remained unhappy with their leader's gentility, his "reasonable" direction of their party, and his blindness to his cousin's foibles. Occasionally they used Sir Frederick as a target, a means to embarrass their chief and demonstrate his ineffectual leadership. Increasingly under pressure from his party to be more aggressive, Robert participated more actively in its morality crusade after 1904.[8] Robert could not remain forever a hostage to family loyalties; nor did Sir Frederick expect his protection, especially as his own private life and business transactions became a subject of public record.

Charges of intemperance had haunted Sir Frederick from his entry into politics. Nor did chivalry confine his affections to courtly love. Stories of Sir Frederick's more exotic private life had been the stuff of speculation and gossip for years, local wags carelessly attributing Kings County's reputation for "brains" to Sir Frederick's extramarital activities! Others enjoyed repeating the local admonition: "Hide your daughters, Dr Borden is coming!"[9] The first serious libellous attack on Sir Frederick's personal behaviour, however, appeared in the *Calgary Eye Opener*, "an amusing but disreputable little weekly"[10] edited by Robert Edwards. The *Eye Opener*'s story, designed to thwart Sir Frederick's rumoured appointment to the high commissionership in London, focused on the minister's alleged "hi-jinks" at a military banquet in Toronto. According to Edwards's story, Sir Frederick had become so intoxicated during the Toronto banquet that he had performed a sword dance on the table to prove that he could dance between the decanters, not an entirely unusual antic during mess dinners! More incriminating was the allegation that after the banquet the titled minister had been sighted in the company of "two ladies of easy virtue," from whose company he emerged two days later without his Windsor uniform and consequently unable to attend a government banquet.

To his friends, Sir Frederick dismissed Edwards's article as lacking "the slightest foundation or justification," attributing it to the work of "a small clique of low down politicians."[11] In his more forthright communication with his solicitor, however, he confessed that he did play the violin and that sometimes at social gatherings he had joined "the boys, playing accompaniments to the singing."[12] Convinced that it was best to give the article as little publicity as possible, especially considering the paper's dubious character, Sir Frederick chose to ignore it,[13] citing the American preacher Dr Lyman Beecher's admonition: "[N]ever go to war with a skunk, for he had once done so ... and the skunk got the best of it."[14]

Given his desire to succeed Lord Strathcona, however, Sir Frederick could not ignore an article entitled "The 'Pure Politics' in Canada

Campaign" that appeared in 1907 in the prominent British journal the *Nineteenth Century and After*. In this sulphurous, muckraking account, its author, H. Hamilton Fyfe, described "the foul and miasmic depths of corruption" that lay behind Ottawa's "apparently tranquil and engaging surface," beginning with the Pacific Scandal.[15] Fyfe then repeated the *Eye Opener*'s attack on Sir Frederick as a more recent example of the Canadian capital's continuing sordid and corrupt private and public life, cautiously omitting the minister's name. The Conservative journal the *Toronto World*, for whatever reason, picked up the British article, giving its accusations further publicity.

Sir Frederick reacted immediately. After consulting Sir Wilfrid Laurier on the article's allegations, the minister placed the matter in the hands of Charles Russell, his legal counsel in London.[16] The *Nineteenth Century and After* responded at once with a full apology, which it published in its December 1907 issue, "withdrawing" the offending article, expressing its "extreme regret that any such unfortunate and scurrilous gossip should have been quoted in these pages," and offering its sincere apologies to Sir Frederick "for any injury which could possibly have accrued to him from such a scandalous story."[17] The magazine's apology was accompanied by a sum of £250 sterling in damages and the payment of court costs. Although Borden initially believed that the article was the work of "low level politicians," he became increasingly convinced that its real target was his cousin, the leader of the Opposition, as least in the case of the Conservative *Toronto World*.[18]

Sir Frederick's trials were far from over. On the last day of December 1907, the month that the *Nineteenth Century and After* published its apology, the irrepressible *Calgary Eye Opener* struck again with another, more-compromising story. The second volley consisted of a letter from a Mrs Maria Allison, who ran the boarding house on Russell Street in Ottawa where Sir Frederick had stayed before joining the cabinet, in which she accused Sir Frederick of inducing her daughter to leave home. Ten days later a second letter from Mrs Allison itemized other alleged misdeeds committed by the minister while he resided in her boarding house. In both cases, Sir Frederick ignored Mrs Allison's charges, treating them and the *Eye Opener* with contempt. His contempt, however, did not banish public doubts and suspicions or silence the wily Mrs Allison and her daughter.

Meanwhile Sir Frederick's public morality, his distribution of Militia contracts and favours to friends and associates, was attracting Opposition scrutiny, despite their leader's apparent sensitivity on the subject. Generally Borden's contemporaries on both sides of the House commended his resistance to partisan interference in military appointments and professional advancements, enumerating the many examples of non-partisan appointments. Even the *Military Gazette*, which was no friend of Borden or the government, concluded in 1904 that Sir Frederick "has shown his good faith [as a non-partisan administrator] in the appointments he has made in connection with both peace and war contingents, and in selecting men for the Permanent Force and the staff."[19]

Borden insisted on professional criteria for military appointments, and even in awarding other, non-essential patronage, he appeared even-handed and non-partisan. For example, in the distribution of honorary titles and positions (such as honorary lieutenant-colonelcies) to rich and pretentious friends and business associates, an innocuous, bi-partisan indulgence in which the rich patron provided private funding to urban Militia units in exchange for colourful uniforms, gold braids and titles, those who were favoured included Liberal partisans such as Sir Henry Pellatt (Queen's Own Rifles) and the Ottawa lumber king J.R. Booth (43rd Regiment), with whom Borden had business and political relations, as well as Conservatives such as H. Montague Allan (5th Royal Scots) and Rodolphe Forget (65th Carabiniers), all wealthy prominent citizens.

Although one recent historian concluded that Borden's management of the public funds entrusted to his department was generally sensible, honest, and effective, a reconciliation of the public good "with the benefits of patronage,"[20] some of Borden's partisan opponents were less confident and probed assiduously for evidence of malfeasance. Hard evidence of malfeasance was often as difficult to establish, however, as suspicions were to allay. Moreover, neither accusation nor suspicion nor lack of evidence alone established guilt or innocence. And those who sought hard evidence frequently faced roadblocks. For example, in 1906–07 the Commons' Public Accounts Committee closely scrutinized the Militia Department's suspicious purchase of 450 shooting galleries from the Ontario Sub-Target Gun Company, since the company's shareholders included Borden's personal secretary, C.L. Panet, and his business associates H.M. Pellatt, F.O. Lewis, J.M. Woods, H.H. Wickwire, and others. But when Borden and Panet testified before the committee, they were both afflicted with a severe case of amnesia. Neither man was able to recall the exact details.[21] The Public Accounts Committee was no more successful in 1908 in its inquiry into the continuing business relationships between Borden's son-in-law, L.S. Macoun, an investment broker and agent, and the government-owned Dominion Arsenal that Macoun supplied with metals and machinery.[22]

Still, the Conservatives continued to probe the Militia Department's annual accounts. They questioned the department's annual contracts with Borden's business partner, J.W. Wood, for "tens of thousands of dollars," to supply "tents and other equipment," since Wood was a large Ottawa property owner, the commanding officer of the Governor

General's Foot Guard, and the Militia Department's landlord.[23] Similarly, they kept a watching brief on his department's contract with the Ottawa Car Company, whose president, Thomas Ahearn, was both Sir Frederick's and the prime minister's personal friend. Borden defended the contract on the grounds that the company had invested in special machinery to produce military equipment, an arrangement the Conservatives continued when they came to power.[24] Still, appearances and perceptions could be misleading and a fertile breeding ground for suspicions. Consequently, while one scholar found no "evidence of patronage for personal or political gain" in Borden's dealing with Charles Ross and his rifle,[25] the minister's close friendship with Vickers-Maxim's Canadian agent, F.O. Lewis, a Montreal banker, merchant, and co-partner in Borden's cold storage business, might well have created concerns, especially as Borden's re-equipment of the Canadian field and garrison artillery required the negotiation of contracts with Vickers for several millions of dollars, and Vickers was the only supplier.

As the 1908 federal election approached, the Opposition accelerated its assault on the government. Its strategy turned the fourth session of Canada's Tenth Parliament into a circus of accusations and recriminations, a spectacle that lasted for 236 days, the longest parliamentary session to that date. The self-appointed crusty old chief of the Opposition's morality squad, George Eulas Foster, still stinging from the 1906 life insurance commission's criticism of his handling of the funds of the Independent Order of Foresters (the commission had called it "shady"), sought revenge and Sir Frederick became his special prey.[26] Foster, sensing the minister's vulnerability, hounded Sir Frederick relentlessly on the minister's administration of his department, his alleged conflicts of interest, and his troubled private life. Borden and Foster were old opponents, and their verbal duel rapidly degenerated into a parliamentary dogfight, occasionally requiring the Speaker's intervention to restore order and decorum.

In May 1908 Foster raised the issue of Sir Frederick's complicity in the New Brunswick Cold Storage deal, reading into the parliamentary record F.E. Williams's bitter press communications charging Sir Frederick with influence peddling and conflict of interest. Then, just as the debate on Sir Frederick's association with the New Brunswick Cold Storage Company began to subside, Foster struck again, asking the minister to respond to the charges raised by Mrs Alison's letters published some five months previous. Although this was a private matter, Foster's question focused attention on an issue that Sir Frederick had hoped to suffocate with silence. The Opposition, however, determined to create an image of a government permeated by "wine, women and graft," regarded it as an opportunity too good to miss.

To enhance the public perception of malfeasance, the Opposition insisted that Sir Frederick's estimates be subjected to meticulous scrutiny. Foster demanded to know the price of the land purchased to expand the Militia's campground at Niagara. He questioned the terms of the contract with the Ross factory for 52,000 bayonets to accompany the controversial rifles, a query that predictably reopened debate on the government's controversial choice of the Ross rifle and its production and delivery difficulties. This Opposition strategy backfired, however, as Sam Hughes intervened to assist Sir Frederick, contradicting or correcting Foster's more extravagant charges.[27] While Sir Frederick appreciated Hughes's interventions, he had little difficulty defending himself. He could obfuscate, insinuate, and confound with the best of them; indeed, his admirers thought he was best when provoked.

Although the Conservatives' morality crusade was less successful than they had hoped, they were beginning to inflict Liberal casualties. To limit the damage, in May 1907 Laurier, convinced that the Opposition's revelations were more the result of archaic administrative structures than corruption, charged John Mortimer Courtney, a recently retired sixty-seven-year-old civil servant, with a royal commission to examine the structures of Canadian government and make appropriate recommendations. As a result of his investigations, in June 1908 the government introduced Bill 189, an amendment to the Civil Service Act, creating a Civil Service Commission designed to establish a professional, merit-based, non-partisan inside civil service.

A history of conflict animated Borden's relations with Courtney. A "choleric," English-born, Gladstonian "liberal radical," Courtney had little sympathy for the Militia.[28] As deputy minister of finance, he had scrimmaged frequently with Sir Frederick over his department's expanding estimates and expenditures, probably acting with Fielding's full support. Courtney resisted and resented Sir Frederick's several successful raids on the public purse, especially his repeated request for supplementary estimates. He had tried to restrain Borden on several occasions, and their battles were often intense. Twice Sir Frederick had to threaten resignation in order to persuade Laurier to overrule the powerful deputy minister.

Courtney had also been critical of Borden's administration of his department. In 1903 he had initiated an investigation into alleged misappropriation of funds and careless accounting practices in the Militia Department. Borden, however, had responded positively to Courtney's criticism. Acutely aware of the power of information and efficient systems and their relationship to control and authority, Borden welcomed the opportunity to reorganize his department's chaotic record-keeping system. Based on a dated British practice, his department's records and communications had been retained, or not, by the individual or unit to whom the communication was addressed or referred. Often lost, misfiled, or discarded, the departmental records possessed little coherence, consistency, or continuity. After canvassing the experience and advice of the British War Office and the American Department of War, Borden chose the more centralized American model. Instituted by 1904, his new record system possessed one central registry, served by a vertical card system, for all departmental records except for secret material.[29] The system subsequently served as a model for other government departments.[30]

Borden's exemplary positive response, however, did not prevent Courtney from revisiting the Militia Department during his 1907–08 investigation or from faulting it for its reporting structures and wasteful practices. Convinced that the recently created Militia Council was responsible for the department's expanding budget demands and careless, extravagant expenditures, Courtney focused his criticism on the council, claiming that it was controlled by its military rather than its civilian members, a strange charge and one in contradiction to the charges of most of Borden's critics, who saw the council as an unfortunate triumph of civilian control. In Courtney's view, the Militia Council had to be brought back under civilian control, along the lines of the British Army Council.[31]

Courtney's severe criticism of the Militia Department irritated Sir Frederick. More disturbing still was his cousin's response. In his opening speech on Bill 189, Robert Borden, pressed by his party to be "less reasonable," had devoted some fifteen minutes to Courtney's strictures of the Militia Department, clearly inviting Foster and others to follow his lead. Although the Opposition had often dismissed Courtney as a "Liberal hack," on the eve of a federal election it was prepared to use whatever ammunition came to hand. Provoked by these criticisms of his department, and at his best when provoked, Borden decided to spike their guns immediately. Courtney's report, Borden countered, was biased, inaccurate, misleading, and prejudiced, grounded on hearsay, faulty newspaper gossip, and unsubstantiated assumptions. More than that, Courtney's criticisms were simply the continuation of a vendetta, a regurgitation of the 1903 criticism of his department's administration of funds (and those departmental flaws had been corrected). Yet Courtney persisted, singling out Borden's department and holding it to higher standards than those held for other departments.

As for Courtney's criticism, Borden continued, that the Militia Council was too powerful, dominated by military members who had emasculated the civilian deputy minister, he was simply wrong, especially when he contrasted the Canadian to the British Army Council. In fact, the only discernible difference between the British Army Council and Borden's Militia Council was that the British Army Council could "make decisions in the absence of the war secretary, [whereas] the Militia Council was purely advisory," thereby enshrining "the Canadian principle of absolute civil supremacy."[32] Contrary to Courtney's assertions, Borden assured the House, the deputy minister's powers remained as they had been defined in the 1886 Militia Act. As for his department's increased budget, all these expenditures had been authorized by Parliament and represented important additional responsibilities, such as the acquisition of the British garrisons, designed to provide military services and safeguard military stores. Moreover, he reminded the House somewhat pointedly that estimates and questions of governance were policy issues that were best settled in Parliament, not by public servants.

Borden went on to explain to the House that he had seen a preliminary draft of Courtney's report in October 1907 and as a consequence had sent Percy Lake to meet with Courtney to correct the report's various errors, especially regarding the workings of the Militia Council, as opposed to the British Army Council, but Courtney had turned a deaf ear and persisted in his errors.[33] Borden's well-documented spirited defence seems to have been effective; certainly it convinced Laurier, who described Borden's intervention as one of his finest speeches in some time.[34] It may even have persuaded the Opposition not to pursue the matter during the coming election, or perhaps they had better ammunition, more sensational issues.

Indeed, the long 1908 parliamentary session was but a dress rehearsal for the 1908 federal election that followed, an election unlike any Sir Frederick had ever experienced. Discouraged by their successive failures to dislodge Borden from Kings, the local Conservative Party had decided not to nominate a candidate. Instead they decided to leave the field open to a recently successful political formation called the Union Reform. Organized by a coalition of some twenty clergymen, whom the Liberal *Morning Chronicle* disdainfully dismissed as "retired" gentlemen, "some in their dotage, willing to walk into the limelight,"[35] the contest attracted national attention.[36] Whatever their age, and not all were old, or their disabilities, in the June 1906 provincial election the Reform Union had elected their candidate in Kings, Charles Alexander Campbell, who defeated Harry Wickwire by less than a hundred votes. Flushed by their success, they anticipated repeating this feat easily in the federal election, given Sir Frederick's "unsavoury" record. Their program had three principal objectives: prohibition, electoral purity, and non-partisan politics. Their candidate, Nathan Woodworth Eaton, was a Canning merchant, closely allied to the Conservative Party.

A fear that the non-partisan claim might dissolve party loyalty made the contest unpredictable and difficult to manage. The clerical coalition, led by the Reverend Beales (Baptist), the Reverend J.A. Spidell

(Baptist), and the Reverend Barrett (Methodist), spared neither press nor pulpit in its effort to demolish Sir Frederick. Its literature of "fear and slander" and anti-Catholicism consisted of copies of the *Eye Opener* and pamphlets reading "Hurrah for Laurier, France and Romanism," appeals to prejudice and fanaticism that Sir Frederick found particularly offensive. Anonymous letters circulated charging Sir Frederick with drunkenness and gross misbehaviour. Rumours that the government maintained a bartender and purchased exorbitantly priced wine glasses were designed to remind constituents of Sir Frederick's intemperate habits and the government's failure to legislate prohibition. Nonetheless, the Union Reform was itself a fragile amateur coalition, and it was up against a seasoned professional fighting to retain his personal reputation and eligibility for future awards.

Initially Sir Frederick approached the election with a resignation bordering on fatalism. Two years before he had failed to persuade H.H. Wickwire to replace him as the Liberal's federal candidate for Kings. Again Laurier had pressed him to remain, reiterating his promise to reward his fidelity should the aged Strathcona ever resign. The targeted and personal focus of his opponents' program made it imperative that Borden stand and clear his personal reputation, especially if he hoped to succeed Lord Strathcona. Except for two or three excursions to adjacent constituencies and one to help the Liberals in Fredericton, Sir Frederick remained grounded in his constituency,[37] canvassing the electorate, confirming the faithful, steadying the faltering, and reconverting the fallen. Anxious to retain one of its most prominent cabinet members, the party sent some of its heavyweights to endorse Sir Frederick's re-election. The strategic issue, however, was how best to confront his pious opponents.

That Sir Frederick had decided to take the offensive became obvious on 17 September 1908, nomination day, when Liberal partisans assembled in Kentville. As soon as the party's local executive ratified Sir Frederick's nomination, they adjourned as usual to address a larger audience of the faithful and the curious. The presence of W.S. Fielding, A.K. Maclean (the able young Halifax Lawyer and MP for Lunenburg), and Charles Marcil (the Commons' deputy speaker) magnified the importance of the occasion. Each of the distinguished guests spoke, lauding the government's record and Sir Frederick's accomplishments, urging the people of Kings to help maintain the province's "solid eighteen" by giving Sir Frederick the largest majority of his career. Fielding's reputation for piety, temperance, and probity offered some reassurance to the Baptist conscience of Kings.

Sir Frederick then took the platform, and after assuring his audience that he prized no honour or distinction more than representing his "native county in the Federal House," he defiantly confronted his

opponents' "slanderous" accusations. He appealed to those who knew
him and his family to decide the truth or falsity of the malicious charges. He reminded his audience that the country owed its only temperance legislation to the Liberal Party. Yet, "good and necessary" as
"temperance and morals" were, he continued, there were other issues
than temperance in "governing a great country like Canada."[38] To
remind his constituents of his recent vindication regarding the libellous charges of the *Nineteenth Century and After,* he announced that the
£250 ($1,250) he had received from the lawsuit in England would be
contributed to the furthering of education in Kings County. Finally, he
challenged any man or woman who wished to face him in the courts to
make a personal accusation. While Borden's defiant declaration of war
appears to have rallied his troops, the battle had only begun.

Sir Frederick's opponents had two obvious disabilities, their lack of
political finesse and their vaunted non-partisanship, disabilities that
Borden intended to exploit. To give their cause weight and visibility,
early in the campaign the Union Reform invited Dr J.G. Shearer, the
Presbyterian president of the Dominion Lord's Day Alliance, to speak
to a presumably non-partisan meeting in Canning on temperance. Dr
Shearer's address was not a Union Reform success. He soon detected
the partisan nature of the meeting and turned the tables on his hosts,
informing the large assembly that government by party was the only
means of administering the country, that national prohibition was not
an issue in this campaign, and that his experience during the past years
had given him "an increased esteem for both the character and ability of our public men."[39] This was not what the Union Reform organizers had come to hear. To make matters worse, the chairman of the
so-called non-partisan meeting then called upon "our own candidate,
N.W. Eaton," to address the gathering and thank the speaker. In a state
of nervous agitation, Eaton, not an experienced speaker, harangued
the audience but in his haste failed to thank Dr Shearer.

Sir Frederick was present and anxious to challenge Eaton, who had
declined or ignored Sir Frederick's previous invitations to debate the
issues. Even on nomination day, traditionally an occasion for the con-
tenders to match wits, Eaton had refused to confront Sir Frederick
directly.[40] Consequently, when Liberal members of the "non-partisan"
temperance rally called for "the doctor," Sir Frederick rose to do what
Eaton had failed to do, to express to Dr Shearer his warm appreciation of his address and to thank him for the work he had done for the
Dominion Lord's Day Alliance and the entire country. Nothing more
was necessary. The contrast between the two candidates, the amateur
and the professional, was not lost on the attentive, pragmatic, and discriminating audience.

The Union Reformers' non-partisan claim offered a double-edged sword, an opportunity as well as a potential danger: it could free traditional voters to support or oppose either side. To rally his constituents' partisan loyalty, Borden decided to press his advantage and expose the hypocrisy of his opponents' non-partisan claims by reminding his constituents that Eaton, the Union Reform candidate, was a Conservative and that all twenty clergymen of the Union Reform party happened also to be Conservatives. According to Borden, the Union Reform's claim to be non-partisan was little more than a dishonest ploy to mask its true partisan character.

Toward the end of the campaign Sir Frederick Borden, confident of the success of his confrontational strategy, decided upon even bolder action. A Kentville merchant, William M. Carruthers, who had been dismissed as Kentville's postmaster and superintendent of the Savings Bank Department and blamed his dismissal on Sir Frederick, took the minister up on his challenge to meet his accusers in court, taunting him by distributing copies of the offending issue of the *Calgary Eye Opener*. Borden immediately secured a warrant for Carruthers's arrest. Carruthers was arraigned on 20 October and charged with criminal libel. At the prisoner's request, he was released on $800 bail and the trial was postponed until after the election. The sensation of the local campaign, Carruthers's arrest drew the attention of journalists throughout the province and sobered, though failed to silence, Borden's critics.

About a week before the election Sir Frederick sensed a reaction in his favour as people began to question and doubt the Union Reform's methods and motives. Wavering Liberals returned to the fold. Some Conservatives disapproved of the Union Reform's tactics, felt absolved from party allegiance, and decided to support Sir Frederick. A few days before the election an enthusiastic, cheering, partisan audience at Wolfville carried Sir Frederick triumphantly from the building. The electoral results confirmed their enthusiasm: he retained his seat with the second largest majority of his career, a surplus of 491 votes, 55 per cent of the votes cast, altogether a very personal victory and a sharp, though temporary, rebuke to his accusers.[41]

"None of us can look very far ahead," Sir Frederick wrote somewhat sombrely to his brother-in-law in the wake of his controversial re-election, "but at the present moment it looks as if I might remain in politics for some time."[42] Little did Sir Frederick realize how prophetic were his words or how difficult would be the years ahead. His most immediate challenge, however, was the Carruthers's trial, an ordeal that would entail a painful public dissection and exposure of his private life. Immediately after the election, on 10 November 1908, Carruthers appeared before the Kentville justice of the peace, E.M. Beckwith, for a preliminary examination. A "true bill" was made out and the case was sent to the Nova Scotia Supreme Court, scheduled to meet in Kentville in June 1909.

The Kentville trial attracted a large, partisan, and curious audience. Prominent legal council represented both parties. Sir Frederick had retained H.H. Wickwire and W.E. Roscoe, and Carruthers had secured R.E. Ritchie, an able Halifax lawyer, and A.E. Dunlop, a Kentville lawyer. The appearance of Mrs Maria Allison, the author of the *Eye Opener*'s offending letters, took Sir Frederick's counsel by surprise. A jury was selected, the charges were read, and the defence gave its plea. Carruthers admitted distributing copies of the *Eye Opener*, "in order that they [the electorate] might fairly and with full knowledge of the facts, determine whether the said F.W. Borden was a fit and proper person to represent the said electoral district."[43] Carruthers based his confidence in the validity of the *Eye Opener*'s allegations on the "general tenor" of Mrs Allison's letters, comparable reports regarding Borden's "misconduct" with women, and his own "knowledge" that Borden "was addicted to the excessive use of intoxicating liquors and that he at such times acted in a highly improper manner."[44]

Borden had good reason to be apprehensive about the outcome of the trial. The previous year his former colleague, Henry Robert Emmerson,[45] Laurier's "alcoholic, womanizing" minister of railways and canals (1904–07), had charged the editor of the Fredericton *Gleaner* with defamatory libel for publishing an article describing the minister as "an intolerable reprobate." According to the *Gleaner,* Emmerson, a former president of the Baptist Convention of the Maritime Provinces, "had been ejected from a Montreal hotel with two women of ill repute." Emmerson, however, dropped the charges, claiming that the judge had decided "that it was in the public interest that statements such as that [of the *Gleaner*] whether true or false, should be published, providing the writer or publisher believed them to be true when published."[46] For Borden, this was a disturbing precedent. To make matters worse, Carruthers was much better represented, prepared, and financed than Borden and his counsel had anticipated. Moreover, during the selection of jurors, the defence lawyers seemed to have worsted the plaintiff's counsel. So successful had they been that Carruthers's lawyers allegedly boasted that they could secure a verdict without calling a witness.[47] Borden himself estimated that at least seven of the jury were Tories.[48] To avoid an embarrassing reversal and to sue for time, Borden's lawyers asked for and received a postponement until the autumn session, to obtain additional evidence and better witnesses.

The postponement purchased time but not public silence. Savouring the sordid details and the pleasant prospect of victory, Borden's opponents were furious with the postponement. Nor did they mince their words or waste an opportunity to turn the titillating details to political advantage. The *Halifax Herald* demanded that Sir Frederick not attend the forthcoming Imperial Naval Conference in London until he had cleared his name.[49] The newspaper also gave prominence to the remarks of the Reverend J.A. Spidell, one of the disappointed leaders of the Union Reform and subsequent Conservative candidate, to a meeting of the Central Baptist Association condemning members of his own congregation who "rose from their knees where they had been praying, 'Thy Kingdom come' ... and went straight to the polling booth and cast their vote for a man whose name ... had become a stench in the nostrils of the right thinking people from Halifax to Vancouver."[50] The Opposition also aired the ranting of Rev. Dr J. Pringle, another clergyman, who during the Presbyterian General Assembly at Kingston in June 1909 launched a fierce critique of the federal government's "corrupt" Yukon administration. In the course of his intemperate attack, Dr Pringle singled out Sir Frederick for special condemnation: "there sitting at the Council table of the nation was Sir Frederick whose name was a synonym for lust."[51] When his reverend colleagues attempted to restrain Dr Pringle, the agitated clergyman challenged the minister "to bring any action against me if he dares." Embarrassed by his opponents' abusive language, Sir Frederick dismissed their "ravings" as unworthy of notice, though he reserved the right to prosecute them if the Carruthers case failed to vindicate his reputation.[52]

When the Carruthers trial resumed on 12 October, it played to a large and attentive audience of spectators within and outside the courtroom. The six-day court drama fed the public with the bizarre and sulphurous details of the case. In Ottawa Sir Frederick's prudish young friend and colleague Mackenzie King read the press reports with growing alarm and fascination. Two days after the trial began, King confided to his diary that things looked "very black for Sir Frederick so much so that I fear Sir Wilfrid will have to take notice of them." During a cabinet meeting about five o'clock that evening, the observant King noted that a "clerk brought him [Laurier] clippings from tonight's journal with today's evidence. He [the prime minister] grew very serious and read it, then got up quietly and walked out." "What," King piously pondered, "has he not had to contend with, what he must know of the weaknesses of men."[53]

Things were less bleak in Kentville than Mackenzie King had feared. To trump Mrs Allison's presence, the prosecution had procured as a witness Mrs Allison's daughter, Miss Charlefour, the "young" lady whom Sir Frederick allegedly had enticed from her home for "improper purposes";[54] this was a surprise appearance that the local press described as creating "quite a flurry."[55] In her initial testimony Miss Charlefour denied under oath that she was "on intimate terms with Sir Frederick or had received him at her apartment or elsewhere" or that she had ever received any financial assistance from the minister. When the defence cross-examined her "rather closely" and presented her with a picture of herself for identification, Miss Charlefour, aware of her role in the courtroom drama, dramatically grasped the photograph from Mr Ritchie's hand and tore it to shreds, sending the "fragments of cardboard flying through the court," meanwhile casting "a look of scorn upon Mr. Ritchie."[56]

When Carruthers took the stand he admitted to the court that he and Sir Frederick had not been "on friendly terms" ever since his dismissal from the Kentville Post Office in 1883 "owing to certain irregularities." Although a member of the Opposition at the time, Sir Frederick had successfully pursued the issue of Carruthers's "irregularities" with the government.[57] More sensational was Mrs Allison's elaboration of her letters to the *Calgary Eye Opener*. Not to be upstaged by her daughter, she explained to the court that Sir Frederick and other Nova Scotia members had resided at her boarding house on Russell Street in Ottawa during the parliamentary sessions from 1894 until Sir Frederick became a minister in 1896. During their stay Sir Frederick and other members of Parliament had signed her daughter's application to enter a nursing program in Montreal, which Mrs Allison interpreted as a means of enticing her daughter to leave home. While her daughter resided in Montreal, Mrs Allison alleged, Sir Frederick had visited her weekly and assisted her with her rent. In support of her claims Mrs Allison submitted a photograph of her daughter and the minister. Sir Frederick's amorous adventures with her daughter, Mrs Allison contended, was not the minister's only marital infidelity; indeed Sir Frederick's alleged relationship with another woman, a Mrs McParland, had "broken up the home." According to Mrs Allison, Sir Frederick used to "hide in a pile of old boxes near the house" until Mrs McParland's husband had left for the evening.[58]

When Mrs McParland took the stand, however, she denied knowing Sir Frederick, asserting that she had seen him only once in her life. Miss Charlefour's return to the witness stand further undermined Mrs Allison's credibility, her daughter representing her mother as a quarrelsome, conniving, and litigious person. Contrary to her previous sworn testimony, however, Miss Charlefour admitted to having had a closer friendship with Sir Frederick than she had previously admitted but added that she had been "on very intimate terms with a number of men."[59] Furthermore, she confessed to having blackmailed Sir Frederick for $2,000 "under her mother's instruction." She explained to the court that she had been thirty-two years old when Sir Frederick had allegedly enticed her to leave home and that she had done so only after she had quarrelled with her mother. In further testimony Miss Charlefour volunteered the information that her mother had been separated from her second husband and that when he had died in 1902, Mrs Allison had refused to attend his funeral. Miss Charlefour also told the court that Mrs Allison, after a quarrel with her son, had had him committed to a mental institution for a few years; when he returned home, she had pressed charges against him for "indecent language."

In light of Mrs McParland's and Miss Charlefour's evidence, the jury's confidence in Mrs Allison's allegations began to crumble. Carruthers himself had admitted in his preliminary testimony that he had based his belief in Mrs Allison's allegations on the "general tenor" of her letters as published in the *Eye Opener*. Since the defence had failed to establish a reasonable foundation for the allegations, the jury took little time to reach a unanimous conclusion: Carruthers was guilty of libel. The defence lawyers pleaded with the judge for a lenient sentence on compassionate grounds: Carruthers was the sole support of a sister, "an elderly lady and subject to heart trouble."[60] The judge's decision was a $100 fine or a six-month prison term.

Relieved by the court's verdict, Sir Frederick dismissed the case as "a blackmailing business from beginning to end." His only regret was his failure to have settled the whole thing when Mrs Allison had first made the charges thirteen years ago. No longer a resident of the boarding house, he had wanted to press charges, but his wife had dissuaded him, as she "dreaded publicity."[61] Fresh from victory, Sir Frederick decided to make a clean sweep of any accusation that might tarnish his public reputation. Consequently, he entered a $25,000 libel suit against William Cotton, then editor of the *Cowansville Observer*, to which Cotton responded with an apology, explaining his actions in terms of his inexperience.[62] The Opposition press gave Sir Frederick a clean bill, perhaps fearing other libel suits. But as Sir Frederick informed a Halifax audience, one rarely won wars against skunks. The odour would remain for a long time, and contribute to his defeat.[63]

In this context the prospects of an escape to London must have seemed attractive indeed. London promised a dynamic, sophisticated environment in which to pursue his personal and material agenda. At the same time it provided a physical and political distance and semi-retreat from the increasingly searching eye of progressive morality and its demanding standards of public and private probity. For the restless and ambitious Borden, the wait for Lord Strathcona to vacate the office of high commissioner must have seemed endless.

CHAPTER 23

Defeat

During his last parliamentary term, and even before, Sir Frederick appeared to be a man marking time to yesterday's tunes, patiently awaiting Strathcona's resignation. A man out of step with his era, he seemed caught between changing worlds, his values and habits arrested in time and space. His pursuit of prestige, place, pleasure, and wealth, his dynastic aspirations, his refusal to be stampeded by contemporary moralists, all seemed but a means to arrest change, to resist a world of growing personal isolation and uncertainty. As time went on, he became more careless of his public image, less careful to camouflage conflicts between his private and his public interests. His conspicuous consumption, his flaunting of moral codes, his alleged weakness for "wine and women," and his increasing resistance to popular moral causes, such as the effort to abolish racetrack gambling,[1] made him appear a man from another era, a person whom his opponents derided as the "eighteenth-century knight."[2]

His wealth and travels, his entertainment of national and imperial persons at Borden Place, their conspicuous arrival in his ministerial railcar, all accentuated the increasing social distance between him and his community. Gradually Sir Frederick became an object of community curiosity, pride, and envy; he grew to be more a spectacle than a participant in his community. Preoccupied and distracted with national and imperial issues, as well as with his private and material pursuits, Sir Frederick spent less time on constituency work. The personal, social, material, and political bonds that had made him so effective a representative of his constituency slowly eroded. Affectionately known as "the doctor" by his older supporters even long after he had been knighted, he increasingly came to be known as "Sir Frederick" by his younger constituents. A hostage of political success, Sir Frederick's personal knowledge of his constituents and his own paternalistic, chivalrous charm and charity bred a corrosive complacency that took for granted his constituents' support and masked the warning signals of his coming defeat. Restless and impatient, Borden sought greater personal freedom and other challenges. There would be a price to pay for his personal and political disengagement.

After twelve years as minister of militia he had enunciated the broad outline of his reform program and accomplished much of his agenda. He had established his authority within his department. He had surrounded himself with a team of competent civilian and military officials with whom he enjoyed a respectful and constructive working relationship He had restructured the Militia and prepared it for service at home and abroad. In many respects his department was on autopilot, a ministry that required minimal ministerial intervention.

Like the prolonged graceful decline of his province's mercantile economy, Borden's political disengagement was neither abrupt nor traumatic. He remained politically productive, and although aging and bruised, he was far from a spent force. Time had not diminished his intellectual curiosity, his faith in progress, and his fascination with industrial and technological innovation; nor had it sapped his enterprise, energy, and imagination. Above all, age had not nullified his political usefulness, especially as time went on and Laurier depended more and more on the few remaining members of his old guard, whom he drew defensively around him. By 1908 only four members of Laurier's original cabinet remained: Borden, Cartwright, Fielding, and Fisher. Of these Borden was probably the closest to the prime minister. None had known Laurier longer than Borden had.

As linguistic and religious tension continued to bedevil Canadian politics, Laurier valued senior colleagues who shared his inclusive, conciliatory perspective and went out of their way to build bridges. Representative of Borden's ecumenical approach to religion was his and Lady Borden's audience with Pope Pius X in January 1909, an honour he listed consistently in his biographical resumé. In September the following year Borden travelled to Montreal to greet the papal legate Cardinal Vannutelli, who was in the city to attend the twenty-first Eucharistic conference. Borden was one of the five federal cabinet members to attend the banquet the government of Canada held at the Windsor Hotel for the conference's distinguished guests. On this occasion he was less than happy when public controversy compelled him to cancel plans for a military guard of honour, his critics citing military orders that forbade the use of the Militia for sectarian purposes, a regulation that Borden would have been happy to ignore. Conscious of the relationship between religion and culture, Borden overlooked the breach in Quebec of the military regulation forbidding soldiers to carry any weapon but side arms during church parades; he viewed the breach as minor and its enforcement as a needless provocation. Irritated by vigilant Protestant criticism of the "defiant" uniformed presence of members of the 65th Regiment during the opening ceremonies of the Eucharistic conference, Borden was content to remind units of the regulation but made no effort to prosecute the offenders.

Borden's conciliatory approach to conflict was not confined to religious and linguistic questions. Within the Militia as well he frequently found himself mending fences, healing wounds, arranging settlements, and negotiating patronage with his opponents. His interventions were numerous: securing Hughes' passage to South Africa, persuading Domville to retire, defending Hutton from the wrath of his cabinet colleagues, or resolving a personality conflict.[3] Conversational, receptive, clinical, and non-confrontational, Borden was slow to anger, ever ready with an anecdote to distract antagonists or break a tense moment, but determined, even stubborn, if pushed too far. It is not surprising, therefore, that Laurier, who seemed to understand his hyperactive friend and colleague and his chronic need for useful employment, asked Sir Frederick to assist Mackenzie King in mediating the bitter Grand Trunk Railway strike in 1910.

Although the strike of Grand Trunk conductors and trainmen has been described as "the most serious strike situation in years,"[4] the company had little difficulty re-establishing its freight service four days after the trainmen walked off the job. But that did not resolve the strike. Begun as an attempt to secure wage parity with trainmen on other lines, notably the Canadian Pacific Railway, the strike soon became a contest of wills between the union and the American-born GTR president Charles Melville Hays, who seemed determined to win at any price to set an example that would leverage his own corporate reputation. Hayes had been hired as general manager in 1895 by the railway's London board, and his mandate was to restructure the GTR by introducing "American methods" to its operations.

The appointment of Borden, a sympathetic friend of business and an elder statesman, solved a number of problems. Principally it reassured the railway's management, the more conservative members of the business community, and the Liberal cabinet (whose impartiality had been compromised by its controversial 1902 decision to back the GTR's decision to build a second transcontinental railway); and it balanced the putative labour proclivities of the young minister of labour, Mackenzie King. Moreover, before and during the subsequent formal negotiations, Borden served as the chief interlocutor with the Grand Trunk's "stubborn," "petty," and erratic president, playing a more active role in the negotiations than historians preoccupied with King's career have acknowledged. At the same time, Borden was a trusted friend of the young minister, in King's view one of his few dependable supporters within Laurier's cabinet. As minister of militia, Borden was also responsible for the armed forces, the chief support to the civil power in the event of violence or its threat. This was not a misplaced consideration, for on two occasions during the fifteen-day strike (18 July–2 August) clashes between the strikers and the strikebreakers required the intervention of the Militia.

A ruthless authoritarian, Hays needed careful handling.[5] Notwithstanding the government's close ties to the railway, it possessed little sympathy for the company's grossly discrepant wage policy and flatly refused Hays's initial request for compulsory arbitration. In Laurier's view, "it was time for the Grand Trunk to start 'paying the same wages as its competitors.'"[6] The failure of the company-union negotiations on 27 July, however, persuaded the government to intervene and mediate the conflict, a process that entailed a week of "protracted and exasperating negotiations."[7]

During these negotiations Borden's role was more than that of an interested observer. Even before its decision to mediate the dispute, the government had sent Sir Frederick to speak to Hays, "urging him to consider either negotiation or arbitration."[8] Furthermore, after the more formal discussions had begun and appeared to have reached a stalemate on issues such as the reinstatement of strikers, Borden's clinical skills were required to reason with the excitable, duplicitous president. So erratic was the behaviour of the fifty-four-year-old Hays during these negotiations that two of his vice-presidents explained apologetically to Sir Frederick and Mackenzie King that Hays "was not himself."[9] Nonetheless, King and Borden worked "unceasingly"[10] and successfully to secure a shaky resolution that ended the strike on 2 August, a settlement that "might have been counted as a qualified victory for workers ... if the settlement had not been violated from the first by the company."[11] Borden's role ended once the initial settlement was reached and the trainmen had returned to work. Monitoring the implementation of the agreement became the responsibility of the minister of labour. As a result, Borden became a passive, though informed and interested, spectator to the tortuous recriminations and betrayals that followed as Hays's violations of the agreement effectively nullified the settlement.

During these years Borden, ever curious, restless, and innovative, dabbled in other activities outside his ministry as well. One extra-ministerial project entailed a scheme that some suspected had been motivated by the prospect of private gain. In the wake of the closely contested and tumultuous April 1908 Newfoundland election, the St John's *Daily News* charged Sir Frederick with being party to a conspiracy to bring Newfoundland into Confederation. According to the *Daily News*, the leader of the newly founded People's Party, Edward Morris, a former justice minister in Robert Bond's Liberal government, was in the pay of the Canadian government, and before breaking with the Liberal Party, had endeavoured to negotiate confederation with Canada. Morris's Canadian conspirators in this nefarious scheme were Harry J. Crowe, a company promoter with a financial interest in Newfoundland, principally timberland, and Sir Frederick Borden, representing the federal government. That there were discussions is almost certain, though the details are difficult to establish. When questioned, Sir Frederick confessed that Harry Crowe was an old friend of his from Bridgetown, Nova Scotia, who had migrated to Newfoundland and with whom he had maintained contact, but Borden insisted, somewhat euphemistically, that his own personal interest was not the prospect of personal gain but simply the "rounding out of confederation."[12] While Newfoundland politicians might retail Confederation as a treacherous act of betrayal,[13] in Canada Sir Frederick's interventions could be marketed as patriotism. This was not bad press.

During these final years, however, Borden's sights remained firmly fixed on London. An escape from the tedious minutia of local issues and the irritants of censorious public scrutiny, the high commissionership (a position that had been occupied by his old political rival, Sir Charles Tupper) promised to match Borden's continuing desire for public service with social advancement and material benefit. Pursuit of the post had kept Borden in politics. His friendship with Strathcona provided a close and perhaps deformed perspective on the position's possibilities. During this era of high imperialism and Canadian influence in London, few high commissioners had wielded more power and influence than Lord Strathcona, who cleverly exploited this position to his personal advantage. But Lord Strathcona also had very deep pockets, deep enough to purchase attention, deference, silence, and complicity, assets that Borden could only dream of matching.

During the South African War Borden had developed a warm and profitable friendship with Lord Strathcona. The Militia Department's supervision of the recruitment of the Lord Strathcona's Horse, the mounted battalion of 500 western Canadian scouts and roughriders that the wealthy high commissioner had offered to finance for service in the South African War, had been a great success, though it had got off to a very frosty start when Lord Strathcona had made his contingent's recruitment and purchases conditional upon the approval of the GOC of the Canadian Militia, an ill-timed, gratuitous slur on Laurier's government then in conflict with General Hutton. But Laurier had been firm. He had informed Lord Strathcona that the ordinary administrative rules governing recruitment would prevail and that all those involved in the recruitment and despatch of the men for his battalion

Lord Strathcona
and Sir Frederick
at the Quebec
Tercentenary,
1908. *Courtesy
Library and Archives
Canada, PA24768*

and the procurement of horses and supplies would act only under the minister's supervision.

Helpful, solicitous, and accommodating, Borden lost no opportunity to reassure the influential high commissioner. His flattering suggestion that the battalion bear Lord Strathcona's name was very well received. So too was his choice of Sam Steele to command the battalion. Sam Hughes, a close friend of both the minister and Lord Strathcona and whom Lord Strathcona initially sought to command his scouts, may have reinforced Strathcona's good opinion of Borden.[14] When the Bordens visited England in the summer of 1900, Lord Strathcona had entertained them at Glencoe. Subsequently, no visit to London was complete without an invitation to spend a weekend at Glencoe. Whatever the reasons for Lord Strathcona's good opinion of Borden, the high commissioner's grateful satisfaction with and generous public appreciation of the minister's efforts formed the bases of a long and productive friendship.

Conscious of the value of the high commissioner's goodwill, Borden continued to solicit and benefit from Strathcona's good offices. Soon after the Strathcona Horse's year of service in South Africa, this temporary unit had been disbanded. At the time, Borden promised to reconstitute the force and make it part of the Permanent Force. As a first instalment of his promise, on July 1900 Borden had the Strathcona Horse's battle honours and customs transferred to "A" Squadron of the Canadian Mounted Rifles (re-designated the Royal Canadian Mounted Rifles in 1903). Then, on 1 May 1911, the squadron was renamed the Strathcona's Horse as a tribute to the aged high commissioner. In return Borden appeared to have an open line to the high commissioner's influence and benevolence, assets that he translated into a number of private and public endeavours, useful advice, letters of introduction, and funding for the Strathcona Trust.

In the early summer of 1911 Borden's dream of succeeding Lord Strathcona came close to fulfilment. While Sir Frederick was in London with Laurier to attend the coronation of George V and the Imperial Conference, the ninety-one-year-old high commissioner informed the prime minister verbally that he wished to be replaced and urged Laurier to announce his replacement at the high commissioner's Dominion Day banquet. Laurier accepted his advice and seized the occasion of the banquet to thank Lord Strathcona for his long years of dedicated public service and to present his successor, Sir Frederick Borden, whom the prime minister praised as "one of his most faithful, as well as capable ministers" in his cabinet.[15]

Laurier's announcement seemed to mark the pinnacle of Sir Frederick's career, a personal coronation and reward for his long public service. A highlight of his career, this occasion was qualified only by a bout of illness that plagued his sojourn in London and an extraordinary heat wave in the city. Otherwise London was a personal triumph for Sir Frederick from start to finish. The *Times* announced his arrival. With him were his sociable, charming wife, his two daughters, and his son-in-law, Leslie Macoun, who was serving as an aide-de-camp to the commander of the Canadian coronation contingent, all resident at the fashionable Hotel Cecil. He was wined and dined by a selection of the titled and powerful. Clubs offered him honorary temporary membership during his two-month stay. His picture appeared in the *Court Journal*. He attended the coronation and had a private audience with the new king and queen. The British Army named him an honorary surgeon general. Delighted with his London reception, Frederick returned home to prepare for his move to the imperial capital, ready for the new challenge.

The political stalemate that confronted Laurier and Sir Frederick upon their return to Canada in mid-July only confirmed the minister's desire to escape to London. The parliamentary session that had begun on 17 November 1910 had been the longest and one of the most acrimonious on record. In January 1911 W.S. Fielding had stunned the Opposition in the House of Commons with his triumphant announcement that he had negotiated a reciprocity agreement with the United States. Once the Opposition had absorbed the shock, it had rallied to reject the agreement, buoyed by growing public criticism inspired and financed by various influential, well-heeled interests groups, including prominent Toronto Liberal businessmen.

Convinced of the agreement's public popularity, Laurier had left things very much in Fielding's competent hands during his absence in London. But all had not gone as Laurier had hoped. Upon his return from London, the prime minister, irritated by the Opposition's persistence, threatened to dissolve the House and submit the agreement to the people, confident of the outcome. When the Opposition called the prime minister's bluff, the governor general dissolved the Eleventh Parliament on 29 July and writs were issued for elections on 21 September 1911. According to the Liberal *Morning Chronicle,* the only question to be decided by the electorate was the size of the government's majority.[16]

Sir Frederick made no plans to contest his seat. He was too preoccupied with his preparations for London, responding to premature letters of congratulations, making arrangements for the care of his houses in Canning and Ottawa, negotiating transportation of his household (including his eighty-three-year-old mother-in-law), procuring suitable living space in London, and preparing for his elder daughter's imminent marriage. Fearful that the arrival of Lord Strathcona's formal letter of resignation during an electoral contest would put him in an awkward position, making his candidacy redundant, even frivolous, Borden wanted to wait as long as possible before announcing his intention, confident that the electoral outcome in Kings was not in doubt. Consequently, three weeks after the dissolution of the House Borden was still in Ottawa, attending to personal affairs, catching up on a backlog of work, and preparing his department for his successor, Edward Mortimer Macdonald, the MP for Pictou whom Laurier had tagged as Borden's replacement.[17] Finally Laurier could wait no longer. Anxious to secure as many safe seats as possible, the prime minister pressed Sir Frederick to stand while awaiting Lord Strathcona's letter. Strathcona's letter never arrived.

Meanwhile Sir Frederick returned to Kings to contest the seat, with every confidence that reciprocity would "carry the country hands down,"[18] an assessment he had made in March and that time and circumstances had not altered. When Borden had made his rash prediction, his constituency had seemed committed to the trade deal. All the signs had been positive. Two months after Fielding had announced his trade agreement, the Kentville Board of Trade had endorsed reci-

procity by a vote of 87 to 3.[19] Since then, the June provincial election
had been fought in Kings on reciprocity and both of the county's Liberal candidates (including Harry Wickwire) were returned with large
majorities, further feeding Sir Frederick's self-confidence.[20] The cities
might be against the trade agreement, Sir Frederick liked to tell his
rural audience, but the masses "if they have any common sense will
favour it," especially "where their material interests were at stake."[21]
Sir Frederick's firm and successful legal action and the passage of
Nova Scotia's prohibition law in 1910 had cleared public discussion of
the troublesome personal issues that had bedevilled his last election,
making the 1911 contest a straight party battle on the trade issue, and
that issue alone seemed sufficient to assure Sir Frederick's re-election.
The Conservatives' nomination of a mere "stripling" to oppose him,
Arthur DeWitt Foster, a twenty-five-year-old Canning schoolteacher
from across the street, only confirmed Borden's confidence in the
outcome.[22]

Convinced of the popularity of reciprocity in Kings, Sir Frederick
treated the contest as though it would be a local version of Laurier's
national strategy and that his own re-election would be a personal coronation for his long and distinguished career. When the Liberals' nom-
inating convention finally met in Kentville on 19 August, the president
of the Kings riding association, I.B. Oakes, introduced Sir Frederick as
their "old and beloved war chief of over a third of a century," language
clearly designed to contrast him with his youthful and inexperienced
opponent. Sir Frederick developed the theme in his acceptance speech,
reminding his audience that only four other members of the House had
comparable years of service. Even Borden's defence of the trade agreement was retrospective and nostalgic. After scolding the Opposition
for its parliamentary obstruction of the trade agreement, he assured his
audience that "everyone, no matter what their politics, was in favour
of reciprocity," none less so than Sir John A. Macdonald, who had
always favoured "a reciprocity clause in the National Policy."[23] Drawing upon his repertoire of rhetorical examples from his days in Opposition, Borden spoke of the region's prosperity during the Reciprocity
Treaty of 1854, adding to his historical argument the geographic logic
of trade that would open an eastern seaboard market of some fifteen
million persons to his province. Why, Sir Frederick asked his audience,
oblige the people of Winnipeg to pay more for their apples when they
may procure them cheaper from the middle states?[24] In conclusion he
warned that if "we turn this chance down another might not come for
fifty years."[25]

To assist Sir Frederick, the prime minister made a triumphant tour
of the Annapolis Valley, flanked by W.S. Fielding and Sir Frederick,

his two tried and true Nova Scotia veterans. As Laurier's train made its slow progress from Halifax to Digby, including a side trip to Canning (where he stayed overnight at Borden Place), it stopped briefly at each station so that the prime minister could greet and address the crowds of curious spectators. The response was overwhelming. People occupied "every available point of vantage ... men climbing upon the roof of the station or on nearby poles and trees to see and hear" the respected, charismatic prime minister. If one could judge from the people's enthusiastic reception of their leader, the Liberals had every reason for confidence.

Their confidence, however, was misplaced. Nationally and locally their party was a disorganized casualty of longevity, complacency, and distraction. Even in Borden's own county, only one ward possessed an organization, and the June provincial election seemed to have sapped the county's human and financial resources. In contrast, their opponents were well organized and well financed. Sir Frederick had also underestimated Foster, the "young stripling," who was roughly the same age as he had been when he had won his first federal contest. Even the Liberals had to admit that Foster was a popular, energetic, witty, and gifted speaker, though they dismissed his oratory as "cheap."[26]

Foster confronted the trade question directly, perhaps more aware than Sir Frederick of the county's opinions and loyalties. He reminded his audiences of a speech Sir Frederick had given in Boston on 27 October 1910 in which the venerable minister had told his American audience that while Canadians would always entertain an American suggestion for freer trade, most Canadians were content "to let well enough alone," and if Americans were unhappy with their own tariff policy, "there is the Canadian tariff, one of the finest in the world. Just copy it."[27] In Parliament and in the press, the Tories made great use of Sir Frederick's Boston speech.[28] Sir Frederick countered that when he had made his Boston speech he had had no idea that Canada could negotiate so favourable an agreement and one that it would be "wicked" for an agricultural county to reject. The Tories, however, persisted, making Borden captive of his earlier assessment of the tariff.

Nor did Foster hesitate to employ nationalist arguments in his appeal to the descendants of His Majesty's Yankees. He rejected Sir Frederick's trivialization of national markets and his call to the county's farmers to substitute their smaller, distant trade in western Canadian for the closer, larger, more logical eastern seaboard market. According to Foster, the market for Annapolis Valley apples in Winnipeg was far from negligible and the Americans' sudden interest in free trade was neither disinterested nor dependable. In Foster's opinion, the Americans' real agenda was to reduce Canadians to hewers of wood and drawers of water. "Do you want your flour to be ground in the United States, your brand and your middlings to be made across the lines," he asked rhetorically, "with the profit on the work all going to another country?" And where, he continued, will fruit growers get wood for their barrels "when the wood is sold to the Yankees for pulp?" Foster's answer was clear and forthright: "[K]eep our raw products for our own people and finish them at home. That was the policy of Sir John A. Macdonald and is the policy of R.L. Borden today." Above all, he warned his audience, "Keep an eye on Uncle Sam with his striped pants."[29]

About two weeks before the election, the *Halifax Herald* prophesied that there was a strong Conservative current running in Kings, one that even "Sir Frederick's long purse does not appear to be able to stem."[30] To counter Laurier's triumphal tour of the valley, R.L. Borden visited Kentville briefly a few days before the election to address the trade issue. True to his custom, he went out of his way to make it clear that he would discuss only policy issues, not the merits of the local candidates.[31]

The electoral results demonstrated how much Sir Frederick had misread his constituency, much as he and his party had misread the country. He and Fielding were both defeated, Borden by only 151 votes. News of his pending appointment to London, his late entry into the contest and lack of organization may well have made the difference between victory and defeat. Although he secured 48.4 per cent of the votes cast, the message was clear. Even more devastating was the defeat of his party, since that loss robbed him of his coveted chance to succeed Lord Strathcona in London. Nevertheless Sir Frederick greeted the electoral results with equanimity, in contrast to his bitter outburst in 1882, though the stakes were higher in 1911. He gamely assured his friends that he did not regard his defeat as "personal in any way"; he was convinced that it "would have happened under similar conditions no matter who my opponent might have been."[32] His health was also a consideration, as his doctors had advised him to escape from public responsibilities "at the earliest possible moment." Less convincing was his comment that given the "overwhelming defeat of the Government" he did not regret his personal defeat, "as it relieves me from further service in Parliament of which I have fairly tired."[33]

In his immediate post-electoral correspondence, Sir Frederick's analysis of his and the party's defeat was remarkably lucid and perceptive. In his view, the party had been poorly organized, overconfident, and out of touch with public opinion. People throughout the country and in his own constituency were very prosperous, with an "enormous crop being gathered." In his opinion, they resented the Americans' past refusal to grant them trade concessions when they needed them and suspected that the Americans' sudden trade offer was motivated by "their own selfish ends." Basically, this was Foster's argument.[34] In Borden's view, Laurier had been defeated by the nationalism he had encouraged. Borden might well have applied his analysis of Laurier's role in the party's general defeat to himself. He may have been defeated by the "Britification" of the valley, its lucrative capital, trade, and cultural links with Britain, which he had fostered and epitomized. When His Majesty's Yankees had been obliged to choose, they had been persuaded by the claims of transatlantic markets and loyalties during this high age of imperialism.

CHAPTER 24

Death

As an aging Sir Frederick assessed his defeat in the autumn of 1911, it must have seemed a long time since the spring of 1874 when the twenty-six-year-old physician first entered Canada's House of Commons, as surprised as others by his own success. At that time he was an ambitious, optimistic, hyperactive young physician, called to help govern a fragile but promising young state beset by enormous challenges. The rawness of the national capital, far from Borden's home and young family, had made it difficult for him to consider the city little more than a temporary lodging, a boarding house address. Over time, however, the city had matured and become the symbol of a dynamic, prosperous country. The city had grown on him and become a home away from home, his new social, political, and economic centre of gravity. By 1911 he was no longer an outsider. Increasingly, trans-regional political and economic interests, friends, associations, and loyalties defined his and Lady Borden's world. Perhaps nothing underscored Borden's transformation more than his decision to remain in Ottawa after his defeat, retain Stadacona Hall, and divide his time between Ottawa and Canning.

As Sir Frederick looked back on his long years of public service, his memory could not have helped but be prompted by the flood of appreciative letters, telegrams, articles, resolutions, and testimonials, from friends and supporters on both sides of the House and beyond, acclaiming his contribution to military reform. His long tenure had imprinted his style and agenda on the Department of Militia and Defence. Among the communications were letters from Percy Lake and D.A. Macdonald, with whom he had worked so long and so well. There was also a "touching letter" from the Conservatives' chief military critic, his old friend Sam Hughes, "expressing his deep regret at your going down."[1] The Militia Council presented him with a gift and a warm testimonial. In praising Sir Frederick, many admirers quoted the British military magazine the *Broad Arrow*'s earlier assessment: "No Minister of Militia has ever done so much towards making the Canadian forces so thoroughly effective and ready for the field as he."[2] These

(LEFT) The marriage of Sir Frederick's elder daughter, Elizabeth, to Gordon Hewitt in October 1911. The small "flower girl" is Rosamond, Julia and Leslie Macoun's only daughter and Sir Frederick's only grandchild. *Courtesy Joan Murray and Ken Bezanson*; (RIGHT) Sir Frederick's younger daughter, Julia Maude Macoun, at her sister's wedding. *Courtesy Joan Murray*

and other appreciative testimonies cushioned the break as he cleared his office for his successor and friend, Sam Hughes.

Although now sixty-four and despite his physician's stern advice to slow down, Sir Frederick had difficulty following his physician's counsel, at least in the short run. Fortunately he had begun to clear his office before the election in anticipation of his move to London. Even so he had scarcely time to complete the task before he was obliged to return to Canning to host the marriage of his elder, thirty-seven-year-old daughter, Elizabeth, to the twenty-six-year-old Charles Gordon Hewitt, on 11 October 1911, less than three weeks after the election. Elizabeth and Charles were married in the Methodist church by its minister the Reverend Arthur Hockin, with Julia Maude and Leslie Macoun serving as witnesses and their small daughter, Rosamond, as the flower girl. Eleven years Elizabeth's junior, Charles Gordon Hewitt, DSC, was a distinguished English-born scientist, educated at the Victoria University of Manchester, where he had lectured from 1902 until 1909, when he had been recruited for the position of dominion entomologist. A reputable scientist, prolific author, and convinced conservationist, he had a "brilliant" career as a civil servant and drafted important conservationist legislation. He was also a "charming" and enthusiastic volunteer, president of the Ottawa Boys Home, a councillor of the Ottawa Humane Society, and advocate of the Boy Scouts movement. An avid gardener, Hewitt shared the Borden family's interests in travel, art, literature, music, and flowers. Borden Place benefited from his horticultural interests and activities.[3]

By remaining in Ottawa, Sir Frederick and Lady Borden would be close to both of their daughters and their families. But Ottawa had become more than a necessary home away from home imposed on him by his political engagements and family obligations. It had become a genteel community of friends and visitors, of concerts, dinners and afternoon teas, a convenient and congenial location that offered access to power and influence across party lines. Closer to Montreal and Toronto than Canning, Ottawa served as an opportune site for Borden's business activities. It was also the destination of those seeking political favours where he could continue to play the role of lobbyist, well connected as he was to both sides of the House. Free at last from the obligations of public life, Borden intended to devote all his time to personal and business interests, and he pursued this object with new vigour and despite his doctor's warnings.

Escaping the sticky tentacles of politics for the corporate world proved harder than he had anticipated, especially since the two worlds were so intertwined. Had Borden really wished to abandon the political world, however, he would not have retained his Ottawa residence. In this relatively small, highly political town, surrounded by old political friends and allies, Borden found it difficult to turn his back on the political world, to reorder his personal and professional routine and relationships, to break old habits, and to renounce the associations and alter the rhythm of the public life that had engaged his time and attention, all of which had aided and abetted his entrepreneurial ventures and structured his personal life and public career for almost four decades.

However firm Sir Frederick's initial resolve to renounce public life may have been, and it did not seem to have been very firm, he was faced with many tempting offers from both his own party and the new Conservative government. As one of a small coterie of Laurier's close

personal friends and advisors, Sir Frederick also possessed a privileged access to his cousin Robert Borden, the new prime minister,
although he had to be careful to compromise neither his own party
nor his cousin. More important than influence was the perception of
influence, and Sam Hughes, for one, believed that Sir Frederick possessed great influence with the new prime minister. Consequently,
in soliciting a place in Robert Borden's cabinet, Hughes immodestly
informed the prime minister that Sir Frederick himself had acknowledged that "the vast majority of the democratic and effective changes"
that occurred in the Militia during Sir Frederick's administration were
"due to my [Hughes's] suggestions."[4] And when Hughes feared that
his direct solicitation had failed to convince his leader, the relentless
supplicant implored Sir Frederick to intervene with his cousin, which
Sir Frederick did, adding the sage proviso that Sam would need to be
controlled, an endorsement that Robert Borden acknowledged to have
persuaded him to include Hughes in his cabinet, despite the governor
general's more astute reservations. But control Hughes, Robert Borden
did not.[5]

Appreciative of Sir Frederick's intervention, Hughes reciprocated
his friend's good offices, ever ready to honour old political debts, a
credit that Sir Frederick was not reluctant to reclaim. For example,
soon after Hughes took office, Sir Frederick advised the new minister against reopening a $1 million contract with Vickers-Maxim that
was being negotiated through its Canadian agent and the recently
appointed president of its Canadian subsidiary, F.O. Lewis, a Montreal hardware merchant, closely associated with Borden's cold storage scheme and other business activities. According to Sir Frederick,
there was "a moral commitment to Vickers,"[6] and Hughes, conceding
the point, signed the contract, "though his departmental officials knew
nothing of such a commitment" and retained some very serious reservations.[7] More than a year later Sir Frederick again drew upon his
credit with Hughes. Unhappy with the quality of the Dominion Arsenal's ammunition and the administration of its superintendent, Colonel
F.M. Gaudet, Hughes had asked two British officers from the Woolwich
Arsenal to inquire into the Dominion Arsenal's operation. Although
the enquiry failed to detect serious misconduct, it pointed to deficiencies. An article in the Montreal *Gazette*, described by Sir Frederick as
"newspaper gossip" inspired by the Conservative journalist and Militia officer Colonel Edward W.B. Morrison, led Sir Frederick and other
Liberals to fear that the press might turn the findings into a critique
of Sir Frederick's administration. After consulting with Laurier, Sir
Frederick wrote Hughes asking for a copy of the report, explaining his
fears, and Hughes responded frankly and cooperatively.[8]

Hughes himself continued to regard Sir Frederick as a friend and counsellor and to seek his advice and assistance. When Hughes convened his second military conference on Paardeberg Day 1913, to discuss military policy, secure bipartisan support for his expanded military program, and silence opposition, he invited Sir Frederick along with the governor general, the Duke of Connaught, to speak to the conference on the importance of cadet training.[9] Similarly, on 4 August 1914, the day war began in Europe, Hughes informed the press that he would call immediately "his predecessor, Sir Frederick Borden, for advice in mobilization and equipment."[10] While this gesture was designed more to validate his own actions and please Sir Robert than to indicate a serious intention to be guided by Sir Frederick's counsel, it nevertheless underscored his continuing respect and confidence in Sir Frederick. And it would not be the last flattering gesture.

Borden's working relations with the Conservative government did nothing to diminish his influence within his own party. Laurier appreciated Sir Frederick's political skills and judgment, his intelligence, energy, and executive ability, and had confidence in his loyalty. And in the wake of his defeat the Liberal leader surrounded himself with a very small group of mostly old and trusted advisors, including Sir Frederick, Sydney Fisher, and Mackenzie King. More than many in the party, Sir Frederick seemed to have absorbed the shock of defeat. He was eager to rebuild the party, reorganize its structure, and rethink its program. Less than three months after the Liberals' defeat, Borden, Fisher, and Mackenzie King agreed to help Laurier rebuild the party, advising him on policy and strategy and preparing the party for the next election.

In all their meetings Borden insisted that organization was the key to the party's future success, both at the provincial and at the federal level. In his view, the party had grown old and careless and had depended upon the country's prosperity and its leader's charm to compensate for its organizational failings. To remedy the party's organizational defects in his own province, early in 1912 Borden met with Fielding and George Murray, the provincial premier, to revive the Nova Scotia Liberal Association, an organization in which he, Fielding, and Murray became honorary presidents. Subsequently Borden and Sydney Fisher persuaded Mackenzie King, then considering his options for useful employment, to become the information officer of an "adequately financed" national Liberal headquarters, to be in charge of the editing of letters, pamphlets, and briefs as well as the rebuilding of the organization of the national party. King's appointment led to the founding of the *Canadian Liberal Monthly*, of which he became editor for a year, a strategic position for an ambitious young man on the make.[11]

Sir Frederick maintained a warm and constructive friendship with Sir William Mulock's protegé, William Lyon Mackenzie King. Both King and Sir Frederick were educated, liberal imperialists, interested in ideas and comfortable in a British world. Sir Frederick seemed to support King's social policies, including King's call for a royal commission on technical education, a subject in which Borden had a particular interest; and King, despite his "aversion" to war, backed Sir Frederick's version of a Canadian navy. The ambitious young deputy minister of labour soon found himself a guest at Sir Frederick's dinner parties, where he enjoyed access to persons of influence and power, opportunities that he readily employed to advance his career. For example, in October 1905, the thirty-one-year-old King "presumptuously" solicited a post in Laurier's cabinet, informing Laurier that he had been encouraged to enter public life by Sir Frederick and L.P. Brodeur.[12]

King seemed to regard Sir Frederick, twenty-seven years his senior, as a "pleasant and congenial companion," a supportive, sympathetic ally in the younger man's search for political influence. To King, Borden was a welcome contrast to some of the older members of Laurier's cabinet, whom King believed to be prejudiced against his youth, men such as Fielding, Cartwright, Scott, and even Aylesworth. Above all, King feared the powerful, "conservative" minister of finance, W.S. Fielding, who had expressed reservations on King's 1910 Combines Investigation Act, apposed Canadian representation in Washington, and, in King's view, exercised too much influence on Sir Wilfrid.[13] Since Sir Frederick had direct access to Laurier, King seemed to see him as a valuable counterbalance to the others, a useful friend in court. Even after the party's defeat King and Sir Frederick remained good friends, a friendship that extended to Sir Frederick's family, with whom King corresponded and whom he would continue to entertain when they visited Ottawa long after Sir Frederick's death.[14] King seemed to enjoy the older gentleman's company despite their quite different private lives and temperaments. As King's diary records, Sir Frederick was a person with whom he felt comfortable having lunch at the Chateau Laurier, then spending the evening together first, "at my rooms & later at the Rideau Club."[15]

Sir Frederick and King agreed that ideas were central to the party's rejuvenation. In their search for ideas Sir Frederick himself wrote to the British Liberal Party for information on its program and organization.[16] In rethinking their party's program, King was delighted to find that Sir Frederick gave priority to ending electoral bribery and corruption. As Sir Frederick confessed to King and Fisher, he had not always practised what he had preached, but he felt strongly that "fighting corruption by every means" was right. While both he and King believed that the ultimate remedy to corruption was education, Sir Frederick

feared that education might not be sufficient in the short run; meanwhile only legislation could eliminate all bribery in money and drink.[17]

Sir Frederick appeared sincere in his intentions. In his private correspondence he affirmed that he had never personally offered a bribe
in his life. Nevertheless he admitted freely that he had not been as careful as he might or should have been: too often he had tolerated the
practice and thereby condoned it. In the future, however, he promised
not to "repeat this error," but "to go further and say that I shall be prepared to expend public money fully to put down, prevent, and expose
as well as punish" violators.[18] His definition of bribery, of course, was
a narrow one, confined to the direct purchase of votes with drink or
money during an election. It did not include party favouritism or benefiting from inside information or government contracts.

Meanwhile Sir Frederick continued to advise Laurier on party policy
and strategy, especially on the Conservatives' controversial naval bill.
Indeed, some Opposition members, recalling Sir Frederick's commitment to the formation of a Canadian navy, exaggerated his influence
on the party's naval policy, holding him personally responsible for persuading Liberal senators to scuttle the Conservatives' naval bill in May
1913.

By 1914 Sir Frederick, Sir Wilfrid, Fisher, and King had made considerable progress in revitalizing the party, encouraging the reorganization of provincial parties, and establishing a national office staffed by
an ambitious, energetic information officer, party organizer, and editor
of a crusading monthly journal. Nevertheless the party remained
largely the fief of its revered elderly leader and his small coterie of
trusted friends, a condition far short of the growing ambitions of some
restless younger Liberals, anxious to exploit the divisions and blunders
of the Conservative government and capitalize on the revived fortunes
of several provincial Liberal parties.

The outbreak of war on 4 August 1914 created a breach in Laurier's
small praetorian guard. Immediately upon the declaration of war, Laurier returned to Ottawa and proclaimed a truce "to all party strife."
He cancelled his planned transcontinental tour, and at the emergency
parliamentary war session later that month he promised to assent to all
war measures so long as there was a danger. One of the first casualties
of Laurier's truce was Mackenzie King, who had been offered the position of head of the Rockefeller Foundation's Department of Industrial
Relations. King had been torn between the lucrative offer from John D.
Rockefeller and his Canadian political ambitions, and the temporary
truce in party hostilities made it easier for him to justify acceptance of
Rockefeller's offer.[19]

Initially the war placed a premium on Sir Frederick's time, not the
least because of his experience and knowledge of military and imperial

issues and his ability to negotiate across party lines. Immediately upon
the outbreak of hostilities in Europe Hughes announced his intention
of seeking Sir Frederick's advice and assistance in managing the war
effort. At the same time Laurier asked Sir Frederick to serve on a very
small wartime advisory committee that included Fisher and King;
"he did not want others."[20] Robert Borden, too, found Sir Frederick
a useful sounding board, confiding in his cousin his frustrations with
"British officialdom" and seeking his advice on how best to cope with
recalcitrant British officials.[21]

But as time went on, neither Hughes nor Sir Robert, overcommitted
and enmeshed as they were in the complexities and changing nature
and magnitude of the war, had the time or need to draw upon Sir Frederick's rapidly dated and limited experience. And in the House of Commons, Sir Frederick's would-be successor as minister of militia, E.M.
MacDonald, became the party's chief military critic. In the spring of
1915 Sir Frederick's party influence diminished further when the fragile truce in political warfare ended and a group of younger Liberals, Newton W. Rowell, Andrew McMaster, Charles Dunning, Thomas
Crerar, and others, sensing the government's vulnerability, pressed for
some greater influence in their party's direction. Their sense of urgency
was fuelled by the expiry of the Conservatives' five-year parliamentary
mandate in September 1916.

Convinced of the pressing need to prepare for a general election,
Adam Kirk Cameron, a Fielding supporter and Laurier confidant, persuaded Laurier to call a convention in Ottawa for this purpose. The
convention's agenda was to address western alienation, explore ways
to exploit the government's bungling war effort, capitalize on the provincial Liberals' revived fortunes, rethink the party's program, and,
above all, enlarge Laurier's circle of advisors. Determined to rejuvenate the party, Cameron and others wanted a more broadly representative national advisory committee composed of younger, more dynamic
party advisors. In December 1915 Laurier reluctantly convened a meeting in Ottawa of Liberal members of Parliament, senators, and other
party advisors to consider Cameron's proposals. During the convention, Laurier agreed to establish a national Liberal advisory committee,
which he seemed to regard at the time as little more than an electoral
war council. Sir Frederick's name was significantly absent from the
initial proposed list of thirty-seven committee members.

Laurier, however, lacked confidence in the committee as a permanent
advisory body and found it awkward to use the large national committee effectively. Moreover, "many of the older Liberals resented the formation of the committee, believing it would disturb existing political
institutions."[22] Nonetheless Laurier consented to a second convention
in Ottawa in July 1916, using that occasion to add twenty-one more

names of his own choosing to his national advisory committee, including that of Sir Frederick. Enlarging the committee made it all the more
unwieldy and redundant. It may even have been Laurier's way of emas-
culating it, especially after he agreed to the prime minister's request to
extend the life of Parliament for an additional year. Committee or no
committee, Sir Frederick retained direct access to Laurier, King, and
Fisher. Yet whatever the appearance and courtesies, his days of effective influence on party policy and direction were over. Increasingly Sir
Frederick became more a party relic, respected, consulted, quoted, and
praised, his virtues contrasted with those of his flamboyant successor.
He was part of the party's past, not its future.[23]

Borden's growing disengagement from active politics gave him time
for his diverse business portfolio. After his defeat in 1911 he remained
president of the Nova Scotia Electric Company, the Nova Scotia Power
and Pulp Company, the Silver Crown Mining Company, the Porcupine
Estates Gold Mine Company, and the King's Park Reality Company;
and chairman of the Butte Central Copper Company's board as well
as that of the Harbourville Reality Company. He served as a director
of the Canadian Cobalt Company, Mutual Life Insurance, the Credit
Clearing House Company, and the Avon Valley Development Company. During this time, and well before his defeat, his most expansive,
remunerative, and controversial endeavour was the ambitious scheme
to electrify Halifax, to light the city and power its tramway with hydroelectricity generated by the Gaspereau River, discussed in an earlier
chapter. This scheme, however, imposed a heavy tax on his physical
energy, resources, and political credit.

Meanwhile time was beginning to take its toll on Sir Frederick's
health. In the fall of 1910, strained and overworked, he had complained
of health problems. His doctor had advised him to slow down and had
"absolutely forbidden [him] to worry about business affairs." But he
had failed to heed this advice, refusing to cut his activities or "to admit
that his mental or physical ability was in the least impaired."[24] Four
months after war broke out in Europe, Mackenzie King, who appeared
to possess a morbid interest in the health of his older colleagues, grimly
noted Sir Frederick's declining health. Three months later King's diary
entry was alarming: "Sir Frederick looks a much shattered man, and I
doubt if he has much longer to live. Certainly he will have to give up
forever the thought of returning to public life."[25]

As it turned out, Sir Frederick's health was more robust than King
had feared. Nor had Sir Frederick relinquished his interest in public
life. Indeed, he had every intention of contesting his constituency. During his constituency association's last convention, the delegates had
"declared their confidence" in and loyalty to "their distinguished lead-

er."[26] Nor did he entertain any doubt but that he would repeat his 1887 victorious return, especially since circumstances in his constituency bore such a striking resemblance to the situation thirty years earlier. The constituency's unfortunate incumbent, Arthur DeWitt Foster, had been implicated in a war-purchasing scandal and had been repudiated by his party for alleged corruption in the purchase of horses. Sir Robert Borden seems never to have forgiven Foster for defeating Sir Frederick and immediately read him out of the party; normally Sir Robert was not so exigent in dealing with his party's numerous sinners!

Only ten days before Sir Frederick died he had been in Halifax, visiting friends and attending to business, including that related to the Nova Scotia Tramways and Power Company. To "the casual observer ... his aspect was that of unusual physical vigour."[27] According to the *Herald*, "none of his friends who met him at that time suspected it was their last meeting"; nor did "even the members of the family circle anticipate his sudden death." A week later, however, he had a paralytic stroke that confined him to his bed. Then, around eight o'clock on Saturday morning, 6 January 1917, four months short of his seventieth birthday, Sir Frederick died suddenly in his sleep. Private telegrams to Sir Robert, Sir Wilfrid, Sydney Fisher, Mackenzie King, and others announced Sir Frederick's death. Major daily papers across the country noted his death, accompanying the notation with a photograph and a biographical resumé of his career. Some carried a brief editorial appreciation of his public contribution, spicing it with personal reminiscences.[28]

On the day of his funeral, flags flew at half-mast in Canning, Kentville, and throughout the county. Official representatives, former colleagues, friends, neighbours, and the curious gathered for the funeral service at Canning's small Methodist church in the early afternoon of Tuesday, 9 January 1917. Special trains ran between Kentville and Canning to accommodate out of town visitors. Only a small number of "the immense crowd" could enter the church, which was draped in floral tributes from friends, colleagues, and public bodies in the region, province, and Ottawa. Among the official representatives was Sir Frederick's friend and colleague A.K. Maclean, the Liberal MP from Halifax and the Canadian government's official delegate; the Honourable E.H. Armstrong, the representative of the Nova Scotia House of Assembly; M.H. George, the delegate of the Nova Scotia Legislative Council; and the county's entire municipal council (it had opened its scheduled semi-annual meeting in Kentville that morning, then adjourned to attend the funeral as a body). The "pressure of public business" only days before the opening of a new – and promising to be tumultuous – parliamentary session prevented Sir Robert from attending the funeral; instead he sent his "favourite" brother Hal, of the Privy Council, as his per-

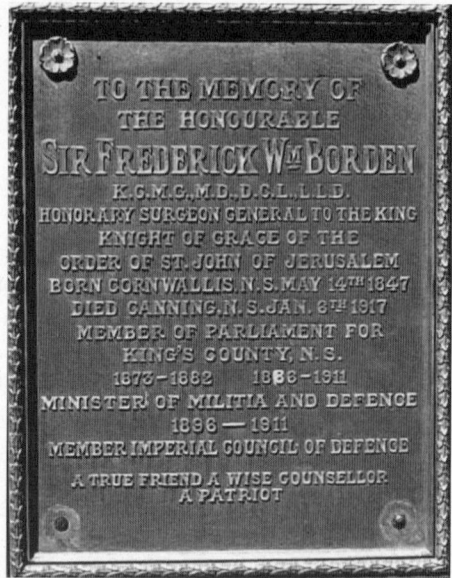

(LEFT) Sir Frederick's monument in the family burial plot. Not shown in the picture are two rectangular stones on either side, marking the burial of Sir Frederick's two wives, and the circular stone cross commemorating Harold, near his mother's tombstone. *Courtesy Fieldwood Heritage Society*; (RIGHT) The bronze plaque at the base of Sir Frederick's memorial. *Courtesy Fieldwood Heritage Society*

sonal representative.[29] Sir Wilfrid was unable to attend the funeral for similar reasons. According to Mackenzie King's diary, only his mother's serious illness, which entailed around-the-clock care, prevented King from going to Canning.[30]

The service was conducted, perhaps predictably, by his cousins the Reverend Dr Byron Crane Borden, the president of Mount Allison University, and the Reverend Dr Arthur Cummings Borden, the distinguished retired Methodist missionary to Japan, assisted by two local Methodist clergy, the Reverend Mr Wright of Kingsport and the Reverend Arthur Hockin of Grand Pre.[31] After the ceremony a long entourage escorted Sir Frederick's remains to the family burial plot in the Hillaton Cemetery (a site that accommodated the Wesleyan Methodist church until it burnt in 1909 and a cemetery that had been enlarged in 1911 thanks to a portion of land conveyed to the church by Sir Frederick),[32] where he was interred beside his first wife, with sufficient space reserved on the other side for her sister, his second wife. Close by was a stone cross memorial to his only son, Harold, who had been buried in South Africa.

Above Sir Frederick's grave the family later erected an impressive stone monument with a bronze plaque affirming his claim to public memory: his place and date of birth and death; his service to the state as a member of Parliament and minister of militia and defence; his medical and honorary degrees; his titles, Knight Commander of St Michael and St George, Knight of Grace of the Order of St John of Jerusalem, honorary surgeon general to the king; his membership in the Imperial Council of Defence; and above all "A True Friend   A Wise Counsellor   A Patriot." Significantly absent was any hint of his material success as a Maritime entrepreneur. Sanitized of its material base, Sir Frederick's claim (and by extension his family's) to memory was based on his professional attainment and public service as a healer, philanthropist, a wise and valued counsellor, a warrior of selfless, patriotic sacrifice, a man of refinement and title – a knight indeed.

In remembering Sir Frederick, friends and colleagues recalled his personal qualities, his love of reminiscences and recollections of old friends, his "broad-minded, generous nature," his sense of fairness and freedom of rancour and bitterness, his chivalry, his paternalism, and his many acts of kindness and beneficence. They remembered his common sense, his "vision and far-sighted judgment," his "executive ability,"[33] his seemingly inexhaustible energy, enterprise, and courage, and his impatience with indecision and inactivity.[34] His community remained fascinated with him, if sometimes awed by and a bit envious of his external symbols of wealth and standing, his house, his guests, his travels, and his motorcar, their curiosity piqued by rumours of his more exotic private life.

Public tributes focused on high policy. Preoccupied by a world war whose outcome was then far from certain, the *Times* reminded readers of Borden's standing as an imperial statesman, his contribution to Canadian military preparedness. In its obituary the London journal recalled that Sir Frederick had been "one of the most eager among his colleagues to send contingents to South Africa and the naval programme had his zealous support," noting as well that under his administration expenditures on Canada's land forces "increased fivefold."[35] Others lauded his reform of the Militia, linking it to the success of Canadian arms in the Great War then raging in Europe. Political partisans hailed him as an "exponent and champion of Liberalism." Mackenzie King, who penned an obituary article for the *Liberal Monthly* after lengthy consultation with Laurier (in some senses it was a joint statement), hailed him as a champion of "complete Canadian autonomy," a cause he pursued with "vigour and unanswerable argument." Above all, King and Laurier remembered Sir Frederick as "a fine fellow, a plucky fighter," "courageous," "never seeking excuses."[36] Since then,

scholars have underlined his political skills, his "genius" for "cooperation and manipulation," and his ability to keep "the machine working
smoothly and criticism at a minimum."[37]

Had Sir Frederick penned his own obituary he might well have drawn
attention to Sir Sam Hughes's recent, apparently generous tribute in
naming the military base at Angus Plains, about eighty kilometres
north of Toronto, Camp Borden in honour of his old friend and predecessor. An initiative enthusiastically endorsed by the prime minister,
Camp Borden was billed as a lasting monument to Sir Frederick's service to the Canadian military forces, then heavily engaged in Europe.
Sir Frederick himself may have been slightly amused by Hughes's gesture and have enjoyed the irony that in 1905 he had rejected Angus
Plains, the sandy site dubbed the "Canadian Sahara," as a central training base in favour of Petawawa.[38] Borden would have been aware that
Hughes's purchase of training camps, often through the good offices
of political friends, had been an object of sharp public and Opposition
criticism. The Liberal press had often reminded its readers that by 1916
Canada possessed one acre of training ground for every recruit, not
to mention Camp Hughes, the large 90,000-acre site that Sir Sam had
modestly named after himself. Nonetheless Sir Frederick had appreciated Hughes's tribute.

Hardened political opponents retained another construction of Sir
Frederick's personal behaviour, character, and public contribution. To
them he would remain a partisan, duplicitous, self-serving parvenu;
a smell in the nostrils of right-thinking people from Halifax to Vancouver; a Nova Scotia country doctor who had had no knowledge of
military affairs, had been interested only in patronage and corruption,
and had turned the Militia into a "Tammany" Hall. They would point
to the continuing deficiencies in Canada's military forces, condemn
his conflation of private and public interests, and censor his untidy private life.

Sir Frederick died in the first week of 1917, the year that marked the
fiftieth anniversary of Confederation. It was a decisive and divisive year
in his country's fragile history, as well as a tense and critical year in the
Great War then raging in Europe. This difficult period had actually
begun the year before, in February 1916, with the destruction by fire of
the central block of the Parliament Buildings, where Sir Frederick had
spent thirty-five years of his public life. Then, in November 1916, Sir
Robert Borden had removed Sir Sam Hughes from the Ministry of Militia and Defence. The following month David Lloyd George's recently
formed National government underlined the alarming stalemate on the
western front and the need for a more concerted political direction of
the war. Sir Frederick's death spared him even more alarming news:

the weakening and the disintegration of the eastern front, Czar Nicholas II's abdication in February, the Bolshevik seizure of power in October, and mutinies in the French army in May and June 1917.

Had Sir Frederick lived he would have applauded Sir Robert's role in framing Article IX of the Imperial Conference of 1917, a resolution that described Canada and the other self-governing dominions as equal with Britain, "autonomous and no way subordinate one to the other," a true commonwealth of nations. In many ways this resolution represented the triumph of Sir Frederick's own imperial vision, and one he shared with his cousin. The Canadian Corps's celebrated success at Vimy and its continuing decisive contribution during the last hundred days of World War I would have been a vindication of his efforts to build a capable, autonomous Canadian military force led by Canadians, a source of great pride, though a pride qualified by his painful appreciation of the war's awful personal cost. He might well have wondered how Canadian naval and air services might have contributed to the war's success had they developed as he had hoped and planned, encouraged by the distinguished contribution of Canada's "Knights of the Air" to the Royal Flying Corps. Last but not least, he would have surely welcomed the belated entry of the United States into the war in April 1917.

Death spared Sir Frederick the tragic and divisive conscription crisis, that uncivil battle within his own country and party, with its appeals to prejudice, its broken friendships, and the spectacle of the deep personal anguish of his old friend and leader, Sir Wilfrid Laurier. The issue had raised its ugly head during the months preceding his death. Already the *Halifax Herald* was campaigning for a national government and compulsory military service. Finally, there was that other awful tragedy so close to home, the Halifax explosion that devastated the city in December 1917 (just before the traumatic federal election), leaving 1,900 dead and 9,000 injured, an explosion, in Hugh McLennan's view, that severed Canada's mid-Atlantic world, weakening imperial ties and strengthening continental imperatives. In other words, it wrought a transformation that would have brought Sir Frederick's world almost full circle.[39]

Tragedy haunted Sir Frederick's family, both before and after his death. It began with his mother's early death from tuberculosis when he was but fifteen years of age. The unfortunate early death of his first wife left him with three small dependent children. His only son's death in battle cut deeply, disrupting and redirecting his dynastic dreams. Then, on 29 February 1920, his son-in-law Charles Gordon Hewitt died at the age of thirty-five from Spanish influenza, a war-bred epidemic that killed some 50,000 other Canadians largely between the ages of

fifteen and thirty-five.[40] Twenty-two years later another war claimed
two more members of his immediate family. In February 1942 the war
censor announced that Sir Frederick's younger daughter, Julia Maude,
and her husband, Leslie S. Macoun, were "among the passengers on
the ill-fated liner *Lady Hawkins* which was recently torpedoed and sunk
in the Atlantic" on 19 January 1942.[41] According to the terse, filtered
wartime report, their boat had been torpedoed off St Kitts on its way to
the Barbados, presumably where they planned to spend the remaining
weeks of winter.

"Lady Elizabeth," as Lady Borden was affectionately called by many
of her friends, lived on another thirty-nine years after her husband's
death, presiding over a lively household. Her mother, aged eighty-nine
at the time of Sir Frederick's death, would live another two years. Julia,
Leslie, and their only child, Elizabeth Rosamond,[42] divided their time
between Ottawa and their Woodside estate, where Leslie "operated a
large fruit farm" and continued to administer the family's finances.[43]
After her husband's death from influenza in 1920, Sir Frederick's elder
daughter, Elizabeth, joined Lady Borden at Borden Place, where they
lived mutually supportive but quite autonomous lives, assisted by a
household staff of some seven persons. Elizabeth, a somewhat eccentric
stepdaughter, maintained a vigilant watch over Lady Borden, enforcing deference and respect, reminding the careless, casual, or forget-
ful of her stepmother's title and standing. To those less familiar, Lady
Borden was known as "the Queen."

The community viewed the younger Elizabeth with respectful amusement and curiosity. A short-tempered, "no-nonsense type of person"
who wore "riding britches all the time," much to Lady Borden's disapproval, Elizabeth, identifying herself as an "apple grower," appears
to have taken charge of the family's "Habitant" commercial orchards
after the tragic deaths of her sister and brother-in-law in 1942, managing them with a shrewd and exacting eye for profit. During the war
she posted one of her agents close to Aldershot to sell apples to the
troops. She loved dogs and horses (which she rode sidesaddle) and
shared her father's affection for cars; she shopped in the neighbouring
town of Kentville by drawing up to a store and honking the horn of her
Hudson for service.

However devoted Elizabeth may have been to her stepmother and
however solicitous of her welfare, for over two decades after her husband's death Lady Borden maintained an independent social routine.
After all, she was not quite fifty-four when her husband died, still
healthy, active, and with an unabated love of serious books, politics,
travel, and entertainment. With her network of friends, she possessed
the time, health, and means to maintain, even indulge, her ambitious

social life. She continued to receive and entertain family, friends, and visitors and to travel within Canada and abroad. In Ottawa Lady Borden stayed with Julia, her stepdaughter; Julia and her husband had purchased a house on 199 Wurtemberg Street, close to "Glensmere," Robert Borden's home (at 201 Wurtemberg Street). While visiting her stepdaughter, Lady Borden met and dined with many of her old friends, including Mackenzie King, with whom she discussed books and politics, and of course Sir Robert and the other Lady Borden.[44] In Toronto she visited the Pellatts, and continued to spend time in London on her way to Florence, where she spent the winters until World War II.

Although the family lost "a lot of money" during the 1929 stock market crash, the family's large orchards proved very profitable during the Depression and war years. The bumper harvests during the early thirties, falling transatlantic freight rates, and their Ontario and Quebec competitors' devastating spring frosts gave Annapolis Valley apple producers an enviable lucrative, competitive edge in the London and Liverpool markets.[45]

World War II, however, brought stark changes to Lady Borden's routine. No longer could she winter in Florence, and since the eight large stone fireplaces at Borden Place failed to provide a comparable warmth, she spent her winters at the Cornwallis Hotel in Kentville. On 11 May 1948 the younger Elizabeth died at the age of seventy-three of coronary thrombosis after only a few days in hospital in Wolfville.[46] Lady Borden lived on another eight years after Elizabeth's death, assisted by her seven servants (paid in cash monthly from the interest income on a trust fund) and surrounded by the household and personal memorabilia of her life. Occasionally, her valuables, including her jewels, which she kept at Borden Place, became casualties of the rather careless household management. Dressed in "long dresses – almost to the floor," her long hair either "in a braided bun or worn in braids wound up and fastened over the top of her head," Lady Borden retained her regal appearance.[47] Mentally and physically active, she exacted respect and deference; only a month before her death the Kings County Women's Liberal Association once again acclaimed her their honorary president.[48] Stoutly refusing to accept the claims of time, on birthdays during the last years of her life, she insisted on subtracting rather than adding a year from her age, a claim that no one dared challenge.

Finally, on 28 February 1956, Lady Borden died after a short illness, less than a week short of her ninety-third birthday. In the early afternoon of a snowy March 3rd, neighbours, friends, and family, including her sole step-granddaughter, Elizabeth Rosamond Green (her step-great-granddaughter, Julia Leslie Green, was at boarding school), gathered in the Trinity United Church in Canning to pay their last solemn respects to "the Queen." This was the church, formerly the Wesleyan Methodist Church, into which she had been baptised, whose ministers had married her, and which had buried her father, mother, sister, husband, and stepdaughter. She and her mother, Mrs J.H. Clarke, and her stepdaughter Elizabeth had been especially active members and benefactors of the church.[49] In a simple service led by the church's minister, Rev. J.W. Barbour, a former pastor, Dr T.W. Hodgson from Digby reminded the congregation of Lady Borden's "Christian character and her life of service to her church and community." In the audience was the premier of the province, Henry D. Hicks, a reminder of her former public stature. Then, in a brief service of committal, Lady Borden joined the other members of her family (this included her mother and father, her stepdaughter Elizabeth, and her husband) in the wrought-iron-fenced family burial plot, a headstone identical in size and design to that of her sister marking her place adjacent to Sir Frederick and not far from the thriving town in which she had been born.[50]

APPENDIX

Corporate Ventures

Note: This list is not definitive; it contains the names of only those companies that were found during the research for the book.

American Farm Products Company
Ames-Holden-McCready
Avon Valley Development Company
Beaver Valley Oil Company
Boland-Thomson Silver Mining Company Limited
British Canadian Lumber Company
Buffalo, Lockport & Rochester Railway Company
Butte Central Copper Syndicate
Canada Finance and Agency Company Limited
Canada Food Company Limited
Canadian Cobalt Company Limited
Canadian Light and Power Company
Canadian Tungsler Mines Limited
Canning Water and Electric Light, Heating and Power Company
Caribou Deeps Limited
Cobalt Central Mines
Credit Clearing House Syndicate
Dominion Box and Package Company
Dominion of Canada Trust Company
East Oregon Light and Power Company
Electrical Development Company
Empire Cobalt Company Limited
Evangeline Fruit Company
Fessenden Wireless Telegraph
Gaspereau Electric Light Company
Gaspereau Lumber Company
Harbourville Realty Company
Havana Central Railway Company
Home Bank
Imperial Trust Company
International Mercantile Agency

International Underwriting Company
Irondale Bancroft and Ottawa Railway Company
King's Park Realty Company, Limited
Maple Leaf Fruit Company
Maritime Coal, Railway and Power Company
Maritime Lumber Company
Maritime Telegraph and Telephone Company Limited
Montreal and Oregon Gold Mines Limited
Montreal Street Railway
Mutual Life Assurance Company
Nicola Lake Horticultural Estates Limited
Nipissing Mines Company
Noiseless Typewriter Company
North Atlantic Collieries Company Limited
Northern Crown Bank
Nova Scotia Carriage Company
Nova Scotia Development Company
Nova Scotia Land Corporation Limited
Nova Scotia Light and Power Company
Nova Scotia Power and Pulp Company
Nova Scotia Power Company
Nova Scotia Telephone Company
Peterson Lake Silver Cobalt Mining Company
Porcupine Estates Gold Mines Limited
Reddick Larder Lake Mines Limited
Republic Mines Company
Richelieu and Ontario Railway
Scheelite Mines Limited
Silver Crown Mining Company Limited
Simplex Medal Box Company
Single Service Package Corporation
Spanish River Pulp and Paper Company
Stadacona Oil and Improvement Company
Stanfield Company Limited
Stewart and Mathews Company Limited
Tri-National Security Company
Tungsten Mines Limited
Union Printing Company
United Railways of Havana and Regla Warhouses, Limited
Victoria Tripolite Company Limited
Western Farm Products Limited
Woodside Electric Light Company

Notes

DUA   Dalhousie University Archives
LAC   Library and Archives Canada
NA (UK)   National Archives, United Kingdom
NARA   National Archives and Records Administration, College Park, MD
NLS   National Library of Scotland
PANL   Public Archives of Newfoundland and Labrador
PANS   Public Archives of Nova Scotia
PRO   Public Record Office, London, England

INTRODUCTION

1 Formerly known as Baltimore, the village was renamed Borden by the Canadian Northern Railway in 1906. The proximity of the village of Fielding, named for Borden's Nova Scotia colleague in Laurier's government, suggests an effort to honour the province's two senior political leaders. See Bill Barry, *Geographic Names of Saskatchewan* (Regina: People Places Publishers, 2005).

2 One might also add Borden, Ontario, a geographic township in the Sudbury district, named in 1905 for Sir Frederick Borden. Nick and Helma Mika, *Places in Ontario* (Belleville, ON: Mika Publishing Company, 1977).

3 Phillips Payson O'Brien, "The Titan Refreshed: Imperial Overstretch and the British Navy before the First World War," *Past & Present* 172 (August 2001): 157.

4 *Halifax Herald*, 29 June 1909.

5 Ibid.

6 C.P. Stacey, *The Military Problems of Canada* (Toronto: Ryerson Press, 1940), 170n17.

7 John Buchan, *Lord Minto: A Memoir* (London: Thomas Nelson and Sons, 1924), 126.

8 Norman Penlington, *Canada and Imperialism 1896–1899* (Toronto: University of Toronto Press, 1965), 57–8; George F.G. Stanley, *Canada's Soldiers* (Toronto: Macmillan, 1960), 297–8; C.P. Stacey, *L'Histoire Militaire* (Ottawa: Queen's Printer, 1964), 22–3, 67, 160–3; James Eayrs, "Canadian Defense Policies Since 1967," in *Special Studies Prepared for the Special Committee of the House of Commons on Matters Relating to Defense* (Ottawa, 1965), 5; and general histories such as W.L. Morton, *The Kingdom of Canada* (Toronto: McClelland & Stewart,

1963), 397; Stephen J. Harris, *Canadian Brass: The Making of a Professional Army, 1860–1939* (Toronto: University of Toronto Press, 1988), 36.

9   If Lady Borden was offended, it did not prevent her from reading and discussing Buchan's *Oliver Cromwell* with Sir Robert Borden and Mackenzie King. See Library and Archives Canada (hereafter LAC), W.L.M. King's *Diary*, 27 January 1935.

10 John Buchan [Lord Tweedsmuir] became Canada's governor general (1935–40).

11 In the early 1920s, Sir Robert had instructed Loring Christie to protest the absence of Borden's own name in an index of the Royal Institute of International Affairs' history of the Peace Conference. See Margaret MacMillan's "Canada and the Peace Settlement," MS 452.

12 LAC, Robert Borden Papers, John Buchan to Sir Robert Borden, 25 August 1932; see also Janet Smith, *John Buchan* (London: Thames and Hudson, 1965), 231.

13 British Library, E.T.H. Hutton Papers, vol. 4 (50,081).

14 Sandra Gwyn, *The Private Capital* (Toronto: McClelland & Stewart, 1984), 421, 427.

15 Paul Bilkey, *Persons, Places and Things* (Toronto: Ryerson Press, 1940), 101.

16 Sir John French, "Greetings and Tributes to Old Comrades in Arms: The Prospect for the Empire," in *The Empire Club of Canada Speeches 1922* (Toronto, 1923), 173.

17 Sam Hughes's eulogy on at least two occasions: *Morning Chronicle* (Halifax), 22 June 1904 and 24 August 1907. See also Canada, House of Commons *Debates*, 10 June 1904, 4657; and LAC, Robert Borden Papers, Sir Robert Borden to John Buchan, 28 July 1932, vol. 262, 14723–34.

18 Norm Marion, ed., *Camp Borden Birthplace of the RCAF 1917–1999* (16 Wing Borden, 1999); Desmond Morton, *Le Billet pour le front histoire sociale des volontaires canadiens 1914–1919* (Outremont, QC: Athena editions, 2005), 21; Robert Craig Brown, *Robert Laird Borden: A Biography*, vol. 2 (Toronto: University of Toronto Press, 1975), 202–4; Henry Borden, ed., *Robert Laird Borden: His Memoirs*, vol. 1 (Toronto: Macmillan, 1938), 22.

19 Donald C. Gordon, *The Dominion Partnership in Imperial Defence, 1870–1914* (Baltimore: Johns Hopkins University Press, 1965), 168.

20 Richard A. Preston, *Canada and "Imperial Defence"* (Durham, NC: Duke University Press, 1967), 406.

21 Desmond Morton, "Authority and Policy in the Canadian Militia, 1874–1904" (PhD thesis, University of London, 1968), 431.

22 Harris, *Canadian Brass*, 80, 92, 117; William Beahen, "A Citizens' Army: The Growth and Development of the Canadian Militia 1904–1914" (PhD thesis, University of Ottawa, 1978), 301n9.

23 Harris, *Canadian Brass*, 32. A knowledgeable contemporary of Borden's was also impressed by Borden's record of reform: C.F. Hamilton, "The Canadian Militia: The Beginning of Reform," *Canadian Defence Quarterly*, April 1930, 338.

24 Desmond Morton, "The Cadet Movement in the Moment of Canadian Militarism, 1909–1914," *Journal of Canadian Studies* 13, no. 2 (Summer 1978): 56.

25 S.J.R. Noel, *Patrons, Clients, Brokers: Ontario Society and Politics, 1791–1896* (Toronto: University of Toronto Press, 1990), 76.

26 http://measuringworth.com/calculators/powerus suggests a multiple of 15 to describe 2005 value, measured by consumer price index.

27 P.B. Waite, "Invading Privacies: Biography as History," *Dalhousie Review* 69, no. 4 (Winter 1990): 479.

28 Geoff Eley, *A Crooked Line: From Cultural History to the History of Society* (Ann Arbor: University of Michigan Press, 2005), 168.

29 Andrée Lévesque, "Réflections sur biographie en l'an 2000," *Revue d'histoire de l'Amérique française* 54, no. 1 (été, 2000): 95.

30 Carl Berger, *The Writing of Canadian History: Aspects of English Canadian Historical Writing since 1900* (Toronto: University of Toronto Press, 1986), 270.

31 Naomi E.S. Griffith, *The Context of Acadian History 1686–1784* (Montreal and Kingston: McGill-Queen's University Press, 1992), 30.

32 William H. Sewell, Jr, *Logics of History: Social Theory and Social Transformation* (Chicago: University of Chicago Press, 2005), 195.

33 Suzanne Morton, "La biographie peut-elle être de l'histoire sociale," *Revue d'histoire de l'Amérique française* 54, no. 1 (été, 2000): 107.

34 Sewell Jr, *Logics of History*, 299.

35 Interview with Mrs Lewis Clarke, June 1989.

CHAPTER ONE

1 Margaret Conrad, ed., *They Planted Well: New England Planters in Maritime Canada* (Fredericton: Acadiensis Press, 1988).

2 John V. Duncanson, *Falmouth Township* (Belleville: Mika Publishing Company, 1983), 20, 184.

3 His future wife's home.

4 Samuel's great-grandfather, Richard, had come to the Massachusetts Bay Colony in 1637, possibly as a Quaker, and settled in Portsmouth at a place known as Quaker Hill. Public Archives of Nova Scotia (hereafter PANS), F.W. Borden Papers (hereafter FWB Papers).

5 PANS, Deeds, Kings County, Reel 18279, Petition, Samuel Borden to Lieutenant-Governor Wilmot, 3 August 1765: seeking permission to sell up to forty-six acres.

6 Arthur Wentworth Hamilton Eaton, *The History of Kings County, Nova Scotia* (Salem, MA: Salem Press Company, 1910), 579.

7 PANS, Wills, Kings County, Horton Township, 1822, Reel 18282, vol. 8, p. 146.

8 PANS, Wills, Kings County, Horton Township, 27 July 1805, Reel 19712, no. 65, p. 267.

9 See Joshua M. Smith, *Borderland and Smuggling* (Gainesville: University Press of Florida, 2006), 50–1.

10 On 26 January 1809.

11 *Provincial Wesleyan*, 1 January and 11 June 1862.

12 Robert Laird Borden, *Memoirs* (Toronto, 1938), 1.

13 Andrew was joint guardian (along with Frederick William Borden) of Jonathan's daughter, Maria Frances, Frederick's half-sister.

14 Colin Howell, "Medical Professionalization and the Social Transformation of the Maritimes 1850–1950," *Journal of Canadian Studies* 27, no. 1 (Spring 1992): 7.

15 PANS, RG 83, vol. 1, p. 111, 3 July 1858.

16 It reputedly had been used as a boarding school between 1840 and 1847.

17 Eaton, *History of Kings County*, 580.

18 PANS, School Papers, Kings County, 1851–82.

19 PANS, FWB Papers, Borden to Byron Borden, 19 January 1906.

20 The evidential silence contrasts with Robert Borden's testimony to his mother's influence upon his formation. See Robert Craig Brown, *Robert Laird Borden: A Biography*, vol. 1 (Toronto: University of Toronto Press, 1975), 5–6.

21 Both carried their mother's maiden name.

22 PANS, MG 9, vol. 188, Parliamentary *Scrapbook*, W.R. Canning, "Appreciation," January 1917.

23 Paul Bilkey, *Persons, Papers and Things* (Toronto, 1940), 101.

24 PANS, FWB Papers, Borden to W.E. Roscoe, 8 November 1907.

25 Eaton, *History of Kings County*, 729.

26 *Nova Scotian*, 22 January 1887.

27 Douglas A. Lorimer, *Colour, Class and the Victorians* (Bristol, 1978), 111.

28 Brown, *Robert Laird Borden*, 7.

29 A Prussian-born, naturalized British subject and a professor of German language and literature, Heinrick Godefray Ollendorff (1803–1865) claimed to teach students to read, write, and speak French (and German) in six months, employing a question-and-answer method based on the principle that each question contains most of the answer to be returned.

30 M.V. Marshall, *A Short History of Acacia Villa School* (Wolfville, NS: Acadia University Institute, 1963), 11–15, 36.

31 Brown, *Robert Laird Borden*, 7.

32 *Presbyterian Witness*, 15 August 1863.

33 Dr Jonathan Borden's sister Amanda had married John Caldwell, Mary (Caldwell) Woodworth's first cousin.

34 *Nova Scotia Census of 1851* and *Canada Census of 1871*, p. 32, no 18. Frederick's stepmother was a staunch Presbyterian. The Bordens seem to have had a somewhat ecumenical approach to religious affiliation. While the first Bordens in Nova Scotia appear to have been Quakers, Perry (junior) Borden's wife, Lavinia Fuller, was probably Presbyterian and attended the Covenanter's Church, where she was buried and where Andrew Borden was a member. Perry's second wife was a devoted Wesleyan Methodist for thirty years, and Perry's obituary notice in the *Provincial Wesleyan*, 11 June 1862, describes him as "long united to the Wesleyan church in Lower Horton." The Browns were also prominent members of the Presbyterian Church, despite the fact that the 1851 Census listed Maria Frances and her husband, Dr Jonathan Borden, as Free Will Baptists; if this was so, their association with the Baptists does not appear to have lasted long, since Maria Frances's death was announced in the *Presbyterian Witness*, 29 November 1862.

35 *The Calendar of Kings College* (Halifax, 1864), 30.

36 Kings College Archives, Matriculation Book, 1863.

37 W.S. Moorson, *Letters from Nova Scotia* (London: Henry Colburn and Richard Bently, 1830), 213.

38 F.M. Vroom, *Kings College: A Chronicle, 1789–1939* (Halifax: Imperial Publishing Company, 1941), 81.

39 University of Kings College Archives, Terminal Examination Grades, C.1.2.2, *Register of Names of Students at Kings Commencing 1861.*

40 University of Kings College, *Calendar*, 1866, 41.

41 Mike O'Brien, "Manhood and the Militia Myth: Masculinity, Class and Militarism in Ontario, 1902–1914," *Labour/Le Travail* 42 (Fall 1989).

42 PANS, FWB Papers, Borden to G.G. Jones, 29 March 1906.

43 Geoffrey Bolton, "The Idea of a Colonial Gentry," *Historical Studies* 13 (1968): 317.

44 *A Catalogue of the Officers and Students of Harvard for Academic Year 1869–70* (Cambridge, 1869), 76–93. The number of Nova Scotia students at Harvard would decline markedly with the opening of the Dalhousie Medical Faculty in 1868 and the increased attraction of McGill's medical school, where Frederick's son would enrol. According to Belcher's *Almanac* for 1885, by 1884 the number of Nova Scotians at Harvard had dropped to fourteen (166–7) .

45 Eaton, *History of Kings County*, 878.

46 S.E.D. Shortt, "Physicians, Science, and Status: Issues in the Professionalization of Anglo-American Medicine in the Nineteenth Century," *Medical History* 37 (1983): 65, 64, 61.

47 PANS, RG 83, vol. 1, 472.

48 Colin Howell, "Medical Professionalization and the Social Transformation of the Maritimes 1850–1950," *Acadiensis* 21 (Spring 1992).

49 PANS, FWB Papers, Borden to Governor-General, 14 March 1911.

50 See S.E.D. Shortt, "Before the Age of Miracles: The Rise, Fall and Rebirth of General Practice in Canada, 1890–1940," in Charles Roland, ed., *Disease and Medicine: Essays in Canadian History* (Toronto: Hannah Institute, 1984); Sasha Mullally, "Unpacking the Black Bag: Rural Medicine in the Maritime Provinces and Northern New England States, 1900–1950" (PhD thesis, University of Toronto, 2005).

51 Borden's 1906 biographical entry states that he practised medicine for "30 years." *The Canadian Parliament* (Montreal, 1906), 17.

CHAPTER TWO

1 See Colin Howell, "Reform and the Monopolistic Impulse: The Professionalization of Medicine in the Maritimes," *Acadiensis* 11 (1981): 3–22. See, too, S.E.D. Shortt, "Physicians, Science, and Status: Issues in the Professionalization of Anglo-American Medicine in the Nineteenth Century," *Medical History* 27 (1983): 51–68.

2 PANS, vertical MS file, Margaret E. Ells, "Canning in the Seventies," 3.

3 *Nova Scotian*, 23 July 1866.

4 *Yarmouth Herald*, 19 July 1866.

5 PANS, vertical MS file, Margaret Ells, "Canning," 10. There was also a small Wesleyan Mission House and later a Church of England.

6 *Yarmouth Herald*, 19 July 1866; *Star* (Berwick), 19 July 1866.

7 *Star* (Berwick), 19 July 1866.

8 *Yarmouth Herald*, 19 July 1866; the *Nova Scotian*, 23 July 1866, estimated the loss at £25,000 sterling of which £5,000 were insured.

9 PANS, vertical MS file, Margaret Ells, "Canning," 6.

10 In 1830 it was renamed to commemorate the recently deceased British prime minister, George Canning.

11 PANS, vertical MS file, Margaret Ells, "Canning," 11.

12 Arthur Wentworth Hamilton Eaton, *The History of Kings County, Nova Scotia* (Salem, MA: Salem Press Company, 1910), 152.

13 Donald Smiley, ed., *Rowell-Sirois Report*, Book 1 (Toronto: McClelland & Stewart, 1963), 18.

14 See Graeme Wynn, *Timber Colony* (Toronto, University of Toronto Press, 1981), 69–72.

15 PANS, vertical MS file, Margaret Ells, "Canning," 12.

16 Dalhousie University Archives (hereafter DUA), Abram Jess, "History of Scott's Bay," MS.

17 Eric W. Sager and Gerald E. Panting, *Maritime Capital: The Shipping Industry in Atlantic Canada, 1820–1914* (Montreal and Kingston: McGill-Queen's University Press, 1990), 77–80.

18 PANS, E.J. Cogswell, "Kentville: A Historic Sketch," 1895 typescript, MS.

19 See Marguerite Woodworth, *History of the Dominion Atlantic Railway* (Kentville, NS: Kentville Publishing Company, 1936).

20 PANS, Nova Scotia Ms *Census* (1860); Canada, *Census* (1871), vol. 1, 73; (1881), vol. 1, 12; (1891), vol. 1, 30. Unfortunately, these official returns are not entirely useful for comparative purposes, since census figures are given for districts rather than towns and the borders of these census districts changed from census to census. In the absence of more accurate statistics, Lovell's *Directory* may provide a clearer picture of what was happening within each village. According to Lovell's *Directory*, Berwick's population grew from 350 in 1871 to 1,500 in 1896; Kentville's from 1,000 to 1,686; and Wolfville's from 900 to 1,200, whereas Canning's remained static at 600 during this period. See *Lovell's Directory* (Montreal, 1871), 1549, 1560, 1669, 1789; *Lovell's Directory* (Montreal, 1896), 197, 229, 275, 445.

21 Canada, *Census* (1871), vol. 3, 90; (1911), vol. 1, 67. See also Alan A. Brookes, "Out-migration from the Maritime Provinces, 1860–1900: Some Preliminary Considerations," *Acadiensis* 5 (Spring 1976): 26–55.

22 *Canada Gazette,* 28 January 1892; *Presbyterian Record,* 22 March 1884.

23 PANS, vertical MS file, Margaret Ells, "Canning," 9.

24 David Alexander, *Atlantic Canada Shipping Project*, vol. 3 (Saint John: Memorial University of Newfoundland), 99.

25 Sager and Panting, *Maritime Capital*, 92; they suggest that the decline in fleet registered at Windsor "was delayed by a decade" (122).

26 W.C. Milner, *The Basin of Minas and Its Early Settlers* (Wolfville, NS: Wolfville Acadian, 1930), 93.
27 Sager and Panting, *Maritime Capital*, 70. This calculation is based on Sager and Panting's claim that a ship was valued at $30 to $35 a ton.
28 Milner, *The Basin of Minas*, 65.
29 He continued to attend the annual militia camp as a military physician in 1896 and 1897. In 1903 he became a member of the Ontario College of Physicians and Surgeon. His constituents continued to refer to him as "the doctor" even after his knighthood.
30 Caldwell was a cousin, the son of Frederick's Aunt Amanda (Borden) Caldwell.
31 PANS, RG 48, Reel 782, Kings County, Administrative Papers. Charles Henry Borden's homestead and about $4,000 went to his widow.
32 PANS, RG 47, Reel 1313, p. 52.
33 By the Reverend Y.H. Pickles.
34 PANS, RG 64/649/1894 Barkhouse, Clement and Bessie Borden.
35 *New Star* (Berwick), 8 June 1888.
36 Betty Hearn to Carman Miller, 20 January 1964. Hearn was the archivist of the Bank of Nova Scotia.
37 *Presbyterian Witness*, 23 January 1892.
38 *Journal of the Canadian Bankers Association* 2 (1895): 667.
39 Supreme Court of Nova Scotia, *David Berteaux vs Frederick W. Borden*, 1891 A. No. 4075.
40 Bank of Nova Scotia Archives, James Forgan to Thomas Fysche, 5 January 1888; Thomas Fysche to F.W. Borden, 11 July 1888. Fyche and Borden later served on the board of Reginald Aubrey Fessenden's Wireless Telegraph Company. PANS, FWB Papers, F. Minden Cole to Borden, 1 December 1910.
41 PANS, FWB Papers, Borden to Arthur F. Borden, 25 January 1901.
42 PANS, FWB Papers, Borden to W.H. Chase, 8 April 1916.
43 Supreme Court of Nova Scotia, *David Berteaux vs Frederick W. Borden*, 1891.
44 *Provincial Wesleyan*, 1 December 1888.
45 *Maritime Merchant*, 4 March 1897.
46 PANS, FWB Papers, Borden to C.V. Anthony, 10 January 1901.
47 Sager and Panting, *Maritime Capital*, 153.
48 Woodworth, *History of the Dominion Atlantic Railway*, 104, 106, 110; Canada, House of Commons, *Debates*, 31 August 1891, 1120.

CHAPTER THREE

1 Thomas H. Ferns and Robert Craig Brown, "John Charlton," in *Dictionary of Canadian Biography*, vol. 8 (Toronto: University of Toronto Press, 1994), 189.
2 S.J.R. Noel, *Patrons, Clients, Brokers: Ontario Society and Politics, 1791–1896* (Toronto: University of Toronto Press, 1990), 18.
3 Noel, *Patrons, Clients, Brokers*; Cathy Matson, *Merchants & Empire: Trading in Colonial New York* (London: Johns Hopkins University Press, 1998).
4 Carman Miller, "Family, Business and Politics in Kings County, N.S.: The Case of F.W. Borden 1874–1896," *Acadiensis* 8 (Spring 1978): 60–75.

5 J.K. Johnson, *Becoming Prominent: Regional Leadership in Upper Canada 1791–1841* (Montreal and Kingston: McGill-Queen's University Press, 1989), 160–1.

6 *Daily Acadian Recorder*, 26 January 1874.

7 *Acadian Recorder*, 14 June 1856, Charles Rohan's comment about Samuel Chipman.

8 PANS, FWB Papers, Borden to S. Blenkhorn, 7 July 1908.

9 Robert Craig Brown and Ben Forster, *Historical Atlas of Canada,* vol. 2 (Toronto: University of Toronto Press, 1993).

10 PANS, MG 9, vol. 188, Parliamentary *Scrapbook*, 176.

11 Donald Swainson, "The Personnel of Politics: A Study of the Ontario Members of the Second Federal Parliament" (PhD thesis, University of Toronto, 1968).

12 PANS, MG 9, vol. 188, Parliamentary *Scrapbook*, 20 April 1874.

13 Canada, House of Commons, *Debates*, 13 March 1875, 690.

14 Ibid., 15 March 1876, 655.

15 From 1885 until 1898, federal elections were governed by the federal Franchise Act.

16 PANS, FWB Papers, Borden to Captain Potter, 11 November 1901.

17 Noel, *Patrons, Clients, Brokers*, 277.

18 Canada, House of Commons, *Debates*, 22 March 1888, 359.

19 Charles Tupper appears to have held £4,000 sterling in company stock under the name C.H.M. Black. See Marguerite Woodworth, *History of the Dominion Atlantic Railway* (Kentville, NS: Kentville Publishing Company, 1936), 74n.

20 In 1875 Borden broke with his party and voted for John Costigan's motion for an address to the Crown respecting common schools in New Brunswick. Canada, House of Commons, *Debates*, 8 March 1875, 613.

21 Ibid., 21 January 1881, 617; 15 May 1882, 1545.

22 Ibid., 11 March 1889, 530.

23 Ibid., 10 May 1892, 2396.

24 Ibid., 11 March 1889, 529ff.

25 Sir Frederick Borden, "The Canadian Militia – Past, Present and Future," *United Service Magazine* 32–4 (1906): 145.

26 Canada, House of Commons, *Debates*, 13 March 1875, 690.

27 Ibid., 689ff.

28 PANS, MG 9, vol. 188, Parliamentary *Scrapbook,* W.R. Canning, "An Appreciation."

29 *Morning Herald* (Halifax), 9 and 11 September 1878.

30 *Western Chronicle* (Kentville), 27 June 1883.

31 *Morning Herald*, 18 September 1878.

32 Two other infants were reportedly born but died within twenty-four hours of their birth. Julia Leslie Green MacKay to author, 13 January 2010.

33 Canada, House of Commons, *Debates*, 20 April 1880.

34 In 1880 the Commons bill was defeated in the Senate; two years later it passed with a comfortable majority. Canada, Senate, *Debates*, 17 May 1882.

35 Carman Miller, "Samuel Chipman," in *Dictionary of Canadian Biography*, vol. 7 (Toronto: University of Toronto Press, 1988), 177; Barry M. Moody, "William

Henry Chipman," in *Dictionary of Canadian Biography*, vol. 9 (Toronto: University of Toronto Press, 1976), 130.

36 PANS, FWB Papers, Borden to H.H. Wickwire, 25 June 1906.
37 Canada, *Sessional Paper, no. 77* (1883), 203.
38 *Morning Herald*, 26 June 1882.

CHAPTER FOUR

1 In 1880 Borden had supported a bill to legalize marriage between a man and the sister of a deceased wife, legislation that aroused the ire of many churchmen, including members of the Presbyterian Church in Canada. *Acts and Proceedings of the 6th General Assembly of the Presbyterian Church in Canada* (Toronto, 1880), 51, 56.
2 PANS, Canning United (formerly Methodist) Church, Reel 1297.
3 "Wives of Cabinet Ministers," unidentified newspaper clipping in the possession of Ken Bezanson, Port Williams.
4 Elizabeth Tupper Clarke outlived Frederick Borden; she died 27 June 1919 at the age of ninety-one.
5 S.J.R. Noel, *Patrons, Clients, Brokers: Ontario Society and Politics, 1791–1896* (Toronto: University of Toronto Press, 1990), 65.
6 Canada, House of Commons, *Debates*, 31 August 1891, 1120.
7 Marguerite Woodsworth, *The History of the Dominion Atlantic Railway* (Kentville, NS: Kentville Publishing Company, 1936), 110.
8 *Morning Chronicle* (Halifax), 3 February 1887.
9 Ibid., 2 and 3 February 1887.
10 Ibid., 15 February 1887.
11 *Nova Scotian*, 19 February 1887.
12 J. Murray Beck, *Politics of Nova Scotia, 1701–1896*, vol. 1 (Tantallon, NS: Four East Publications, 1985), 218.
13 Canada, House of Commons, *Debates*, 6 April 1894.
14 *Morning Herald*, 2 and 16 February 1887.
15 For a fuller discussion of the repeal issue, see Colin D. Howell, "W.S. Fielding and the Repeal Elections of 1886 and 1887 in Nova Scotia," *Acadiensis* 8 (Spring 1979).
16 Paul Bilkey, *Persons, Papers and Things* (Toronto: Ryerson Press, 1940), 101.
17 He had been appointed assistant surgeon to the 68th Battalion on 22 October 1869, promoted to surgeon on 22 October 1879, and was named principal medical officer of the brigade camp at Aldershot on 1 September 1887. See Geo. McLean Rose, *A Cyclopedia of Canadian Biography* (Toronto, Rose Publishing, 1888), 317–18.
18 Canada, House of Commons, *Debates*, 21 January 1881, 616ff.
19 Ibid., 17 May 1887, 509.
20 H.V. Nelles, *The Art of Nation-Building: Pageantry and Spectacle at Quebec's Tercentenary* (Toronto: University of Toronto Press, 1999), chap. 10.
21 Canada, House of Commons, *Debates*, 3 June 1887, 768; 15 March 1876, 655.
22 LAC, Ernest Pacaud Papers, Laurier à Pacaud, 7 fevrier 1898.

23 Canada, House of Commons, *Debates*, 21 January 1881, 617; 14 March 1890, 1963. For example, Borden disagreed with A.G. Jones's criticism of a $3,000 subsidy to the Churchill brothers for the maintenance of a Minas Basin ferry service.

24 Robert Craig Brown, *Robert Laird Borden: A Biography*, vol. 1 (Toronto: University of Toronto Press, 1975), 31.

25 PANS, FWB Papers, Bordon to C.R. Bill, 28 March 1898; L.V.D. Chipman to Bordon, 18 August 1896.

26 DUA, Jonathan Steele Papers, H.H. Steele to his father, 9 January 1894.

27 A. McKim, *Canadian Newspaper Directory* (Montreal, 1892), 161. When the *Western Chronicle* ceased publishing in 1916, it was controlled by the Union Printing Company, and its two chief shareholders were Sir Frederick Borden and H.H. Wickwire. See *Kentville Advertiser*, 8 December 1916.

28 P.B. Waite, "Becoming Canadians: Ottawa's Relations with the Maritimes in the First and Twenty-first Years of Confederation," in *National Politics and Community in Canada*, edited by Kenneth Carty and W. Peter Ward (Vancouver: University of British Columbia Press, 1986), 165; P.B. Waite, *The Man from Halifax* (Toronto: University of Toronto Press, 1985), 285.

29 *Nova Scotian*, 21 February 1891.

30 *Morning Chronicle*, 24 September 1903.

31 Brown, *Robert Laird Borden*, vol. 1, 31.

32 Canada, House of Commons, *Debates*, 31 March 1893.

33 Ibid., 31 March 1892.

34 See Supreme Court of Nova Scotia, *David Berteaux vs Frederick W. Borden*, 1891.

35 Canada, House of Commons, *Debates*, 8 July 1891, 1951; 22 June 1892, 4082; 6 April 1892, 1032; 13 June 1895, 2605; 11 June 1895, 2484; 11 March 1896, 3272.

36 Beck, *Politics of Nova Scotia*, 248.

37 *Official Report of the Liberal Convention* (Toronto, 1893), 18.

38 *The Newspaper Reference Book of Canada* (1903), 164.

39 During Borden's first parliamentary interventions, one Conservative paper accused him of reading his speech "like a child reading a spelling book" (a charge that he angrily denied). Canada, House of Commons, *Debates*, 15 March 1876, 654.

40 Ibid., 17 January 1896, 281–2.

41 Canadian Institute for Historical Reproduction (CIHM), Frederick Borden MP on Budget, Ottawa, 6 April 1894, FC 36, no. 01029, Thomas Fisher Rare Book Room, University of Toronto.

42 Canada, House of Commons, *Debates*, 12 June 1894, 4130–42; Alan A. Brookes, "The Golden Age and the Exodus: The Case of Canning, Kings County," *Acadiensis* 10 (Spring 1981): 57–82.

43 Sir Richard Cartwright, *Reminiscences* (Toronto: William Briggs, 1912), 325–6, 402–5.

44 Canada, House of Commons, *Debates*, 24 March 1896, 4480–508.

45 *Morning Chronicle*, 8 May 1896.

46 Brown, *Robert Laird Borden*, vol. 1, 44.

47 *Morning Chronicle*, 30 April 1896.
48 PANS, FWB Papers, Borden to David Mills, 4 January 1901.
49 *Morning Chronicle*, 5 June 1896.
50 Ibid.
51 Ibid., 4 June 1896.
52 Ibid., 14 May 1896.
53 Borden informed Laurier in April 1897 that the election in King's had turned on reciprocity, not the Manitoba Schools Question, but the timing of his communication with the prime minister seems to suggest that the purpose of his message was to persuade Laurier to proceed with trade negotiations with the United States rather than undertake a considered analysis of the 1896 election. LAC, Laurier Papers, Borden to Wilfrid Laurier, 5 April 1897.

CHAPTER FIVE

1 Jones lacked a seat in the House but the party did not feel him sufficiently important to make a seat available to him as it did for W.S. Fielding.
2 *Canada Year Book* (Ottawa, 1911), 258–9. This does not include the $2,256,709 budget for the newly created Naval Services.
3 *Globe* (Toronto), 8 January 1917.
4 Quoted in John Buchan, *Lord Minto: A Memoir* (London: Thomas Nelson and Sons, 1924), 119.
5 In 1902 Laurier cautioned Lord Dundonald: "You must not take the Militia seriously." Cited in C.P. Stacey, *The Military Problems of Canada* (Toronto: Ryerson Press, 1940), 68. Even Borden's imperialist former colleague, Sir William Mulock, believed that "the strength of the nation lay in its peaceful and happy homes ... [not in its] battleships and engines of destruction." *Morning Chronicle* (Halifax), 26 January 1907.
6 PANS, FWB Borden Papers, Borden to W.S. Fielding, 8 October 1902; Borden to Laurier, 19 November 1908; National Library of Scotland (hereafter NLS), Minto Papers, Minto to Brodrick, 23 November 1902.
7 Canada, House of Commons, *Debates*, 10 April 1902; *Gazette*, 15 February 1901; Stephen J. Harris, *Canadian Brass: The Making of a Professional Army, 1861–1939* (Toronto: University of Toronto Press, 1988), 37.
8 LAC, Laurier Papers, 4775ff.
9 Desmond Morton, *Canada and War: A Military and Political History* (Toronto: Butterworths, 1981), 19.
10 Canada, House of Commons, *Debates*, 20 August 1891, 4235; 10 February 1893, 600; 22 April 1896, 7007ff.
11 Harris, *Canadian Brass*, 86.
12 Carman Miller, "The Montreal Militia as a Social Institution before World War I," *Urban History Review* 19, no. 1 (June 1990): 57–64.
13 Desmond Morton, *Ministers and Generals: Politics and the Canadian Militia, 1868–1904* (Toronto: University of Toronto Press, 1970), 168.
14 The other occasions were a fire, a Montreal student riot, conflict surrounding the kidnapping of a young girl, and sabotage. See Jean Pariseau, "Forces

armées et maintien de l'ordre au Canada, 1867–1967: Un siècle d'aide au pouvoir civil," vol. 3 (PhD thesis, Université Paul Valery, III, Montpellier, 1981). My count includes the Yukon Field Force, omitted by Pariseau.

15 J.E. Brown, a surveyor; J.M. Brown, 2nd class clerk; B.P. Brown, 1st class clerk; and Robert Brown, inspector of saddlery.
16 PANS, FWB Papers, Borden to W.T. White, 23 November 1901.
17 PANS, FWB Papers, Borden to T.H. Morse, 29 March 1904.
18 PANS, FWB Papers, N.Y. Gascoigne to Borden, 14 July 1896.
19 C.F. Hamilton, "The Canadian Militia: The Beginning of Reform," *Canadian Defence Quarterly*, April 1930, 338.
20 NLS, Minto Papers, Minto to Lord Seymour, 1 April 1899.
21 Norman Penlington, *Canada and Imperialism* (Toronto: University of Toronto Press, 1965), 72.
22 Canada, House of Commons, *Debates*, 25 June 1900, 8231.
23 Harris, *Canadian Brass*, 60–1.
24 *Morning Chronicle*, 7 September 1904.
25 Above all, his respect for the PF was not the result of a post–Boer War repentance; quite the contrary, the Boer War confirmed his faith in the citizen soldier. Harris, *Canadian Brass*, 35.
26 Canada, *Debates*, 10 July 1899, 7024.
27 PANS, FWB Papers, Gerald Kitson to Borden, 1 February 1897.
28 Canada, *Debates*, 8 April 1897, 667.
29 Canada, *Sessional Paper,* no. 35a (1898).
30 Canada, House of Commons, *Debates*, 25 June 1900, 8260–1.

CHAPTER SIX

1 See Desmond Morton, *Ministers and Generals: Politics and the Canadian Militia, 1868–1904* (Toronto: University of Toronto Press, 1970).
2 See Jacques Gouin and Lucien Brault, *Legacy of Honour* (Toronto, 1985), chap. 4.
3 LAC, Wilfrid Laurier Papers, C-758, p. 25890.
4 *Morning Chronicle* (Halifax), 27 January 1897.
5 *Berwick Register*, 2 June 1897.
6 John Buchan, *Lord Minto: A Memoir* (London: Thomas, Nelson and Sons, 1924), 126.
7 *Ottawa Free Press*, 27 June 1904. For a more detailed discussion of this question, complete with documentary references, see my "F.W. Borden and Military Reform, 1896–1911," *Canadian Historical Review*, September 1969, 267–8n14.
8 NLS, Minto Papers, Minto to Joseph Chamberlain, 15 February 1900.
9 PANS, FWB Papers, J.D. Edgar to Borden, 31 October 1896.
10 PANS, FWB Papers, Gibson to Borden, 15 December 1896.
11 PANS, FWB Papers, Borden to James Sutherland, (?) November 1901.
12 PANS, FWB Papers, Borden to Laurier, 28 December 1899; Borden to Oliver Mowat, 9 December 1899; Hutton Papers, Borden to Hutton, 30 January 1899.
13 PANS, FWB Papers, Borden to E.C. Borden, 28 December 1896.

14 Canada, House of Commons, *Debates*, 3 April 1900, 3103.
15 S.J.R. Noel, *Patrons, Clients, Brokers: Ontario Society and Politics, 1791–1896* (Toronto: University of Toronto Press, 1990), 288.
16 George Stanley, *Canada's Soldiers, 1604–1954: The Military History of an Unmilitary People* (Toronto: Macmillan, 1960), 298.
17 PANS, FWB Papers, Borden to A.G. Blair, 22 November 1899.
18 Canada, House of Commons, *Debates*, 25 September, 1896, 1993.
19 Canada, *Sessional Paper*, no. 1 (1899): 23; *Sessional Paper*, no. 1 (1901): 121.
20 W.A. Beahen, "A Citizens' Army: The Growth and Development of the Canadian Militia 1904–1918" (PhD thesis, University of Ottawa, 1978), 301n9.
21 Canada, House of Commons, *Debates*, 10 July 1899, 7091.
22 Ibid., 22 April 1897, 1083.
23 They were Captain E.M. Beckwith, William Dorman, and Harold Borden, all Liberals.
24 J.B.B. Brebner, *The North Atlantic Triangle* (New York: Columbia University Press, 1945), 165.
25 PANS, FWB Papers, Borden to A.G. Blair, 22 November 1899.
26 *Halifax Herald*, 23 March 1898.
27 Canada, House of Commons, *Debates*, 20 June 1899.
28 PANS, FWB Papers, H.W. Brown to Borden, 14 April 1897.
29 Canada, *Sessional Paper*, no. 35a (1903), 94.
30 J. Castell Hopkins, ed., *The Canadian Annual Review of Public Affairs, 1902* (Toronto: Annual Review Publishing Co., 1903), 170. See, too, Carman Miller, *Painting the Map Red: Canada and the South African War, 1899–1902* (Montreal and Kingston: McGill-Queen's University Press, 1993), chap. 28.

CHAPTER SEVEN

1 See Desmond Morton, *Ministers and Generals: Politics and the Canadian Militia, 1868–1904* (Toronto: University of Toronto Press, 1970).
2 *Revised Statutes of Canada*, 1886, 46 Victoria, chap. 41, section 37.
3 This position was taken by the governor general, Minto: see NLS, Minto Papers, Minto to Dundonald, 24 March 1903; as well as by Frederick D. Monk, the Conservative member of Parliament for Jacques Cartier: see Canada, House of Commons, *Debates*, 23 June 1904, 5411ff.; and occasionally by Sam Hughes: see Canada, House of Commons, *Debates*, 10 June, 1904, 4588ff.
4 NLS, Minto Papers, Minto to Borden, 12 July 1904.
5 *Statutes of Canada, 1867–68*, 31 Victoria, chap. 40, section 2.
6 Cited in Canada, House of Commons, *Debates*, 24 June 1904, 5544.
7 PANS, FWB Papers, Borden to J.W. Laurie, 5 March 1900.
8 In Borden's view this was one of the more serious deficiencies in the position; see Canada, House of Commons, *Debates*, 5 May 1903, 2405.
9 National Archives, United Kingdom (hereafter, NA [UK]), Colonial Office 42 (875), Minute, John Anderson, 7 February 1900.
10 British Library, H.O. Arnold-Forster Papers, *Diary*, 27 February 1904, commenting on Hutton's difficulties in Australia.

11 Canada, House of Commons, *Debates*, 5 May 1898, 4932.
12 PANS, FWB Papers, N.Y. Gascoigne to Borden, 29 July 1897; N.Y. Gascoigne to Borden, 16 April 1897.
13 PANS, FWB Papers, Borden to F.L. Berque, 22 March 1898.
14 Canada, House of Commons, *Debates*, 5 May 1903, 2405.
15 H. Strachan, *The Politics of the British Army* (Oxford: Clarendon, 1997), 104.
16 See Richard J.R. Lehane, "Lieutenant-General Edward Hutton and 'Greater Britain': Late-Victorian Imperialism, Imperial Defence and the Self-Governing Colonies" (PhD thesis, University of Sydney, 2005).
17 Ibid.
18 NA (UK), Colonial Office 42 (875), Minute, John Anderson, 7 February 1900.
19 British Library, Hutton Papers, "Memorandum of the Hutton-Wolseley Interview," 29 July 1898.
20 PANS, FWB Papers, Borden to Laurier, 5 March 1900.
21 Carman Miller, *Painting the Map Red: Canada and the South African War, 1899–1902* (Montreal and Kingston: McGill-Queen's University Press, 1993), 231–3.
22 British Library, H.O. Arnold-Forster Papers, *Diary*, 27 February 1904.
23 British Library, E.T.H. Hutton Papers, Hutton to Ardagh, 21 November 1898.
24 British Library, E.T.H. Hutton Papers, Hutton to Nathan, 9 January 1899, 1044.
25 PANS, FWB Papers, Borden to Hutton, 20 October 1899.
26 Cited in Canada, House of Commons, *Debates*, 23 June 1904, 5428.
27 PANS, FWB Papers, Borden to J.W. Laurie, 5 March 1900.
28 PANS, FWB Papers, Borden to Hutton, 20 October 1899.
29 PANS, FWB Papers, Borden to Clifford Sifton, 9 October 1899.
30 PANS, FWB Papers, Borden to Hutton, 28 December 1899.
31 PANS, FWB Papers, Borden to Hutton, 28 December 1899.
32 PANS, FWB Papers, Richard Cartwright to Borden, 16 April 1900.
33 NLS, Minto Papers, Minto to Joseph Chamberlain, 17 February 1900.
34 Canada, House of Commons, *Debates*, 25 February 1901, 385.
35 Desmond Morton, "Authority and Policy in the Canadian Militia, 1874–1904" (PhD thesis, University of London, 1968), 431.
36 NLS, Minto Papers, *Draft of Toronto Club Speech*; *Globe* (Toronto), 15 December 1898; LAC, John Willison Papers, George Simpson to Willison, 24 November 1898.
37 Morton, *Ministers and Generals*, 146.
38 PANS, FWB Papers, Borden to J.V. Ellis, 9 February 1899.
39 NLS, Minto Papers, Minto to Hutton, 9 June 1899.
40 LAC, Laurier Papers, Minto to Bordon, 11 June 1899.
41 British Library, Hutton Papers, Hutton to Sir Redvers Buller, 18 June 1899.
42 PANS, FWB Papers, Richard Scott to Borden, 14 April 1899.
43 Morton, "Authority and Policy," 431.
44 NA (UK), Colonial Office 42 (876), Seymour to Selborne, 18 September 1900.
45 NA (UK), Colonial Office 42 (875), Minute, John Anderson, 6 March 1900.
46 Quoted in R.A. Preston, *Canada and "Imperial Defense"* (Durham, NC: Duke University Press, 1967), 256.

47 See Ronald G. Haycock, *Sam Hughes: The Public Career of a Controversial Canadian 1885–1916* (Waterloo, ON: Wilfrid Laurier University Press, 1986), chap. 5; Carman Miller, *The Canadian Career of the Fourth Earl of Minto* (Waterloo, ON: Wilfrid Laurier University Press, 1980), chap. 5.
48 NLS, Minto Papers, Minto to Hutton, 10 August 1899.
49 LAC, Laurier Papers, Hubert Foster to Hughes, 24 August 1899.
50 *Globe* (Toronto), 4 October 1899.
51 *Halifax Herald*, 23 March 1900.
52 Hutton described Lord Roberts, the commander-in-chief of British forces in South Africa, as a "military Gladstone," not meant to be a flattering comparison. Lehane, "Lieutenant-General Edward Hutton," 206.
53 *Globe* (Toronto), 4 October 1899.
54 *Canadian Military Gazette*, 3 October 1899. See also NLS, Minto Papers, Minto to Laurier, 6 October 1899.

CHAPTER EIGHT

1 *Halifax Herald*, 4 November 1899.
2 See Carman Miller, *Painting the Map Red: Canada and the South African War, 1899–1902* (Montreal and Kingston: McGill-Queen's University Press, 1993), chaps 1–3.
3 Jonathan Lewis, introduction to *The Boer War,* by Tabitha Jackson (London, UK: Channel Four Books, 1999), 7.
4 Gordon Heath, "A War with a Silver Lining: Canadian Protestant Churches and the South African War 1899–1902" (PhD thesis, St Michael's College, 2004).
5 Although Laurier did not call an election for another year, he was considering doing so.
6 Miller, *Painting the Map Red*, chap. 2.
7 Ibid., 438–9.
8 PANS, FWB Papers, Borden to J.H. Gibson, 21 October 1899; Borden to Kerr, 3 November 1899.
9 LAC, William Otter Papers, E.T.H. Hutton to Otter, 4 September 1899; Oscar C. Pelletier, *Mémoires, souvenirs de famille et récits* (Quebec, 1940), 307.
10 *Montreal Star,* 6 September 1899.
11 LAC, Laurier Papers, Laurier to Borden, 5 September, 1899.
12 LAC, Laurier Papers, Borden to Laurier, n.d.
13 Laurier LaPierre, "Politics, Race and Religion in French Canada: Joseph Israel Tarte" (PhD thesis, University of Toronto, 1962), 373.
14 *Montreal Star*, 4 October 1899.
15 *Gazette* (Montreal), 6 October 1899.
16 LAC, J.S. Willison Papers, Borden to Willison, 10 October 1899.
17 NA (UK), Colonial Office 42 (869), Chamberlain to Minto, 13 October 1899.
18 Laurier Papers, "Memorandum of the Privy Council Session," 13 October 1899.
19 *Halifax Herald*, 17 October 1899.

20 For fuller details on fielding the force, see Miller, *Painting the Map Red*, chap. 4.

21 NLS, Minto Papers, L. Drummond to Minto, 30 October 1899.

22 University of Birmingham Archives, Joseph Chamberlain Papers, Chamberlain to Lansdowne, 14 October 1899; Lansdowne to Chamberlain, 15 October 1899.

23 For more details, see Miller, *Painting the Map Red*, chap. 4.

24 PANS, FWB Papers, Borden to J.H. Gibson, 21 October 1899.

25 PANS, FWB Papers, Borden to Hutton, 8 November 1899.

26 British Library, Hutton Papers, MS, "Memoirs," 159.

27 *Gazette* (Montreal), 31 October 1899.

28 PANS, FWB Papers, Borden to H.G. Thrasher, 6 January 1912.

29 *Halifax Herald*, 4 November 1899.

30 Glenbow Museum Archives, Samuel B. Steele Papers, Steele to Laurier, n.d.

CHAPTER NINE

1 PANS, FWB Papers, Borden to Hutton, 18 December 1899.

2 See Carman Miller, *The Canadian Career of the Fourth Earl of Minto* (Waterloo, ON: Wilfrid Laurier University Press, 1980), 106–8.

3 *Quebec Mercury*, 2 December 1899.

4 Glenbow Museum Archives, Sam Steele Papers, Strathcona Horse *Diary*, 28 February. Dr Duncan McEachern of Macdonald College, chosen especially by Lord Strathcona, also used Beith to inspect horses for the Strathcona Horse.

5 PANS, FWB Papers, Borden to J.I. Tarte, 15 December 1899; R. Cartwright to Borden, 9 October 1899; Borden to C. Sifton, 9 October 1899.

6 For a fuller description of this dispute, see Miller, *The Canadian Career*, 108–18.

7 NLS, Minto Papers, Memorandum of Laurier-Minto interview, 30 January 1900.

8 NLS, Minto Papers, Minto to Chamberlain, 17 January 1900.

9 NLS, Minto Papers, Memorandum of Laurier-Minto interview, 27 January 1900.

10 NA (UK), Colonial Office 42 (875), Chamberlain to Minto, 1 February 1900.

11 PANS, FWB Papers, Hutton to Borden, 11 December 1899.

12 NLS, Minto Papers, Hubert Foster to W. White, 29 January 1900; Foster to White, 1 February 1900.

13 NA (UK), Colonial Office 42 (875), Minto to Chamberlain, 7 February 1900.

14 NA (UK), Colonial Office 42 (875), Minto to Chamberlain, 7 February 1900.

15 LAC, Laurier Papers, Strathcona to Laurier, 13 February 1900.

16 Canada, House of Commons, *Debates*, 13 February 1900, 330.

17 NLS, Minto Papers, Minto to Seymour, 20 March 1900.

18 NLS, Minto Papers, Minto to Lady Minto, 13 June 1904.

19 NA (UK), Colonial Office 42 (896), Minto to Brodrick, 19 November 1900.

20 *Halifax Herald*, 26 June 1900.

21 Ibid., 18 June 1900.

22 PANS, FWB Papers, F.E. Devlin to Borden, 31 July 1899.

23 *Halifax Herald*, 23 June 1900.
24 Ten Liberal members of Parliament opposed the majority report, and six MPs were sufficiently unhappy with its exoneration of Devlin, effectively shielding him from prosecution, that they voted for the minority report. Three of the ten, Dominique Monet, Henri Bourassa, and Arthur Putte, opposed any monetary expenditure on the war, Puttee, the Labour member from Winnipeg, because he was a pacifist. Two others, Harris George Rogers and William Pettet, were former Patrons of Industry; another, Duncan Graham, was an Independent Liberal; and Robert Lorne was on his way to becoming an Independent and would not be returned in the next election. The rest, John Valentine Ellis, Joseph Ethier, and Frank Oliver, continued to enjoy the party's favour.
25 PANS, FWB Papers, Bordon to D.A.P. Clarke, 11 January 1900.
26 PANS, FWB Papers, Borden to R.W. Kinsman, 28 December 1900.
27 Robert Borden, quoted by Roy McLaren in "Harold Borden," in *Dictionary of Canadian Biography,* vol. 12 (Toronto: University of Toronto Press, 1990), 114–15.
28 *Halifax Herald*, 18 July 1900; *Globe* (Toronto), 18 July 1900; *Montreal Star*, 18 July 1900; and *Manitoba Free Press*, 18 July 1900.
29 For more details on Harold Borden's death, see Carman Miller, *Painting the Map Red: Canada and the South African War, 1899–1902* (Montreal and Kingston: McGill-Queen's University Press, 1993), 248–9.
30 *Halifax Herald*, 18 July 1900.

CHAPTER TEN

1 Adamantly opposed to Macdonald's Franchise Act, in 1898 the Liberals reverted to the provincial electoral lists.
2 *Halifax Herald*, 30 October 1900.
3 Ibid., 6 November 1900.
4 PANS, FWB Papers, H. Brown to F. Ronan, 17 October 1900.
5 *Halifax Herald*, 1 November 1900.
6 PANS, FWB Papers, W.S. Fielding to Borden, 12 December 1899.
7 Robert Craig Brown, *Robert Laird Borden: A Biography*, vol. 1 (Toronto: University of Toronto Press, 1975), 47.
8 Ibid., 46.
9 John Coldwell Adams, "The Other Borden," *Atlantic Advocate*, August 1979, 22.
10 PANS, FWB Papers, R.L. Borden to F.W. Borden, 23 April 1910; R.L. Borden to F.W. Borden, 20 December 1910; Henry C. Borden to F.W. Borden, 28 March 1911, re. Canadian Tungsten Mines Limited and the Scheelite Mines Limited. Frederick and Robert invested in a consortium to purchase Parc St Denis in Montreal. See D.J. Hall, *Clifford Sifton: A Lonely Eminence 1901–1929*, vol. 2 (Vancouver: University of British Columbia Press, 1985), 214.
11 Canada, House of Commons, *Debates*, 11 July 1904, 6390.
12 R.L. Borden to John H. McIntyre, 4 April 1908; F.W. Bordon to William McIntyre, 26 February 1901, in the private collection of Ken Bezanson.

13 Canada, House of Commons, *Debates*, 29 May 1905, 6656.

14 Not only did Workman "head the list" of investors in Borden's Butte Central Copper Company, but he also became a director and vice-president; nor did Borden hesitate to call upon Workman to advance him money "for a short time," to cope with the financial difficulties of his Supply Company, giving him stocks and notes as collateral. PANS, FWB Papers, Freeman I. Davison to Borden, 23 March 1910; L.S. Macoun to Borden, 19 July 1910; Borden to Freeman Davison, 9 November 1910.

15 For a fuller description of the house, see Courtney C. Bond, *City on the Ottawa* (Ottawa: Queen's Printer, 1961), 61.

16 Sir Frederick Borden, "The Canadian Militia – Past, Present and Future," *United Service Magazine* 32–4 (1906): 150.

17 Duff Crerar, *Padres in No Man's Land* (Montreal and Kingston: McGill-Queen's University Press, 1995), 17–23.

18 Ibid., 23.

19 Ibid., 28.

20 Canadian Militia Council, *Minutes*, 30 May 1905.

21 Sixteen of the Militia's 85 battalions and 570 of its 4,270 officers were francophone.

22 Canada, House of Commons, *Debates*, 23 June 1904, 5443ff.

23 NLS, Minto Papers, Minto to Lord Dundonald, 20 March 1902.

24 NLS, Minto Papers, Minto to St John Brodrick, 27 May 1902.

25 PANS, FWB Papers, Borden to Colonel Percy Lake, 31 May 1902.

26 NLS, Minto Papers, Minto to Richard O'Grady-Haly, 18 October 1901.

27 NLS, Minto Papers, Minto to St John Brodrick, 29 May 1902.

28 NLS, Minto Papers, E.T.H. Hutton to Minto, 19 July 1900.

29 By comparison, New Zealand, a county with a fraction of Canada's population, provided an equal number. Australia contributed at least 16,000 men, over twice Canada's number of volunteers.

30 For additional information on Howard's Canadian Scouts, see Neil Speed, *Born to Fight* (Melbourne: Caps & Flint, 2002).

31 J. Castell Hopkins, ed., *Morgan's Annual Register* (Toronto: Annual Review Publishing Co., 1902), 286–7.

32 *Canadian Military Gazette*, 16 February 1901.

33 PANS, FWB Papers, Borden to Laurier, 21 January 1901.

34 See Carl Berger, *A Sense of Power* (Toronto: University of Toronto Press, 1969).

35 G.M. Grant agreed: "We are henceforth a nation." Cited in T.G. Marquis, *Canada's Sons on Kopje and Veldt* (Toronto: Canada's Sons Publishing Co., 1900), 7.

36 *Ottawa Citizen*, 14 April 1900.

37 G.T. Denison, *The Struggle for Imperial Unity* (Toronto: Macmillan, 1909), 268; *Globe* (Toronto), 28 July 1900.

38 LAC, Richard E.W. Turner Papers, *Diary*, 20 July 1900.

39 E.W.B. Morrison, *With the Guns in South Africa* (Hamilton: Spectator Print Co., 1901), 258, 290.

40 For more information on these tensions, see Carman Miller, "The Unhappy Warriors: Conflict and Nationality among Canadian Troops during the South African War," *Journal of Imperial and Commonwealth History* 23, no. 1 (Janu-

ary 1995); and Carman Miller, "The Crucible of War," in *The Boer War: Army, Nation and Empire,* edited by Peter Dennis and Jeffrey Grey (Canberra: Army History Unit, 2000).

41 *Mail and Empire,* 6 November 1900.

42 S.M. Brown, *With the Royal Canadians* (Toronto: Publishers Syndicate, 1900), 6; Marquis, *Canada's Sons on Kopje and Veldt,* 71; J. Douglas Borthwick, *Poems and Songs of the South African War* (Montreal: Gazette Publishing Company, 1901), 125.

43 See John F. Owen, "The Military Forces of Our Colonies," *Fortnightly Review,* March 1900; Richard Jebb, *Studies in Colonial Nationalism* (London: E. Arnold, 1905), 127; Arthur Conan Doyle, *The Great Boer War* (London: Smith, Elder and Co., 1903), 742; Rudyard Kipling, "The Captive," in *Traffics and Discoveries* (London: Macmillan, 1904); John Stirling, *The Colonials in South Africa, 1899–1902* (Edinburgh: Blackwood, 1907).

44 Paula M. Krebs, *Gender, Race and the Writing of Empire* (Cambridge, UK: Cambridge University Press, 1999), 170–1.

45 *Manchester Guardian,* 9 November 1900; John Hobson, *Canada Today* (London, 1906), 101, 105.

46 Stephen Leacock, "Greater Canada: An Appeal," *University Magazine* 6, no. 2 (1907): 132–41.

47 Jeanette Duncan, *The Imperialist* (Toronto: McClelland & Stewart, 1971), 229.

CHAPTER ELEVEN

1 J. Castell Hopkins, ed., *The Canadian Annual Review of Public Affairs, 1903* (Toronto: Annual Review Publishing Co., 1904), 476.

2 Stephen Harris, *Canadian Brass: The Making of a Professional Army, 1860–1939* (Toronto: University of Toronto Press, 1988), 11–12.

3 NA (UK), Colonial Office 42 (875), Minto to Chamberlain, 24 March 1900; NLS, Minto Papers, Minto to Gerald Kitson, 10 April 1900.

4 *Saturday Night,* 14 May 1900; *Montreal Herald,* 4 May 1900; *Globe* (Toronto), 3 May 1900.

5 NA (UK), Colonial Office 42 (875), Minute, John Anderson, 7 April 1900.

6 NLS, Minto Papers, Minto to Laurier, 11 April 1900.

7 NA (UK), Colonial Office 42 (875), Minto to Chamberlain, 2 May 1900.

8 NLS, Minto Papers, Minto to George Parkin, 26 September 1904; Minto to Joseph Chamberlain, 5 December 1900.

9 Quoted in T. Robert Fowler, *Courage Rewarded* (Victoria, BC: General Store Publishing House, 2008), 47.

10 Laurier Papers, Borden to Laurier, 17 December 1900.

11 Hopkins, *Canadian Annual Review of Public Affairs, 1903* (1904), 476.

12 See Desmond Morton, *The Canadian General* (Toronto: Hakkert, 1974), 244.

13 J.E. Collins, *Canada under the Administration of Lord Lorne* (Toronto: Rose Publishing, 1884), 262n.

14 Canada, House of Commons, *Debates,* 13 February 1900, 339.

15 Minto objected that Aylmer's Liberal Party associations would make him a creature of the minister.

16 Harris, *Canadian Brass*, 64–5; Desmond Morton, *Ministers and Generals: Politics and the Canadian Militia, 1868–1904* (Toronto: University of Toronto Press, 1970), 142.

17 For a fuller discussion, see Carman Miller, *The Canadian Career of the Fourth Earl of Minto* (Waterloo, ON: Wilfrid Laurier University Press, 1980), 140–1.

18 Hopkins, *Canadian Annual Review of Public Affairs, 1903*, 476.

19 NLS, Minto Papers, Kitson to Minto, 9 April 1900.

20 NA (UK), Colonial Office 42 (886), G. Fleetwood Wilson to CO, 31 August 1900.

21 NA (UK), Colonial Office 42 (886), Minute, G.W. Johnson, 19 May 1901.

22 NLS, Minto Papers, Minto to Lansdowne, 31 August 1901; Miller, *Canadian Career*, 142–3.

23 NA (UK), Colonial Office 42 (886), War Office to Colonial Office, 9 March 1901; Minute, C.T. Davies, 17 May 1901.

24 Hopkins, *Canadian Annual Review of Public Affairs, 1903*, 481.

25 Ibid., 476.

26 NA (UK), Colonial Office 42 (892), Minute, A.B. Keith, 14 April 1903.

27 NA (UK), Colonial Office 42, Minto to Chamberlain, 28 May 1903.

28 NA (UK), Colonial Office 42 (883), Minute, E. Wingfield, 8 June 1901.

29 NA (UK), Colonial Office 42 (896), Dundonald to Nicholson, 8 June 1903.

30 O.D. Skelton, *The Life and Letters of Sir Wilfrid Laurier* (Toronto: Oxford University Press, 1921), 114.

31 British Library, H.O. Arnold-Forster Papers, *Diary*, 8 December 1903.

32 NA (UK), Cabinet, 38/D/no. 82, "Minute of the 26th meeting of the Committee of Imperial Defence," 11 December 1903.

33 NLS, Minto Papers, *Diary*, 3 January 1904.

34 NLS, Minto Papers, *Diary*, 2 March 1904.

35 Max Beloff, *Imperial Sunset,* vol. 1 (London, UK: Methuen & Co., 1971), 83; Franklyn Arthur Johnson, *Defence by Committee: The British Committee of Imperial Defence 1885–1959* (London, UK: Oxford University Press, 1960), 58.

36 Johnson, *Defence by Committee*, 48–9; W.S. Hamer, *The British Army: Civil-Military Relations, 1885–1905* (Oxford: Oxford University Press, 1970), 199.

37 See John Edward Kendle, *The Colonial and Imperial Conferences, 1887–1911* (London, UK: Longmans, 1967), chap. 10.

38 For additional information, see Johnson, *Defence by Committee*; Donald C. Gordon, *The Dominion Partnership in Imperial Defence, 1870–1914* (Baltimore, MD: Johns Hopkins University Press, 1965).

39 NA (UK), War Office, 32 (266), Admiralty to War Office, 19 April 1902.

40 British Library, Balfour Papers, Selborne to Balfour, 5 April 1903.

41 Samuel F. Wells, Jr, "British Withdrawal from the Western Hemisphere," *Canadian Historical Review*, December 1968, 340.

42 NA (UK), Cabinet, 38/31, no. 79, "Minutes of the 25th meeting of the Committee of Imperial Defence," 4 December 1903.

43 NA (UK), Colonial Office 42 (896), Borden to Minto, 1 March 1904; PANS, FWB Papers, Borden to Lyttelton, 1 March 1904.

44 NA (UK), Colonial Office 42 (896), Minute, Lyttelton, 12 January 1904.

45 NA (UK), Colonial Office 42 (896), John Anderson to M.F. Ommanney, 2 February 1904.
46 NA (UK), Colonial Office 42 (896), A.F. to H.B. Cox, 23 March 1904.
47 NA (UK), Colonial Office 42 (896), A.F. to H.B. Cox, 23 March 1904.
48 Hopkins, *Canadian Annual Review of Public Affairs, 1903*, 469.

CHAPTER TWELVE

1 University of Birmingham, Joseph Chamberlain Papers, Brodrick to Chamberlain, 26 December 1901.
2 NLS, Minto Papers, Minto to Dundonald, 26 March 1902.
3 John Buchan, *Lord Minto: A Memoir* (London, UK: Thomas Nelson and Sons, 1924), 271.
4 NLS, Minto Papers, Minto to Lady Minto, 2 July 1904; Diary, 20 April 1903; Minto to Arthur Elliot, 13 August 1904.
5 LAC, Laurier Papers, Minto to Laurier, 5 February 1902.
6 Canada, House of Commons, *Debates*, 23 June 1904, 5432.
7 Desmond Morton, *Ministers and Generals: Politics and the Canadian Militia, 1868–1904* (Toronto: University of Toronto Press, 1970), 181.
8 PANS, FWB Papers, 5 March 1904.
9 PANS, FWB Papers, Borden to Dundonald, 21 February 1903.
10 Canada, House of Commons, *Debates*, 30 March 1903, 209.
11 PANS, FWB Papers, Borden to H.O. Arnold-Forster, 4 August 1904.
12 NLS, Minto Papers, Minto to Parkin, 26 September 1904.
13 J. Castell Hopkins, ed., *The Canadian Annual Review of Public Affairs, 1903* (Toronto: Annual Review Publishing Co., 1904), 476.
14 PANS, FWB Papers, Borden to T.D.B. Evans, 12 April 1904.
15 Carman Miller, *The Canadian Career of the Fourth Earl of Minto* (Waterloo, ON: Wilfrid Laurier University Press, 1980), 149.
16 Canada, House of Commons, *Debates*, 10 June 1904, 4583; NLS, Minto Papers, Minto-Borden interview, 9 June 1904.
17 NLS, Minto Papers, Minto-Dundonald interview, 10 and 11 June 1904.
18 Ibid.
19 NLS, Minto Papers, Minto to Mary Minto, 2 July 1904.
20 NLS, Minto Papers, Arthur Guise to Lady Minto, 26 June 1904; Douglas M.B.H. Cochrane, Earl of Dundonald, *My Army Life* (London: Edward Arnold and Company, 1926), 226–7, 258.
21 NA (UK), Colonial Office 42 (896), Minto to Lyttelton, 14 June 1904.
22 NLS, Minto Papers, Laurier-Minto interview, 17 June 1904.
23 NLS, Minto Papers, Minto to Lady Minto, 5 June 1904.
24 The House was dissolved on 29 September and the general election held on 3 November 1904.
25 Canada, House of Commons, *Debates*, 23 June 1904, 5405.
26 Dundonald, *My Army Life*, 243.
27 NLS, Minto Papers, *Diary*, 22 July 1904.
28 British Library, H.O. Arnold-Forster Papers, *Diary*, 11 August 1904.

29 NA (UK), Colonial Office 42 (897), M.F. Ommanney to H.B. Cox, 16 June 1904.

CHAPTER THIRTEEN

1 Mark Moss, *Manliness and Militarism* (Don Mills, ON: Oxford University Press, 2001), 107.
2 Robert H. MacDonald, *Sons of the Empire: The Frontier and the Boy Scout Movement, 1890–1918* (Toronto: University of Toronto Press, 1993), 17–20; John Gooch, *The Prospects of War: Studies in British Defence Policy 1847–1942* (London: Allen and Unwin, 1981), 35–51.
3 MacDonald, *Sons of the Empire*, 82.
4 Ibid., 79.
5 Ibid., 85, 112, 117.
6 Canada, House of Commons, *Debates*, 26 June 1900, 8293.
7 Ibid., 10 April 1902, 2534; *Globe* (Toronto), 28 July 1900; the *Journal* (Ottawa), 20 December 1900, contains a detailed description of Boer defence system; *Mail and Empire*, 19 January 1901.
8 The idea drew heavily upon a civic humanism deeply ingrained in British and American history.
9 Sir Frederick Borden, "The Canadian Militia – Past, Present and Future," *United Service Magazine* 32–4 (1906): 145.
10 Stephen Harris, *Canadian Brass: The Making of a Professional Army, 1860–1939* (Toronto: University of Toronto Press, 1988), 35–7. The paternity of Canada's citizen army is at best contestable. Dundonald claimed paternity in an article published a year after his unceremonious departure from Canada in 1904; in a plea for the adoption of a citizen army in Britain, he drew heavily upon the Canadian example. Borden, however, had announced his preference for a citizen army and its objective of training 100,000 men well before Dundonald's arrival in Canada. Moreover, Dundonald's subsequent use of anatomical language to describe the force ("skeleton," "flesh and blood") replicates the language of (Dr) Borden's major policy outline of October 1903. Compare Dundonald, "Notes on a Citizen Army," *Fortnightly Review* 78, new series (July–December 1905): 627–39, with Borden's Commons speech.
11 Canada, House of Commons, *Debates*, 25 June 1900, 8239.
12 Ibid., 8 October 1903, 13402.
13 Ibid., 10 April 1902, 2514.
14 Ibid., 19 April 1901, 3777.
15 Earl of Dundonald, "Notes on a Citizen Army."
16 J. Castell Hopkins, ed., *Canadian Annual Review of Public Affairs, 1908* (Toronto: Annual Review Publishing Co., 1909), 284.
17 Canada, Department of Militia and Defence, *Annual Report*, 1905–6, 40.
18 William Beahen, "A Citizens' Army: The Growth and Development of the Canadian Militia, 1904–1914" (PhD thesis, University of Ottawa, 1978), 213.
19 Ibid., 214.
20 J.D.P. French, "Report," Canada, *Sessional Paper*, no. 35a (1911), 13.
21 Canada, House of Commons, *Debates*, 8 October 1903 [F.W. Borden], 13387.

22 The number of cavalry regiments increased from 16 to 36; the number of infantry battalions from 85 to 103; and the number of artillery batteries from 48 to 61 during this period. For example, in 1905 Saskatchewan possessed no military units; ten years later it had four infantry battalions, four cavalry regiments, "and corps of artillery and support troops." Beahen, "A Citizens' Army," 195.

23 Ibid., 270.

24 Ibid., 200–3.

25 Canada, House of Commons, *Debates*, 8 October 1903, [F.W. Borden], 13405.

26 Beckles Willson, *The Life of Lord Strathcona and Mount Royal* (Toronto, 1915), 560.

27 Hopkins, *Canadian Annual Review, 1904*, 472.

28 Moss, *Manliness and Militarism*, 92.

29 Sir Frederick Borden, "The Canadian Militia – Past, Present, and Future," *United Service Magazine* 32–4 (1906): 145.

30 Ibid.

31 Some authors have seen this as an intrusion into provincial jurisdiction, despite its authorization by the Militia Act (1868); if so, it did not appear to alarm Borden or attract a great deal of public commentary at the time.

32 Desmond Morton, "The Cadet Movement in the Moment of Canadian Militarism, 1909–1914," *Journal of Canadian Studies* 13, no. 2 (Summer 1978): 59.

33 See *Militia Act* (1904), sections 64–7.

34 Canada, House of Commons, *Debates*, 10 July 1905, 9119.

35 PANS, FWB Papers, Borden to Sam Hughes, 15 April 1909.

36 Beahen, "A Citizens' Army," 322.

37 PANS, FWB Papers, Borden to Lord Strathcona, 28 June 1911.

38 *Canadian Military Gazette*, 10 October 1911.

39 Morton, "The Cadet Movement," 63.

40 Hopkins, *Canadian Annual Review of Public Affairs, 1909*, 63.

41 *Morning Chronicle* (Halifax), 8 April 1903.

42 Ibid.

43 According to Desmond Morton, *Ministers and Generals: Politics and the Canadian Militia, 1868–1904* (Toronto: University of Toronto Press, 1970), Appendix A, Table 2, 201, there were only eight officers or former officers in the House of Commons after the 1900 general election.

44 Canada, House of Commons, *Debates*, 8 October 1903, 13430.

45 Ibid., [Sam Hughes], 13436.

46 Earl of Dundonald, "Notes on a Citizen Army," *Fortnightly Review,* October 1905.

CHAPTER FOURTEEN

1 Desmond Morton, "The Cadet Movement in the Moment of Canadian Militarism, 1909–1914," *Journal of Canadian Studies* 13, no. 2 (Summer 1978): 56–68; William Beahen, "Filling Out the Skeleton: Paramilitary Support Groups, 1904–1914," *Canadian Defence Quarterly* 13 (1884): 34–41; Mike O'Brien, "Manhood and the Militia Myth: Masculinity, Class and Militarism in Ontario,

1902–1914," *Labour/Le Travail* 42 (Fall 1998): 115–41; Mark Moss, *Manliness and Militarism: Educating Young Boys in Ontario for War* (Don Mills, ON: Oxford University Press, 2001).

2　Keith Walden, *Becoming Modern in Toronto: The Industrial Exhibition and the Shaping of a Late Victorian Culture* (Toronto: University of Toronto Press, 1997), 268, 272.

3　Ronald Rudin, *Founding Fathers* (Toronto: University of Toronto Press, 2003), 205–6; H.V. Nelles, *The Art of Nation-Building: Pageantry and Spectacle at Quebec's Tercentenary* (Toronto: University of Toronto Press, 1999), chap. 9.

4　Carman Miller, "The Montreal Militia as a Social Institution before World War I," *Urban History Review* 19, no. 1 (June, 1990): 57–64; Walden, *Becoming Modern*, 37.

5　W.T. Barnard, *The Queen's Own Rifles of Canada, 1860–1960* (Toronto: Ontario Publishing Co., 1974), 81–91.

6　Some employers, however, were opposed to using the citizen militia as strike-breakers, since citizen soldiers were often their workers, friends of the strikers, or sympathetic to the strikers' cause. Employers preferred to use the PF.

7　Others such as Montreal's Ogilvie Flour Mill offered an extra week's holiday to any man attending a militia camp; in Hamilton 800 "commercial and industrial leaders" pledged their support for training camps; and in Toronto the Canadian Manufacturing Association recommended similar support. William Beahen, "A Citizens' Army: The Growth and Development of the Canadian Militia 1904–1914" (PhD thesis, University of Ottawa, 1978), 225.

8　Thomas Socknat, *Witness against War* (Toronto: University of Toronto Press, 1987), 11–42.

9　Ibid., 32.

10　As Desmond Morton has pointed out, these sentiments were not new. In 1875 Liberal MP Malcolm Cameron declared that he "would as soon think of teaching his child to drink whiskey or steal, as to be a soldier." Morton, "The Cadet Movement," 57, 63.

11　O'Brien, "Manhood and the Militia Myth," 121.

12　Socknat, *Witness against War*, 37; O'Brien, "Manhood and the Militia Myth," 135.

13　Thomas P. Socknat, "Canada's Liberal Pacifists and the Great War," *Journal of Canadian Studies* 18, no. 4 (Winter 1983–84): 30.

14　Canada, *Statutes,* 31 Vic. (1868), CAP 40, item 59.

15　K.B. Walmsley, "Significance and National Ideologies: Rifle Shooting in Late Nineteenth Century Canada," *Social History* 20, no. 1 (1995): 63–72.

16　In 1898 Borden's ministry gave the DRA a special additional subsidy of $5,000 to establish a permanent headquarters in Ottawa. Canada, *Sessional Paper,* no. 35 (1898).

17　See Beahen, "A Citizens' Army," 326–38.

18　Sandra Gwyn, *The Private Capital* (Toronto: McClelland & Stewart, 1984), 327.

19　J. Castell Hopkins, ed., *Canadian Annual Review of Public Affairs, 1905* (Toronto: Annual Review Publishing Co., 1906), 565.

20　Peter Hanlon, "Sara Galbraith Beemer," in *Dictionary of Canadian Biography*, vol. 14 (Toronto: University of Toronto Press, 1998), 53. See also Canada, House of Commons, *Debates*, 11 July 1899, 7152.

21 Beahen, "A Citizens' Army," 121.

22 Ibid., 217–18.

23 PANS, FWB Papers, Borden to H.H. McLean, 6 May 1909.

24 Beahen, "A Citizens' Army," 312; *Canadian Military Gazette*, 14 March 1905.

25 Canada, House of Commons, *Debates*, 25 June 1900, 8238.

26 Beahen, "A Citizens' Army," 236.

27 Canada, House of Commons, *Debates*, 3 April 1907, 5864.

28 Ibid., 9 December 1911, 1021, 1029.

29 Beahen, "A Citizens' Army," 237.

30 Canada, House of Commons, *Debates*, 29 May 1903, 3769; PANS, FWB Papers, Borden to A.G. Jones, 28 April 1903.

31 *Statistical Year Book of Canada*, 1911.

32 Beahen, "A Citizens' Army," 314–15.

33 See *Revised Statutes of Canada*, 1906, vol. 1, Militia Act, 4E.VII, c. 23, items 62 and 63.

34 E.J. Hobsbawm, *The Age of Capital* (London, UK: Weidenfeld & Nicolson, 1975), 94–7.

35 LAC, RG 24, Strathcona to Borden, 27 March 1909.

36 Hopkins, *Canadian Annual Review of Public Affairs, 1909*, 145, 281.

37 Donna McDonald, *Lord Strathcona: A Biography of Donald Alexander Smith* (Toronto: Dundurn, 2002), 461.

38 LAC, RG 24, Borden to all premiers, 29 January 1909.

39 LAC, RG 24, Borden to Scott, Hazen, and Rutherford, 30 December 1909.

40 Morton, "The Cadet Movement," 67n63.

41 Robert H. MacDonald, *Sons of the Empire* (Toronto: University of Toronto Press, 1993), 196.

42 PANS, FWB Papers, Borden to J.C. Gardner, 7 December 1909.

43 Sir Frederick Borden, "The Canadian Militia – Past, Present and Future," *United Service Magazine* 32–4 (1906): 146.

44 Carman Miller, "The Montreal Militia as a Social Institution before World War I," *Urban History Review* 19, no. 1 (1990): 57–64.

CHAPTER FIFTEEN

1 Canada, House of Commons, *Debates*, 18 July 1908, 13561.

2 For a fuller discussion of this unit, see Bill Rawling, *Death Their Enemy: Canadian Medical Practitioners and War* (n.p.: n.p., 2001).

3 Apart from Osborne, two doctors, C.W. Wilson and Eugene Fiset, were attached to the first contingent.

4 Four served two separate terms.

5 The son of Borden's former colleague A.G. Jones, Guy Carleton Jones, was the assistant quarantine officer at Halifax.

6 *Ottawa Citizen*, 4 June 1900.

7 Rawling, *Death Their Enemy*, 54.

8 For a fuller comparison, see Susan Mann, *Margaret Macdonald: Imperial Daughter* (Montreal and Kingston: McGill-Queen's University Press, 2005), 68–9.

9 Borden sent a five-man "Canadian postal contingent" to South Africa that worked within the British Army Postal Corps to look after Canadian post. Carman Miller, *Painting the Map Red: Canada and the South African War, 1899–1902* (Montreal and Kingston: McGill-Queen's University Press, 1993), 456–8.
10 *Globe* (Toronto), 8 January 1917.
11 The Quebec-born father of the wireless, Reginald Aubrey Fessenden (1866–1932), achieved two-way voice transmission and the first public broadcast of music on Christmas Eve, 1906. See O. Raby, *Radio's First Voice* (Ottawa: Canadian Communications Foundation, 1970).
12 Mary Vipond, *Listening In: The First Decade of Canadian Broadcasting, 1922–1932* (Montreal and Kingston: McGill-Queen's University Press, 1992), 12.
13 William Beahen, "A Citizens' Army: The Growth and Development of the Canadian Militia 1904–1914" (PhD thesis, University of Ottawa, 1978), 206.
14 Ibid., 204.
15 Henry Green, *The Silver Dart: The Authentic Story of the Hon. J.A.D. McCurdy, Canada's First Pilot* (Fredericton: Atlantic Advocate, 1959), 197.
16 *Halifax Herald*, 17 June 1909.
17 Canada, House of Commons, *Debates*, 25 November 1909, 446; Beahen, "A Citizens' Army," 206.
18 Canada, House of Commons, *Debates*, 19 April 1901, 3391.
19 Ibid., 11 July 1904, 6458.
20 Ibid., 10 July 1905, 9123–4.
21 PANS, FWB Papers, Borden to Earl Grey, 17 April 1909.
22 Graham D. Taylor, "A Merchant of Death in the Peaceable Kingdom, Canadian Vickers, 1911–1921," in *Canadian Papers in Business History*, vol. 1, edited by Peter Baskerville (Victoria: Public History Group, 1989), 219.
23 Canada, House of Commons, *Debates*, 18 July 1908, 13560.
24 Ibid., 21 May 1908, 8959.
25 Ibid., 14 February 1900, 437–8.
26 Randolph Carlyle, "Our National Arm," *Canadian Magazine,* September 1908.
27 PANS, FWB Papers, Borden to W.D. Otter, Sam Hughes, F.M. Gaudet, and J.M. Gibson, 13 August 1901.
28 John Swettenham, *To Seize the Victory* (Toronto: Ryerson Press, 1965), 162.
29 LAC, MG 30, A 95, vol. 3, Papers of the Ross Rifle Company, Sir Charles Ross to F.W. Borden, 23 June 1902. See A.F. Duguid, *The Official History of the Canadian Forces in the Great War, 1914–1919,* vol. 1 (Ottawa: King's Printer, 1938), app. 3, 77; Ronald Haycock, "Early Canadian Weapons Acquisition: 'That Damned Ross Rifle,'" *Canadian Defence Quarterly* 14 (1984–85): 48–57.
30 Maurice Olivier, ed., *Colonial and Imperial Conferences from 1887 to 1937* (Ottawa: Queen's Printer, 1954), 180; Canada, House of Commons, *Debates*, 8 October 1903, [F.W. Borden], 13436.
31 Richard Preston, *Canada and "Imperial Defense": A Study of the Origins of the British Commonwealth's Defense Organization, 1867–1919* (Durham, NC: Duke University Press, 1967), 294.
32 *Halifax Herald*, 30 April 1902.
33 PANS, FWB Papers, Borden to Ross, 16 May and 4 July 1904.

34 Canada, Militia Council, *Minutes*, 3 July 1905.

35 Ibid., 13 June 1906.

36 Ibid., 14 and 17 July 1906.

37 Ronald G. Haycock, *Sam Hughes: The Public Career of a Controversial Canadian* (Waterloo, ON: Wilfrid Laurier University Press, 1986), 121–2.

38 See ibid., 132–3n29.

39 PANS, FWB Papers, Borden to Lewis, 3 December 1907; Borden to Nesbitt, 29 March 1907; Borden to K.R. Dans, 30 March 1908.

40 LAC, Laurier Papers, Borden to Laurier, 27 December 1907; Laurier to Borden, 31 December 1907.

41 H.V. Nelles, *The Art of Nation-Building: Pageantry and Spectacle at Quebec's Tercentenary* (Toronto: University of Toronto Press, 1999), 75.

42 Canada, House of Commons, *Debates*, 21 May 1908, 8911.

43 PANS, FWB Papers, Borden to Nesbitt, 1 March 1909.

44 Canada, House of Commons, *Debates*, 14 January 1907, 1403–9; 26 February 1907, 3732–802; 18 July 1908, 13561.

45 Haycock, *Sam Hughes*, 120.

46 Canada, House of Commons, *Debates*, 3 April 1907, 5887, 5895.

47 Haycock, *Sam Hughes*, 127.

48 PANS, FWB Papers, Sam Hughes to Borden, January 1911, confidential memo, Re. coal, iron, and aluminium properties.

49 Canada, House of Commons, *Debates*, 8 October 1903, 13434.

50 Canada, Militia Council, *Minute*, 24 December 1907.

51 The Department of Militia's Small Arms Committee consisted of nine officers, including its chairman, Sam Hughes, and four associate experts.

52 *Canadian Military Gazette*, 12 March 1907.

53 Ibid., 14 June 1910; J. Castell Hopkins, ed., *The Canadian Annual Review of Public Affairs, 1908* (Toronto: Annual Review Publishing Co., 1909), 276.

54 Quoted in Beahen, "A Citizens' Army," 283.

55 Beahen, "A Citizens' Army," 274, 276, 284–5. And as some writers have pointed out since, its difficulties may have been magnified by the use of British ammunition.

56 Canada, Department of Militia and Defence, *Annual Report*, 1908–09, 77.

57 Ibid., 1911–12, 1–3.

CHAPTER SIXTEEN

1 It had gone from 1,000 when he became minister, to 2,000 in 1904, to an authorized 5,000 in 1906 but with an actual strength of 3,500.

2 Stephen Harris, *Canadian Brass: The Making of a Professional Army, 1860–1939* (Toronto: University of Toronto Press, 1988), 74–5.

3 Canada, Militia Council, *Minutes*, 24 and 27 April 1905.

4 Harris, *Canadian Brass*, 86.

5 In 1900 Borden became a corresponding member of the Military Surgeons of the United States, and in 1903 he joined the Ontario College of Physicians and Surgeons.

6 Sir Frederick Borden, "The Canadian Militia – Past, Present and Future," *United Service Magazine* 32–4 (1906): 146.

7 Canada, House of Commons, *Debates*, 8 October 1903, 13399.

8 Canada, *Sessional Paper,* no. 35 (1907), 2.

9 Canada, House of Commons, *Debates*, 8 October 1903, 13401.

10 Canada, *Sessional Paper,* no. 35 (1904), 12.

11 Canada, House of Commons, *Debates*, 17 February 1910, 3735.

12 Borden, "The Canadian Militia," 146.

13 Canada, *Sessional Paper,* no. 35 (1908), 27.

14 Borden, "The Canadian Militia," 146

15 Canada, House of Commons, *Debates*, 12 July 1904, 6528.

16 Canada, Department of Militia and Defence, *Annual Report*, 1905, 22; NA (UK), Governor General Records, Lyttelton to Grey, 17 April 1905; 26 August 1905.

17 Canada, House of Commons, *Sessional Paper,* no. 35a (1907), 13.

18 Harris, *Canadian Brass*, 35.

19 In fact, the West remained organized into districts.

20 Canada, House of Commons, *Debates*, 11 July 1904.

21 This is a strikingly contemporary example of "representative bureaucracy." See Donald Savoie, "Intrastate Federalism in Canada and the Civil Service," in *Continuity and Change in Canadian Politics,* edited by Hans J. Michelmann and Cristine de Clercy (Toronto: University of Toronto Press, 2006), 85.

22 PANS, FWB Papers, Borden to Justice Martin, 4 January 1903; Borden to A.G. Jones, (?) December 1902.

23 *Halifax Herald*, 25 October 1905.

24 Canada, House of Commons, *Debates*, 11 July 1899, 7152.

25 PANS, FWB Papers, Borden to R. Dandurand, 2 January 1904; LAC, Raoul Dandurand Papers, 30 December 1903; *Star* (Montreal), 22 February 1904.

26 PANS, FWB Papers, Borden to Alfred Lyttelton, 1 March 1904.

27 *Ottawa Citizen*, 9 December 1904.

28 Roger Sarty, "Canada and the Great Rapprochement, 1902–1914," in *The North Atlantic Triangle in a Changing World: Anglo-American-Canadian Relations, 1902–1956,* edited by B.J.C. McKercher and Lawrence Aronsen (Toronto: University of Toronto Press, 1996), 27.

29 *Morning Chronicle* (Halifax), 21 February 1905.

30 Ibid.

31 *Nova Scotian*, 1 December 1905.

32 Borden, "The Canadian Militia," 147.

33 J. Castell Hopkins, *The Canadian Annual Review, 1905* (Toronto: Annual Review Publishing Co., 1906), 563.

34 Canada, House of Commons, *Debates*, 14 March 1910, 5499.

35 Canada, House of Commons, *Sessional Paper,* no. 35a (1909), 6.

36 Harris, *Canadian Brass*, 71.

37 James Robert Laxer, "French Canadian Newspapers and Imperial Defence, 1899–1914" (MA thesis, Queen's University, 1967), 2.

38 *Times*, 19 June 1897; Canada, House of Commons, *Debates*, 5 February 1906, 1216.

39 For a fuller discussion of this issue, see Carman Miller, *Painting the Map Red: Canada and the South African War, 1899–1902* (Montreal and Kingston: McGill-Queen's University Press, 1993), 51–2.

40 Harris, *Canadian Brass*, 60–1.

41 Howard D'Egville, *Imperial Defence and Closer Union* (London, P.S. King and Son, 1913), 127.

42 Canada, *Revised Statutes*, 4 Edward VII, 1904, s. 70.

43 Donald C. Gordon, *The Dominion Partnership in "Imperial" Defence* (Durham, NC: Duke University Press, 1967), 276.

44 *Documents relatifs aux relations extérieures du Canada*, vol. 1 (1909–18) (Ottawa, 1967), 232–3.

45 NA (UK), Cd 4475 (1909), 7.

46 W. Beahen, "A Citizens' Army: The Growth and Development of the Canadian Militia, 1904–1914" (PhD thesis, University of Ottawa, 1978), 196.

47 Harris, *Canadian Brass*, 37.

48 Canada, *Sessional Paper,* no. 35a (1909), 9.

49 Ibid., 8.

50 Hopkins, *Canadian Annual Review of Public Affairs, 1908* (Toronto: Annual Review Publishing Company, 1909), 279.

CHAPTER SEVENTEEN

1 Canada, Department of External Affairs, *Documents Relating to Canada's External Relations*, vol. 1: *1909–1918* (Ottawa, Queen's Printer, 1967), 229.

2 A challenge that continued to face Canadian politicians and soldiers in both world wars: Paul Dickson, "Colonials and Coalitions," in *Leadership and Responsibility*, edited by Brian Farrell (Montreal and Kingston: McGill-Queen's University Press, 2004), 237.

3 Quoted in Max Beloff, *Imperial Sunset,* vol. 1 (London, UK: Methuen and Co., 1971), 77.

4 See Edward Kohn, *This Kindred People: Canadian-American Relations and the Anglo-Saxon Idea, 1895–1903* (Montreal and Kingston: McGill-Queen's University Press, 2005).

5 Bernard Porter, *Journal of Imperial and Commonwealth History* 34, no. 3 (September 2006): 466.

6 Thomas H. Raddall, *His Majesty's Yankees* (New York: Doubleday, 1942).

7 Canada, House of Commons, *Debates*, 8 October 1903, 13436.

8 *Documents Relating*, 231.

9 Mike O'Brien, "Manhood and the Militia Myth: Masculinity and Class in Ontario, 1902–1914," *Labour/Le Travail* 42 (Fall 1998): 115–41.

10 "The Honourable Sir Frederick Borden," *Liberal Monthly*, January 1917, 73. This obituary, written by Mackenzie King, was vetted and approved by Laurier, more particularly King's assessment of Borden's contribution toward Canadian autonomy. See LAC, Mackenzie King, *Diary*, 12 January 1917.

11 Such as O.D. Skelton, J.W. Dafoe, L.-O. David, and others.

12 Carman Miller, *The Canadian Career of the Fourth Earl of Minto* (Waterloo, ON: Wilfrid Laurier University Press, 1980), 122–4.

13 John Edward Kendle, *The Colonial and Imperial Conferences, 1887–1911* (London, UK: Longmans, 1967), 35–6.

14 Laurier appeared genuinely committed to a broadly based "profitable imperialism," if one can judge by his December 1901 proposal to meet with the Australasian colonies to discuss a Pacific cable and subsidized steamship service.

15 Howard D'Egville, *Imperial Defence and Closer Union* (London, UK: P.S. King and Son, 1913), 129–31.

16 The Coefficients, formed by Sydney and Beatrice Webb following the Colonial/Imperial Conference of 1902, consisted of a cross-section of prominent literary, political, and academic persons who met to discuss public affairs. A similar group, the Compatriots, founded in 1904 by Leo Amery, focused on imperial relations, as did the Pollock Committee, which had grown out of the Imperial Federation (Defence) Committee and the Round Table movement. Composed of overlapping membership, these organizations publicized their views in revues, the press, lectures, and debate. While few advocated a formal political union of the Empire, they sought more-effective imperial consultation through a significant reordering of imperial governance. See Kendle, *The Colonial and Imperial Conferences*, 55ff.

17 Ibid., 106.

18 Ibid., 53.

19 Ibid., 198.

20 See James A. Colvin, "Sir Wilfrid Laurier and the Imperial Problem, 1896–1906" (PhD thesis, University of London, 1954).

21 D'Egville, *Imperial Defence and Closer Union*, 130n; Kendle, *The Colonial and Imperial Conferences*, 79.

22 "The Honourable Sir Frederick Borden, K.C.M.G.," *Canadian Liberal Monthly*, January 1917, 73–4.

23 Ibid., 73.

24 D'Egville, *Imperial Defence and Closer Union*, 150.

25 Oscar Douglas Skelton, *Life and Letters of Sir Wilfrid Laurier*, vol. 2 (Toronto: McClelland & Stewart, 1965), 114.

26 Ibid., 213n1.

27 *Globe* (Toronto), 8 January 1917.

28 "The Honourable Sir Frederick Borden, K.C.M.G.," *Canadian Liberal Monthly*, 73.

29 Kendle, *The Colonial and Imperial Conferences*, 73–4. In 1908 Lord Grey complained to the colonial secretary, Lord Elgin, that there were only two unnamed Canadian cabinet ministers who had any detailed knowledge of "foreign relations." Of the two, the anonymous one that "drinks at times" was probably Borden. Quoted in John Hilliker, *Canada's Department of External Affairs*, vol. 1 (Montreal and Kingston: McGill-Queen's University Press, 1990), 33.

CHAPTER EIGHTEEN

1 John Edward Kendle, *The Colonial and Imperial Conferences, 1887–1911* (London, UK: Longmans, 1967), 53, 65. As Kendle points out, after the failure of the 1911 Imperial Conference, the CID became the central objective of the Round Table movement and the *Times*. See his chapter 10. The CID was even seen as

a model for imperial conferences. See Maurice Pope, ed., *Public Servant: The Memoirs of Sir Joseph Pope* (Toronto: Oxford University Press, 1960), 169–70.

2 Kendle, *The Colonial and Imperial Conferences*, 169ff.
3 J. Castell Hopkins, ed., *The Canadian Annual Review of Public Affairs, 1903* (Toronto: Annual Review Publishing Co., 1904), 476.
4 Canada, Department of External Affairs, *Documents Relating to Canada's External Relations*, vol. 1: *1909–1918* (Ottawa: Queen's Printer, 1967), 139.
5 Canada, House of Commons, *Debates*, 10 February 1910, 3346.
6 Marc Milner, *Canada's Navy: The First Century* (Toronto: University of Toronto Press, 1999), 11.
7 Milner, *Canada's Navy*, 13.
8 Oscar Douglas Skelton, *Life and Letters of Sir Wilfrid Laurier*, vol. 2 (Toronto: McClelland & Stewart, 1965), 213.
9 Kendle, *The Colonial and Imperial Conferences*, 83ff.
10 Phillips Payson O'Brien, "The Titan Refreshed: Imperial Overstretch and the British Navy before the First World War," *Past & Present* 172 (August 2001): 150, 157.
11 Cited in ibid., 159.
12 Milner, *Canada's Navy*, 12.
13 Canada, House of Commons, *Debates*, 21 May 1908, 8958.
14 Stephen Harris, *Canadian Brass: The Making of a Professional Army, 1860–1939* (Toronto: University of Toronto Press, 1988), 75.
15 *Times* (London), 12 March 1911.
16 *Proceedings of the Imperial Conference of 1907*, 30 April 1907, GG Records, RG 7, G 21, file 251, vol. 1, 1900–34.
17 *Canadian Liberal Monthly*, January 1917, 74.
18 Hopkins, *Canadian Annual Review of Public Affairs, 1909*, 85.
19 Harris, *Canadian Brass*, 75.
20 Ibid., 71.
21 C.P. Stacey, *Canada and the Age of Conflict: A History of Canadian External Policies*, vol. 1 (Toronto: University of Toronto Press, 1981), 82.
22 H.V. Nelles, *The Art of Nation-Building: Pageantry and Spectacle at Quebec's Tercentenary* (Toronto: University of Toronto Press, 1999), 212.
23 O'Brien, "The Titan Refreshed," 160.
24 Nelles, *Art of Nation-Building*, 213.
25 Canada, House of Commons, *Debates*, 29 March 1909, 3584ff.
26 Canada, Department of External Affairs, *Documents*, Grey to Colonial Office, 4 May 1909, 225.
27 LAC, Laurier Papers, Laurier to Borden, 17 July 1909.
28 Hopkins, *Canadian Annual Review of Public Affairs, 1909*, 85.
29 Ibid., 80.
30 Ibid., 85.
31 According to Kendle, during this 19 August 1909 meeting between the CID and dominion representatives "nothing of importance occurred," since neither Asquith nor the Admiralty could uncouple defence from foreign affairs; consequently, they were unprepared to concede any dominion participation in foreign affairs, though pressed by imperialists to do so. Kendle, *Colonial and Imperial Conferences*, 192.

32 Canada, Department of External Affairs, *Documents*, 229.
33 Ibid., 231.
34 Milner, *Canada's Navy*, 15.
35 Canada, House of Commons, *Debates*, 10 February 1910, 3339.
36 Canada, Department of External Affairs, *Documents*, 229.
37 Ibid., 234.
38 Hopkins, *Canadian Annual Review of Public Affairs, 1909*, 80.
39 Ibid.
40 Ibid., 80.
41 The Royal Navy's "one flag, one fleet" mentality died slowly. It seemed that the Royal Navy continued to regard the Canadian force as a subordinate, as it refused a Canadian request to fly a slightly modified version of its white ensign that would have had a small "green maple leaf centred on the Cross of St George" (a design suggested by the governor general, "Lord Grey, and approved by Laurier's Cabinet") and it only reluctantly agreed to the insertion of a "C" in HMCS. See Milner, *Canada's Navy*, 22.
42 Canada, House of Commons, *Debates*, 3 February 1910, 2954.
43 Ibid., 2963.
44 Ibid., 10 February 1910, 3306, 3343.
45 Ibid., 10 February 1910, 3310ff.
46 Ibid., 19 April 1910, 7434.
47 In her biography of Lord Strathcona, Donna McDonald suggests that Laurier was reticent about announcing Lord Strathcona's retirement; if so, his reticence was quickly overcome. Donna McDonald, *Lord Strathcona: A Biography of Donald Alexander Smith* (Toronto: Dundurn, 2002), 483.

CHAPTER NINETEEN

1 David Cannadine, *Ornamentalism: How the British Saw Their Empire* (Oxford: Oxford University Press, 2001), 10.
2 If one uses the consumer price index, a multiple of 15 ($4.5 million) would describe its 2005 value. See http://measuringworth.com/calculators/powerus/.
3 NLS, Minto Papers, Lord Minto to Joseph Chamberlain, 19 August 1900.
4 PANS, FWB Papers, Borden to A.T. Clarke, 12 January 1901.
5 Michael Bliss, "George Albertus Cox," in *Dictionary of Canadian Biography*, vol. 14 (Toronto: University of Toronto Press, 1998), 251.
6 Desmond Morton, *Wheels: The Car in Canada* (Toronto: Umbrella Press, 1998), 13.
7 Given Borden's apparent profit from the controversial Nova Scotia Power deal, this figure may understate the value of his estate at death.
8 For example, Sir Wilfrid Laurier's estimated worth at death in 1919 was $25,000. See Réal Bélanger's "Wilfrid Laurier," in *Dictionary of Canadian Biography*, vol. 14 (Toronto: University of Toronto Press, 1998).
9 Horst K. Berz and E.K. Hunt, "Methodological Problems in Contrasting Economic Systems," *American Journal of Economics and Sociology*, October 1970, 355.

10 Quoted in P.L. Payne, *British Entrepreneurship in the Nineteenth Century* (London : Macmillan, 1974), 25.

11 Thorstein Veblen, *The Portable Veblen* (New York: Viking, 1950), 270.

12 Pierre Bourdieu, *Outline of a Theory of Practice* (Cambridge, UK: University of Cambridge Press, 1977), 184.

13 See Christopher Armstrong and H.V. Nelles, "Getting Your Way in Nova Scotia: 'Tweaking' Halifax, 1909–1917," *Acadiensis* 5 (Spring 1976): 106–7.

14 Douglas Lorimer, *Colour, Class and the Victorians* (Bristol, UK: Leicester University Press, 1978), 111.

15 H. Perkin, *The Rise of Professional Society: England since 1880* (London, UK: Routledge, 1989).

16 Payne, *British Entrepreneurship*, 25–6.

17 Anthony D. Smith, *National Identity* (London, UK: Penguin, 1991), 160.

18 Ibid., 163.

19 Ibid., 95–9.

20 Mark Girouard, *The Return to Camelot: Chivalry and the English Gentleman* (New Haven, CT: Yale University Press, 1981), 131.

21 PANS, MG 9, vol. 188, Parliamentary *Scrapbook*, W.R. Canning, "An Appreciation."

22 Henry Borden, ed., *Robert Laird Borden: His Memoirs* (Toronto: Macmillan, 1938), 1.

23 PANS, FWB Papers, Borden to J.A. Glen, 18 March 1901; T. Borden to F.W. Borden, 29 October 1909.

24 See M. Brook Taylor, *Promoters, Patriots, and Partisans: Historiography in Nineteenth-Century English Canada* (Toronto: University of Toronto Press, 1989), 204.

25 Geoff Eley, *A Crooked Line: From Cultural History to the History of Society* (Ann Arbor: University of Michigan, 2005), 151–2.

26 P.B. Waite, "Invading Privacies: Biography as History," *Dalhousie Review* 69, no. 4 (Winter 1990): 480.

27 Mike O'Brien, "Manhood and the Militia Myth: Masculinity, Class and Militarism in Ontario, 1902–1914," *Labour/Le Travail* 42 (Fall 1989): 121.

28 Sir Frederick Borden, "The Canadian Militia – Past, Present and Future," *United Service Magazine* 32–4 (1906).

29 Sandra Gwyn, *The Private Capital* (Toronto: McClelland & Stewart, 1984), 421.

30 NLS, Minto Papers, Bordon to Minto, 2 October 1901.

31 The difference was that Turner came under fire.

32 NLS, Minto Papers, Roberts to Minto, 28 May 1901.

33 J. Castell Hopkins, ed., *The Canadian Annual Review, 1903* (Toronto: Annual Review Publishing Co., 1904), 548.

34 PANS, FWB Papers, Borden to Robert E. Finn, 9 January 1901.

35 Hopkins, *The Canadian Annual Review for 1903*, 548.

36 In 1951–52 Elizabeth Hewitt's estate bequeathed funds to Mount Allison University to establish two Harold Borden–Maude Macoun entrance scholarships worth $300 each, in memory of her deceased brother and sister. In 1958–59 Lady Borden's estate established three Harold Lothrop Borden entrance scholarships, each worth $500.

37 Nelles, *Art of Nation-Building,* chap. 10.
38 Payne, *British Entrepreneurship,* 44–5.
39 Cannadine, *Ornamentalism,* 21.
40 Stephen Archibald and Sheila Stevenson, *Heritage Houses of Nova Scotia* (Halifax: Formac, 2003), 87.
41 For an excellent description of the Old Place and its natural environment today, see Merritt Gibson, *The Old Place: A Natural History of a Country Garden* (Hantsport, NS: Lancelot Press, 1997).
42 Julia Leslie Green MacKay to author, 13 January 2010.
43 Karl Baedeker, *The Dominion of Canada* (London, UK: T. Fisher Unwin, 1907), 74.
44 Interview with Joan Elizabeth (Starr) Murray, 2 February 2004, the great-granddaughter of Dr Jonathan Borden, who grew up in Upper Canard in the Georgian house purchased by Dr Jonathan Borden.
45 Julia Leslie Green MacKay to author, 13 January 2010.
46 PANS, FWB Papers, L.S. Macoun to Borden, 19 February 1910.
47 See Courtney C. Bond, *City on the Ottawa* (Ottawa: Queen's Printer, 1961), 61, for a fuller description of the house. Formerly the Belgian Embassy, it is currently (2009) occupied by the High Commission of Brunei Darussalem; at the time of its sale in the early 1990s its listed price was $1.7 million.
48 PANS, FWB Papers, Charles Panet to L.S. Macoun, 31 December 1908.
49 "The Wives of Cabinet Ministers," unidentified newspaper clipping in the possession of Ken Bezanson.
50 PANS, FWB Papers, Borden to H.M. Pellatt, 22 November 1901.
51 PANS, FWB Papers, J.O. Smith to Borden, 27 May 1911.
52 Patricia Seed, *Ceremonies of Possession in Europe's Conquest of the New World, 1492–1640* (Cambridge, UK: Cambridge University Press, 1995), 8.
53 For a discussion of contemporary industrial leaders' membership in social organizations, see T.W. Acheson, "Changing Social Origins of the Canadian Industrial Elite, 1880–1910," in *Enterprise and National Development: Essays in Canadian Business and Economic History,* edited by Glenn Porter and Robert D. Cuff (Toronto: Hakkert, 1973).
54 *Times* (London), 17 June 1911.
55 Donna McDonald, *Lord Strathcona: A Biography of Donald Alexander Smith* (Toronto: Dundurn, 2002), 446.
56 PANS, FWB Papers, Borden to J.W. Orde, 24 May 1911.
57 Hopkins, *Canadian Annual Review of Public Affairs, 1909,* 175.
58 Interview with Joan Murray, 2 February 2004.
59 Esther Clark Wright, *Blomidon Rose* (Toronto: Ryerson Press, 1957), 54.
60 Ibid.
61 Gwyn, *The Private Capital,* 327.
62 Sir Frederick Borden, "The Canadian Militia – Past, Present and Future," *United Service Magazine* 32–4 (1906): 150.
63 PANS, FWB Papers, Borden to A.S. Burgess, 13 December 1909.
64 *Wolfville Acadian,* 6 February 1942.
65 Cannadine, *Ornamentalism,* 98.

CHAPTER TWENTY

1 Lewis Fischer and Eric Sager, *The Enterprising Canadians: Entrepreneurs and Economic Development in Eastern Canada, 1820–1914* (St John's, NL: Maritime History Group, 1979); Judith Fingard, "Paradoxes of Progress," in *Atlantic Provinces in Confederation*, edited by E.R. Forbes and D.A. Muise (Toronto: University of Toronto Press, 1993).
2 Roy E. George, *A Leader and a Laggard: Manufacturing Industry in Nova Scotia, Quebec and Ontario* (Toronto: University of Toronto Press, 1970), chaps 9 and 10.
3 Christopher Armstrong, *Blue Skies and Boiler Rooms: Buying and Selling Securities in Canada, 1870–1940* (Toronto: University of Toronto Press, 1997), 24. See also Christopher Armstrong, "Making a Market: Selling Securities in Atlantic Canada," *Canadian Journal of Economics* 13 (1980): 438–54.
4 T.W. Acheson, "The National Policy and the Industrialization of the Maritimes, 1880–1910," *Acadiensis* 1, no. 2 (Spring 1972): 48.
5 PANS, FWB Papers, Borden to Willard Ilsley, 16 January 1904.
6 Keith Walden, *Becoming Modern in Toronto: The Industrial Exhibition and the Shaping of a Late Victorian Culture* (Toronto: University of Toronto Press, 1997), 85.
7 Patrick Chapin, "Late-Victorian Gentlemen Entrepreneurs Venturing into New Worlds of Canadian Business: The Nestegg Mining Company, 1896–98," *Journal of the Canadian Historical Association* 16, no. 1 (2005): 169.
8 PANS, FWB Papers, Borden to Boak, 6 November 1901.
9 PANS, FWB Papers, Borden to Fred L Lordley, 2 March 1909; D.H. Tolmie to Borden, 1 March 1909; Borden to C.A. Henderson, 10 May 1909.
10 PANS, FWB Papers, Borden to R.W. Kinsman, 5 February 1900; Borden to R.W. Kinsman, 3 May 1901.
11 PANS, FWB Papers, Borden to R.W. Kinsman, 1 February 1902; Borden to R.W. Kinsman, 3 March 1902; Borden to Martha Kinsman, 3 February 1901; Borden to R.W. Kinsman, 17 January 1908.
12 PANS, FWB Papers, Borden to W.T. White, 23 November 1901.
13 PANS, FWB Papers, Borden to R.W. Kinsman, 5 February 1900.
14 PANS, FWB Papers, Borden to R.W. Kinsman, 3 May 1901.
15 PANS, FWB Papers, Borden to R.W. Kinsman, 19 June 1899.
16 Borden estimated that his net loss was $3,000, as the insurance covered only $20,000. See PANS, FWB Papers, Borden to C.V. Anthony, 10 January 1901.
17 PANS, FWB Papers, Borden to H.H. Wickwire, 29 November 1901. Wickwire owned $16,500 in preferred stock.
18 PANS, FWB Papers, Borden to H.H. Wickwire, 11 November 1901.
19 PANS, FWB Papers, H.H. Wickwire to Borden, 27 December 1899.
20 PANS, FWB Papers, Borden to R.W. Kinsman, 9 January 1900.
21 PANS, FWB Papers, Borden to Sinclair, 2 February 1900.
22 Nova Scotia, *Laws*, 1901, 293–7.
23 PANS, FWB Papers, Borden to W.T. White, 23 November 1901.
24 PANS, FWB Papers, Borden to James Robertson, 22 November 1901.

25 PANS, FWB Papers, Borden to J.W. Wood, 20 November 1901.
26 Of the company's $100,000 bonds, Borden held $85,000; Lady Borden $500; Alfred Potter $1,500; W R Potter $2,000; and George Boak $500. PANS, FWB Papers, L.S. Macoun to Borden, 9 May 1911.
27 Nova Scotia, *Laws* (1899), 442.
28 *Halifax Herald*, 9 January 1917.
29 Nova Scotia, *Laws* (1912), 622.
30 Canada, *Sessional Paper*, no. 29 (1912), 413–15.
31 PANS, FWB Papers, Borden to W. R. Potter, 21 April 1908.
32 PANS, FWB Papers, L.S. Macoun to Borden, 30 March 1911.
33 In fact there may have been moments of real tension and threats of legal action, Sir Frederick believing that Macoun was "skimming off the top." Julia Leslie Green MacKay to author, 13 January 2010.
34 PANS, FWB Papers, L.S. Macoun to A.S. Burgess, 25 March 1911.
35 PANS, FWB Papers, L.S. Macoun to Borden, 9 May 1911.
36 PANS, FWB Papers, L.S. Macoun to Borden, 30 March 1911.
37 PANS, FWB Papers, *Report of Nova Scotia Technical College on Survey of Railway from Canning to Cape Blomidon*.
38 PANS, FWB Papers, Charles Panet to L.S. Macoun, 3 November 1910. One of the directors was E.A. Robert, who had plans to electrify Halifax.
39 Nova Scotia, *Statutes*, 1911, chap. 3.
40 Christopher Armstrong and H.V. Nelles, *Southern Exposure* (Toronto: University of Toronto Press, 1988). The book describes George Cox, George William Ross, William Thomas White, Edward Clouston, B.F. Pearson, H.M.A. Whitney, J.N. Greenshields, among others.
41 Armstrong, *Blue Skies*, 34.
42 Ibid., 51.
43 For example, a $50,000 loan from the Bank of Montreal (PANS, FWB Papers, Bank of Montreal to Borden, 28 July 1911) and his decision as president of the King's Park Reality Company to finance a purchase of land in Hull for $121,200, $25,000 in cash, the rest secured by a mortgage at 6 per cent, in three equal payments (PANS, FWB Papers, R.V. Sinclair to Borden, 2 December 1910).
44 Borden seems to have been involved in gold speculation in the Klondike. D.J. Hall, *Clifford Sifton: The Young Napoleon*, vol. 1 (Vancouver: University of British Columbia Press, 1985), 168.
45 PANS, FWB Papers, Freeman Davison to Borden, 23 March 1910.
46 PANS, FWB Papers, Freeman Davison to Borden, 19 November 1910.
47 PANS, FWB Papers, Borden to Freeman Davison, 21 November 1910.
48 Gregory P. Marchildon, *Profits and Politics: Beaverbrook and the Gilded Age of Canadian Finances* (Toronto: University of Toronto Press, 1996), 150.
49 PANS, FWB Papers, F. Minden Cole to Borden, 1 December 1910.
50 PANS, FWB Papers, L.S. Macoun to Borden, 9 May 1911 and 26 May 1911.
51 Borden had investments in the Nicola Lake Horticultural Estates Ltd, the British Columbia Development Association Ltd, the Winnipeg-based Stewart and Mathew Company Ltd, and the King's Park Reality Company, headquartered

in Ottawa and of which he was president – all dealt in real estate; he also held land northeast of Calgary. PANS, FWB Papers, L.S. Macoun to Borden, 13 December 1910.
52 Armstrong, *Blue Skies*, 57.

CHAPTER TWENTY-ONE

1 See Christopher Armstrong and H.V. Nelles, *Southern Exposure: Canadian Promoters in Latin America and the Caribbean* (Toronto: University of Toronto Press, 1988).
2 See Margaret Conrad, "Apple Blossom Time in the Annapolis Valley, 1880–1957," *Acadiensis* 9, no. 2 (Autumn 1980): 5–9.
3 Gregory P. Marchildon, *Profits and Politics: Beaverbrook and the Gilded Age of Canadian Finance* (Toronto: University of Toronto Press, 1996), 63.
4 The Dominion of Canada Trust Corporation Ltd denoted shares in sterling, established a Canadian board in Toronto in 1906, and managed stock for a number of small Nova Scotia companies (e.g., the Alfred Dickie Lumber Company, the Musquodobit Lumber Company, and the Empire Construction Company). PANS, FWB Papers, J.P. Murray to shareholders, 8 February 1911; A. Collard to Borden, 10 July 1910.
5 PANS, FWB Papers, H.P. Hill to Charles Panet (Borden's secretary), 2 May 1910: a request for a letter of introduction to Lord Strathcona; Hill wished to establish an English company to promote the noiseless typewriter company.
6 PANS, FWB Papers, Borden to Charles Fitzpatrick, 21 January 1901; Borden to Hon. R.R. Dobell, 14 January 1901.
7 PANS, FWB Papers, Borden to F.W. Hodson, 29 November 1901: a request to assess the value of his Ayrshire, Jersey, and Guernsey herd.
8 Canada, House of Commons, *Debates*, 17 January 1910, 1969.
9 Christopher Armstrong and H.V. Nelles, "Getting Your Way in Nova Scotia: 'Tweaking' Halifax, 1909–1917," *Acadiensis* 5, no. 2 (Spring 1976): 105–31.
10 PANS, FWB Papers, Borden to C.A. Henderson, 28 May 1906.
11 *Canada Gazette*, 13 October 1906, 807. Graham possessed 50 per cent of the stock of the Evangeline Fruit Company, in which Borden had a sizable investment. PANS, FWB Papers, L.S. Macoun to Borden, 26 May 1911.
12 *Maritime Grocer*, 31 October 1895.
13 *Monetary Times*, 1 February 1901; see, too, Norman H. Morse, "The Economic History of the Apple Industry of the Annapolis Valley" (PhD thesis, University of Toronto, 1952), 28.
14 PANS, FWB Papers, Borden to R.J. Graham, 25 June 1907.
15 In fact, the Order-in-Council of 2 August 1907 granting the subsidy specified a sum of $30,000.
16 PANS, FWB Papers, L.S. Macoun to Borden, 23 July 1910.
17 Canada, House of Commons, *Debates*, 27 May 1908, 9308–9.
18 Ibid., 9313.
19 Ibid., 9311.
20 PANS, FWB Papers, L.S. Macoun to Borden, 19 July 1911.

21 T. Pringle and Son Archives, Montreal, Century File, Electrical Power Contracts and Other Reports, "Estimate of Developing Hydraulic Power, Transmission and Distribution," 24 November 1899.

22 Nova Scotia, *Journal of the Legislative Council*, Provincial Secretary's Report, app. 12, 33, 1908.

23 They included W.G. Ross, F. Howard Wilson, William P. Webster, O.A. Smith, J.A. Neville, J.E. Wood, and P.J. McIntosh.

24 PANS, FWB Papers, Borden to W.G.A. Lambe, 3 May 1909.

25 PANS, FWB Papers, E.A. Robert to W.G.A. Lambe, 20 June 1910; Memorandum of Agreement between L.G.A. Lambe and E.A. Robert, October 1910.

26 PANS, FWB Papers, Borden to W.G.A. Lambe, 5 February 1910; 10 March 1910.

27 PANS, FWB Papers, Borden to W.G.A. Lambe, 10 March 1910; W.G.A. Lambe to E.A. Robert, 14 March 1910.

28 PANS, FWB Papers, Borden to W.G.A. Lambe, 10 March 1910.

29 In November 1909 Borden had purchased 100 first mortgage bonds of $1,000 in Robert's Canada Light and Power Company, with two calls of 10 per cent. FWB Papers, E.A. Robert to Borden, 29 November 1909.

30 PANS, FWB Papers, E.A. Robert to Borden, 1 March 1910. According to William Fong, at this time Borden purchased fifty preferred shares in Ames-Holden-McCready from George F. Johnson, J.W. McConnell, and Hudson Joshua Allison, and subscribed to $25,000 in preferred stock in the British Canadian Lumber. This may have been part of the deal. See William Fong, *J.W. McConnell* (Montreal and Kingston: McGill-Queen's University Press, 2008), 127.

31 PANS, FWB Papers, Borden to W.G.A. Lambe, 16 May 1910. Roscoe's services from March 1908 until April 1910 amounted to $1,406, a cost to be shared between Lambe and Borden.

32 PANS, FWB Papers, Borden to E.A. Robert, 10 May 1911.

33 J. Castell Hopkins, ed., *The Canadian Annual Review of Public Affairs, 1913* (Toronto: Annual Review Publishing Co., 1914), 498.

34 PANS, FWB Papers, Borden to G.H. Murray, 26, 27, and 30 March 1911.

35 PANS, FWB Papers, E.A. Robert to Borden, 30 May 1911.

36 Hopkins, *Canadian Annual Review of Public Affairs, 1913*, 498.

37 Armstrong and Nelles, "Getting Your Way in Nova Scotia," 122.

38 Ibid., 498. This initiative would be headed by the Conservative Montreal businessman D. Lorne McGibbon.

39 The Liberals held twenty-seven of the assembly's thirty-eight seats.

40 Robert Craig Brown, *Robert Laird Borden: A Biography*, vol. 1 (Toronto: University of Toronto Press, 1975), 130–1.

41 PANS, FWB Papers, C.R. Bill to E.N. Rhodes, 27 March 1914.

42 Armstrong and Nelles, "Getting Your Way," 126.

43 *Halifax Herald*, 9 January 1917.

44 Ibid., 128–9.

45 Armstrong and Nelles, "Getting Your Way," 103–1.

46 PANS, FWB Papers, W.G.A. Lambe to Borden, 5 May 1909.

CHAPTER TWENTY-TWO

1 PANS, FWB Papers, Borden to Edgar M. Smith, 10 November 1904.

2 PANS, FWB Papers, Borden to E.C. Curry, 9 July 1906.

3 *Morning Chronicle* (Halifax), 10 and 19 October 1904.

4 PANS, FWB Papers, Borden to B. Nason, 15 November 1904; see, too, *Morning Chronicle,* 5 November 1904.

5 PANS, FWB Papers, Borden to H. Magee, 30 November 1904; C. Panet to A.M. Mackay, 8 August 1904.

6 PANS, FWB Papers, Borden to Edgar M. Smith, 10 November 1904.

7 Robert Craig Brown, *Robert Laird Borden: A Biography,* vol. 1 (Toronto: University of Toronto Press, 1975), 123.

8 Ibid., 122.

9 Julia Leslie Green MacKay to the author, 13 January 2010.

10 H. Hamilton Fyfe, "The 'Pure Politics' Campaign in Canada," *Nineteenth Century and After,* no. 368 (1907): 665.

11 PANS, FWB Papers, Borden to Charles Russell, 26 October 1907.

12 PANS, FWB Papers, Borden to Charles Russell, 26 October 1907.

13 PANS, FWB Papers, Borden to W.E. Roscoe, 8 November 1907.

14 PANS, FWB Papers, Borden to Charles Russell, 3 February 1908.

15 Fyfe, "The 'Pure Politics' Campaign in Canada," 672.

16 PANS, FWB Papers, Borden to Charles Russell, 26 October 1907.

17 Apology, *Nineteenth Century and After,* no. 370 (1907): 1030.

18 PANS, FWB Papers, Borden to J.S. Willison, 5 December 1907.

19 *Military Gazette,* 10 May 1904.

20 William A. Beahen, "A Citizens' Army" (PhD thesis, University of Ottawa, 1978), 267, 301n9.

21 Canada, Journal of the House of Commons, *Appendix V,* 42, 1906–07, and *V,* 43, 1907–08.

22 Canada, House of Commons, Public Accounts Committee, *Journals,* app. 5, 43.

23 Beahen, "A Citizens' Army," 230, 295.

24 Ibid., 272.

25 Ibid., 284.

26 Brown, *Robert Laird Borden,* 123.

27 Canada, House of Commons, *Debates,* 18 July 1908, 13558.

28 His brother, Leonard Courtney, a British MP, was one of the most influential British pro-Boers during the South African War (as was Leonard's wife, Kate Courtney, the sister of Beatrice Webb). Arthur Davey, *The British Pro-Boers, 1877–1902* (Cape Town: Tafelberg, 1978), 87; see, too, John A. Turley-Ewart, "John Mortimer Courtney," in *Dictionary of Canadian Biography,* vol. 14 (Toronto: University of Toronto Press, 1998), 241–3; Maurice Pope, ed., *Public Servant: The Memoirs of Sir Joseph Pope* (Toronto: University of Toronto Press, 1960), 113.

29 Canada, *Sessional Paper,* no. 35, 1904, 107.

30 Paul Marsden, "Shaping the Canadian Record of War in the 20th Century," in *Canadian Military History Since the 17th Century*, edited by Yves Tremblay, (Ottawa, 2001), 456.

31 Canada, House of Commons, *Debates*, 9 July 1908, 12505ff.

32 Roger Sarty, "Canada and the Great Rapprochement," in *The North Atlantic Triangle in a Changing World: Anglo-American-Canadian Relations, 1902–1956*, edited by B.J.C. McKercher and Lawrence Aronsen (Toronto: University of Toronto Press, 1996), 24.

33 Canada, House of Commons, *Debates*, 9 July 1908, 12505ff.

34 PANS, FWB Papers, Borden to W.E. Roscoe, 21 July 1908.

35 *Morning Chronicle*, 30 October 1908.

36 On 17 September 1908, the *Cowansville Observer*, edited by William Cotton, published an article entitled "A Vote for Laurier Endorses Fred Borden," for which Cotton later apologized to avoid a $25,000 libel suit. PANS, FWB Papers, William Cotton, 6 December 1910.

37 PANS, FWB Papers, Borden to D.C. Cameron, 6 November 1908.

38 *Morning Chronicle*, 18 September 1908.

39 Ibid., 2 October 1908.

40 Ibid., 10 October 1908.

41 PANS, FWB Papers, Borden to D.A. Armstrong, 13 November 1908; Borden to William Rand, 13 November 1908; Borden to L.G. Power, 13 November 1908; *Morning Chronicle*, 30 October 1908.

42 PANS, FWB Papers, Borden to A.T. Clarke, 10 November 1908.

43 *Halifax Herald*, 3 June 1909.

44 Ibid.

45 Henry Robert Emmerson (1853–1914) was premier of New Brunswick from 1897 to 1900.

46 Wendell Fulton, "Henry Robert Emmerson," in *Dictionary of Canadian Biography*, vol. 14 (Toronto: University of Toronto Press, 1998), 342.

47 PANS, FWB Papers, Borden to Curry, 21 June 1909.

48 PANS, FWB Papers, Borden to Justice Forbes, 22 October 1909.

49 *Halifax Herald*, 5 June 1909.

50 Ibid., 29 June 1909.

51 Ibid., 14 June 1909.

52 Ibid., 14 and 29 June 1909.

53 LAC, Mackenzie King *Diary*, 14 October 1909.

54 *Morning Chronicle*, 11 November 1908.

55 Ibid., 14 October 1909.

56 Ibid.

57 Ibid.

58 Ibid., 15 October 1909.

59 Ibid.

60 Ibid., 18 October 1909.

61 PANS, FWB Papers, Borden to Justice Forbes, 22 October 1909.

62 PANS, FWB Papers, William Cotton to Borden, 6 December 1910.

63 PANS, FWB Papers, Borden to Charles Russell, 3 February 1908.

CHAPTER TWENTY-THREE

1　J. Castell Hopkins, *Canadian Annual Review of Public Affairs for 1909*, Toronto: Annual Review Publishing Co., 1910, 242.

2　Canada, House of Commons, *Debates*, 27 May 1908.

3　For example, in 1905 Borden negotiated a peace between Lieutenant-Colonel Roper, the commanding officer of the Governor General's Foot Guards, and his regimental officers and NCOs, who refused to turn out for Friday-night drill. Although the Militia Council fretted about mass insubordination, Borden negotiated a settlement allowing the officers to withdraw their resignation. William Beahen, "A Citizens' Army: The Growth and Development of the Canadian Militia 1904–1914," 235.

4　R. MacGregor Dawson, *William Lyon Mackenzie King* (Toronto: University of Toronto Press, 1958), 179.

5　Theodore D. Regehr, "Charles Melville Hays," in *Dictionary of Canadian Biography*, vol. 14 (Toronto: University of Toronto Press, 1998), 462–4.

6　J.H. Tuck, "Union Authority, Corporate Obstinacy and the Grand Trunk Strike of 1910," *Historical Papers/Communications Historiques, 1976*, 177.

7　F.A. McGregor, *The Fall and Rise of Mackenzie King: 1911–1919* (Toronto: Macmillan, 1962), 41.

8　Tuck, "Union Authority," 179.

9　Dawson, *William Lyon Mackenzie King*, 210.

10　Ibid., 210.

11　Tuck, "Union Authority," 188.

12　J. Castell Hopkins, ed., *The Canadian Annual Review of Public Affairs, 1908* (Toronto: Annual Review Publishing Co., 1909), 215.

13　Peter Neary, *Newfoundland in the North Atlantic World, 1929–1949* (Montreal and Kingston: McGill-Queen's University Press, 1988), 5.

14　This assessment runs counter to that found in W.T.R. Preston, *The Life and Times of Lord Strathcona* (Toronto: McClelland, Goodchild and Stewart, 1914), 261, in which Preston, who had high esteem for Sir Frederick Borden, though an unflattering view of Strathcona, claimed that Strathcona so disliked Borden that he was prepared "to do everything to prevent" his becoming high commissioner, including delaying his formal resignation – which he did but perhaps not for that reason. Although the long-serving high commissioner talked frequently of relinquishing the post, he seemed to enjoy the position and was reluctant to leave. Of course, Strathcona may have preferred other persons over Borden, such as his protegé, Sir Edward Clouston, a Conservative and a former general manager of the Bank of Montreal, but quite apart from his politics, Clouston's ill health and business reversals made him a very unlikely choice. In fact, Borden's relations with Strathcona were cordial, and there is no reason to believe that Strathcona wished to block his appointment. See Carman Miller, "Edward Clouston," in *Dictionary of Canadian Biography*, vol. 14 (Toronto: University of Toronto Press, 1998), 219–22; Gregory P. Marchildon, *Profits and Politics* (Toronto: University of Toronto Press, 1996), 176–8, 198, 229–32.

15 Ibid., 263.
16 *Morning Chronicle* (Halifax), 1 August 1911.
17 E.M. Macdonald, *Recollections, Political and Personal* (Toronto: Ryerson Press, 1938), 521. Macdonald was tagged to succeed Sir Frederick as minister of militia and defence.
18 PANS, FWB Papers, Borden to F.C. Curry, 15 March 1911.
19 *Morning Chronicle*, 9 March 1911.
20 Ibid., 14 June 1911.
21 PANS, FWB Papers, Borden to F.C. Curry, 15 March 1911.
22 PANS, FWB Papers, Borden to E.S. Crawley, 5 October 1911.
23 *Morning Chronicle*, 21 August 1911.
24 Ibid., 21 August 1911.
25 *Halifax Herald*, 1 September 1911.
26 *Morning Chronicle*, 15 September 1911.
27 *Halifax Herald*, 28 October 1910.
28 Canada, House of Commons, *Debates*, 21 March 1911, 5752.
29 *Halifax Herald*, 18 September 1911.
30 Ibid., 6 September 1911.
31 Ibid., 18 September 1911.
32 PANS, FWB Papers, Borden to J. Russell, 2 October 1911.
33 PANS, FWB Papers, Borden to W.M. Ainley, 27 September 1911.
34 PANS, FWB Papers, Borden to A.S. Magee, 25 September 1911.

CHAPTER TWENTY-FOUR

1 Ronald G. Haycock, *Sam Hughes: The Public Career of a Controversial Canadian, 1885–1916* (Waterloo, ON: Wilfrid Laurier University Press, 1986), 130.
2 *Broad Arrow*, December 1901.
3 Paul W. Riegert, "Charles Gordon Hewitt," in *Dictionary of Canadian Biography*, vol. 14 (Toronto: University of Toronto Press, 1998), 487. Among his several other distinctions, Hewitt was president of the Entomological Society of Ontario, honorary treasurer of the Royal Society of Canada, and a member of the advisory board of the Wildlife Protection Society. In 1918 he received the gold medal of the Royal Society for the Protection of Birds. A prolific writer, he was the author of *Houseflies and How They Spread Disease* (Cambridge: University of Cambridge Press, 1914).
4 Robert Craig Brown, *Robert Laird Borden: A Biography*, vol. 1 (Toronto: University of Toronto Press, 1975), 203; Haycock, *Sam Hughes*, 129.
5 Haycock, *Sam Hughes*, 131.
6 PANS, FWB Papers, F.O. Lewis to Borden, 5 December, 21 December, 29 December 1911, 9 January 1912; Borden to F.O. Lewis, 23 January 1912. Frederick Orr Lewis had been named president of Canadian Vickers, incorporated in June 1911; the company's future in Canada depended upon the maintenance of this lucrative contract. See Graham D. Taylor, "A Merchant of Death in the Peaceable Kingdom," in *Canadian Papers in Business History*, vol. 1, edited by Peter Baskerville (Victoria: Public History Group of the University of Victoria, 1989).

7 William Beahen, "A Citizens' Army: The Growth and Development of the Canadian Militia 1904–1914" (PhD thesis, University of Ottawa, 1978), 272.

8 *Gazette* (Montreal), 28 July 1913; PANS, FWB Papers, Borden to Laurier, 4 August 1913; Borden to S. Hughes, 4 and 13 August 1913; S. Hughes to Borden, 7 and 13 August 1913.

9 J. Castell Hopkins, ed., *The Canadian Annual Review of Public Affairs, 1913* (Toronto: Annual Review Publishing Co., 1914), 716.

10 Hopkins, *Canadian Annual Review of Public Affairs, 1914*, 145.

11 F.A. McGregor, *The Fall and Rise of Mackenzie King, 1911–1919* (Toronto: Macmillan, 1962), 79–80.

12 R. MacGregor Dawson, *William Lyon Mackenzie King* (Toronto: University of Toronto Press, 1958), 178, 179.

13 McGregor, *Fall and Rise of Mackenzie King*, 40–1.

14 LAC, Mackenzie King *Diary*, 26 January 1922, 19 April 1932, 27 January 1935, 21 September 1932.

15 LAC, W.L.M. King Papers, *Diary*, 17 August 1914.

16 PANS, FWB Papers, Borden to H. Greenwood, 2 February 1912.

17 LAC, W.L.M. King Papers, *Diary*, 4 March 1912.

18 PANS, FWB Papers, Borden to F.G. Curry, 2 January 1912; Borden to I. Oakes, 31 January 1912.

19 Dawson, *William Lyon Mackenzie King*, 227ff.

20 Ibid., 81.

21 LAC, Robert Borden Papers, Robert Borden to F.W. Borden, 15 September 1915, vol. 26, nos 115686–87.

22 Deborah Harflett, "The Public Career of Adam Kirk Cameron 1874–1867" (MA thesis, McGill University, 1975), 43–4.

23 *Canadian Liberal Monthly*, August 1916.

24 PANS, FWB Papers, Borden to Freeman Davison, 23 November 1910.

25 LAC, W.L.M. King Papers, *Diary*, 31 December 1914.

26 *Morning Chronicle* (Halifax), 8 January 1917.

27 *Halifax Herald*, 9 January 1917.

28 *Globe* (Toronto), 8 January 1917; *Halifax Herald*, 9 January 1917.

29 *Globe*, 8 January 1917.

30 LAC, W.L.M. King Papers, *Diary*, 12 January 1917.

31 *Wolfville Acadian*, 12 January 1917.

32 PANS, Canning United (formerly Methodist) Church, Reel 1297, Bordon to Rev. J. Hockin, 6 November 1911.

33 *Liberal Monthly*, January 1917, 73.

34 PANS, MG 9, vol. 188, 176, Parliamentary *Scrapbook*, newspaper clipping, 30 January 1917.

35 *Times* (London), 8 January 1917.

36 LAC, W.L.M. King Papers, *Diary*, 13 January 1917.

37 Beahen, "A Citizens' Army," 121.

38 *Liberal Monthly*, August 1916, 155.

39 Hugh MacLennan, *Barometer Rising* (Toronto: McClelland & Stewart, 1989), 257, 267, 279.

40 Paul W. Riegert, "Charles Gordon Hewitt," in *Dictionary of Canadian Biography*, vol. 14 (Toronto: University of Toronto Press, 1998), 487.

41 *Wolfville Acadian*, 6 February 1942.

42 Elizabeth Rosamond, married to Edmond Green, died at the age of seventy-nine on 29 November 1985, succeeded by one daughter, Julia MacKay; Rosamond occupied Borden Place until her removal to the Blanchard Fraser Memorial Hospital. According to the *Chronical Herald*, 5 February 1986, "She lived most of her life in the Valley area."

43 *Wolfville Acadian*, 6 February 1942.

44 LAC, W.L.M. King Papers, King, *Diary*, 27 January 1935.

45 Julia Leslie Green MacKay to author, 13 January 2010.

46 *Nova Scotia Historical Vital Statistics*, Book 1948, p. 3615; PANS, Canning United (formerly Methodist) Church, Reel 1297.

47 Julia Leslie Green MacKay to the author, 13 January 2010.

48 *Kentville Advertiser*, 9 February 1956.

49 Although the 1891, 1901, and 1911 censuses list Sir Frederick as a Methodist, his name does not appear on the Canning Methodist Church's (Trinity United Church's) annual membership roll. PANS, Canning United (formerly Methodist) Church, Reel 1297. The church was destroyed by fire in 1909; when it was rebuilt and reopened in 1910, Lady Borden donated the chimes and carpet, and her mother, Mrs John Clarke, donated the pulpit.

50 *Kentville Advertiser*, 1 and 8 March 1956.

Index

Skelton, O.D., 248
Small Arms Standing Committee, 222
Smart, Charles A. (Col.), 182
Smith, Adam, 275
Smith, Anthony D., 276
Smith, Henry (Col.), 169
Smith-Dorrien, Horace (Gen.), 176
Society of Friends, 206. *See also* Quakers
Sommerville, William (Rev.), 22, 26
Sons of England, 198
Soulanges Canal scandal, 71
South African Constabulary, 155, 187
South African War, 78, 99, 113, 117, 124, 197, 215, 221, 224, 278; and Borden, 241, 283, 342; business, 79, 299, 313; chaplains, 152; contingent crisis, 97, 146; expeditionary force, 236–7; garrisons, 231; Hughes, 110; Hutton, 99–100, 133, 241; militarism, 197, 201; nationalism, 156–7; Permanent Force, 191, 224; rations, 139–40, 215; reform, 228, 154, 156, 158–9, 161, 178, 186–7, 191, 196, 212, 215, 278; rewarding of veterans, 153, 163–5, 227, 229, 262–3; Ross rifle, 223
Southern Exposure, 304
Spanish American War, 94
Spanish influenza, 363
Spanish River Pulp and Paper, 305–6, 314
Spender, Harold, 157
Spidell, J.A. (Rev.), 330, 335
Springfield rifle, 220
Stacey, C.P., 263
Stadacona Hall, 151, 283, 285–6, 290, 350
Stairs, William J., 26
Stanfield, Frank, 304, 317, 319
Stanfield Co., 306, 317
Stanley Barracks (Toronto), 193
Steele, Jonathan, 36, 40, 65
Steele, Sam B. (Lt-Col.), 93, 158, 343
Stone, F.G. (Col.), 85, 164, 167
Stoney Creek Battlefield, 202

Strathcona, Lord, 3, 120, 127–8, 191, 206–7, 273, 287, 293, 308, 321; and Borden, 287, 342–4; high commissionership, 308, 324, 331, 337, 342, 344, 348
Strathcona Horse, 134, 177, 191, 342–4
Strathcona Medical Building (McGill), 279
Strathcona Trust, 195, 206–7, 344
Sub-Target Gun Co. *See* Ontario Sub-Target Gun Co.
Sudan, 237
Sun (Saint John), 104
Supreme Court of Canada, 73
Supreme Court of Nova Scotia, 68, 334
Sutherland, James, 89, 121, 134
Sweetsburg (QC), 182
Swiss system, 188, 195

Tanner, Charles Elliott, 318–19
Tariff Commission, 74, 88
Tarte, Israel, 73, 133–4, 321; and contingent crisis, 117–22
Taylor, Norman W., 296
temperance, 44, 48, 62, 144, 199–200, 202, 323, 331–2
Temperance and General Life Insurance Co., 299
Temperance Society (Canning), 44, 62, 147
Thompson, John S.D., 64, 66–7
Tilley, Leonard, 48
Times, 216, 254, 287
Tiverton (Massachusetts), 12–13
Toronto, 60, 180, 229, 279, 345, 352, 365; and Borden, 275, 286, 297, 301, 304; South African War, 117, 120–1
Toronto, University of, 195, 208
Toronto Banquet, 161, 164, 169, 254, 324
Toronto Club, 103
Toronto News, 187
Toronto Veterans Association, 292
Toronto World, 325
Trades and Labour Council. *See* labour unions